SOCIOLOGY

▲ ADDISON-WESLEY PUBLISHING COMPANY

Reading, Massachusetts ● Menlo Park, California ● London ● Amsterdam ● Don Mills, Ontario ● Sydne

Ronald C. Federico/Janet S. Schwartz

Iona College   American University

THIRD EDITION
SOCIOLOGY

Sponsoring Editor: *Ronald R. Hill*
Production Editors: *Stephanie Argeros-Magean*
Mary Clare McEwing
Copy Editor *Nancy F. Farrell*
Text Designer: *Margaret Ong Tsao*
Illustrator and Art Coordinator: *Susanah H. Michener*
Cover Designer: *Ann Scrimgeour Rose*
Cover Photographer: *Mark Solomon/The Image Bank*
Production Manager: *Karen M. Guardino*
Production Coordinator: *Peter Petraitis*

The text of this book was composed in Bembo
by Monotype Composition Company

Library of Congress Cataloging in Publication Data

Federico, Ronald C.
  Sociology.

  1. Sociology.   I. Schwartz, Janet.   II. Title.
HM51.F39   1983   301   82-11375
ISBN 0-201-12030-5

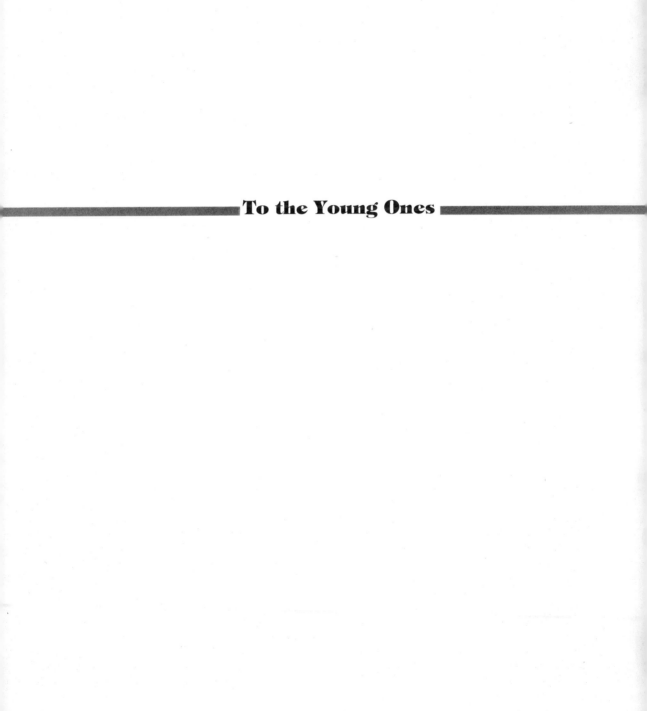

To the Young Ones

PREFACE

A student went to see a favorite teacher to ask what courses he would be teaching the next semester. The teacher replied that he would be teaching *the* course, meaning that whatever the title, he was going to teach what he knew. This anecdote illustrates a problem confronted by teachers of introductory sociology. The introductory course is supposed to help the student understand and appreciate a wide-ranging and constantly changing discipline. Most sociologists are more knowledgeable about some parts of the field than about others, yet we have to teach a whole discipline. Our lives are further complicated by students whose interests change from year to year. How, then, can we make *the* course the right one for our introductory students?

This book has been revised to try to address this need. It adopts a number of strategies in working toward this goal.

BALANCE

As in previous editions, all the major areas of sociological thought are covered concisely but thoroughly. Four major theoretical perspectives are used throughout: structural-functionalism, conflict theory, symbolic interactionism, and exchange theory. The result is a balanced treatment of all subjects, and content sound enough to provide support for students even in areas which faculty may not feel are their special strength.

NEW TOPICS

Several areas of sociological study are introduced for the first time in this edition. These include a new chapter on sex roles and content on medical sociology, applied sociology, unions, the quality of life, biotechnology, family violence, leisure, the changing nature of the workplace, and new approaches to community development. The material on sociological research methods has been greatly expanded in the chapter devoted to that subject, and it is also reinforced throughout the text by way of Reminder Boxes. The material in the Appendix, all of which is new, introduces students to sociology as a career. It provides information on the American Sociological Association, including its membership and publications, and also addresses prospects for employment in the discipline. The inside of the front cover introduces sociology as a social science and provides a chart relating sociology to the other social sciences.

CROSS-CULTURAL MATERIAL

This edition broadens readers' sociological world by building in regular comparisons between the United States and other contemporary societies, especially the Soviet Union, Israel, Japan, Sweden, and Yugoslavia. As in previous editions, comparisons are also made to less industrialized societies when appropriate. This comparative perspective will help students grasp the idea that social life is collectively negotiated, and that societies structure their activies in many different ways. It also links the student to societies beyond their own, and helps them to understand better the global concerns frequently discussed in the mass media.

SOCIAL ISSUES AND INTERVIEWS

The Social Issues have been revised and updated, enabling students to see in-depth applications of sociological thinking to a variety of areas. They include

Women in the 1980s by Laurel W. Richardson, Ohio State University

Homosexuality by Thomas K. Fitzgerald, University of North Carolina at Greensboro

The Elderly as a Minority Group by Robert J. Havighurst, University of Chicago

The Mass Media by Muriel G. Cantor, American University

Death and Dying by Robert Fulton, University of Minnesota

Work and Leisure by Janet S. Schwartz, American University

Social Welfare as a Social Institution by Ronald C. Federico, Iona College

Science and Social Change by Norman W. Storer, Baruch College, The City University of New York

The Interviews have been completely redone in an exciting way. In each case, a respected sociologist is interviewed about an area of contemporary concern which he or she has studied. These interviews expose students in a very personal way to contemporary sociologists and their thinking about some of the major issues of our time. They include

Kurt Finsterbusch, University of Maryland, on scarcity and social organization;

Rosabeth Moss Kanter, Yale University, on power in the workplace;

Jennie J. McIntyre, University of Maryland, on family violence;

Joseph Schwartz, Columbia University, on social inequality in industrial societies;

Gerald D. Suttles, University of Chicago, on the urban community in its social context;

Robin M. Williams, Jr., Cornell University, on racial and ethnic inequality in America;

Jacqueline P. Wiseman, University of California at San Diego, on marriage and the family in a changing world.

SUPPLEMENT PACKAGE

The text is reinforced through excellent supplemental materials. The *Instructor's Manual, Student Study Guide,* and *Test Item File* provide opportunities for faculty and students to enrich their teaching and learning. The text is also keyed to *Experience with Sociology,* a set of ten modules addressing ten current social issues, which is a unique and new feature of this edition. Each module engages students in the analysis and use of data to understand an issue, and asks them to make decisions based on their analysis. The needed data are provided in each module, and the statistical analysis does not require special mathematical skills or electronic equipment. Through the modules, students actually "do" sociology, so theories and issues of methodology come alive and are made immediate and meaningful. The modules will enable instructors to bridge the often lamented gap between theory and data in introductory courses, and they do so in a way that is easily accessible to every instructor and student. The modules also expose the students to applied aspects of sociology since they demonstrate how the discipline can be used in practical, day-to-day decision making.

IN-TEXT TEACHING METHOD

Summaries and study questions at the end of each chapter have also been expanded and revised. To assist the students in learning new material

and preparing for exams, the "key terms" discussed in each chapter have been set in boldface type on first usage. These key terms are then collected at the end of each chapter, where they may be reviewed in context. They appear again in the glossary at the back of the book. Consistent with the substantial amount of new content in this edition, this glossary has been expanded and revised.

FURTHER IMPROVEMENTS

This edition has been greatly improved in format and writing style. The use of color is substantially increased. The writing is less formal and incorporates more examples from events covered in the mass media. We believe the book will be more attractive to a wide range of students because of its greater visual appeal and the ability of students to relate more directly to its illustrations of sociological concepts.

Making extensive revisions on a book of this size and scope is a complex undertaking, and it has been possible only because of the help and cooperation of many people. The social scientists who prepared social issues and participated in interviews have contributed their specialized expertise and insights; they are listed earlier in this preface. Dr. Gai Berlage and Dr. William Egelman, both at Iona College, have provided valuable teaching and learning resources for users of this edition. They are the authors of the *Instructor's Manual* and the innovative *Experience with Sociology*. Professor Donn Murphy of West Valley College, who developed the *Test Item File*, has provided a tool for instructors which should make their instructional tasks a bit easier. Further information about computerized testing and customized test preparation is available on request from Addison-Wesley or your local sales representative. Professors Harold Cox and Linda Larkin of Indiana State University have developed a comprehensive study guide, which we hope will further facilitate students' introduction to our exciting discipline. The American Sociological Association has been very helpful by allowing us to use data compiled by them about the discipline.

The staff at Addison-Wesley Publishing Company has also been critical to the success of this book. Under the able leadership of editor Ronald R. Hill, many specialized staff people have contributed their expertise, including Linda Bedell, Mary Clare McEwing, Jo-Ann Caratell, Stephanie Argeros-Magean, and Debra Hunter. Without their help, the important work of carefully checking content, style, and details could not have taken place.

Several other groups and individuals have also contributed significantly to this book. The following sociologists critiqued drafts of the manuscript and made extremely helpful suggestions: Stan Albrecht of Brigham Young University; William Cross of Illinois College; M. Jay Crowe of the University of Colorado at Denver; Donna Darden of the University of Arkansas; Irwin Kantor of Middlesex County College; Gwinn Lovell of Southeast Missouri State University; Guinevere Norman of Los Angeles Pierce College; Howard Robboy of Trenton State College; Paul Sharp of Oklahoma State University; T. P. Schwartz of Coventry, Rhode Island; Steven Stack of Pennsylvania State University; Kenrick Thompson of Northern Michigan University; and Charles Van Middlesworth of Kansas City, Kansas Community College. Mary Bruno, Nancy Girardi, Dorothy Bowers, Larry Paulette, and Carol Angelilli helped prepare the manuscript, often working under great time pressure. Finally, without the support and encouragement of family and close friends, the energy to complete such a large project would have been exhausted long before it was completed. To each and every person who has helped us, we express our deepest thanks and appreciation.

Yonkers, New York　　　　　　　　　　　R.C.F.
Chevy Chase, Maryland　　　　　　　　　J.S.S.
January 1983

BRIEF CONTENTS

CONTENTS

PART ONE

THE SOCIAL INDIVIDUAL

1

INTRODUCTION TO SOCIOLOGICAL THOUGHT

- The Sociological Imagination
- The Nature of Sociology
- Patterned Behavior
- The Study of Groups
- The Individual and the Group
- Sociology and the Social Sciences
- The Development of Sociology
- The Sociological Imagination Revisited
- SUMMARY

Sociology—the science of society—permits us to look at our everyday lives as if we were strangers seeing our society for the first time. Observing our social lives with greater clarity enables us to understand the patterns of our own lives and those of others.

THE SOCIOLOGICAL IMAGINATION

Regardless of the grade you receive, this course will have been worthwhile if you leave it with what is known as "the sociological imagination"—a way of looking at your experiences that can help you see yourself and others in new ways. This new perspective can also help you to deal with, solve, and understand problems you face every day and major crises that come along once in a while.

In 1959, sociologist C. Wright Mills first used the term **sociological imagination.** This is how he described the concept:

Nowadays men often feel that their private lives are a series of traps. They sense that within their everyday worlds, they cannot quite overcome their troubles, and in this feeling, they are often quite correct . . . yet men do not usually define the troubles they endure in terms of historical change and institutional contradiction. . . . They do not possess the quality of mind essential to grasp the interplay of man and society, of biography and history, of self and world. What they need, and what they feel they need, is a quality of mind that will help them to use information and to develop reason in order to achieve lucid summations of what is going on in the world and what may be happening within themselves. It is this quality of mind, I am going to contend . . . [that] may be called the sociological imagination. (Mills, 1959: 3–5)

This special understanding of the interplay of people and society is the primary goal of sociology.

THE NATURE OF SOCIOLOGY

As a science, sociology is only about 150 years old. Through many of these years it remained the subject of sometimes wild misunderstandings. Although some of these misunderstandings still persist today, in recent years the sociologist has won a respected place in the public mind. Newspapers cite social scientists as experts on everything from race relations to the disappearance of the family farm, from childhood suicides to the population explosion. Journalists ask sociologists for authoritative opinions on why so many people are moving to the Southwest and how day care centers will affect the development of young children. During elections, public opinion polls designed by sociologists make headlines. But do you know exactly what sociology is or what sociologists do when they go to work?

Sociology is the scientific study of the structure, the functioning, and the changes in human groups. As you can readily see, this definition says only that sociologists *examine* society. It does not mean that they necessarily enter the field of social work. It does not mean that sociologists try to overthrow capitalism by becoming socialists. These areas of social concern are not the same thing as sociology. All the definition says is that sociologists study groups of people and that they are scientific in their approach.

If this definition does not seem very specific, perhaps it is because sociology is such an enormous field of study. Sociologists look for the reasons behind all the things people are (students, mothers, teachers, cigarette smokers, boyfriends) and all the things people do (work, wear clothes, smoke pot, get married, drink too much) as they live in a society.

No group of people is beyond the interest of sociologists. They explore street gangs, drug addicts, skid row alcoholics, prostitutes, and criminals, groups that most people would rather forget about. They also study the worlds of executives, politicians, doctors, and generals. They have few inhibitions about turning their spotlight on churches and clergy, political parties and presidents, or mothers and fathers. Church sermons, voting in Wichita, and giving birth are all social phenomena.

PATTERNED BEHAVIOR

While most people consider their lives unique, sociologists take the somewhat unpopular view that people behave in fairly predictable ways. For example, it is unlikely that a student entering the first class of a semester would walk up and kiss the instructor. It would be equally unlikely for the student not to kiss a long-lost aunt who had just returned home after years of missionary work in Honduras. Kissing mothers, aunts, and lovers is expected; kissing children—anybody's children—is permissible but voluntary; kissing authorities and strangers is not done, except at parties or on certain holidays. In short, whom the average student will embrace is quite predictable.

Given a few simple facts about individuals—say, their incomes, religion, and levels of education—a sociologist can predict with considerable accuracy where they live (that is, in what part of town), what kinds of jobs they hold, how long they can expect to live, how many children they have, how they talk to them, what they think of the president and chamber music, what they do on Sundays, even how they make love. Then the sociologist asks why. Why do ad executives drink martinis and construction workers drink beer? Why are women employed as secretaries, and men as executives? Why do people talk to children one way and to old people another way?

This is not to say that sociologists have no respect for individuality. The truth is quite the contrary. Sociologists are fascinated by the fact that despite vast individual differences, people tend to relate to one another in predictable ways.

And they have some ideas about why this is so. Knowing how other people will behave toward you and how you are expected to behave toward them eliminates the need to consider countless alternatives and make decisions every time you step outside your door. Without this predictability, life would be a maze of problems and conflicts.

Sociologists consider patterned behavior the glue that holds people and families and societies together. Without it, few of us could function. Sociologists study that glue: what it is made of, how it works, and why it sometimes fails.

THE STUDY OF GROUPS

In the course of a lifetime, each of us joins or is put into a wide variety of groups. Nearly everyone is born and raised in a family. During our early years we join play groups in our neighborhoods and schools. This process continues throughout life as we join other friendship groups, work groups, recreational groups, and so on.

Sociologists study the origins, growth, and activities of groups much as psychologists study the childhood, development, and behavior of individuals. For the sociologist, a group has a personality of its own. It is more than the sum of its individual members. Knowing the individual psychological characteristics of five or twenty people does not enable the sociologist to predict how they will act when they work together as a group. For a variety of reasons, people seem to behave differently in groups than they do by themselves, and to behave differently in different groups. The man or woman who is aggressive and demanding at work may be gentle and even passive at home.

A classic example of the effect of a group on individuals can be found in the civil rights movement of the 1960s. Until the late 1950s, most blacks in the Deep South more or less accepted the back seat in the bus, literally and figuratively. Of course, there had been rebellions against

Seiji Ozawa conducts a rehearsal of the Boston Symphony orchestra. For the sociologist, such a group exhibits a personality of its own that transcends the characteristics of individual members and encourages patterns of predictable behavior.

making a concerted effort to change society—that inspired individuals to risk their jobs and personal safety.

In studying a group, the sociologist tries to understand: (1) its organization or structure—the way it distributes authority and responsibility, the way members typically act toward one another; and (2) the group's function—the needs it fills for individual members, and its role in society as a whole. Sociologists also study changes in these structures and functions and the effects such changes have on group members as individuals.

THE INDIVIDUAL AND THE GROUP

Although sociologists focus on group behavior, they do not ignore individuals. Groups are composed of individuals and are influenced by them. For example, a family group will be affected if one of its members becomes seriously ill. Individuals, in turn, are influenced by the groups to which they belong as can be seen when a self-help group like Alcoholics Anonymous helps one of its members to stop drinking. Sociology, therefore, sees an important reciprocal interaction between groups and individuals. While its primary interest is in groups, it correlates closely with social and biological sciences like psychology and biology, which are primarily the study of individual behavior.

While emphasis on individual and group behavior among the social and biological sciences is a matter of degree, each contributes to our understanding at both levels. Sociology's interest in, and concern for, individuals will be seen at many points throughout this book. For now, an illustration may help clarify the linkages between sociology and individual and group behavior. While much of daily life depends on individuals acting according to social expectations, the rules of behavior vary from group to group and from situation to situation. Imagine, for example, that

discrimination since the beginnings of slavery, but these had been isolated instances. It was not until masses of black people joined forces in organized groups that protest efforts began to have a real impact on the lives of most blacks in the United States. During the 1950s and 1960s, many individuals who once would have been afraid to speak out became vigorous protesters, often risking injury for their defiance of discriminatory laws and practices. They demanded front seats on buses and in white restaurants and hotels, demands that would have been unthinkable a few years earlier. It was in large part the existence of a movement—large numbers of blacks and whites

you are a black child in Montgomery, Alabama, in the 1950s. You have always been taught to respect and obey adults, especially the police. But your parents, acting with the support of the civil rights movement, are now telling you to ignore the white adults who try to prevent you from entering school. They also want you to break the law, to disobey the police when they tell you to leave a segregated restaurant. Discovering how individuals handle such conflicts and how they fit the different parts of their lives together—sometimes adjusting to the group, sometimes making the group adjust to them—is one of the aims of sociology.

SOCIOLOGY AND THE SOCIAL SCIENCES

It must be obvious that a science that studies street gangs and presidents is different from a science that studies atoms, rocks, or frogs. Sociology is one of the group of **social sciences**: sciences that study the various aspects of human society. Anthropology, psychology, economics, and political science are other social sciences. Biology, chemistry, physics, astronomy, and geology are examples of **natural sciences:** sciences that study the physical features of nature and the ways in which they interact and change.

But one thing all sciences have in common is that they are based on the assumption that there is order in the universe and regular patterns and rules that the curious can discover and understand. The astronomer looks for the rules that explain the composition and the movements of things in space. The geneticist looks for the chemical rules that cause babies to resemble their parents. The sociologist looks for the regularities in human behavior which occur in our societies. Although the social sciences and the natural sciences study different phenomena, they share many philosophical and methodological characteristics.

At this point we should again emphasize that sociologists study the group behavior of human beings. This focus on the interaction between people sets sociology apart from other social sciences with their own particular focuses. For instance, psychology also studies human behavior, but psychologists are more concerned with the mental processes of particular individuals than they are with the organization of people in groups.

Political science studies the aspects of human life that relate to power and to governments. Economics limits its focus to the ways that humans exchange money, resources, and services. Anthropology and sociology are very much alike, and they have moved closer together in recent years. The difference is that, in general, anthropologists usually study preliterate cultures of the past and preindustrial cultures in the modern world, and they tend to take a broad overview of cultures as a whole. Sociologists, on the other hand, tend to focus on specific segments of social organization and spend most of their time on current concerns within their own societies.

It should be clear that these areas of interest overlap. Political science is incomplete without an understanding of the ways in which economics contributes to power and government. Sociologists, in turn, learn from anthropologists about the many ways people construct their societies, and understand from psychologists how an individual comes to think and to act in certain ways. We have developed many social sciences because no one science can study every aspect of human life in depth.

THE DEVELOPMENT OF SOCIOLOGY

As far as we know, people have always sought to understand social life in order to predict and control it. We can imagine that preliterate humans, without being scientific, recognized the protection that groups gave their members, and saw that leadership of these groups required certain essential skills. But the first records of social understanding are found among the writings of such Greek philosophers as Plato and Aristotle. By today's standards, their thinking was not much more than the recorded observations of curious minds. It was neither scientific nor free from prejudice. Sociology as a discipline did not truly leave the realm of "casual observation" until the Industrial Revolution in England in the mid-1700s.

The Industrial Revolution

The Industrial Revolution was a time of great social unrest in Western society. Knowledge of physics and mathematics had reached the point where "the machine" became a possible and practical answer to many of society's problems of work and scarcity. Most people spent their lives on small farms, raising their own food and making their own clothing. Such a life leaves little time for anything but work. With the advent of machines, human time and energy could be used for other things.

But the machine became more than a useful step forward: it also became a passion. All jobs, from harvesting and planting to weaving and sewing, were examined to see how a machine might be invented to do them. Jobs that had previously been done by hand on small farms, in little shops, or in the home were, by the mid-1800s, being performed in the factory, the home of machines. Machines could do the work of many people in less time and at less expense. And mechanization had another consequence: it led to the establishment of large farms that began to drive the small farmer out of business. Where before, children had learned the crafts of their parents, now the family farm or small craft shop could no longer compete with "the mighty machine."

This economic pressure caused the young to move to the cities, looking for work and opportunity. For the first time, the traditional ways of

The Industrial Revolution threatened the social and economic stability of European society. The plight of these tobacco strippers, working late into the night in violation of child labor laws, emphasized the need for a better understanding of society as a means for confronting social problems.

life of European society were undermined. Families were broken up. In the impersonal cities, people lost their old identities and their networks of friendship and family. The "rational" approach to life was very much in style. Religion, based as it is on feelings for community and the spiritual, began to lose its influence over peoples' ideas about themselves and their destinies. In the cities, people faced new psychological, social, and physical problems. In this new and confusing time, the need to understand, predict, and plan social life became more urgent than ever.

The Social Philosophers

The first "social philosophers" looked at society in purely philosophical terms. According to the French philosopher Jean-Jacques Rousseau, the natural and simple happiness in which primitive humans had once lived was destroyed as soon as one of them joined labor with another to make life easier. At that point of social union, humankind was caught in a web of cooperation and competition.

A man with possessions is a man with something to lose, and a man who is dependent on the activities of others is also dependent upon their dispositions. . . . The poor man needs the help of the rich: the rich, the services of the poor. All are enmeshed in a web of . . . dependence and . . . comparison. (Smelser and Warner, 1976: 29)

The keen observations of such philosophers as Rousseau were useful, but as the Industrial Revolution and "rational" thinking gained momentum, social thinkers began to use scientific methods to learn more about the life they observed around them. Charles Darwin's theory of evolution was particularly influential. Until Darwin's time, the study of human life had been the interest of philosophers and the church, not scientists. Today, in the modern world, we are so used to science and rapid change that it is hard for us to conceive of the effect Darwin had on

his world. Try to imagine the impact of a scientific study that denied everything that people believed about human creation. The Bible had been the basis of morality and of the authority of the church for generations. Suddenly, a new book, *Origin of Species,* written by a scientist, questioned its truth. This sudden boost in the respectability of science encouraged other thinkers and scholars to break with tradition and to seek scientific explanations of human behavior in society.

The First Sociologists

A French mathematician, Auguste Comte (1798–1857), was the first to suggest that scientific methods should be used to study society. He is responsible for giving the name "sociology"— the science of society—to this new branch of knowledge. Late in life Comte abandoned his family and his career as a mathematics teacher to preach a new religion he called "positive philosophy," a science of thinking based on hard facts.

Auguste Comte

Herbert Spencer

Karl Marx

He believed that in the industrial age the world would look to science to explain the universe and to guide individual decisions. Comte himself did little in the way of practicing his new religion. But while he did no social research himself, he planted the idea that society in all of its variations is a proper topic for scientific investigation.

It was an English intellectual named Herbert Spencer (1820–1903) who popularized this new science with the publication of *The Study of Sociology* in 1873. Spencer, a retired engineer turned philosopher, believed that sociology should study *all* aspects of society together, not just individual parts such as the family or religion. Spencer compared society to a giant organism in which all the parts and all the processes are related

in complex ways. He also borrowed from Darwin and suggested that civilizations, like organisms, go through a process of adaptation or *social* evolution. But, like Comte, Spencer was convinced that nineteenth-century Europe—especially England—had reached the pinnacle of cultural and social development. This belief biased his research and colored his conclusions. From Spencer's perspective, all other cultures were "backward" and should emulate England.

Contrary to Comte and Spencer, Karl Marx (1818–1883), did not see an evolutionary development of society. Instead, Marx saw a revolutionary movement from one stage of history to another which he perceived as progressive. Central to this analysis was the concept of social class. For Marx classes were not determined by one's ranking on the basis of income, prestige, and power, as sociologists generally measure and define social classes today. Social class meant one's relationship to the means of production, such as factories, tools, and capital. In a capitalist system those who own the means of production constitute the ruling class and are called the **bourgeoisie.** The propertyless workers, whom Marx called the **proletariat,** must sell their labor power in order to survive. Under capitalism, the bourgeoisie is the ruling class. In prior history, there have been other ruling classes in each of several economic systems, of which slavery and then feudalism were the most important. In each case, a new class emerged which struggled to wrest power from the ruling class, thereby establishing a new historical stage. Capitalism emerged from feudalism, and Marx asserted that communism would emerge from capitalism.

According to Marx, the class which controls the means of production controls all of the existing institutions in society: political and legal systems, education, religion, the arts, and so forth. Thus, no institution is independent of the ruling (property-owning) class. For example, political power in the Marxist framework is the power of the ruling class to oppress the others. The ideas which justify the capitalist system and attempt to give it legitimacy are diffused through all social institutions, including education, religion, and the arts: "the ideas of the ruling class are in every age, the ruling ideas." What Marx implied is that the values, beliefs, and norms of society reflect the interests of the ruling class. As Parkin, a British sociologist, points out: "Dominant values are in a sense a representation of the perceptions and interests of the relatively privileged; yet by virtue of the institutional backing they receive, such values often form the basis of moral judgements of underprivileged groups. In a way, dominant values tend to set the standards for what is considered to be objectively 'right' " (1971: 83). Thus, for example, we seldom if ever question why some live in substandard housing, and others have several mansion-like homes. We

simply accept the situation as right, because the occupants deserve it.

In the Marxist framework, to accept the values and ideas of the dominant class and not to recognize that they are merely a means to legitimize the existing social order constitutes "false consciousness." Marx argued, however, that conditions under capitalism will inevitably worsen because of the greed of the bourgeoisie. Workers become conscious of their position in society as they get increasingly exploited. They then will organize politically for a revolutionary challenge to the ruling class. The revolutionary conflict between the proletariat and the bourgeoisie brings a new social order in which private property ceases to exist. Since a class society is based on private property, its elimination brings about a classless society in which no one person exploits others.

Marx did not anticipate that a full-fledged communist system would emerge following the revolution. Before communism becomes a reality there is a period of revolutionary transformation from one system to another. This intermediate or transitional stage is a socialist society, which moves society to communism. Marx never set out a blueprint of what this communist society was to be like. From his prolific writings it is clear nevertheless that this was to be an egalitarian society which would provide vast opportunities for the development of each person. Communism was to be highly productive since each person would work eagerly and willingly. For Marx, work was the essence of the man or woman; only through work does one create and fulfill oneself as a person, and cooperate with others. In a capitalist system work is dreaded, because the labor is imposed and the worker exploited. The worker is alienated (detached) from the product of his or her labor which is seen as simply a commodity.

Karl Marx was not what one might call a value-free sociologist. He abhorred capitalism and regarded it as vile and exploitative. Social change required that men and women take an

Emile Durkheim

and developing techniques for truly scientific research is generally given to the Frenchman Emile Durkheim (1858–1917). In all of his books, Durkheim concentrated on two general ideas: first, that a society is more than the sum of its parts and must be studied as a separate entity with a life of its own; and second, that people are a product of their society with feelings and attitudes created by social forces.

In contrast to Marx's concern with conflict and change, Durkheim saw the moral order as of primary importance. Less developed societies were characterized by **mechanical solidarity** in which homogeneous, intertwined groups were highly integrated into the community and a common moral order. The modern world is characterized by **organic solidarity,** the integration that results from many specialized activities being coordinated to work toward a common goal. For example, doctors and bus drivers have very different skills and activities, but each contributes in a special way to people being able to function effectively in society. Durkheim called this specialization of tasks the **division of labor.**

The division of labor in contemporary societies was to Durkheim a panacea to the problems of industrialization. To illustrate, in the modern factory organic solidarity involves interdependence of many specialized roles. This not only assures a state of well-being among workers since they know what is expected of them and their workmates, but it also provides individual workers with the feeling that they serve a higher goal (producing goods needed by others in society). Hence the individual acts toward ends that are not strictly his or her own, taking into account higher interests and/or the interests of the state. The state, for Durkheim, was "a neutral representative or the embodiment of the general interest" (Bottomore, 1981: 907), and as such, individuals tend to depend more and more on the state "to remind us of the sentiment of common solidarity" (Durkheim, 1960). The group ensures moral discipline: "A group is not only a moral authority which

active part in changing the social system. As psychologist Erich Fromm (1964) noted, Marx was a humanist for whom freedom, dignity, and activity were basic factors to a "good society." As Marx saw it, communism was to be a society which enables men and women to live in harmony with others, a society which enables every person to develop his or her full potential. However, such a society could only be achieved through the revolutionary overthrow of capitalism.

While Marx's approach had a clear value base, other sociologists began more and more to employ the fact-gathering methods and the objective stance that had yielded so much growth in the other sciences. The credit for refining sociology, trying to eliminate value judgments,

dominates the life of members; it is a source of life sui generis."

The problem of integration was real to Durkheim, who feared that lack of integration and a strong moral order would lead to **anomie, a condition in which people feel isolated and rootless.** In his study *Suicide* (1897), Durkheim demonstrated that suicide rates were related to social conditions. Family men who lived in stable, traditional communities commited suicide much less frequently than single men who lacked a sense of belonging to a family and a community. Durkheim found that suicide rates were highest among unmarried, enlisted soldiers. By using **quantitative methods,** procedures intended to collect accurate measurements, Durkheim disproved many old conceptions about suicide. After analyzing his statistics, Durkheim concluded that suicide could no longer be considered a unique, individual act, but was instead closely related to the degree to which an individual feels a part of one or more groups. Durkheim's study demonstrated the enormous extent to which each person is influenced by society. But more important to the future of sociology, he demonstrated the usefulness of applying quantitative methods and an empirical approach to sociological inquiry. Instead of speculating on broad observations, Durkheim drew his conclusions from collected facts.

Max Weber (1864–1920), not unlike Durkheim, did not show much enthusiasm for a socialist type of society. Weber, a prolific German intellectual with far-ranging interests, seems to have argued with the ghost of Marx in many of his works. For Marx, as we noted earlier, the ownership of the means of production constituted the moving part of history. Social change came with economic changes, and ideas and values were reflections of the existing social order. For Weber, however, ideas and values were independent of economic forces. In *The Protestant Ethic and the Spirit of Capitalism* (1904), Weber argued that the early Calvinist code of puritan ethics created the values supportive to the rise of

Max Weber

capitalism in England, northern Europe, and the United States. The Calvinists believed in hard work, self-discipline, and individuality, and these religious values spilled over into their economic life. Thrifty, hard working, and renouncing worldly pleasures, the Calvinists saved their money and reinvested it in their work. They considered economic success as a sign of God's grace. Weber attempted to demonstrate how such ideas, values, and beliefs have a strong influence on people's behavior. This, of course, was an attempt to refute Marx's position. Another area in which Weber differed from Marx was in his view of the role of sociologists. A "value free" social science was the primary objective for Weber. Sociologists, he argued, should be neutral in their analysis of social phenomena; they should stand apart from what they are examining; and they should not permit their values to influence their work.

Weber also disagreed with Marx with respect to social class. For Weber, class was multidimensional. Its base was not merely economic, but included social prestige and power as well. While these three factors are generally interdependent, they need not be so. One could have a high prestige without economic resources as, for example, is true of some deposed members of the nobility. Similarly, practitioners of organized crime may have considerable economic resources, but these resources are not sufficient to rank them high in social prestige. Distinctive to Weber's view of modern society was the rational legal organization, or what we call the bureaucracy. Bureaucratic organizations, whether in the form of a hospital, university, or industrial organization, are characterized by efficiency, rationality, and routine. Work is standardized, and the em-

ployee easily replaced. Weber, while generally less than enthusiastic about bureaucratic organizations, recognized their importance as the most efficient way of getting things accomplished. By placing individuals in the hierarchy of the organization, the main concern is with their technical proficiency and not their personal characteristics, such as physical attractiveness, personality, and so on. Education and technical training, or "merit," become the major criteria for a place in the bureaucracy.

Modern Sociology: The American Contribution

During the twentieth century, developments in sociology have, for the most part, taken place within the United States. In this context, the science developed a two-pronged tradition. Under the influence of William Graham Sumner (1840–1910), sociologists began to study the features of ordinary, day-to-day life. Simultaneously, the work of Lester Ward (1841–1913) influenced the application of sociology to social reform efforts. It will be clear in the theoretical perspectives to be discussed shortly how these interests were incorporated into the development of the discipline. In its early period, concern with current problems and issues was especially strong—alcoholism, crime, child labor, the new immigrants, and so on, dominated sociological thinking. Between 1918 and 1935 there were major contributions to social psychology (Mead, 1934; Cooley, 1902) and to human ecology (Park, 1925). Sociologists at the University of Chicago were preeminent in the field during the first half of the century, but it was Talcott Parsons (1902–1980) at Harvard, and his students, who forged the theoretical framework of structural functionalism, which until recently has been the major theoretical underpinning of most American sociology. Before turning to this theory, we will look at theoretical perspectives as a part of sociology.

Talcott Parsons

Theoretical perspectives. When young adults play popular music, they hear the performance of human beings with talent and sensitivity. When people of middle age hear the same music, they hear important traditions and standards of good taste being violated by irresponsible youngsters. The group's agent hears a show biz routine that is aimed to please a certain type of audience and improve everybody's income.

What accounts for the difference in the way these people hear the music? The melody has not changed; the volume is the same; the words emerge the same way each time. In other words, the *facts* of the group's performance have not changed. What *is* different, of course, is each person's point of view while observing the facts. And each of these points of view leads to different interpretations.

In the sciences, a point of view is called a **theoretical perspective,** and it can be defined as a systematic explanation of the relationships between experimental facts. A theory makes sense out of an assortment of facts by helping the scientist to look for underlying principles that tie them together. Because facts don't speak for themselves, a theory can help researchers organize their thinking about the facts they have gathered. In addition, theories can suggest future experiments and procedures that can be used in gathering information and facts of varying types. Sociologists have given names to the different theoretical perspectives, or ways of looking at a sociological problem. There are many such schools of thought, but the four that have gained the most respect among sociologists are *structural functionalism, conflict theory, symbolic interactionism,* and *exchange theory.* Let us now look at each in turn.

Structural functionalism. The image of society as it emerged in structural functionalism bears the mark of Spencer and Durkheim, and uses a biological analogy of society as an organism. According to **structural functionalism,** the different parts of society comprise a whole, acting and reacting to each other and to the whole. The interdependence of the different parts means that change in one part will lead to changes in other parts of the system, thus causing dislocation or even major changes in society. Functionalists argue that if certain phenomena, such as religion, are to continue to exist in society they must contribute to its well-being. Otherwise these structures will disappear. Thus, religion continues because it provides people with something they are unable to get on their own, or which is not provided by other social institutions. Fundamental to functionalism is the maintenance and stability of the social order. For example, the family is seen as a highly functional institution for the maintenance and support of the social system. The family ensures the preparation of the younger generation for future roles; it ensures the physical well-being of its members; it regulates sexual activity; and it provides a social identity from birth.

The focus on stability and interdependence suggests that change is something to be avoided, or, at the very best, that change has to be slow in order not to disrupt the system. However, a structural functionalist perspective also recognizes that functions might be viewed differently. What is functional for one group may be dysfunctional for another group (Merton, 1957). This raises questions about how an activity can be functional for society as a whole. The Columbia University sociologist, Robert Merton (1957), addressed this issue by distinguishing between **manifest functions** "which are intended and recognized" and **latent functions** which "are neither intended nor recognized." Thus, for example, a manifest function of the family is to care for the young, but a latent function is to preserve existing power relationships that favor adults and, at times, permit child abuse or neglect. Pope (1942), on the basis of his study of a North Carolina mill town, found that some Baptist manufacturers supported Protestant sects because they provided an outlet for frustrations arising from low wages and poor working conditions.

Religion distracted the mill workers from economic and political organization that might have been more functional in resolving their frustrations.

Functionalists tend to view social systems as cooperative arrangements whose stability rests on common norms and values. But it is questionable whether such uniformity exists and, more important, whether social behavior is simply a manifestation of commonality of values and norms.

Conflict theory. An alternative explanation for social interaction is that it is motivated by the quest for power. In this process, conflict is created. The preeminent conflict theorist, as noted previously, was Karl Marx. Largely ignored in American sociology during the first half of the

C. Wright Mills

century, **conflict theory** and its proponents have been the subject of increasing interest among American and other sociologists in the last two decades. In part, this renewed interest might be attributed to the stormy decades of the sixties and seventies, when the theoretical framework of functionalism and its emphasis on order, stability, and shared values provided little explanation for the sudden emergence of conflict and strife.

Contemporary conflict theorists like C. Wright Mills (1956), Lewis Coser (1956 and 1967), and Ralf Dahrendorf (1969) do not necessarily follow in the footsteps of Marx, in either anticipating a world revolution or seeing the emergence of a class-conscious proletariat ready to challenge the capitalist system. Contemporary conflict theorists tend to focus less on large-scale confrontation and more on conflict within or between groups. Coser (1956), for example, sees conflict between management and labor as leading to positive consequences for both. Dahrendorf (1959), a German sociologist, has argued that Marx's analysis of class conflict may have been valid for the nineteenth century when industrial and political conflict was merged. Today, however, industrial conflict is isolated from political conflict, confined to industry, and "robbed of [its] influence on other spheres of society." More significant to Dahrendorf today is the issue of authority: those who have it by virtue of their position in industry, labor unions, government, and so forth, and those who issue orders to those who lack authority. For Dahrendorf, conflict and consensus are part of society and sociologists should be cognizant of both.

While the issue of conflict and consensus will be subject to continuing empirical studies as well as debate, sociologists today are branching out in their studies of conflict. The Marxist framework is used by some (Wright, 1976; Wright and Perrone, 1977), but others apply the concept of power to other areas of social life. Collins (1975) has applied this approach to the role of

Conflict theorists argue that tension is an integral part of social life and that conflict is essential to change in society. During the unrest of the 1960s and 1970s, the conflict perspective gained popularity as minority groups seized opportunities to demand increased social power.

women. Wilson (1978) regards class as more important than race in explaining the position of black Americans in contemporary society, as well as explaining the conflict that results between blacks and whites. So after a period of relative disfavor in American sociology, conflict theory has reasserted its claim as an important theoretical perspective. In part, this is occurring by broad-

ening of the theory to explain behavior at many levels rather than just in societies as a whole.

Symbolic interactionism. **Symbolic inter- action theory** focuses on interaction between people as the basic unit of social life. Rather than seeing social structures as heavily determining people's behavior (as do the structural functional and conflict theorists), the symbolic interactionists focus on the way social structure itself emerges from the daily interaction between people. Through their interaction people develop a self-identity, a sense of belonging to larger social units (families, communities, a society, and so on), and belief systems. These identities are all subject to renegotiation in the course of day-to-day living. Since most people have fairly routine contexts in which to interact with others (their family, jobs, and friendship groups, for example) a social structure does emerge which has some stability and some influence over ongoing behavior. Nevertheless, symbolic interactionists see daily interaction as a prerequisite to social structure.

George Herbert Mead (1863–1931) is generally considered to have established symbolic interactionism as a sociological theory. He began with the biological fact that humans have the capacity to create symbols and use them to communicate with each other. The creation of symbols with shared meanings, which makes communication possible, occurs through interaction. For example, a child usually learns the meaning of the word "hot" by interacting with his or her parents. This word is a symbol which is then used to refer to a whole range of objects and situations having to do with heat. Mead went on to point out that we also learn to symbolize ourselves. We develop a sense of ourselves by interacting with others and watching their responses (which are, of course, expressed through the use of symbols like smiles or words of praise). In this way, the self becomes both an *object* (our conception of how others react toward us, which Mead called the "me") and a *subject* (our conception of ourselves, the "I"). A young woman who is considered very pretty by others, and related to by others on the basis of her looks (the "me"), may wish others would instead respond to her on the basis of the intelligence which she values in herself (the "I").

Symbolic interactionism, then, focuses on interaction between people and the negotiations which occur through these interactions. In the example above, the young woman might choose to respond to others in ways that reinforce their definition of her: she might dress stylishly, wear a lot of makeup, and seek a career in the entertainment field. She could, of course, choose instead to negotiate interactions that are closer to her preferred view of self. The important point is that behavior (hers and others) will *emerge* through this interaction and manipulation of symbols.

The negotiations which enable social life to emerge have several important characteristics, according to the symbolic interactionists. One is that people do not automatically react to situations they face. Instead, they assess situations and think about the choices they have. William I. Thomas (1863–1947) called this **defining the situation.** Once defined, the result becomes the reality as perceived by the people involved. A teacher, for example, may define a student as unwilling to learn because of inattention in class. The teacher may then ignore the child, thereby ensuring his or her failure, even though the reason for the child's inattention may have been a hearing problem rather than lack of interest.

Many factors go into defining a situation, and several have been explored by symbolic interactionists. Charles Horton Cooley (1864–1929) talked about the **looking-glass self.** This is the reflection of ourselves we get from others as we observe their reactions to our behavior (similar to Mead's concepts of the "I" and the "me"). Erving Goffman (1922–   ) focused on ways people are stigmatized because of their appearance (a disfigured person, for example), a handicap (such as blindness), or their social standing (a prisoner, for instance). In order to negotiate interactions with others in ways which minimize our disadvantages from such stigmas, we compose a fascinating array of strategies which Goffman identifies and discusses within the context of a staged performance (much like a theatrical performance is carefully planned). For example, we may interact with certain people only at

Human beings have the ability to create a self-image by manipulating symbols in their interactions with others. Entertainer Rod Stewart, for example, chooses to project a somewhat bizarre and androgynous image that confirms his fans' expectations of how a rock star behaves.

specific times when we know we will make the best self-presentation. Herbert Blumer adds to the theory the importance of the social and cultural environment for interpersonal negotiations (see Johnson, 1981). He suggests that people carry learned sets of ideas and values which may influence their particular perception of various situations. Encountering a police officer on the street may be reassuring to a middle-class white person but be perceived as a threat to a person who is a member of a minority group.

Focusing on social patterns as emerging from social interaction provides an alternative view to a structural functionalist approach. Social structure is a context for behavior but people are seen as constantly in the process of negotiating specific aspects of their everyday lives. Change can occur in social structures through these negotiations. Nevertheless, social interaction theory has been criticized for being too person-focused and reducing social structure to individual behavior. As a result, a fourth theoretical approach devel-

"Careful, now. I don't like the looks of this."

Drawing by Ed Fisher; © 1977,
The New Yorker Magazine, Inc.

oped to help observers better understand the nature of social interactions and to establish a better linkage between individual interaction and the development of social structure. It is called exchange theory.

Exchange theory. **Exchange theory,** like symbolic interactionism, sees social life as emerging from interpersonal interactions; however, it focuses on the exchange of valued services and benefits and the costs and rewards of these exchanges. In this sense it has economic and psychological perspectives since it sees people as actors who seek to avoid pain and maximize pleasure. People enter into the behavioral exchanges that generate rewards for them, have the least costs involved, and lead to treatment which is relatively similar to that enjoyed by persons similar to themselves (this is called *distributive justice*). In other words, people exchange things with each other (money, labor, affection, and so on) as part of their effort to meet their needs.

George Homans (1910–   ), working at Harvard, was an early exchange theorist whose work was done primarily with small groups. He noted that groups encompassed both internal and external exchanges among their members. Internally groups are concerned with interaction, activities, and sentiments. For example, members of a work group carry out work activities together but in the process they develop interaction patterns which include sentiments or feelings about each other and the activities they share. A work group also is affected by an external environment, the workplace itself. This imposes expectations on group members which, along with the nature of the internal interaction, determine the nature of the costs and rewards to members of the group. Indeed, society as a whole exerts pressure for people to meet certain expectations. Homans noted that at all levels—internal, external, and societal—people calculate rewards and costs and negotiate behavior patterns accordingly. Therefore, exchange theory specifies one of the bases on which social interaction occurs and out of which patterns of behavior (including social change) emerge.

Exchange theorists have attempted to show how the basic process of exchange can be used to organize larger group behavior as well as dyadic (two-person) relationships. Social psychologists John Thibaut (1917–   ) and Harold Kelley (1921–   ) suggest that as groups increase in size the patterns of exchanges will become more complex and indirect. Nevertheless, all the parties involved will be calculating their rewards and costs. At work, for example, supervisors and workers enter into exchanges that include their own behaviors related to each other—the supervisor may authorize a worker to take an extra day off in return for the worker's assumption of a particularly difficult assignment. Yet both function within company rules that are basic to keeping their jobs.

In the process of exchange there is generally a **norm of reciprocity.** This refers to the expectation that there will be a reasonably equal exchange between the people involved. Peter Blau (1918–   ) uses situations in which there is unequal exchange to explain how power and authority develop in relationships and groups. The person receiving more benefits than he or she gives eventually assumes a position of subordination in the relationship. In a group, the person who can provide the most benefits to the other group members becomes the leader. Eventually shared values emerge which give the leader the *right* to expect compliance. This same process of unequal exchange can similarly lead to dominant and subordinate relationships among groups. The ability of oil-producing nations to dominate exchange relationships with other nations is a case in point. The value of their exchange could not be matched by many other nations with whom they interacted. The oil-producing nations derived power over these other nations as a result.

By looking at the way individuals and groups exchange resources desired by each, exchange theorists have attempted to account for both interpersonal and large-scale interaction. A social structure emerges from these sets of exchanges. Like symbolic interactionists, exchange theorists emphasize the subjective definition of what is desirable. Food is only desired by someone who is hungry, after all. They also refer to societal values which in part govern appropriate expectations between parties to an exchange. The two theories—exchange and symbolic interaction—both attempt to link individual behavior with patterns of behavior that are on one hand stable and enduring and on the other hand subject to renegotiation and change.

A look at the historical development of sociology as a discipline emphasizes the core concerns of this social science. Understanding *why* and *how* individuals establish patterns of group behavior is basic to sociology. Why don't we all do only what we want to do? How do we develop structures which organize people in ways that make certain aspects of their behavior highly predictable? A second major concern in sociology is how social patterns can be both enduring and changing. How can women redefine sex roles and still get married? Why do workers want job security, yet complain about boredom at work? The four major theoretical approaches discussed above attempt to address these concerns. None is right or wrong. Each contributes to our understanding. Throughout the rest of the book these theories will be used as part of our exploration of the various areas of sociology. They are fundamental parts of sociology's distinctive perspective on human life.

THE SOCIOLOGICAL IMAGINATION REVISITED

After you study sociology for a while, you will become more aware of how and why people live as they do. You may criticize some elements of society and feel a desire to correct them. This critical spirit has been a major stimulus in the career of a sociologist mentioned earlier in this chapter, C. Wright Mills.

In the middle of the 1950s, Mills took a look at the growing middle class that was prospering during the peacetime that followed the Second World War. His book, *White Collar: The American Middle Class,* demonstrated that this economic class, which had no leadership or common sense of identity, mistakenly believed that it had power and status because it had economic security. Instead, Mills argued in *The Power Elite,* the true power was held by a small, tightly knit group of the population who controlled politics, diverse areas of the military, and big business, and who regularly cooperated with each other.

Responding to his sense of the powerlessness of the average individual, Mills outlined the role he felt sociology should play. He distinguished social problems or "issues" from "personal trou-

On election day, Victoria Woodhull, the "terrible siren," asserts her right to vote at the polls. Frustrated by their place in society, champions of women's rights attempted to improve their lives by making others aware of the circumstances that oppressed many women.

bles" in the following way: if one person in a city of 100,000 loses his or her job, it is a personal trouble; when 1,000 people are out of work, it is a social problem. The distinction is one of degree: a social issue involves a group, not just a single individual. But Mills made an important observation: average people in trouble are most likely to believe that their problems are merely personal troubles. They do not have the sense of belonging to a group. They do not have the ability to see beyond their own lives; therefore, they do not realize there are thousands like them. Mills called on sociologists to show individuals that *they are the products as well as the creators of their times*. He felt that as sociology develops and wins the respect of the public, the consciences of professional sociologists must also develop, keeping the science honest in its methods and relevant to society's need for objective understanding.

It was in urging this heightened consciousness for sociologists and for society at large that Mills outlined the perspective we discussed earlier, "the sociological imagination." He believed that with sociology "the individual can understand his own experience and gauge his own fate only by locating himself within his period—he can know his own chances in life by becoming aware of those of all individuals in his circumstances" (Mills, 1959: 5).

At the beginning of the chapter we noted that sociology differs from social work. As sociologists have sought to respond to Mills' vision, they have done so in ways other than providing social services to people as social workers do. Traditionally, sociologists have taught and done research in colleges and universities. Educating people is a powerful way of making them aware of their relationships with their social world.

Now sociologists are moving more into planning, policy, and consultation. These roles have given them access to societal decision making, informing that process with a knowledge that is uniquely sociological. More detail about the place of sociology and sociologists in the contemporary world may be found on the inside back cover of this book. Here it is sufficient to say that the sociological imagination continues to enrich our social world, and in increasingly varied ways.

SUMMARY

1. The purposes of this chapter are: to define and explore the nature of sociology; to trace the development of sociology and its various theoretical perspectives; and to look at the place of sociology in the contemporary world.

2. Sociology is the scientific study of the structures, functions, and changes in human groups. As a result of such study, sociologists have shown that people relate to each other in predictable patterns of behavior that enable society as a whole, individuals, and groups to function together.

3. As the traditional foundations of European society were undermined with the onset of the Industrial Revolution, there was an increased need to understand and predict social life. The social philosophers tried to understand society in terms of philosophical concepts. As "rational" thinking became more influential, however, social thinkers began to apply the scientific method to the study of society. Sociologists such as Comte, Spencer, Marx, Durkheim, and Weber added more information to the body of sociological knowledge and developed increasingly better and more accurate techniques for gathering and interpreting this information.

4. The theoretical perspectives most commonly adopted by sociologists are outlined below.

   Structural functionalism. Structural functionalists assume that all parts of society are related to all other parts, and they are interested in understanding how each part performs a useful function for society.

   Conflict theory. Conflict theorists interpret social interactions in terms of struggle rather than cooperation, and they link conflict to social change.

   Symbolic interactionism. Symbolic interactionists focus attention on the way patterned behavior emerges from day-to-day human interaction.

   Exchange theory. Exchange theorists use the process of exchange between people and groups to understand how patterned behavior—as well as power and authority—develops.

5. Sociologists work in increasingly diversified settings. In addition to the traditional roles of sociologists as college professors and social researchers, they are now found in government, marketing, personnel, policy, and planning positions.

REVIEW

Key Terms

Sociological imagination

Sociology

Social sciences

Natural sciences

Bourgeoisie

Proletariat

Mechanical solidarity

Organic solidarity

Division of labor

Anomie

Quantitative methods

Theoretical perspective

Structural functionalism

Manifest functions

Latent functions

Conflict theory

Symbolic interaction theory

Defining the situation

Looking-glass self

Exchange theory

Norm of reciprocity

Review and Discussion

1. What most distinguishes sociology from the other social sciences? Which social science is most appealing to you? Why?

2. Why are you taking a course in sociology? How do you hope it will be useful to you in your present or future plans and activities?

3. Why does sociology have so many different theories? Would it be desirable to have one "master" theory? Explain your answer.

4. Think of a social problem (such as crime, spouse abuse, or drug use) and analyze it from one of the four theoretical perspectives discussed. Does it help you gain new insights into the problem?

5. Which theoretical perspective is most like your personal view of society? Which do you think is least valid? Why?

References

Blau, Peter (1964). *Exchange and Power in Social Life.* New York: John Wiley.

Bottomore, T. B. (1981). "A Marxist consideration of Durkheim." *Social Forces* 59: 902–917.

Collins, R. (1974). *Conflict Sociology: Toward an Explanatory Science.* New York: Academic Press.

Cooley, Charles Horton (1902). *Human Nature and the Social Order.* New York: Scribners.

Coser, Lewis A. (1956). *The Functions of Social Conflict.* New York: Free Press.

———— (1967). *Continuities in the Study of Social Conflict.* New York: The Free Press.

Dahrendorf, Ralf (1959). *Class and Class Conflict in Industrial Society.* Palo Alto, Ca.: Stanford University Press.

———— (1969). *Essays in the Theory of Society.* Palo Alto, Ca.: Stanford University Press.

Durkheim, Emile (1897). *Suicide,* transl. by John A. Spaulding and George Simpson. New York: Free Press, 1951.

———— (1960). *The Division of Labor in Society.* Glencoe, Ill.: Free Press.

Fromm, Erich (1964). Foreword, in Karl Marx, *Early Writings,* translated and edited by T. B. Bottomore. New York: McGraw-Hill.

Goffman, Erving (1959). *The Presentation of Self in Everyday Life.* New York: Doubleday.

Homans, George (1961). *Social Behavior: Its Elementary Forms.* New York: Harcourt, Brace and World.

Johnson, Doyle Paul (1981). *Sociological Theory.* New York: John Wiley.

Mead, George Herbert (1934). *Mind, Self and Society,* edited by Charles D. Morris. Chicago: University of Chicago Press.

Merton, Robert (1957). *Social Theory and Social Structure.* Glencoe, Ill.: Free Press.

Mills, C. Wright (1951). *White Collar.* New York: Oxford University Press.

———— (1956). *The Power Elite.* New York: Oxford University Press.

———— (1959). *The Sociological Imagination*. New York: Oxford University Press.

Park, Robert E., with **E. W. Burgess, R. D. McKenzie,** and **Louis Wirth** (1925). *The City*. Chicago: University of Chicago Press.

Parkin, F. (1971). *Class Inequality and Political Order*. New York: Praeger.

Pope, Liston (1942). *Millhands and Preachers*. New Haven: Yale University Press.

Smelser, Neil J., and **R. Stephen Warner** (1976). *Sociological Theory*. Morristown, N.J.: General Learning Press.

Thibaut, John, and **Harold Kelley** (1959). *Social Psychology of Groups*. New York: John Wiley.

Thomas, W. I., and **Florian Znaniecki** (1918). *The Polish Peasant in Europe and America*. Boston: Richard G. Badger.

Tucker, Robert C., ed. (1972). *The Marx–Engels Reader*. New York: W. W. Norton.

Weber, Max (1904). *The Protestant Ethic and the Spirit of Capitalism,* translated by Talcott Parsons. New York: Scribners, 1958.

Wilson, J. W. (1978). *The Declining Significance of Race*. Chicago: University of Chicago Press.

Wright, Erik O. (1976). "Class boundaries in advanced capitalist societies." *New Left Review* 98: 3–41.

Wright, Erik O., and **Luca Perrone** (1977). "Marxist class categories and income inequality." *American Sociological Review* 42: 32–55.

2

THE
SCIENCE OF
SOCIOLOGY

We read about the debate over the value of busing as an effective strategy for school integration quite regularly in the newspaper. Some say it works, while others disagree. Others reject the whole idea of busing on the basis of their moral or religious beliefs. Still others don't particularly care whether it works or not; their concern is simply to avoid long bus trips for their children, and to protect the quality of the schooling their children are currently receiving and which they fear will deteriorate if busing is implemented. Who is right? As it turns out, everyone is. Studies have shown that busing both is and is not effective. Moral and religious beliefs are not usually subject to "proof"—people simply believe what they have been taught is morally or spiritually correct. And one can hardly blame parents for wanting the best for *their* children without taking responsibility for the well-being of everyone else's children. Yet society has a problem. How is a collective decision to be made about the wisdom of accepting or rejecting busing as part of an effort to achieve greater equality of educational opportunity for all?

It is precisely this kind of situation in which sociology can be helpful. Sociological thinking is based on *data,* facts that are systematically collected in the real, observable world. The close link between knowledge and the data which support it is a fundamental characteristic of sociology or, indeed, of any science. In this chapter, we will summarize the most common research techniques used by sociologists to collect and analyze data. We will also look at some of the issues that arise when sociologists try to use data and knowledge to help solve specific social needs, such as a decision about school busing. Ultimately, sociological (or any type of scientific) knowledge is only one part of the process societies use in addressing fundamental concerns. People's values and beliefs usually enter in, as do efforts by groups with vested interests to protect themselves. Still, sociology's contribution can be significant.

THE SCIENTIFIC APPROACH

If you will recall, we defined sociology as the scientific study of the structure, the functioning, and the changes in human groups. An important word in this definition is *scientific.* Sometimes people who are not acquainted with sociology claim that it is just a lot of common sense dressed up in fancy words. "Anybody," they say, "can see what's going on in the world if they'd open their eyes and use a little common sense." But let's take a quick look at this kind of knowledge we call common sense and decide how reliable it really is.

COMMON SENSE AND SCIENCE

"Look before you leap" is a very good piece of common sense that warns us to be cautious. But "He who hesitates is lost" is an equally good piece of common sense that encourages us to act boldly. We know that "Absence makes the heart grow fonder," but we've also heard, "Out of sight, out of mind." Common sense, it seems, can change to fit the situation as we see it.

The term "common sense" refers to the whole range of traditional sayings and popular assumptions we use to support our own view of the world. But that's not science. For example, in the Middle Ages, people noticed that the sick did not have lice like everybody else. The lice, parasites that draw their nourishment from the blood stream, had abandoned their infected and feverish hosts. However, common sense led doctors to conclude that if lice were a sign of health, the way to cure fever was to infect the ill with lice. In our own time, children see violence portrayed on TV as a common way of resolving disputes or handling anger. They could easily conclude that violence is an acceptable—or even desirable—way of behaving when angry or when disagreements arise. Both the Middle

Ages doctor and the young TV viewers have applied common sense to their personal observations. But neither had the advantage of complete and accurate information, and so they drew wrong conclusions. By being scientific, sociology attempts to avoid the pitfalls of common sense by seeing beyond what *seems* obvious.

As a science, sociology is an accumulation of systematically collected data and concepts, and theories related to these data. The term **data** refers to facts collected by means of the research techniques that will be described in this chapter. Whether they are astronomers, biochemists, or sociologists, scientists deal in fact, focusing on phenomena that can be counted, measured, or tested. The astronomer follows the movements of the stars with a telescope, recording observations in precise mathematical terms. The biochemist submits material to microscopic examination and chemical tests, recording each change in temperature, volume, color, and so on. The sociologist studies group behavior by gathering statistics, administering questionnaires, observing and recording group activities, and conducting interviews and laboratory experiments. Precision and systematic collection and analysis of data are essential to the scientific method. Such data collected through the scientific method then become the building blocks for future studies, as well as ways to help us describe and understand existing social life. Naturally, mastery of the scientific method requires specialized training. Table 2.1 presents data about the number of persons receiving degrees in sociology during 1979–80.

Many have pointed out that sociology—and the companion social sciences of psychology, political science, economics, and anthropology—are different from the physical sciences, such as physics, chemistry, and biology. This difference was recently described by a prominent sociologist in the following way:

In physics, the phenomena under study are fixed, at least in the sense that, though they may be in

TABLE 2.1 / GRADUATES WITH SOCIOLOGY DEGREES, 1979–80

Degree	Men	Women	Total
Bachelor's	33.3 (6,383)	66.7 (12,781)	100.0 (19,164)
Master's	49.7 (667)	50.3 (674)	100.0 (1,341)
Doctorate	60.9 (355)	39.1 (228)	100.0 (583)

Source: Scientific Manpower Commission, *Manpower Comments* 18 (October, 1981): 20 (based on statistics compiled by the National Center for Education Statistics). Cited in American Sociological Association, *Footnotes* 10, no. 1 (February 1982): 2.

constant movement, they follow a reasonably standard orbit. The physicist is experimenting on the basis of a highly developed and coherent body of theory. And finally, since the phenomena are under the control of the investigator, he does not require their active participation in the experiment. This model is much less appropriate in sociology. . . . The phenomena we study are in movement, and new combinations of phenomena are constantly emerging. Our theory base is much less firm, and our links from data to theory are often exceedingly shaky. Furthermore, we are dealing with active human beings, who can contribute to our study if we allow them to participate." (Whyte, 1982: 20)*

How can disciplines which study such different phenomena be in any sense alike? The answer lies in the research process itself. The social and physical sciences use the same steps when studying phenomena of interest, even though the phenomena may be quite different. We will

---

*From the presidential address to the American Sociological Association, 1981. By permission of William F. Whyte. Reprinted from William F. Whyte, "Social inventions for solving human problems." *American Sociological Review* (February 1982): 20. By permission of The University of Chicago Press.

examine these steps in the next section. However, we should keep Whyte's analysis in mind, because later we will see that the nature of the phenomena being studied may influence the way the steps are carried out.

THE SCIENTIFIC METHOD

The **scientific method** is a systematic series of steps that scientists use to investigate a problem and to gather information. Through years of trial and error, it has become accepted as the most reliable procedure for gathering information while ensuring maximum objectivity and consistency. But the scientific method is more than just the series of procedural steps. It is also a spirit of curiosity and intellectual adventure that enjoys the work of digging up facts which help us better understand the world around us.

Sociology's use of the scientific method does not mean that sociology neither recognizes nor values other sources of knowledge. Science is only one way of knowing, one which is based on facts (called data) collected using specific research techniques. These techniques have been developed to reduce as much as possible the influence of the scientist's personal values on the collection of facts. The data are, therefore, objective indicators of social reality rather than the researcher's subjective interpretations of reality. Other sources of knowledge include the values and personal beliefs of the thinkers involved. For example, artists have very individual, although often brilliantly insightful, perspectives on human life. Religious thinkers work within an accepted set of beliefs about the human experience. Visionaries and mystics contribute their own highly idiosyncratic but often exciting perspectives to our view of the world. While all types of knowledge can be useful, only scientific knowledge is objective and therefore open to scrutiny by anyone who wishes to challenge the accuracy with which facts were obtained. As we

will see later, the focus on empirical fact also makes scientific data compatible with contemporary techniques of statistical analysis and computer manipulation. Thus, while sociologists recognize and respect alternative ways of knowing, they are committed to following the scientific method as rigorously as possible in their own research.

What exactly is the scientific method? We can begin by briefly describing its four major parts. When carrying out scientific research, the sociologist uses all four of them.

Born a simple peasant girl, Joan of Arc was inspired by visions and voices she believed came from heaven to liberate her oppressed countrymen from the English. She embarked upon her mission at the age of seventeen and subsequently led the French army to victory at the siege of Orléans.

I. Formulating the Problem

The researcher first chooses the question to be answered by scientific investigation. After examining the existing knowledge on the particular topic, the researcher identifies a specific problem about which more must be discovered.

Formulating the hypothesis. At this point, the scientist forms a **hypothesis,** a tentative relationship that experimentation will seek to prove or to disprove. This is a precise statement that can be tested for specific results. Examples of hypotheses might be, "Television violence stimulates aggressive behavior in children," "Students who smoke marijuana have a greater tendency to engage in premarital coitus," or "Adolescents whose parents are divorced are more apt to have attempted suicide." Note that in each case a single and specific relationship is to be examined. It can be just as valuable to disprove a hypothesis as it is to prove it. The work is never lost. In either case, the researcher has gained a building block upon which to construct further experimentation.

II. Collecting the Data

The scientist must first identify the kind of data that will best suit the requirements of the hypothesis: hours of television watched and programming, observed behavior, or personal testimony about marijuana use and/or sexual experience, to cite a few examples.

Choosing a research design. Next, the manner for gathering these data must be selected. Sociologists regularly use questionnaires, interviews, public records, prearranged laboratory situations, and observations to gather the information they require. Of all the steps, choosing the research design is the most crucial. Data collection is the heart of the scientific method, and it requires both creativity and ingenuity.

III. Analyzing the Data

The scientist summarizes and organizes the data in terms of the hypothesis. In smaller studies, the scientist may look over the assorted data as they are printed on paper, but more and more researchers are using computers as tools to reduce time and to eliminate errors. Usually, data can be interpreted in several ways and the researcher must be careful not to overlook any of the possibilities. If, for example, it is found that students who smoke marijuana have a higher rate of premarital sex, it cannot be concluded that one causes the other. Perhaps both are the results of still other factors yet to be identified.

IV. Drawing a Conclusion

Finally the scientist reports on the experiment in the clearest terms possible. He or she states what concrete information was gained by the research, or if the results were inconclusive; demonstrates how the work has added to knowledge in the particular area; and indicates further research that might be pursued in the same field.

Verifying the findings. If possible, scientists do the same experiment several times to see if they get the same results more than once. Scientific objectivity requires that they maintain a skeptical attitude about their findings. But the more times scientists obtain the same results, the more confidence they have in their discoveries. For this same reason, they publish their experiments in professional journals so that others who wish to may verify the results for themselves.

THE TOOLS OF SOCIOLOGY

For each of the steps of the experimental procedure discussed above, sociologists have a number of "tools" or strategies available to them. We can organize some of them into the following chart.

Formulating the problem
Control of variables

Collecting the data
Laboratory studies
Field studies
Participant observation
Surveys
Case studies

Analyzing the data
Statistics
Tables and charts

Verifying the findings
Determining the validity and reliability

We will introduce each of these tools in the next few sections of the text. First, a brief definition and description will be provided. This will be followed by an in-depth example, often taken from the sociological literature. Finally, methods reminder boxes will appear throughout the text. These will summarize the method and its use as exemplified in various areas of sociology.

We hope that this three-part approach will help you to understand sociological methodology better. However, we also hope the fascination of the process of scientific research will engage your interest and that you will realize how critical research is for enriching the sociological imagination.

FORMULATING THE PROBLEM

Variables

Describing and explaining social phenomena are complex tasks. True, sociologists are concerned with gathering facts and statistics. But "social facts" are extremely complicated. Several factors—group size, ethnic background, religion, education, and so on—may contribute to the occurrence of any behavior in social life.

To describe and explain any social behavior, the sociologist must try to identify as many significant or relevant variables as possible. A **variable** is any measurable quality or condition that is subject to change from individual to individual, group to group, time to time. A variable, in turn, is subdivided into attributes that distinguish and classify people with respect to that category. For example, one such variable is *sex,* and the attributes for sex are *male* and *female.* Another common variable would be *social class,* and specific attributes might be *lower class, middle class,* and *upper class.*

It is important, of course, that the attributes for any variable be mutually exclusive. In other words, each person must exhibit one of the possible attributes of the variable, but no person can exhibit two attributes at the same time. Hence, an individual who may be classified as lower class and female cannot also be described as upper class and/or male. If it is found that subjects of an investigation do exhibit more than one attribute of a particular variable, the researcher has not correctly defined the attributes or the variable in question.

In sociology, as in all sciences, the researcher tries to determine the interaction of one variable with another: of income with divorce rate, for example. The phenomenon being studied is called the **dependent variable,** or the variable that changes in response to changes in the independent variable. Usually the dependent variable is an attitude (such as racial feelings or political beliefs) or a behavior (such as divorce or delinquency). It is called "dependent" because it is influenced by, or depends on, other variables.

The variable that the researcher controls for experimental purposes is the **independent variable.** The sociologist tests for the effect that the independent variable has on the dependent variable. A basic scientific assumption is important to the logic of such experimenting: *the independent variable always precedes the dependent variable in* *time;* a person's behavior today cannot be caused by some unknown factor that will happen tomorrow. In the complexity of human behavior, however, this time sequence is often not easy to determine.

The independent variable can be manipulated by the researcher. He or she can select families with high, low, or median incomes in order to determine the effect of income on divorce rate, for example, or choose males or females to test the effect of sex on racial attitudes. Because racial attitude does not cause sex, we say that sex is independent of this attitude. Since sex (the independent variable) may influence racial attitude (the dependent variable) the **causal variable** in research is the independent variable (Cole, 1976: 33–34).

COLLECTING THE DATA

There are a number of methods commonly used by sociologists to collect data. Each has its particular advantages and disadvantages. We will look at these methods in turn and try to identify the research situations in which each would be especially useful.

Laboratory Studies

Laboratory studies are experiments conducted in an environment that the sociologist controls. This ranges from the way subjects are introduced to the experiment, to the size and arrangement of the room in which the study takes place, to the distance between subject and subject, and subject and experimenter. Experimenters can record subjects' responses exactly with tape recorders, video tape, and other equipment. Once they have agreed to participate in the experiment, subjects are a captive audience. Intrusion and other outside interferences are reduced. In the laboratory, very little is left to chance.

The usual laboratory study involves two groups of subjects to be tested. One set, the **experimental group,** is a group whose behavior in response to a specific variable is to be observed and measured. The other, the **control group,** is one that experiences everything experienced by the experimental group except the independent variable.

For example, a researcher may want to investigate the relationship between frustration and aggression: when people are frustrated, do they tend to behave more aggressively toward others? After she selects twenty children as her subjects, her first step will be to divide them into two groups: a control group and an experimental group. The experimental group includes subjects whose behavior is observed and measured under conditions precisely controlled by the experimenter. As we saw above, the control group is a group of subjects whose behavior is not affected by the experimental conditions, but who are included for purposes of comparison with the experimental group. Unless the control and experimental groups are as similar as possible, the results of the experiment will not be valid. For example, if all the children in one group came from low-income families, while all those in the second group came from middle-income families, the results of this study might be distorted by the influence of an extraneous variable: social class. The researcher would not be able to tell if her results were caused by differences in social class or by the independent variable that she has chosen to test experimentally.

In this experiment, Group A, the control group, will be invited to the laboratory, taken to a room full of toys, and allowed to play as they like. Group B, the experimental group, will also be taken to the same room where they too may play as they like. After a few minutes the researcher will return, yell at the children in Group B for touching the toys, and take the toys away. (The children's frustration is the independent variable.) Then the researcher will return, leave a large stuffed bear, and retire behind a two-way mirror to see what, if any, new behavior these events may have provoked. (Aggression is the dependent variable.) The presence of a control group enables the researcher to eliminate the possibility that some unanticipated conditions are causing the observed behavior, instead of the independent variable. For example, the researcher might want to eliminate the possibility that all children become aggressive when they participate in an experiment. If the frustrated children in the experimental group *do* behave aggressively, but the children in the control group *do not,* the researcher can conclude that frustration does provoke aggression.

If carefully designed and executed, laboratory experiments can provide extremely useful insights into different kinds of social behavior. It would be difficult to measure aggression so precisely without laboratory controls. However, there are obviously limits to the usefulness of laboratory studies. For instance, not all the behavior sociologists wish to study can be brought into the laboratory. A riot, a day's work, or a spontaneous family quarrel cannot be artificially created. In addition, laboratory subjects often exhibit changes in behavior known as the *researcher effect* (similar to the Hawthorne effect, to be discussed in the following section). Aware that they are in a special environment for experimental purposes, subjects will sometimes try to figure out what is expected of them and perform accordingly. They change their usual behavior in an effort to be "good" subjects, thereby unwittingly distorting the data the researcher is trying to collect. For this reason, among others, it is necessary for the researcher to examine even tight controls carefully to see that they do not allow for behavior other than that which is the object of the experiment.

Field Studies

Sometimes sociologists are able to find a natural setting "in the field" where variables can be controlled much as in a laboratory environ-

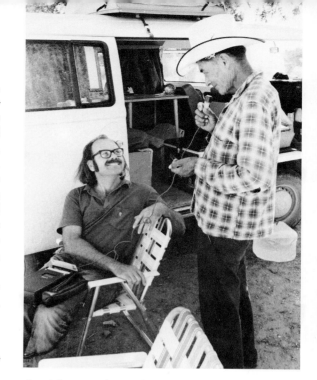

A sociologist conducts a field interview on an American Indian reservation.

ment. In a sense, a field study tries to maximize both spontaneity and control. People are observed in their daily routines, yet these can be controlled in ways which minimally disrupt the ongoing behavior of interest. Field studies have been carried out in prisons, hospitals, offices, and factories. As in laboratory experiments, the sociologist observes both an experimental and a control group. Field studies, then, avoid the artificial atmosphere of laboratory experiments and attempt to take advantage of natural settings which also allow for the control of the variables being studied.

In a classic study known as the Hawthorne experiments, researchers from Harvard moved into a manufacturing plant of the Western Electric Company at Hawthorne, Massachusetts. Many separate studies were carried out in order to study what factors influenced worker output and efficiency. But the results of one experiment—

designed to determine the effect of illumination on worker efficiency—are especially intriguing.

Researchers selected workers who were similar with respect to characteristics which could affect the outcomes of the research: age, length of time with the company, and type of task performed, for example. This is called *matching* subjects. These workers were then divided into a control group and an experimental group. While illumination level was held constant for the control group, the lighting was varied for the test group, and the productivity of each worker was then recorded. To the surprise of the experimenters, not only did the production of both control and test groups increase at the same rate, but the production increases of the test group seemed unaffected by the amount of lighting. Workers kept producing more even when they were working almost in darkness.

Apparently some factor other than lighting was operating to produce these effects. Named the **Hawthorne effect,** this "unknown" factor turned out to be the effect of the investigation itself. Productivity increased in both control and experimental groups because workers, conscious of participating in an experiment and being observed, changed their normal behavior patterns. They were responding to the personal attention received from the investigators.

In order to avoid the Hawthorne effect, field researchers have devised various procedures to prevent their subjects from ever finding out that they are participating in a research study. In a study of homosexual activity in men's rest rooms, Laud Humphreys (1970: 11–25) took down the license plate numbers of the men he observed, and after tracing their identities, conducted interviews with them, gathering information as part of a survey whose major purpose was the assessment of health care. (Naturally he took precautions to protect the names of the men in his study.)

While the use of deceptive or unobtrusive methods raises serious ethical questions, the rich possibilities of field research continue to make it a popular form of sociological research. Field researchers are acutely aware of the need to consider thoroughly the possible consequences of their study before designing their research. When these ethical considerations can be resolved in a professionally responsible manner, field studies make possible the study of behaviors that can rarely be studied successfully in laboratory settings.

Participant Observation

Rather than observing their subjects under controlled conditions, some sociologists actually take part in the activities they want to study, joining a gang, or the Army, or a ballet troupe, and assuming the role of a group member. This is called **participant observation.** By living and interacting on a daily basis with a group of people, the sociologist can gain valuable insight into the behavior, attitudes, and social organization of the group being studied.

Such in-depth information could probably not be acquired through other methodological techniques, such as interviews or laboratory experiments. The information obtained through the use of these methods is limited to the questions the interviewer asks or to the design of the experiment. In other words, the researchers select in advance the behaviors they wish to study. Obviously, then, the use of such methods is possible only when the researcher has some previous knowledge of the phenomenon to be studied. However, the participant observer is open to discovering details of social behavior of which he or she has little or no prior knowledge.

Generally, a sociologist doing a participant-observation study will live and interact with the group under study, participating as much as possible as a member of the group, for an extended period of time. For example, in his classic study of life in an Italian ghetto (which

John Howard Griffin, author of Black Like Me, *posed as a black man in order to experience firsthand what it was like to be a member of a minority group during the late 1950s.*

he called "Cornerville"), William Foote Whyte spent three and a half years in the community. He roomed with a local family, joined clubs, worked for a local politician, and "hung-out" with the street people. In his words:

. . . I spent a great deal of time simply hanging around with them and participating in their various activities. I bowled, played baseball and softball, shot a little pool, played cards, and ate and drank with my Cornerville friends. This active participation gave me something in common with them so that we had other things to talk about

besides the weather. It broke down the social barriers and made it possible for me to be taken into the intimate life of the group. (Whyte, 1955: 256)

Before the publication of Whyte's *Street Corner Society,* sociologists knew relatively little about street gangs and life in urban ethnic neighborhoods. Most researchers assumed there was a high degree of social disorganization in the ghetto. To the contrary, Whyte found that relationships were remarkably stable in Cornerville; friendships which developed in childhood often continued through adult life. Street gangs were organized in terms of a very explicit hierarchy; mutual obligations between gang members were clearly defined. Gangs provided a wealth of social services to members, and leaders acted as a link between the gang and the outside world, which most gang members knew little about.

The researcher who actually joins the group being studied faces the problem of remaining objective. Being used to daily activities in the group, the researcher may take them for granted and lose the objectivity necessary to accurately describe and observe behavior. The researcher may also accept the group's own values, protecting and defending them rather than examining their development and functions in the group. When the sociologist over-identifies with the group being studied, he or she is less likely to benefit from studying the group as a participant observer. In the final analysis, the quality of participant-observation study depends on the researcher's ability to organize observations in a systematic way, to combine sensitivity with objectivity, and to interact fully with his or her subjects. Such studies cannot be duplicated and verified as easily as laboratory experiments, but they provide unique opportunities for intimate observations and deep insights.

Surveys

The **survey** is a technique that enables a researcher to gather information about a social phenomenon involving large numbers of people. This kind of "overall" information about populations is extremely important in mass societies, and it underlies much of the decision-making process within governments, businesses, and civil organizations. Surveys may be used to describe populations in terms of such demographic characteristics as age, sex, and race, or in terms of such socioeconomic characteristics as income, residence, and education. Surveys are also done which question people about their attitudes, opinions, and preferences. In all cases, surveys help the observers of a society to describe that society in a general way.

The total category of people who are to be investigated is known as the **population** of the survey. Later in the book we will look at the results of a survey done to understand student sexual activity on college and university campuses in the U.S. The population in such a survey would be respondents from all college and university campuses. When all of them had answered the questions comprising the survey, we would have data from the whole population with which to describe the behavior of its members. If, as is most often the case, the population is so large that a study of all its members is impractical, a researcher may choose to study only a small **sample:** a specific group of subjects drawn from a larger population. In the survey mentioned above, this was the case. Only 150 campuses were studied so that respondents were drawn from this subpart of the total population. Whereas surveys are generally done using samples because of time and money factors, a very famous survey uses the total population rather than a sample: the United States Census taken every ten years. Here, every member of the United States population is supposed to be included in the survey.

Survey researchers who utilize a sample usually wish to generalize from the sample to the entire population of their study. In order to do so with any degree of confidence, the researcher must choose a sample that is representative: one that contains a cross section of all the major characteristics present in the larger survey population. For example, if the survey population is to be joggers in the Chicago area, and it is known that 30 percent of this population are female or that 15 percent of these joggers are over the age of fifty, the sample should also contain proportionate percentages of people with these characteristics. Sex and age would be considered major characteristics in an athletic population. By contrast, hair color or national origin might not be factors to be considered in drawing a representative sample of joggers.

Once the sample is selected, the researcher begins to conduct interviews or to administer questionnaires. This may be done in a number of different ways: by phone or mail, or person-to-person, either on the street, in an office, or house-to-house. It is extremely important that each individual selected to be included in the sample respond to the survey; otherwise the sample will no longer be representative. Depending on the characteristics he or she wishes to study and to measure, the sociologist may ask either *structured* or *unstructured questions*. Unstructured questions allow respondents to answer in their own words and in whatever depth desired; for example, "How do you feel about abortion?" Structured questions require respondents to fit their answers into a predetermined set of choices; for example, "Please complete the following: I feel abortion is morally acceptable: (a) under no circumstances; (b) only when the mother's life is at stake; (c) any time before pregnancy has advanced three months; (d) any time at the mother's discretion."

While surveys enable researchers to measure certain kinds of behavior and attitudes with precision, they also have limitations. There is always the possibility that the researcher may misinterpret answers or influence a response to a question. In addition, there is no way of making sure that respondents take the survey seriously or that they will understand the questions. Interpretations of questions may vary from one person to the next, and these interpretations will

One of the first scientists to study human sexual behavior, Alfred C. Kinsey (far right) founded the Institute for Sexual Research. In personal interviews, he and his colleagues conducted a pioneer survey of the sexual activities of thousands of men and women in the United States and Canada.

affect the answers that are given. For example, some students who are asked about incidents in which they defied their parents may list events like drinking beer. Others may consider such events as too insignificant to mention. Surveys must also define whether the purpose is to find out about attitudes or about behavior, since the two are frequently different. For example, knowing that a person believes in racial equality does not necessarily mean that he or she does not practice racial discrimination. Researchers may survey attitudes, behaviors, or both, but knowledge about one of these cannot be used to generalize about the other. Similarly, attitudes may vary greatly over a short period of time. For example, when polling public opinion before a national election, the Gallup and Harris polls obtain a running series of surveys from week to

week as actions or statements by the candidates affect the public's evaluations. Thus, while surveys are valuable when we seek to understand and to describe the behavior or characteristics of a large group of people, researchers must exercise great care in developing questions and procedures that will obtain the needed information as precisely as possible.

Case Studies

A **case study** is an attempt to look at a research problem in depth. While the researcher conducting a survey seeks general knowledge about a large number of people, the scientist who undertakes a case study seeks detailed knowledge of a more limited population: a person, a family, an organization, a culture group, a community.

The case study may combine several of the research techniques already discussed—participant observation and questionnaires when studying a community, for example. The challenge of this research technique is to choose the mix of different methods which will best combine to provide answers to the research question.

Case studies have often been done with social phenomena which occurred in the past. Historical events have been pieced together through intensive investigation of public records, letters, diaries, folklore, and the recollection of any eyewitnesses who might still be living. For example, a modern urban riot or other sudden event cannot be adequately studied in progress even if the sociologist is lucky enough to witness it. Interviews and participant observation could be done during the riot, but afterwards other information about its causes and effects would also be needed to make it a case study.

Many exciting case studies have also been conducted on social phenomena in progress over an extended period of time. For example, Susan Sheehan conducted extensive interviews with a professional criminal (and others) to understand his life both in and out of prison. She also collected voluminous other information about his prison and the whole prison system in order to put the facts of his life in social context. Friends and personal records were also consulted. *A Prison and a Prisoner* (1978), the edited version of these interviews, traces the progress of the life of a professional thief from early initiation to the skills of the trade through recollections of specific crimes and personalities, arrests, prison, and the problems of rehabilitation. At the same time, this intimate personal account also offers a look at the social forces that encourage people to take up a life of crime.

While case studies can provide a deeper understanding of a particular topic, it is not clear how far their findings should be generalized. For example, to what degree are the details of a specific criminal career helpful in understanding the behavior of all other criminals? The results of a case study may or may not be representative of any larger population. The strength of these studies is that they offer a mixture of data that can suggest what kinds of other representative investigations are needed.

ANALYZING THE DATA
Statistics

Statistical analysis is one of the most important tools available to researchers. If the data collected are quantified or expressed numerically, the sociologist can make statistical measurements. Statistics can provide methods for describing, summarizing, and organizing data—**descriptive statistics**—as well as for making predictions and estimations—**inferential statistics.** Statistical analysis is especially important when large amounts of data have been collected, and when one wishes to make decisions with a known probability of accuracy on the basis of the data.

Measures of central tendency. Three types of descriptive measures are commonly used in statistical analysis: the mean, the median, and the mode. These measures of central tendency identify what is "average" or "typical" of a set of data and the people from whom they were obtained. Each type of measure goes about this in a slightly different way, and hence has certain advantages and disadvantages.

You are already familiar with the **mean** because it is the same thing as the *average* you learned in elementary arithmetic. It is calculated by adding up all the scores in a particular list to obtain a sum and then dividing that sum by the total number of scores. Because the mean includes all the scores, it can be distorted by any extreme values. Therefore, when there are extreme scores in a sample, some researchers prefer to use the median as a measure of central tendency. The **median** is the middle value in a set of scores.

For example, the following numbers represent the incomes of seven members of a group:

$2,000–$5,000–$5,000–$8,000–$9,000–
$10,000–$37,000

The middle value of this series is $8,000 (there are three values above it and three below it). Note that the mean in this example is $10,857 (a $76,000 total divided by seven incomes). In this example, the mean is a less accurate representation of most of the incomes than the median because of the one unusually large income ($37,000) in the list. The score that occurs most frequently is called the **mode.** In the example above, the mode is $5,000 because it is the income that occurs most often (twice, while all the others occur only once).

As this example shows, different measures of central tendency may yield different results. The researcher must choose the one that is most likely to provide the descriptive summary of the data which will be most helpful for understanding the data. Measures of central tendency are useful because they describe a characteristic of a group in terms of a single number. However, note that they do not tell us much about the individual members of a group.

Variability

When sociologists want to know more about the attributes of individual members in a set of data, they use a measure called **variability** (also known as dispersion). A measure of variability indicates the degree to which scores are scattered around the center point of the data. For example, the average income of both doctors and actors may be $40,000. But, while most doctors' incomes may cluster close to the average of $40,000, the incomes of actors may be more widely scattered, reflecting, perhaps, the difference in income between small-part actors and movie stars. The distribution of income for actors, then, has *more* variability than the distribution of income for doctors.

Variability is an important aspect of sociological statistical analysis because the potential range of human social behavior is so great. The sciences that investigate physical phenomena often show a lesser degree of dispersion in their measurements. Central tendency, therefore, is most useful in sociological analysis when it is accompanied by measures of the variability of the data.

Correlation

Whereas measures of central tendency and variability are examples of descriptive statistics, correlation exemplifies inferential statistics. Correlation is the degree to which events or variables are related. For example, a sociologist may have noted a tendency in his or her data for people with large incomes also to be highly educated, or for smoking to be related to lung cancer. In each of these cases, it would be desirable to have a precise measure of the relationship between these factors. Correlational analysis provides a tool for this kind of measurement.

The degree of association between two variables is often conveniently summarized in the form of a single number known as a **correlation coefficient.** To illustrate how this works, suppose that couples with the highest incomes also have the highest divorce rates. In other words, divorce rates increase as incomes increase. This sort of one-to-one correspondence between two variables is called a perfect **positive correlation.** On the other hand, if the data showed that divorce rates increase as incomes decline we would have a perfect **negative correlation.**

Once a correlation is established, however, it does not necessarily identify a causal relationship between the variables. Two variables might, in fact, be entirely independent of one another and still have a high correlation. For example, executive salaries and marijuana smoking are both increasing and therefore show a high positive correlation. But this does not prove that high salaries encourage marijuana use, nor does it prove that the use of marijuana increases executives' salaries. Further investigation of other variables is required to understand this simplistic correlation more accurately.

Statistical techniques are important tools for sociologists in their effort to understand the empirical data they collect. Such techniques can become highly complex and an in-depth description of them is inappropriate at this point in your study. Nevertheless, the concepts and examples summarized here should help you to understand and to appreciate statistics as a part of the sociologist's work.

VERIFYING THE FINDINGS

Validity and Reliability

Sociologists often seek to invent measuring devices to assess the variables of people's behavior. Such techniques as questionnaires, scales, tests, and indices are useful ways to describe behavior in the form of empirical data which can be analyzed statistically. If a researcher wanted to study prejudice, for example, he or she probably would not obtain accurate results by asking the subjects if they are prejudiced. The researcher might instead ask subjects to rate various racial and ethnic groups on a numerical scale as to which group is most intelligent, which is second, third, and so on. In this fashion, opinions can be translated into data which lend themselves to statistical analysis.

In using one of these techniques, the sociologist must take precautions to ensure that the measuring procedure is both valid and reliable. **Validity** is the degree to which a research device actually measures the variable it has been designed to measure. For example, does an instrument that was intended to measure prejudice really measure prejudice, or does it in fact measure some other related variable, such as educational level? **Reliability** is the degree to which a research device yields consistent results each time it is used. In other words, a scale, index, test, or

"That's the worst set of opinions I've heard in my entire life."

Drawing by Weber; © 1975,
The New Yorker Magazine, Inc.

questionnaire is said to be reliable when repeated use of its measurements will give similar results. Ideally, a reliable research device will give similar results regardless of the subjects studied, the researcher administering the device, or the setting in which the research is done. One way to check the reliability of a questionnaire, for example, is to have several people coding answers to the questions. If there are significant differences in the ways different people interpret the responses, the questionnaire is unreliable.

In his book, *Questionnaire Design and Attitude Measurement,* A. N. Oppenheim uses the following metaphor to illustrate the differences between reliability and validity:

. . . a clock is supposed to measure "true" time. If it were to show the wrong time, we would say that

Reminder Box / HOW TO READ A TABLE

Sociologists often display data in the form of tables so that important variations in these data may be quickly identified for analysis and interpretation. Therefore, the ability to read and to understand tables is a necessary skill for the student of sociology. Tabular formats vary considerably, yet there are features common to all tables, and following certain steps to reading tables will enable you to get the most information from them.

The first step is to read the *title*. A good title tells you precisely the kind of information you can expect to find in the body of the table. In the case of the Table A, the title indicates that information is presented on deaths due to homicide or suicide, reported by race and sex of victims for the years 1940 through 1975.

The next step is to check for explanatory notes. A *headnote* may be included after the title to explain how the data were collected, how variables were defined, or reasons for choosing certain categories for arranging the data in a specific way. Our table has a headnote explaining that the rates summarized in the second half of the table are based on every 100,000 residents of the country who are over 14. Similarly, *footnotes* may explain such things as incomplete data or possible inaccuracies, as well as give the source of the data. The source given for our sample table is the United States Bureau of the Census. These explanatory notes help the reader judge the accuracy and usefulness of the table.

Next, look at the *units of measurement* that are used. In this table, the figures are presented in absolute numbers in the top of the graph and then as rates (per 100,000) in the lower half. Often, too, the unit of measure will be in thousands or millions and careful reading of *all* the units will avoid confusion about the values presented.

The fourth step is to read the *labels* for each horizontal *row* and vertical *column*. These labels indicate what data are contained in the table and how the researcher subdivided the totals into smaller categories. The totals of the homicides and suicides are arranged by race and sex and by year. (Note, however, that not all years have been included.) Breaking down the totals into subcategories helps in comparing the data. If it is important to know how the categories were defined, the information should be given in the footnote.

Next, check to see what *variability* there is in comparing one column or row with another. By looking at the numbers and rates under the label "Total," for example, we can see that there has been a large increase in homicides and suicides over the years summarized in our table. However, the population has also increased and a simple count does not tell the whole story. Checking the "rates," we see that indeed there are more homicides per 100,000 of the population, but that suicides have occurred at a fairly steady proportionate frequency over the 35 years covered in the table.

Comparing columns, we see that the numbers of female homicide victims in both racial categories are quite similar, but that these numbers represent a much greater rate of victimization for the "Negro and other" females. (A similar comparison may be made for the male homicide victims.) In addition, we can see that whites (both male and female) have been committing suicide in far greater numbers and at greater rates than their minority counterparts. The rates for all categories have increased only slightly over time, with the exception of a more rapid increase among minority males.

Critically examine all of the figures in a table, comparing them in both rows and columns, and draw conclusions from them. Does a comparison of the figures in one row or column show significant differences? Furthermore, carefully consider the source of the

Reminder Box / (continued)

figures presented. Many sources are heavily biased, even though they may be "official." Sources that will in some way benefit from the conclusions drawn from the table should be closely examined. Question also if the categories are useful in gaining insight into the data. Most important, what sociological questions are answered or raised by the data?

TABLE A / HOMICIDE VICTIMS AND SUICIDES, BY RACE AND SEX: 1940 to 1975

Rate per 100,000 resident population, fifteen years old and over

	Homicide victims					Suicides				
		White		Negro and other			White		Negro and other	
Year	Total	Male	Female	Male	Female	Total	Male	Female	Male	Female
Number										
1940	8,329	2,977	796	3,670	886	18,907	13,990	4,294	476	147
1945	7,547	2,759	791	3,210	787	14,782	10,374	3,920	380	108
1950	7,942	2,586	952	3,503	901	17,145	12,755	3,713	542	135
1955	7,418	2,439	922	3,191	866	16,760	12,430	3,662	531	137
1960	8,464	2,832	1,154	3,437	1,041	19,041	13,825	4,296	714	206
1965	10,712	3,660	1,379	4,488	1,185	21,507	14,624	5,718	866	299
1968	14,686	5,106	1,700	6,417	1,463	21,372	14,520	5,692	859	301
1969	15,477	5,215	1,801	6,951	1,510	22,364	14,886	6,152	971	355
1970	16,848	5,865	1,938	7,413	1,632	23,480	15,591	6,468	1,038	383
1971	18,787	6,155	2,106	8,357	1,869	24,092	15,802	6,775	1,058	457
1972	19,638	6,820	2,156	8,822	1,840	25,004	16,476	6,788	1,292	448
1973	20,465	7,411	2,575	8,429	2,050	25,118	16,823	6,589	1,285	421
1974	21,465	7,992	2,656	8,755	2,062	25,683	17,263	6,660	1,332	428
1975	21,310	8,222	2,751	8,331	2,006	27,063	18,206	6,967	1,416	474
Rate										
1940	8.4	6.7	1.8	79.9	18.5	19.2	31.3	9.6	10.4	3.1
1945	7.7	6.8	1.7	71.4	15.2	15.1	25.6	8.2	8.5	2.1
1950	7.2	5.3	1.9	67.4	16.2	15.6	26.0	7.4	10.4	2.4
1955	6.4	4.8	1.7	57.8	14.4	14.5	24.5	6.9	9.6	2.3
1960	6.9	5.3	2.0	56.2	15.6	15.4	25.7	7.6	11.7	3.1
1965	8.0	6.3	2.2	66.6	15.9	16.1	25.3	9.2	12.9	4.0
1968	10.5	8.5	2.6	90.0	18.2	15.2	24.2	8.8	12.1	3.8
1969	10.9	8.6	2.7	95.1	18.3	15.7	24.4	9.3	13.3	4.3
1970	11.6	9.5	2.9	95.9	18.5	16.2	25.3	9.6	13.4	4.3
1971	12.6	10.2	3.1	105.9	20.7	16.2	25.0	9.9	13.4	4.8
1972	13.0	10.6	3.1	108.3	19.7	16.5	25.6	9.7	15.9	4.8
1973	13.3	11.3	3.6	100.7	21.4	16.3	25.7	9.3	15.4	4.4
1974	13.7	12.0	3.7	101.7	20.9	16.4	26.0	9.3	15.5	4.3
1975	13.4	12.2	3.8	93.9	19.7	17.0	27.0	9.6	16.0	4.6

Source: U.S. Bureau of the Census, *Statistical Abstract of the United States: 1977* (98th edition) Washington, D.C., 1977.

it was invalid. If it were sometimes slow and sometimes fast, we would call it unreliable. (Oppenheim, 1966: 70)

As with a clock, the validity and reliability of research devices are essential to the accurate measurement of sociological data.

ETHICAL CONCERNS

Because sociology investigates the details of people's lives and habits, it runs the risk of violating numerous ethical considerations. First, the gathering of personal information may be interpreted as invasion of privacy. Earlier, we mentioned the Hawthorne effect, the change in subjects' behaviors when they know they are being studied. But if researchers conceal their identities in order to acquire accurate information, they become open to accusations of deception.

A second ethical consideration concerns how the research results will be used. Information about people and groups is often power over those people and groups. Furthermore, because research requires financial support, those who provide the money can determine what information will be gathered and to what use that information will be put. This has been a particularly sensitive topic when research is supported by the government.

To address these concerns, the American Sociological Society adopted a code of ethics to which its members are expected to adhere. Among others, the code sets forth the following principles.

1. *Scientific objectivity in research.*
2. *Integrity in research.* Sociologists must seek expert assistance or refuse to carry on research that is beyond their competence.
3. *Respect for the subjects' rights to privacy and dignity.*
4. *Protection of subjects from personal harm.*
5. *Protection of confidentiality of research data.* Although research information is not "privileged communication" in a legal sense, the sociologist must protect both subjects and informants as much as possible.
6. *Honesty in reporting research findings.* Findings must be presented without distortion and no data should be omitted that might significantly alter the interpretation of the findings.
7. *Misuse of research role.* Sociologists must not use research as an excuse to obtain information unrelated to professional purposes.
8. *Report of sources of financial support.*
9. *Disassociation from unethical research.* Sociologists must not enter into research agreements that violate the principles of this code, and they must resign from any arrangement if they discover violations that they are unable to correct.

Through such efforts of sociologists to ensure the ethical nature of their research, the scientific stature of their work is protected, along with the rights of those they study. This balance is always a delicate one. Research that violates the rights of those it studies will ultimately be rejected legally and morally. Biased research purposefully seeking to justify the beliefs or interests of those who paid for the research will be scrutinized by other scientists and exposed as propaganda rather than research. On the other hand, research that is so limited by efforts to be completely acceptable to everyone may lack access to needed data and hence be ineffective.

Many topics which sociologists study are highly controversial. A recent example is the controversy over how much human intelligence is influenced by heredity and how much by the environment. The implications of such research are very great. If heredity is especially important, efforts might be made to control who may have children. If the environment is critical, social programs to improve such things as nutrition,

One controversial topic examined by sociologists has been the impact of heredity and environment on human intelligence. Many feel it is unfair to attribute IQ differences in children from impoverished backgrounds to heredity, for they have never been exposed to the language and values of the middle class that writes intelligence tests in this country.

housing, and schooling would be logical. In the first instance, moral and ethical issues are numerous while in the second, financial issues dominate. In either case, sociological research findings take on tremendous societal significance.

There is a tendency for the people presenting information to be associated with its content, and this has often happened to sociologists. When their research findings do not support "common sense" or people's moralistic stance or the wishes of special interest groups, sociologists—and sociology itself—are sometimes attacked as too radical or merely pseudoscientific. The only rational response to such personal attacks lies in the scientific method. If the researchers can demonstrate the care and accuracy with which their research was done, the results should be accurate descriptions of reality. That is the sociologist's (or any scientist's) responsibility: to describe the world accurately. Many people don't like the picture that emerges. The sometimes desired result—changing the picture—involves affecting political and economic decision-making structures rather than interfering with sociology's efforts to study social behavior scientifically.

THE FUTURE OF SOCIOLOGICAL RESEARCH

In the early 1960s, a large-scale study was carried out by a prominent sociologist for the U.S. Department of Education (Coleman, 1966). Its purpose was to assess the state of equality of education in the United States, and to identify the factors influencing educational equality and inequality. It was a massive and costly study which involved over 4,000 schools throughout the country, 645,000 students, and 20,000 teachers (Ryan, 1976: 44). Yet the report generated more controversy than social change. Criticisms of the report included attacks on both the methodology and the whole research design. For example, a particularly critical observer notes the following:

This massive exercise in statistical purism, in 737 pages of huge double columns, has managed to disguise as findings *what amounts to nothing more than an enormously inflated* restatement of the problem. *(Ryan, 1976: 48)*

At another point this same critic observes:

Despite all of Coleman's confirming evidence (which is spelled out in an inordinate number of pages, graphs and tables), he doesn't reach the heart of the problem. Why don't black children perform as well? On this question Coleman's report is most disappointing. (Ryan, 1976: 45)

These kinds of critiques of sociological research are not at all unusual. For some time there has been a debate between sociologists who emphasize the scientific nature of the discipline and those who feel that the scientific method as it is used in sociology must be tempered with common sense and humanistic values (recall our discussion earlier in the chapter about the differences in the phenomena studied by the physical and the social sciences). Some years ago, C. Wright Mills warned against what he called **abstracted empiricism,** focusing so completely on the collection and analysis of data that one loses sight of the fact that sociological research should contribute in some way to the betterment of society (Mills, 1959). A similar question was raised by Lynd when he asked "Knowledge for what?" (Lynd, 1939). This debate is still very much alive in the discipline (see Table 2.2). Indeed, as the universities of today are pressured to provide concrete, practical solutions to social problems the debate has intensified. No longer, it seems, can sociologists be content simply to study human behavior in order to increase our knowledge. Increasingly there is the expectation that the knowledge will be put to use.

Two recent events help to clarify the issues with which sociology is struggling as it attempts to chart its future. In a book called *Why Sociology Does Not Apply,* a distinction is made between research done from a disciplinary perspective and that done from a policy perspective (Scott and Shore, 1979: 2). The disciplinary perspective adapts the problem being studied to the scientific method (discussed earlier in this chapter). Even more significantly, "The final product is often private in the sense that the results are brought home to the discipline. Often they remain unnoticed by policy-making bodies" (Scott and Shore, 1979: 2). The focus is on knowledge for knowledge's sake, carefully but rather rigidly following a predetermined research procedure. The policy perspective reverses all this, starting instead with the problem to be studied, then developing an appropriate research strategy (based on the scientific method, of course). Then, "Only after policy implications have been stated would one consider (from quite a different point of view) theoretical implications for sociology" (Scott and Shore, 1979: 2). Ob-

TABLE 2.2 / DOCTORATES IN SOCIOLOGY: WHO ARE THEY?

One of the reasons there is such healthy debate in sociology is the diversity of background among sociologists and the varied work activities in which they are engaged. The following data note that less than 60 percent of sociologists with Ph.D.s have bachelor's degrees in sociology. This provides for many points of view in the discipline. The fact that sociologists work in different types of organizations also promotes diversity.

Social Characteristic	1974–75		1979–80	
	Men	Women	Men	Women
Marital Status				
Married	71.9	52.2	68.0	48.6
Not married	23.1	44.7	26.9	49.4
Not known	5.0	3.2	5.1	2.0
Median Age at Doctorate	31.8	31.4	32.8	33.1
Median Time Lapse from BA to Doctorate				
Time in years	8.5	8.7	9.8	9.9
Registered time in years	6.0	6.5	7.3	7.3
Percent with Degree in Same Field as Doctorate				
Bachelor's	54.2	59.4	58.1	55.8
Master's	85.4	86.7	87.8	89.1
Primary Postdoctoral Work Activity				
Teaching	75.5	72.6	56.5	55.7
Research and development	14.5	19.3	29.6	28.3
Administration	2.0	1.9	6.5	5.7
Professional service to individuals	1.2	0.9	1.9	2.4
Other	0.4	1.4	1.9	1.9
Activity unknown	6.5	3.8	3.7	6.0
Total	(734)	(345)	(566)	(405)

Sources: National Research Council, *Summary Report 1975: Doctorate Recipients from United States Universities*. Washington, D.C.: National Academy Press, 1976. National Research Council, *Summary Report 1980: Doctorate Recipients from United States Universities*. Washington, D.C.: National Academy Press, 1981, pp. 32–35. The 1975 figures also appear in: D. Wilkinson, "Percentage of Women Doctorates in Sociology Increases," *Footnotes* 5 (December, 1977): 8. Cited in B. J. Huber, "Sociology Ph.D. Production Declines in Late 70s," *Footnotes* 10, no. 1 (February 1982): 2.

viously this approach focuses much more on the purpose of the research, thereby building in a direct link to application—Lynd's "Knowledge for what."

This same issue was addressed by a recent president of the American Sociological Association. In his presidential address, William Whyte made a plea for more attention to social inventions for the solution of social problems (Whyte, 1982). He, too, noted that much sociological research is too inwardly focused and methodologically rigid (Whyte, 1982: 10). He suggests that an alternative approach is likely to be more fruitful. Using sociological methodology rigidly can actually limit one's insight rather than expand it since procedures and ways of thinking may be

TABLE 2.3 / THE USES OF RESEARCH

The following data report the use of the results of research projects funded by the United States Administration on Aging (AoA). It shows how sociologically relevant scientific research can have many uses.

Type of Use	Number of Uses	Percent of Total (N = 228)	Number of Awards (N = 99)*
Uses by Knowledge Distributors (N = 19 Awards)			
Newspaper article (by others)	50	21.9	13
Newsletter article	11	4.8	5
Magazine article	3	1.3	3
TV or radio coverage (not involving appearances)	13	5.7	4
Other	7	3.1	5
Subtotal	84	36.8	
Uses by Practitioners, Policy Makers, Other Researchers (N = 32 Awards)			
Cited in others' courses	7	3.1	4
Contributed to or cited in other researchers' work	31	13.6	19
Used as a basis for a conference	9	3.9	6
Used as a basis for legislative action (federal)	5	2.2	5
Used as a basis for legislative action (nonfederal)	12	5.3	5
Used as a basis for new or different practices in program management or personnel training by practitioners	41	18.0	18
Used by AoA for subsequent research agenda	3	1.3	2
Other	1	0.4	1
Subtotal	109	47.8	
Uses by Original Researchers (N = 16 Awards)			
Follow-on grant from AoA	8	3.5	8
Related grant from another agency	16	7.0	9
Related grant from AoA	5	2.2	4
Other	6	2.6	3
Subtotal	35	15.3	

* This column lists the number of awards for which each type of use was reported.
Source: Kristina Peterson and Deborah Leinbach, "The Products and Uses of Research Sponsored by the Administration on Aging" (Washington, D.C.: American Institutes for Research, 1981), p. 8.

accepted—and applied—unthinkingly. Whyte feels that often a sociologist's task is to creatively reorganize and interpret already existing data rather than to collect new data. Another important task is to illuminate the social principles underlying behavior rather than only to describe it (recall Ryan's criticism of Coleman's study discussed above). Like Scott and Shore, then, Whyte sees a number of opportunities for sociologists to have more of an impact on social policy by using established research methods in more creative and flexible ways (see Table 2.3).

This creative ferment in sociology has spawned a new area of specialty in the discipline. Variously called **applied sociology,** clinical sociology, or sociological practice, the thrust is the same: to expand into areas where there are clients, people, or groups who contract with sociologists to solve specific problems (Foote, 1981). No longer are sociologists restricting their area of expertise only to *studying* behavior. Now they also see a role for themselves in solving problems by the skillful application of sociological research, including the creative analysis and interpretation of data and knowledge. This idea of applying sociology to the solution of specific social problems is not new: Louis Wirth discussed it in the first half of this century. But it is undergoing a renaissance in terms of the energy being devoted to developing the idea. Already sociologists work for businesses like Xerox and Prudential Life Insurance, helping them to understand better the needs of their workers and customers, and to solve specific organizational problems. The opportunities for future growth seem almost limitless.

Finding a Balance

Not all sociologists are happy about talk of applying sociology. They fear that the rigor of the scientific method will be compromised. Using methodology more flexibly and creatively is one thing, but using it sloppily is another. They are also concerned that sociologists will become enmeshed in ideological and political battles that will result in the loss of scientific objectivity. And, as sociology becomes linked to policy making, support for sociological research may depend more on the wishes of those in power. Funding sources might try to prevent projects they feel will not support their positions, actions that are less likely if sociology is seen as oriented toward pure knowledge rather than practice.

There are, of course, no easy answers. As a growing, living discipline, sociology and the methodology it uses must change and adapt to its environment. If sociology becomes excessively in-grown and detached from reality it loses some of its objectivity and methodological vigor. If it focuses too heavily on practice, it may also lose its ability to illuminate social behavior in a thoughtful, systematic, and objective way. A balance is needed and will probably emerge as sociologists of both persuasions work together to chart the future of the discipline. We hope that your studies will enable you to capture some of the excitement generated by this creative exchange of differing viewpoints within sociology.

SUMMARY ▬▬▬▬▬▬▬▬▬▬

1. Like all scientists, sociologists use the scientific method to investigate a problem and gather information. The scientific method consists of the following steps: formulating the problem; collecting and analyzing the data; and drawing a conclusion.

2. Sociologists use many "tools" to gather information: variables (independent and dependent); laboratory, field, and case studies; participant observation; surveys, statistics, tables, and charts; and methods for ensuring validity and reliability. Each of these tools has a particular role to play in the rigorous application of the scientific method to the wide range of human behavior studied by sociologists.

3. Because sociologists investigate the details of people's lives and habits, they adhere to the highest ethical codes with respect to research methods and use of their findings.

4. Sociology is being seen increasingly as a problem-solving as well as a knowledge-generating discipline. This shift has important implications for the use of methodology, since a problem-oriented focus is thought to require more methodological flexibility and creativity. At present, sociologists are working to find a balance between problem solving and knowledge generating within the discipline.

REVIEW

Key Terms

Data	Control group	Inferential statistics	Negative correlation
Scientific method	Hawthorne effect	Mean	Validity
Hypothesis	Participant observation	Median	Reliability
Variable	Survey	Mode	Abstracted empiricism
Dependent variable	Population	Variability	Applied sociology
Independent variable	Sample	Correlation	
Causal variable	Case study	Correlation coefficient	
Experimental group	Descriptive statistics	Positive correlation	

Review and Discussion

1. How scientific do you think sociology is? On what facts do you base your opinion? How is the scientific stature of sociology affected by the kind of behavior it studies?

2. Have you ever participated in social research? For example, have you ever filled out a questionnaire? Responded to a telephone survey? What were your feelings: Did you like the process? Did you feel you were doing something worthwhile? Did you learn anything from your research experience?

3. How valid do you think newspaper reports of events are? How reliable are they? Explain your answers.

4. Which of the several research techniques discussed in this chapter interests you the most? Why? What kind of questions that you would like answered would your preference help you to answer?

5. What role do you see for computers in sociological research? What dangers can you see in the use of computers for sociological research? On balance, do you think sociologists should be encouraged or discouraged in the use of computers in their research?

References

Cole, Stephen (1976). *The Sociological Method*. Chicago: Rand McNally.

Coleman, James S. (1966). *Equality of Educational Opportunity*. Washington, D. C.: U. S. Office of Education.

Foote, Nelson N. (1981). The theory of sociological practice. Paper presented at the 76th Annual Meeting of the American Sociological Association, August 1981.

Humphreys, Laud (1970). Impersonal sex in public places. *trans*Action 7 (January 1970): 11–25.

Lynd, Robert S. (1939). *Knowledge for What?* Princeton: Princeton University Press.

Mills, C. Wright (1959). *The Sociological Imagination*. New York: Oxford University Press.

Oppenheim, A. N. (1966). *Questionnaire Design and Attitude Measurement*. New York: Basic Books.

Ryan, William (1976). *Blaming the Victim,* rev. ed. New York: Pantheon Books, a Division of Random House, Inc.

Scott, R. A., and **A. Shore** (1979). *Why Sociology Does Not Apply*. New York: Elsevier.

Sheehan, Susan (1978). *A Prison and a Prisoner*. Boston: Houghton Mifflin.

Whyte, William Foote (1955). *Street Corner Society: The Social Structure of an Italian Slum,* rev. ed. Chicago: University of Chicago Press.

———— (1982). Social inventions for solving human problems. *American Sociological Review* (February 1982): 1–13.

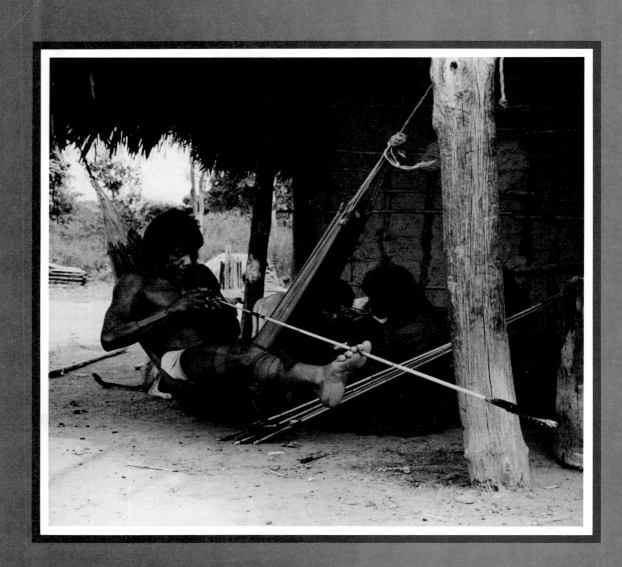

3

CULTURE, SOCIETY, AND HEALTH

Culture and society are interrelated. The patterns by which people live and the values that justify those patterns are learned from infancy until we can hardly imagine any other way. Our culture "dictates" that we marry for love, and never more than one partner at a time. In many African societies people assume that a man will have many wives. In China at the turn of the century, marriages were arranged by the couple's families. American middle-class children are socialized to value competitiveness. The Zunis think little of personal success, and they will only accept positions of leadership if they are forced to do so (Benedict, 1934). For Americans a cow is a source of dairy products and, when slaughtered, steak. In India, the cow is sacred and beef taboo.

As these examples show, every society has its distinctive customs and practices. Social scientists use the term **culture** to refer to a population's characteristic values, beliefs, behaviors, and artifacts which are preserved and transmitted from generation to generation. This definition is rather different from everyday usage in which the word culture suggests refinement, or "class." We say people are cultured if their grammar and their clothes are impeccable, if they prefer classical music and ballet to TV, if they are familiar with Shakespeare and can order their dinner in French. To the sociologist, however, the person watching the afternoon soap operas and the Ozark mountain man possess as much culture as the person watching *King Lear* or listening to an opera. The way people talk to their children and what makes them feel proud or ashamed are as much a part of their culture as sculpture, music, and dance.

In sociology, the concept of culture includes all those aspects of human life that are learned and shared by the members of a society. Shaking hands upon meeting, for example, is part of our culture, as is our belief in romantic love or the idea that hard work brings success. Sociologists sometimes refer to these more intangible aspects of culture as nonmaterial culture. The material elements of culture include all created objects, such as tools, buildings, paper, furniture, in fact, anything that people have constructed or altered to fill a need. Culture is transmitted from generation to generation, a phenomenon unique to humans. We might say that culture takes the place for humans of genetically programmed behavior to cope with the environment in other living species. Culture, however, is infinitely superior as a means of coping with the environment and forming social relations. Culture is more flexible and adaptable than genetically programmed behavior.

Culture, of course, is learned. In the United States, no child is born believing in the virtue of hard work, just as no Zuni child is born with a distrust of ambition. We begin to learn these attitudes and beliefs in infancy. In the process of growing up, we acquire the skills to use the material aspects of our culture—how to read a newspaper, hunt with a bow and arrow, or drive a car. We also develop certain tastes—for beef, or raw fish, or seal blubber. And we acquire certain beliefs and values—progress is good, humility is a virtue, wealth is admirable or desirable. In fact, we learn all of the spoken and unspoken rules that tell us how to behave and how we can expect others in our society to behave.

Many societies share components of the same culture. In fact Western societies have long shared an enormous amount of material and nonmaterial culture. England, Canada, and the United States are thought by some to be virtually the same culturally. The three nations share the same language and have a common heritage of cultural traditions, but there are also significant cultural differences. Each of these societies also has distinct subcultures. They will be discussed later in this chapter.

LANGUAGE

A **language** is a system for communicating facts, ideas, and feelings by using standardized symbols in a grammatical framework recognized by a

Because the Plains Indians kept no written records, oral storytelling and artistic depiction of history and legend became an important means of preserving tradition. Today the cultural heritage of native Americans continues to be preserved by individuals like Sioux artist Calvin Larvie. His dramatic painting, "People of the Sky," portrays the myth of the happy hunting ground where warriors on dappled steeds found the answers to their prayers.

particular society. "Symbols" should not be confused with simple "signs." A *sign* has a direct, unchanging relationship with the thing it represents. For example, dark clouds are a sign of rain recognized by people in any culture. In contrast, the relationship between a *symbol* and what it represents depends only on the agreements people have made. A symbol bears no direct connection to what it represents. The word "rain" does not sound or look like rain, but it does make us think of rain. In French, "pluie" is the word symbol for what we call rain; in German it is "Regen."

Language and Culture

Language is essential to the development and transmission of culture. It records the components of a culture—its knowledge, beliefs, and values. Members of a society use language to share their skills and experiences, not only with those around them, but also across distance and time. Language enables them to recall the past and to plan for the future. Through language, societies transmit their cultures from generation to generation.

Human and Animal Communication

Only human beings have spoken and written language. Other animals can use sound to signal danger, to threaten enemies, and to attract mates, but they lack the ability for abstract thought and the intricate physiological mechanisms necessary for understandable speech. Attempts in the 1950s and earlier to teach chimpanzees to speak were almost all complete failures (Kellog, 1968). One chimp, raised from infancy in a human environment, succeeded in voicing a few barely understandable words (Hayes and Hayes, 1952). Trying to teach chimps to speak is like trying to teach human beings to fly by flapping their arms like wings.

Some experiments have shown advances over what scientists had previously assumed chimps can learn. But how much more they can learn is uncertain. Existing research indicates that their limits are at a level vastly below the language capability of humans.

The Sapir-Whorf hypothesis. Studying the languages of various cultures, anthropologist Edward Sapir and his student Benjamin Lee Whorf observed striking differences in the ways that members of different societies talk about the world. They concluded that language does more than simply provide a means of expression for human thought—language actually determines how an individual from a particular society will think. In each language the world is categorized in different ways. Because each language gives importance to different things in the environment, people from two cultures actually live in two distinct worlds.

One of Sapir and Whorf's most striking examples involves the word "snow." Those who speak English have only one word for it. Although active skiers refer to "powder," "base," and maybe "slush," most people in our culture, most of the time, say "snow." Eskimos, on the other hand, have no general word for snow. Instead, they know between twenty and thirty different kinds of snow, each expressed by a different word. Since snow is such an important element in their lives, they are forced to make distinctions that are meaningless to us.

In a similar way, we have many words to describe our cars. Where a person from another culture might see a roadway full of vehicles of many shapes and sizes, in the United States we distinguish among sedans, station wagons (and woodies), sports cars, compacts, subcompacts, hatchbacks, two doors, four doors, vans, panel trucks, trailer trucks, pick-ups, buses, and jeeps—not to mention particular make and model names. Snow is important to the Eskimos, and we depend on our vehicles a major part of the time. If you were to stand beside an Eskimo and look at a highway covered with snow, each of you would be seeing a different world and each would interpret the scene according to the features that hold the most meaning.

But language/thought differences go still deeper. Whorf compared the language of the Hopi Indians with English. Unlike English, the Hopi language contains no words referring to time. It does not have names for such concepts as days, weeks, or months. And it does not have tenses for verbs: no past (was), present (is), or future (will be). Instead, the Hopi see all things as "becoming." A thing or event has already become (objective or manifest) or it is becoming (subjective or manifesting).

The objective or manifested comprises all that is or has been accessible to the senses, the historical physical universe, in fact, with no attempt to distinguish between present and past, but excluding everything that we call future. The subjective or manifesting comprises all that we call future, but not merely this; it includes equally and indistinguishably all that we call mental—everything that appears or exists in the mind. (Carroll, 1956: 59)

As a result, the Hopi lack the strong consciousness of time and of time passing that is so central to the thoughts and expressions of English-speaking people. We tend to think of time as a straight line, and we continually choose the correct verb form to show when and in what order events happened. To the Hopi, such distinctions are of little importance since, for them, all things are in a constant state of becoming.

The Use and Abuse of Language

The study of how language affects society is called **sociolinguistics.** As we have seen, a people's language reveals much about their chief concerns. In the same way, it can define the way people relate to one another.

English, for example, has few words to distinguish family relationships. A word like "uncle" is used for all the brothers and brothers-in-law of one's mother and father. But in some societies, people feel that it is important to know exactly whose brother is meant and, sometimes, whether it is an older or a younger brother. A person has different obligations to different uncles in such societies. Their language has evolved to express these social values.

Similarly, English has been criticized for the way it supports male dominance. For example, we say, "Each student opened *his* book" and "A person must discipline *himself.*" We speak of *manpower* and *manmade,* and we call ourselves *mankind.* Many argue that such patterns of our

language support sexism in English-speaking societies.

This power of language to direct people's thought is well understood not only by sociologists, but also by politicians and advertisers. In fact, anyone who wants to win an argument or give a certain impression chooses his or her language for the effect it has.

In 1949, George Orwell explored this idea in his novel *1984.* In it he imagined a future society where all aspects of life, including the use of language, were determined and controlled by a totalitarian government. A new language, Newspeak, was devised so that "undesirable" thoughts could not be expressed.

The word free *still existed in Newspeak, but it could only be used in such statements as "This dog is free from lice" or "This field is free from weeds." It could not be used in its old sense of "politically free" or "intellectually free," since political and intellectual freedom no longer existed even as concepts, and were therefore of necessity nameless.*

A person growing up with Newspeak as his sole language would no more know that equal *had once had the secondary meaning of "politically equal," or that* free *had once meant "intellectually free," than, for instance, a person who had never heard of chess would be aware of the secondary meanings attached to* queen *and* rook.

A great many words were euphemisms. Such words, for instance, as joycamp *(forced-labor camp) or* Minipax *(Ministry of Peace, i.e., Ministry of War) meant almost the exact opposite of what they appeared to mean. (Orwell: 303–304)*

We are not approaching Orwell's 1984, but there are some interesting parallel examples of language usage in the 1970s and 1980s. During the Vietnam war, an army colonel complained to reporters that "You always write it's bombing. It's not bombing! It's air support!" Bombing also became "surgical air strikes"; burning jungles "resources control program"; and killing became "termination with extreme prejudice" (Chasin and

Chasin, 1974). Language is also used to enhance status: the garbage collector is a "sanitary engineer," the janitor a "superintendent," and so on. In 1981, tax reduction was the motto of the administration. But when a tax increase became necessary in 1982, the public was told that what was needed is "revenue enhancement." Language, then, becomes an important way for humans to organize their world and, at times, to manipulate it.

ADAPTATION

Although we humans are intellectually superior to the rest of the animal kingdom, we are physically inferior and extremely vulnerable to the environments we inhabit. In fact, without culture—our collective know-how and forms of organization—we would be poorly equipped for survival. The greatest advantage that we humans have is our ability to change our behavior to suit any environment. Although we lack a thick hide or fur to protect us from the elements, we know how to take the animal's skin and put it on our own backs. Though we lack the sharp teeth of a predator, we can make weapons. To protect ourselves and our offspring, who take years to mature, we have developed many kinds of families and societies. Without these cultural solutions to the basic biological problems of obtaining food, keeping warm, defending ourselves, and reproducing, we would be relatively helpless.

In a sense, then, for us, culture takes the place of instincts and specific biological adaptations. Using the only material available—snow—Eskimos build igloos which can withstand the most violent blizzard. In a different environment, the Indians of the Great Plains invented tepees, which provided shade in the summer and warmth in the winter and could be disassembled quickly when the tribe moved to follow the buffalo herds. And in densely populated urban centers, modern architects have looked upward for space and

One significant advantage of the human species is the ability to adapt to different environments. In the harsh tundra of northern Europe, for example, the Lapps have developed a lifestyle centered around the great herds of reindeer, their all-important source of food and materials for clothing.

perfected the art of building skyscrapers. These solutions are the cumulative result of generations of experience with a particular habitat. Most people from Chicago could not step off a plane in the Arctic and hunt a walrus; nor could most Eskimos get around in the subways of Chicago.

Each of them has learned to survive well within a specific environment. Of course, we should also add that each could learn the other's way of life. Cultures are specific and organized around environmental facts. But human beings are flexible and able to adjust to new cultures.

In fact, when viewed in their environmental contexts, most customs that seem exotic and even "unnatural" begin to make sense. In many tropical societies, women refrain from sexual activities with their husbands for as long as three years after a child is born, a custom few Western couples would applaud. This is an adaptive custom important to the culture. The only way infants can obtain the protein they need for growth is through their mothers' milk. If a woman became pregnant soon after giving birth, her milk supply would cease, and the child could develop a protein deficiency (Whiting, 1964). Of course, primitive people would not have known about protein, but they may have believed that they had been given a crying, weak, or sickly child as punishment for their sexual activity.

Not all cultural developments are adaptive in the sense that they improve a people's chances for survival. Industrialization, for example, has had negative as well as positive consequences. On the positive side, it has provided jobs for growing populations and has generated wealth that could be invested in medical research, mass education, and other socially useful projects. Nevertheless, we have recently begun to realize its negative consequences in terms of polluted air and poisoned waters.

Some cultural practices create as many problems as they solve. In the long run, a culture must be sufficiently adaptive that individuals can at least survive, reproduce themselves, and keep their society going. But certain traditions and beliefs may actually serve to prevent a society from solving its biological and social problems. This happened to the Plains Indians when many of them refused to give up their nomadic way of life, even after white hunters had killed off the buffalo that were the Indians' main source of food, clothing, and shelter. Yet, to the Plains Indian, settling down was alien, unthinkable.

Most cultures, of course, do far more than simply provide for people's bare physical existence. They also provide for various psychological and social needs—the need for intimacy and friendship; the need to build and create; and the desire for security, personal honor, and social recognition, for example. Although these needs are intangible, they are as real and as necessary to the human animal as food and shelter are.

Animals do not panic in response to rumors, plants do not grow lush because the gardener promised to add fertilizer to the soil next week, nor do stones roll uphill because other stones believe it more honorable to be located higher on the mountain. . . . Only man behaves as though "society," "honor," "the buying public" and a host of other intangibles were real things. . . . (Storer, 1973: 14)

THE CONTENTS AND ORGANIZATION OF CULTURE

In every culture there is a complex interrelationship of material objects, skills, rules, and values, all working together. A good example of this is our modern highway system. When Henry Ford invented a way to mass-produce the "horseless carriage," he was solving a practical problem in transportation. Today cars are an integral part of our lives. Of course, they would be useless if there were no roads. In the United States we have a well-developed highway system because as a society we value mobility, including the freedom to travel, enough to have devoted vast amounts of time and money to building roads. Of course, these highways would be chaotic if one driver did not know what to expect from the next. So we also have rules concerning how to drive. The rules and values that pattern behavior in society are the subject of this section.

Norms

As we suggested earlier, in every society there are right and wrong ways to drive a car or guide a plow, to organize a family, to speak to one's parents and children, to dress, to earn a living, to gain political power. Sociologists use the term **norms** to refer to these cultural standards that define correct and incorrect behavior. We call behavior that conforms to these standards *normal*.

Folkways. Informal customs regarding the correct way to behave are called **folkways.** In the United States, people usually shake hands when they are introduced, eat dinner with knives and forks, cover their mouths when they cough, dress formally for religious services, wait in line to buy a ticket to a movie. These customs simplify routine encounters.

Mores. In contrast to folkways, **mores** are the norms that a culture considers to be essential. So basic are mores to a society's way of life that they perpetuate themselves from generation to generation virtually unquestioned. In the Western world, nearly everyone considers cannibalism and infanticide not only immoral but unnatural. We view a person who dines on human flesh as something less than human, although cannibalism is practiced in other cultures. We find it difficult to believe that a parent would intentionally kill his or her child, although this practice is acceptable in some societies. Mores are so ingrained, so laden with emotions, that even the thought of transgressing them is often outrageous. People who violate the mores of their societies are usually subjected to the most severe punishment: death, complete ostracism, a life sentence to prison, or a stay in a mental hospital. They may also suffer the internal penalties of guilt, shame, and self-disgust.

Laws. In most societies, some of the mores are formalized into a body of laws. But laws

Although the Moslem custom requiring women to hide themselves from public view may seem outlandish to us, it is completely proper within the context of Moslem culture. Without such a cultural perspective, an outsider cannot objectively judge the customs of other societies.

may also be created to set forth simple and practical rules for order, conduct, and expediency. Generally, **laws** are formalized norms enforced through specific penalties by designated authorities. In small, close-knit societies, laws are usually unnecessary. Everybody knows everybody else, and everybody knows the rules. If one person steals another person's cow, the theft cannot be concealed. In such societies, social pressure—the threat of being ostracized or shamed—keeps most people in line. Indeed, in some preliterate cultures ostracism is such an overwhelming experience that it can be fatal.

In larger, more complex societies, social pressure is not so effective. A person can go to a different neighborhood, steal a purse, and return home in a new set of clothes without any of his or her friends or family knowing. In dormitories, social pressure normally keeps residents from stealing, but not outsiders. When someone breaks into a dorm, the police are called. Laws take over where social pressure fails.

The close connection between laws and a particular society's way of life can be seen in laws that have lost their significance over time. In colonial Boston, for example, a central field was reserved for the grazing of cows. The law has never been removed from the books, and today you could still bring a herd of cows into the large downtown park known as Boston Common. You would receive much criticism for violating modern folkways, but a formal law would still support your action. As with all norms, laws lose their significance when viewed outside of their particular cultural context.

Norms and reality: the double standard. Of course, people do not always obey the law or even their consciences. Norms suggest ideal ways of behaving and what ideal relationships should be. But they do not necessarily describe reality.

For example, for years nearly everyone in the United States condemned sex outside marriage. But over thirty years ago, in his now famous report, Kinsey found that of those sampled one in four married women and one in two married men had committed adultery, and that 20 percent of the women interviewed had experienced premarital sex before the age of twenty (Kinsey, Pomeroy, and Martin, 1948). The Mae Enga of New Guinea believe that women are unclean and that sexual relations are dangerous. But Mae women miraculously continue to bear children (Meggitt, 1964). Young Mexican males spend much of their leisure time seducing young ladies—yet this does not affect their faith that their sisters are absolutely chaste (Severo, 1973).

To some extent, norms can be stretched to fit reality. In the United States, we believe that "all men are created equal"—even though the situations of blacks, Chicanos, Indians, Puerto Ricans, migrant farmers, welfare recipients, communists, and women indicate otherwise. We also believe that our country is a true democracy, governed by freely elected public servants who are responsible to the people—yet we are not shocked when corruption in government is exposed, for we suspect that in truth most politicians are slightly dishonest. Nevertheless, norms can only be stretched so far before some people

begin to rebel. And some norms are inviolable—such as, for example, the norms that forbid murder. Table 3.1 looks at norms considered important by Americans.

Values

Societies expend considerable effort teaching children and reminding adults that there are right and wrong ways to behave. But norms alone do not make a culture, any more than rules alone make a game. A chess match would be intolerably dull if neither player cared whether he or she won and neither appreciated the other's style and cleverness. Norms are the rules of the game; values are the goals and ideals that make the game meaningful.

Sociologists call people's ideas about what is important, admirable, good, beautiful or ugly, exciting or dull, holy or profane their value system. **Values** can be defined as cultural goals and criteria for evaluating people, behavior, experiences, and objects. To a large extent, values,

TABLE 3.1 / BEHAVIORS CONSIDERED DESIRABLE AMONG AMERICANS, 1978

Behavior	Percent Stating Very Important
Good Health	97
Family Life	92
Peace of Mind	91
Respect from Others	76
Having Friends	71
Being Educated	69
Being Employed	60
Having a Religion	58
Having Money	47
Sexual Activity	38
Romantic Love	33

Source: U.S. Bureau of the Census, *Social Indicators III*, Washington, D.C.: U.S. Government Printing Office, 1980, p. LV.

like norms, are culturally determined. The experiences that make people laugh or cry, love or hate, cower or explode in anger vary markedly from culture to culture. Williams (1970) identified a series of "value orientations" in American society. Williams did *not* suggest an American national character, or a basic American personality type based on American values. The enormous diversity of American society would make such an effort hazardous at best. The value orientations identified by Williams are: achievement and success; activity and work; moralism; humanitarianism; efficiency and practicality; progress and material comfort; equality and freedom; democracy; conformity; science; and rationality.

We merely have to look at how middle-class parents socialize their children to recognize how these values shape our lives and experiences. To strive to achieve in school, sports, or interpersonal relations, to defer gratification, and to save and be thrifty are evident in a legion of overt and covert rules. Work and achievement are not simply the domain of the occupational sphere: they are all-encompassing values. Even marriage manuals tell us to work hard and to experiment and eventually every male and female will be a perfect lover. Recreation is not only fun and games; recreation is hard work: "I had a good workout" is the standard by which a game is evaluated. Tennis partners, for example, are matched fairly evenly. There is no fun in playing with a weak partner. Efficiency and practicality coalesce with technology and rationality. The car is the most efficient and practical means of transportation and the assembly line is the most efficient and practical production method, without regard for the consequences. As Williams notes, progress has been an integral part of the nation. But the belief in the capacity of men and women to reason, to create a better life, centered by the late nineteenth century primarily on the economic and technological realms. Progress, achievement, and success were based on scale

and size. On the individual level they meant more, and bigger. The bigger the house, the car, the television set the greater the achievement and success. Note, for example, the difference between the trade unions in the United States and in West European nations. In the latter trade unions were deeply involved in the political realm. In the United States, Samuel Gompers centered the goal of the American worker on "more and more" economic rewards. The more the better: "business unionism" was the trademark of the American labor movement. Table 3.2 presents data about recent values expressed by Americans as interpreted through the national priorities they considered important.

Ethnocentrism. People everywhere are emotionally attached to their folkways and mores. In the United States, not only do we value cleanliness, we tend to look down on people who do not bathe regularly, or purify their water, or confine the exercise of bodily functions to well-scrubbed bathrooms with flush toilets. Sociologists call the tendency to consider the norms and values of other groups inferior to one's own **ethnocentrism.**

Some degree of ethnocentrism is probably necessary to group life. The conviction that we are doing the right thing, that our values and manners are correct, makes a difference in how well we do them. Ethnocentrism helps to hold families, professions, universities, and societies together by strengthening the belief that the practices of one's own culture are the best solutions to life's problems.

For this reason, ethnocentrism may also make us feel that other people's customs are strange and sometimes disgusting. Horace Miner (1956) described the habits of a North American tribe called the Nacirema from the viewpoint of the ethnocentric observer:

*The daily body ritual . . . includes a mouth-rite.
Despite the fact that these people are so punctilious*

TABLE 3.2 / AMERICANS EXPRESS THEIR VALUES, 1971–80

Type of Expenditure by the Nation (U.S.)	Percent of Respondents Who Felt Expenditure Important, Averaged over Period 1971–80
Halt the Rising Crime Rate	65.1
Improve and Protect the Nation's Health	58.8
Deal with Drug Addictions	58.8
Improve and Protect the Environment	53.1
Improve the Nation's Education System	48.9
Solve Problems of the Big Cities	44.2
Improve Conditions of Blacks	27.3
Military, Armaments, and Defense	22.9
Welfare	16.9
Space Exploration	9.0
Foreign Aid	3.8

Source: U.S. Bureau of the Census, *Social Indicators III,* Washington, D.C.: U.S. Government Printing Office, 1980, p. LIX.

about care of the mouth, this rite involves a practice which strikes the uninitiated stranger as revolting. It was reported to me that the ritual consists of inserting a small bundle of hog hairs into the mouth, along with certain magical powders, and then moving the bundle in a highly formalized series of gestures.

In addition to the private mouth-rite, the people seek out a holy-mouth-man once or twice a year. These practitioners have an impressive set of paraphernalia, consisting of a variety of augers, awls, probes, and prods. The use of these objects in the exorcism of the devils of the mouth involves almost unbelievable ritual torture of the client. . . . In the client's view, the purpose of these ministrations is to arrest decay and to draw friends. The extremely sacred and traditional character of the rite is evident in the fact that the natives return to the holy-mouth-men year after year, despite the fact that their teeth continue to decay. (pp. 504–505)

Although Miner was describing our own customs of toothbrushing (spell Nacirema backward), they seem bizarre and foreign because they are removed from the framework of values within which we normally view them. So it is when we look at other cultures. Our reactions to foreign customs are based primarily on our own culture's attitude toward those behaviors. The customs themselves are neutral.

Like most things, ethnocentrism carried to an extreme can prove destructive and maladaptive. The Nazis' belief in the superiority of the "Aryan" race and culture led ultimately to the death of millions of non-"Aryans."

Cultural relativism. Although sociologists as people are no less human and no less ethnocentric than anyone else, they try to suspend their biases when looking as scientists at their own or other cultures. Most sociologists are probably monogamous, but they do not therefore condemn polygamy (the practice of marrying more than one spouse). When sociologists study a polygamous culture, they try to see how this family system interacts with other customs and what functions it performs, in the sense of providing for the biological and the emotional needs of family members. This recognition that a society's norms and values should be examined objectively within their particular cultural context is termed **cultural relativism.**

Quite simply, the point is that, taken out of its cultural surroundings, *any* custom may appear ridiculous or even unnatural. Cultures are highly integrated systems of technology, norms, and values. One has to look at the entire picture to understand the meaning and the function of brushing teeth or polygamy.

It is important to understand that the sociologist remains nonjudgmental. This, however, does not mean that because we understand how various patterns fit together into a system that we condone genocide in Nazi Germany, or the extermination of Native Americans, or the slaughter of millions of people in the Soviet Union in the name of socialism. As private citizens, sociologists no less than other people condemn such behavior. Furthermore, sociological research documents the destructive effects of such behavior on the social structure and social relationships of these societies.

Cultural Integration

Small preindustrial societies tend to be highly integrated; these societies are homogeneous cultures in which values are shared, and there is little room for deviation. Consequently, however advantageous change appears to be, it has major consequences for such societies. In several Australian aborigine societies, the introduction of the steel axe by Europeans undermined age-old myths that described the aborigines' history and place in the universe. Old men once revered for their knowledge of traditions lost prestige and authority; trading relations with neighboring tribes, based on the ceremonial exchange of stone axes, dissolved (Arensberg and Niehoff, 1964).

This situation is not unique to preindustrial societies. While our large, complex society can absorb some changes more easily, there are always adjustments to be made. Contraceptives liberated women from the fear of pregnancy and enabled the family to plan the number of children desired. For some Catholics this freedom of choice led to conflicts with the church and undermined the authority of the priest. Adjustments to change can be seen in other areas as well. The introduction of the car led to changes in dating patterns—and at least in part undermined the role of parents. The decision of the government that

Some cultural practices create as many problems as they solve. In India, for example, cattle, long regarded as sacred animals, are given a great deal of freedom and often cause problems in the industrial context of that developing nation.

poor people could decide how the resources allocated to fight poverty should be used challenged the long-standing cultural belief that professionals and political role-incumbents knew best what was "good" for the poor, thus threatening their authority and power.

As these examples suggest, the different elements of a culture—a people's technology, customs, and beliefs—are intertwined. Everyday routines, ways of earning a living, sex roles, and cherished values are interdependent parts of a culture. One cannot be changed without affecting the others.

Sociologists consider a culture integrated when there are few contradictions between norms and reality, and when norms are relatively consistent so that individuals do not face severe conflicts in different areas of their lives. If a man can fulfill his roles as father and businessman without having to sacrifice one for the other, we would say these norms are consistent.

Degrees of cultural integration vary widely from one society to another. Our society is extremely heterogeneous. Folkways and institutions change as one moves from region to region, from city to country, from rich to poor, from church to boardroom, from labor to management, and from one occupation to another. Ethnic and religious diversity, economic inequality, and specialization all contribute to the complexity and inner contradictions of United States society. The diversity can be stimulating, but it also makes cultural integration more difficult to achieve. The longing some people have for earlier, less complex periods in this nation's history, and the volumes that have been written on the difficulties many have had adjusting to society, attest to the difficulty of achieving high levels of integration in complex cultural systems.

In summary, a culture is a more or less integrated system of norms and values that guides social interaction. People who share a culture know what to expect from one another. But norms, values, and behavior patterns are rarely uniform throughout a society. In our own country, manners, morals, family structure, and so on vary markedly from group to group, for, like all complex societies, ours contains numerous subcultures.

SUBCULTURES

To speak of French, Japanese, or our own culture in the singular, as one way of life, is somewhat misleading. Any New Yorker can spot out-of-towners by the way they dress or talk or act during rush hour on the subway. At a party, a psychiatrist can recognize another psychiatrist after a few minutes of conversation. Students dress, talk, and, to some extent, think differently than people who are functioning in the "real" world outside of school. All of these people, and more—New Yorkers, psychiatrists, the young, the middle-aged, workers, ad executives, homosexuals, soldiers, and inmates—belong to what is loosely called the "American" culture. But each is also part of a distinctive subculture.

Subcultures are variations on the dominant culture, adaptations of majority norms and values. A culture is not a rigid system: People modify norms and values to fit their backgrounds and current needs. When a group of people, consciously or unconsciously, voluntarily or involuntarily, establishes a "cultural island" for itself, acting in ways that distinguish it from other groups and give it a sense of group identity, and when these distinctive thought and behavior patterns are passed on to new members, sociologists consider such a group to be a partially separate culture in its own right, existing within a larger dominant culture.

A subculture may form around race, ethnic or religious background, geographic regions, age, sex, socioeconomic status, profession, or life style. Some people are born into subcultures—into the Little Italys and Chinatowns of our cities, for example. Others choose subcultures, deciding, for example to become a doctor or a Born Again Christian. All subcultures develop ways

Although still part of the larger culture, people who share a particular ethnic heritage with its distinguishing norms and values may interact as a subculture. Here a group of Chinese Americans celebrates the New Year with lion dancing in the streets of New York City.

of expressing their togetherness. Symbols, jokes, customs, distinctive dress, food, neighborhoods, and words create a sense of "us." Nearly everyone in the United States has some subcultural affiliation, some in-groups with which he or she identifies. In the following section, we focus on three—the adolescent subculture, socioeconomic subcultures, and countercultures (a rather unique type of subculture).

The Adolescent Subculture

Adolescence in this and other industrial societies is a difficult, ambiguous time of life. Thirteen- and fourteen-year-olds are beginning to break away from their parents and family, but the day when they will establish households of their own is still years away. The transition is slow and sometimes painful; their parents are ambivalent about their growing independence.

In small towns, especially, adolescents depend on their friends for support, advice, and "social rewards" (praise and prestige). The in-group develops its own standards for dressing, talking, music, dancing, spending Saturdays, and fending off adults. In effect, adolescents create a subculture.

In *The Adolescent Society* (1961), James S. Coleman argued that the isolation of young people in high schools and school-related activities for so long a period has definite countercultural effects. For example, the avowed purpose of going to school is to learn, because society needs educated, skilled people. But Coleman's interviews and questionnaires suggested that a large proportion of high school students in both cities and small towns do not value academic achievement very highly. They may study hard to satisfy their parents and teachers, but among themselves team spirit, athletic achievement, clothes, cars, keeping up with the "in" crowd, and friendliness (or "personality," as it used to be called) are far more important. In this case, the adolescents' values directly contradict those of the school.

The good student may have to choose between alienating friends by getting straight As or lowering his or her standards in order to fit in. But what if the student does not enjoy sports and is not interested in ecology or politics? What if he or she has an overwhelming passion for poetry or the stock market? This kind of student is unlikely to find encouragement from friends, and may become shut out of his or her friends' social life. This is not to say that all adolescents are conformists, but that nonconformists may be stranded between parents and peers who do not understand. Because adolescents are so isolated and interdependent, the chances for individuals to feel good about themselves—to feel acceptable—are limited. As a result, they are especially vulnerable to group pressures.

Today, there are new subcultures in the high school, although the patterns of the 1950s are reemerging as well, with some modification. Peer pressures have led to alcoholism and the use of drugs. The number of out-of-wedlock pregnancies has increased among teenagers, and the proportion of births out of wedlock has also grown rapidly among teenagers. In New York City in 1980, for example, close to 86 percent of the births were to women in their early teens. Many attribute this rise to peer pressure to be active sexually.

Class Subcultures

Adults, too, are segregated. Often they choose a home in a neighborhood with people more or less like themselves, and pick friends among their neighbors, coworkers, and church members. In other words, they live and form ties with "their own kind."

In 1962, sociologist Herbert J. Gans studied the West End of Boston, a low-income, Italian-American community. At first, he assumed that the community's Italian heritage would strongly influence its cultural patterns. As his study progressed, though, he found that little of the Old World culture survived beyond the second generation, and he gradually began to see that the subculture of the West End was an adjustment to working-class economic conditions, and not an extension of the "Italian way of life."

Gans developed this point by comparing the attitudes of the members of the various economic subcultures (lower class, working class, middle class, and upper middle class) toward family, friends, education, and the outside world (Gans, Chap. 11). He found that working-class men tend to see their jobs primarily as the way to provide for their families—they work because they have to, not for self-fulfillment or because their work is satisfying in itself. The working-class man plays a decisive role in his family's life, and often spends his leisure time with his male cronies. The working-class woman is usually responsible for home and child care (although with more women joining the labor force, this situation is gradually changing). She frequently spends her spare time with female relatives. Thus, wives and husbands share a roof and children, but tend to lead separate lives. Romantic expectations in a working-class marriage are low: husbands and wives do not really expect their spouse to understand or listen to their troubles, and they do not spend time discussing their relationship (see Komarovsky, 1964). Their children are expected to be seen but not heard, and education is regarded primarily as a way of keeping children off the streets and out of trouble. For the members of the working class, the family is the center and sanctuary of their lives, and they tend to view the outside world with suspicion (see Table 3.3).

In contrast, Gans found that the middle classes make little or no distinction between the family and the outside world. Family members see themselves as partners in the effort to improve their position in society and believe that, for the most part, society is on their side. Wife and husband devote themselves to job and family in the hope of improving their family's way of life

TABLE 3.3 / EVALUATION OF LIFE IN THE U.S.

The following data demonstrate class differences in the views of respondents to their lives in American society. Education and income are used as indicators of class in this table. It is clear that the higher the social class, the more likely people are to feel that their lives are improving.

Characteristics	Percent Who Think Life in the U.S. Is Getting Better	
Education	*1971*	*1978*
8 years or less	12	11
9 to 11 years	11	14
12 years	17	15
13 to 15 years	22	20
16 years or more	27	26
Income		
Less than $4,000	12	14
$4,000 to 7,999	13	16
$8,000 to 11,999	15	16
$12,000 to 15,999	17	17
$16,000 to 22,999	16	18
$23,000 to 29,999	20	17
$30,000 and over	24	20

Source: U.S. Bureau of the Census, *Social Indicators III*, Washington, D.C.: U.S. Government Printing Office, 1980, p. LX.

and standard of living. Job success is a prime concern because the family's status depends on it.

The middle-class family is child-centered. Husband and wife spend a lot of time with their children. A great deal of attention is paid to giving the children a good education, encouraging them to work hard, and helping them with homework so that one day they may have a prestigious and secure career. In the area of friendships, the middle-class husband and wife entertain together and associate with other families who share their interests.

After suggesting that the sharp differences in outlook and values between the economic subcultures make moving up the social ladder extremely difficult, Gans concluded:

Each subculture (lower class, working class, middle class, and upper middle class) is an organized set of related responses that has developed out of people's efforts to cope with the opportunities, incentives, and rewards, as well as the deprivations, prohibitions, and pressures which the natural environment and society—that complex of coexisting and competing subcultures—offer to them. (p. 249)

Gans thus suggested that economic opportunities affect the way individuals perceive the world around them, their jobs, and even their families. Parents pass on to their children the values they have developed in response to social conditions. In Gans's view, the Italian-American West Enders (and, by implication, other working-class people) "were not simply frustrated seekers of middle-class values. Their way of life constitutes a distinct and independent working-class subculture that bore little resemblance to the middle class" (p. x).

Countercultures

Subcultures are adaptations to the realities of life, and a subculture may modify the dominant cultural patterns in an effort to adapt to a culture, as many new immigrants have done. A subculture need not reject the dominant culture, but countercultures do. Almost on principle what the existing culture accepts as "good," the counterculture invariably sees as bad.

Sociologist Kenneth Westhues states that there are two ways to define a **counterculture:**

. . . an ideological level and . . . behavioral level. On the ideological level, a counterculture is a set of beliefs and values which radically reject the dominant culture of a society and prescribe a sectarian alternative. On the behavioral level a counterculture is a group of people who, because they accept such beliefs and values, behave in such a radically

nonconformist way that they tend to drop out of the society. (1972: 9–10).

Utopian communities constitute a counter-culture ideologically and behaviorally. Members of the Oneida community, for example, rejected the values of the dominant culture, "dropped" out, and established their own community. The cultural patterns of the Oneida community were clearly contrary to the larger society; in fact, they were highly offensive to it. Among the Oneidians the type of family structure most of us take for granted was nonexistent. Sexual relations were open, but emotional ties to a specific member of the opposite sex were forbidden. An older male was assigned as a sexual partner to a young woman, and an older woman to a young man. The dominant values were egalitarianism and allegiance to the community.

Not all counterculture groups drop out; some remain and hope to change the culture and its values. A variety of countercultures prolifer-ated during the 1960s. And while in one way or another all appeared to be opposed to the values and norms of the dominant culture, there were considerable variations. Some emphasized the sensual and spontaneous; others, opposed to the dominant values of wealth, material accumula-tion, hierarchy, and dominance, aimed for a new social order. The motto of the so-called flower children was love. The radical left and the Black Panthers wanted to eliminate racism and the culture of capitalism. They sought to change the existing culture, and to establish a new and what they perceived as a "just" normative system.

Yinger (1977) points out that the United States (and England) has a strong tradition of dissent. France and Germany—with less of a tradition of dissent—have experienced revolu-tionary and counterrevolutionary cycles. But the strong tradition of the legitimacy of dissent in the United States does not mean that widespread

The United States remains a nation with a strong tradition of dissent. This photo shows New Hampshire state police attempting to break up a 1979 demonstration staged by the Clamshell Alliance, an antinuclear group that tried to block delivery of a nuclear-reactor containment vessel to Seabrook.

countercultural challenges do not create strains and value conflicts. The counterculture of the 1960s was not limited to the radical left or Black Panthers. It was also a conflict between the "hard hats" and the "long hairs"; between the peace groups and the supporters of the war in Vietnam; between students and administrators; between youth and elders.

The end of the war in Vietnam, the abolition of discriminatory laws against blacks, increased integration, and changed norms about the propriety of long hair and other patterns of behavior suggest that some of the values of the counterculture have become part of the normative structure. This has helped reduce the strain and allowed for cultural reintegration.

The decade of the 1980s is not without its counterculture, but the changes of the last two decades have made the counterculture less value-laden. It is instructive to compare the hostility encountered by the members of the Oneida community with the proliferation of communes in the cities and rural areas of America in the 1970s. Today's communes may not be viewed by their neighbors as desirable, but many are tolerated or seen as alternative life styles.

Members of one counterculture, for example, wanted to establish a commune based on brotherhood and love, but their effort had a tragic ending. Jim Jones led a tight collective of followers to Guyana to escape the evils of American society. Members shortly discovered that the commune was based neither on love, nor on brotherhood. The commune was firmly controlled by the leader, Jones, who required each member to hand over his or her financial resources, to work long hours on little food, and to live in primitive conditions. People who wanted to leave were punished, and when an investigative team led by a member of the United States Congress arrived to inquire about some of these reports, the Congressman was killed, and close to 1000 people were forced to commit suicide. Clearly, the commune established by Jim

Jones was at least in the beginning a counterculture in its fullest meaning. Of course, most communes and countercultures are experienced by their members as useful and good. Jones's Peoples Temple was a tragic exception to this rule.

CULTURE AND CHANGE

In every culture, customs are affected by attitudes about what is civilized and uncivilized, what is right and wrong, and what is possible and impossible. To the extent that parents and societies pass these norms and values on from generation to generation, culture is a conservative force. But there is at the same time another force—cultural change—as, for example, the countercultures discussed above. Change is usually slow but constant. Nowhere in the world is life exactly as it was hundreds of years ago. Mexican peasants may still use the same kind of farming methods, looms, or potter's wheels that were used centuries ago, but they may also send their children to government schools, get vaccinations in a modern health clinic, and wear factory-made clothes.

Innovation and Borrowing

Technological innovations are a major source of cultural change. They invariably affect the way people live—often in unforeseen ways. The most obvious source of these innovations is inventions, but more often the source of cultural changes is contact with other cultures. A nation sends out a few ships in search of a new route to India, where spices are abundant. The explorers stumble onto America and return with tobacco, corn, and potatoes (all indigenous American crops). Or a people are conquered and forced to accept the conqueror's customs. In these ways technology and cultural traits spread around the world.

Ralph Linton has suggested the extent of cultural borrowing in a description of the morning rituals of the typical American:

On awakening he glances at the clock, a medieval European invention, uses one potent Latin word in abbreviated form, rises in haste, and goes to the bathroom. Here, if he stops to think about it, he must feel himself in the presence of a great American institution; he will have heard stories of both the quality and frequency of foreign plumbing and will know that in no other country does the average man perform his ablutions in the midst of such splendor. But the insidious foreign influence pursues him even here. Glass was invented by the ancient Egyptians, the use of glazed tiles for floors and walls in the Near East, porcelain in China, the art of enameling on metal by Mediterranean artisans of the Bronze Age. Even his bathtub and toilet are but slightly modified copies of Roman originals. The only purely American contribution to the ensemble is the steam radiator.

In this bathroom the American washes with soap invented by the ancient Gauls. Next he cleans his teeth, a subversive European practice which did not invade America until the latter part of the eighteenth century. He then shaves, a masochistic rite first developed by the heathen priests of ancient Egypt and Sumer. The process is made less of a penance by the fact that his razor is of steel, an iron-carbon alloy discovered in either India or Turkestan. Lastly, he dries himself on a Turkish towel. (1937: 427–28)

Today science and technolgy are the major forces of change. Scientific knowledge is common "property," and technological developments diffuse rapidly throughout the world. Television creates a mass world culture. The Soviet city teenager as a member of a relatively closed society knows almost as much about rock as his or her Western counterpart. For years Western social scientists have been discussing how the centrally contolled Soviet system can, or will, change. More recently computer science

is seen as the major force of change in the Soviet system. Sociologists Alex Inkeles and David Smith, for example, have argued that the industrial organization imposes similar values and beliefs on people wherever it appears: ". . . men become modern through the particular life experiences they undergo . . . employment in complex, rationalized, technocratic organizations . . . has particular capabilities to change men so that they move from the more traditional to the more modern pole in their attitudes, values, and behavior" (1974: 6). This does not mean that all industrial societies will become identical, and the Japanese experience suggests the the industrial organization can be adapted—at least in part—to the culture. But for how long is uncertain.

SOCIETY AND CULTURE

People are social animals; without other humans they do not survive. Infants depend on other people to provide for their physical and emotional needs and to teach them the rules and values of their society. Old people become apathetic and ill when isolated from other people; they care little about themselves, what they eat, or how they spend their time. For humans to interact with other humans, the ability to establish social relations is imperative.

Many animals also lead intensely social lives. Lions, for example, live in families (called prides) consisting of one dominant male, perhaps one or two other males, several breeding age females, and their offspring. The members of a pride share territory and food, and they cooperate in raising the cubs. After several years, the young go off to join prides of their own. A few species of birds choose mates for life. Ant societies are based on a complex division of labor, with fighters, workers, drones, and queens each playing a distinct role in the construction of a hill, the gathering of food, and procreation. Similarly, fish live in schools, bees in hives, sheep in herds, and wolves in packs.

This resemblance between animal and human society is only superficial. While both have structures that organize behavior, nonhuman species are genetically programmed to create their social organization. The ants in the United States do not create a capitalist society and the social organization of ants in the Soviet Union shows no dissidents. The ants in Poland were building their anthills oblivious to the courageous efforts of Polish workers to restructure their society. Thus **society** refers to a group of people, living in a specific geographical area, who share a culture which serves as the basis of organization of their society. Society is rarely static; change is a continuous process and each generation leaves society a little different than it was before.

All societies have a **social structure.** Its components are statuses, roles, groups, and institutions. Let us look at each in turn.

Social Structure

Structure is a term most of us use frequently. We speak of the structure of a building, bridge, table, or chair. We are well aware that the structure of a building consists of a foundation, floors, walls, a roof, windows, and we know that the different parts have to fit together into a whole. If a new building deteriorates after a few years, we will assume that there was something wrong with the structure. If it sags, we will say that the foundation was poor. If the rain makes its way into the building and ruins the walls and ceiling of a room, we assume that there was something wrong with the fitting of the different parts.

The structure of a building is obvious. But social structure is far less obvious. One might ask: How can we apply the concept of social structure when it involves human behavior? People are not inanimate parts of a foundation, a wall, or a roof. People are individuals. There is

no denying that there is something unique about each person; nevertheless, there is a structure, or a continuing pattern of relations in a group or society. As Williams observes,

To demonstrate structure one need only show a recurrence of elements related in definite ways. In the interest of realism it is best to speak of the structure of social phenomena only where there is an important degree of continuity, where human activities are so patterned (recurrent) that we can observe a growing standardization persisting, although changing over a considerable time (1970: 22–23)

Consider, for example, the college or university that you attend. Do you usually worry that the professor will not show up for class? that the student cafeteria will not serve lunch? that there is no library? that you or your parents will not receive a bill for your college tuition? Clearly, you have no such concerns. This does not mean that you will think the professor is brilliant; that you will love the cafeteria food; that the library will have a collection of books on a highly obscure topic; or that you will look forward to the tuition bill. What it does mean is that there is patterned behavior. The professor is in class; food is served; books are in the library; and the bill arrives promptly each semester. There is regularity, coordination, and predictability (Williams, 1970).

Even the class in sociology shows a social structure, a fairly regular pattern after a relatively short time. Within two weeks of the the beginning of the semester everyone will have "a regular seat." Several students will invariably ask questions. Students will begin to expect Jane or Joe to ask questions, and perhaps even feel that the class is not quite "right" without the questions. Jane or Joe may emerge as bright or a "pest," and may be sought for advice before an examination. In a lecture hall of 500 students, the social structure of the class will differ, but close observation will reveal recurrent patterns of behavior.

The Concept of Status and Role

We sometimes refer to a person as having high status or low status, meaning that someone has much or little prestige. While we do not quarrel with this notion, analytically the term **status** refers to a position in a set of relationships. The term **role** refers to the rights and obligations, to the behavior and attitudes of a particular status (see Fig. 3.1). According to Linton (1936), one occupies a status, but plays a role; a role is the dynamic part of the status. Status then is fixed, but a role can be modified. Thus, for example, the nine Supreme Court Justices occupy the same status (though one is the chief justice), but there may be differences in how each justice perceives his or her role. The status of father specifies a man's relationship with his child, but the role of father has ample room for variation. The role of father entails the right to guide the child, and the obligation to support the child. But guidance may take a variety of forms. To some it may mean "guiding" the child into the father's footsteps, and for others guiding may mean to let the child develop to its fullest potential, even if the child as an adult chooses a different life path than what the father had hoped for. Similarly, obligation may take varied forms: for some it may mean material support and provision of necessities, and for others it may mean psychological support. Today the role of the father is fluid; in a divorce, increasing numbers of fathers assume custody of a child and perform the role of father and "mother." Such role behavior would have been deviant a mere 20 years ago.

Each status generally contains more than one role. For example, in the status of Supreme Court Justice, the justice maintains a wide range of roles with others whose status requires them to interact with him or her, e.g., lawyers, colleagues, law clerks, typists, and so on. The case of professor,

Fig. 3.1 / Statuses and Roles

Statuses and roles do not exist isolated from other statuses and roles. Instead, they cluster in role sets. In this diagram, the circles are statuses and the lines are corresponding roles. In the status of professor, for example, a faculty member maintains a wide range of roles with others whose social positions require them to interact with him or her.

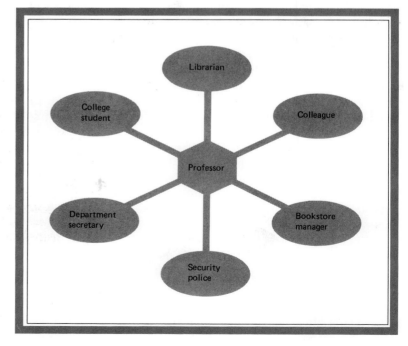

In the film Kramer vs. Kramer, *Dustin Hoffman portrayed a father who moved beyond the stereotypical role of financial provider to become the primary nurturing parent of his child.*

student, or any other status is similar. The cluster of roles attached to a status is called a **role set** (Merton, 1957).

Role relationships involve expectations held by the various role occupants. The behavior of a mother is in part defined by the expectations of her husband and children. Their behavior in turn is partly shaped by the expectations of their mother. As a rule each expectation is shaped by the culture and institutionalized through the norms. Family relations, for example, are expected to be highly personal and emotionally intense. But relationships in large organizations are expected to be emotionally neutral and focused on the performance of work activities. Thus, it is normative for the mother to be concerned with the whole child, and the mother-child relationship "ought" to be based on love. On the other hand, the role of the supervisor and worker "ought" to be objective and focused on the work to be done. There is no norm which requires the supervisor to "love" the worker. In fact, as

Chapter 11 illustrates, the normative patterns of large-scale organizations, or bureaucracies, are built on relations that are neutral and impersonal.

Role strains. Because people occupy numerous statuses and accompanying role sets at the same time, the possibilities for problems in carrying out role expectations are numerous. These problems are called **role strains,** and may be of many kinds: role ambiguity, role discontinuity, changing roles, and role conflict. We will look briefly at each.

The strain that occurs because role expectations are unclear or poorly defined is called **role ambiguity.** For example, we have come to expect young adults in the United States to experience emotional turmoil, stress, and confusion. Part of our teenagers' confusion arises because our culture does not clearly specify when the transition from adolescence to adulthood occurs. Is a person an adult at age 21? after graduating from high school or college? when he or she marries? when he or she is economically self-sufficient? Many societies have **rites of passage,** social events that mark the passage of an individual from one status and role to another. Our society has few of these. Graduation ceremonies, marriage ceremonies, and retirement parties help to serve this function, but still they generally don't provide absolutely clear social statements about an individual's new social standing. Role ambiguity, then, can make it difficult for the individual to know what his or her role is, and which role expectations he or she should meet.

A woman who has been married to the same man for fifty years often experiences role discontinuity when her husband dies. **Role discontinuity** is a shift from one role to another in which there is inadequate preparation or acceptance of the new role, and in which there may also be a sense of loss in regard to the old role. Unless people are prepared to move from one role to another, they often find such transitions difficult and unpleasant. The routine of their lives is altered—they no longer know what to do, and they may feel uncomfortable in the new behaviors expected of them. To some degree, anticipatory socialization helps, but in many cases there simply is no preparation for movement between roles.

In a society dedicated to technological innovation, new social statuses and roles emerge regularly and older ones are discarded or modified. Computer programmer, space scientist, and astronaut are just a few of many recently developed statuses, while we rarely hear about blacksmiths or coopers (barrel-makers) any more. Whenever new statuses and roles are created, **role change** occurs, and people are faced with learning and unlearning appropriate behaviors. As with role discontinuity, planned efforts by society to help people prepare for role changes are helpful.

Role conflict is the kind of role strain that occurs when an individual is expected to perform one role with built-in inconsistencies or two roles that are incompatible.

The college professor who must counsel students on a personal level as well as evaluate their academic performance objectively and impersonally performs a role with a built-in conflict. Similarly, the military chaplain who must preach Christian love and charity while sanctioning war may also experience role conflict. The foreman in a factory occupies a role that requires mediating between the expectations of superiors who want increased production and the demands of the workers who want to maintain a stable output. The foreman may become caught in the middle, exposed to pressure from both directions.

Role strains are usually perceived by people as unpleasant. Roles help people to know what they are to do, what is expected of them. They also help people know what to expect from others, thereby removing a lot of uncertainty and anxiety from day-to-day interactions. Consequently, social structures build in mechanisms to reduce role strains as much as possible. Role sets do this by automatically triggering off certain role behaviors. When around his child, for example, a father will generally act like a parent. In other words, his parental role will be his **dominant role,** and all his other roles (welder, tennis player, Democrat, and so on) will be **latent roles** (that is, not performed at that particular time). When he is at work, of course, that role will be dominant and his parental role latent. Roles can also be clarified and separated by being rigidly defined and automatically assigned to certain types of people. When people can select their own statuses and roles there is much more opportunity for strain and conflict. We will look at this issue of choosing statuses and roles in the next section.

Ascribed Statuses and Roles

An **ascribed status** is a status assigned by society without reference to personal ability, effort, choice, or accomplishment. Almost every society ascribes statuses and roles by sex and age. Race, ethnicity, and family background are also often used as criteria to assign people to certain statuses. Allocated at birth, regardless of capacities or preferences, ascribed statuses determine an individual's present and future roles.

Ascription by sex. All societies clearly differentiate statuses and roles for each sex. In Western culture, the woman's role has traditionally been associated with her family and household, while practically everything else has been labeled "man's work." A woman cares for her children, cooks, cleans, sews, and does the family wash while her husband leaves home to earn a living for the family. A man is expected to provide an adequate income for his wife and children, but he has considerable choice about how he fills the role of breadwinner. He may work as a taxi driver, architect, upholsterer, or college professor, for example. The opportunities and choices open to women, on the other hand, have been more narrowly assigned. The major occupation of most married women is that of housewife. Even wives who work full time usually continue to handle homemaking and child care responsibilities (Malbin, 1972). Women's changing roles are discussed in greater detail in Chapter 5.

Ascription by age. Everyone passes through different stages of life and is ascribed certain roles according to age. Some of these assignments are based on biological distinctions that are shared by all human beings. But, like sex-role distinctions, age roles are based on more than merely reaching a certain level of physical maturity. Age roles are closely tied to a society's system of values, beliefs, and attitudes.

In our own society, for example, many believe that a person is an adult simply because he or she has reached the age of 21. Just as arbitrarily, at 65 or 70 an individual is judged "too old" to work, and is required to "retire" from full social participation. Yet, however vague, abrupt, or arbitrary the transition from one age level to the next, every individual is expected to learn new roles associated with each age. In the last chapter, we discussed this process of social-

ization throughout the life cycle. But what are the various roles we play?

A person in our society under the age of 14 is socially defined as a child and has a whole series of obligations and rights that flow from that social definition. The child's principal business is learning to become a member of his or her society. Accordingly, children are expected to follow the reasonable demands of their parents, teachers, and others in positions of authority. In return, they are loved, fed, clothed, and otherwise cared for. Dressing and feeding themselves, discovering through play how to get along with other children, learning how to read, write, and count—all are part of growing up.

Children in our society are not expected to work for a living. Their "chores" around the house are seen as educational and are not an essential part of the household's economy. Our norms say that regular employment of children for pay is immoral, and our laws make child labor illegal except under limited conditions. We are shocked when we read the descriptions in Charles Dickens's novels of underfed children toiling 16 hours a day in the cotton mills of nineteenth-century England.

As children grow up and enter adolescence, their role changes. Since at this point they are neither child nor adult, they may face conflicting expectations. Teenagers are expected to behave in a more mature and responsible fashion than children, but not to become completely independent of their parents. In general, teenagers in our society are expected to be boisterous and loud, to be rebellious and confusing, and generally to tax the patience of their elders. Albert Bandura (1971) suggests that this role is imposed by society on adolescents, and is not simply a biological or psychological phase:

If a society labels its adolescents as "teenagers" and expects them to be rebellious, unpredictable, sloppy, and wild in their behavior, and if this picture is repeatedly reinforced by the mass media, such cultural expectations may very well force adolescents into the role of rebel. (p. 30)

To become an adult in most societies is to assume the role of a responsible working member of society. As we have seen, may adult roles are ascribed on the basis of sex. However, as young adults, individuals in our culture generally are allowed more freedom in selecting their own roles than at any other time in life. Once they have reached middle age, the possibilities become more limited. The middle-aged man or woman who wishes to start a new career at that point in life often has a hard time of it. Many employers do not regard the middle-aged "beginner" as a good investment. Moreover, society's current emphasis on youth and glamour often makes it difficult for people to accept themselves as middle-aged. When we label someone *over the hill,* we are expressing a general societal attitude that the later years of life are *declining* ones, in which individuals must accept an ever-*diminishing* role.

In many nontechnological societies, people can look forward to a peaceful and full old age surrounded by children and grandchildren and respected for their years of experience. But in a society that values rapid progress, the old are not generally respected for their accumulated knowledge and skills and are not consulted for guidance. They are often regarded as obsolete and are discouraged from playing a productive economic role. Many are abruptly cut off from their former roles and responsibilities by compulsory retirement policies or by social pressure to step down from their jobs and make room for younger people. While many older people are unable to keep up with the pressures of a full day's work and are glad to retire, others, who are still healthy and competent, resent enforced inactivity.

The elderly in our society are also cut off from active roles in family life. In societies where several generations live together in the same household, old people have important roles to play in raising grandchildren and helping to run the household. But in most industrialized societies, children move away from their parents to start separate families of their own. In-laws or grandparents are not usually welcome additions to the household. Many older people, having been self-reliant and independent adults, do not want to become dependent on their children or risk being regarded as a nuisance or an economic drain. Many move to retirement communities, or they may be placed in a nursing home where they are segregated with other old people.

Ascription by race. The practice of ascribing roles on the basis of race has been normative in American society until fairly recently. The pattern of racial separation which began with slavery and was continued through legal segregation marked a black person for virtual servitude and poverty from the moment of birth. This is discussed in Chapter 9 in more detail.

Achieved Statuses and Roles

In contrast to statuses ascribed at birth on the basis of characteristics that a person did not choose, an **achieved status** is a status acquired through personal effort, choice, or accomplishment. Examples in our society include those of lawyer, governor, champion cross-country runner, and president.

*Although it was often said that Lyndon Baines Johnson was born for the Presidency, it seemed quite unlikely that he would ever attain it. . . . Lyndon Johnson was born in the three-room Johnson home at Hye. . . . The Johnson family was extremely poor. Money was scarce in the backcountry hills, . . . and the oil boom had not yet come to Texas. . . . Water was a problem, and . . . farming was not, as the future President was to put it, "worth a cotton-pickin' damn." (*The New York Times, *Jan. 23, 1973)*

Every American is steeped from childhood in similar stories of success. Abraham Lincoln, the popular Horatio Alger tales, LBJ—all symbolize the "self-made man," whose success is achieved through hard work and talent. The "new world" invited settlers to choose from an abundance of occupations and promised a society in which an individual's achievements would be limited only by ability and luck.

The constant necessity of choosing one's goals and the insecurity of competing for them also create certain difficulties. In societies that stress achievement, individuals are free to utilize all their abilities and ambitions. Like Lyndon Johnson and Richard Nixon, they can dream and work and propel themselves from a simple, poor background to the heights of power and wealth.

Yet, should they aim and fail, they must also bear the full burden of that responsibility. The sometimes desperate struggle for wealth, status achievement, and public acceptance is an integral part of contemporary Americans' heritage. Believing that "the Lord helps those who help themselves," we seek "self-improvement," study at night, slim down, shape up, deodorize ourselves, and attend "cultural affairs," all in an unending determination to reap the promises of open opportunity. We stigmatize those who have failed as lazy and irresponsible. Those who can

Mikhail Baryshnikov and Judith Jamison performing in "Pas de Duke." Early in his career, Baryshnikov chose to defect from Russia to the United States, where he eventually achieved the status of ballet superstar, father, and director of the American Ballet Theater.

not earn their own way may be classified as shirkers:

A person can be expected to act responsibly only if he has responsibility. This is human nature. So let us encourage individuals at home and nations abroad to do more for themselves and decide more for themselves. . . . Let each of us remember that America was built not by government but by people—not by welfare, but by work—not by shirking responsibility, but by seeking responsibility. (President Nixon's Second Inaugural Address. The New York Times, *Jan. 21, 1973)*

Behind such an exhortation lies the conviction that anyone who is not afraid of a little effort and self-discipline can make it "like the rest of us." Yet, in reality, the truth is not so simple. In theory, all Americans are equal, but in practice, as we noted earlier, some are "more equal" than others. Although Americans can climb the occupational ladder through their own achievement, as other chapters in this book show, "winning" is not quite as simple as it is sometimes suggested.

GROUPS AND SOCIAL INSTITUTIONS

Social behavior usually means group behavior. In everyday speech, group usually means a collection of people. In sociology we distinguish several types of groups. For the moment we will define a group as two or more people who interact regularly and identify with one another. Groups are an essential part of the social structure of a society. Groups are discussed in detail in Chapter 10. Here we will note only the main types: *primary groups* and *secondary groups.*

A **primary group** is characterized by face-to-face relationships over a long period of time. Examples of primary groups are the family, the peer group, work groups, and friends. **Secondary groups** consist of large numbers of people

who relate to each other in an impersonal and formal manner. Their relationships center on specific tasks, and they are goal oriented. An example of a secondary group is any large-scale organization, such as United States Steel, the United States Post Office, the Ford Motor Company, and so on. Modern industrial societies are characterized by secondary groups; simple, or less (industrially) developed societies are characterized by primary groups.

Groups are an important part of a culture's translation into an operating social structure. Specific norms, statuses, and roles apply to numbers of people who interact together. Workers, for example, share norms and roles in their daily activities. This is what makes it possible for them to work together harmoniously. Similarly, family members share norms and have interlocking roles so that they can function as a unit. Groups, then, enable society to organize large numbers of status and role occupants. As we will see shortly, these groups are further organized into social institutions. In this way social organization includes people individually and collectively.

Institutions

We devote several chapters to institutions later in this book, but for the time being, you should understand that sociologists do not use the word institution in the everyday sense of referring to a building or an organization such as a school, prison, or hospital. To a sociologist an **institution** is a system of norms, values, statuses, and roles that develop around a basic societal goal (see Fig. 3.2). No society could survive for long if certain basic prerequisites for group life were not fulfilled. Among these are the reproduction and nurturance of children; the affirmation and celebration of the society's most cherished values; the perpetuation of cultural knowledge and skills; the distribution of goods and services; leadership and protection of society's members. These basic prerequisites are fulfilled by the institution of the family, religious

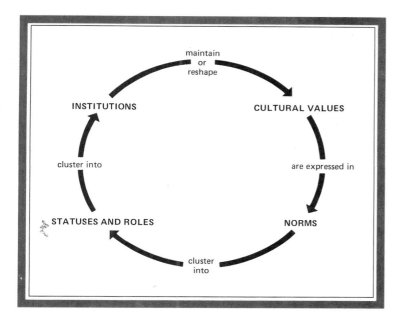

Fig. 3.2 / Culture and Social Structure

institutions, the institution of education, and economic and political institutions.

We may look at social institutions as the last organizational step of social elements discussed in this chapter. A culture expresses itself in terms of its norms and its values; in turn, these cluster to define statuses and roles which individuals come to occupy within their specific society. Finally, the individuals in these statuses and roles coordinate in institutions to meet a specific goal.

Take, for example, the family that we will discuss at length in a later chapter. Concepts of the family include cultural ideas about how individuals should select a mate (or mates), the ceremonies that transform people into a family, norms about how the husband and wife should relate to one another and to their offspring, and laws regulating these relationships.

The institutions discussed in this book are distinct, but not unlike cultures, they are integrated to fit together. This is not meant to suggest that we have achieved maximum institutional integration; change is continuous, and institu-

tions, despite their quest for stability and continuity, experience change. The continuity and change of institutions is the subject of many chapters in this book.

THE SOCIOLOGY OF HEALTH: CULTURE AND SOCIETY IN INTERACTION

To conclude this chapter, we will examine health in the United States as an example of the way culture shapes the development of specific norms, statuses and roles, and institutional structures. **Medical sociology** studies the behavior of physicians, patients, and nurses, as well as the organizational structures in which they interact (Wilson, 1970: 1). Sociologists are concerned with our health care system because "Many of our society's problems, such as inflation, poverty, unemployment, and even foreign affairs, are associated with aspects of our health-care system.

The growing economic and social importance of the system guarantees it will be of major importance to our political processes" (Enos and Sultan, 1977: 3). The far-reaching web of the health care system is illustrated in Fig. 3.3.

Health and Culture

Like any part of a society, health is very much affected by culture. Our conceptions of

well and sick are part of our culture's definition of categories of behavior. For example, on the Navajo Reservation a congenital dislocation of the hip is fairly common. It is not considered a serious problem by the Navajo, since people with the condition lead relatively normal lives and are accepted in the community. Anglo doctors, however, have favored surgery in order to avoid additional joint deterioration later in life. Unfortunately, the surgery creates hip stiffness and

Fig. 3.3 / The Economics of Health

Source: From Victor R. Fuchs, "The Contribution of Health Services to the American Economy," in Victor R. Fuchs, ed., *Essays in the Economics of Health and Medical Care* (New York: National Bureau of Economic Research, 1972), p. 23.

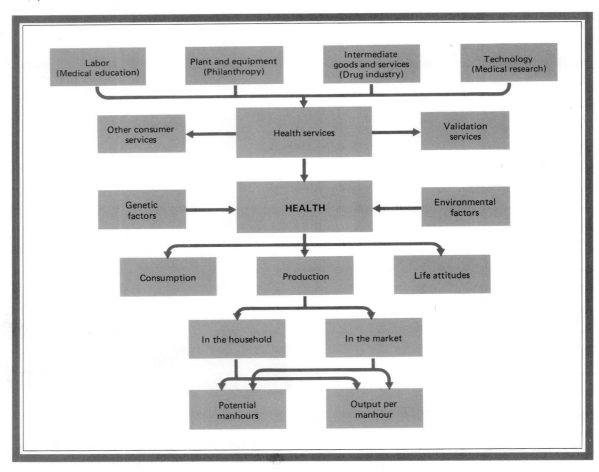

impedes such things as horseback riding, important in Navajo reservation life (Brownlee, 1978: 175). Definitions of the acceptable parameters of health clearly vary between these two cultures. A study of Mexican-Americans in the Southwest reinforces the significance of culture in defining illness. The researchers note that the members of the group they studied considered health care as necessary only when someone was too emaciated or pain-wracked to be able to work (Bullough and Bullough, 1972). The concept of preventive health care suggests a degree of control over one's life that these people—and many others who face poverty as a daily reality—do not believe is possible.

Cultures also define appropriate treatment for illness. Talcott Parsons (1951) did a classic study of the role of the sick person in our society. His study showed that we have clear expectations about what a sick person is expected to do—cooperate with the doctor, for example. Yet we are very reluctant to allow certain kinds of medical personnel to treat us in particular ways, and would consider ourselves perfectly justified in *not* cooperating under those circumstances. For example, acupuncture is not widely accepted in the United States, as it is in many other societies. Chiropractors, too, are distrusted by some people, who would avoid treatment from them even if surgery were the only alternative. Cultural values may also take precedence over medical treatment. People often refuse to change their ethnic food habits in spite of orders to do so from a physician who may be concerned with cholesterol or calories.

The Structure of Health Care

Once cultural values have established approaches to defining health and illness, as well as appropriate societal responses to illness, specific social structures are created—the health care system. It may be having a medicine person who performs rituals to cure illness, and who knows

and uses herbs for curing purposes. The family is very commonly involved in health care, performing roles ranging from identifying illness, to providing care, to supporting people's efforts to locate and use more specialized health care structures like hospitals and clinics (Brownlee, 1978: 80–93). In complex, industrial societies like our own, other social institutions also become involved in health care. Schools include health education in their curriculums, and provide limited nursing services as well as nutritional lunch programs. Politicians debate various programs to support health care delivery in society. The economic institution has a substantial interest in such things as pharmaceuticals, hospital construction, health insurance plans, and so on. And religion is often an important component of people's ability to cope with illness and death.

Structures to organize health care can be grouped into four categories: epidemiology, professions, service delivery structures, and structures to finance health care. Let us look at each in turn.

Epidemiology. **Epidemiology** is the identification of types of diseases within a population and its subgroups. Our society is very concerned with identifying diseases so that they can be controlled. A vast range of structures is involved in locating diseases: private physicians, the public schools, the public health service, the military, and many others. Once located, diseases have to be correctly identified. This entails an extensive network of research facilities at universities, in hospitals, and at all levels of government. The recent dramatic rise of the incidence of a rare cancer, Kaposi's Sarcoma, in the gay male community is a case in point. The Federal Centers of Disease Control were instrumental in diagnosing the disease, and in subsequent efforts to understand why it was suddenly appearing in such a deadly form among gay men (Mass, 1981).

Health care professions. Medical professions have been notable for their growth in

In complex societies like our own, various social institutions—including family members, educators, and political figures—may become involved in health care. Recently, Nancy Reagan visited Atlanta schools as part of a program to discourage drug abuse by informing parents and children of its dangers.

number and specialization (Enos and Sultan, 1977: 20–37). In addition to specialized types of doctors and nurses, there are physician's assistants, nurses' aides, physical therapists, anesthesiologists, X-ray technicians, pharmacists, radiotherapists, medical social workers (themselves specialized in dealing with renal dialysis, oncology [cancer], and so on), and many others. Issues involved in teamwork among these many professions have become highly visible and very important. They relate to both the quality and cost of health care. Adding the mental health network into this analysis further illuminates the complexity of the web of health care professions.

Service delivery structures. Unlike earlier days when doctors routinely made house calls,

babies were often delivered at home, and people even remained in their own homes to die, today health care is centralized. We go to clinics and hospitals, nursing homes and mental hospitals, dentists' offices and rehabilitation centers. These structures utilize the skills of several types of professionals. They are complex, costly structures that, while usually efficient, remove the patient from his or her regular environment during the treatment period. Additional issues are raised regarding preserving the patient's basic right to control his or her own body, and to decide when he or she is ready to die. It is little wonder that medical ethics is such a rapidly growing concern in society. Before looking briefly at health care financing, we will review the medical care delivery system in Fig. 3.4.

Financing health care. Enos and Sultan (1977) note the following:

In the 12 months ending June 1975, each person in the United States had spent $547 for health care. For this same period, personal income per capita was $5,633. For an average family of four, then, health-care expenditures were $2,188. In effect, each individual was spending a startling 9.7 percent of his personal income for health services. . . . [during] the first three months of 1976, medical-care services rose at an annual rate of 14 percent. . . . This contrasts sharply with the annual index rate for all consumer purchases of only 3.9 percent for the same period. (p. 38)

Obviously, health care is big, big business. The costs are only bearable because the government pays for more than 42 percent of them, and, of the remainder, health insurance plans pay for more than two-thirds (Enos and Sultan, 1977: 39). There is growing concern that health care costs

Fig. 3.4 / The Medical Care Delivery System
Source: Darryl D. Enos and Paul Sultan, *The Sociology of Health Care.* New York: Praeger, 1977, p. 327. Adapted from "The Delivery of Medical Care," by S. Garfield. © 1970 by Scientific American Inc. All rights reserved.

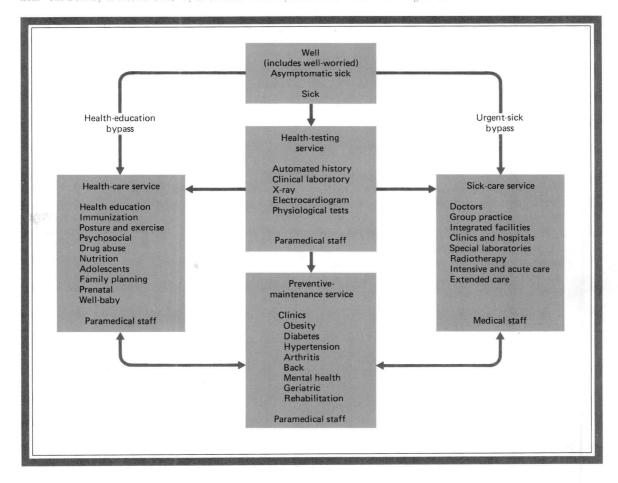

have to be controlled if individual and societal bankruptcy are to be avoided. There is considerable debate over how to accomplish this, however (Enos and Sultan, 1977: 233–379).

Summary and Conclusion

The health care system in the United States is a good example of the way culture directs a society's efforts to develop and implement its goals. The elaborate, specialized, and costly health care system in our nation reflects values implemented through the structure of social institutions. As a result, our health care system differs from those in other countries. Sociologists, of course, would expect this, since each society has its own distinctive culture.

SUMMARY

1. The main purposes of this chapter are: to introduce and explain the concepts of culture and society; and to examine the various aspects and components (language, norms, values, statuses, roles, groups, and institutions) of culture and society.

2. Every society has a distinctive culture which is preserved and transmitted from generation to generation. The concept of culture includes all aspects of human life that are learned and shared by members of society. Sociologically, society and culture are two different concepts: society refers to a group of people living in a geographical area who share a culture.

3. Resemblance between human and animal societies is superficial since most human behavior is learned and most animal behavior is guided by instinct. In a sense, culture takes the place of instincts and specific biological adaptations for humans.

   Language, a system for communicating facts, ideas, and feelings, seems to be the primary factor that has enabled humans to develop and transmit their culture to following generations. The Sapir-Whorf hypothesis suggests not only that language gives human thought a means of expression, but that it actually determines how a human from a particular society will think. Sociolinguists study the power of language to direct people's thoughts and thus its effects on society.

4. Every culture has rules that define correct and incorrect behavior in a particular society. These rules, called norms, include folkways, mores, laws, and institutions. In addition, every culture has values that are the criteria for evaluating people, behavior, experiences, and objects. Although people often consider another society's norms and values inferior to their own (ethnocentrism), objective evaluation of that society's norms and values (cultural relativism) is more helpful in understanding that society.

5. Subcultures are variations of the dominant culture in which adaptations of majority norms and values distinguish one group from another. Countercultures are opposed to the dominant culture; they can withdraw from society and form their own community, or remain and attempt to change the culture.

6. Cultures are constantly changing due to innovations (mainly science and technology) from within the culture itself as well as those borrowed from other cultures.

7. The statuses and roles of individuals are the basic units of interaction. People occupy a status, but play a role. Roles are the rights and obligations of a status. Role behavior is partly defined by the expectation of others in a role set, but in every society role behavior is primarily derived from a

society's norms. A society assigns statuses and roles by ascription and achievement.

8. Institutions are systems of norms, values, statuses, and roles that develop around a basic societal goal. Some of the major institutions of society are the family, economic, political, or religious institutions. The health care system was used as an example of the way culture gets translated into social structures.

REVIEW

Key Terms

Culture	Ethnocentrism	Role set	Latent roles
Language	Cultural relativism	Role strains	Achieved status
Sociolinguistics	Subcultures	Role ambiguity	Ascribed status
Norms	Counterculture	Rites of passage	Primary group
Folkways	Society	Role discontinuity	Secondary group
Mores	Social structure	Role change	Institution
Laws	Status	Role conflict	Medical sociology
Values	Role	Dominant role	Epidemiology

Review and Discussion

1. How has the culture in which you were raised influenced your behavior? What differences do you see between the way you think and act compared to friends of yours who come from different racial or ethnic backgrounds?

2. Think of an American myth, legend, or folktale (for example: Johnny Appleseed, Davy Crockett, or George Washington and the cherry tree). What cultural values does the story reflect? Do you think the myth, legend, or folktale is as relevant today as it used to be?

3. Make a list of all the statuses you occupy. For each, identify at least one role expectation. Which two of your statuses do you find conflict the most? Why?

4. Make a schedule of the things you have to do today. Which activities are part of your ascribed statuses, and which are part of your achieved statuses? Which do you least like to do?

5. Would you describe yourself as ethnocentric? What evidence would you use to support your analysis?

6. To what degree do you think our health care system truly reflects American values? For example, based on our values, do you think doctors should make house calls? Or should the government pay such a large chunk of health costs?

Experience with Sociology

This chapter makes the point that health care is closely tied to culture. Situations that are defined as illnesses vary from culture to culture, as do conceptions of how and why people become ill. Our highly technological society has come to rely increasingly on sophisticated medical procedures and equipment to diagnose and treat illness. There is little doubt that most Americans consider our medical technology desirable, and that it is very effective in preventing death and illness in many cases.

Nevertheless, our approach to medical care also has its drawbacks. Unlike less technologically developed societies where health care is organized around the family and the local community, our medical care is often impersonal and isolates the ill person from his or her loved ones. Our health care system is also very expensive, and costs continue to climb rapidly. In Module 8 of *Experience With Sociology*, you will have a chance to explore the costs of our society's approach to health. It will help you to see that cultural values are made operational through social structures. Those structures, in turn, affect cultural values. We can see this in our own struggles to decide *who* should have access to very expensive health care, and *how* society can provide access.

References

Arensberg, Conrad M., and **Arthur H. Niehoff** (1964). *Introducing Social Change.* Chicago: Aldine.

Bandura, Albert (1971). The stormy decade: Fact or fiction? In *Adolescent Behavior and Society,* ed. Rolf E. Muuss, 1971, pp. 22–31. New York: Random House.

Benedict, Ruth (1934). *Patterns of Culture.* Boston: Houghton Mifflin.

Brownlee, Ann Templeton (1978). *Community, Culture, and Care.* St. Louis: C. V. Mosby Co.

Bullough, Vern, and **Bonnie Bullough** (1972). *Poverty, Ethnic Identity, and Health Care.* New York: Appleton-Century-Crofts.

Carroll, John B., ed. (1956). *Language, Thought, and Reality: Selected Writings of Benjamin Lee Whorf.* Cambridge, Mass.: M.I.T. Press.

Chasin, Barbara, and **Gerald Chasin** (1974). *Power and Ideology.* Cambridge, Mass.: Schenkman.

Coleman, James S. (1961). *The Adolescent Society.* New York: Free Press.

Enos, Darryl, and **Paul Sultan** (1977). *The Sociology of Health Care.* New York: Praeger.

Gans, Herbert J. (1962). *The Urban Villagers.* New York: Free Press.

Hayes, K. J., and **C. Hayes** (1952). Imitation in a home-raised chimpanzee. *Journal of Comparative and Physiological Psychology* 45: 450–459.

Inkeles, A., and **D. H. Smith** (1974). *Becoming Modern.* Cambridge, Mass.: Harvard University Press.

Kellog, W. N. (1968). Communication and language in the home-raised chimpanzee. *Science* 162: 423–427.

Kinsey, Alfred C., Wardell B. Pomeroy, and **Clyde E. Martin** (1948). *Sexual Behavior in the Human Male.* Philadelphia: Saunders.

Komarovsky, Mirra (1964). *Blue-Collar Marriage.* New York: Random House.

Linton, Ralph (1936). *The Study of Man.* New York: Appleton-Century-Crofts.

———— (1937). One-hundred percent American. *American Mercury* 40: 427–429.

Malbin, Nona G. and **Helen Y. Waehrer** (1972). *Woman in a Man-made World.* Chicago: Rand McNally.

Mass, Lawrence (1981). Cancer in the gay community. *New York Native* 17 (July 27–August 9 1981): 1ff.

Mead, Margaret (1968). *Coming of Age in Samoa.* New York: Dell (originally published in 1928).

Meggit, M. J. (1964). Male-female relationships in the Highlands of Australian New Guinea. *American Anthropologist* (Special Issue): 204–224.

Merton, Robert (1957). *Social Theory and Social Structure.* Glencoe, Ill.: Free Press.

Miner, Horace (1956). Body ritual among the Nacirema. *American Anthropologist* 58: 503–507.

Orwell, George (1949). *1984.* New York: Harcourt.

Parsons, Talcott (1951). *The Social System.* Glencoe, Ill.: Free Press.

Ruesch, Hans (1950). *Top of the World.* New York: Harper & Row.

Severo, Richard (1973). Mexicans talk of romance: A love affair with tradition. *The New York Times,* January 10, 1973, p. 46.

Storer, Norman W. (1973). *Focus on Society.* Reading, Mass.: Addison-Wesley.

Westhues, Kenneth (1972). *Society's Shadow: Studies in the Sociology of Countercultures.* Toronto: McGraw-Hill Ryerson.

Whiting, John W. M. (1964). Effects of climate on certain cultural practices. In *Explorations in Cultural Anthropology,* ed. W. Goodenough, pp. 511–514. New York: McGraw-Hill.

Williams, Robin M., Jr. (1970). *American Society.* New York: Albert A. Knopf.

Wilson, Robert N. (1970). *The Sociology of Health.* New York: Random House.

Yinger, Milton, M. (1977). Countercultures and social change. *American Sociological Review* 42: 625–635.

4

SOCIALIZATION AND PERSONALITY

Most of us are familiar with a certain kind of situation. While a parent tries to grocery shop at the supermarket, a youngster keeps suggesting items to buy: a favorite cereal, ice cream, or perhaps a brand of toothpaste the child saw on televison. Occasionally the youngster's pleas are heeded, but many times they are not. Why? Certainly it isn't because parents wish to deprive their children of things they want. Instead, the refusal reflects the responsibility parents feel to teach their children what they will need to know as they grow up. They need to learn that some foods are nutritionally preferable to others; that cost is an important factor when shopping; and that most of the time we can't have everything we want—we need the discipline to make wise choices as consumers. For children, these can be difficult lessons that may take years to learn.

However commonplace the above situation may be, it illustrates two important sociological concepts that will be the focus of this chapter: socialization and personality. **Socialization** is the process of social learning through which we internalize culturally approved ways of thinking, feeling, and behaving. It is primarily through social learning that we develop a sense of self through the formulation of attitudes, beliefs, values, and patterns of behavior which characterize our thinking and relationships with others. These consistent, relatively predictable characteristics that distinguish people from each other comprise each person's **personality.** We will see in more detail later in this chapter that socialization occurs in two ways: informally and formally. When a parent in a supermarket explains to a child why a desired item is not a good buy, informal social learning is taking place. We are all familiar as well with more formal socialization which occurs in school and other contexts purposefully structured to teach people something.

It would be a mistake to think of personality as resulting only from social learning. Our behavior is a combination of social learning and genetic programming, but humans are far more influenced by socialization than by genetic factors. This is unlike the tendency of other members of the animal kingdom which are far more governed by their genetic programming. The degree to which humans are influenced by their biological inheritance is a question receiving intensive study with even factors like psychological depression, violent behavior, and sexual preference being studied for possible genetic components (Johnson, 1980). But we know that they also have significant social elements. In addition, most of our daily tasks have been learned, reflecting the enormously versatile and adaptive nature of the human species.

For these reasons, socialization is critical for

At an early age, children begin to learn appropriate adult behavior by observing their parents. This young boy, watching his father make arrows, belongs to a society in which hunting is the male's responsibility.

both the individual and society. People learn how to participate in society and how to use their physiological capabilities to develop and work toward life goals for themselves. Socialization is also important for society, since when people learn how to act in socially approved ways they are less likely to violate society's expectations. Now we will look more closely at the process of socialization.

THE PROCESS OF SOCIALIZATION

Some years ago, a young deaf-mute woman managed to escape from a dark attic room where she had been confined with her illegitimate daughter for six and a half years. The child, Isabelle, behaved like a wild animal at first. She could barely walk and made only strange croaking sounds; she was terrified of strangers, particularly of men. Isabelle was placed in an institution and given special training. Within two and a half years she had reached a normal level of development and was able to attend school. Obviously, Isabelle was biologically normal, as evidenced by her rapid progress once she was given attention and instruction. Her strange initial behavior resulted from the fact that for six years her physical world was limited to a darkened room, and her social world to her imprisoned, confused deaf-mute mother. Not until she was exposed to the outside world and had begun to interact with other people did Isabelle truly join the human community and thus acquire an individual identity (Davis, 1947).

In a sense, we, like Isabelle, have all undergone the process of learning to be "civilized." We are also dependent on others, especially the members of the families in which we are raised. For most of us, "civilization" begins much earlier than it did for Isabelle, and in an environment which is far more benign. However, as a society we are becoming increasingly aware of dangers such as child abuse and neglect which interfere with efforts to socialize youngsters to grow up healthy physically and psychologically (Chase, 1976). We also know that socialization is influenced by social conditions, for example, various forms of prejudice and discrimination (Billingsley and Giovannoni, 1972; Sheehan, 1975). We will look at these specific factors later in the chapter.

Newborn babies are completely self-centered: all that matters to them is having their needs satisfied. For the first year or so of life children cry whenever they are hungry or uncomfortable, burp and throw up without regard for those around them, wet their beds or the persons holding them, and fall asleep whenever they are tired. Babies have no manners, no morals, no shame, no regard for other people. If they are to survive and become civilized members of their society, someone (usually their parents) must feed them, wash and clothe them, and tame them. Somehow children must be convinced not only that they should use the toilet, say "please" and "thank you," eat with a knife and fork, control aggressive impulses, say their prayers, brush their teeth, and so on—but that they *want* to do these things.

Each of these "lessons" represents an imposition on the child, who must give up some freedoms and some pleasures in the process of socialization. Sociologists generally agree that these lessons are learned as children pass through several critical periods as they are growing up. The way they are handled during these periods influences their personalities. All infants must be nursed or bottle-fed for at least a few months and then weaned. All must be diapered for a period and then toilet trained. All must learn to regulate their sexual and aggressive impulses. (No known society advocates total promiscuity, and uncontrolled aggression would be chaotic.) Finally, all must at some point give up their dependence on the people who care for them and begin to act on their own.

Informal (Primary) Socialization

Most socialization occurs without the subject being very aware of it. Children observe the behavior of their parents and siblings and generally begin to imitate what they see. Those around them react to their efforts at imitation, encouraging some and discouraging others (Clarke-Stewart, 1977). The learning of sex roles is one example. In a household where the woman does most of the cooking and cleaning chores, the children imitate her behavior. When young, they enjoy being "mother's helper" and making a game out of their helping efforts. Children do the same for activities they observe their father does. Gradually, however, most adults will encourage girl children to continue imitating their mothers but reward boy children more for imitating their fathers. Through this process, sex roles get learned so that eventually certain things will "feel" right and others will not (Bernard, 1981: 123–151).

Considerable research supports the view that informal socialization begins at birth (Clarke-Stewart, 1977). From the very first interaction of the newborn with those around him or her, learning is occurring. The world gradually emerges as a comforting or a hostile and difficult place depending on whether or not stroking, feeding, soothing, and cuddling occur. As we will see when studying personality development later in the chapter, this early learning is thought to influence later development. Earliest socialization, then, is probably especially significant for developing a sense of self in a physical and social environment, and a generalized sense of well-being (Turner, 1980). Gradually the infant learns to distinguish his or her primary caretaker(s), usually the parent(s), and then to focus on this person or persons. As a result, the actions of these people gradually become significant in the socialization process.

Socialization is more than just learning what to do. It is also learning what is "right" and "wrong." When behavior is observed or taught, and then performed, people's reactions usually carry with them some evaluative component: "good boy!" or "naughty boy!" As a result, we tend to learn behavior and values at the same time, gradually coming to feel good about ourselves when we have done the "right" thing— and bad when we have acted "wrongly" (Gordon, 1976). In other words, through socialization we internalize society's demands, accepting societal beliefs about appropriate and inappropriate behavior, and judging our own actions by these standards. This, of course, is why socialization and personality development are so closely related.

Formal (Secondary) Socialization

Unlike informal socialization, which usually occurs without our knowledge, formal socialization is purposeful and obvious. Whereas the family and the peer group are the most common contexts in which informal socialization occurs, school, church, and the workplace are important sources of formal socialization. Part of their societal mission is to prepare people to function effectively as members of society in particular behavioral areas. We all learn to read, write, perform mathematical computations, and obey rules in grade school. In other schools, we can also learn to fix cars, cook, program computers, style hair, and do a host of other useful things. In church we learn religious dogma and procedures, while at work we learn specific skills and procedures needed for a particular job.

An interesting example of the power of secondary socialization in schools is provided by the author, James Clavell. In a magazine article he told of the time his daughter came home from first grade excitedly reciting the pledge of allegiance. " 'What's pledge mean?' asked her father, not yet an American citizen. "Pledge'illigience is pledge'illigience,' she replied with impatience.

Not only had (her) teacher neglected to explain what the words meant, but Clavell found upon asking his adult friends that none of them knew who wrote the pledge, or when it became an obligatory ritual in schools, or why it was considered so important" (Bernstein, 1981: 47ff). This learning of information considered important for maintenance of social structures is characteristic of secondary socialization, even if we don't always learn why it is important.

Formal socialization is important for enabling people to *do* things, but it tends to be less closely tied to their sense of *being* someone. In part, this is because formal socialization usually occurs after informal socialization in the family. Children already have a sense of self, and they have begun to develop standards of "right" and "wrong." Formal socialization extends, modifies, and solidifies what has already been learned, but it is unlikely that there will be radical changes. There are exceptions, of course. Goffman's analysis of total institutions is a case in point (1961). A **total institution** is an organization that has total control over its members for an extended period of time. Examples include prisons, mental hospitals, and the army. In such settings, socialization can be exceptionally effective, even to the point of changing earlier learning. The reason is that the organization becomes the source of both informal and formal socialization; the members are cut off from the groups that supported their earlier behavior. Goffman notes that total institutions often practice *mortification rituals* that serve to strip the subject of his or her previous sense of identity. When army recruits have their heads shaved, and prisoners have to wear uniforms, they are being forced to acknowledge that their prior identities are being changed. They are now soldiers who must learn to obey, even to kill on command; or prisoners who have forfeited a number of basic rights and comforts.

Most formal socialization is not as extreme as what occurs in a total institution. The socialization of new members of a profession is a more

Total institutions often practice mortification rituals, such as shaving the heads of military recruits, as a means of stripping individuals of their prior identities.

common example. There is an extensive literature in sociology about how professionals—doctors, nurses, lawyers, and so on—absorb the knowledge, values, and skills that characterize their professions (Becker et al., 1961; Ritzer, 1977; Vollmer and Mills, 1966). The socialization of ballet dancers provides a vivid example of the process (Federico, 1974). Training begins early, usually by age eight. It includes formal classes to learn technical skills and the human physiology on which they are based. The young dancers also learn the history of ballet, which includes its development as an art form rather than just technical skill. In addition to their own classes, students observe more advanced dancers as they study and perform, and gradually they get involved in performances themselves. By the time they are ready to dance professionally, they have been gradually socialized to ballet as a way of life as well as a work activity (Federico, 1982).

Anticipatory Socialization

By its very nature socialization is future oriented. It teaches people what they will need to know at some future time: how to dress, eat, find employment, raise a family, and so on. In other words, **anticipatory socialization** is socialization that prepares people for future roles and statuses. Much of it is informal and generalized, as when we learn sex role behavior as a young child. However, as we get closer to entry into specific statuses, such as marriage or a particular job, more formal socialization usually occurs. Preparation for marriage may include religious instruction, sex education, and explicit efforts by one's parents to provide information about useful activities—cooking, child rearing, money management, and so forth. Similarly, entry into a new job frequently entails formal training, either on the job or prior to the start of work. Keep in mind, however, that these formal kinds of anticipatory socialization occur against the backdrop of more informal and more generalized socialization such as ideas of what marriage ought to be, or of what is appropriate behavior at work.

SOCIALIZATION AND THE LIFE CYCLE

The process of socialization does not end with childhood, marriage, a job, or retirement. From our births to our deaths, we are continually involved in learning how to play our part in society. For example, when a young man takes a job in a factory, he exchanges the role of student for that of worker. Gradually he begins to learn the ropes: how to handle machinery, when to say yes to the boss, where to draw the line in jokes about his girlfriend. Similarly, when a young woman marries, she exchanges her single role for that of wife and eventually perhaps that of mother. Such changes in role and status require learning new behaviors and attitudes, and learning to think of oneself in a new way. What does society expect of a child? Of a newlywed? Of a parent? Of a dying patient in a nursing home? As we assume each one of the stages of life, we learn new ways of interacting with the people around us. Socialization continues throughout life.

At different points in the life cycle, different agents of socialization are of special importance. An **agent of socialization** is a social unit which has recognized responsibility for carrying out socializing activities. The family socializes children; schools socialize young people; peer groups socialize their members; work organizations socialize workers; churches socialize members of their congregations. All of these are examples of agents of socialization. Some are influential throughout the life cycle, from birth to death. Others, like schools, are of particular importance at certain points during the life cycle. Assessing the importance of socialization throughout life is complicated by the anticipatory nature of socialization. Schooling occurs at one or more particular points in the life cycle, yet it establishes values, knowledge, and skills which influence behavior throughout one's life. While we can look at the particular influence of various agents of socialization at various points in the life cycle, keep in mind that their influence may be very far-reaching.

The Family

Mothers are not machines. They do not dispense love and comfort and food automatically, unconditionally. From the first time a mother picks up her newborn infant, she reacts to its behavior. If while nursing it bites or sucks so hard that it seems about to choke, she pulls back; if it cries incessantly, she may get angry or worry that her child is sick. At first the infant does not sense it's mother's reactions—in fact, it does not even recognize her. All it cares about is being full and comfortable. However, at about six months, the infant becomes more discriminating. It begins to distinguish between different people and to realize that its mother (or the primary caretaker) is the one who brings it pleasure and eases pain. The infant's attachment to her grows and extends to the father and perhaps to siblings over the next year and a half. The infant starts to shy away from strangers and to cry when its mother goes away (Ainsworth, 1974; Schaffer and Emerson, 1964).

Early human contact. Socialization begins when children sense that the way they act influences the way their parents react to them. If they smile, their parents smile; if they cry, their parents bring food; if they grab, their parents push them away. Insofar as they are able, they adjust their actions to their parents' feelings. Spitting food, wetting on adults, and knocking ashtrays off tables make parents angry. Smiling and imitating sounds make them happy. Children thus learn the most elemental social norms well before they are able to understand why they should behave in certain ways. At this stage, they are thinking practically. They know certain actions are dangerous because they make their parents angry, but they have no sense of right and wrong, pride and shame.

Early socialization seems to depend on the parent (or parent-substitute) first, being loving and nurturing with the child; and second, evaluating the child's behavior according to more or less adult standards. If the child does not receive love and affection, if his or her parents greet every action with annoyance or hostility, the child has no reason to behave well. The moti-

vation is missing; the child has nothing to lose. The same is true for the child whose parents' love and approval are unconditional. Unless parents make some demands, the child will not learn that his or her actions influence the way people respond. Continuing interaction with an adult who loves the child and cares how he or she behaves is a prerequisite for socialization.

Learning social norms. The parents of many families are quite explicit about how their children should and should not behave, and they enforce their rules in a variety of ways. Research has shown that a family's social class is the most important factor in determining how parents will raise their children. Most of children's values about work and education, for instance, are determined by this first orientation (Cook-Gumperz, 1973). Furthermore, parents in different social classes use different strategies to shape children's behavior. Middle-class parents in the United States usually encourage good behavior with affection and praise rather than with material rewards, which they believe give children the wrong idea. They stress initiative, self-control, and inner motivation. Children should "be good for goodness' sake." They try to reason with their children, explaining the consequences of eating too much candy or of running into the street. When these methods fail, they often punish their children with deliberate withdrawal of affection and with isolation, rather than with a beating. Working-class parents, on the other hand, focus on conformity, obedience, and external behavior. They favor discipline by more direct methods of physical punishment (Clausen and Williams, 1963; Duberman, 1976; Kohn, 1963).

Gradually, through identification, children begin to consider their parents' attitudes and values their own, and to judge their own behavior according to those standards. The development of a conscience involves the transformation from conformity (children obeying their parents because they want to please them) to morality (children developing an inner sense of right and wrong and following the rules to please themselves).

The Peer Group

A **peer group** is made up of friends and associates who are usually of similar age and social standing. Children who play or attend school together are peers, as are adults who regularly socialize and who share generally similar interests and other characteristics. While all peer groups function as agents of socialization, they are especially important for youths. People in the Western world tend to regard children as fragile beings who must be shielded from the facts of life (including sex, death, and loss of prestige or money), and parents rarely discuss their work, social life, or personal problems with children. Young people are effectively shut out of the adult world: from kindergarten on, children spend most of their time with their peers—that is, with other children in classrooms, after-school activities, neighborhood play groups, and street gangs.

The withdrawal of parents creates a vacuum that peer groups fill. From sixth grade through adolescence (when most young people still live at home), children in the United States often spend about twice as much time with their peers as they do with their parents. On weekends, for example, the average twelve-year-old may spend only two to three hours a day with his or her parents. In one survey, most sixth-graders indicated they preferred friends to family—not so much because peer activities were so attractive, but because they received relatively little attention at home (Bronfenbrenner, 1970). Parents are busy with their own lives; fathers are usually away from the house much of the time. In addition, parents and schools reward popularity, ability to get along with others, team spirit. The shy, introverted child—the loner—is often labeled "maladjusted," or is simply ignored (Fricke, 1981).

Like all groups, peer groups develop their own norms and values. Sometimes these norms conform with those of society as a whole: the preference of adolescents for friendly, outgoing individuals who adapt easily to the group and who show leadership potential mirrors the norms of business and professional life in the United States. But peer-group norms may also conflict with those of society. Peer values tend to subvert the purpose of schools: bright adolescents often disguise their abilities in order to gain admittance to the in-crowd. And perhaps with good reason. Young people who do not get along with their peers have few other places to turn for companionship, advice, and the kind of information parents think they are too young to have. One study of peer-oriented youngsters (those who value their friends' approval more than that of their family or teachers) suggested that they have a less favorable self-concept and less hope for the future than children who communicate well with adults and that they are more likely to engage in antisocial behavior, such as delinquency (Bronfenbrenner, 1970). These observations suggest that, as socializing agents, peer groups are less than desirable substitutes for adult interest and concern.

Nevertheless, peer groups perform an important socializing function (Collins, 1981). Youth is prolonged in industrial societies, where the labor market demands more and more education. Young people are economically dependent on their families for an extended period. But, no matter how democratic parents may be, a child is never on an equal footing with them. In the family, children may get what they need and want (from attention to college tuition) by learning how a powerless person manipulates a powerful person. In peer groups, however, children learn how to establish egalitarian relationships—how to deal with equals. Crying and pouting may work with parents, but not with friends. In school, on the playground, and in the street, the children learn to fight for their rights. In adolescence, the peer group serves as a bridge to

Peer groups perform the important socializing function of teaching people how to deal with equals. Such groups continue to serve as a source of emotional support, values, and information throughout life.

independence: while parents still see fifteen-year-olds as children, their friends see them as autonomous persons.

The School

Just as peer groups give children experience in interacting with equals, schools introduce children to impersonal relationships. Kindergarten or first grade is the child's first encounter with "the system." However demanding parents may be, they are involved with the child's overall behavior and development. The school system, in contrast, is mainly interested in the child's concrete achievements. While mothers adjust their demands and rewards to the child, teachers, who are responsible for 30 or 40 children at a time, are less flexible. To succeed in school or even to pass, the child must learn to obey those

in authority and to follow rules that were not designed with him or her in mind. For the first time, the child is one in a crowd.

The avowed purpose of education, of course, is to teach children the information and skills they will need to become productive members of their society. Today schools in the United States teach not only reading, writing, and arithmetic, but also sex education, child care, cooking, sewing, carpentry, driving, sports, and often specific occupational skills, such as typing or auto mechanics. But the education system is also designed to produce good citizens. Values are taught explicitly in civics classes, and implicitly through student governments, debating societies, team sports, and the like. Schools teach the young to adjust to impersonal systems of authority and to value social approval—qualities that are adaptive for people who live in complex technological societies.

Some children adapt easily to classroom discipline and find school extremely rewarding; others do not. Often it is the child who is somewhat different from the norm who does not adjust well to classroom life. Lower-class children, for example, are frequently misunderstood by the average middle-class teacher committed to such middle-class values as neatness, punctuality, emotional restraint, and achievement (Ryan, 1976: 31–62). Similarly, teachers are often baffled and annoyed by creative children. The child who is labeled odd or troublesome at age six or seven has difficulty changing that image in the eyes of teachers and administrators. And there is a real danger that these children may come to accept the school's verdict and begin to regard themselves as inadequate (see Friedenberg, 1959, 1965, and Ogbu, 1978).

On the other hand, schools provide children with a number of alternative routes to self-esteem. The modern family is small. Children's opportunities for approval are limited to their parents and siblings; they have only a few examples of adult behavior to emulate. In school they have contact with many adults who may be quite different from the children's parents. In addition, they can seek support from their classmates. A child who does poorly in academic work may win praise on the sports field or gain prestige among peers by defying authority and violating the rules. Informal networks are often as important to the student as formal educational structures.

The Mass Media

The mass media (television, radio, books, newspapers, magazines, records, movies) supply a large quantity of social information to our lives every day. Even though the direct human contact of the family, the peer group, or the school is not provided, the media's power to socialize is enormous (Gumpert and Cathcart, 1979). Television, the most obvious example, is perhaps the most popular and effective medium because it presents living images, and so it comes closest to real human contact. With a TV set in 97 percent of the households in America, the influence of television is not only instantaneous, but almost totally pervasive.

Through the mass media, we receive news, information, and entertainment, and we are introduced to new fashions and consumer products. We are kept up-to-date with the rest of our society, and we are encouraged to adjust our values to match society's values. In this respect, we are at the mercy of those who control the choices and the regulations of the subject matter and the advertising that appear in the various media. Often their selections are motivated by profit alone.

"What a TV battle! . . . The politicans fighting for our minds and the cosmetic people battling for the rest of our bodies, faces and hair!"

Grin and Bear It by George
Lichty. © 1971 Field Enterprises, Inc.
Courtesy of Field Newspaper
Syndicate.

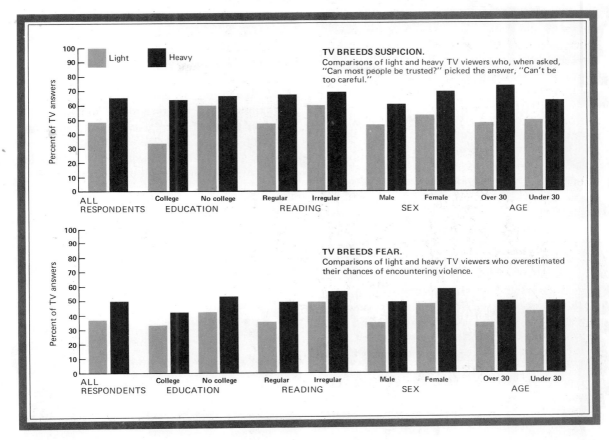

Fig. 4.1
Reprinted from *Psychology Today* magazine. Copyright © 1976
Ziff-Davis Publishing Company.

Indeed, there has been increasing public concern over the nature of the values expressed by televison programming. Consumer groups such as ACT (Action for Children's Television) protest the images of violence and sexual behavior to which children are exposed. The problem drew widespread attention in the 1977 court case of Ronny Zamora, a fifteen-year-old boy who murdered his neighbor when the elderly woman discovered him robbing her home. His lawyer argued that Zamora was under the influence of prolonged exposure to television police-show violence and was therefore unable to tell right from wrong.

Another effort of the media has been to make it more and more possible for everyone to experience what the rest of our society is experiencing. All youth are simultaneously aware of the latest releases and information about top recording stars. The whole country may enjoy the same movie within the period of one summer. On any given day, a person from New York and a person from Los Angeles could discuss a flood in Colorado, the details of a particular football play in Dallas, or Archie Bunker's latest dilemma. Thus the media socializes not only by teaching us what our society expects of its members, but also by making us more like one another because of our shared media experiences (Klapper, 1960).

The Workplace: Learning to Work and Retire

The workplace interacts with other socializing agents at the same time that it performs socializing functions of its own. Kohn and Schooler (1969, 1973) have shown that the family is important in teaching attitudes toward work, achievement, and work gratification. The higher the social class, the more there are expectations that work should be personally gratifying and allow for self-direction. Lower social classes tend to view work as primarily a source of income, and expect to follow orders. These views of work relate to more general values emphasizing long-range planning and self-responsibility for higher social classes, and feelings of less control over one's environment among members of lower classes.

Since most adults have to work to support themselves, success on the job is important. Socialization to work takes two major forms. One is learning how to do the job itself. Many businesses spend considerable time and effort formally socializing their employees to their work (Reed, 1981). For example, airlines have special schools where flight attendants learn safety and passenger service procedures in simulated aircraft. There are also more informal procedures to teach new workers how to navigate successfully in specific workplaces—who to watch out for, where the coffee is kept, how to process sick leave requests, and so forth.

Aside from the work itself, an important aspect of any job is relationships with co-workers. Since most people spend a great deal of their adult life at work, the coworker peer group becomes very important to them. Studies of men working in a machine shop have shown how workers get socialized to the norms of the work group (Roy, 1954). Similar socialization has been documented in such widely diverse occupations as hairdressers (Schroder, 1978), professional baseball players (Charnofsky, 1974), physicians (Becker and Geer, 1958), and ballet dancers (Mazo, 1974). The 1981 air traffic controllers strike in the U.S. exemplifed the importance of work socialization. Many controllers went on strike primarily because of loyalty to their co-workers and their desire to maintain good interpersonal relations. Even most of those who decided not to strike indicated that they experienced painful conflicts between what they thought they should do as government employees, and what they believed their co-workers expected of them.

Retiring from the workplace is generally considered to be the clearest indicator of entry into the old age phase of the life cycle. The workplace helps to socialize retiring workers by helping them plan for income and health needs through pension and other retirement plans. Retirement ceremonies help retirees acknowledge their movement into a new phase of life, as well as providing the support of friends and co-workers during their transition. Unfortunately, there are relatively few other agents of socialization to help people prepare for old age and, eventually, death. As a result, beliefs learned earlier may poorly prepare people for the last stages of the life cycle. Stereotypical views of the elderly as asexual, feeble, senile, and cranky often prevail, even though they are inaccurate for many of the elderly (Kalish, 1975).

As a result, anticipatory socialization may create problems for the elderly. They may fear the aging process and not learn how to adapt to it. This can accelerate normal physiological degenerative processes, as well as generate psychological problems that make old age a period of

Programs that enable senior citizens like these "foster grandparents" to keep active and productive can help make the transition from work to retirement a positive one.

anxiety and isolation. The transition from work to retirement should be one which, as much as possible, emphasizes continuing opportunities for the aging person to remain active and productive. The workplace, and peer-group relationships established at work, can help socialize retiring workers to see their retirement in this way. However, other supports are needed, especially to counteract earlier socialization which may have been more negative about old age. Peer support groups like the National Association of Retired People and the Gray Panthers can help people move from the workplace into a healthy, happy retirement.

SOCIALIZATION AND PERSONALITY

Love and hate, joy and sorrow, pride and shame, enthusiasm and boredom are universal human emotions. Everyone has moments of intense anger and hours filled with excitement and joy. But some people seem to be angry most of the time, just as some usually seem to be happy, some apathetic, and some shy. As we saw earlier in the chapter, personality refers to the way a person typically behaves—to the consistent, relatively predictable characteristics that distinguish people from each other and make each one a unique individual. We also noted that the personality has both social and genetic components. We will now look at these two dimensions of personality.

Nature and Nurture

People are both biological and social beings. The human species has tremendous adaptive potential as part of its genetic structure. Unlike most other forms of life, humans have few genetically programmed patterns that guide behavior. We have all tried to approach a wild squirrel, rabbit, or bird with the intention of feeding or petting it; however, the wild creature automatically flees from human contact, and has no way to determine whether any particular human will be helpful or hurtful. People are much more flexible. When approaching a strange person or situation, we have a number of ways to try to determine whether or not we are likely to be hurt. We ask questions, observe behavior, listen, smell, and so on. We then process the information we receive and make a decision whether to proceed ahead or to flee. Humans, then, are decision-making creatures, while most other life forms operate much more on the basis of genetic programming that automatically dictates behavior in various situations.

Our decision-making abilities result from the ability to think, learn, and communicate with elaborate types of symbols (such as language); however, when we are born, we have *potential* rather than *ability*. We can learn how to talk, but cannot do so automatically (a dog can bark automatically but cannot learn to talk). Our potential can only be fulfilled if we are placed in a social environment that nurtures us and that teaches us how to use the ability with which we were born. Naturally, we are all born with different genetically inherited potential. Some will grow to be larger than others; intellectual capacity will vary; physical coordination differs; hearing and sight are different; and on and on.

Sociologists have conceptualized the physical and social characteristics of humans in terms of nature and nurture. **Nature** refers to the genetic potential with which we are born and which can be modified only slightly, if at all, by the environment. Each of us, for example, has a genetically programmed maximum height. No matter how well we eat and exercise, we will not exceed it, although we will see shortly that poor nutrition and physical care can stunt growth. **Nurture** is the set of socially determined experiences people have which facilitate or block the development of their genetic potential. Obviously nature and nurture are related, although we do not yet know all of the ways one influences the other. Nor is it clear how much behavior is genetically programmed and how much is subject to environmental conditions. An example of current efforts to better understand the relationship between nature and nurture is the debate around race and intelligence, described in Chapter 16. An important subpart of sociology which focuses on nature-nurture relationships is sociobiology, to which we will now turn.

Sociobiology

Sociobiology has been defined as "the study of the biological basis of social behavior in every kind of organism, including man, pieced together with contributions from biology, psychology, and anthropology" (Wilson, 1975a: 39). As an example of how sociobiologists think, consider their analysis of the genetic basis for altruistic or unselfish behavior in animals. When a bird gives up its life to alert the flock to danger, the bird is ensuring the survival of the other birds, some of whom are its relatives and therefore have some of the same genes it has. Over the course of evolution, birds who squawk when in danger (thereby alerting others) will survive better than those who don't. What appears to be heroism in the bird's actions sociobiologists attribute to the effect of mathematical chance over millions of years.

Sociobiology first came to the attention of the general public in 1975 with the publication of Edward O. Wilson's *Sociobiology: The New Synthesis,* and this popularization has given rise to heated and emotional reactions in many academic communities across the United States. The attacks on Wilson and sociobiology fall into two basic categories: science and politics.

While there is scientific evidence that genes may influence animal behavior, many opponents of sociobiology believe that applying this evidence to human behavior is not scientifically sound (Altman, 1975). They feel that sociobiologists do not take into account that behavior is transmitted to humans through culture, which can strongly influence or change the behavior outlined by a person's genetic makeup. Opponents also argue that there is little actual evidence to support the theory that human behavior is genetically based. Moreover, any serious efforts to obtain this evidence would require controlled human breeding and rearing experiments in which most people would be unwilling to participate.

The questioning of the scientific foundations of sociobiology has been accelerated by some of the work of Lorenz (1966), Tiger (1972), and Ardrey (1966). They attempt to demonstrate that humans—and especially men—have an innate biologically inherited sense of territoriality and aggressiveness. They believe that this accounts for much of the conflict that is observed in human interaction. This thesis has not been supported by scientific research, although experimentation is underway to look at the effects of crowding on behavior. A stimulating new work by Lopez (1979), *Of Wolves and Men*, also seeks to address the degree to which animal behavior is carried over into human behavior. For the most part, however, popularized versions of sociobiology have simply tended to reinforce doubts that evidence of genetically based animal behavior can be readily transferred to human behavior.

Politically, many opponents feel that sociobiology may lead to a popularization of genetic determinism and be used to rationalize social inequality for certain races and genders. People might support such actions by reasoning that you can't correct social inequality because you can't correct or change what's in a person's genes. For example, many feminists have been upset by Wilson's "guess" that the "genetic bias (in men and women) is intense enough to cause a substantial division of labor even in the most free and most egalitarian societies," and that "even with identical education and equal access to all professions, men are likely to continue to play a disproportionate role in political life, business and science" (Wilson, 1975a: 48, 50).

Sociobiologists, including Wilson, have answered most criticisms. Many admit that research is needed and that the theory will probably change as evidence becomes available (Barchas, 1976). They also believe that to condemn sociobiology because it *might* be misused politically contradicts the spirit of scientific research. Wilson has said that the misuse of the idea should be discouraged, not the idea itself.

But Wilson's main defense against the attacks on him and his book is that he has clearly stated his belief that *culture,* and not genetics, is the strongest factor shaping human behavior:

What the genes prescribe is not necessarily a particular behavior but the capacity to develop certain behaviors and, more than that, the tendency to develop them in various specified environments. . . . It is this pattern of possibilities and probabilities that is inherited. To make such a statement wholly meaningful, we must go on to compare human beings with other species.

Which behavior a particular human being displays depends on the experience received within his own culture, but the total array of human possibilities, as opposed to baboon or termite possibilities, is inherited. It is the evolution of this pattern which sociobiology attempts to analyze: (1975a: 46, 48)

It cannot be said that one side is right or one side is wrong and, of course, justice cannot be done to either side of the conflict in such a limited discussion. The nature-nurture controversy over the origin of human behavior can still arouse considerable emotion and debate and will probably continue to do so for some time.

Culture and Personality

The culture in which a person is raised greatly affects the development of his or her personality—the way a person typically behaves. By restricting some tendencies and encouraging others, the cultural environment influences the possibilities that are open to any of its members. You will recall that culture is the storehouse of knowledge, values, and objects that is available to any society. Therefore, the socialization which occurs in a society will be built around the cultural elements its members need to learn. There is a considerable amount of sociological and anthropological data to support this point. A summary of some of it follows.

Cultures tend to restrict some behavioral tendencies while encouraging others. For example, although it is unusual for men in our society to embrace, in other countries physical demonstrations of affection and emotion are quite common.

In general, all babies have the same biological needs and all require social teaching; nevertheless, techniques of child rearing vary widely among the societies of the world. Whiting and Child (1953) documented differences in child rearing among 50 nontechnological societies. For example, toilet training practices ranged from the Dahomeans who frightened and shamed their children to the Siriono of South America who pay little attention to bladder and bowel training until between the ages of 4 and 6. Treatment of the elderly is similarly differentiated. Among the Eskimo, old people are expected to end their lives when they can no longer be productive and independent (Townsend, 1977). Yet Mexican-Americans value their older members and go to great lengths to protect and support them (Valle and Mendoza, 1978). All of these studies imply that different societies meet various individual requirements in different ways. As we would expect, socialization prepares people to act in ways that are considered desirable in the society in which they live (Munroe and Munroe, 1975). The result is that personality development is influenced by the way in which socialization occurs.

Reminder Box / **STATISTICS**

Statistics provides methods for describing, summarizing, and organizing data (*descriptive statistics*) as well as for making predictions and estimations (*inferential statistics*). As noted in Chapter 2, statistical analysis is especially important when large amounts of data have been collected, and when one wishes to make decisions based on data collected with a known probability of accuracy.

In this Reminder Box, we will illustrate the utility of one descriptive statistic, the mode. Other frequently used descriptive statistics are the median and mean, and, along with the mode, they are measures of central tendency. That is, they all seek to identify what is typical of a set of data, although each takes a different mathematical approach to this task. The mode, for example, is simply the value in a set of data which occurs most frequently.

Let us use the mode to better understand the concept of the modal personality. In any group there will be a range of personalities. Some people will be relatively more aggressive; others more passive. Some will express their emotions freely, while others will be more controlled. Some will use logical cognitive thought processes, and others will find it difficult to think in a logical, problem-solving way. Since personality refers to the organized collection of such behavioral, emotional, and thought processes, we can expect to find many kinds of personalities represented in any group.

Yet anthropologists and sociologists have also discovered that each culture has a modal personality. That is to say, in each culture certain ways of behaving, feeling, and thinking are more common than others. White Anglo-Saxon males in the United States are, on the whole, relatively aggressive in contrast to males in some Native American tribes. Modal personality is not a measurement of whether something is good or bad, but simply of what is most common. Often that which is most common is a good clue to what a group values, but not always. Just because the modal cause of death is heart disease doesn't mean that heart disease is highly valued! However, it may reflect what social patterns are valued and illustrate the (unanticipated) effect of these patterns in causing heart disease. We can see, then, how a statistic like the mode summarizes large amounts of data in a way that enables us to better understand some aspect of human behavior.

MODELS OF PERSONALITY DEVELOPMENT

The link between socialization and personality development has been explored by both sociology and psychology. This is an area where there is continuing study and few firm conclusions. A number of social scientists have been influential in expanding our knowledge in this area. Each has contributed concepts and theoretical frameworks that help explain personality development and the place of socialization in this process. We will now review the ideas of a few of the most prominent thinkers. Keep in mind that each believes that the quantity and quality of our interactions with others is of primary importance in personality development.

Freud's Theory of the Unconscious

The famous Viennese doctor, Sigmund Freud (1856–1939), constructed a theory of personality development which has influenced Western ideas for the last half-century. Although his popularity has diminished in recent years, his idea that we are affected by strong and primitive forces working in the subconscious is still influential.

The forces Freud described are sexual desire and aggression which struggle constantly with the rules and the demands of the social order. The process of socialization, Freud argued, is a continuous and unhappy battle between opposing forces. The infant is an instinctive, pleasure-seeking creature who is totally absorbed in obtaining bodily gratification. Society is a complex arrangement of cooperation with others. During the "growing up" process the child learns to bury selfishness in favor of order.

Freud called the part of the psyche that seeks immediate gratification of physical and emotional needs the *id*. Infants are totally dominated by the id. As children grow, however, they begin to discover that the world will not always satisfy their desires. Older people have rules and regulations: children must play by the rules to get what they want. Gradually they develop the ability to reason; they learn to gratify their needs in socially approved ways. Freud called this rational part of personality the *ego*.

Finally, as children are socialized to the norms of their society, they develop what Freud called a *superego,* or conscience. In effect, the superego is an internalization of others' (primarily one's parents') ideas about right and wrong. Freud believed that the id and superego are forever at odds. Their struggle between desire and morality is never resolved; socialization is never complete. The ego, the rational mind between these two forces, tries to reconcile them by redirecting impulses from the id into channels that the superego finds acceptable. Freud went on to suggest that if the individual's needs are not sufficiently satisfied in infancy and early childhood, and if socialization is too harsh, the child will not develop the "ego strength" necessary for a happy and satisfying adult life.

Cooley's Theory of the Looking-Glass Self

Charles Horton Cooley (1864–1929), an early social psychologist, suggested that the "self" is largely a social product, and he outlined a process that differed from Freud's. Cooley was puzzled by the fact that so many people's self-concepts have little or no relation to reality. Intelligent, well-read women go through life thinking themselves dull; successful businessmen attribute their triumphs to luck, not skill; stern parents see themselves as kind, loving, and permissive; homely individuals flirt and parade about as if they were magnificent. How, Cooley asked, do people acquire the sense that they are intelligent or dull, warm or hostile, beautiful or ugly?

Like Freud and others, Cooley looked for an answer in childhood experiences. He suggested that at an early age, children begin to sense that their parents are *evaluating* their looks, moods, and behavior. Each feels perceived as a particular *kind* of child, as one who may or may not live up to his or her parents' hopes. With the realization that people are judging them, children rather suddenly become aware of themselves as distinct persons. They begin scanning their parents' faces for clues to their identity. If their parents and siblings tell them over and over that they are independent and assertive, they will probably grow up believing that they are and feeling quite positive about themselves. On the other hand, as the following letter suggests, not all parents help their children develop a positive self-concept.

Dear Ann Landers:

I could never talk to anyone about this problem and I must tell it to somebody. It is getting me down.

My husband and I have been married ten years. Our son, who is now eight, is a handsome boy. . . . Our daughter is two years old, and I am sorry to say she is the homeliest child I have ever seen. Nature really played a dirty trick on us. It would have been much better if the boy was homely and the girl had been good looking. A girl needs beauty—a boy doesn't. . . .

When our daughter is older we can have her protruding ears fixed, her chin built up, and her nose remolded. Hopefully, she will have a good figure. If she doesn't there are several things a girl can do. But the growing up years are going to be hard on this pathetic child. Please tell me how to face the future cheerfully. If you could name some movie stars who were homely youngsters, it would help a lot.

*Star Crossed**

---

*From Ann Landers, in the *Washington Post*, April 15, 1971. Courtesy of Field Newspaper Syndicate.

It is disturbing to imagine the self-concept this child will develop on the basis of the "clues" she will gather from her mother's treatment. However, another mother in another society might find the same child exceptionally beautiful. Criteria vary, but all societies evaluate their members, and the way other people react to a person's looks or behavior will affect that person's self-concept.

In some cases, hair and skin color influence both social standing and self-concept. For years black children growing up in the United States learned that their skin color and hair texture were not considered attractive by whites. Consequently, many black people straightened their hair and used skin bleach. Similarly, many Americans— white and black—believe that "blondes have

"I have a good sense of my body in a bathing suit around people who appreciate what I'm doing, like in a contest. Then I'm proud. But on a beach most people are not experts. The general public doesn't know how to look. How proud can you be when they don't even know what they're looking at?"—Arnold Schwarzenegger

Charles Gaines, *Pumping Iron* (1974). New York: Simon and Schuster.

more fun.'' The dark-haired girl may, as a result, grow up thinking she is plain compared to her blonde friend.

Cooley called this the **looking-glass self**—the self-concept all individuals form by observing other people reacting to their behavior.

> *Each to each a looking glass*
> *Reflects the other than doth pass.*

As we see our face, figure, and dress in the glass, and are interested in them because they are ours, and pleased or otherwise with them according as they do or do not answer to what we should like them to be; so in imagination we perceive in another's mind some thought of our appearance, manners, aims, deeds, character, friends, and so on, and are variously affected by it.*

It is important to note that Cooley used the word imagination to describe the individual's perception of his or her appearance to others. One's self-concept, then, does not necessarily reflect reality. S. Frank Miyamoto and Sanford M. Dornbusch (1956) demonstrated that people frequently misjudge the way others see them. These researchers divided 195 subjects into ten groups, and asked them to rate themselves and the other members of the group on intelligence, self-confidence, physical appearance, and likableness. They were then asked to guess how the other members of the group rated them. In nearly every case, the subjects' self-conceptions were closer to what they thought the group felt about them than to the group's actual ratings. More recent research supports these findings (Banks and Grambs, 1972; Fitzgerald, 1977). In checking the social looking glass, people tend to see what they want and have come to expect to see as a result of the cues they have received from others.

---

*From Charles H. Cooley, *Human Nature and the Social Order* (New York: Charles Scribner's Sons, 1902). Reprinted with the permission of Charles Scribner's Sons.

Mead's Theory of the Generalized Other

Young children who are almost entirely dependent on their mothers are especially vulnerable to what they believe their mothers think of them. However, as they grow, the number of **significant others**—people whose evaluations matter enough to affect one's self-esteem—increases. They begin to interact more with their fathers and siblings; they start to play with neighborhood children; they go to school, where they encounter teachers and classmates; they begin to hang out with particular cliques of friends. Adults are somewhat more selective than children or adolescents in their choice of significant others. They look to friends for an appraisal of their home, teachers for an evaluation of their children, business associates for an assessment of their talents. Some of these circles may serve as a **reference group**—any group that individuals take into account when they evaluate their own behavior or self-concept. Medical students, for example, in learning to become doctors, do not consider outsiders capable of evaluating their work, but they try to meet the standards set by other doctors, their professional reference group.

George Herbert Mead (1863–1931) introduced the term *symbolic interaction* to sociology (see Chapter 1). He saw society as a continuous mixing of information, attitudes, and impressions exchanged between people in the form of reactions, gestures, and facial expressions. It was from this point of view that he approached the problem of personality development.

Mead's collected work (1934), published after his death, used the term **generalized other** to describe the impression a person has of society's overall expectations. Mead believed that individuals internalize the attitudes of others; they judge themselves and their behavior according to the general expectations of the others in society.

This awareness of others and their attitudes

develops slowly through the process of role playing. At the age of two or three, children often imitate their parents. They dig with a toy shovel in the garden beside their father or mimic the way their mother sits down in her chair with the newspaper. But they do not really understand the role they are imitating. At about age four, children begin to pretend that they are their mothers or fathers. They go off by themselves or with friends and try on adult roles, switching happily from one to another. In a single afternoon, they can be a father, a fireman, a dancer, an Indian, even a baby. This role playing enables them to discover where they stand in relation to others, but their play is still only imitative. True games are possible only when children become aware of the roles of other players. Team sports, for example, require an understanding of the roles of the other players and of their expectations of you. To play outfield on a baseball team, the child must be able to see the game from the batter's point of view; must be aware of what the batter may do and what the batter expects the outfielder to do. At about age six or seven, children develop this ability, not only in sports but in all areas of life; and they begin to expect of themselves what others expect of them. In

other words, they internalize the team, the coach, the rule-book—the expectations and values of society—in the form of a *generalized other*.

Erik Erikson: Eight Stages of Human Development

Erik Erikson, an eminent American psychologist, has suggested theories of personality development that provide useful guides to the study of the processes of socialization and social interaction. Erikson, a pupil of Freud's, concentrated his own study on the various choices the ego makes between the desires of the id and the social know-how of the superego. This analysis led him to identify eight stages in the ongoing development of the self. At each stage, the personality has the ability to move in either of two general directions. Viewed sociologically, Erikson's scheme illustrates the course of an individual from the most personal concerns to the most sweeping of compromises with the social environment.

1. Infancy (trust vs. mistrust). In their earliest stages, children are completely dependent

TABLE 4.1 / ERIKSON'S EIGHT STAGES OF HUMAN DEVELOPMENT

Stage	Approximate Age	Psychological Crisis
Infancy	0–3	Trust/mistrust
Early childhood	3–5	Autonomy/shame and doubt
Play stage	4–5	Initiative/guilt
School age	6–12	Industry/inferiority
Adolescence	12–	Identity/confusion
Young adulthood		Intimacy/isolation
Young adulthood and middle age		Generativity/stagnation
Old age		Integrity/despair

on others for their place in the world. They are helpless and everything around them is new. At this point they come to judge the world according to the quality of the treatment they receive. If they are warmly cared for, they will develop the basic feeling that the world is essentially trustworthy and reliable. If they are treated haphazardly, they will develop feelings of mistrust.

2. Early childhood (autonomy vs. shame and doubt). By the age of three, children have begun making major attempts to take responsibility for their own bodies. Naturally, they are bound to fail or go beyond their own capacities quite easily. For example, they may urinate on furniture, climb too high and become frightened, or experiment with electrical outlets. At this point they may develop feelings of autonomy (self-confidence) or of self-doubt. Parents who encourage the child's explorations without exposing the child to unnecessary danger or dismay will foster self-confidence.

3. The play stage (initiative vs. guilt). By the age of five, children are beginning to try out their feelings about the world and about themselves in the form of games and fantasies. If the products of their imaginations are met with respect, they will grow to have confidence in the things they initiate. If they are ridiculed, they will tend to develop feelings of guilt.

4. School age (industry vs. inferiority). In school, children confront the need to fit in and to be evaluated by strangers whose attitudes are largely impersonal. At this stage, they may either come to feel that they are acceptable to the world beyond their families or that they are somehow inferior.

5. Adolescence (identity vs. confusion). Adolescents are in a stage between childhood and adulthood. Most important at this time is that individuals feel a sense of progression and of continuity from life's early orientations to the general plans they are beginning to see for their futures. Furthermore, they need to establish a continuity between who they feel they are and the reactions they receive from other people. If they are unable to coordinate these various factors, a clear sense of self may not develop.

6. Young adulthood (intimacy vs. isolation). The ability to make commitments of friendship or love to other people poses another crisis of opposites. To be intimate is to be under the partial control of another person, but to maintain the self untouched is to lose the ability to be intimate. The ability to establish commitments of the self is established or rejected at this point.

7. Young adulthood and middle age (generativity vs. stagnation). *Generativity* means to be doing something of significance, creating something. With the possibilities of childhood gone and the path of the future fairly well established beyond any major changes, individuals begin to commit themselves to productive and giving activities. Parenthood and job commitments answer these needs in most people. This time of life is actually marked by several alternating periods of activity and stagnation.

8. Old age (integrity vs. despair). Finally, unable to begin anything new, individuals review their lives and judge the quality of their contributions and choices. They may accept their lives as meaningful or they may fall into despair as they evaluate all their past as many lost chances.

All of these theories emphasize the importance of socialization in the process of personality development. Regardless of the biological inheritance with which one begins life, the process of growth will be influenced by the social environment. In learning *how* to behave, the person develops a sense of *who* he or she is. This idea affects what will be seen as appropriate behavior. For example, women who are overprotected may develop a sense of themselves which emphasizes

During young adulthood and middle age, people often commit themselves to productive and giving activities. Many satisfy their desire to feel significant and creative through parenthood or through their jobs—like this music teacher helping her students fashion instruments out of natural objects.

what they cannot do. As a result, they may not even try to do certain things—their socialization has taught them that it would be inappropriate and futile to do so. Thus, we can see the interaction between socialization, personality, and society. Socialization prepares people to do certain things and to think of themselves in a certain way. It determines how they will try to participate in society, and whether or not their efforts will be successful.

SOCIALIZATION AS CONTROL

Thus far we have looked at socialization as a process helpful to individuals and society; however, it can also be analyzed from a very different perspective: socialization as a mechanism of social control. As noted in Chapter 1, Karl Marx felt that all of the institutions of society functioned to support its dominant ideology. This, he felt, ensured that those in power would preserve their privilege. As a result, schools, churchs, political parties, and the economic system all functioned to support the existing social structure. Yet it is through these social institutions that socialization occurs. Most people, then, learn behaviors and ideas that are actually counter to their own best interests. In our own society, for example, we learn to value competition, and believe that if we work hard enough we will be successful. Conflict theorists would point out that this work ethic is very useful for employers, but it is unlikely to result in economic success for those members of society lacking education, skills, or connections (Auletta, 1981). In effect, then, socialization may serve to control people's behavior so that they don't challenge the existing social structure.

Other factors may also make socialization a less than liberating and enriching experience for many members of society. Take Luis Guzman, for example.

Like many other young criminals, Luis grew up in a family with little structure. The family moved from one dilapidated tenement to another. Neither parent paid much attention to the children. Meals and bedtimes could come at any time. Sometimes there was no food at all in the house. Once, one of Luis's sisters was bitten by a rat as she slept. . . . Keeping track of Luis was beyond either parent. . . . They remember some, but not all the institutions he has lived in, beginning with a brief stay in a Roman Catholic home when he was five years old . . . the arrests and his escapes are a jumble in their minds. (Treaster, 1981)

Luis is obviously an extreme example, but the increase in incidences of child and spouse abuse attests to the fact that many families are troubled. Similarly, many schools are plagued by crime and lack of resources. Peer groups often reward drug use and the crime needed to support drug habits.

Children raised in institutions also encounter limited socialization opportunities. Comparisons between children raised in institutions and children raised at home by their parents indicate that even very basic motor skills are in part learned behavior. In most orphanages and hospitals, children receive adequate but minimal care: they are washed, changed, fed, and turned in their cribs. But attendants rarely have time to play with the infants, talk to them, or help them to sit up or grasp a toy. Researchers have found that institutionalized children are between two and twelve months behind normal children in their ability to sit, grasp objects, and walk (Munroe and Munroe, 1975).

The research of Jack and Barbara Tizard provides another example. They report that their studies of institutional and family children suggest that a major difference in the personality development of the children they studied was related to the *quality* of the relationships they were allowed to form with the individuals who raised them. Those who were able to develop close relationships (adopted children and those who were finally returned to their parents) showed more maturity than those who were raised in institutions where even their favorite nurses came and went according to shifts and job changes (Tizard and Tizard, 1974).

To illustrate the way in which social control and fragmented socialization can reinforce each other, consider the case of homosexuals. A society like our own strongly emphasizes the family, male dominance, and fairly narrowly defined, heterosexually oriented sex roles. Homosexuals are perceived as a potential threat to these existing values and social structures in a number of ways. Familylike relationships exist among homosexuals, but they do not emphasize children and formal legal bonds. Homosexuals can relate to each other in ways which mix conventionally "masculine" and "feminine" feelings and activities, challenging conventional sex roles. All of this leads to opportunities to rethink male and female roles, and to increase individual freedom of life style and ways of relating to others. Yet it also questions conventional social patterns, especially those which value things "masculine" more than things "feminine." This view, of course, supports efforts of many women's groups to eradicate sexism in general. It is little wonder, then, that dominant groups in society discourage homosexuality, and attempt to control opportunities to be socialized as a homosexual.

The family is a good example of how socialization of homosexuals is controlled. Most homosexuals are raised in heterosexual families. From an early age, they learn that heterosexual behavior is desirable, even though their own feelings are homosexual. They are taught conventional heterosexual patterns of relating to others: male-female roles, dating, and so on. Homosexual behavior is usually punished when it occurs, either informally through ridicule and shame, or more formally through being ejected from the family home or even forced into psychiatric treatment. Places for homosexuals to socialize are not popularized in the mass media, so homosexuals often have difficulty making contact with peers who could provide support for them. Yet it is only through such contact that socialization as a homosexual is really possible.

The experiences which homosexuals have are not that uncommon. Since socialization prepares people for acceptable participation in society as defined by dominant power groups, all members of minority groups will be subject to control through socialization. The handicapped learn they are stigmatized and are encouraged to be docile and dependent. The poor are encouraged to work harder rather than to question an economic system built on competition among people with vastly different resources. Racial and ethnic minorities are taught that they talk, eat, and dress "funny," and that they need to become like

everyone else. Women who aspire to careers learn to "dress for success" by emulating men. In many ways, then, socialization becomes a complex process of human development mixed with social control.

To summarize, there is no doubt that socialization is fundamental to human beings if they are to develop their genetic potential. It is also basic to the establishment of patterns of social behavior that make social order possible. Yet agents of socialization are very susceptible to manipulation by power groups in society, and they vary greatly in their ability to prepare people for fulfilling lives in society. It is little wonder, then, that some see socialization as a mechanistic process which limits freedom of choice and individuality. We will consider this issue in the next section.

CONFORMITY VERSUS FREEDOM

Commenting on "the incredible fact" that most people grow up to be relatively predictable human beings living well within the norms of their society, sociologist Peter Berger (1963) wrote:

Our imprisonment in society . . . appears as something effected as much from within ourselves as by the operation of external forces. . . . Society not only controls our movements, but shapes our identity, our thoughts and emotions. The structures of society become the structures of our own consciousness. (p. 121)

What Berger suggested is that socialization is more than simply learning to conform to society's rules; it is growing to *like* doing what one is supposed to do. When children in the United States are first taught to use the toilet, no doubt they are puzzled by the significance their parents attach to so uninteresting an object. But they realize that it is very important to parents and eventually they learn to use the bathroom like an adult. They conform. In fact, it is only a matter of time before they start to prefer using the toilet to their former state of freedom. People in other parts of the world are perfectly content to relieve themselves by the side of the road; most of us would find this practice distasteful.

But conformity to social norms is never total. In theory, all people in the United States believe that it is wrong to steal. Private property is sacred in this country. Nevertheless, thousands of people commit burglary every year. Of course, most people do not steal. But the temptations are there; we all experience them, and some of us give in. We tend to treat some norms pragmatically, weighing the chances and consequences of getting caught against the rewards of "getting away with it."

Throughout this chapter we have stressed society's role in personality development. The evidence of the dehumanizing effects of isolation presented at several points indicates that people cannot by themselves build and maintain a sense of individual human identity. Genetic endowment and varied life experiences make individuals different; but all people internalize many of their society's rules. Does this mean that society holds the strings and that people are only puppets?

Is Freedom an Illusion?

The classic statement of American individualism comes from Henry David Thoreau's *Walden*:

If a man does not keep pace with his companions, perhaps it is because he hears a different drummer. Let him step to the music which he hears, however measured or far away.

But what if everyone marched to a different drummer? If we want to live alone, we can live as we like. But if we want and need other people,

we have to create some common ground of mutual expectations. To live in a family, to have friends and get along with peers, to participate in society as a student or worker, we must compromise our own personal needs and desires to some extent. People are complex beings, full of uncertain and contradictory thoughts and feelings, personal fantasies, drives, ambitions, fears. Conflicts arise whenever two or more people get together. But does this mean that individuals must sacrifice their freedom to survive?

The real question seems to be where to draw the line between individuality and social demands. At what point do people begin to place their own needs above society's needs? At what point do social demands exceed social rewards? Is the conflict between the individual and society necessary, or does the much-talked-about alienation of people today suggest that something is wrong with society—or with the individuals who compose society?

Freud believed that conflict between the individual and society is built into the human condition, and that it can never be resolved completely:

The development of the individual seems . . . to be a product of the interaction between two urges, the urge towards happiness . . . and the urge towards union with others in the community . . . the two urges . . . must struggle with each other in every individual; and so, also, the two processes of individual and of cultural development must stand in hostile opposition to each other. . . . (1961, p. 134)

Freud argued that "civilization and its discontents" are necessary. By nature, people are self-centered, lazy, irrational, antisocial: without being forced they would never consent to follow social rules. Nevertheless, he felt that oversocialization—the complete submission of the self to social demands—was destructive. People become neurotic when they give up too many of their desires and impulses in order to become what they believe they are expected to become.

Although many of us seldom question the patterns of behavior we have learned through socialization, others, like the "hippies" of the 1960s, challenge society's rules and make choices that clearly run counter to societal norms.

The Quest for Freedom and Dignity

The psychologist B.F. Skinner is known as a behaviorist. He believes that people do not shape the world, rather that it shapes them. "People have assumed from the beginning of time that they initiate their own actions . . . To suppose this is a great mistake. Geneticists would say that the individual acts to maximize his survival, but actually it is the other way around:

the environment causes us to select behaviors; if behaviors are successful, we will act that way in the future" (Greenberg, 1981: C3).* Skinner goes on to dispute sociobiologists who believe that some behaviors may be genetically influenced. To Skinner, social experiences are far more significant determinants of behavior than genes. For example, when one person goes to another's aid

*© 1981 by The New York Times Company. Reprinted by permission.

it is because earlier learning has taught the good samaritan that he or she will be rewarded for this behavior. Rewards might take the form of social praise, monetary rewards, or even benefits in an afterlife. Behaviorists believe that all behavior is influenced by rewards and punishments: we do what we get rewarded for. Of course, rewards may be of many different kinds. However, Skinner feels that the distribution of rewards and punishments in our society is carried out in a haphazard way that leads as often as not to chaos and antisocial behavior.

Parents have little understanding of what they are doing with their children; children are subject to conflicting standards from different adults. For adults, there is no stable community to reinforce socially desirable behavior. "Why should anyone be affected by the praise or blame of someone he will never see again?" (Skinner, 1971: 155) In *Beyond Freedom and Dignity* (1971), Skinner questioned those who believe people's dignity depends on their independence, that goodness exists because people are free to do evil but choose otherwise. In his view, freedom is an illusion. If people are products of their environment, he argued, the only sensible course is to engineer a social environment in which people would be rewarded consistently for desirable behavior.

Although Skinner is highly respected for his experimental work in the use of rewards and punishments as part of learning, not all social scientists agree with his suggestions for the future of society. Most of us accept some degree of manipulation of rewards and punishments with mental patients, in part because we assume they are suffering. But what about punishing students or employees when they are late for class or work by administering electric shocks to them? In addition, Skinner does not address himself to the question of who would decide what is normal and socially desirable. No doubt a good deal of our behavior is shaped by rewards from parents, friends, teachers, the media; but that is not the same as deliberate, controlled manipulation of all areas of life.

The issue of choice. Although many would disagree with the concept of total control suggested by Skinner, all of us can see that much of our behavior is already controlled. Through socialization we learn patterns of behavior that we never even think to question. This is true even though many times what we learn—and accept—is damaging to us. For many years the physically handicapped accepted society's description of them as helpless, and they rarely challenged the lack of facilities that then effectively made them helpless. We are all controlled in other ways as well: the poor simply do not have access to good quality housing, schooling, and medical care simply by virtue of their poverty. They may want a better life, but their income denies their wishes.

Are we, then, really captives who have little choice and control over our own lives? If we look back a few years, we can recall a period when "hippies" were common. These people challenged many social rules and rejected much of their socialization. Even today, we see change all around us. People are choosing to divorce in spite of vows that marriage is forever; others are changing their participation in organized religion in spite of their religious upbringing; still others are moving to the suburbs although they never thought they could do without the stimulation of city life. Clearly, people do make choices that run counter to their upbringing and even to common societal norms. How is this possible if society exerts such strong controls on us?

In truth, we have more freedom of choice than appears possible at first glance. For one thing, norms are not rigid—they allow some flexibility and variation, which can gradually lead to change. Also, the fact that socialization is lifelong means that we sometimes join new groups which help us to rethink some of our earlier socialization. Studies of recruitment into sects and cults, for example, show that this is an important element in that process (Stark and Bainbridge, 1980). Then, too, the structures and institutions of society change and exert pressure for change on those within them. The fast-paced, impersonal supermarket makes it less likely that the weekly grocery shopping will be the social occasion that it often used to be when shops were small and customers known by name.

Perhaps the most important point of all is to remember that society is the people who populate it. Social structures are developed which tend to foster predictable behavior, but the structures themselves exist because people have created them. If the structures become too confining, they can be changed. When enough people perceive that society is not meeting their needs, it can be changed. Socialization works to teach us what we—through the intermediary of social structures—have decided we ought to know. Collectively, we can change our mind, as we did when we outlawed racial segregation and discrimination. We can also change our mind one by one. The young man who decides to study ballet rather than marketing is defying convention. So is the social activist who marches in protest of nuclear power or killing whales. Even crime can be used as a way to rebel against societal conventions when they are perceived as being inequitable and personally disadvantaging—"hustling" may be far more satisfying and rewarding. These individual choices often carry costs—being unpopular in one's peer group, being jeered by bystanders, or being imprisoned, for example. But choice is possible, and can even develop into a social movement (discussed in detail in Chapter 19).

Most of us will rarely choose to reject what we have been taught. It is easier not to, and we may be basically satisfied with our lot. But it is important to remember that we can, and to understand that doing so is not so unusual. Part of society is change; part of socialization is relearning and new learning. Such possibilities make the study of sociology so endlessly fascinating—society is never static, never dull!

SUMMARY

1. The main purposes of this chapter are: to discuss the processes involved in socialization (social learning); to examine formal and informal agents of socialization such as the family, peer groups, school, mass media, and the workplace; to discuss the importance of socialization for personality development, including a review of major theories; and to consider the possibilities for freedom and individuality in society.

2. Socialization is the process of learning and internalizing culturally approved ways of thinking, feeling, and behaving. One aspect of socialization is the development of a self-concept, which many theories try to explain and predict: Freud's theory of the unconscious, Cooley's theory of the look-ing-glass self, Mead's theory of the generalized other, and Erikson's eight stages of human development

3. Socialization and development occur throughout the life cycle. They occur through contact with other socialized human beings in social structures which serve as agents of socialization: the family, peer groups, school, the mass media, and the workplace. Each of these tends to have particular significance at different points in the life cycle.

4. For centuries people have debated the question of whether personality is determined by inheritance (genes/nature) or environment (experience/nurture). The general belief among sociol-

ogists today is that people are born with certain genetically determined needs, potentials, and limits, and learn to satisfy their needs and develop their potential within a particular social environment. Environment is important to humans because they lack the genetic programming that guides the behavior of other animals.

5. Socialization can be viewed as both liberating and confining. It allows human beings to develop their genetic potential, yet it tends to shape this potential so that it fits into prevailing standards of what is desirable. Many people are socialized in social structures that are harsh or disorganized, creating substantial obstacles to learning social roles and internalizing them into a healthy self-identity.

6. Balancing conformity and freedom is a difficult task for the individual and society. Socialization emphasizes conformity, yet there are opportunities to choose alternative behaviors. Often, however, choosing to act differently entails paying social costs. Nevertheless, these options can be important sources of personal satisfaction and useful social change.

REVIEW

Key Terms

Socialization	Agent of socialization	Nurture	Significant others
Personality	Peer group	Sociobiology	Reference group
Total institution	Nature	Looking-glass self	Generalized other
Anticipatory socialization			

Review and Discussion

1. Try to remember how your parents got you to obey their rules. Did they reason? Threaten and carry out punishment? If you decide to have children, what might you do differently? If you have children already, how have your methods differed from your parents' and why?

2. Have you ever experienced any times in your life where you felt your socialization was inadequate; e.g., you didn't know how you were supposed to act? Think about specific instances, and try to understand why they may have occurred.

3. How important is your current peer group as an agent of socialization? Do you learn things from your friends? Do they exert a noticeable influence on your behavior? In general, are you satisfied with the influence of your peer group on your life? Why or why not?

4. How important are the mass media in your life? Do you read a newspaper regularly? Watch TV? Listen to the radio? Why do you do each? Do you feel that you are influenced by each? If so, in what ways?

5. How would you describe your personality? Are you similar to others in your family, or quite different? Why do you think this is so?

6. In *The Pursuit of Loneliness* (1971), Philip Slater wrote: "One of the major goals of technology in America is to free us from the necessity of relating to, submitting to, depending upon, or controlling other people. Unfortunately the more we have succeeded in doing this the more we have felt disconnected, bored, lonely, unprotected, unnecessary, and unsafe" (p. 26). Do you agree or disagree with Slater's remarks? Why?

References

Ainsworth, Mary (1974). Phases of the development of infant-mother attachment. In *Culture and Per-*

sonality: Contemporary Readings, ed. Robert A. Levine, pp. 61–64. Chicago: Aldine.

Altman, Irwin (1975). *Environment and Social Behavior.* Monterey, Cal.: Brooks-Cole.

Ardrey, Robert (1966). *The Territorial Imperative.* New York: Atheneum.

Auletta, Ken (1981). The underclass. *The New Yorker,* November 16, 1981, pp. 63ff.

Banks, James W., and **Jean D. Grambs,** eds. (1972). *Black Self-Concept.* New York: McGraw-Hill.

Barchas, Patricia (1976). Physiological sociology: Interface of sociological and biological process. In *Annual Review of Sociology,* eds. Alex Inkeles, James Coleman, and Neil Smelser, pp. 299–334. Palo Alto, Cal: Annual Reviews, Inc.

Becker, Howard S., and **Blanche Geer** (1958). The fate of idealism in medical school. *American Sociological Review* 23, no. 1 (February 1958): 50–56.

Becker, Howard S., with **Blanche Geer, Everett Hughes,** and **Anselm Strauss** (1961). *Boys in White.* Chicago: University of Chicago Press.

Berger, Peter L. (1963). *Invitation to Sociology.* New York: Anchor Books.

Bernard, Jessie (1981). *The Female World.* New York: Free Press.

Bernstein, Paul (1981). Making of a literary shogun. *The New York Times Magazine,* September 13, 1981, pp. 46ff.

Billingsley, Andrew, and **Jeanne Giovannoni** (1972). *Children of the Storm.* New York: Harcourt Brace Jovanovich.

Bronfenbrenner, Urie (1970). *Two Worlds of Childhood.* New York: Russell Sage Foundation.

Charnofsky, Harold (1974). Ballplayers, occupational image and the maximization of profit. In *Varieties of Work Experience,* eds. Phyllis I. Stewart and Muriel G. Cantor, pp. 262–73. New York: John Wiley.

Chase, Naomi (1976). *A Child Is Being Beaten.* New York: McGraw-Hill.

Clarke-Stewart, Alison (1977). *Child Care in the Family.* New York: Academic Press.

Clausen, John A., and **Judith R. Williams** (1963). Sociological correlates of child behavior. In *Child Psychology,* 62nd Yearbook of the National Society for the Study of Education, Part I, ed. H. W. Stevenson, pp. 68–100. Chicago: University of Chicago Press.

Coleman, James (1961). *The Adolescent Society.* New York: Free Press.

Collins, Glenn (1981). Stressful world of adolescent. *The New York Times,* December 7, 1981, p. B18.

Cook-Gumperz, Jenny (1973). *Social Control and Socialization.* Boston: Routledge and Kegan Paul.

Cooley, Charles R. (1902). *Human Nature and the Social Order.* New York: Scribners.

Davis, Kingsley (1947). Final note on a case of extreme isolation. *American Journal of Sociology* 52: 432–37.

Duberman, Lucile (1976). *Social Inequality: Class and Caste in America.* Philadelphia: J. B. Lippincott.

Federico, Ronald (1974). Recruitment, training, and performance: The case of ballet. In *Varieties of Work Experience,* eds. Phyllis Stewart and Muriel Cantor. New York: John Wiley.

———— (1982). Factors affecting the decision by ballet dancers to end their performing careers. In *Performers and Performances,* eds. Jack Kamerman and Rosann Mortorella. South Hadley, Mass.: J. F. Bergin Publishing Co.

Fitzgerald, Thomas K. (1977). *Education and Identity.* Wellington, New Zealand: New Zealand Council on Educational Research.

Freud, Sigmund (1961). *The Future of an Illusion, Civilization and Its Discontents, and Other Works.* London: Hogarth.

Fricke, Aaron (1981). *Reflections of a Rock Lobster.* Boston: Alyson Publications.

Friedenberg, Edgar Z. (1959). *The Vanishing Adolescent.* Boston: Beacon Press.

———— (1965). *Coming of Age in America.* New York: Random House.

Goffman, Erving (1961). *Asylums.* Chicago: Aldine.

Gordon, Chad (1976). Development of evaluated role

identities. In *Annual Review of Sociology,* eds. Alex Inkeles, James Coleman, and Neil Smelser, pp. 405–33. Palo Alto, Cal.: Annual Reviews, Inc.

Greenberg, Joel (1981). B. F. Skinner now sees little hope for the world's salvation. *The New York Times,* September 15, 1981, pp. C1ff.

Gumpert, Gary, and **Robert Cathcart,** eds. (1979). *Inter/Media: Interpersonal Communication in a Media World.* New York: Oxford University Press.

Johnson, Harriette C. (1980). *Behavior Psychopathology and the Brain,* vol. I. New York: Curriculum Concepts.

Kalish, Richard A. (1975). *Late Adulthood: Perspectives on Human Development.* Belmont, Cal.: Wadsworth.

Klapper, Joseph (1960). *The Effects of Mass Communication.* New York: Free Press.

Kohn, Melvin (1963). Social class and parent-child relationships: An interpretation. *American Journal of Sociology* 68: 471–80.

Kohn, Melvin, and **Carmi Schooler** (1969). Class, occupation and orientation. *American Sociological Review 34* (1969): 659–678.

——— (1973). Occupational experience and psychological functioning. *American Sociological Review 38* (1973): 97–118.

Lopez, Barry (1979). *Of Wolves and Men.* New York: Scribners.

Lorenz, Konrad (1966). *On Aggression.* New York: Harcourt, Brace, and World.

Mazo, Joseph (1974). *Dance is a Contact Sport.* New York: E. P. Dutton.

Mead, George Herbert (1934). *Mind, Self, and Society,* ed. Charles W. Morris. Chicago: University of Chicago Press.

Miyamoto, Frank S., and **Sanford M. Dornbusch** (1956). A test of interaction hypothesis of self-conception. *American Journal of Sociology* 61: 399–403.

Munroe, Robert, and **Ruth Munroe** (1975). *Cross-cultural Human Development.* Belmont, Cal.: Wadsworth.

Ogbu, John (1978). *Minority Education and Caste.* New York: Academic Press.

Reed, Sally (1981). The basic skills, company style. *The New York Times Survey of Continuing Education,* August 30, 1981, p. 20.

Ritzer, George (1977). *Working: Conflict and Change,* 2nd ed. Englewood Cliffs, N.J.: Prentice-Hall.

Roy, Donald (1954). Efficiency and "The Fix": Informal intergroup relations in a piecework machine shop. *American Journal of Sociology* 60 (November 1954): 255–66.

Ryan, William (1976). *Blaming the Victim,* rev. ed. New York: Vintage Books.

Schaffer, H. Rudolph, and **Peggy E. Emerson** (1964). The development of social attachments in infancy. Monographs of the society for Research in Child Development, no. 3.

Schroder, David (1978). *Engagement in the Mirror: Hairdressers and Their Work.* San Francisco: R. & E. Research Associates.

Sheehan, Susan (1975). *A Welfare Mother.* New York: Mentor.

Skinner, B. F. (1971). *Beyond Freedom and Dignity.* New York: Alfred A. Knopf.

Slater, Philip (1971). *The Pursuit of Loneliness.* Boston: Beacon Press.

Stark, Rodney, and **William Sims Bainbridge** (1980). Networks of faith: interpersonal bonds and recruitment to cults and sects. *American Journal of Sociology* 85, no. 6: 1376–95.

Tiger, Lionel (1972). *Men in Groups.* New York: Random House.

Tizard, Jack, and **Barbara Tizard** (1974). The institution as an environment for development. In *The Integration of the Child into a Social World,* ed. M. Richards. London: Cambridge University Press.

Townsend, John R. (1977). *Top of the World.* Philadelphia: J. B. Lippincott.

Treaster, Joseph (1981). Young life of crime: The violent streets of Luis Guzman. *The New York Times,* November 9, 1981, pp. B1ff.

Turner, Johanne (1980). *Made for Life.* New York: Methuen.

Valle, Ramon, and **Lydia Mendoza** (1978). *The Elderly Latino.* San Diego, Cal.: Campanile Press.

Vollmer, Howard, and **Ronald Mills,** eds. (1966). *Professionalization.* Englewood Cliffs, N.J.: Prentice-Hall.

Whiting, John W. H., and **Irvin B. Child** (1953). *Child Training and Personality.* New Haven, Conn.: Yale University Press.

Wilson, Edward O. (1975a). Human decency is animal. *The New York Times Magazine,* October 12, 1975, pp. 38–50.

——— (1975b). *Sociobiology: The New Synthesis.* Cambridge, Mass.: Belknap Press of Harvard University Press.

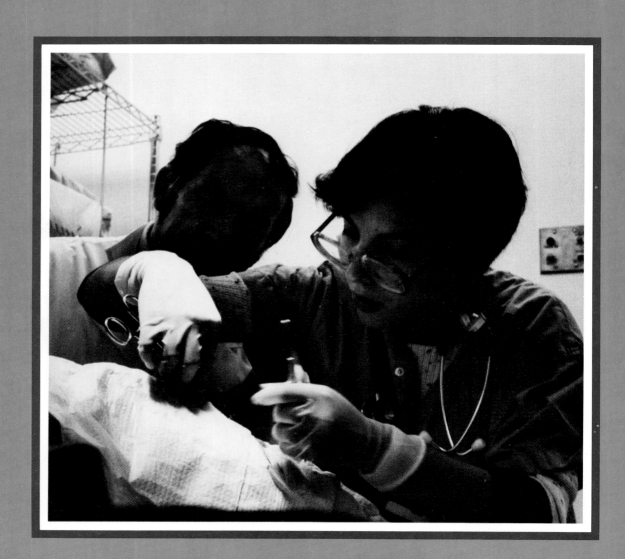

5

WOMEN, SEX ROLES, AND SOCIETY

Several years ago a college instructor posed the following riddle to a class of 35 students. A father and his son were in a serious car accident. The father was killed instantly, and the severely injured son was rushed to the hospital for emergency surgery. A surgeon was called who, approaching the patient, exclaimed: "I cannot operate on this boy, he is my son!" How is this possible?

None of the students could supply an answer to the question. The inability of 35 college students (male and female) to solve the riddle illustrates not merely the stereotype of who is supposed to be a surgeon, but the different worlds of men and women. Whether at school, church, work, or play, boys and girls and men and women are governed by different norms, expectations, and rewards. (Bernard, 1981: 4).

The rules governing the behavior of men and women are not universal and not necessarily consistent within or between societies. In some societies, a woman can be an astronaut. On June 12, 1963, Valentina Tereshkova, a Soviet woman, became the first and so far only woman astronaut. In World War II, both American and Soviet women served in the Armed Forces, but the American women were excluded from combat. Israeli women fought side by side with men in their war of independence, but today, while Israeli women are still subject to military service, they are limited to white-collar work in the military.

Throughout history, what woman could or could not do has been explained in a variety of ways, although biology has remained the central factor in most views. Let us look at some of the biological characteristics of men and women.

BIOLOGICAL DIFFERENCES

All humans have 23 pairs of chromosomes, which carry the genetic material which they have inherited. Each pair of chromosomes is the same, with the exception of the pair responsible for the sex of the individual. Females have two X chromosomes, while males have an X and a Y chromosome. During conception the embryo receives one X chromosome from the female, and either an X or Y chromosome from the male. If the chromosome from the male is an X the sex of the infant is female, but if the chromosome is a Y, the sex is male. Both men and women have the same chemical substances, called hormones, although in different proportions. Men have greater amounts of androgens and testosterone, women greater amounts of estrogen and progesterone. On the basis of available studies, injection of the male testosterone produces more aggressive behavior in animals; however, its effects on humans is still under study.

So far the most basic known functional differences between men and women are women's capacities to reproduce and to lactate (pro-

Shown are the chromosomes of a normal human male. All the pairs are composed of similar shapes except the sex-chromosome pair (lower right corner), which is composed of the large X (female) and smaller Y (male) chromosome.

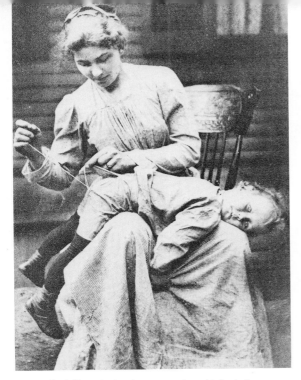

Sex-role differentiation is not merely a biological phenomenon but a reflection of the expectations of different historical periods and different social organizations. For example, how many traditional homemakers of the 1890s had access to other career options? How many could have envisioned the technological and social advances that would open the path for women astronauts in the twentieth century?

duce breast milk). But neither the differences in the chromosomes and hormones, nor the capacity to bear children and lactate provides evidence which would enable us to claim that men or women are inherently better equipped to care for the young or to assume household responsibilities. Similarly, there is no evidence to suggest that a man should be a carpenter or electrician and a woman a seamstress or a telephone operator. If role differences were based on biology, women would not have been—at different periods of history—denied a variety of rights and privileges, e.g., the right to vote, education, jobs, and so forth. Sex role differentiation is not a biological phenomenon. Instead, it is a *social* reflection of the culture and social organization of particular societies. The social nature of **sex role** differentiation is evident also in the *differences of what is considered proper or right for women and men to do,* or not to do, as well as in what it is thought women and men are capable of doing.

SEX ROLE ALLOCATION IN SUBSISTENCE SOCIETIES

Secondary sex differences between males and females show men to be generally stronger, to have a more massive skeleton, a higher muscle-to-fat ratio, and more body hair. These secondary characteristics are not universal, however. As

127

D'Andrade noted, secondary characteristics are affected by cultural, environmental, and technological factors. In Bali, males do not do heavy lifting work, preferring instead to spread a heavy load among many men. As a result, both males and females have slender bodies. But Balinese men who work as dock coolies develop heavy musculature typical of males (D'Andrade, 1966: 176). Therefore, the generally greater size and strength of men may be at least partly the result of the genetic adaptations to generations of men performing heavy labor.

There is some evidence for this theory in subsistence economies where the division of labor corresponded to the physical differences between men and women. Murdock's (1937) cross-cultural studies show men generally engaging in pursuit of sea mammals, hunting, herding, and fishing. Women generally performed such activities as grinding grain, carrying water, cooking, and preserving meat and fish. But not all activities performed by men and women in the 224 societies studied by Murdock were related to the greater strength of men. For example, metal working and weapon making and the manufacture of musical instruments were nearly always male tasks, whereas the manufacture and repair of clothing, pottery making, mat making, and weaving were predominantly tasks allocated to women.

D'Andrade relates physical and social bases for sex role allocation in yet a different way. He suggests that division of labor by sex comes from activities directly related to physical differences but then spreads to activities only indirectly related to physical differences (1966: 178). For example, weapon making as a male activity may precede activities which involve physical strength, like hunting. The reproductive functions of women, which require nursing of the young infant, limit the physical mobility of women; consequently tasks near the domicile only indirectly related to the care of the young become allocated to women.

What may have begun as a functional division of labor, based on physical strength and child-bearing capacity, evolved into a social division of labor. These sex role divisions were buttressed during various periods of history by ideology, Judeo-Christian traditions, laws, and a variety of pseudoscientific theories of women as inferior, subordinate, or less capable than men.

IDEOLOGY AND SEX ROLES

Ideology is a system of beliefs held by members of a group. This common belief system serves as a means to legitimize existing social patterns. Ideologies are ingrained through the process of socialization and education. Parsons has noted that ideologies promote social integration and acceptance of existing structural arrangements as proper and right. Slavery, for example, ultimately rested on the power of the dominant group. However, most of the time little overt force was required to keep slaves subjugated because there was a prevailing ideology of white supremacy, the alleged superiority of whites which justified their enslavement of blacks.

Historically, the subordinate position of women has not been unlike the position of the slaves. It has been supported by an ideology of male supremacy and notions of the natural place of women. The demands of the abolitionists for the emancipation of slaves and for women's rights brought the following response. ". . . If our women are to be emancipated from subjection to the law which God has imposed upon them, . . . if, in studied insult to the authority of God we are to renounce in the marriage contract all claim to obedience, we shall soon have a country over which the genius of Mary Wollstonecraft [an eighteenth-century feminist] would delight to preside, but from which all order and all virtue would be speedily banished . . . there is no deformity of human character from which we turn with deeper loathing than from a woman forgetful of her nature, and clamorous for the vocations and rights of men" (Bledsoe, 1857: 223–25 quoted by Myrdal 1944: 1074).

It would be erroneous to assume that such beliefs were held only by men. Many women also accepted the notions of their own inferiority as God's will. They were content to remain subordinate as the weaker sex, requiring men to care for them.

Hacker (1951) has called attention to the similarities in the caste-like status of both women and blacks. Hacker pointed to the ascribed attributes of women and blacks such as inferior intelligence and smaller brain size; emotionalism of women and blacks; that women and blacks were "contented" with their lot. Both women and men accommodated the image created by this ideology. Men acted graciously and women deferred to them, many times concealing their real feelings by pretending ignorance and by appealing for guidance. Both women and blacks endured discrimination each in their own way. For women, it meant confinement to traditional jobs, deprivation of political influence, etc. To be sure, men married women, but the fact of marriage did not alter the inequality. Love, as Hacker argues, does not mean equality; one may love those who are either inferior or superior, and one may love a person without understanding the person.

Given the vast social and political changes in our society, and the significant educational achievements of women, it should come as no surprise that women are increasingly rejecting the traditional ideologies. However, by no means is this response uniform among all women. Beliefs about the so-called natural place of women are centuries old, and the sociocultural patterns

Many women are rejecting traditional ideologies and entering formerly male-oriented professions and activities. Some, like power-lifter Jan Todd, manage to balance both worlds. When not setting deadlift records (424 lbs.), Jan teaches high school in Nova Scotia, where she and her husband run a 75-acre farm.

have become embedded in the social structure. For example, in the occupational sphere, there is a dual labor market in which low paying jobs are regarded as the domain of women and high paying jobs the domain of men. Sociocultural patterns have also become embedded in personality traits of men and women through the process of socialization. Characteristic of the personality of men are such traits as dominance, independence, and leadership. Men are said to be aggressive, rational, and decisive, not given to emotionalism or tears. It is asserted that women, on the other hand, are indecisive, passive, emotional, dependent, and affectionate. They lack leadership qualities and a rational approach to the world and to things in general. They cry easily, and sulk, and they perform best in interpersonal relations with people, preferably with children and other women. They are fickle and unreliable. Men view the world scientifically, but women rely on intuition.

Parsons (1955) did not attribute inherent personality traits to men or women. But he viewed the division of labor between men and women as functional. Parsons dichotomized the role of women and men into the **expressive,** which focuses on caregiving and providing emotional support, and the **instrumental,** concerned primarily with task performance and getting ahead. He argued that such a division of labor was functional for American society as a whole and for the family in particular. Regardless of how the social division of labor evolved, "there can be little doubt about how the ways in which differentiation plays into the structure and functioning of the family as we know it" (1955: 23). The focus on the male as the primary breadwinner leads naturally to assigning the leadership role—the instrumental role—to the husband. The bearing and early nursing of children establish a primacy on the mother-child relationship, which in turn leads naturally to the mother assuming the expressive role. According to Parsons this ensures the proper socialization of future generations of men and women.

The division of labor into two separate spheres ensures that the economic performance of men will not be hindered by the need to be the primary provider of emotional nurturance and support to the family. It also removes the woman from the instrumental domain, precluding possible competition between men and women in the economic sphere. In Parsons's functional framework, the crucial distinction between male and female roles is not whether women are engaged in paid employment, but the fact that women do not have jobs "which are in basic competition for status with those of their husbands" (1955: 94). Fundamental to the functional framework is that the man has a job which determines his social status or standing. This shows up in differential earnings for men and women (Table 5.1). The woman, whose primary role is that of mother and wife, does not require an independent status. It is sufficient for the wife to be dependent on the status of the husband. As a child, she derives her status from the position of her father, and as a wife from the position of her husband. For the large segment of women who worked, their work did not supply them with a status of their own. It was simply viewed as a useful source of supplemental income for the family. Middle-class women generally held positions lower than their husbands, and there was no reason to treat the husband and wife as independent.

In such a view women, as a category, could not aspire or aim for a position in which they competed with men. Women who did try to compete with men in the occupational world were viewed as deviant. The functional framework was in essence an ideology serving to perpetuate the authority and power of men. It was legitimized by notions of child care as natural to women, and necessary if we are to protect the family and society. Not all women subscribed to these notions, and not all women were willing to accept their condition in society. However, women who aspired to careers encountered a variety of obstacles. They were generally con-

TABLE 5.1 / MEDIAN EARNINGS OF FULL-TIME, YEAR ROUND WORKERS BY SEX: 1955—79

| Year | Median Earnings | | | | Women's Earnings as Percent of Men's |
| | Current dollars | | 1979 dollars | | |
	Women	*Men*	*Women*	*Men*	
1955	$ 2,719	$ 4,252	$ 7,369	$11,523	64
1960	3,293	5,417	8,071	13,277	61
1965	3,823	6,375	8,789	14,655	60
1970	5,323	8,966	9,950	16,759	59
1975	7,504	12,758	10,127	17,217	59
1979	10,168	17,062	10,168	17,062	60

Source: Linda J. Waite, "U.S. Women at Work," *Population Bulletin* 36, no. 2 (May 1981): 30. Published by Population Reference Bureau, Inc., Washington, D.C.

sidered neurotic, aggressive, and castrating. And even if they ignored the public opinion about their deviant roles, married women experienced considerable role conflicts between their roles as women, employees, wives, and mothers. Now let us turn to the process through which men and women learn sex role expectations and behaviors.

SOCIALIZATION

Before the socialization process creates an American or Russian, before we learn that we are Catholic or Protestant, Jew or Mormon, and long before we learn that the president of the United States is elected every four years, the socialization process establishes a gender identity which remains the basic identification for the duration of one's life. **Sex** is a biological fact but **gender** is a social and psychological identity, irrespective of the biological fact of sex. Males, if socialized as females, will socially and psychologically identify as females. Similarly girls, if reared as boys, will identify with the male gender (Money and Ehrhandt, 1972). As a result, societies may practice **sex differentiation,** in which males and females are treated differently simply

because of their biological characteristics. Societies may also engage in **gender differentiation,** treating men and women differently because of sex-role expectations. When gender differentiation is practiced, and sex roles are very clearly defined, **sex role stereotyping** occurs. Men and women are expected to act in specified ways, regardless of whether they want to or even are able to. Like any stereotype, sex-role stereotypes tend to ignore individual preferences or characteristics. That is why in the past women were expected to defer to their husbands even if the women were in reality more intelligent, more skillful, or more highly trained.

All infants, whether reared in the United States or China, require physical care and emotional sustenance. In principle, infants—whether boys or girls—receive the required care, usually from their mothers. Recent studies, however, suggest that male infants receive less immediate attention and less cuddling than girl infants (Lewis, 1972). The mother, as the major and immediate agent of socialization, is not likely to think in terms of "I am socializing a female (male) child." However, the cultural beliefs that girls are less strong, or more delicate than boys, may elicit greater attention and more nurturing behavior for girls than boys. Rubin et al. (1974) found

that first-time parents rated their daughters as
softer, smaller, and less attentive than sons.
Whether girls in reality are softer or weaker is
not the issue, but the perception and perhaps
expectation that girls should be smaller or softer
may encourage dependency in girls but not in
boys.

Sociocultural patterns have long imposed
symbolic images of boys in blue and girls in
pink, alerting all to a normative response: "she
is beautiful," "he is big." The five-month-old
infant is rewarded with a smile or hug when
capable of pulling itself to a standing position,
but the male infant is more likely to be told,
"You are a big strong boy," and the female
infant, "You are a good girl." As the child grows
older, the praise and rewards will have continued
to reflect the normative patterns of appropriate
future roles for boys and girls. The three-year-
old boy who skins his knee may be told, "Boys
do not cry," but girls are permitted to express
their discomfort in tears. In fact, a girl's tears are
not only symbolic of discomfort and pain, but
represent her supposed fragility, sensitivity, and
emotionalism.

At an early stage of the child's development,
scripts anticipating the differential roles in adulthood prevail for boys and girls (Kohlberg, 1966).
Children internalize their gender through differential rewards and punishments: behavior culturally appropriate for male or female gender is
rewarded. A girl playing with a doll will elicit
approval; a comparable choice by a boy will
result in disapproval, particularly from the male
parent. Differential rewards are dispensed by
parents, peers, and adults in general. To be sure,
there are class and subcultural differences in
socialization (Kohn, 1978), but regardless of class
variations, the boy is expected to master an
occupation eventually, whereas the ultimate role
for the girl is wife and mother. By the age of
five, on the basis of its experience and intelligence,
a child is able to self-categorize cognitively as a
male or a female. "Once the boy has stably
categorized himself as male, he then values pos-

*The different socialization of boys and girls begins early in
life. While girls tend to be rewarded for pursuing passive,
domestic activities, boys are encouraged to be active and to
be aggressive problem solvers.*

itively those objects and acts consistent with his gender identity" (Kohlberg, 1966: 89). The same is true, of course, for girls. By the age of five, gender identity is irreversible.

Socialization is direct and indirect, implicit and explicit. The games children play and the toys they use are gender differentiated. Girls play with dolls, sewing machines, brooms, stoves, and carpet sweepers. They sew and jump rope. In games, boys are the doctors and the girls the nurses. Toy trains, model airplanes, erector sets, and soldiers are boys' toys. Laws (1979), having reviewed a number of studies on toy preferences, concludes that this cultural process leads boys and girls to different destinations. Laws regards this as an illustration ". . . of one of the major functions of sex role socialization, which is to create sex [role] differences of taste and temperament, of ambition and outlook" (1979: 248).

Toys and games are not the sole example of stereotypical notions of role appropriateness. Preschool children's books portray men and women in gender differentiated activities that have no basis in reality. In a study of award-winning books for preschool children, Weitzman et al. (1972) found that women are underrepresented in central roles. The portrayal of boys is of active, independent, inventive, and fearless people; they are the leaders. Girls are portrayed as passive and followers. Women's activities take place indoors; they cook, set the table, nurse, and serve others. Women are passive; men lead and women follow, men rescue, and women are rescued (see Table 5.2). The limited roles portraying women are dramatically contrasted by the variety and options available to males: housebuilders, store keepers, story tellers, monks, fishermen, soldiers, police officers, judges, etc.

The lack of reality in these books as noted by Weitzman et al. is exemplified by the fact that at a time when 40 percent of adult women in the United States were in the labor force, no woman in the sample of books examined was portrayed as holding a job. The coeducational school system would lead us to assume that boys and girls

TABLE 5.2 / WOMEN AND CRIME

Statistics have traditionally shown far lower crime rates for women than for men. This reflects their socialization, as well as the fact that they tend to spend less time out of the home. The following data show the percentage of men and women who were estimated to be inmates in state correctional facilities in 1974. They also show percentages of inmates from traditionally female occupational groups.

Characteristics	Percent of Inmates
Sex	
Male	97
Female	3
Occupation at Time of Arrest	
Salesworkers	2
Clerical workers	4
Machine operators	2
Service workers	11

Source: U.S. Dept. of Justice, *Sourcebook of Criminal Justice Statistics 1980* (Washington, D.C.: U.S. Government Printing Office), p. 500.

receive the same education and training. Each is expected or required to master in the early years an elementary knowledge of reading and arithmetic. But the early educational process is not merely learning to read or write, it is also a process of learning how to interact with others, what behavior is appropriate in different situations, what language should be used, and how games are to be played. In all of these realms, there are different scripts for boys and girls.

These scripts have tended to be remarkably durable. For example, between 1930 and 1970 major and dramatic changes took place in the United States and the world at large: a depression, unemployment, World War II, the "Black Revolt," Vietnam. During these years, ever larger numbers of women entered the labor force. During World War II, 200,000 American women served in the Armed Forces. Jobs traditionally considered male, symbolically represented by "Rosie the Riveter," were performed by women. Yet, elementary school readers portrayed women in 1970 not unlike the way they were presented in 1930 (Child et al., 1946; Saario et al., 1973). The educational experience neither begins nor ends with the textbook used. As one proceeds from grade to grade, gender appropriate occupations continue as an integral part of the learning process. Vocational courses prepare boys for skilled occupations and apprentice programs prepare them for such technical and remunerative jobs as plumbers and electricians. The vocational courses offered to girls are in homemaking.

In the past decade, efforts to change some of the most excessive forms of gender differentiation have been initiated in the school system. Textbooks today portray men and women in less stereotyped roles; primary textbooks no longer show women as only mothers. Title IX of the Educational Amendment Act of 1972 prohibits a gender differentiated curriculum. Vocational programs providing women only with home economic programs and men with courses and training in skilled jobs have been curtailed. But television and television commercials—even if somewhat more moderate than in the past in the portrayal of women in stereotypical roles— nevertheless continue to portray women as the "weaker" sex. Judging by their television images, women are pliant and lacking independence. In shows for child audiences male characters predominate. Men are still shown working in a variety of occupations; women are still shown as either not working, or working in stereotypically female occupations (Levinson, 1975). Television commercials also continue to perpetuate the portrayal of women as concerned primarily with home, children, and cleanliness, while men are shown as more concerned with their careers (McArthur and Resko, 1975). It is clear, then, how people get socialized into sex roles. But how well does their socialization prepare them for the contemporary social world?

WOMEN AND WORK

The overwhelming emphasis on women as wives and mothers would seem to suggest that women seldom, if ever, step outside the threshold of their homes for paid jobs. Even in the Victorian era the image of women as sheltered ladies ignored the reality that in 1890 women constituted 17.2 percent of the labor force.

For the majority of these working women, work was a dire financial necessity. Industrialization created new jobs in the cities, and increasing numbers of women entered gainful employment. In 1900, the United States census bureau classified 9000 women as professionals, i.e., primarily religious, charity, and welfare workers. In 1880 there were 75 women lawyers and by 1910 their numbers increased to 1341; the proportion of women doctors increased from 2000 in 1880 to 5 percent of all doctors in 1910 (Filene, 1974).

The induction of men into the Armed Forces during World War II created vast labor shortages; women were welcomed into jobs from which they had only recently been excluded. They worked in the steel mills and in defense production, on railroads and in factories. To work was to be patriotic. With the end of the war, women continued to work, although in declining numbers. In 1950, for example, 34 percent of women aged 16 and above were employed. However, their work experience was usually different from that of men. Women generally worked prior to marriage and before the arrival of children. They returned to work on a part-time basis when their children entered school. With the exception of the span of the war period, women with preschool children generally remained outside the labor market.

This pattern changed. Between 1970 and 1980, the most rapid increase in the labor force occurred for women with children under the age of six years. The percentage of women in the labor force aged 25–34, the prime childbearing years, increased from 43 percent in 1970 to 65

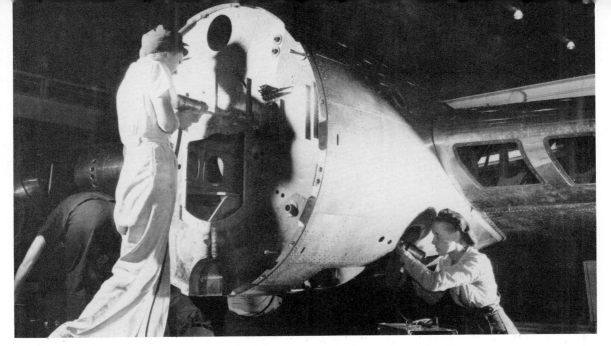

Women's slacks, which made their appearance just before World War II, gained general public acceptance during the 1940s when millions of women entered the work force, taking over jobs formerly held by men.

percent in 1980; 45 percent of mothers of pre-school children under the age of six were working or looking for work, compared to 12 percent in 1950. Over 50 percent of women aged 16 and older are currently employed (or looking for work), and close to 70 percent of these work because of economic necessity. The majority of working women are single mothers with children, and women whose husbands earn less than $7000 per year. The notion that women work only to secure some luxury items for the family is clearly erroneous (Waite, 1981). See Table 5.3 for a breakdown by marital status and age of children.

Women have traditionally found employment in "female" occupations such as secretarial work, library work, social work, and nursing. Today, more are branching out into traditionally male dominated, high-prestige occupations. The percentage of women lawyers and judges rose from 4 percent in 1960 to 13 percent in 1980 (Waite, 181: 26). Similar changes are occurring in science. In 1970, there were 3569 full-time women students enrolled in engineering; in 1980 the number increased to 49,000. In 1970, women constituted 0.8 percent (358) of graduating engineering students; by 1981 the number increased to 10.4 percent (6545). Current estimates suggest that in 1984, women will constitute 14 percent of the graduating engineering class (Vetter, 1981: 1314). Between 1965 and 1980, there has also been an increase in the number of women scientists: women achieving doctorate degrees in mathematics increased from 50 in 1965 to 116 in 1980; in the physical sciences from 127 to 386, and in life sciences from 263 to 1342 (Vetter, 1981).

The rising number of women in the professions reflects the progress women have made in entering new fields and competing for advanced degrees. Women, however, continue to have greater difficulties than men in finding employment and advancing in careers. With the exception of a B.A. in engineering, women's initial

TABLE 5.3 / U.S. WOMEN'S LABOR FORCE PARTICIPATION, BY MARITAL STATUS AND PRESENCE AND AGE OF CHILDREN: MARCH 1980

			Percentage of Women Working			
			With children under age 18			
					Under age 6	
Marital status	Total	With no children under 18	Total	Age 6 to 17 only	Total	Under age 3
Total	51.1	48.0	56.6	64.4	46.6	41.7
Never married	61.2	61.8	51.5	67.3	43.4	41.1
Married, husband present	50.2	46.1	54.2	61.8	45.0	41.1
Married, husband absent	59.4	58.7	59.9	66.4	51.8	42.0
Widowed	22.5	19.9	58.8	61.1	45.6	n.a.
Divorced	74.5	71.4	78.1	82.3	68.0	56.5

n.a. = not available

Source: Linda J. Waite, "U.S. Women at Work," *Population Bulletin* 36, no. 2 (May 1981): 22. Published by Population Reference Bureau, Inc., Washington, D.C.

"*I really enjoyed dinner at your place last night, Marge. Your husband is a marvelous cook.*"

From the *Wall Street Journal*. By permission of Cartoon Features Syndicate.

salaries are lower than the salaries offered to men, and the differences increase with age (Vetter, 1981: 1320).

The progress of women in achieving professional jobs has not altered the type of job most women hold, however. The majority of working women perform the same jobs they have performed throughout the century. In 1900, almost all domestics, seamstresses, and dressmakers were women and the situation remains the same today. Secretaries, nursery school teachers, practical nurses, typists, child care workers, and telephone operators are positions allocated almost solely to women. In fact, the percentage of stenographers, typists, and secretaries who are women has increased from 72 percent in 1900 to almost 100 percent in 1980 (Waite, 1981; see Table 5.4). Women working full-time and year round earn on the average about 60¢ compared to each dollar earned by men with similar hours and work experience. Median earnings of full-time workers who are women have remained considerably

TABLE 5.4 / MOST SEGREGATED "FEMALE" OCCUPATIONS: 1900, 1950, 1980

| | 1900 | | | 1950 | |
Occupation	Percent of Female Labor Force in Occupation	Females as a Percent of Total in Occupation	Occupation	Percent of Female Labor Force in Occupation	Females as a Percent of Total in Occupation
Dressmakers and seamstresses	7.8	100	Nurses	2.9	98
Milliners	1.4	100	Dressmakers and seamstresses	0.9	97
Private household workers	28.7	97	Telephone operators	2.2	96
Nurses	0.2	94	Attendants, physicians' and dentists' offices	0.2	95
Attendants, hospitals and other institutions, midwives and practical nurses	1.8	89	Private household workers	8.9	95
Operatives, paperboard containers and boxes	0.3	84	Stenographers, typists, and secretaries	9.5	94
Charwomen and cleaners	0.5	84	Milliners	0.1	90
Boarding and lodging housekeepers	1.1	83	Librarians	0.3	89
Attendants and assistants, library	0.0	80	Office machine operators	0.8	82
Telephone operators	0.3	80	Sales workers, demonstrators	0.1	82
Operatives, knitting mills	0.6	78	Operatives, mfg., apparel and accessories	4.0	81
Housekeepers and stewards, except private household	0.5	78	Bookkeepers and cashiers	4.7	78
Teachers	6.1	75	Counter and fountain workers and waitresses	4.0	78
Librarians	0.0	72	Housekeepers and stewards, except private household	0.5	78
Stenographers, typists, and secretaries	1.8	72	Teachers	5.2	75
Operatives, misc. fabricated textile products	0.3	71	Attendants and assistants, library	0.1	74
Operatives, apparel and accessories mfg.	3.0	70	Spinners, textile	0.4	74
Total	54.4		Operatives, knitting	0.7	72
			Operatives, misc. fabricated textile products	0.2	72
			Boarding and lodging housekeepers	0.1	72
			Dancers and dancing teachers	0.1	71
			Religious workers	0.2	70
			Operatives, tobacco mfg.	0.3	70
			Total	46.4	

(Continued)

TABLE 5.4 / (Continued)

Occupation	1980	
	Percent of Female Labor Force in Occupation	Females as a Percent of Total in Occupation
Secretaries	9.3	99.1
Dental assistants	0.3	98.6
Pre-kindergarten teachers	0.6	98.4
Private household workers	2.5	97.5
Practical nurses	0.9	97.3
Dressmakers	0.3	97.2
Lodging quarters cleaners	0.4	97.0
Typists	2.4	96.9
Telephone operators	0.7	96.9
Demonstrators	0.2	96.7
Registered nurses	3.0	96.5
Receptionists	1.5	96.3
Child care workers	1.0	96.1
Keypunch operators	0.6	95.9
Sewers and stitchers	1.8	95.7
Teacher's aides	0.9	93.7
Bank tellers	1.2	92.7
Bookkeepers	4.2	90.5
Billing clerks	0.4	90.2
Bookkeeping and billing machine operators	0.1	90.0
Total	32.2	

Source: Linda J. Waite, "U.S. Women at Work," *Population Bulletin* 36, no. 2 (May 1981): 27. Published by Population Reference Bureau, Inc., Washington, D.C.

behind male earnings. As is evident in Table 5.1, between 1955 and 1979 women earned at the most 64 percent of what men earned, and by 1979, the proportion declined to 60 percent.

Women's consistently lower earnings are said to be a result of the choice of jobs which pay little, unwillingness to be committed to jobs which require more than set hours, unwillingness to assume responsibility, frequent dropping out from jobs when family responsibilities demand presence at home, lack of professionalism, and a host of similar reasons. But as Waite (1981) and others have pointed out, women who are committed to continuous full-time work do not fare any better than women who are less serious about their jobs; they neither earn more, nor do they have greater opportunities for promotion than their counterparts who work part-time.

The clustering of women in lower level white-collar jobs and in unskilled and poorly paid jobs reflects the socialization process, stereotypes, cultural beliefs, and discrimination. It reflects the **dual labor market.** The **primary labor market** provides good and stable jobs, with opportunities for advancement. Jobs in the primary labor market are assigned to men. Women are assigned to the **secondary labor market,** to jobs which are unskilled, poorly paid, temporary, and provide no opportunity for advancement (Piore, 1970, cited by Laws, 1979: 24–25). The recent work of McLaughlin (1978), demonstrates that occupational pay scales are directly related to gender. Professions in which males predominate are significantly better paid than professions in which women predominate.

Being the token woman among managers of professionals is not a path to success either, as Kanter (1977) has noted. The token woman, not unlike the token member of any minority group, encounters pressures not experienced by men who blend in to the organization. Superiors watch closely over the performance of the token member both on the job and in behavior external to the job. Her visibility as one among many can not be missed. A token represents a challenge to the dominant group. She is excluded from the informal social interactions and the informal process of socialization. If the token individual woman leaves the job, she is then regarded as unwilling or unable to make it in the world of men, and the stereotype about the place of women is reinforced.

MALE GENDER ROLES

It would be erroneous to assume that sex role differentiation hurts women only. The establishment of separate domains, male and female, has profound effects on both men and women. In this section, we will focus on male sex roles.

The rigid patterns of developing a "man" to conform to unique and distinctive sets of gender roles imposes a psychological dimension on men which denies them a variety of experiences and options. The expectation is that "boys do not cry," that boys are expected to be "heroes," stoic or cool in the face of danger. The boy is tough; he plays cowboys and Indians; boys are expected to fight back and to show their manliness through aggressive acts. Young male teenagers are most often involved in gang wars when they think their manliness and status as men are threatened (Short and Strodbeck, 1976).

The idealization of sports for boys as good, valuable fun and a means to learn how to be competitive may be far from what many men experience as pleasurable. The participation of boys in various sports activities provided in the school or neighborhood does not invariably mean

Industrialized society, with its de-emphasis of physical labor, is experiencing the breakdown of many traditional sex roles. John Collins was the first male in the United States to become a certified midwife.

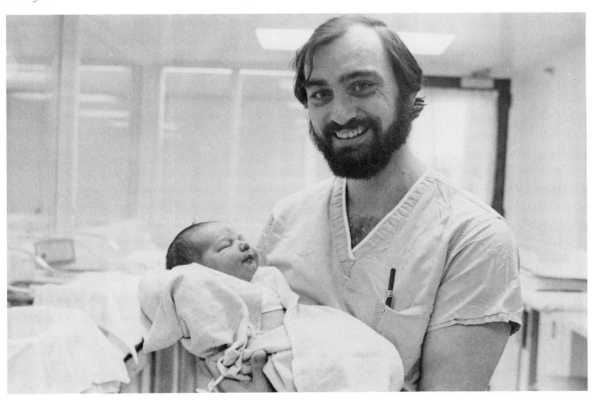

that they would not rather do something else. The pressure of the father and the peer group is often as much of a factor for such participation as the desire of the male child. Pleck (1976) vividly describes his experience with sports, which left him "feeling distant from my body." We can see, then, how expectations related to being "manly" can require a man to wear a mask to hide his feelings.

Success is a source of status in society which may take a variety of forms: wealth, fame, power, etc. The signs of success are material possessions, consumption, and other symbols which inform the world that the bearer has made it: a briefcase instead of a lunch pail, a suit and tie instead of workers' overalls. Of course relatively few men achieve "success." The majority of men merely have jobs which provide a modicum of well-being for themselves and their families. But what they lack in material success is made up through other "status" achievements, e.g., the fastest beer drinker in the local saloon, the best dart thrower in the neighborhood (David and Brannon, 1976).

But the very same men who derive their "success" from dart throwing or beer drinking lose their status in a dismal fashion when unemployment strikes. Work is central to the male role. Men are expected to be the "breadwinners" who support themselves and their families. A man's job is a significant part of his identity. So unemployment presents not merely a problem of how to feed the family, but it also generates feelings of failure as a man and fears of loss of respect from peers and the community. As Parsons (1955) has pointed out, it is the exceptional "normal" male who can have a respected place in society without a job. Numerous studies have demonstrated the dire consequences of unemployment for men as well as for women. But the prevalent definitions of male and female roles leave only the unemployed man with a generalized feeling of failure as a person. It might be said that for a man a job is tantamount to a moral obligation. Sex role differentiation determines

opportunities not only for women, but for men as well. Because women are not expected to have a job outside the home, unemployment has relatively little effect on their sense of identity (although it may have significant financial effects). For men, though, being expected to work links employment to self-worth.

The dominant position of men throughout the world should not obscure the fact that the roles imposed on men are difficult and complex. Consider, for example, the fact that insurance companies require higher premiums on car insurance for males aged 18–25 than for comparably aged females. This reflects the higher accident rate of males. Speed, risk taking, and daring are what we socialize men to attempt. These characteristics become an expression of manhood, or macho qualities, for which they often pay with their lives. Similarly, crime rates are significantly higher for men than for women. Nearly a century ago Durkheim found suicide rates to be higher for men than for women. Life expectancy has been consistently lower for men than for women; for a man born in 1979, for example, life expectancy was 68.7 years, and for a woman, 76.5 years.

Analyses of gender roles enables us to look behind the so-called natural attributes of men and women. When we do so, we discover social arrangements that create differences between the sexes. Each sex suffers as a result, although in rather different ways. By being restricted in what they may do outside the home, women live longer than men and are involved in fewer aggressive acts. Yet the cost of this "protection" is dependence and lack of opportunity. Men have greater access to desirable social resources: money, power, and prestige. Yet they pay a price in terms of rigid emotional control, aggressive behavior, and shorter life spans. Examining possibilities for modifying sex roles to better serve both sexes—and therefore society as a whole—can be facilitated by looking at the experience of other societies. We will now turn to this task.

CROSS-CULTURAL DIFFERENCES

Research by Margaret Mead (1935, 1972) in three New Guinea tribes shows patterns of sex role allocation that differ significantly from those encountered in American society. According to Mead, among the Arapesh, men and women alike were expected to be "succoring" and "cherishing." Both men and women were concerned with child rearing tasks. Among the Mondugumor, on the other hand, both men and women were aggressive, hostile, and competitive. The traits usually associated with women in American society, e.g., being gentle, warm, helpful, and caring, were absent in Mondugumor women. Among the Arapesh and Mondugumor "both men and women were expected to conform to a single type: the ideas of behavioral styles that differentiated men and women was wholly absent" (Mead, 1972: 224). Mead found a still different pattern among the Tchambuli. In that society, sex role behavior was the reverse of what is found in American society: women were the traders and economic providers, while men were artists who spent much of their time gossiping.

Yet another pattern of sex role differentiation is found in the kibbutzim in Israel. These settlements began in the early 1900s as agriculture communities founded on an ideology of complete equality between men and women. Both sexes were required to participate in production activities which meant that they worked long and gruelling hours in the fields. The kibbutzim were highly successful in achieving economic self-sufficiency as well as equality between men and women. In the 1950s, however, many of the kibbutzim became wealthy communities, and

Although both men and women of the kibbutzim originally worked together in the fields, a sex-based division of labor evolved as the wealth of the communities increased. Men increasingly took on the heavy agricultural chores, while women concentrated on domestic jobs in the nurseries, schools, and kitchens.

work in the fields was said to be too difficult for the women. Harvesting and driving tractors became the domain of men, and women took on jobs in the nursery, the schools, the kitchen, and the laundries. While women do not appear to be very happy working eight hours a day doing laundry, or cooking for several hundred people, it is suggested that they nevertheless prefer it (Spiro, 1979).

Some sociologists and anthropologists (e.g., Spiro, 1979) argue that the emergent role differentiations in the kibbutzim are natural, reflecting not only the preferences of the women, but the physical difficulties encountered in these jobs. But what may also explain the return to the more traditional task of women's work in the kibbutz is the fact that the larger Israeli society provides traditional role models for men and women. The kibbutz is not an isolated outpost in Israeli society cut off from the mainstream of life in Israel. There is constant interaction between the kibbutz inhabitants and the larger society. Kibbutz women serve in the Israeli Armed Forces where they are placed in service rather than combat positions. The patriarchal ideology of the Jewish religion coupled with a large population influx of bearers of this traditional ideology after World War II may have contributed to a return to the more traditional sex role patterns. Hence, the experiences of women in the kibbutzim may exemplify the way in which social factors take precedence over biological ones.

To continue our cross-cultural comparison of sex roles, we will look in some detail at sex roles in contemporary Russia and Sweden. These societies provide an interesting contrast to life in the United States. As we will see, Russia has achieved greater occupational diversity for women, yet it also maintains a belief system similar to that in the United States which emphasizes the role of women in the family whether or not she also works. In Sweden, however, some far more fundamental changes seem to be underway.

WOMEN IN OTHER INDUSTRIAL SOCIETIES

Sex Roles in the U.S.S.R.

In the Soviet Union, women are represented in all occupations, ranging from the most menial to the most prestigious. As is evident in Table 5.5 women are streetsweepers and clerks, doctors and scientists, economists and journalists, tractor drivers and milkmaids. Biology has not prevented women from participating in role domains seldom if ever occupied by women in other societies, yet role differentiation is as much part of the sociocultural arrangements in Soviet society as it is in American society. The Marx-Engels thesis that the abolition of private property will end the subordinate position of women has not been borne out in the Soviet and the East European socialist systems.

While women are found in all sectors of the occupational system, women remain a minority in the most prestigious and powerful sectors. Throughout the history of the Soviet state, there have been conspicuously few women in the Soviet political elite. The underlying cause for the poor representation of women in the arena of the political decision-making process, in their token representation in the halls of the Academy of Science, and in the upper levels of management is embedded in the tumultuous and tragic history of the Soviet socialist state. Nevertheless, some specific causal factors emerge quite clearly.

The legal statutes promulgated by the new Soviet state in 1917 ensured women equal rights to work and equal pay and access to educational institutions. Women were given the right to keep their own names and could have separate homes. As citizens, they had equal rights to participate in all social and political institutions. In order for these rights to become a reality, vast resources were required to build a network of child care institutions, supportive services, and consumer

IN FOCUS/The Changing Roles of Women

Every society differentiates between men and women, holding different expectations for the behavior patterns of each sex. Although women have traditionally been granted lower status than men in most cultures, the inferiority of women as a biological fact of nature has been vigorously challenged in modern times. This photo essay traces the changing roles of women in American society.

(a)

(b)

(a,b) Prior to industrialization, the average American believed that a woman's place was in the home. Considered dependent and delicate, women were expected to busy themselves with domestic activities such as childrearing, sewing, and getting the family wash spanking clean.

(c)

(c) As women became more active in the work force and took advantage of new educational opportunities, they began to demand greater equality as well. The National American Woman Suffrage Association, formed in 1890, met with considerable internal and external opposition. By 1914, only eleven states had given women the vote, and it was not until 1920 that the Nineteenth Amendment was finally ratified.

(d)

(f)

(e)

(g)

(h)

(d) Many young people of the 1920s aspired to be rebellious, pleasure-seeking individualists. With bobbed hair and daring short skirts, the smoking, drinking, uncorseted flapper soon became the symbol of her generation's moral revolution.

(e) "Rosie the Riveter" became the symbol of the millions of American women who entered the work force during World War II. Taking over jobs formerly reserved for men, they read blueprints, serviced airplanes, greased locomotives, and ran municipal bus lines.

(f) During the 1950s, millions of veterans returned to their wives and sweethearts and, once again, the majority of Americans accepted the view that women could best find fulfillment by devoting themselves to home and family. The mass media encouraged Mom to click her heels over getting the family wash really clean!

(g,h) The 1960s ushered in a new period of unrest and activism. Inspired by the black civil rights movement, women again pressed for social and economic equality. As the number of working women increased, they began making inroads into formerly male-dominated occupations.

(j)

(i)

(i) *Although gains made by the women's movement have recently come under attack, many women continue to pursue new opportunities and to explore new roles. In 1981, Sandra Day O'Connor—judge, housewife, and mother—was appointed a Justice of the Supreme Court.*

(j,k) *Women are pursuing sports not as the cheerleaders of the past but as serious participants. As a byproduct of the 1980s preoccupation with fitness, many women have begun to literally reshape the notion of female beauty. An article in* Time *magazine (August 30, 1982) reports that "to be in condition is not only healthy, it is sexy—and inseparable from a strength of the self and the spirit," and that the emerging ideal form is slimmer, graceful, and speaks assurance.*

(k)

goods. However, Stalin's focus on industrialization and the commitment of resources to heavy industry greatly limited the development of these facilities and services. Even as late as 1975, only 37 percent of Soviet preschool children were accommodated in child care facilities. A possible response to limited facilities and services could have been to redefine the roles of men and women, allocating equal responsibilities for child care and homemaking to both men and women. This option was never selected, however.

The ideology which supported women's entrance into the occupational sphere did not challenge, or even question, the traditional familial obligations of women. The Soviets superimposed a set of occupational roles on women and buttressed these roles with a belief system that spoke of the importance of women in production. This ideology, while new and dramatic in its proclamation of equality of men and women, retained the traditional values, which assign primacy to the role of women as mothers and homemakers. Soviet intellectuals and social scientists promulgate these images at scientific meetings and conferences. Notions such as "the more feminine the woman the greater her value" or "to make the woman ashamed of feminine impulses and inclinations is to impoverish the life of men and women" are widely disseminated in the Soviet mass media.

The Russian socialization process differs from American society only in the fact that male and female children are socialized for gainful employment. But as in the American society, toys for female and male children are highly differentiated. Girls may play with a doll or a tractor, but boys are not given such options. The doll, symbolic of the potential role of mother, remains the domain of the girl. Mothers are advised to praise girls when they play with dolls, for being good conscientious mothers, for taking good care of their children, and for keeping them neat and clean (Nechaeva and Markova, 1975: 232). Posters of boys and girls in various children's

settings portray them in highly differentiated roles: boys are seen in metal working classrooms, and girls in sewing classrooms; girls are portrayed as petting animals, and boys as saving a drowning person.

Soviet children grow up in homes in which they experience a division of labor not much different from what we see in the West. Emotional nurturance and support are expected from mothers; women—not men—provide warmth and affection. According to research by Soviet sociologists, the expressive domain is the woman's (Kharchev, 1974; Kon, 1973).

Analysis of the children's readers used in the first and second years of Soviet Russian schools shows women in roles not unlike those in American society. Women are overwhelmingly identified as mothers and grandmothers, performing traditional household jobs. They are portrayed as naive, careless, passive, and politically inactive. Men are seen in directing, leadership roles, politically involved, and constructive. Their self-image is favorable; they aim to achieve (Rosenhan, 1977).

In secondary schools, teachers evaluate occupations in terms of which are more appropriate for boys and which for girls. Studies have shown that teachers identified professional occupations as "very good" for boys, and "good" for girls. Skilled jobs were rated "very good" for boys and "poor to medium" for girls. Other studies have shown that there is general agreement among seniors in secondary schools that physicist, mathematician, and doctor are among the most attractive professions, yet girls choose occupations in the humanities significantly more often than boys, while boys tend to the scientific and technical fields (Vodzinskaia, 1973).

The dual labor markets in the USSR resemble the sex segregated system in the United States. Over 95 percent of secretaries, typists, nurses, dressmakers, child care workers, and teachers' aides are women in the Soviet Union. But contrary to other industrial societies, including

TABLE 5.5 / WORKING WOMEN IN THE SOVIET UNION

Profession	Percentage Who Are Female
Economists, planners	82
Physicians	74
Dentists	77
Engineers	40
Designer draftsmen	57
Technical personnel on railroad	43
Teachers in higher educ. institutions	43
Scientific personnel and heads of science research institutions and organizations	40

Source: Based on data in Schwartz (1979). Reprinted by permission.

the United States, women are well represented among the professions (see Table 5.5).

The figures in Table 5.5 are impressive relative to women in capitalist countries. It is worth noting that while 82 percent of economists and planners are women in the Soviet Union, few women participate in major economic policy decisions. Women scientists are infrequently found as heads of institutes, and most of the female teachers in higher educational institutions occupy positions low in rank. In 1975, only 2 percent of the professors and academicians of the prestigious Academy of Science were women. Women physicians, while 74 percent of all physicians, constitute but a small percentage (10 percent) of the Academy of Medical Sciences. Generally, the rule seems to be that the higher the level of a position the fewer women will reach it. Soviet explanations for the relatively small number of women at the upper levels of the professions and administration invariably center on women's double burden. Women, in addition to holding full-time jobs, are also responsible for child care and home responsibilities. Indeed, women devote 2½ times more hours than men do (27 hours and

11 minutes per week for women and 11 hours and 40 minutes for men) to home and children in addition to a full-time job. Soviet studies also show that promotion of women to higher level positions occurs at a rate significantly slower than similar progress for men. It takes women two to three years longer than men to be promoted to similar positions (Feigin and Golovanova, 1973).

The Soviet case suggests that despite claims to the contrary sex role differences do not diverge from the functionalist framework of the capitalist United States. Soviet sociologists do not formally dichotomize male and female roles into instrumental and expressive, but by "reinforcing the family as a fundamental social institution based on the sexual division of labor" (Lapidus, 1977: 136) society forces the same end result. Soviet policy regarding the roles of men and women is, as in other societies, not simply a question of education and jobs. It is also a question of the nature of support for equality in the roles of men and women. So far, at least, there is no indication that the Soviets are intent on changing the roles of men. As stated recently by Soviet sociologists, "the goal of socialism is not equality in home responsibilities of men and women" (Gordon and Klopov, 1972: 319).

Sex Roles in Sweden

In the early 1950s, economic development in Sweden brought large-scale shifts in population from rural to urban areas, and the familiar pattern of women entering the labor market in response to economic demands. The number of women seeking jobs was particularly high among women in their forties. Having reared their children these women sought opportunities in the world of work. The patterning of roles for men and women thus did not differ from that in the United States.

Full employment, a considerable shortage of labor, and the rising proportion of women in paid jobs, coupled with an egalitarian ideology of the Swedish social democratic government, gradually led to significant changes in policy regarding the roles of men and women. Contrary to the Soviet system which never redefined the roles of men and merely superimposed the role of worker on the role of mother-homemaker, in Sweden the goal is to redefine the roles of men and to change the structure of the family. Swedish society is attempting to change past traditions which tied men to jobs and women to home and family.

The Swedish educational system is developing a curriculum which does not assign men and women to separate domains. Boys and girls receive training in home and child care, as well as in sewing and woodworking. Textbooks are evaluated, and a factor in the selection of a book is the portrayal of men and women in egalitarian roles at home and at work. The Swedish educational system confronts the existing patterns of role allocation. It uses education as a means to counteract past traditions of sex role inequality in all spheres of life.

The schools should assume that men and women will play the same role in the future, that preparation for the parental role is just as important for boys as for girls, and that girls have reason to be just as interested in their careers as boys. (Baude, 1979: 153)

In most contemporary industrial societies, there have been efforts in varying degrees toward a more equitable allocation of roles. Sweden, however, appears to have moved toward this goal to a greater extent than other societies. The Swedish seem to have recognized that while only women can bear children, men and women can perform the roles of socializer and homemaker equally well.

In 1974, a law was passed providing either the father or mother with a right to a paid leave of absence of seven months following the birth or adoption of a child. Who remains in the home to care for the child is a decision made by the parents. They can decide that either parent will

take the full seven months, or that they will take turns, dividing the time equally, or both will work part-time. The Swedish insurance system provides compensation from 12 to 18 days (depending on the age of the child) to either parent to care for a sick child.

Swedish policies that support equal roles for men and women have been implemented only recently. These policies have received widespread support in society, but it would be naive to assume that legal supports will immediately change social patterns that have existed for centuries. It

Swedish society is actively trying to encourage equality of roles in men and women and to promote the view that men can perform just as well in the roles of socializer and homemaker.

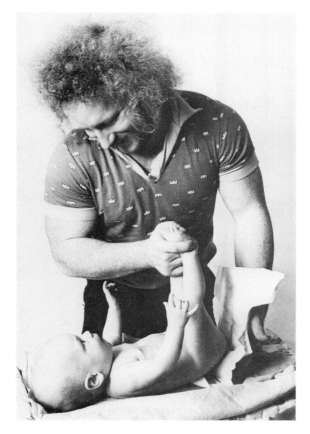

SOCIAL ISSUE/Women in the 1980s:

Laurel W. Richardson /Ohio State University

The fact that this essay is being written is in itself a statement that the "place" of women is still problematical, not only for sociologists, but for most men and women in contemporary society. The need to discuss the "future of women" testifies not only to the social and cultural changes that have occurred during the past 15 years, but to the persistence of a "double standard" that pervades all areas of social life. No article on "Men in the 1980s" will appear in this volume because men and what men do are still considered normative, the standard against which women and what women do are evaluated and measured. This double standard will continue to have consequences for the life opportunities and life strategies of women throughout this decade. Before discussing these opportunities and strategies, however, it will be useful to briefly review the nature of the sex-gender system in which we work and play, live, and love.

All known societies classify and stratify their members as either male or female, based on their biological role in reproduction. And, all known societies evaluate males and male-associated activities (whether those be making money or making poetry), masculine-associated personality traits (whether those be aggressivity or gentleness, rationality or emotionality), and male-centered goals (whether those be splitting atoms or seeking grace), more highly than they evaluate females and female-associated activities, personality traits, and goals.

Socialization practices—from differences in parental interaction with male and female children to educational and religious training to films, books, and television—confirm and reconfirm the cultural belief that males and females are not only different, but that the male and the masculine are more important and valuable. Agents of social control such as the church, law, science, and medicine bear down on adults to accept the accustomed differential evaluation and the accustomed division of labor as right, moral, and proper.

In contemporary American society, the division of labor assumed moral, right, and proper is still one that holds men primarily responsible for the economic well-being of women and children, and holds women primarily responsible for the domestic sphere—its accoutrements, meals, cleanliness, children, and emotional stability. In this way, the institutions of paid labor in the marketplace and unpaid labor in the home are intertwined, and the career success of the man is at least partially dependent upon the woman taking care of the home, the children, the laundry, the cholesterol levels.

In brief, *androcentrism* or male-centeredness and *patriarchal* institutions or institutions that perpetuate female subordination and male superordination are persistent, pervasive, and highly interwoven and interdependent upon one another.

A decade or so of scholarship and research have documented and demonstrated the extent of androcentrism and patriarchal institutions. At this point, no serious scholar questions that males have been and continue to be accorded more privileges and opportunities than females, and that these are perpetuated through both the structure and the ideology of the society. Similarly, however, scholars recognize that there has been over the past 15 years a persistent and steady challenge to that structure and ideology. This challenge has been made through the collective activity of women and men engaged in the feminist social movement.

The consequences of this social movement activity have been felt at institutional, associational, and personal levels. For example, due to the collective efforts of movement activists, a national policy emerged during the seventies that favored legal equality of rights and protections for men and women. Legislation at the national, state, and local levels was passed including laws prohibiting sex discrimination in credit, employment, and educational opportunities, as well as laws to protect displaced homemakers and abused spouses. At the association-

Life Opportunities and Life Strategies

al level, women's spaces, coffee houses, art galleries, bookstores, film companies, publishing firms, and college curricula emerged. And at the personal level, the struggle to have "nonsexist" relationships and living arrangements, and to raise children free of limiting sex-stereotypes commenced.

Thus, we are at a point in history when, although androcentrism and patriarchy persist in all arenas of social life, some avenues for change have been opened. What, then, might we expect in the near future? What might be the life opportunities and life strategies of women during the 1980s?

Historically, changes in women's lives toward greater equity have occurred during periods of general social unrest, periods in which the political and legal climate is attuned to correcting injustices and inequities in general. At this point in time, however, we are immersed in a period of economic, political,

and social conservatism. Thus, to discuss the future of women means discussing their present, for in all likelihood the trends that are currently in motion will persist. To do this, I will first discuss some demographic and economic baselines as they affect the life-opportunities of women; I will then discuss some of the more important life strategies that women will employ throughout this decade.

Females constitute 53 percent of American society. Although most women are married at some point in their lives, nearly all of them can expect to live without the company of a husband for a *major* portion of their lives. Thirty-seven percent of women over 18 are single; the average age of the American widow is only 53; approximately 30 percent of marriages end in divorce. With more females than males and the cultural preference of older men for younger women, it is likely that women of all ages,

and especially those over 40, will be living increasingly on their own throughout this decade—indeed, throughout this century.

Nearly all women will continue to work outside the home for a *major* part of their lives. For most women, paid-labor is not a choice: It is an economic necessity. Single, divorced, and widowed women's financial support comes primarily from their own paid-labor. For a married couple to even hope to pretend to a middle-class life style requires that both partners be employed outside the home. Right now, 54 percent of all mothers with children at home and 45 percent of mothers of preschoolers are in the paid labor force. The "ideal" American family of the breadwinning father/breadbaking mother and their two children constitutes less than 7 percent of American households.

Not only will women continue to work outside the home, they will continue to be less financially rewarded for their labors than men. They will continue to be slotted into occupations which are sex-typed female—such as office worker, elementary school teacher, waitress, and household worker. These jobs have low prestige, few fringe benefits, and low salaries. Only 7 percent of American women earn over $15,000 a year—in contrast to 46 percent of men. A woman with a college degree can expect to earn what a man holding an eighth-grade certificate earns. There is no reason to assume these inequities will abate during this decade.

Women who are highly trained executives and professionals will continue to experience severe discrimination in job placement and advancement throughout the decade. Not only is it true that the more prestigious the career, the fewer the women, but also that the more prestigious the career, the greater the discrepancy in financial and other rewards. For example, seven years out of a Harvard graduate school finds a woman twice as likely to be non-volitionally unemployed as her male counterpart; and finds her salary, if she is an educator or public health administrator, approximately 40 percent less than her male co-graduate. Indeed, in many

of the professions, the rate of financial disparity between the sexes has been increasing. Again, there is no reason to assume this trend will attenuate over this decade.

Throughout the decade, women will not only work outside the home, they will continue to work inside the home. Employed women spend another 34 hours on domestic responsibilities—in contrast to the four hours their husbands spend; that is, employed women have two full-time jobs. All studies indicate that even in the most egalitarian of marriages, the woman takes the primary responsibility for the home and the children, and greater preference is given to her husband's career.

Most women, then, can expect to live a major part of their lives unmarried, to work outside the home and inside the home, to earn low wages in low prestige occupations, to have their careers take second-place to their husbands, and face the probability of raising children on their own—emotionally and financially. These are the base-line realities of women's lives—now and into the near future.

Consciously and nonconsciously realizing these life constraints, women have been devising strategies they believe will improve their chances for well-being. These strategies share in common that they are *responses* to the *same* social conditions: they are attempts to make meaningful and satisfying lives with a system of sex-based inequality.

Some women have chosen the Careerist strategy. They defer marriage (or remarriage), children, and social activities placing practically all of their energies and motivations into "making it" in their chosen career. For many of these women, the underlying belief is that if they adopt male-associated activities, personality traits and goals, and suppress the female-associated ones, they will find success and happiness in the male imperium. Rather than marrying a man, they have decided to become one. "Assertiveness training," "dressing for success," "playing games mother never taught them," are cant for some of these women, as well as 75 hour work weeks. Except for a very small number of such women, however, this strategy is not wholly effective. This is so, because the double standard is operative. Even if a woman adopts behavior identical to a man's, it is not perceived of as identical; she is not judged equally competent or dedicated because her sex-status, female, is still salient. Examples of this abound in our language practices:

He's aggressive; she's pushy.

He's hard-nosed; she's hard to work for.

He's ambitious; she's power mad.

He's a king-maker; she's a queen bee.

He's close-mouthed; she's secretive.

He climbed the ladder to success; she slept her way to the top.

A second strategy which women have adopted is the Superwoman strategy. Superwomen want to believe they can do everything and anything—leap into the establishment with a single bound, stop speeding adolescents with a single word, soothe Superhusband with a single touch. They want everything at the same time, and they want everything done to near perfection. They see themselves as androgynous, or able to incorporate simultaneously the activities, personality traits, and goals associated with both males and females. The television perfume ads are addressed to them: executive by day, mother by eveningtide, and seductress by night. Attempting to do everything superbly, these women tend to be constantly plagued by self-doubts and are susceptible to premature exhaustion, heart disease, and alcoholism. Because this strategy is so demanding and requires extraordinary motivation, stamina, and energy, and because other options are available, I believe this Superwoman strategy has mostly run its course, and that fewer women will adopt this strategy into the eighties.

Emerging now, and promising to gain momentum over the next few years is a third strategy we might call the neo-Cinderella one. The new Cinderella is not a girl-child. She does not want to be saved from a wicked stepmother, and she knows there are no Prince Charmings out there. Rather, she is likely to be a woman in her late twenties or early thirties who wants to be "saved" from her meaningless low-paying job, a life of supposed independence which has become one of economic hardship, fatigue, loneliness, and fear. She is not looking for a Prince Charming, a perfect man, but only for a "good husband," a man who will provide for her financially while she raises children. But, she does expect, if she finds him, to live happily ever after. Given the demographic realities discussed earlier, however, it is highly likely that many women will not find Mr. Good Husband, and many of those who do will find themselves "ex-Mrs. Good Husband" within seven years—single mothers this time back on their own. Therefore, although this strategy may provide a kind of temporary relief for women, it is not likely to provide the life-long satisfaction they seek.

A fourth strategy is being devised by women we might call "Balancers." Such women may want "everything"—love-life, children, careers—but unlike Superwomen they see life as possibly led in a series of phases or stages: that not everything has to be had right now; and, they do not demand of themselves peak performance at every task. Balancers might devote their early twenties to their education and careers, their late twenties to establishing a love-relationship, their early thirties to children, and their late thirties to renewed career dedication. Women who adopt this strategy seem to have a realistic appraisal of their life-opportunities and they use tactics to increase the probability that their life-strategy of balancing will bring the desired rewards. For example, they are likely to retain their name upon marriage, refusing to have their identity linguistically incorporated into their husband's. They look for partners who are "equals"—equally trained, equally committed to careers, and equally concerned with the nurturance of their home-life. Because these women are struggling toward a balanced life, should either their marriage or their career give way, they will not suffer the same kind of decimation that accrues to women who have only one set of aspirations. Moreover, the sociological and psychological research suggests that this strategy is most likely to provide women with a sense of well-being. I believe the number of Balancers will increase over this decade, and that, in fact, many of the neo-Cinderellas will opt for that strategy at a later point in their lives.

Each of these strategies—Careerist, Superwoman, neo-Cinderella, and Balancer—are reactions to the constraints women experience because they are women in an androcentric and patriarchal society. Implicit in these four life strategies is the tension between "home and work." Determining where and when to place one's aspirations and energies—in careers, in homes, in both—remain salient issues which will continue to engage women's life energies.

More broadly, however, this tension between home and work for contemporary women can be understood as tension between one's need for achievement—to be recognized for one's accomplishments, and one's need for affiliation—to have close and meaningful relationships with others. Although home vs. work has been the field upon which this "tug-of-war" has been played, a new playing field has been excavated, tempered, outfitted, and populated. We might call this field a "Women's Stadium." This Stadium will be an increasingly important symbolic and pragmatic arena for women throughout this decade. More women will be turning to other women as a major part of their life strategy for the attainment of both success and succorance, financial rewards and friendship, achievement and affiliation. Not only will women continue to "bond" with men, they will increasingly "bond" with other women. The Women's Stadium is one of the major legacies of the women's movement. Its presence gives women a new resource for devising life strategies.

Today, women and women-associated activities, personality traits, and goals have been upgraded

in the eyes of women. This means, most importantly, that a woman evaluates herself more highly, as well. Mental health surveys for example, show that women growing up during the height of feminist social movement activity are freer of mental-illness and fuller of self-esteem than women have been in the past. Because women feel better about themselves and each other, associating with women for economic, social, or political reasons will be increasingly viewed as a legitimate and valued enterprise. Although women have always been "friends," what will be different is that these friendships can have a high priority in women's lives; they will not be

viewed as "second-best" or "make-do." For many women freed from competition with each other for men, or involved in relationships with men that lack emotional intimacy, female friendships will be the primary way in which affiliative needs will be met. The oversolicitous waiter who asks women dining together on a Saturday night, "What are such good-looking women like you doing out alone?" can be answered truthfully, "We are not alone. We are with each other."

Second, the feminist movement has created a number of groups, organizations, and women's spaces—galleries, bookstores, theaters. These organizations and spaces are not "women's auxilaries" nor called pejoratively "just" for women. Rather, they provide a structural opportunity for women with similar goals, problems, issues, or interests to congregate, collaborate, and move toward meeting their need for both affiliation and achievement.

Third, because there are some women in the businesses and professions who are strongly committed to helping other women, opportunities for women newly entering those arenas have expanded. These opportunities include *networking*—or establishing ties with other women, professional *caucussing*—or using the collective voice to confront sexual harassment and sex discrimination, and the existence of female mentors. Not only does this mean that women will be increasingly able to depend on other women to teach them the ropes, it means there are some women braiding new ones. Such women are challenging the overidentification with the male-associated model of doing business, research, medicine, law, and social service, and are finding ways to change the structure of their work worlds. For example, a group of saleswomen for a national computer company began to meet informally. Soon, despite their company's sales philosophy which encouraged competition between the salespersons, the women began to share their sales-strategies and marketing ideas. Two things happened. First, their individual sales records soared—they far outdistanced the sales records of their male counterparts; and second, they became close friends—persons they could turn to and count on in crises and jubilations. Having women-identified-women in businesses and professions means, then, that women have the opportunity into the future of embracing a life-strategy that allows them to meet their needs for achievement and affiliation simultaneously.

Throughout this decade, then, we might expect the life-opportunities of women to change little, and we might expect these life-strategies to continue to be responses to the social conditions in which they live. Women will continue to focus on the dilemma of home versus work, and will continue to recognize that other women can play a major role in their search for achievement and affiliation. Although it is unlikely that major social movements directed toward equality and justice will emerge during this decade, I believe it is equally unlikely for a conservative backlash to totally undo the changes already set in motion. Rather, the early years of this decade will be a period of consolidation, of relative quietude and entrenchment; however, during the next decade, if the social and political cycle repeats itself—as it always has—we should be entering a period newly attuned to equality and justice, a period in which new life-opportunities and life-strategies for all society's members can flourish.

is unlikely that large proportions of fathers of newborn infants will avail themselves of the opportunity to care for their child during the first few months of life. Nor is it likely that all Swedish mothers are ready to relinquish their role as primary caretaker of the child. The "impact" of the educational system and other policies have no doubt created vast changes in the image of roles appropriate for men and women. But education is only one of the institutions affecting concepts of what is right and proper. Changes in other institutions, in the belief systems of the older generations, in work, and in daily human interactions are less likely to keep pace with the purposely enacted policies in the educational realm.

Conclusion

There is no question that sex roles have been changing for both men and women. These changes have been enmeshed in societal ideologies and structures of socialization, resulting in patterns of sex role changes that vary from society to society. These changes have special sociological significance because they affect not only how individuals think of themselves, but also how they act. Sex role changes also lead to changes in the societal structures governing power and authority. This, of course, lies at the very heart of a society, and helps to explain why who stays home and who goes to work affect a lot more than how well the dinner gets cooked!

SUMMARY

1. The purposes of this chapter are to explore sex role differentiation; to examine and discuss, on the basis of available studies, sex role differentiation as a biological and social phenomenon; to examine the process of socialization and ideology cross culturally, and to explore its effect on gender roles; to explore cross culturally the impact of legal changes, past traditions, and social policy on the occupational experience of women.

2. Role differentiation may have begun as functional differentiation based on the greater physical strength of men and lactation of women, which enabled men to hunt large animals and women to nurse their infants. These practices appear to have led to the development of a system of beliefs, an ideology, supported by religion and pseudoscientific theories justifying the subordinate position of women. With time, this ideology became accepted as "natural."

3. Socialization (the process of learning and internalizing culturally approved modes of behavior), ensures gender appropriate roles for males and females. Girls internalize values and norms appropriate to their future roles as mothers and wives; boys on the other hand internalize values appropriate to their future roles as wage earners.

4. Cross-cultural studies show that gender role allocation is variable, depending on the social and cultural definitions of role appropriateness. Women can be soldiers, scientists, and steel workers (and even astronauts); men can rear children and engage in home making activities.

5. Legal changes providing women with equal access to education and work are crucial to equality of men and women. But the continuity of traditional social patterns, socialization, and education on the basis of gender roles creates, as the Soviet experience shows, continuing obstacles in achieving social, political, and economic equality.

6. Role differentiation on the basis of gender is costly to men and women; it denies women access to social, economic, and political resources, but it also limits the development of men as people. The high rates of violence, suicide, and assault among men and their shorter life expectancy suggest that a number of costs are directly associated with the male gender role.

REVIEW

Key Terms

Sex role	Instrumental role	Sex differentiation	Dual labor market
Ideology	Sex	Gender differentiation	Primary labor market
Expressive role	Gender	Sex role stereotypes	Secondary labor market

Review and Discussion

1. How did your mother view her role as a woman? Did she seem content, or did she ever express impatience or anger with her role? What do you think contributed to her view of her role, and her reactions to it?

2. Did your mother work while you were growing up? If so, what adjustments were made in the family to accommodate her job? If not, did your family have to forgo things that you might have been able to have had she worked? How do you feel about your mother either working or not working?

3. Do you believe there are biological differences in the innate abilities of men and women? What do you base your belief on?

4. If you are a woman, have you ever wished you were a man? Why? If you are a man, have you ever wished you were a woman? Why? If you could choose your sex, knowing what you now know about sex roles, which sex would you want to be?

5. Do you favor our society moving toward either a Soviet or a Swedish model of sex role definitions? What do you see as the advantages of whichever model you choose, e.g., either retaining our own, adopting a Soviet approach, or following the Swedish model?

6. What does women's liberation mean to you? Would it affect male sex roles? If so, how?

Experience with Sociology

This chapter has discussed sex roles at length, focusing on the socialization processes that maintain sex-role differences. In spite of substantial similarities between men and women in terms of what they are biologically *able* to do, their socially defined *behaviors* are usually quite different. Women are most often concerned with the home, children, and interpersonal relationships. In contrast, men's activities tend to revolve around work and instrumental behaviors. In other words, in our society—and others as well—sex role is a more important determinant of behavior than are the biological characteristics of each sex.

Module 6 in *Experience With Sociology* enables you to assess for yourself the importance of sex roles in contemporary American society. The media are full of stories about changes in the role of women in our society. Women today seem to have more choices regarding marriage and childrearing, as well as more opportunities to pursue advanced education degrees and to enter prestigious professions like law and medicine. As you do Module 6, you will have an opportunity to examine data in order to reach your own conclusions about whether male and female roles are still sex-typed.

References

Baude, A. (1979). Public policy and changing family patterns in Sweden, 1930–1977. In *Sex Roles and Social Policy,* eds. J. Lipman Blumen and J. Bernard. Beverly Hills: Sage.

Bernard, J. (1981). *The Female World.* New York: Free Press.

Child, I. L., E. H. Potter, and **E. M. Levine** (1946). Children's textbooks and personality development. *Psychology Monographs* 60:1–54.

D'Andrade, R. (1966). Cross-cultural differences of sex differentiation in behavior. In *Development of Sex Differences,* ed. E. Maccoby. Stanford: Stanford University Press.

David, Deborah, and **Robert Brannon,** eds. (1976). *The Forty-Nine Percent Majority: The Male Sex Role.* Reading, Mass.: Addison-Wesley.

Dobson, Richard B. (1977). Mobility and stratification in the Soviet Union. *Annual Review of Sociology* 3: 297–330.

Feigin, S. E., and **M. A. Golovanova** (1973). The evaluation of qualifications of scientific cadre. In *The Scientific Cadre of Leningrad,* eds. S. A. Kugel and D. B. Lebin. Leningrad: Nauka (in Russian).

Filene, P. G. (1974). *Him, her, self.* New York: Harcourt Brace Jovanovich.

Gordon, L. A., and **E. M. Klopov** (1972). *Man after Work.* Moscow: Progress.

Hacker, Helen (1951). Women as a minority group. *Social Forces* 30: 60–69.

Kanter, Rosabeth (1977). *Men and Women of the Corporation.* New York: Basic Books.

Kharchev, A. G. (1974). Women's Career Work and the Family. Paper presented at the VIII World Congress of Sociology, Toronto, Ontario, Canada.

Kohlberg, L. A. (1966). A cognitive developmental analysis of children's sex role concepts and attitudes. In *The Development of Sex Differences,* ed. E. E. Maccoby. Stanford: Stanford University Press.

Kohn, M. (1978). *Class and Conformity.* Chicago: University of Chicago Press.

Kon, I. S. (1973). Youth as a social problem. In *Society and Youth.* ed. V. D. Kobetskii. Moscow: Molodaia Gvardia (in Russian).

Lapidus, G. W. (1977). Sexual equality in Soviet policy: A developmental perspective. In *Women in Russia.* eds. D. Atkinson, D. Dallin, and G. W. Lapidus. Stanford: Stanford University Press.

Laws, J. L. (1979). *The Second Sex.* New York: Elsevier.

Lebin, B. D., and **I. I. Leiman** (1972). The woman scientist: Her professional and family role. In *The Production Activities of Women and the Family.* ed. I. N. Lushchitskii. Minsk: Izd. BGU. (in Russian).

Levinson, A. (1975). From Olive Oyl to Sweet Polly Purebread: Sex role stereotypes and television cartoons. *Journal of Popular Culture* 8: 561–572.

Lewis, M. (1972). Parents and children: Sex role development. *School Review* 80: 229–240.

McArthur, L. Z., and **B. G. Resko** (1975). The portrayal of men and women in American television commercials. *Journal of Social Psychology* 97: 209–220.

McLaughlin, S. D. (1978). Occupational sex identification and the assessment of male and female earning inequality. *American Sociological Review* 43: 909–921.

Mead, M. (1935). *Sex and Temperament in Three Primitive Societies.* New York: Mentor.

—— (1972). *Blackberry Winter.* New York: Morrow.

Money, J., and **A. Ehrhandt** (1972). *Man and Woman: Boy and Girl.* Baltimore: Johns Hopkins Press.

Murdock, G. (1937). Comparative data on the division of labor by sex. *Social Forces* 15: 551–553.

Myrdal, Gunnar (1944). *An American Dilemma.* New York: Harper.

Nechaeva, V. G., and **T. A. Markova** (1975). *Moral Education in the Nursery School.* Moscow: Prosveschenie (in Russian).

Parsons, T., and **R. F. Bales** (1955). *Family Socialization and Interaction Process.* Glencoe, Ill.: Free Press.

Pleck, Joseph (1976). My male sex role—and ours. In *The Forty-Nine Percent Majority: The Male Sex Role.* ed. Deborah David and Robert Brannon. Reading, Mass.: Addison-Wesley.

Rosenhan, J. M. (1977). Images of male and female in children's readers. In *Women in Russia,* eds. D. Atkinson, A. Dallin, and G. W. Lapidus. Stanford: Stanford University Press.

Rubin, J. Z., F. J. Provenzano, and **Z. Luria** (1972). The eye of the beholder: Parents' views on sex of newborns. *American Journal of Orthopsychiatry* 44: 512–519.

Saario, T., C. N. Jacklin, and **C. K. Tittle** (1973).

Sex role stereotyping in the public school. *Harvard Educational Review* 43: 386–416.

Schwartz, Janet S. (1979). Women under socialism: Role definition of Soviet women. *Social Forces* 58: 67–88.

Short, James F., and **Fred L. Strodbeck** (1976). Why gangs fight. In *The Forty-Nine Percent Majority: The Male Sex Role*. eds. Deborah S. David and Robert Brannon. Reading, Mass.: Addison-Wesley.

Shubkin, V. N., and **G. M. Kochetov** (1968). Leader, colleague, subordinate. *Social Research* 2: 143–155 (in Russian).

Spiro, M. E. (1979). *Gender in Culture: Kibbutz Women Revisited*. Durham, N.C.: Duke University Press.

Titma, M. Kh. (1975). *Occupational Choice as a Social Problem*. Moscow: Mysl (in Russian).

Vetter, B. M. (1981). Women scientists and engineers: Trends in participation. *Science* no. 4527, 1313–1321.

Vodzinskaia, V. V. (1973). Orientations toward occupations. In *Social Stratification and Mobility in the USSR.,* eds. and translators Murray Yanowitch and Wesley Fisher. White Plains: International Arts and Sciences Press.

Waite, Linda J. (1981). "U.S. Women at Work." *Population Reference Bureau* 36, no. 2.

Weitzman, L., D. Eifler, E. Hokada, and **C. Roll** (1972). Sex role socializations in picture books for preschool children. *American Journal of Sociology* 77: 1125–1149.

PART TWO SOCIAL INTERACTION

6

SOCIAL PROCESSES

- *Exchange*
- *Cooperation and Competition*
- *Conflict and Conflict Resolution*
- *SUMMARY*

Starting in the summer of 1980, workers in Poland began to challenge the nation's political and economic systems. Eighteen days of strikes culminated in the formation of the union called Solidarity, led by Lech Walesa. As the union's power grew, virtually every part of Polish society was changed in some way: there was greater freedom of the press, more worker participation in decision making, a stronger role for the Catholic church in social affairs, and so on (Darnton, 1981). Yet the people of Poland were well aware of the fact that similar efforts in Czechoslovakia in 1968 resulted in a Soviet-led invasion by Warsaw Pact forces. Indeed, many people feared a Soviet invasion, especially as Solidarity escalated its demands. Sociologically, a very interesting situation existed. On one hand, Polish workers were banding together against Communist party leaders and factory managers in order to improve their lives. At the same time, however, the leaders of Solidarity were working together with these same party leaders and managers both to achieve change and to avoid a Soviet invasion.

The situation in Poland illustrates the four basic social processes to be discussed in this chapter: exchange, cooperation, competition, and conflict. **Social processes** refers to the important recurring patterns of social behavior that characterize the interactions between individuals and groups. It is through these social processes that a social structure is able to function.

These four social processes pervade the structures of society through which human behavior is organized. Socialization, described in detail in Chapter 4, teaches people how and when to use various social processes. For example, women learn that dating is a situation in which men compete with each other for their attention. After the courtship period, however, women are not expected to encourage competition for their attention. Instead, they are supposed to develop cooperative and exchange relationships with one man—their husband. If a woman's relationship with her husband deteriorates into one characterized by conflict, she is encouraged to consider separation or divorce. Learning how to use the four major social processes selectively is an important function of socialization.

Internalizing values and techniques of exchange, cooperation, conflict, and competition is also a basic part of a society's stratification system (described in more detail in the next two chapters). Stratification involves the ranking of people according to socially determined criteria: rich and poor, powerful and weak, desirable and undesirable, and so on. We usually learn that we should cooperate with people like ourselves—they share our values and understand our needs. Our "inferiors" in a social stratification system are often seen as threatening, and relationships with them are based on competition and even conflict. Interracial conflict is a good example. The nature of the exchanges we have with people at different levels in a stratification system also varies. Exchanges with peers are likely to be more equal, while those with inferiors are more frequently exploitative or unequal (they are not "worth" as much).

Social processes, then, are basic to understanding the way people are taught to relate to each other, and why certain types of relationships exist and are maintained. While this chapter will focus on patterns of social behavior, it is important to note that this does not mean that these patterns are unchangeable. Indeed, we will look at some of the forces for change throughout the chapter. Now, however, let's look at the first of the four basic social processes: exchange.

EXCHANGE

Almost all human interactions may be defined in terms of **exchange,** a mutually rewarding social relationship in which individuals or groups supply each other with desired goods or services. A worker receives wages in exchange for her labor; she trades her wages for goods and services—food, clothes, medical treatment, housing,

In prehistoric times people often formed cooperative exchanges that enabled the group to successfully hunt game, which was then shared by all. Thus, by working together, individuals accomplished more than they could by hunting alone.

a car, a vacation. If she opens a savings account, the bank will pay her interest in exchange for the use of her money; if the bank lends her money, she must pay the bank interest in exchange for the use of *its* money. She may ride to work in a car pool, whose members exchange driving services on a rotating basis; on the way to work, they exchange information and ideas on everything from the latest movies to the idiocy of politicians and the state of the world.

Exchange is also a factor in the most intimate relations of marriage and family life. A loving relationship is based on mutual affection and respect (a type of social exchange). And a marriage is also made up of a very real and practical exchange of services (an economic exchange). The wife who does not hold an outside job contributes her services—caring for the children, cooking, cleaning, doing the laundry—in exchange for the economic support of her husband, who also usually performs small duties of house-

hold maintenance. Parents provide their children with economic and emotional support in exchange for affection and respect, hoping that when they are old their children will help support them (Blau, 1964; Heath, 1976).

Exchange relationships are found in every society in every age and characterize the interactions between groups as well as between individuals. The hunting bands of prehistoric times survived by cooperative exchanges of goods and services. When individuals were successful in hunting or gathering, they shared the food with other members of the band; if they came home empty-handed the next day, luckier individuals shared with them. No one went hungry. With the development of agriculture and the rise of cities, forms of exchange became more complex. People with specialized skills—metalworkers, pot makers, weavers, merchants, and artists—traded their services for goods or money. Farmers provided food to city dwellers in exchange for manufactured products. Trade developed over great distances. From very ancient times, people of sub-Saharan Africa traded gold and ivory for salt from areas north of the Sahara. The people of the city-states of Phoenicia, where agricultural land was scarce, developed special skills as manufacturers and merchant seamen; their products and services were exchanged for food and raw materials. Figure 6.1 looks at a more recent type of geographical exchange.

Fig. 6.1 / Population Shifts, Regional Competition, and Exchange

Changes in population are important, since population is accompanied by growth, economic development, and political power. Cities and regions have begun to compete with each other for population in order to get the rewards that population growth brings. Sociologically, we might note that growth also brings problems, so in fact elements of exchange are also involved in population shifts.

Source: The *New York Times*, December 18, 1981. © 1981 by The New York Times Company. Reprinted by permission.

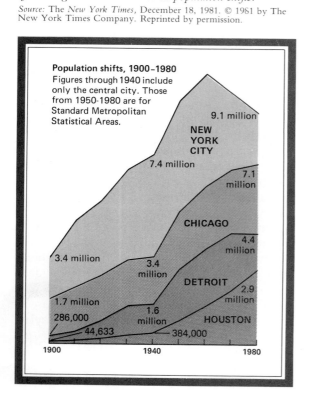

Of course, not all exchanges are positive. Two prehistoric hunters—or two modern city dwellers—may exchange insults and blows as well as food and assistance. Throughout history clans, tribes, and nations have engaged in economic rivalry and outright warfare. Family members can and do hurt one another—physically and emotionally. Both positive and negative exchanges can be found in all periods, in all societies, and on all levels. Let us look for a moment at negative exchanges in more detail.

Exploitative Exchange

Some exchange relationships are based on mutual exploitation. In these cases, the basic exchange process still works, but the result is some level of loss by both parties. A classic example is spouse abuse, especially wife-battering (Norman and Mancuso, 1980). A woman may submit to physical abuse by her husband in return for his financial support. The husband, in turn, gratifies his need to feel "manly" and in control. Yet both are also hurt in this type of exploitative exchange. The woman can be physically injured, and she is almost invariably psychologically humiliated and made to feel inadequate. The man gradually destroys his ability to have a loving relationship with his wife (and children, in many cases), and he avoids dealing with the pressures that threaten his sense of well-being and which have led to this aggression.

Groups, too, sometimes use exploitative exchanges. Employers who hire illegal aliens because they will work long hours for low wages maximize their short-run profit. The aliens may be grateful to get work and not be reported to the immigration authorities. However, the aliens have no legal protection and little opportunity to move into the major institutional structure of society, remaining chronically vulnerable to deportation. The employers never develop a stable, skilled labor force that allows for long-range economic success. In addition, they are subject to fines and other legal actions.

Why do exploitative exchanges exist if they are so destructive? In part, the answer lies in fear and ignorance. Often people don't recognize that they are being exploited, or they are afraid to assert their rights (battered wives and exploited aliens tend to feel very vulnerable in a male-dominated and complicated legal system). Sometimes no one recognizes that an exchange is exploitative, or definitions of what is exploitation change. Wives used to be grateful for whatever they got: some physical abuse was not considered so bad if other needs were being met. The women's movement has changed these beliefs among many women, and helped to identify the exploitative aspects of abuse relationships between spouses. And finally, conflict theorists would remind us that dominant groups tend to perpetuate ideologies that disguise ways in which exchanges are exploitative in order to maintain a social order that preserves their own privileges. In this sense the exploitation works to the advantage—materially and psychologically—of those in power.

Formal and Informal Exchange

Types of exchange may be seen as representing a continuum. At one end are highly formalized patterns of exchange. Merchants expect to be paid in money for their goods, either in cash or through the use of credit. Customers expect to receive full value for their money. They interact on an impersonal basis as buyer and seller. Either can go to court if he or she feels cheated. In industrialized societies much exchange is formal, usually codified through laws and specific procedures. This is because of the complexity of exchange in societies like our own. The diner who sits down to a roast beef dinner in a restaurant, for example, is the ultimate beneficiary of a chain of formalized exchange relationships. It stretches from the rancher, the meatpacker, and the wholesaler to the restaurant owner, all of whom employ many people who are part of the exchange network. Yet the diner usually has direct contact with only one person in the chain: the server in the restaurant.

At the other extreme are very informal patterns of exchange. These are generally characterized by **reciprocity,** voluntary and informal social exchanges which seek to ensure some degree of equality in the value of what is exchanged (Johnson, 1981, 364–66; Titmuss, 1971). In the United States, the partners in a marriage do not keep accounts of how much each has contributed in terms of financial support, labor,

The formal transactions that take place in a store are examples of exchange. Although modern industrial societies have eliminated most forms of direct bartering, each party in an exchange still must evaluate what conditions will make the exchange rewarding.

or affection, although a persistent imbalance may eventually destroy the marriage. As sociologist Peter Blau put it, "Neighbors exchange favors; children, toys; colleagues, assistance; acquaintances, courtesies; politicans, concessions; discussants, ideas; housewives, recipes" (Blau, 1964: 88). Informal exchange exists in all societies. Even in our own society, which has many areas of formalized exchange patterns (such as in business), there are also areas of social life characterized by informal exchanges (like the family and friendship groups). Nevertheless, our society would have more formalized exchanges than preindustrial societies in which the minimal division of labor and emphasis on small groups usually makes formalized legal sanctions unnecessary. Even in those societies persistent shirkers may find themselves the object of powerful social pressure. In this way, reciprocity is maintained (Freuchen, 1975; Lee, 1969).

In between the two extremes of formal and informal patterns of exchange is a whole range of behaviors that have elements of both. The family provides a good example. We have already noted that the family generally operates on the basis of informal exchanges. But consider what happens when divorce occurs. Much more formal patterns of exchange are created, such as visiting rights in exchange for child support payments. And, because the family as a social institution is changing, so are patterns of exchange. Michelle Triola successfully sued actor Lee Marvin for what was dubbed "palimony" even though they were not married. The court reasoned that a relationship of several years duration entailed exchanges; Ms. Triola, for example, said she had given up a career in order to be with Mr. Marvin. Therefore, when the relationship ended, he was ordered to pay her a sum of money to compensate her for what she had forgone on his behalf. The

Fig. 6.2 / What do children owe their parents?

Exchange within personal relationships (a family, for example) is more difficult to define than in business matters. Do children owe their parents for all the years of caring? Or are parents obligated to their children, regardless of future repayments?

Source: *The General Mills American Family Report—1966–77*, "Raising Children in a Changing Society," Yankelovich, Skelly, and White, Inc. Copyright General Mills, Inc., 1977, Minneapolis, Minn. Used by permission.

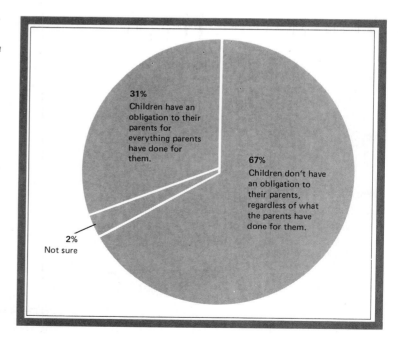

31% Children have an obligation to their parents for everything parents have done for them.

67% Children don't have an obligation to their parents, regardless of what the parents have done for them.

2% Not sure

increasing popularity of **prenuptial agreements** is another example of the greater formalization of exchange relationships in marriage. In such documents both parties itemize exactly how their possessions are to be distributed in the event the marriage is terminated.

The Functions of Exchange

Perhaps the chief function of exchange is to strengthen social bonds, thereby helping to ensure a group's survival. Exchange promotes social solidarity by creating alliances and establishing bonds within and between families and groups.

For instance, in many traditional societies, marriages involve exchange relationships that encompass both the economic and social life of the society. The bridegroom and his family are expected to pay a "bride price" to the bride's family in exchange for future services to her husband's family: childbearing and domestic duties, helping in the fields, and other economic activities. Relatives and friends of the groom are expected to help him raise the bride price; in return, he may be expected to work for his relatives to pay off the debt and to help his friends when it is their turn to marry. Marriages are often arranged between families, or wives are exchanged between villages and clans specifically to promote friendly relations and cooperation in times of danger or economic hardship (Hoebel, 1972).

Similar functions can be seen in more industrialized societies. Canada, a federation of provinces similar to our federation of states, provides a good example. The western provinces of Alberta and Saskatchewan have rich oil reserves of great value to the other provinces. The other provinces, in turn, provide a labor supply

Marriage traditionally includes some form of ceremonial exchange, whether it involves a dowry or the more symbolic exchange of rings and vows.

and markets for the western—primarily agricultural—enterprises of the oil-rich provinces. During the early 1980s, Alberta and Saskatchewan negotiated with the central government to set a price for domestic oil that would bring a fair return to the oil producers at the same time that costs were controlled for oil users throughout the nation. In this way everyone benefitted, and the sense of all Canadians working together toward a common national purpose was reinforced. We should recall, however, that not all exchanges are helpful. Exploitative exchanges may have hurtful as well as helpful effects, as discussed earlier in this chapter.

COOPERATION AND COMPETITION

In premodern societies, people hunt, fish, build houses, and fight together. In the United States or other technologically advanced countries, members of a labor union band together to protect their interests in terms of wages and working conditions; members of a political party join forces to get their candidate elected; members of a social club work together simply to provide opportunities for recreation and entertainment for the membership.

Cooperation—the joining of effort for a mutual goal—is one of the basic social processes. **Competition**—the effort of individuals or groups to surpass each other in order to obtain rewards that are in limited supply—is the opposite of cooperation. Two men may vie for the same woman, or the same job; politicians compete for an elective office; rival companies try to outsell each other; countries compete for oil, cotton, wheat, military superiority. Of course, the rewards of competition need not be material; individuals and groups regularly compete for prestige or status, or simply for the psychological satisfaction of winning.

Competition differs from conflict (the topic of the next section) in two ways: first, it is usually impersonal; second, its goal is to surpass—not eliminate or destroy—the other person or group. For example, a member of a basketball team competes against players on other teams in the league year in and year out, yet feels no personal animosity toward members of the other teams; in fact, members of different teams may be close friends off the playing court. Competition is limited by the rules of the game and the players' willingness to abide by the rules; a player cannot win by fouling an opponent, running with the ball, or putting the referee out of action. However, fierce competition may lead to conflict—as when a disputed call leads to an angry brawl between players.

The rules which govern competition are taught by the agents of socialization: the family, school, peer group, and so forth. These rules become internalized, and they can be differentiated as those applying in general (never cheat in one's effort to get ahead) and those applying to specific situations (members of minority groups are more vulnerable, and may be easier people to compete against because they may lack needed resources, such as education or political power). The conditions under which competition takes place generally reflect the ability of dominant groups to set the rules. When blacks were excluded from voting and good quality schools, they had little ability to participate in societal policy making or to be successful competitors in social situations requiring education and political influence (Ryan, 1976). As a rule, competition favors groups that already have access to resources. People do not start the "race" from the same point, nor are they even necessarily using the same rules since their socialization has often been quite different (Ogbu, 1978).

Cultural Influences

The relative importance of cooperation and competition varies greatly from one culture to another. Anthropologist Margaret Mead has studied many of the tribes of New Guinea. She has found that different child-rearing practices produce distinct patterns of behavior in these societies. Among the Arapesh, for example, children are encouraged to "get along" with one another from the time they are very young. Cooperation is rewarded, and competition is discouraged. As a result, there is little competition in adult Arapesh society. In other New Guinea societies, however, Mead found children being taught that only by competing with one another could they obtain material or emotional rewards (such as respect and approval).

The Kwakiutl child learns that prestige and social status are obtained first by competing to acquire material goods and then by competing to give away or destroy those goods in dramatically staged potlatch ceremonies. On the other hand, the Zuni Indian child in the southwestern United States learns to cooperate with others and is rewarded for blending with the group. Zuni children play group games, with no individual winners or losers. The individual who acquires wealth or possessions is not admired, but is expected to distribute any surplus wealth among members of the community. However, unlike the Kwakiutl, the Zuni does not acquire prestige or a reputation for generosity by giving possessions away; giving things away is considered "natural" behavior, to be carried out without boasting and unaccompanied by special ceremonies (Goldman, 1937).

Among advanced industrial societies, the United States and China are good examples of a highly competitive society and a highly cooperative society. Children in the United States learn to compete for good grades in school, for prestige and leadership among peers, for awards, honors, and scholarships. Success is admired, and failure is despised. While our society values individual autonomy, achievement, and competition, Chinese society prizes discipline, loyalty, and cooperation (Sidel, 1972). Children in China are taught to work for the good of the group and to see individual competition as selfish and immoral. In school, for example, Chinese chil-

dren are encouraged to work together on group projects and, in winter, to help one another in taking off and putting on heavy outdoor clothing. They strive not for individual rewards but for the success of classmates or teammates.

No society, however, is completely competitive or cooperative. Despite the emphasis on cooperation in China, there are frequent struggles for power among rival political leaders. In our own country, family members are expected to help one another while still competing with others to get ahead economically. Athletes are urged to cooperate with teammates in order to compete with other teams. While societies can be categorized as generally more oriented toward either cooperation or competition, both efforts play a part in every society. Like any other aspect of social life, acting cooperatively or competitively is generally determined by social norms that define when such behavior is appropriate.

The Effects of Cooperation and Competition

Patterns of competition and cooperation within societies have consequences both for individuals and for the larger society. In Chapter 3, we mentioned that parents will encourage their children to be competitive or cooperative, depending on which type of behavior is more adaptive for their particular culture. Cooperation may be more advantageous in some circumstances; competition, in others.

The advantages of cooperation. By cooperating, groups of people can accomplish together what no single individual could accomplish alone. In ancient times enormous groups of people working together built the pyramids, the Great Wall of China, and the massive irrigation works that made possible the birth of civilization in Mesopotamia. The building of a modern skyscraper requires the cooperative efforts of real estate experts, architects, engineers, construction

The barn-raising custom of years past was an example of cooperation on a community-wide scale. The efforts of many multiplied the size of the task that could be accomplished.

workers, plumbers, electricians, and many other specialists.

People of all times and places have learned that cooperation with others is often the best way of serving their own interests. Consider, for example, the strike by the faculty at a large midwestern university in the Fall of 1979. Like all faculty, individual scholars were concerned about their ability to create and maintain a viable learning atmosphere at the university. Such factors as class size, criteria for faculty promotion and retention, support for scholarly research, and faculty salaries are involved in this goal. Yet in an era of declining public funds for higher education in many states, it is difficult to decide how to cut expenses in ways that will least disrupt the university's educational function. When the university decided to control costs by strictly limiting faculty salary increases, as well as reducing their role in policy making in the University, the faculty rebelled.

Although it had threatened to strike before, the faculty, in spite of being unionized, had never done so. Individual faculty members who disagreed with university policies might rebel, but the cost of such action could be not having one's contract renewed. When the faculty finally decided to take collective action in 1979, they were successful in changing university policy and protecting each other—the university could hardly afford to fire 70 percent of the faculty! As a result, cooperative action had a number of positive collective *and* individual results. Collectively, the university benefitted from a stronger faculty voice in administrative affairs which related to the creation and maintenance of a sound learning environment. Individually, faculty received higher salaries, protection from being fired for disagreeing with university policies, and greater control over their own work activities. The strike demonstrated how collective and individual interests are often closely related.

Cooperation plays an important part in the economic life of even highly competitive industrial nations (see Table 6.1). Within a corporation, every employee, from a janitor to the president, is essentially engaged in a cooperative endeavor. In 1980 and 1981, the employees of Continental Airlines banded together with the president and other executives to purchase the airline to avoid having it taken over by another company. Their effort, although ultimately unsuccessful, illustrates an especially high level of corporate cooperation. In all cases, however, large-scale production and distribution are made possible only through the cooperation of producers, middle people, retailers, and consumers.

Groups that emphasize cooperation also provide certain psychological and emotional benefits for their members. Heavy tasks may seem lighter if the work is shared, whether the task is clearing

TABLE 6.1 / BUDGETING AS COOPERATION

The U.S. budget represents an effort to distribute societal funds so that all the nation's needs are met. It is in the best interest of the society as a whole for each of its subparts to ensure the survival and well-being of all the other subparts. The following data represent the results of this process as expressed in federal expenditures in May 1979. Figures are in millions of dollars.

Category	Expenditures
Total	41,618
National defense	9,965
International affairs	743
General science, space, technology	442
Energy	737
Natural resources and environment	969
Agriculture	69
Commerce and housing credit	16
Transportation	1,326
Community and regional development	787
Education, training, employment, social services	2,559
Health	4,258
Income security	13,558
Veterans benefits and services	1,694
Administration of justice	364
Other	4,855

Source: Federal Reserve System, *Annual Statistical Digest 1970–1979*, March, 1981, p. 213.

a field of weeds or organizing a space program to put people on the moon. The Wolof are quite conscious of the benefits of group labor: companionship, joking, singing, and working rhythmically to the beat of a drum helps members of agricultural work groups forget the stifling heat, the dust, the tedium, and the difficulty of their work. Cooperative arrangements also provide security for group members. A Bushman hunter knows he will have a meal even if he has been unsuccessful that day in hunting. In cooperative societies, such as the Wolof, the Manus, or the Mossi, an individual is assured of group support to meet financial or social obligations and aid when he or she is ill or disabled. For members of advanced industrial societies, unemployment compensation, old-age pensions, and government aid to the disabled provide the same kind of security.

Cooperative groups may be more efficient and more productive than groups that emphasize competition. Morton Deutsch demonstrated this fact in a series of experiments. He organized members of a psychology course into five-member cooperative and competitive groups. For six weeks each group spent three hours per week working on a series of puzzles and human relations problems. In the cooperative groups, each student's grade depended on the quality of the group's solutions. In the competitive groups, students were graded on their relative contribution to the group's solutions. Thus, it was to the advantage of each member of the cooperative groups to contribute to the group goal, while in the competitive groups each member could achieve a high grade only by competing with other members of the group. Deutsch found that the cooperative groups solved the puzzles more rapidly than the competitive groups and produced better and more detailed suggestions about how to handle the human relations problems (Deutsch, 1949).

Many real-life problems are more amenable to cooperative than to competitive solutions. For example, dismantling a circus tent, preparing and serving a banquet for 500 people, or carrying out a successful bank robbery requires careful coordination of cooperative participants. If anyone fails to carry out his or her proper role at the correct time and in the correct manner, the whole system may break down.

A drawback of cooperation.

While cooperative arrangements can benefit groups and individuals, the same arrangements can present what some might view as a handicap to a society: a strong emphasis on cooperation may stifle individual initiative and produce a society that is too rigid to adapt to changing conditions. For example, among the Arapesh, cooperation is encouraged so strongly that individuals who show special skills or creativity are not rewarded; in fact, they may be viewed with suspicion because they are "putting themselves forward." Compared with some of their more assertive neighbors, the Arapesh—both as individuals and as a group—are relatively passive and uncreative. Arapesh society is static, and few innovations are adopted even though they are in contact with outside societies with more "progressive" ways of doing things. Of course, it should be noted that many cooperative groups choose to remain "static" because they don't want the "progressive" way with its accompanying pollution, corruption, and conflict.

Competition as a positive dynamic.

Competition can be beneficial in many areas of life—economics, the arts and sciences, politics, and religion. In the United States, for instance, competition spurs individual and group initiative, creativity, and achievement by rewarding these traits. In socialist societies, production is directed by central planning boards. Officially this eliminates economic competition; however, some socialist economic planners have found that introducing competition between factories leads to increases in productivity. Competition seems to encourage people to greater efforts in industry—and in other areas as well, such as science and religion.

Competition is also one way for a society to allocate scarce rewards on a merit basis. Other methods, such as equal division of goods or distribution according to need, could work but might cause ill feelings—those with little or no ability or ambition would receive the same benefits as those who worked harder and produced more. In the United States, this aspect of competition has resulted in an open class system which offers the possibility of upward mobility

The fast-growing computer industry is marked by strong competition among computer producers who vie for a major share of the market. Such a competitive climate is one way that societies encourage productivity and provide a means of allocating scarce rewards on a merit basis.

TABLE 6.2 / BUDGET CUTTING AS COMPETITION

Budget cutting reduces monies available to various programs. This frequently results in increased competition among program users and administrators for the reduced resources available. The Reagan administration's proposed severe cuts in expenditures for social welfare had this effect, especially in the areas of health and social services, where funds for numerous programs were consolidated into block grants for which local programs will have to compete.

Service	Fiscal Year 1981 (before block grants) in millions	Fiscal Year 1983 (after block grants) in millions
Health		
Community health centers	327.0	
Migrant health	41.6	
Black lung	3.5	$416.7
Family planning	182.4	
Total	554.5	
Social Services		
Child welfare services	172.7	
Child welfare training	5.2	
Foster care	327.8	$380.1
Adoption assistance	0	
Total	505.7	

Source: Human Services Insider 1, no. 3 (Feb. 12, 1982): 3.

and betterment of one's social position through achievement and steady, productive work. In societies where power, wealth, and status are allocated at birth or on some other nonmerit basis, some individuals will never have an opportunity to compete for a larger share of societal rewards.

The negative consequences of competition. Competition has its drawbacks too. What some people may see as challenging, others may regard as a discouraging obstacle. Where competition is overemphasized, group cohesiveness may be destroyed and individuals may suffer. Economic competition in the United States has sometimes been called a "rat race," inhuman in that it distorts normal human relations and inhumane in its effects on individual lives (see Table 6.2)

In a highly competitive society, some people will always be more successful than others. And the successful may become contemptuous of "losers" or insensitive to their problems. With our emphasis on individual initiative and personal success, we tend to assume that people who do not hold prestigious, well-paying jobs are somehow inadequate, incompetent, or irresponsible. Thus, many believe that people on welfare are simply lazy—even though study after study has shown that most of those who receive welfare are truly unable to work: young children, their mothers, the old, and the physically disabled (U.S. Dept. of Health, Education and Welfare, 1972). Moreover, most adults who receive welfare payments would overwhelmingly prefer to be working and consider welfare degrading. "Losing" in a competitive society may seriously damage the individual's self-esteem and even affect his or her ability to compete. Thus, children who are unsuccessful academically during their first years in school may come to hate school and become even less able to compete there; they may drop out before graduating and thereby further handicap their chances of successfully competing in the economic sphere. We want also to note that one need not be poor to feel like a loser. In the summer of 1981 the president of Continental Airlines committed suicide after he "lost" the battle to keep the airline from being taken over by another company—we can see that for some people competition never ends. There is always the next higher rung to achieve.

In some activities, competition is less efficient than cooperation. As you will recall, Deutsch discovered that cooperative groups were more productive than competitive groups in solving relatively complex intellectual problems. Also, the spirit of competition may lead to unnecessary duplication of effort. In the United States, local, state, and national governments sometimes refuse to cooperate on common problems because officials at each level of government jealously guard their prerogatives. But possibly the greatest disadvantage of competition is that it may easily turn into another common social process—conflict.

CONFLICT AND CONFLICT RESOLUTION

Conflict is a step beyond competition. **Conflict** is a form of competition in which the competitors seek not only to surpass their rivals, but to eliminate them from competition, to injure them, to control or deprive them of something against their wills (Williams, 1970). Competition can escalate into conflict when the competing parties fail to follow the "rules." A boxing match is a competition; if a fighter loses his temper, however, and deliberately fouls his opponent, a conflict situation has developed. A company that

puts a competitor out of business by burning its warehouse has obviously gone beyond the bounds of competition.

Some conflicts involve violence and serious damage to one or both parties; some do not. There are conflicts between individuals and conflicts between groups. Because sociologists are most concerned with conflicts between groups, most of our discussion will deal with intergroup conflicts. In the last section we will look at the processes for eliminating or modifying conflicts.

The Escalation of Conflict

Initially, the members of competing groups may feel little hostility toward one another. Yet, as both groups compete more vigorously, individuals may find their loyalties to their own group and their hostility to the opposing group growing. Each group develops self-righteous condemnations of its opponent's conduct. Emotional reactions intensify, and the conflict escalates.

For example, at the beginning of a strike, union members and management representatives may feel relatively friendly toward one another. If the strike is not settled quickly, however, the groups grow more and more hostile. Each regards its own demands as perfectly fair—it is the other side that is being unreasonable. Each begins to form fixed and usually oversimplified impressions of the other (stereotypes), until each regards the other group as selfish, irresponsible, calculating, and untrustworthy. Social pressure reinforces individual loyalty to the group. A worker who would like the strike to end and suggests a compromise solution may be squelched by fellow union members; the same process takes place on the side of management.

Under these circumstances, the resolution of the conflict—an agreement settling the strike—may be very difficult. When the United States air traffic controllers went on strike in 1981, positions hardened quickly on both sides. President Reagan fired all of the strikers, since as federal employees they could not legally strike. Once the controllers were fired, there technically was no strike since there were no employees. The strikers retaliated by seeking the support of air traffic controllers in other nations, encouraging them to refuse to handle American planes. Stories appeared in the papers about how strikers and their families were suffering economically, yet were determined not to settle for less than their earlier demands. Controllers who crossed the picket lines to work told of harrassment and fearing for their safety. With both sides so firmly entrenched, it was difficult to find a resolution which "saved face" for both sides. This illustrates how the processes that escalate a conflict make it more difficult for either side to make concessions and reach a compromise agreement.

In time of war, hostility between in-groups and out-groups may be particularly bitter. When the United States entered World War I in 1917, for example, most Americans felt little hostility toward the German people. Attitudes quickly changed, however, partly as a result of government propaganda. All Germans were seen as cruel and beast-like "Huns" who regularly raped women and murdered children. Americans of German descent were harassed; pacifists who refused to support any war were denounced for disloyalty, and some were imprisoned. Many Americans decided that it was unpatriotic to play the music of Bach and Beethoven; sauerkraut was renamed "liberty cabbage." On the German side, much the same process took place: patriotism and propaganda produced bitter hatred toward the Americans, the British, and the French. The mutual attitudes of mistrust and bitterness engendered by the war made it more difficult to reconcile the combatants when it was over. German bitterness over the terms of the peace treaty ultimately helped bring about the rise of Nazism and World War II.

As these examples illustrate, conflicts between groups sometimes escalate beyond the

In time of war, propaganda is often used to generate patriotism. It focuses on the national good and emphasizes ways that people can and should act selflessly on behalf of the whole nation.

control of either group and inflict hideous damage on both sides. However, just as competition does not always turn into conflict, conflicts do not escalate automatically. Conflicts may be peacefully resolved, and even serious conflicts may have positive results. Precisely what are the effects of conflict?

The Divisive Aspects of Conflict

When conflict escalates into violent confrontations, it usually means that communication has broken down and irrational forces have taken over. For thousands of years, most thoughtful people have deplored the cruelties and destructiveness of wars. Twentieth-century weapons of mass destruction have made war even more terrible. Over 50 million lives were lost during World War II; the destruction of property and other accumulated social wealth was incalculable. Today the United States and the Soviet Union have stockpiled enough nuclear weapons to wipe out all life on earth many times over. Year in and year out, riots, revolutions, civil wars, and wars of aggression cause untold human suffering. Under these circumstances, it is difficult to see violent conflict as anything but senseless destruction.

Conflict within a group may interfere with the attainment of group goals and seriously injure the conflicting parties. Recent events in Iran provide a good example. After the Shah was deposed and went into exile, there was a resurgence of religious extremism under the leadership of the Ayatollah Khomeini (Kifner, 1981). Turning its back on many social and economic policies developed under the Shah, the Iranian economy deteriorated rapidly. Groups whose power and personal freedom were curtailed—such as women and moderates of every religious affiliation—became unhappy. Purges of perceived enemies by the Khomeini regime created an atmosphere of fear and rebellion. Gradually the society became divided into two major groups: the ruling

"Mainly I attribute my old age to getting out of Iran while the getting out was good."

Source: The *Wall Sreet Journal*.
By permission of Cartoon
Features Syndicate.

Islamic extremists and revolutionaries (although each was composed of a number of smaller, diverse groups). The ongoing economic decay and widespread purges were increasingly supplemented by attacks in which revolutionaries killed high officials, including the nation's premier and chief of police (*The New York Times,* 1981). With such widespread conflict and destruction, the nation was essentially paralyzed. Yet neither group would retreat from its professed goals, even though whichever was victorious would inherit a society in shambles.

The hostilities engendered by conflicts between groups can persist over generations and cause serious damage in terms of group cohesion. The American Civil War left social wounds that over a hundred years later are still not healed. The present-day conflict between Catholics and Protestants in Northern Ireland has its roots in the religious conflicts of the seventeenth century and in the centuries-old struggle between the British conquerors and the conquered Irish natives. Conflict can drain away resources and energies that might be used in more constructive ways. Because of the struggles between groups in Northern Ireland, the Middle East, and many parts of Asia and Africa, desperately needed economic development is neglected. In the United States and the Soviet Union each year billions of dollars are diverted from peaceful pursuits and budgeted for defense. Conflicts can be costly to individuals and groups.

The Integrative Aspects of Conflict

Common sense tells us that conflict, by its very nature, is divisive. Nevertheless, sociologists have shown that conflict can also serve an integrative function. Conflict with outsiders often promotes unity within a group. In meeting the external threat, members of a group tend to draw together and to offer one another mutual support. Internal antagonisms that previously threatened to disrupt the group may be overcome in the face of a serious external threat (Simmel, 1955). An example of this would be when members of a labor union forget their individual differences to present a united front against management.

Conflict can clarify issues and focus attention on serious social problems. A direct confrontation may be necessary before bonds of communication and understanding can be established. An example is the civil rights movement of the 1950s and 1960s. Although it created serious animosity between groups of Americans, it also focused public attention on the problems of racial prejudice and the injustices suffered by black Americans. The civil rights movement brought political and economic reforms that might never have been instituted without a direct assault on discriminatory practices. Conflict can also provide a powerful stimulus for social change as seen in the conflict between labor and management in the United States. This conflict has led to a completely altered life style for most workers: reasonable hours, paid vacations, retirement plans, and safe working conditions are now taken for granted. This was not an easy victory, but

involved much suffering and bloodshed in a long history of industrial conflict.

The same mechanisms that ensure peace by limiting competition and conflict may prevent creative confrontations between people with new ideas and different interests. In a small static community—whether it is in New Guinea, or medieval France, or a small town in the United States—there is often little overt conflict because group norms reinforce conformity. In cities, on the other hand, social control is usually looser, and conflict between individuals and groups is more common. Out of this instability, however, have come new forms of political, social, and economic life and new ideas in the arts and the sciences. As Lewis Coser (1956) wrote, "The clash of values and interests, the tension between what is, and what some groups feel ought to be . . . have been productive of vitality" (p. 153).

Conflict Resolution

Although conflict may be beneficial under certain circumstances, there is always the danger that it will get out of hand. Societies try to minimize the damaging consequences through ritualization, accommodation, assimiliation, and superordination.

Ritualization. Serious conflicts may be avoided through formal, stylized, or carefully contained hostile exchanges which social scientists call **ritualization.** Nations in conflict may feel that honor is satisfied by the exchange of strongly worded diplomatic messages; in that case, verbal hostilities take the place of physical hostilities. Certain tribes in Africa and Australia engage at regular intervals in ritual combats. Threatening gestures are made and insults exchanged, but no actual fighting takes place.

Accommodation. The permanent or temporary end of a conflict which allows opposing parties to function together without open hostility, but does not necessarily resolve or settle

The long-standing conflict between Israel and its Arab neighbors often generated open warfare that led to death and destruction. The Camp David Accords, negotiated while Jimmy Carter was president and involving Anwar Sadat and Menachem Begin, sought to resolve the conflict through formal, ritualized procedures.

the causes of the conflict is known as **accommodation.** By agreeing to accommodate one another, each side can retain its beliefs unchanged. However, since accommodation reduces conflict, it gives hostile parties a chance to reexamine the issues and paves the way for friendlier relations and, perhaps, a final settlement of differences.

Compromise is one form of accommodation in which each party makes certain concessions, but keeps the right and power to engage in conflict secretly. Labor unions and management generally compromise on a contract settlement: both sides may regard the settlement as temporary, and when the old contract runs out, conflict may be renewed, thus requiring the negotiation of a new contract. But, for a time, the two sides agree to coexist peacefully. Nations may agree to a compromise settlement when neither side is strong enough to defeat the other. One of the strengths of our political system has been the ability to prevent divisive conflict by finding compromises between opposing interests.

A second form of accommodation is *tolera-*

tion. With toleration, there is no formal agreement to end the conflict. Instead, parties informally agree to put up with each other rather than continue the conflict. Thus, a factory assembly line may include members of many different ethnic, religious, and political groups who might be in serious conflict with one another under other circumstances. Because they must work together, however, they tacitly agree to tolerate individual differences for the duration of the workday.

Assimilation. With accommodation, neither party gives up its goals, values, or sentiments. Instead, both agree to avoid conflict. **Assimilation,** on the other hand, refers to the gradual merging of differing groups so that the distinguishing features of the groups become less and less identifiable as common interests come to outweigh points of difference. For example, women favoring a woman's right to decide whether an abortion is appropriate for herself have not necessarily considered themselves feminists in the sense of wanting a complete reexamination of the role of women in society. However, the similarity of the opposition that feminists and proabortion women face has led the groups to merge in order for each to help the other achieve its goals. Because it focuses on the way sex roles limit women's choices and self-control, the right to an abortion comes to be seen as part of a larger issue.

Groups often merge in this way when they face an external threat, such as a natural disaster or an attack by a third group. However, assimilation is sometimes forced on one group by another, more powerful group. When this happens, the similarity of objectives may be irrelevant, and the assimilated group may not wish to be absorbed. This forced assimilation occurred in much of Eastern Europe following World War II, when Russia absorbed such groups as the Latvians and the Lithuanians.

Superordination. Sociologists have begun to study methods of conflict reduction in controlled laboratory experiments as well as in field observations. They have discovered that one of the most effective ways of reducing conflict is by providing overriding goals. This method of conflict resolution, called **superordination,** involves presenting conflicting groups with a situation in which they can gain certain rewards only by abandoning competitive or conflicting behavior and cooperating with one another.

In a laboratory situation, the emphasis is on structuring the situation so that the conflicting individuals or groups realize that conflict is unproductive and that both groups can "win" only by cooperating. In the "Acme-Bolt Bargaining Game," for example, two players compete as if they were rival trucking companies. The game is played on a board representing trucking routes, and one section of "road" must be used by both players in order to reach their goal. Each player may delay the opponent by blocking the road, or both players may decide to take turns using the road. Because points are scored on the time needed to complete the route, persistent road-blocking reduces the scores of both players. The players eventually realize that it is to their mutual advantage to take turns on the single road (Deutsch and Krauss, 1960).

One of the most interesting experiments in conflict reduction was performed by Sherif and Sherif (see Chapter 10). At a summer camp, groups of boys were organized into two teams; the situation was structured so that competition developed into serious, even violent intergroup conflicts. Then the social scientists who were monitoring the situation set out to test various methods of reducing conflict. Enforced social contacts had no effect on the conflicting groups, nor did verbal encouragements to be more cooperative. The Sherifs found that providing superordinate goals was the only effective method. The groups were presented with a situation in which they could reach mutually desirable goals only be cooperating. After an all-day hike, for example, the boys discovered that the supply truck was stuck in a ditch. Unless the groups cooperated to get the truck out of the ditch, there would be no food and water that night. As the groups learned to cooperate to attain these mutual goals, conflict was virtually eliminated (Sherif and Sherif, 1956).

This method of conflict reduction has implications for conflicts at all levels of human life. If conflicting groups can be brought to realize that cooperation is in their own self-interest, serious human conflicts may be brought under control. Many political commentators believe that the great powers of the world—the Soviet Union, the United States, and China—have at last realized that peace and prosperity are possible only if the three countries cooperate with one another in reducing world tensions. In any case, now that humankind has developed nuclear weapons capable of destroying the world several times over, the problem of finding effective means to resolve international conflicts becomes of greater concern to social scientists, politicians, and ordinary citizens alike.

SUMMARY

1. The main purpose of this chapter is to define and explain, using cultural examples, the functions and consequences of social processes (exchange, cooperation, competition, conflict, and conflict resolution).

2. Social processes are recurring patterns of social behavior that characterize interactions between individuals and groups. All human interaction may be defined in terms of the social process exchange (formal or informal) in which individuals or groups supply each other with desired goods or services. A society's primary type of exchange is related to the size and complexity of that society, and is important because it strengthens social bonds and governs the economic and social life of the society.

3. The importance of cooperation and competition varies from culture to culture, and each has advantages and disadvantages for individuals and society. Among the many advantages of cooperation are that a group can accomplish more than an individual and it is a better way to attack certain problems. One drawback of cooperation is that when creativity and special skills are not rewarded, the society may become static and uncreative. Competition can benefit society by encouraging and rewarding initiative and creativity. However, it can be less efficient than cooperation and it may lead to the destruction of group cohesiveness or erupt into a conflict.

4. When studying conflict, sociologists are mainly concerned with intergroup conflict which occurs when groups compete with increasing hostility and emotion. Conflict can be divisive or integrative. For example, conflict is divisive when it occurs within a group and interferes with the attainment of group goals, or when it drains resources and energies away from more productive projects. Conflict can be integrative if it focuses attention on social problems or provides a stimulus for social change.

5. Societies try to minimize the damage of conflict through four types of conflict resolution: ritualization, accommodation, assimilation, and superordination.

REVIEW

Key Terms

Social processes	Cooperation	Accommodation
Exchange	Competition	Assimilation
Reciprocity	Conflict	Superordination
Prenuptial agreements	Ritualization	

Review and Discussion

1. How many different exchanges were you involved in yesterday (classroom, romantic, political, economic)? Explain whether they were informal or formal exchanges.

2. In what way has the fact that the United States is a highly competitive society affected your life?

Would you prefer to live in a less competitive society? Why or why not?

3. In what daily situations is it advantageous for you to cooperate? Compete? Explain why you feel it best to cooperate or compete in each situation.

4. Can you think of any personal or international situations where cooperation would have been

more efficient and productive, but where the people did not cooperate? How might the result have been different than it was?

5. Explain the difference between an athletic contest and a street fight using the terminology learned in this chapter.

6. Have you ever been in a conflict with anyone as an individual or as part of a group? What circumstances led to the conflict? What forms of resolution finally emerged: ritualization, accommodation, assimilation, or superordination?

References

Blau, Peter (1964). *Exchange and Power in Social Life.* New York: John Wiley.

Coser, Lewis (1956). *The Functions of Social Conflict.* New York: Free Press.

Darnton, John (1981). Poland, one year later, is a society transformed. *The New York Times,* August 31, 1981, p. A4.

Department of Health, Education, and Welfare (1972). *Welfare Myths vs. Facts.* Washington, D.C.: U.S. Government Printing Office.

Deutsch, Morton (1949). The experimental study of the effects of cooperation and competition upon group process. *Human Relations* 2: 199–391.

Deutsch, Morton, and **Robert M. Krauss** (1960). The effect of threat upon interpersonal bargaining. *Journal of Abnormal and Social Psychology* 61: 181–89.

Freuchen, Peter (1975). *Book of Eskimos.* New York: Fawcett World Library.

Goldman, I. (1937). The Zuni of New Mexico. In *Cooperation and Competition among Primitive People,* ed. Margaret Mead. New York: McGraw-Hill.

Heath, A. (1976). *Rational Choice and Social Exchange.* New York: Cambridge University Press.

Hoebel, E. Adamson (1972). *Anthropology: The Study of Man,* 4th ed. New York: McGraw-Hill.

Johnson, Doyle Paul (1981). *Sociological Theory.* New York: John Wiley.

Kifner, John (1981). Khomeini seems to be force that is holding the regime together. *The New York Times,* September 6, 1981, pp. 1ff.

Lee, Richard (1969). Kung bushmen subsistence: An input-output analysis. In *Environment and Cultural Behavior: Ecological Studies in Cultural Anthropology,* ed. A. J. Vayda. New York: Natural History Press.

The New York Times (1981). Two more of Teheran's leaders die as challenge to revolution grows. September 6, 1981, pp. 1ff.

Norman, Elaine, and **Arlene Mancuso, eds.** (1980). *Women's Issues in Social Work.* Itasca, Il.: F. E. Peacock.

Ogbu, John (1978). *Minority Education and Caste.* New York: Academic Press.

Ryan, William (1976). *Blaming the Victim.* New York: Vintage.

Sherif, Muzafer, and **Carolyn W. Sherif** (1956). *Outline of Social Psychology,* rev. ed. New York: Harper & Row.

Sidel, Ruth (1972). Social services in China. *Social Work* 17 (November): 65–72.

Simmel, Georg (1955). *Conflict and the Web of Group Affiliations.* New York: Free Press.

Titmuss, Richard (1971). *The Gift Relationship.* London: Allen and Unwin.

Williams, Robin, Jr. (1970). *American Society,* 3rd ed. New York: Alfred A. Knopf.

7

DEVIANCE AND SOCIAL CONTROL

181

Deviants are the people whose behaviors are noticeably different from those of the majority of people in a society. They may be the criminals or the farsighted innovators. How does a society decide what is normal, and how are the deviants treated?

Some years ago, a young man who had inherited a small fortune announced to the press that he intended to give his money away—and proceeded to toss bills out of his hotel window in midtown New York. With only a moment's hesitation, the public pronounced him mad. "Nobody in his right mind would throw money away." On the surface, this young man's eccentricity seemed harmless, but on a deeper level, it was a distinct threat. Societies, and the individuals who compose them, have a definite stake in people behaving predictably. We base our lives on certain ideas about how things are supposed to happen, how people are supposed to act. The work ethic—the idea that people must contribute to society by working, and that only then are they entitled to its rewards—is one of our basic values. Day after day people go to work in the firm belief that they are doing the right thing and that, in any case, there is no alternative. When money falls from the sky, when someone treats more money than most people earn in a year with abandon and disrespect, they are understandably upset. Deviations from the work ethic make the tiresome commute to work and the long hours spent earning money for a modest savings account seem meaningless.

Social order depends on people behaving in the way we expect them to behave and conforming to social rules. In one sense, social order is an ideal. All people do not follow all the rules all the time in any society. In America, drivers speed, millions smoke pot, successful madams write best sellers about prostitution, the numbers racket flourishes, politicians accept bribes, and students cheat on exams—to choose some of the more obvious examples of breaking the rules. But, amazingly enough, most people *do* follow most of the rules most of the time. In this sense,

social order is very real. If people did not behave predictably for the most part, life would be chaotic, and getting through a single day would be a monumental task (as we suggested in Chapter 1).

DEVIANCE AS A CONCEPT

In everyday conversation we use the word "deviance" to describe behavior that seems strange or unacceptable. For some of us, a college student who spends hours in the library rather than playing baseball will be valued as a scholar; to others, he or she is an "oddball." Business people who become wealthy by selling people products that are poorly made or harm their health are esteemed by some for their wealth and their success; to others, they are crooks who should be put out of business. People who patronize prostitutes value their help in meeting the need for physical closeness; to others, their work is immoral and "dirty." Deviance, then, is always relative: a single act may be considered deviant or acceptable depending on who is evaluating it and under what circumstances. In entails a *stigmatizing process* whereby one group defines another as deviant. Since deviance is a negative label, it is often used to disadvantage groups stigmatized as deviant (Cuzzort and King, 1976:230–34). For example, "bag ladies" are ignored by most people who encounter them on the street since they are routinely labeled as "crazy" and hence unable to be helped. Similarly, ex-convicts find it difficult to get jobs because the criminal label which they carry is used to justify feelings which people have that they are dangerous and untrustworthy.

How can sociology help us to understand better a process that seems so personal and relative? There are a number of ways, including relating deviance to normative behavior, applying the concept of subculture to the phenomenon of deviance, and analyzing situational factors which affect whether behavior is considered a social problem. We will look at each approach in turn.

Sociologists define **deviance** as any behavior that violates social expectations. Durkheim made the important point that deviance can only be understood with reference to the concept of norms (Cuzzort and King, 1976:31–36). It is only because societies define certain behaviors as desirable and important that it is possible for others to be seen as undesirable or threats to social stability. The sociological theoretical perspectives discussed in Chapter 1 further illuminate this view of deviance. Structural-functional theories see deviance as a manifest threat to the social order, although it may serve latent functions (as when prostitutes help people meet sexual needs which might otherwise be disruptive to stable family relationships). Conflict theories view deviance as a significant part of the efforts of dominant groups to control others seeking power. By labeling some people as deviant, power groups justify their own actions to control and even destroy them.

Exchange theories emphasize reciprocal relationships that enable members of groups defined as deviant to organize and to relate to other groups. For example, groups of unwed parents have organized to share resources and to help members live satisfying lives. At the same time, relationships between unwed parents and other groups in society—such as in the workplace— can be better understood by looking at the exchanges which occur and the power differentials which result. Unwed mothers who work often have special needs for time off and variable hours in order to carry out their parenting responsibilities. They frequently have to accept lower wages and less job security in return for flexible work time. The firms for which they work have more power in the exchange relationship and can impose their own conditions for allowing flexible hours.

Finally, the symbolic interactionist perspective is helpful in showing the way labeling and definitions of deviance emerge through interac-

tion. In now-classic research, Becker (1963) showed how marijuana users and jazz musicians established their own definitions of normative and deviant behavior with respect to smoking marijuana and playing jazz. More recently, Plummer (1975) and Fitzgerald (1981) have shown how homosexuals have developed their own definitions of normative behavior as well as strategies to influence the sex-related norms of the larger society.

Subcultures

The sociological concept of deviance focuses on ways in which social expectations get defined. We have seen that different groups affect general societal definitions, and that power is often an important element in the part various groups play in this process. However, the symbolic interactionist theoretical perspective highlights the importance of the internal organization of groups defined as deviant. When people who engage in certain behaviors organize on their own behalf, new normative standards and definitions may result. The group may also seek to have the larger society accept its own definitions, thereby affecting the way the group gets labeled. Let us look at this process.

As we saw in Chapter 3, a subculture is a group which, while accepting most aspects of the larger culture, modifies others. To be a subculture rather than simply a group, the modified cultural elements have to be passed on from generation to generation among members of the group. This happens among members of an ethnic group, for instance, but not among people who work together and form a friendship group. However, Fine (1979) notes that groups also have their own knowledge, beliefs, behaviors, and customs which are shared by members and which give the group its distinctive character. He calls this an **idioculture.** These groups may be parts of subcultures as, for example, when a national organization like the Gray Panthers has chapters across the country. Each is unique, yet each

Although the norms of subcultures like this motorcycle gang may be regarded as deviant by the larger society, they may also lead to changes in societal norms. For example, the current popularity of leather clothing with the middle and upper classes indicates that earlier perceptions of such apparel have changed from "deviant" to "fashionable" over time.

subscribes to knowledge, beliefs, values, and behaviors which the national organization preserves and enforces. In this way a subculture of the elderly is created, with characteristics that are passed on between generations of older people (who belong to the Gray Panthers). Each group's idioculture allows for adaptation to local conditions as well as providing a change mechanism; individual groups can create new knowledge or push for changes in existing values.

As subcultures are formed and become an important part of their members' identity, they form part of the interaction between individ-

uals and society (Fine and Kleinman, 1979). Someone who is strongly identified with and commited to a subculture will generally act according to its knowledge, beliefs, values, and behaviors. Puerto Ricans will preserve their language, and orthodox Jews will continue to eat only Kosher food. To the degree that society responds negatively to these subcultural behaviors, the label of deviant will be borne by individual subcultural members—it may be ridicule for speaking Spanish or difficulty finding Kosher food when traveling. Society may also respond to the subculture itself as being deviant. In such cases, action is likely against the group as a whole, not just its individual members. What happened to the Jews in Nazi Germany is an extreme example, but present day efforts to outlaw homosexuality or to cut off public funding for bilingual education also exemplify societal efforts to define whole groups as wholly or partially deviant. A number of sociological variables influence how and when the larger society will define behavior as deviant. Let us look at some of them.

Deviance and Social Problems

Society tolerates young men "sowing wild oats," young women becoming hysterical over rock stars, and joggers appearing scantily clothed on the street. Other forms of deviance are more than tolerated: they are ignored. Walking through a downtown area, most people will simply walk around a derelict who is sleeping on the sidewalk. Yet others are closely watched and punished for deviant behavior, such as a child who skips school or an exconvict who violates a condition of his or her parole. Why is society so erratic in its response to behaviors considered deviant?

All societies tolerate eccentricity and innovation within certain limits. Remember in our discussion of social norms how we noted the frequent discrepancy between real and ideal norms, and the flexibility in role performance which results. This looseness helps members of society, and society itself, to adapt to changing conditions as well as to find new ways of meeting ongoing needs. Yet when a behavior or condition becomes defined as a social problem, society takes action. Social problems have the following characteristics:

1. The activity occurs frequently. Marijuana was not a cause for widespread public concern when its use was confined to migrant labor camps, minority neighborhoods in big cities, and out-of-the-way places frequented by jazz musicians and other artists. Attitudes changed dramatically when large numbers of middle-class people began smoking pot and thereby breaking the law. Even with the subsequent increased tolerance for marijuana smoking, its use remains deviant in most places and in the opinion of most people.

2. The activity has a widespread impact on society. Alcoholism would not be such a serious issue if heavy drinkers never got behind the wheel of a car, never lost their jobs, and didn't fail to meet their responsibilities toward their families. Because they do, society has developed a range of programs to solve the problem of alcoholism and its effects.

3. The activity violates widely held norms and values. Child abuse has been recognized as a social problem because of its dramatic violation of commonly held beliefs about children. In a society which believes children are valuable and vulnerable, adult roles focus on protecting and nurturing the young. Child abuse directly violates these social expectations and is therefore considered seriously deviant behavior as well as a major social problem.

As these examples suggest, a **social problem** is a condition that a significant number of people believe is undesirable and should be changed, either because it violates accepted values or because it interferes with their ability to achieve individual and group goals. The important point is that for a situation to be defined as a social problem, a number of people must believe that a problem exists and agree that "something should be done." As with other sociological concepts, the subjective element—the belief that a situation is a problem and should be changed—is as important as the objective existence of the condition itself.

Source: The Washington Post Writers Group, 1150 15th Street N.W., Washington, D.C. 20071. Reprinted with permission.

The Relativity of Deviance

Deviance, then, is always relative, A single act may be deviant or acceptable depending on the social context in which it occurs. Particularly in complex heterogeneous societies such as ours, groups have different ideas about what is right and what is not. Deviance is also relative because norms are constantly changing: behavior that is deviant today may be conforming tomorrow. Spouse abuse was until fairly recently something about which women could do little. Today they have a number of legal protections and alternative living options available to them. Finally, deviance is relative because our judgment of what is deviant varies with the circumstances: conduct that is considered deviant in one situation is acceptable, even mandatory, in another. Wearing a bathing suit to the beach is expected, but it is deviant at a symphony concert. During wars, the pacifist—not the killer—is considered "out of step."

The relativity of deviance is what makes it such a complex sociological phenomenon. While some commonly shared set of expectations clearly facilitates social life, it becomes difficult to draw limits beyond which behaviors disrupt the fabric of society. Will particular behavior be disruptive

In the classic comedy Some Like It Hot, *Tony Curtis and Jack Lemmon masqueraded as members of an all-female band to escape a gang of mobsters. Although our society generally disapproves of men dressing as women, the conditions under which such a deviation occurs affect its acceptability—as in a survival situation or in a Broadway performance requiring cross-dressing.*

or creative, and thus productive? And who is to judge? In fact, dominant groups in a society usually make these decisions and impose their judgments through the use of deviance as a label to stigmatize and control the behavior of others. Because there are many areas of dispute in this process, social control is an important part of maintaining prevailing definitions of deviance. We will look at social control in more detail later in this chapter. For now, we want to reinforce the point that definitions of deviance are con-stantly changing in response to other changes in a social structure. Thus, there is nothing inherently wrong or evil with an act labeled as deviant—it simply violates an existing societal norm. But, just as women now wear pants, so men may in the future wear dresses and be quite in style. Behavior itself isn't deviant. It only becomes deviant—or normative—when it is defined as such by society. And societies are noted for changing their minds! Table 7.1 illustrates an area of behavior in which there is considerable am-

TABLE 7.1 / WHAT IS DEVIANCE?

The assessment of what is deviant varies with the social context. The vertical columns of this table group people with like opinions about gays having equal job rights. The horizontal rows show how those same people felt about specific occupations. For example, of the people who said gays should have equal job rights, 50 percent did not want them to be elementary school teachers. Such gross inconsistencies demonstrate the difficulties in defining deviance.

		Should Gays Have Equal Job Rights?		
		Yes	*No*	*No opinion*
Should gays be hired as:				
Doctors:	Yes	65%	16%	22%
	No	25	78	37
	No opinion	10	6	41
		100%	100%	100%
Clergy:	Yes	56%	10%	13%
	No	36	86	47
	No opinion	8	4	40
		100%	100%	100%
Elementary school teachers:	Yes	44%	3%	10%
	No	50	95	57
	No opinion	6	2	33
		100%	100%	100%
Sales persons:	Yes	88%	42%	43%
	No	7	51	17
	No opinion	5	7	40
		100%	100%	100%
Armed forces:	Yes	71%	26%	26%
	No	23	66	34
	No opinion	6	8	40
		100%	100%	100%

Source: The Gallup Poll, Princeton, N.J. 08540. Used by permission.

TABLE 7.2 / AMERICAN CRIME RATES (PER 100,000 INHABITANTS)

America has been experiencing increased crime, as this table shows.

Year	Murder	Rape	Robbery	Aggra-vated Assault	Burglary	Motor Vehicle Theft
1967	6.2	14.0	103	130	827	334
1970	7.9	18.7	172	165	1,085	457
1975	9.6	26.3	218	227	1,526	469
1979	9.7	34.5	212	279	1,499	498

Source: Adapted from U.S. Bureau of the Census, *Statistical Abstract of the United States 1980:* Washington, D.C., p. 182.

biguity about the judgment of deviance. Table 7.2 and Fig. 7.1 provide data about behaviors virtually everyone would agree are deviant.

THE CAUSES OF DEVIANT BEHAVIOR

Most of us tend to believe that a genius is born, not made. We assume that Mozart, who began composing symphonies at age four, had far more innate talent and intelligence than normal children. But what about criminals: Are they born or made? What compels an otherwise upstanding citizen to rob a store? What made Mrs. Rosa Parks of Montgomery, Alabama, refuse to take a back seat in the bus, as was expected of blacks in those days? How does one explain Jane Fonda's risk of a profitable career as a movie star to take controversial positions in behalf of women's liberation and equality? In short, why—for better or for worse—do some people ignore the pressures that make the majority of us conform to social expectations?

Biological Causes

In looking for the sources of deviant behavior, it is important to distinguish between people who choose to violate norms and those who are biologically incapable of living up to social expectations. Inherited genetic defects, brain damage from disease or injury, and extreme malnutrition in infancy can limit a person's ability to learn social norms and carry out usual adult roles in society. In most cases, mental retardation is incurable. Some retarded people are able to work and to care for themselves; others spend their lives in institutions.

Attempts to locate physiological causes of emotional disorders are as old as psychiatry. Symptoms of infant autism, a childhood disorder, often appear when the baby is only three to four months old, suggesting inherited or biological problems. Statistics on schizophrenia indicate that this psychological disorder tends to run in families. Children of schizophrenic parents are more likely to become schizophrenic than are other children, and there is one chance in four that if one identical twin becomes schizophrenic the other will as well (Heston, 1970). In recent years, several researchers have discovered biochemical differences between well and mentally ill patients. When R. G. Heath (1960) injected a protein from schizophrenics (taraxein) into monkeys, he found that the animals' behavior changed dramatically. But to date, no one has been able to determine whether these differences are the cause or the result of emotional disorders. In general, psychologists suspect that some people inherit a biological predisposition to mental illness, which may or may not be activated by their environment (Golden, 1981).

The possibility of a link between biology and criminal deviance has also received a good deal of attention. At the turn of the century, Cesare Lombroso (1911) suggested that criminals

Fig. 7.1 / Violent Death in International Perspective

The chart compares homicide rates of major Western industrial societies. The strikingly higher rates in this society support media assertions that ours is a relatively violent social system.

Source: World Health Organization, *World Health Statistics Annual,* 1970–1978, vol. 1, "Vital Statistics and Cause of Death." Reproduced by permission of WHO, from *Social Indicators III,* U.S. Government Printing Office, 1980, p. 235.

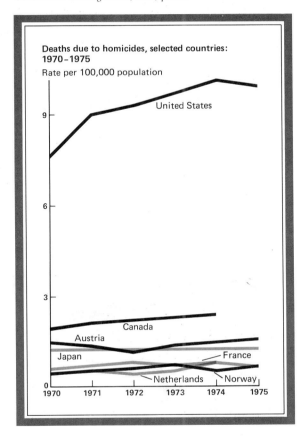

were physiological degenerates, throwbacks to an earlier stage of evolution. In the late 1940s, William Sheldon updated this theory by suggesting that temperament is inherited, like body type, and that criminal tendencies are linked to a stocky build (Sheldon, 1949). By modern standards, neither of these theorists was very rigorous in collecting evidence and their theories have now been completely discredited. However, Amir and Berman (1970) caused quite a stir when they published the results of a study of individuals convicted of violent crimes. A large percentage of these men had a rare *XYY* chromosome pattern. (Most males have an *XY* pattern.) Soon the extra *Y* chromosome was called the "criminal chromosome." Since then, however, much of the early research in this problem has been sharply criticized for its methodology, and biologists generally do not accept that there is any major difference between these two groups of males. In fact, most return the problem of criminality to the areas of environment and socialization.

Psychological Causes

Psychological explanations of deviant behavior focus on the individual and his or her ability to cope with external and internal pressures. A summary of relevant theories is beyond the scope of this chapter (the literature on this topic is vast). For this reason, we will examine only two: the Freudian theory and the frustration-aggression theory.

The Freudian theory. The Freudian interpretations of deviant behavior are somewhat complex. As discussed in Chapter 4, Freudians see life as a struggle between infantile, antisocial impulses, which are largely unconscious, and society's demands, which are internalized in the form of a conscience or superego. Deviance occurs when the individual has failed to resolve conflicts between the two. Take, for example, violence. All societies limit the expression of aggression. Most individuals are able to cope

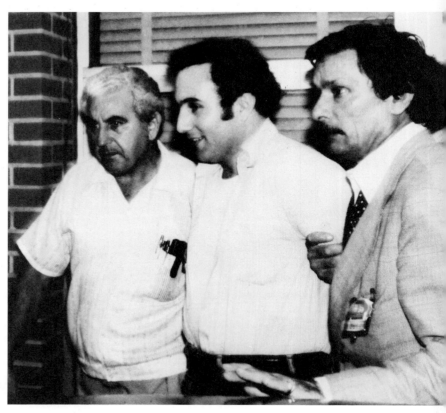

David Berkowitz, alias Son of Sam, was convicted as the murderer of several young women. Drawings and notes found in his apartment indicate that he was a lonely person suffering from paranoia and that serious psychological problems led to his extreme deviant behavior.

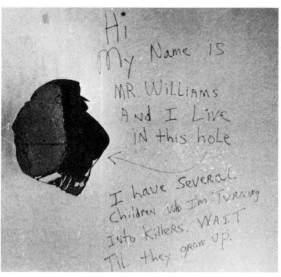

with aggressive impulses, either by directing their feelings into acceptable channels (for example, into sports) or by carrying out terrible vengeance in fantasy. However, those who fear that they are unable to control their impulses will try (unconsciously) to deny that they exist. They may, for example, project their feelings onto those around them, imagining that everyone is out to destroy them. Eventually they lash out in response to a totally innocent remark. This is what psychologists call "acting out": the individuals are acting from unconscious motives; their behavior is compulsive, uncontrollable.

The frustration-aggression theory. The frustration-aggression theory, put forward by the social psychologist John Dollard and colleagues, is quite simple. Dollard was primarily interested in violent behavior. He argued that aggression is a direct response to frustration. When individuals are unable to fulfill their needs or to gratify their desires, they sometimes strike out at whomever or whatever stands in their way. The intensity of their reactions depends on the intensity of their desires and the amounts of frustration. For example, a man who has been fired from a job that he needs badly is more likely to wait in the dark for the foreman who fired him than is a man who has a sizable savings account and numerous contacts who can help him to get a new job.

When people cannot identify the obstacles that stand between them and their goals, or when they realize that their frustraters are far more powerful than they, they may direct their anger at substitute victims. The student who realizes that it is too late to catch up in her reading for an exam picks a fight with her roommate. This is what psychologists call "displacement": in reality, the student is angry at herself. Dollard's point is that when a person is frustrated, he or she will strike out in one way or another. The furstration-aggression theory makes good sense. But it does not explain why some people are able to control aggressive impulses and others are not.

However intriguing, psychological theories of deviance do not explain completely why large numbers of people drift into deviance. In fact, the criminologists Schuessler and Cressey (1959) found very little difference between law-abiding people and convicted criminals in psychological tests for emotional stability, maturity, temperament, and character. In addition, there is little evidence that most criminals are mentally ill. Most mentally ill people do not commit crimes—retardates, for example, are usually insecure when they are taken out of their safe, predictable routines and thus are too *ritualistic* to commit crimes.

Social Causes

Rarely, if ever, are sociologists satisfied with individualistic explanations of social phenomena. Psychologists approach deviance with the question "How and why has this person failed to adapt?" but sociologists ask "When and why does society make adaptation difficult or impossible?" Over the years, a number of sociological theories of deviance have been suggested. These theories are based on analysis of the data available on deviance and on observations about the way people interact in different settings, as well as on interviews with individuals who are pursuing ways of life labeled as deviant.

Social disorganization. When a club or a business or a society is working well, people have a clear sense of where they stand in relation to other people, a clear sense of how to behave and what to expect. Members feel they have a stake in following the rules. They are committed to the group and its goals. The term **social disorganization** describes a breakdown in norms, communication, and commitment in parts of the institutional structure of society. For example, in a well-organized meeting, individuals focus on the person who holds the floor, wait for their turn to speak, obey the chairperson or the group's decisions, and genuinely try to achieve the group's goals. When the group breaks down into small cliques talking among themselves, when individuals ignore the rules, or when several attempt to turn the meeting into a party, the meeting, as such, is over. Disorganization has set in. Breakdowns in social institutions have much the same effect on society.

Robert Merton (1938) attributed widespread deviance to social disorganization. In his view, nonconforming behavior is an attempt to adapt to conflicts in the social structure. Specifically, he attributed deliberate violations of norms and the development of deviant subcultures to a gap between the goals which culture prescribes and

TABLE 7.3 / MERTON'S MODEL OF DEVIANCE

Methods of Adaptation	Culture Goals	Institutionalized Means
Conformity	Accept	Accept
Innovation	Accept	Reject
Ritualism	Reject	Accept
Retreatism	Reject	Reject
Rebellion*	Accept/Reject	Accept/Reject

* Rebellion reflects an attempt to change the social system, that is, an attempt to institutionalize new cultural goals and new means.

Source: Reprinted with permission of Macmillan Publishing Co., Inc., from *Social Theory and Social Structure,* revised and enlarged edition. Copyright © 1957 by The Free Press, a Corporation.

the socially approved means for attaining those goals. For example, American culture instills in most young women a strong desire to get married and raise a family. Wifehood and motherhood are primary goals. But suppose young women outnumbered men by two to one. Merton suggested four ways in which individuals could adapt to situations of this kind. (They are listed in Table 7.3.)

The first is **innovation,** or the development of new means to attain conventional, socially approved goals. The innovative young woman might decide to have a child without getting married (thus fulfilling one goal), commit bigamy (achieving perhaps both goals but irregularly), or murder as much of the competition as she can. Theft is another example of innovation. Our culture advocates the pursuit of wealth, but not by taking other people's property.

The second form of adaptation in Merton's scheme is **ritualism,** or strict adherence to socially approved means without regard to goals. The ritualistic young woman would, for example, spend most of her time sewing a trousseau and discussing wedding plans with her mother, ignoring the scarcity of men. The bureaucrat who clings to procedures at the expense of results is the classic example of ritualism.

Merton used the term **retreatism** to describe rejection of both the means and goals society

prescribes—for example, the young woman who decides to remain single and never date. Drug addicts, alcoholics, streetcorner men, and a large proportion of the emotionally disturbed are retreatists.

The fourth possible solution to social conflicts is **rebellion,** or the development of new means and new goals. Women's liberation, in attempting to redefine the woman's role in our society, is one example of rebellion. Of course, political rebellions provide numerous historical examples of this social response.

Merton argued that the gap between culturally induced ambitions and socially approved routes to success is greatest for the urban poor in our society, but he noted that poverty alone does not promote deviance. Rather, it is the contradiction between the myth of opportunity and the reality of social inequality. (In other societies, large numbers of people accept poverty as their fate.) This contradiction is most obvious in major cities where the populations include the very rich and the very poor and where stores display the rewards of wealth in great variety.

Although Merton talks about individual responses, it is important to remember that social disorganization is a social phenomenon. When normative structures break down, individuals become caught in socially created uncertainties and strains. Take the woman executive, for example. Data indicate that she typically faces job discrimination, sexual harrassment on the job, and criticism from neighbors if traveling is part of her work (Gates, 1981). These individually experienced strains result from the social disorganization created by changing norms about women's roles, especially in the economic sphere. Women are caught in socially created ambiguity which makes it almost impossible to be other than deviant in one way or another. No matter which of Merton's individual solutions is selected, the woman is still deviant. This includes conformity where, should the woman decide to stay home and forego her business career, she is then subject to criticism by proponents of equality for women as well as gnawing doubts within herself as to the wisdom of her "choice." Indeed, when a female executive chooses conformity it is often seen as an indication of a woman's lack of choice: she is simply giving in to intolerable

conflicts and pressures. Social disorganization, then, is a socially created source of deviant behavior that generates individual adaptive efforts.

Anomie. Testifying at a Senate subcommittee on juvenile delinquency, Henry McKay (1954) emphasized the importance of social change and *anomie* to the presence of deviance in society. A term coined by Emile Durkheim (Chapter 1), **anomie** refers to a state of confusion that occurs when members of a group do not feel bound to or supported by any set of norms and values. Durkheim observed that in complex, modern societies, individuals are faced with a bewildering array of different, conflicting norms. Different groups have different ideas about what is right and wrong, valuable and worthless. The individual is not bound to any one group or any one set of norms. The result, as Talcott Parsons (1954) saw it, is a high degree of personal

In complex industrial societies, norms are often in conflict. The two groups shown here have very different attitudes and norms regarding relationships between racial groups.

insecurity. McKay linked anomie to deviance. He suggested that in rapidly changing societies such as our own, social institutions tend to lag behind technological innovations. New problems arise for which there are no cultural solutions. (For example, society is still poorly prepared for breakdowns and accidents in nuclear power plants.) Adults, whose lives reflect the social conditions of the past, and children, who identify less with the past, live in somewhat different worlds. The generation gap is most severe when parents have recently emigrated to the city from rural areas or from foreign countries. Often their old-world values conflict with those of their Americanized, citified children, creating problems within the family (see Shaw and McKay, 1931). In addition, children growing up in urban ghettos encounter two distinct moral worlds: the conventional, respectable world of parents, school, and church, and the underworld of hustlers, pushers, and pimps. Different groups compete for the children's allegiance: they behave one way at home, another at school, another on the street with peers. Norms are blurred; they lack the clear sense of right and wrong that exists in small homogeneous communities. McKay suggested that anomie is most severe among teen-age males, who are pressured to demonstrate their masculinity, but prevented—by law—from becoming autonomous adults until late adolescence.

Several researchers have linked emotional disorders to anomie and social disorganization. Some years ago, Robert Faris and H. Warren Dunham (1938) found that a large proportion of the patients in Chicago's mental hospitals came from poor heterogeneous neighborhoods—the skid rows, the rooming-house districts populated by unattached transients, the communities inhabited by recent immigrants to the city. The midtown Manhattan study (Srole et al., 1962), a random survey of 1160 adults living in a relatively unstable section of New York City, revealed that more than 20 percent were suffering an extreme personal disorganization that prevented them from functioning adequately, while 60 percent showed signs of less severe psychological problems.

We will see in more detail in Chapter 12 that recent research suggests that urban life is not necessarily as anomic as earlier sociologists thought. Nevertheless, many people do experience anomie, which increases the probability that they will engage in behavior labeled as deviant. The recent further development of the concept of subcultures has helped sociology better understand the way anomie relates to deviant behavior. Subcultures, as noted earlier, help establish norms and a sense of personal identity for their members. When the larger society is successful in challenging and weakening subcultural bonds, or when the formation of subcultures is prevented, the result may be an increase in anomie (Fine and Kleinman, 1979). The history of immigration in this country is a good example. Traditionally, the "melting pot" idea was interpreted to mean that immigrant groups should relinquish their ethnic subculture and become "American." However, being American means many different things and takes time. The result was that people got lost in the transition; they gave up what they had and did not yet have an identity in their new cultural and subcultural roles. This process continues with current immigrant groups (Hornblower, 1980).

The elderly have also experienced increasing degrees of anomie and deviant behavior. As family patterns have changed, and a new emphasis on youth has developed, the elderly have been forced into isolation and confusion. Old people who live in poverty, stop eating due to psychological depression, and barely survive with practically no human contact are not uncommon in our society. These are deviant behaviors, but they have resulted from anomie, a sense of being outside the mainstream of society. People like Maggie Kuhn are trying to clarify roles in society for the elderly (Klemesrud, 1981), but in the meanwhile many will experience confusion and pain. Anomie, then, is also a social process with individual costs. When societal changes create ambiguity in a particular area of social norms, people will lack social anchors. Their efforts to survive in such situations will often result in behavior which is considered deviant.

Socialization to Deviance

Although anomie and social disorganization influence deviant behavior, these factors alone cannot explain why some people habitually break social rules. Other sociologists have suggested alternative causes of deviance. Sociologists Richard Cloward and Lloyd Ohlin hypothesized that individuals begin to consider conventional norms illegitimate only when they attribute their personal difficulties and failures to society, not to themselves, and when they have an opportunity to communicate regularly with other alienated individuals. According to this view, antisocial behavior results from socialization to a deviant subculture. People do not become deviant on their own. A woman has to learn the tricks of prostitution (handling customers, the police, and her own emotions) before she turns professional; a boy has to learn how to pick locks, hot wire engines, and dispose of a car before he becomes an auto thief.

In his autobiography (1966), Malcolm X described his initiation into the underworld of Harlem after losing a job with the railroad:

Every day in Small's Paradise Bar was fascinating to me. And from a Harlem point of view, I couldn't have been in a more educational situation. Some of the ablest of New York's black hustlers took a liking to me, and knowing that I was still green by their terms, soon began in a paternal way to "straighten Red out."

Plainclothes detectives soon were quietly identified to me, by a nod, a wink. Knowing the law people in the area was elementary for hustlers, and like them, in time I would learn to sense the presence of police types. . . .

What I was learning was the hustling society's first rule: that you never trusted anyone outside of your own close-mouthed circle, and that you selected with time and care before you made any intimates even among these.

The bartenders would let me know which among the regular customers were mostly "fronts," and which really had something going; which were really in the underworld, with downtown police or political connections; which really handled some money, and which were making it from day to day; which were the real gamblers, and which had just hit a little luck; and which ones never to run afoul of in any way. (pp. 85–87)

For many, the street corner, or the local pimp or bookie, provides instruction in deviant roles. (Like all businesses, the numbers racket, dope rings, and other arms of organized crime have to recruit new members to remain competitive.) For others, jail is a training ground. In prison, first-time offenders find that social approval depends on their exaggerating their crimes and minimizing their respectable side. Old-timers teach them the tricks of burglary or con games, and they emerge learned criminals with connections (Badillo and Haynes, 1972; Sheehan, 1978).

But why do some individuals who live in areas where organized crime and street gangs are prominent adopt a deviant life style, while others do not? In *Principles of Criminology* (1966, chap. 7), the criminologists Sutherland and Cressey point out that all people are exposed to a number of groups with different values. Most of us have the tendency to internalize the norms of the group in which we spend most of our time, or the group that is most significant to us—what Sutherland called **differential association.** The prisoner may have conventional family and friends on the outside, but if he or she is in jail long enough, these people may fade in importance. The adolescent cares more about status in the peer group than for his or her reputation with teachers, social workers, and other adults. It is the norms of the groups to which individuals relate most closely that determine whether their behavior is deviant or not.

Lack of Deterrence

Some sociologists have theorized that deviant behavior results when people have learned that it will not be punished. Eleanor Maccoby and colleagues (1958) argued that young people become delinquent, in part, because adults in their communities fail to apply social rules, not because they are confused about what the rules are (anomie). Others have supported Maccoby's basic point that deviant behavior will tend to increase unless it is actively discouraged (see Greenberg et al., 1979, for a review of such findings). However, recent research is questioning and modifying beliefs about the importance of deterrence. In studying homicide rates, for example, Parker and Smith (1979) found that the certainty and severity of punishment were effective deterrents in only some circumstances. They were better predictors of nonprimary homicide (homicide which occurs during the commission of another crime) than they were in predicting primary homicide (an act of passion involving family members or friends).

The complexity of the relationship between deterrence and deviant behavior is further supported by Greenberg et al. (1979). They note many intervening variables, among them whether people know and/or believe that their deviant behavior will be punished. This can be very uncertain because, as Hagen et al. (1980), found, different types of deviant behavior are responded to in different ways. For example, common crime (acts such as theft, assault, and so on) tends to be responded to more directly and more harshly than **white-collar crime** (crime within business organizations, such as embezzlement). Finally, Beck, Lenihan, and Rossi (1980) have done research to show that deterrence should be coupled with opportunity. Earlier we noted Merton's thesis that blocked opportunity will tend to generate deviant behavior. Beck et al. looked at the other end of this relationship, showing that giving people opportunities to achieve their goals will tend to reduce deviant behavior. So, deterrence can be a factor in the incidence of deviant behavior, generally serving to reduce it. However, the relationship is a far more complex one

Large industrial societies rely on formal agents of social control because their populace lacks the close personal relationships that support informal controls. A police officer enforces the law whether or not he or she knows the person suspected of breaking it.

than the simple belief that increasing deterrence will decrease deviant acts.

Labeling Theory

The driver who slips through a stop sign because she is late to work does not think of herself as a criminal, even though she knows that she is breaking the law. The student who is lying when he tells a professor his term paper is late because he had the flu does not place himself in the same category as students who copy answers during an exam. Nor do the many people who take drugs to help them through the day think of themselves as addicts. Although all of these individuals are breaking social rules, neither they nor their friends consider them "deviant." Similarly, many individuals who enjoy sexual activity with members of the same sex do not think of themselves as homosexuals, and many women who accept money for sex do not see themselves as prostitutes.

In recent years, a number of sociologists have become interested in the identity changes that accompany the transformation of respectable people, who occasionally deviate (what Lemert [1967] called *primary deviance*), into confirmed deviants, who think of themselves as outsiders (*secondary deviance*). At what point does an individual first see himself or herself as a criminal or addict or hooker? What leads such a person to accept deviant behavior and reject conventional norms?

Sociologists Howard Becker, Erving Goffman, and others felt that the key is **labeling**—the assignment of an inflexible social identity to an individual. (Such labels as bum, freak, hooker, and even bad boy are examples.) In *The Outsiders* (1963), Becker wrote:

Deviance is not *a quality of the act the person commits but rather a consequence of the application by others of roles and sanctions to an "offender." The deviant is one to whom that label has been successfully applied. . . . (p. 9)*

People treat known addicts, ex-convicts, and ex-mental patients as if they were *different*. So long as they escape "detection," they can carry on their lives in a respectable, conforming way. However, once their past is learned, people begin to interpret their actions differently.

D. L. Rosenhan learned this firsthand when he and seven colleagues contrived to have themselves admitted to several mental hospitals (1973). None of the eight had any history of emotional disturbance or psychiatric treatment. By almost any standards, they were quite sane. To gain admittance, each reported hearing voices. Otherwise, they were completely honest about their histories and current emotional states. Once in the hospital, they stopped simulating emotional disorder and reported the voices had ceased. The length of time they spent in each hospital ranged from seven to 52 days. Daily visitors could not detect any difference between their behavior and that of other patients. Most spent their time taking notes and talking to patients. Although a number of patients realized that they were impostors, no staff member detected their sanity.

In a second study, Rosenhan told the staff of one hospital that one or more pseudopatients would seek admittance during the next three months. Members of the staff identified 41 impostors. Actually, no pseudopatient appeared for an interview during this period.

Rosenhan concluded that once a person has been labeled insane, people are inclined to view his or her behavior in terms of this diagnosis, unconsciously distorting the facts. For example, one doctor noted to students that "oral-acquisitive" behavior was a symptom of a particular mental illness, pointing to patients who arrived at the dining hall a half hour early. Rosenhan suggested that patients arrived early simply because there is little else to do in a hospital: meals are an event. He also found that when a patient became upset, the staff assumed he or she was having "an episode"—without bothering to see if something had happened to upset the patient. In addition, since patients were assumed to be irrational, staff members often did not bother to speak intelligibly to them. A typical reply to the question "When will I be eligible for ground privileges?" was "Good morning, Dave. How are you today?" Sometimes the doctor would move off without waiting for an answer. Rosenhan found that patients were occasionally regarded as nonpeople. For example, one researcher observed a nurse in the dayroom of a male ward adjusting her bra, as if no one was there.

In many cases, the application of a deviant label becomes a self-fulfilling prophecy. For example, ex-convicts often have trouble finding jobs. They return to the community fully expecting others to see that they have changed, that they are straight. Often, friends, family, and neighbors fail them. People talk behind their backs; they watch them and ask if they are really "trustworthy." Unable to become respectable in other people's eyes, they may gradually accept the popular stereotype "once a criminal, always a criminal," and drift back into the crime subculture. Here, at least, they are insiders. As a result, they may return to criminal means of supporting themselves and thus confirm society's diagnosis. Similarly, the family and friends of people who have been hospitalized for psychological problems see every sign of tension, every unclear remark as evidence of an imminent breakdown. Without support for a healthy self-image, such persons may well withdraw from reality—not because they are incurably "sick," but because society has labeled them so.

In essence, what Becker and Rosenhan suggest is that society *produces* the very behavior it seeks to prevent by defining homosexuality as perversity, drug addiction as depravity, a single crime as a sign of character defects, and "problems in living" as mental illness. For example, society defines heroin as a social menace and outlaws its use. Because heroin is outlawed, addicts must deal with the underworld to obtain drugs; because addiction is stigmatized, they stop associating with nonaddicts. The result? Heroin does indeed become a social menace. As W. I.

Thomas wrote years ago, "If men define situations as real they are real in their consequences" (Thomas, 1928:572).

In this section, we have described several possible answers to the question of why people violate social expectations. No single theory gives the one and only correct answer since the term *deviance* encompasses so many types of behavior. Each theory can only partially explain why people deviate. And throughout the several theories, we can detect the recurring theme that definitions of deviant behavior are relative and changeable. As we will see in the next section, socialization to basic societal values and norms is a powerful counterforce to pressures toward deviance, and, when all else fails, society has mechanisms specially intended to control deviant behavior.

SOCIAL CONTROL

Some degree of conformity is necessary in every society. People could not live together if they did not know more or less what to expect from themselves and others. This is why the first day at college, on a job, or in a foreign country is usually a bit frightening. We do not know what to expect. The term **social control** refers to the ways in which society encourages and enforces conformity to its norms and expectations. The methods of social control include socialization, group pressures, formal rules and laws, and authorities (such as the police) who ensure compliance.

A look at professional athletics provides an overview of social control mechanisms. In sports, as in all areas of life, the game cannot go on if players refuse to follow the rules or suggest that there is another way to play. One way to ensure conformity in sports is to appoint referees who prevent players from cheating or fighting during a game by dispensing penalties for infractions. But this is only part of the story. Suppose a quarterback whose receivers were covered meekly handed the ball to the opposing team to avoid

Reminder Box / PARTICIPANT OBSERVATION

Participant observation was defined in Chapter 2 as a research strategy in which the sociologist lives and interacts on a daily basis with the people being studied. By recording observations in a systematic way about the activities in the group which surrounds him or her, the sociologist can gain valuable insights into the behavior, attitudes, and social organization of the group.

Unlike surveys which obtain data from a large number of people, participant observation is limited to the number of people and interactions which the researcher encounters as a group member. On the other hand, there is minimal influence by the researcher on the group's behavior. He or she observes behavior more or less as it occurs naturally in the group.

Participant observation is especially useful in groups that feel they are devalued by others. Stigmatized groups like homosexuals, the handicapped, and persons engaged in illegal or quasi-legal activities like bookies and hustlers are cases in point. However, even members of some racial or ethnic groups or workers in certain occupations like sanitation or ballet dancing may feel that they are misunderstood and devalued. Groups with such a sense of isolation are often very reluctant to be studied by sociologists, fearing that the result will be further denigration or unwelcome exposure.

In such cases, participant observation may allow the group to feel less self-conscious about being studied because the process is less visible and intrusive. Another factor is the trust that often develops in a researcher who shares the life of the group. Such a person is more likely to understand better the nuances of behavior, the meanings of events, and the full scope of activities. As a result data are more complete and often sympathetic to the group. For example, data which show both the independent as well as the dependent actions of the handicapped lead to an understanding of what it means to be handicapped that goes well beyond the usual focus on disabilities alone. As a result, our knowledge is more complete and accurate and the group itself may be more willing to participate in sociological research.

being tackled. After all, his career and livelihood depend on remaining in good health. The crowd would surely boo this man off the field—if his teammates did not get to him first. This is one of the reasons quarterbacks do not capitulate in mid-game: social pressure. But there are other reasons. Football players resist the temptation to give up because they believe, *inside,* that it is wrong to let their teammates down and unmanly to show fear of injury. In fact, most professional athletes never even experience such temptations. By the time a quarterback reaches the NFL,. his attitudes toward himself and his profession are such that he would not think of giving the ball away. This is no longer an alternative: he has been socialized to win. Social order depends on this combination of internal and external controls. On and off the field, in public and in private, people police themselves as well as each other.

Socialization

As we discussed in Chapter 4, socialization is a process that begins in childhood and continues

Groups establish norms that are remarkably effective in controlling the behavior of their members. These men are probably unaware of how they are conforming to group norms regarding dress and behavior.

throughout life. Children learn many rules from their parents, who enforce the rules with rewards, punishments, and explanations. They acquire other rules of behavior by observing the way people around them behave and by testing the way others react to their own behavior. Gradually they develop an inner sense of right and wrong—a conscience. Whereas they once controlled the impulse to steal because they knew it would make their mothers hurt or angry, they now resist temptations because they would *feel guilty* if they took something that was not theirs. They refrain from stealing even when there is no chance that they will be caught and punished. Thus, children learn to *want* to do what they are *supposed* to do.

Later, as adults, people conform out of habit. Only rarely do we stop to think about why we are waiting obediently in line for a movie ticket, dressing up for a party, or being polite to someone we do not like. Conformity in these instances is more or less automatic. In large part we do things the way we have always done them, without thinking. Unless someone calls attention to our behavior, we are not aware that we are either following or breaking a rule. Social order depends on this kind of automatic conformity.

In the privacy of our homes and the anonymity of the streets, opportunities abound for violating social norms without being caught or punished. But most people would feel guilty if they continually took advantage of these opportunities. They police themselves. Social order also depends on the fact that most people value the rewards of feeling respectable more than they value a stolen record, the gratification of forbidden desires, or violent revenge.

The degree to which people internalize certain norms is easily demonstrated. A few years ago, the Office of Economic Opportunity (OEO) designed a study to test the effects of a guaranteed annual income on work incentive. Thirteen hundred families with incomes below $5000 a year were chosen. OEO raised their incomes to exactly $5000, providing the full amount if no family member was employed; $1000, if family members earned $4000 a year, and so on. The money was given without qualifications. Family heads were not required to look for work, as they must under many state welfare laws. In fact, since their income was guaranteed and they would lose payments if they worked, there was no economic advantage in getting a job. At the end of the year, however, OEO found that 53 percent of the families had increased their incomes (as opposed to 43 percent of similar families who had not received subsidies). Why did recipients work? As one put it, "It is an honor to work" (Cook, 1970). These families had been socialized to believe in the work ethic. Similar results have been obtained in more recent studies (Socolar, 1981).

Of course, the degree to which norms are internalized varies. The average person would never think of murdering someone, no matter how good his or her chances for getting away with the crime. In fact, the idea of killing another human being is so alien to most people that the military must virtually strip recruits of their civilian identity before it begins to train them to fight under conditions where killing is socially approved. But the man who would never think of killing his wife may respond to an attractive coworker's advances during a period when his marriage is less than blissful. Adultery may be against the law, and it may violate Judeo-Christian morals, but it is not beyond the imagination. Many married people do not have affairs, because they have internalized norms about fidelity. But many do, just as many people speed, smoke pot, or cheat a little in business or in school. Socialization is never complete.

Social Pressure

Often individuals conform, not because their conscience dictates a particular course of action, but because they fear their family and friends would disapprove, or because they fear being caught and jailed or fined.

In George Orwell's novel *1984,* cameras and hidden microphones enabled authorities to keep the entire population under constant surveillance. An individual never knew when the Ministry of Information might tune into his or her office or home. So most people obeyed all norms and laws. But Big Brother is a fantasy. In reality, most people do obey rules most of the time. The police could never maintain order on the streets by themselves. Social pressure fills the gap between individuals' consciences and the law. People want the respect and approval of their family and peers; they need to feel that they belong. Group pressure is a primary source of social control.

There is little doubt that groups exercise a strong influence over individuals. In a fascinating experiment, Solomon Asch (1955) demonstrated that group pressure even affects our senses. Asch invited groups of seven to nine students into his laboratory, giving prior instructions to all but one of the students in each group. Asch showed the group two cards: the first one had a single line and the second one had three lines of different lengths. The subjects were asked to select the line on the second card that matched the length of the single line on the first card. After several sets of cards, the students who had been coached began giving the same wrong answer. The student who had received no prior instruction then had to choose between answering correctly and going along with the majority. In most cases, this student gradually succumbed to group pressure. When Asch discussed the experiment with the students some days later, few realized how often they had conformed. After a certain point, they had begun to *see* the lines as the group saw them.

Sociologists distinguish between two kinds of group pressure: the informal controls exercised by small intimate (or primary) groups, and the formal controls used in large impersonal (or secondary) groups, such as a business or a university.

Informal (or primary) group controls. How do primary groups exercise control over members? Imagine a group of friends sitting in the cafeteria over coffee on a Friday morning. All of them want to go upstate the next day to demonstrate against the construction of a nuclear power plant. Susan is the only one who has a car, but she does not want to go. The group can pressure her to change her mind in several ways. They can offer her a reward for compliance—for example, they will go swimming on Sunday if she will drive 70 miles on Saturday. Or they can try to reason with her, pointing out the "error of her ways." After all, it is not very fair of her to prevent all of them from demonstrating just because she does not want to. Where is her social conscience? Shaming is a third alternative. One of the group who knows Susan well might expose her true motives: she wants to begin studying for exams. (Many students do not enjoy being caught taking their studies too seriously.) Another possibility is for other members of the group to swear never to speak to her again. The threat of ostracism is an extremely effective means of enforcing conformity. If all this fails, the group can make life very unpleasant for Susan by ridiculing her so loudly that everyone in the room can hear. She knows, of course, that they will stop if she gives in.

Small primary groups thus pressure individuals to conform by offering rewards, reasoning, shaming, threatening ostracism, and applying ridicule (or, in some cases, physical pain). The techniques are much the same as those used by parents with children. (In effect, groups socialize members to their norms.) But often it is not necessary for the group to act at all. After a person has been shamed or ostracized several times, he or she realizes the consequences of nonconformity. For example, many Americans feel that aiding the poor simply rewards what they consider to be laziness and fraud (see Table 7.4). This helps account for the social disapproval many poor people encounter in our society.

But suppose that Susan is only visiting the campus and never expects to see these people again. This lack of connection would insulate her from the threat of ostracism and from ridicule. Informal group pressure is only effective when the individual is involved in ongoing relationships with other members of the group and cares what they think. Or suppose that Susan is a forty-year-old housewife who has returned to college now that her children are in high school. She will probably laugh off the group's threats. Small groups are able to enforce conformity only when the individual is sensitive to the demands that they make.

Finally, suppose that Susan's favorite uncle is the chief of police in the town where the demonstration is to be held. If she joins her friends, her uncle will be furious: she will lose her status as a serious, respectable young lady in her family's eyes. On the other hand, if she refuses to go, she will lose status among her friends. By conforming to one group's norms, she automatically violates those of another group that is equally important to her.

As a method of enforcing social norms, informal group pressure is most effective in small homogeneous societies where everybody knows everybody else. For example, when children in the small villages of contemporary Greece misbehave, adults ask, "Don't you have a brain?" "Aren't you ashamed?"—emphasizing their ridicule with laughter. By age five or six, most children have learned not to make an "unseemly exhibition" of themselves (Friedl, 1965). The Navajo had no formal system of social control, no laws or police. But in order to survive in their barren desert homeland, the Navajo had to cooperate with one another economically. Individuals were dependent on the good will and respect of their neighbors. Under such conditions, the threat of ostracism alone is enough to keep most people in line (Kluckhohn and Leighton, 1962). This is not true in more complex societies.

TABLE 7.4 / PUBLIC VIEWS ON AID TO THE POOR

"Do you think that most of the poor people in the United States who have been getting help from the Government through food stamps and aid to dependent children could get along without this money if they tried, or do you think they really need this help?"

"Does providing Government benefits to poor people encourage them to remain poor, or does it help them until they begin to stand on their own?"

Get Along Without	Really Need		Remain Poor	Help Until On Own
33%	56%	**NATIONAL TOTAL**	47%	35%
		RACE		
36	51	White	50	31
10	85	Black	29	55
		INCOME		
40	48	**Over $40,000**	66	21
36	54	**$30–40,000**	59	30
34	55	**$20–30,000**	50	28
31	57	**$10–20,000**	42	39
29	59	**Under $10,000**	32	50
		SELF-DESCRIBED POVERTY		
35	54	Those who DO NOT consider selves poor	49	33
24	64	Those who consider themselves poor	38	43
		PARTY IDENTIFICATION		
43	47	**Republican**	56	29
35	54	**Independent**	48	31
24	63	**Democrat**	41	43
		THOSE SEEING POVERTY AS DUE TO:		
56	35	**"Lack of effort"**	73	18
16	75	**"Circumstances"**	26	56
		THOSE WITH VIEW ON CUTS IN PROGRAMS FOR POOR		
50	40	**Willing to cut**	67	23
25	65	**Not willing to cut**	38	42

This poll of 1545 adults was conducted March 11–15, 1982.
Source: The New York Times, March 19, 1982, p. A20. © 1982 by The New York Times Company. Reprinted by permission.

Formal (or secondary) group controls. Anonymity, mobility, and conflicting values make it relatively easy for individuals to escape informal social pressures. Anonymity is a fact of life in complex societies. As often as not, individuals are beyond the surveillance of family and friends. A woman who casually drops a candy wrapper on the street would never think of doing this in her own or her neighbor's backyard. But who notices or cares what she does on a crowded street? Our society has laws against littering and imposes fines for violators because the possibility of disapproval from *strangers* is not enough to make individuals conform.

Mobility also weakens social pressure as a means of control. If a Navajo stole a friend's wife, he could not conceal the fact. Everyone in their society knows them. In the United States if a man and a friend's wife become involved, they can move to another neighborhood or town and start a new life. In addition, young people are exposed to many pressures which may question or contradict what they learn at home. Schools may expose students to scientific research which questions parental beliefs; the mass media contradict parental teachings about the virtue of love versus sex. Bombarded on all sides by forces outside the family, the youngster sees the family as only one of several controlling forces. These

are a few of the reasons why the family has recently lost some of its effectiveness as an agent of social control.

In addition, complex societies include numerous subcultures whose norms and values sometimes conflict with those of society as a whole. Not all groups condemn littering, philandering, cheating, or even stealing. Adolescent peer groups sometimes discourage academic achievement (Coleman, 1961); street gangs condone theft and violence; work groups may cooperate to keep individual output low. And small groups usually close ranks to protect a deviant member. A student who would feel guilty about cheating on an exam might also feel guilty about reporting another student to authorities. Thus, from society's point of view, group pressure can be subversive. In conforming to peer or work groups, the individual may deviate from the norms of the larger society.

Whenever it is possible for people to violate social norms without risking significant personal relationships and group affiliations, formal social controls are necessary. This is true in complex societies, in large businesses, and in universities— all of which are secondary groups. Relationships in secondary groups are relatively formal and impersonal; disapproval is not as effective as it is in small groups. In our society, the police and

TABLE 7.5 / NUMBER OF PERSONS ARRESTED, 1970, 1975, 1979

As would be expected given rising crime rates, arrest rates are also increasing. Note that crime and arrests are far more common among men and among the young.

	1970	1975	1979
Total Number Arrested	6,257,000	7,671,000	9,468,000
% Men	85.6	84.3	84.3
% Women	14.4	15.7	15.7
% Under Age 18	25.3	25.9	22.5

Source: U.S. Bureau of the Census, *Statistical Abstract of the United States 1980:* Washington, D.C., p. 190.

the courts enforce conformity by threatening individuals with the loss of liberty and with fines (see Table 7.5). Businesses control workers by awarding raises and promotions to those who conform and by firing those who do not. Universities use grades and diplomas to encourage academic achievement and the threat of expulsion to prevent cheating. These formal, standardized methods of social control compensate for the lack of fixed standards and the anonymity of complex societies.

THE PROBLEMS OF SOCIAL CONTROL

What can society do when the usual social control mechanisms—socialization and social pressure—fail? There are essentially two approaches to social control. The first is to punish or to isolate deviants in order to protect society. The second is to seek ways to rehabilitate deviants and bring them back into society.

Punishment and Isolation

People are punished in many ways when society feels that formal social controls are necessary. Two examples are losing a job or being denied promotion due to the lack of proper behavior. But prisons are used to punish criminally deviant behavior, and they do so in a drastic manner. Prisons are multipurpose institutions. They are designed to isolate deviant individuals, thus protecting society; to serve as a deterrent to potential offenders; and, to some extent, to rehabilitate the convict. (Mental hospitals are designed to serve the first and last functions—isolation and rehabilitation.) But does prison work? There is considerable evidence that it does not. Approximately 65 percent of the people who have been arrested and jailed return to prison within five years (Federal Bureau of Investigation, 1971). "Repeaters" greatly outnumber new

criminals in all prisons, indicating that the threat of prison is not a terribly effective deterrent. Why?

The deterrent theory of social control has been attacked from several angles, as we noted earlier. For the threat of punishment to be effective, the punishment must be perceived as personally meaningful to the individual, and as likely to be imposed if the prohibited act is committed. In many places, economic cutbacks have reduced the number of police and judges. As a result, it is more likely that crimes will go unpunished, reducing the deterrent effect of formal social control mechanisms (Meislin, 1981). In addition, deterrents influence only premeditated crimes, when the person stops to weigh the risks of getting caught against the benefits of his or her actions. Murder and other violent crimes are usually unpremeditated. Most often people commit murders when they are carried away with rage, or when they panic. In neither case do they stop to think about the consequences (Parker and Smith, 1979). Studies of states that abolished the death sentence some years ago indicate that the electric chair had little or no effect on murder rates (Clark, 1970). Finally, if a person cannot find a job because he or she was once convicted of a crime, that person has little to lose by attempting another crime (Berk et al., 1980).

Other critics of the penal system focus on its effects on the convicted person. In prison, the individual associates exclusively with other convicted criminals. A subculture develops as prisoners attempt to justify their degraded position by assigning prestige to antisocial acts and downgrading the "straight" world. One-time offenders may emerge from prison with many more skills and underworld contacts than they had when they entered (Sheehan, 1978). In addition, prisons deprive people of responsibility for their lives. Every hour of every day is planned, a situation that does not encourage individuals to learn how to cope with personal and social problems. When they are released, exconvicts may find that the stigma of having been in prison

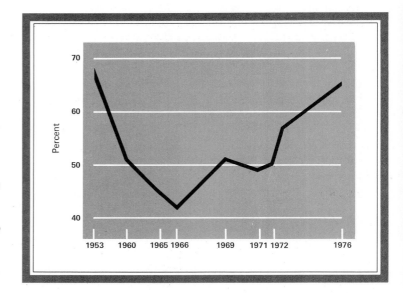

Fig. 7.2 / Death penalty for murder?
Percent saying yes.

Over the years, the average citizen has
varied greatly in his or her willingness to
see the death penalty applied as
punishment for murder.

Source: The Gallup Poll, Princeton, N.J. 08540.
Used by permission.

prevents them from finding legitimate jobs (Berk et al., 1980; Vorenberg, 1972).

Added to these problems is the fact that the police, in accordance with the laws, arrest thousands of people for **crimes without victims**** (for example, prostitution) and for activities many people do not consider deviant or criminal (for example, gambling). Such laws may foster disrespect for other laws. A young person arrested for possession of marijuana, when thousands of people smoke grass and go free, is more likely to vow revenge on the system than to "repent." As former New York Police Commissioner Patrick V. Murphy said, "By charging our police with the responsibility to enforce the unenforceable, we subject them to disrespect and corruptive influences, and we provide the organized crime syndicate with illicit industries upon which they thrive" (in Morris, 1973). When people who feel they have been arrested unjustly enter the prison system, they add substantially to the atmosphere of anger, frustration, and self-righteousness that pervades correctional institutions.

Patients in mental hospitals experience many of the pressures that arise in prisons, with one addition. The mental patient's "sentence" is indefinite. Once committed, the patients are at the mercy of professionals who decide whether or not they should be drugged and whether or not they are ready to return to society. Within the hospital, they associate exclusively with other disoriented people and with attendants and doctors who believe they are sick. They are deprived of their freedom, their privacy, and all responsibility. (If people are sick, they cannot be held responsible for their behavior.) In time patients learn to behave as others expect them to behave (Goffman, 1961). When they are released, they may find that they are stigmatized, much like criminals. Given the choice, most companies would rather hire people who have not been hospitalized. Family members may watch them for signs of recurrence. On the outside, ex-mental patients are more isolated than exconvicts: there is no society for the "previously insane."

---

* A crime without a victim is one which both parties engage in willingly and feel they have benefitted from. A prostitute gets income and her client gets sexual pleasure. Nevertheless in most places prostitution is still illegal.

Rehabilitation

Realizing that the practice of locking up "drunks," addicts, criminals, and emotionally disturbed people often backfires, a number of public and private agencies have begun to experiment with a variety of self-help, medical, and community programs. These programs are designed not to punish or deter deviance, but to bring individuals back into the mainstream of society.

Self-help programs. By far the best known of the self-help programs in this country is Alcoholics Anonymous (A.A.), a voluntary organization started by two men who realized that they themselves had a drinking problem. People who go to A.A. for help are encouraged to face themselves ("my name is ———, and I'm an alcoholic") and to admit their problems and failings in public meetings that closely resemble religious confessionals. At the same time, A.A. provides them the opportunity to meet other alcoholics who have been converted to sobriety. These people make themselves available in times of crisis for advice and moral support. A.A. is based on the belief that ex-alcoholics are better able to help problem drinkers than people who have never experienced alcoholism. Similar community-based programs also exist for drug addicts.

Medical programs. Seeking a different route to drug control, a number of cities have organized methadone clinics. Methadone is a synthetic

Prostitution is the classic example of a victimless crime and for this reason has long been the topic of legal debate.

INTERVIEW/ Jennie J. McIntyre

On family violence: *"The phenomenon of wives getting beaten also was a long time in coming to the public attention. I think earlier we had assumed that the only families in which this happened were very poor, very low-class families."*

Jennie J. McIntyre is Associate Professor of Sociology at the University of Maryland. Her research interests include marriage and the family, sex and gender roles, and majority–minority group relations.

■**Q.** What is your definition of family violence?

■**A.** Well, in a real sense, violence is a use of any force that hurts and that is intended to hurt, that can range from a very small kind of slap that's not supposed to hurt very much, up to and including physical force that results in death.

■**Q.** Which kinds of family members tend to be involved in this continuum of family violence?

■**A.** What generally happens is that the bigger and stronger uses some form of physical force against someone who is smaller or weaker. Parent-child violence is a frequent case. Now, most often this is the matter of spanking that is not intended to seriously hurt the child. It's intended to discipline the child, or to drive home a lesson to the child. But the dividing line between a spanking that doesn't really hurt very much and a beating that really does hurt is very thin. What starts with a spanking or a slap can end up to be much more serious, and the child is seriously hurt. Generally, that kind of violence on the part of a parent toward the child stops well before the child reaches adolescence. When he or she can fight back, there's not that great imbalance of physical strength anymore. So adolescents are less likely to get struck or slapped than smaller children are. However, sometimes there's violence then in both directions, where children who are now bigger and stronger use violence against their parents.

Another type of family violence is an adult child hitting an older person. Sometimes the violence is less direct, such as depriving the older per-

son of medication, or overmedicating them. There have also been cases of grown children abandoning their aging parents. Again, this is a matter of people who are bigger and stronger committing the violence against people who are unable to defend themselves. Sometimes this is related to simply being irritated with the older person who doesn't think or act as quickly as he or she should. And sometimes it's really wanting to have power over the older person, or control of the older person's pension or whatever assets the person has.

■**Q.** What about husband/wife violence?

■**A.** Well, both husbands and wives use violence against each other, and if you're just talking about the absolute numbers of occasions, it might be more or less the same. The big difference is that husbands are usually bigger and stronger and they can do much more damage. So that if you talk about battered spouses, it's usually battered wives. Wives may slap their husbands, but there usually isn't any damage done. However, if it becomes more serious, then the rate of homicides with wives killing husbands is almost the same as that of husbands killing wives. And that is because when wives simply want to hit or strike somebody it really doesn't have much effect. She doesn't have the physical strength. So, if things get to the point where she's really determined to do something, she's more likely to use a weapon . . . and then it's likely to be a real tragedy.

■**Q.** Is rape a part of family violence?

■**A.** Yes. It's a part of family life that people really don't even want to think about. We'd rather think of families as loving and caring and not think of family members as hurting one another, psychologically or physically. And rape tends to hurt both

psychologically and physically. Sometimes it's a very young girl assaulted by her father. Sometimes it's a matter of a wife being assaulted by her husband.

■ **Q.** Do you think there's been an increase in family rape?

■ **A.** It's not at all clear that there's an increase. I think it's very recently come to our attention, and it's very recently that we've been able or even willing to acknowledge that such things could happen. We knew about incest all along, and we always thought of that as a father or stepfather attacking a young girl. We tended not to think of sexual assault as assault. Until recently, wives were not raped in a legal sense because they had the obligation to pro-

vide sexual services to their husbands and so it was generally not considered rape. That legal definition is changing. We find things that are now happening, happened before and nobody thought of it as rape. But it's not only husbands and wives. There are any number of incidents where a family member assaults another.

■ **Q.** You mentioned that the family violence that we're experiencing in this society is a very common phenomenon.

■ **A.** Oh yes. There's no question about it. It was in England that people first started paying attention to wives being beaten. But I think it was in this country that we first started paying attention to children being abused by their parents. And the movement toward providing shelters for battered wives started in England. It has spread to this country and also on the continent of Europe. And feminists in Japan are just now getting interested in this subject. But what's going to happen there is just so very uncertain; of course, that's a very different culture. To some extent, violence is accepted in some cultures, more than it is in our own. Even when we've accepted it in the sense of not paying attention, it was not so much an explicit approval of violence, but not interfering with family privacy.

While we're seeing a great deal of attention being paid to family violence, I don't think that necessarily means that there is more violence in the family now. If you look at the history of childhood and families more generally, children used to be treated not very well. They worked very hard, they were harshly disciplined, and it was generally felt that the head of a family had the right to do whatever he felt he should do in order to handle things. He had the right to beat his wife as well. Under English Common Law the phrase "rule of thumb" comes from a rule that says that a man could beat his wife as long as he used a stick no bigger around than his thumb. And even that was some sort of progress, in that they were saying that there was some limitation on the extent to which he was allowed to use violence. We now have come much further and say that there shouldn't *be* such violence.

We're still very ambivalent about it, however. On one level we say that there should not be such violence. But we still look in the other direction and say, "Well, what goes on within a home is that family's business and we shouldn't interfere." For a long time even professionals took no steps when they saw children that we now would immediately recognize as being battered.

■ **Q.** What was the common professional reaction to being confronted with a battered child?

■ **A.** Well, a pediatrician or somebody in the emergency room would listen to a parent's explanation that the child had fallen or had been in an accident and would simply accept that explanation, rather than to pursue it. So, it was a long time before we even recognized that child abuse did exist. In the nineteenth century when child abuse first came to public attention, we were not interested in parents beating their children. We assumed that parents would only do what was good for their children and would beat them just to teach them right from wrong, and they wouldn't do any harm that way. Rather there was a concern with children who were informally adopted into families where they were expected to work. They were more or less apprenticed to somebody to learn how to do something. There was concern with the well-being of those children. But the assumption was that children in their own families didn't need the protection of outsiders. It's only recently that, as a society, we are willing to look at incidents of that sort and to say that we *should* intervene, even though it is the family. The phenomenon of wives getting beaten also was a long time in coming to the public attention. I think earlier, we had assumed that the only families in which this happened were very poor, very low-class families. It really wasn't something that happened in more respectable or middle-class families. A middle-class woman didn't want to tell somebody else that her husband had hit her, partly because of that feeling that it only happened in lower class families. Women were very careful to hide it when it happened. The first book on this subject was published in England and entitled, *Scream Quietly So the Neighbors Don't Hear*. The author was referring to that very phenomenon: The reluctance of women to let other people know.

■ **Q.** Why does family violence occur?

■ **A.** . . . Yes, I think we would wonder why things like this would happen in families. After all, parents are concerned with the well-being of their children, husbands and wives are supposed to be concerned with each other's well-being, and to a lesser extent, with the well-being of other relatives. Why would things like this happen in those circumstances? In part, it has to do with the nature of family living. Families live together under one roof and it's a relationship that entails all aspects of their lives, not just for a certain number of hours every day or every week, but for 24 hours a day and seven days a week. Even when people are away from each other, the family relationship is still very important. And so it's harder to ignore aspects of family members' behavior that are irritating or that we might consider wrong, because we can't just say, well, some people do that and some people don't. Everything a member of the family does, we think, affects us as well. That's the kind of family we're in, that's the kind of image other people will have of us as a family. So, the occasions for one person being irritated with another are just much greater in family living than in other aspects of our daily lives.

Also, another characteristic of living in the same household with other family members is that there are very few ritual or automatic means of getting away from each other. Perhaps early in the morning, when members might be leaving for work or school is the only time when leaving is easy.

■ **Q.** And this can help avoid a situation that could lead to violence?

■ **A.** Well, if there's an argument in the morning and the husband goes off to work, by the time he comes home, they both have had a chance to think about it and to cool down and to start over again. Or a child goes off to school, and by the time the child comes home from school, things have, again, cooled off and they start over. However, for the rest of the day, people are almost trapped in their own homes and it's not that easy to leave, and that's particularly true late in the evening, and especially after a couple has retired to the bedroom at night. There simply isn't any easy or automatic way of taking one's leave in that kind of situation. I'll contrast that with being irritated or unhappy or angry at what somebody else says. Imagine that two people are talking on the street, and one of them says something that makes the other one angry or at least irritated. They can have good reasons for going in opposite directions. They can say, Well, I'm sorry, I have to leave now. If I don't leave now I'll be late for work, or something of that sort. It's just so much easier for people to get away from each other when things are unpleasant. Within the family, these opportunities are more limited and, as a result, violence may occur.

■ **Q.** How has society responded to family violence?

■ **A.** To some extent, the way in which we responded to the knowledge that children are sometimes abused by their parents, and that some wives get hit by their husbands, was to see it as a medical issue. The first article in a medical journal on child abuse gave doctors a term to use in diagnosis. It talked about the "battered child syndrome," and once it was put in those terms, it was much easier for the doctors to start paying attention and to think about it. But we medicalized it further in that we say that the abuser is sick, and if the abuser is sick, then what we have to do as a society is to find a means of treating this sickness and protecting the child. We are doing much the same thing with husbands who hit their wives. We ask, what's wrong with the husband who does something like this? . . . He's sick. And if he's sick, we must look for ways for treating him so that he will be able to get along in his family life. Treating it in that fashion has many advantages. It's much easier to deal with it. Whereas a professional, such as a doctor, might be hesitant about reporting a patient or a patient's husband as having done something that was illegal, and

something for which he or she could be prosecuted, the doctor would have no hesitation at all about saying this is a man who is sick, who needs help. Professionals also are willing to take a stand. We must ensure that the people who have been abused, whether they be children or adults, receive protection.

■ **Q.** Can you give some examples of what wives, for example, can do to avoid being beaten repeatedly?

■ **A.** Some sociologists are collecting information on women who had gone to court and asked for a court order enjoining their husbands from beating them again. In other words, if a man beats his wife once, he can't be arrested for that. If, however, she gets a court order which says that he must not beat her and he does it again, then he could be arrested. Well, in this study a sociologist followed up on those who did and those who did not get a court order, and found that the women who were not given court orders were more likely to have been beaten again. This suggests that when society is willing to take some kind of action and intervene, we can protect children and other family members from family violence. ■

narcotic that allows addicts to stop taking heroin without experiencing withdrawal, enabling them to return to the community. While addictive, methadone blocks the effects of heroin without producing a high—or so doctors thought. The growing black market in methadone suggests this may not be true. Nevertheless, methadone does relieve addicts of the necessity for obtaining illegal drugs by illegal means. Drugs are also used to control emotional disorders, so that the individual who might otherwise be institutionalized is able to remain in the community.

Halfway houses. Still another approach to rehabilitation is to provide the exconvict or the ex-mental patient with a place to go when he or she leaves the institution. Halfway houses are designed to reintegrate people into society by gradually allowing them to participate in everyday life in a carefully supervised and limited way and with the support of others who share their problems. The individual has a chance to develop a new identity as a respectable and self-respecting person. In essence, halfway houses focus on resocialization.

Examples are California's work-furlough program, which enables prisoners to leave jail daily to go to work (Vorenberg), and the Highfields Project in New Jersey. Instead of sending juvenile delinquents to reform school, some are placed in small, homelike centers staffed by a director, a married couple (who function as surrogate parents), and a caretaker. Both of these programs have proved successful in lowering rearrest rates, but this may be because the participants were chosen very carefully.

The shelters for battered women that are springing up across the country are a different kind of halfway house. Unlike the halfway houses discussed above, these are for the victims of deviant behavior rather than for those performing it. The increasing recognition of the number of women who are battered by their husbands or boyfriends, tied to the realization that women are often financially dependent on the men who

abuse them (Bernard, 1981), has led to the creation of halfway houses for such women. They provide a refuge where a woman and her children who are without other resources can go until she can think through her situation and make plans for her future. For many women, it is a transition from dependence and helplessness to more autonomy over her own life and greater feelings of accomplishment and satisfaction. The halfway house at least provides the physical protection and emotional support basic to the survival of the woman and her children. Like other halfway houses, women's shelters help people move from a constrained environment toward one in which personal freedom and self-responsibility are possible.

The Costs of Social Control

Because it guides an individual toward rewards rather than punishments, socialization is the kindest and perhaps the easiest form of social control. Socialization, unlike imprisonment, has a generally positive and constructive effect on an individual's self-worth and dignity. When subjected to constant restrictive social controls, individuals often begin to feel that they lack control over their own lives. In extreme forms, social control can have extreme consequences.

In *Asylums,* Erving Goffman described how the inmates of prisons, juvenile institutions, mental hospitals, and the like are deliberately stripped of all signs and sense of personal identity, a process he called "mortification." The staff, usually responsible for maintaining order in a large group of people, begin immediately to break the individual's will. Obedience tests are part of the entrance ritual; compliance is rewarded. The individuals' clothes and personal belongings are taken away and replaced with standard drab uniforms and materials. In some cases, they must learn to respond to a number instead of their names. Privacy is denied them; contacts with the outside world are strictly limited. Beatings and

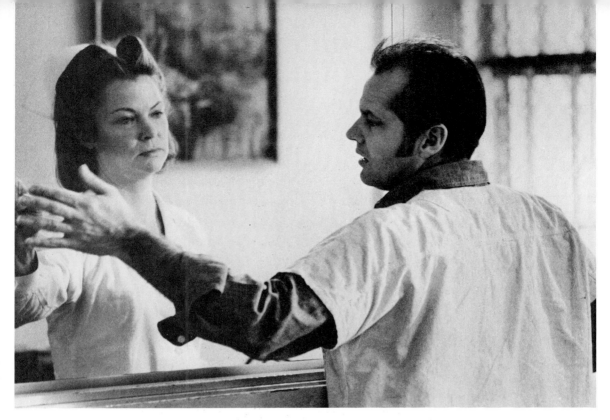

The film One Flew over the Cuckoo's Nest *dramatized the impersonal treatment of mental patients. Whether the main character is truly insane is not clear, but that the hospital routine is dehumanizing is unmistakable.*

isolation in prison and drugs and shock therapy in mental hospitals destroy their sense of physical integrity. Depersonalization is most acute in mental hospitals where, by definition, the inmates' behavior is seen as "involuntary, nonresponsible, and nonculpable" (Goffman, 1961). In sum, the individuals are deprived of their identity, of their roles as father or mother, brother or sister, neighbor, coworker, and normal person. Goffman suggested this is counterproductive:

Although some roles can be reestablished by the individual if and when he returns to the world, it is plain that other losses are irrevocable and may be painfully experienced as such. It may not be possible to make up, at a later phase of the life cycle, the time not now spent in educational or job advancement, in courting, or in rearing one's children. (Goffman, 1961:364).

Goffman also argued that when every aspect of a person's life is controlled, as is the case in total institutions, the person loses the will and sometimes the ability to be responsible for himself or herself. The overwhelming impression of wards in mental hospitals is one of extreme apathy.

Often overlooked is the psychological effect of such institutions on the controllers. In 1970, U.S. Attorney General Ramsey Clark wrote, "Many prison guards are slowly brought to brutality by the environment of the prison itself." He suggested that this is, in part, because most prisons are located in out-of-the-way places where trained personnel are scarce. (The same is true of mental hospitals.) But, Clark continued, "it could happen to anyone" (p. 216). Several years later, social psychologist Philip Zimbardo demonstrated this (1973).

Zimbardo divided a group of 21 college students, selected because tests showed them to be "emotionally stable, physically healthy, mature, and law-abiding," into two sections. Half would be prisoners; half, guards. A mock prison was set up in the basement of a university building, and the ten prisoners were "arrested" in a simulated raid. Both groups were given appropriate uniforms. Guards were told in strong language that they must maintain order. The first day went smoothly, but the second day the prisoners rebelled. The guards reacted with totally unexpected brutality—spraying the rebels with freezing carbon dioxide from fire extinguishers, forcing them to strip naked, and placing ringleaders in solitary confinement. From then on, brutality was the rule: guards made prisoners perform senseless and debasing tasks (such as cleaning toilets with their hands), forced them to vilify fellow prisoners, and so on. Not once did a guard speak up directly in a prisoner's behalf. The inmates became extremely apathetic; one broke down and was convinced to leave.

In their diaries, some of the guards reported enjoying their newfound sense of power. One, however, did not. He wrote the following about how he felt being a guard:

It's almost like a prison that you create yourself—you get into it, and it becomes almost the definition you make of yourself, it almost becomes like walls, and you want to break out and you want just to be able to tell everyone that "this isn't really me at all, . . . I'm not the sadistic kind of person that enjoys this kind of thing." (Zimbardo et al., 1973:49).*

But he stayed, as did the others—all of them regular, healthy college students. As Clark wrote, "It could happen to anybody." Thus, it seems the process of locking up some individuals is damaging to both the controlled and the controllers.

---

* © 1973 by The New York Times Company. Reprinted by permission.

Finally, social control is expensive in monetary costs (see Fig. 7.3). Even socialization is expensive; consider how much it costs to operate the public school system, for example. However, since socialization is a building process as well as a form of social control, it seems like a wise investment. People learn how to be happy, productive members of society as well as learning what behavior is acceptable. Methods of social control that involve force and placing people in places like prisons and mental hospitals have fewer benefits. Expenditures, for police forces, prison guards, psychiatric staffs, and others are very high. While society feels social control is necessary, it comes at a high cost in human as well as economic terms. To the degree that social control can occur through socialization, the payoff to society will be greatest. But society can also reduce the need for social control by defining as deviant only behaviors that are real threats to the social order. Eliminating from definitions of deviance behaviors that are desired by large numbers of people will reduce the need for the most expensive types of physical control.

THE FUNCTIONS OF DEVIANCE

In reckoning the costs of social control, it is important to keep in mind the fact that in some instances deviant behavior actually benefits society. Often deviance serves as an outlet for drives and desires that do not fit within society's norms. Prostitution and gambling are obvious examples. Gambling provides relief from the work ethic—from the drudgery of going to work every day, from the nagging sense of frustration that seems to accompany moderate incomes, from otherwise inescapable poverty. Between the time an individual places a bet and the time winners are announced, he or she can engage freely in extravagant fantasies. Similarly, the prostitute satisfies primarily the person who seeks variety without commitment. Prostitution and

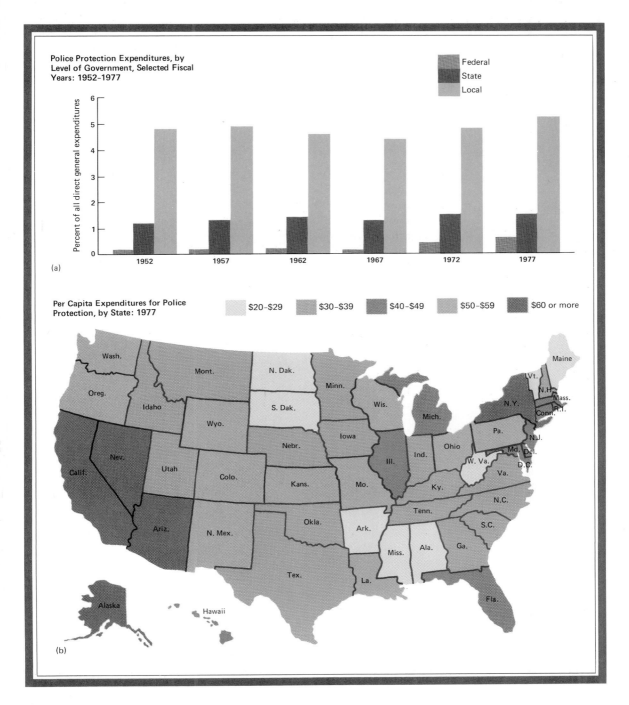

Fig. 7.3 / The Corrections Scene

Illustrations (a) and (b) document how expensive it is to provide formal social control services.

Source: U.S. Bureau of the Census, *Social Indicators III*, Washington, D.C.: U.S. Government Printing Office, 1980, p. 212.

SOCIAL ISSUE/Homosexuality:

Thomas K. Fitzgerald /*University of North Carolina at Greensboro*

LABELS AND REALITY

Homosexual men and women comprise approximately 10 percent of the population, yet they represent one of the most misunderstood minorities in American society. The label "homosexual" has been used to stereotype a group of people who are in reality as different as any other group. What they share is a sexual orientation, not the range of diverse characteristics supposedly attached to same-sex orientation. Homosexuals are no more uniform as a group than are heterosexuals. Some like to dance, and others don't; some are promiscuous, and others are not; some are doctors, and some are laborers; some are married, and others are not; some have Ph.D.s, and and others dropped out of high school. Two researchers at the Kinsey Institute, Bell and Weinberg (1978), entitle their book *Homosexualities* (in the plural), recognizing that homosexual adults are a remarkably diverse group. They warn us that we must consider factors such as race, age, sex, education, and occupation before we can draw conclusions about gay and lesbian people. Further, it is suggested that homosexuals are best understood when seen as whole human beings, not simply in terms of sexual orientation. Barbara Gittings calls this "putting love back in the scientific equations."

In the past, researchers most often studied homosexuals in prison or in therapy. This is, of course, a very biased sample, and it is hardly surprising that researchers concluded that all homosexuals are guilt-ridden, psychological misfits. Evelyn Hooker (1956) was the first to study a non-patient homosexual population. She recognized what she called the "iceberg phenomenon," in which most homosexuals were ignored by studies that looked only at gay and lesbian people who were experiencing problems. Modern research increasingly documents that most homosexuals are indistinguishable from the heterosexual majority with respect to nonsexual aspects of their lives (Marmor, 1980; Woodman and Lenna, 1980). Using a somewhat narrow psychobiological approach, Masters and Johnson even found little fundamental difference in sexual physiology and sexual responses between homosexuals and heterosexuals. The latest Kinsey Institute publication, *Sexual Preference: Its Development in Men and Women* (1981) tests the more common social science theories about origins of homosexuality and concludes: "No particular phenomenon of family life can be singled out . . . as especially consequential for either homosexual or heterosexual development." (Bell, Weinberg, and Hammersmith, 1981).

Modern opinion clearly does not see homosexuality per se as a type of pathology (Marmor, 1980; Masters and Johnson, 1979). Rather, particular social and psychological adaptations largely depend on the types of adjustments possible within socially prescribed contexts. What are the social contexts which confront homosexual persons? How do gay and lesbian people cope with negative labels? And why do the stereotypes about lesbians and gay males persist?

In the remainder of this essay we will examine these questions within the context of the United States society, as well as cross-culturally.

BEYOND THE LABELS

Much of what people associate with the term "homosexual" is, in fact, no more than stereotypes maintained in order to justify behavior that discriminates against gays and lesbians. These *extreme, often pathological reactions against homosexuality,* called **homophobia,** have taken dramatic forms throughout history. In Hitler's Germany, for example, between 50,000 and 200,000 homosexual men perished in Nazi concentration camps for no reason other

The Myth of the Composite Portrait

than having a sexual orientation that was defined as deviant (Heger, 1980: 14). In the United States, a number of gay people have been attacked and killed in the name of symbols like Anita Bryant, fundamentalist religions, and/or the Moral Majority.

Part of the discovery of self for persons in a sexual minority is the realization that one is considered a "devalued person." Barry Adam, in *The Survival of Domination,* suggests that acknowledging this fact is a significant psychological rite of passage for any stigmatized individual. Homosexuals, then, must deal not only with coming to understand their sexual orientation, but also with society's stigmatization of that orientation. Gays are not different because they are homosexual; they differ primarily because they are stigmatized and therefore treated differently.

Let me make clear, however, that not all societies have punished or even have feared homosexual behaviors. Anthropologists have documented that, in over 64 percent of a sample of world societies, homosexuality in one form or another has been considered normal and socially accepted for certain members or at certain periods of life (Ford and Beach, 1951). In some cultures, male homosexuality may be expected of all young men in connection with initiation ceremonies. Shamans (medicine men) frequently have been homosexual, and both male and female homosexuals have had their unions recognized as legal marriages in certain cultures (Fitzgerald, 1977). In the Trans-fly region of New Guinea, as recently as 1977 ethnographers discovered tribes where homosexuality, rather than heterosexuality, was the *cultural preference!* (Kelly, 1977; Van Baal, 1966). These authors relate this preference to the need of these societies to regulate the population.

To love someone of the same sex is, after all, hardly so extraordinary. Same-sex behaviors would be remarkably inconsequential if society did not make them so important. When defined in this way, however, the "inferior" group is disqualified from full participation in society. Its members are subjected to categorical treatment through an externally.

imposed identity. Names become insults in themselves: fag, fairy, queer. Opression against sexual minorities, sociologist Barry Adam suggests (1978: 43), is maintained by "the myth of the composite portrait," which embodies three related axioms: (1) presumably, gays and lesbians are always a "problem"; (2) they are all alike; and (3) they are supposedly recognizable. These axioms are played out in an all-too-familiar script: "They," it is assumed, are animal-like (but, oddly enough, not "natural"). Subhuman categorization is reinforced by pseudoscientific labels like "regressive," "fixated," or "immature." "They," of course, are all hypersexual. Over half the persons in a United States survey agreed with the statement, "homosexuals have unusually strong sex drives" (Levitt and Klassen, 1974: 32). Gays have become the modern-day witch doctors with mysterious sexual powers. "They" are all too visible, meaning that failure to be totally invisible provokes resentment from the larger society. Yet trying to make oneself invisible denies one's own sense of self and well-being, leading to personal fear and anxiety.

Internationally, it has been estimated that there may be upward of 300 million lesbians and gay men, making homosexuals the largest and most far-flung minority on earth. It is also one of the most oppressed (Gitech, 1980: 15). In a number of countries today, homosexual acts remain illegal. Gays have been executed (Iran, Uganda), sent to "rehabilitation" camps (Cuba, Mozambique), sentenced to long-term hard labor (Pakistan and the Soviet Union), and committed to mental institutions or prisons (China, United States). A large number of recent refugees from Cuba were gays fleeing the oppressive conditions on that island (Gitech, 1980: 15). Abhorrence of homosexuality is only too prevalent, and homosexuals are still subjected to blatant discrimination as well as mental and physical abuse.

There are a number of results of such oppression. One is insecurity and fragmentation of identity—what sociologists call *ambiguity of identity*. Having fewer psychological or social supports than majority group members, homosexuals sometimes cope with stigmatization through promiscuity. The important point is not that some gays are promiscuous, but that promiscuity is one among several strategies for coping with being treated as inferior. Another coping device is denial of self, or "flight from identity." There is often as much as a six-year gap between first homosexual experiences and self-identification as a gay or lesbian person (Dank, 1971: 182). Other ways of dealing with oppression include various forms of social or psychological withdrawal—often from potentially positive supports from the gay community itself. Hence, many gay people adopt the kind of low-profile conservatism that they believe is characteristic of the dominant group. This is an attempt to be—as it were—more respectable than the respectable, even if this means joining heterosexuals in punishing other gay people for being "different." Homophobia is not limited to straights.

Homosexuals have also developed more positive ways to survive and cope in repressive societies. Sexual minorities have always employed some *positive* challenges to subordination. Probably the first step toward self-liberation is a sort of internal rage reaction, a resentment about one's status (Adam, 1978: 116). Liberation implies a deep psychological need to assert "self." Unfortunately, the dominant group is apt to interpret such assertiveness as an affront to its authority. Gay humor, or "camp wit," becomes a symbolic means of using language and gesture to destroy some of the worst types of oppression imposed by society. Gay and lesbian people have also begun creating a sense of community which helps reaffirm their identities and protects them from some of the most hurtful oppression and restrictions imposed by a homophobic environment. Indicators of these communities are gay and lesbian residential areas (gay ghettos, as they are sometimes called), community centers, gay and lesbian business groups, religious groups for homosexuals, and so on. Many of these gains have been achieved through the self-help movement. We will look at the way the gay self-help movement develop in Sweden, tradi-

tionally thought to be a relatively liberal society with respect to sexual identity and behavior.

A CASE STUDY: GAY SELF-HELP GROUPS IN SWEDEN*

Self-help groups in general have been defined as "voluntary small-group structures for mutual aid and the accomplishment of a special purpose" (Katz

---

*Much of this summary is taken from a larger research project on "Suicide Prevention and Gay Self-Help Groups in Sweden and Finland" (Fitzgerald, 1981).

and Bender, 1976: 9). Major attributes include a relatively small size and formation by peers rather than from external influences. Hence, such associations minimize referrals to professionals or other agencies; instead, they stress the personal responsibility of members in face-to-face interactions. Assistance, however, is not perceived as being met by existing social institutions. Self-help groups provide a reference point for bringing about desired personal and social changes. Such groups, then, offer various emotional "supports." Frequently, they are "cause-oriented," enhancing a sense of personal identity for their members (Borman, 1976).

Gay self-help groups are only special examples within the widespread self-help movement. In the United States alone, there are more than one-half million self-help groups (e.g., sensitivity groups, consciousness-raising, consumer groups, and medically-oriented associations). Such groups tend to coincide with the breakdown of traditional care-giving structures which once met the needs of certain individuals in a society. Homosexuals, for example, are sometimes thrown out of their families. Lesbians and gay men have joined the ranks of those who have discovered strengths in working together in small personalized groups where they can be themselves. Self-help groups, in essence, are a specialized type of "support system."

The self-help movement is virtually unknown in Scandinavia. This is not accidental as the concept of social welfare is much more firmly established than in the United States (De Cocq, 1976: 203). Most people are already adequately cared for. As a result, the self-help idea in Sweden exists primarily for groups such as gays and lesbians toward whom society has remained somewhat indifferent.

The first gay group in Sweden officially started in 1950. It was a local chapter of a Danish gay organization, and it was begun in response to persistent scandals and persecutions of homosexuals in Sweden. Twelve individuals banded together to form a self-help group that, in this case, took the form of a protest movement. The initial aim of the

"Association for Sexual Liberation" (RFSL) was simply to provide a safe meeting place for lesbians and gay males. From the beginning these were separate associations for men and women, operating under the same umbrella structure. Today, total membership amounts to about 5000, with 13 chapters throughout Sweden. As the original group is now too large to act as a true self-help group, the working committees within RFSL have taken over the self-help function. The parent organization coordinates such mutual-aid groups as the gay Christians, a gay counseling group, the gay socialists, and—the latest—a gay Alcoholics Anonymous.

The gay Christians will serve as a brief example of how these-self-help groups work. Formed in 1977 by a gay man studying for the priesthood, the gay Christian group attracts individuals seeking to resolve conflicts between religion and sexuality. Many such people feel rejected by society. The self-help group offers them a sense of community, certain psychological supports, and more acceptable alternatives to the commercial gay outlets (bars, discos, gay saunas, etc.). This group, however, never intended to be a separate church. Individual members continue to worship in their own churches, joining together only for the purpose of exploring the relationships between homosexuality and the Church. In one sense, such mutual-aid associations act as "broker institutions," helping to interpret the gay situation to the larger society and vice versa. Such a function is the opposite of separatism based on sexual orientation.

Other services provided by these groups include social activities; RFSL operates its own gay club, run by and for its members. Consciousness-raising, or identity, functions are always paramount. Certainly "the befriending service," or the gay outreach, is another important feature of such associations, including a gay switchboard, peer counseling, a gay radio station in Stockholm, and several educational activities.

Some major advances achieved in Sweden since the 1950s include the following: (1) the removal of the laws against homosexual activity between consenting adults (the age of consent is 15 years in Sweden); (2) the placement of same-sex unions on the same footing as common-law heterosexual unions through a custom known as "sammanboende," a kind of quasi-legal marriage (this privilege of equality is extended even to gay immigrants "married" to Swedes); (3) the achievement of a completely modern program of sex education, wherein homosexuality is treated undramatically as simply another way of having potentially meaningful relationships; (4) finally, in November 1979, the removal of the "sickness" label—and, then, only after a large number of Stockholm men and women phoned their employers to say they were "too sick from homosexuality to come to work." This event is in keeping with the 1973 decision of the American Psychiatric Association to remove its sickness label from homosexuality in this country.

Through these local self-help groups, lesbians and gay men are allowed more social alternatives and more humane choices. They also serve as vehicles for social changes. Ultimately one can argue that such grass-roots activity is what participatory democracy is all about: "people in action on their own behalf" (Katz and Bender, 1976: 241). Such organizations can continue to contribute to the adoption of more enlightened and human attitudes toward sexual minorities.

THE PERSISTENCE OF STEREOTYPES

Despite real strides in overcoming oppression, gay and lesbian people worldwide have been relatively unsuccessful in educating the public about real gay issues. The "myth of the composite portrait" still exists in the minds of many people, and stereotypes about lesbians and gay men abound. Why?

Most researchers stress the role of minorities in syphoning away potentially threatening accumulations of unrest in the established orders. Adam calls this function "the lightning rod" theory: stigmatized people serve as "lightning rods" for the discontent and aggression that ebb and flow with historical ups and downs (pp. 28–29). Hence, the economic insecurities of the 1980s parallel the revival of racism, the Ku Klux Klan, anti-Semitism, the neo-Nazis and an anti-gay backlash. There is competition over political and economic control of goods and resources, but political access usually remains the monopoly of nonstigmatized people. The politics of homosexuals as victims, or scapegoats, is translated into discrimination and restricted life opportunities. The ideal goal would be to educate the dominant society to accept a degree of diversity in life styles, while avoiding more ego-destructive myths and stereotypes. The result would be removing from minorities the scapegoat functions that they traditionally have performed. This goal remains for the future, but progress through such techniques as self-help groups is already being made.

References

Adam, B. D. (1978). *The Survival of Domination*. New York: Elsevier.

Bell, A. P., and **M. S. Weinberg** (1978). *Homosexualities: A Study of Diversity Among Men and Women*. New York: Simon and Schuster.

Bell, A. P., M. Weinberg, and **S. Hammersmith** (1981). *Sexual Preference: Its Development in Men and Women*. Bloomington: Indiana University Press.

Borman, L. (1976). Self-help and the professions. *Social Policy (Sept./Oct.): 46–47.*

Dank, B. (1971). Coming out in the gay world. *Psychiatry* 34 (May): 182.

De Cocq., G. A. (1976). European and North American self-help movements. In eds. A. H. Katz and E. I. Bender, *The Strength in Us*. New York: New Viewpoints.

Fitzgerald, T. K. (1977). A critique of anthropological research on homosexuality. *Journal of Homosexuality* 2, no. 4 (Summer): 385–97.

——— (1981). Suicide prevention and gay self-help groups in Sweden and Finland. *Crisis: International Journal of Suicide and Crisis Studies* 2, no. 1 (April): 58–68.

Ford, C. S., and F. A. Beach (1951). *Patterns of Sexual Behavior*. New York: Harper & Row.

Gitech, L. (1980). Gays around the globe: The issue is everywhere. *The Advocate* 296 (July): 15.

Heger, H. (1980). *The Men with the Pink Triangle*. Boston: Alyson Publications, Inc.

Hooker, E. (1956). A preliminary analysis of group behavior of homosexuals. *The Journal of Psychology* 42: 217–25.

Humphreys, L. (1970). *Tearoom Trade: Impersonal Sex in Public Places*. Chicago: Aldine-Atherton.

Internation Gay Association (1981). Press release: Council of Europe to fight discrimination against homosexuals. Dublin: I.G.A.

Katz, A., and E. I. Bender, eds. (1976). *The Strength in Us: Self-help Groups in the Modern World*. New York: New Viewpoint.

Kelly, R. C. (1977). *Etoro Social Structure*. Ann Arbor: University of Michigan Press.

Levitt, E. E., and A. D. Klassen, Jr. (1974). Public attitudes toward homosexuality: Part of the 1970 National Survey by the Institute for Sex Research. *Journal of Homosexuality* 1, no. 1 (Fall): 29–43.

Manderson, L. (1980). Self, couple, and community: A review article of recent writings on lesbian women. *Hecate: Lesbian Studies* 6, no. 1: 67–79.

Marmor, J., ed. (1980). *Homosexual Behavior: A Modern Reappraisal*. New York: Basic Books.

Masters, W. H., and V. E. Johnson (1979). *Homosexuality in Perspective*. Boston: Little, Brown and Co.

Van Baal, J. (1966). *Dema: Description and Analysis of Marind-anim Culture*. The Hague: M. Nijhoff.

Woodman, N. J., and H. R. Lenna (1980). *Counseling with Gay Men and Women*. San Francisco: Jossey-Bass.

gambling, outlets for some people's needs, are functional in a positive way.

Deviant behavior becomes accepted conforming behavior when it brings about needed social change (as with the civil rights movement); when it proves more functional than traditional behavior (for example, women wearing pants); and when it wins the support of a large number of people (as smoking marijuana has).

In a subtle analysis of the balance of deviance and social control, Emile Durkheim suggested that deviance indirectly contributes to social stability by encouraging group unity. An unusual example of this point occurred in Skidmore, Missouri. The town bully, Kenneth McElroy, was notorious for his abuse of townspeople. He seemed to be able to flaunt his violation of community norms, and no one in the small town was able to do anything about it. One day, however, the town confronted Mr. McElroy during one of his attacks against a townsperson. Someone shot and killed him. Yet no one among the 60 or so townspeople watching would admit to having seen who fired the shot (*The New York Times*, August 22, 1981, p. 14). This is an extreme case of shared feelings of anger and frustration uniting a group in defense of the norms of social behavior, even though the group resorted to a deviant act itself to accomplish its goal.

Perhaps more significant, deviance is an important source of social change. In holding her seat on a Montgomery bus, Mrs. Rosa Parks was violating social expectations and was therefore deviant. But she was also demonstrating an alternative to black acquiescence. Deviance can prove to be an innovative response to a social problem. The leaders of the American Revolution—in fact, all revolutionaries—were also violating social expectations. So, too, were the individuals who launched Christianity, discovered germs, invented the airplane, and began campaigning for women's rights. Yet without such innovations, even in the face of threatened punishment, society would be the poorer. Deviance, then, always has a kernel of potential for useful social change.

SUMMARY

1. The purposes of this chapter are: to define deviance; to explore the causes of deviance; to discuss the means by which society controls deviant behavior; and to highlight the difficulties associated with social control.

2. Deviance is any behavior (good or bad) that violates social expectations and norms. The decision of what is or is not deviant is relative to changing norms and to the social context in which judgments are made. Once a behavior is defined as deviant, society can respond to it with approval, disapproval, isolation, or punishment.

3. There are three main factors that influence deviant behavior: biological (due to genetic defects, brain damage, or extreme malnutrition), psychological (due to conflicts between personal and social realities), and social (due to social disorganization, anomie, socialization to deviance, and labeling).

4. Society encourages and enforces conformity to norms and expectations through social controls such as socialization and social pressure (informal/primary group controls and formal/secondary group controls).

5. When the usual social controls fail, there are two additional control measures that can be used:
   Punishment and isolation: Punishment can include losing a job, being denied a promotion, or being put in a mental institution or a prison.

Rehabilitation: Many programs have been designed to bring deviant individuals back into the mainstream of society. These include self-help programs, medical programs, and halfway houses. There are costs as well as benefits to social control, and in determining them, we must consider that deviance can benefit society by providing outlets for desires that do not fit society's norms, by bringing about social and behavioral changes, and by encouraging group unity.

REVIEW

Key Terms

Deviance	Ritualism	Differential association	Social control
Idioculture	Retreatism	White-collar crime	Crimes without victims
Social problem	Rebellion	Labeling	Homophobia
Social disorganization	Anomie		
Innovation			

Review and Discussion

1. Think of opportunities you have had to violate social expectations (speeding, cheating, stealing, dressing oddly). What, if anything, made you conform: internalized norms? social pressure? formal sanctions?

2. Can you think of any instance where you thought a type of behavior was acceptable and another person (parent, child, grandparent, friend) thought the behavior was deviant, or vice versa? Why did each of you feel the way you did about the behavior? What influenced your feelings: social class, gender, race, or other factors?

3. How would your neighbors at home or at school react if a halfway house for exconvicts, exaddicts, or exmental patients was built across the street? What would you expect from the individuals who lived in the halfway house?

4. Make a list of behaviors you consider deviant. Then rank these behaviors from those you find least to most bothersome. For each item on your list, try to think through reasons why people might engage in that type of deviant behavior.

5. Have you ever conformed because of group pressure? Was the control exerted by the group informal or formal? Do you now wish you had behaved differently? If so, why?

6. Can you think of a situation where deviance contributed to social stability? How did it do so?

Experience with Sociology

The great value and fascination of sociology lie in the holistic view it takes. It probes behind the obvious to explore the unintended and the unrecognized, noting that behaviors are none the less real for being hidden. Changing sex roles are a case in point. The focus in this text has been on some obvious questions: How can sex role stereotyping be broken during socialization? How can economic opportunities be broadened for women? What life style choices are now available to women that used to be denied them? These are important questions that underlie our society's efforts to treat women with greater equality, justice, and concern.

Module 4 in *Experience with Sociology: Social Issues in American Society* looks at one of the hidden aspects of sex role redefinitions. Bringing women into the mainstream of the economic institution and freeing them from many of the stereotypes which kept them in the home have had some unanticipated consequences. Women are beginning to experience problems that previously were suffered by men: higher stress levels, more cancer from smoking, and so on. In this module, another problem area is addressed—rising crime rates among women. It will present data to help you examine crime rates and types of crimes committed by women. This analysis will be tied to the changing societal conditions which may lead you to question whether all women are best described as "sugar and spice and everything nice!"

References

Amir, Menachem, and **Yitzchak Berman** (1970). Chromosomal deviation and crime. Federal Probation 34: 55–62.

Asch, Solomon E. (1955). Opinions and social pressure. *Scientific American* 193: 4–8.

Badillo, Herman, and **Milton Haynes** (1972). *A Bill of Rights: Attica and the American Prison System.* New York: Outerbridge and Lazard.

Becker, Howard S. (1963). *The Outsiders: Studies in the Sociology of Deviance.* New York: Free Press.

Berk, Richard A., Kenneth J. Lenihan, and **Peter H. Rossi** (1980). Crime and poverty: Some experimental evidence from ex-offenders. *American Sociological Review* 45 (Oct. 1980): 766–86.

Bernard, Jessie (1981). *The Female World.* New York: Free Press.

Clark, Ramsey (1970). *Crime in America.* New York: Simon & Schuster.

Coleman, James S. (1961). *The Adolescent Society.* New York: Free Press.

Cook, Fred J. (1970). When you just give money to the poor. *The New York Times Magazine,* May 3, 1980.

Cuzzort, R. P., and **E. W. King** (1976). *Humanity and Modern Sociological Thought.* Hinsdale, Il.: Dryden Press.

Faris, Robert E. L., and **H. Warren Dunham** (1938). *Mental Disorders in Urban Areas: An Ecological Study of Schizophrenia and Other Psychoses.* Chicago: University of Chicago Press.

Federal Bureau of Investigation (1971). *Uniform Crime Reports for the United States, 1971.* Washington, D.C.: Government Printing Office.

Fine, Gary Alan (1979). Small groups and culture creation: The idioculture of little league baseball teams. *American Sociological Review* 44 (Oct. 1979): 733–45.

Fine, Gary Alan, and **Sherryl Kleinman** (1979). Rethinking subculture: An interactionist analysis. *American Journal of Sociology* 85, no. 1 (July 1979): 1–20.

Fitzgerald, Thomas K. (1981). Suicide prevention and gay self-help groups in Sweden and Finland. *Crisis* 2, no. 1 (Apr. 1981): 58–68.

Friedl, Ernestine (1965). *Vasilika: A Village in Modern Greece.* New York: Holt, Rinehart, and Winston.

Gates, Anita (1981). Lockout at the boarding gate? *Frequent Flier* (Aug. 1981): 42–45.

Goffman, Erving (1961). *Asylums.* New York: Anchor Books.

Golden, Frederic (1981). Shaping life in the lab. *Time,* March 9, 1981, pp. 50ff.

Greenberg, David F., Ronald C. Kessler, and **Charles H. Logan** (1979). A panel model of crime rates and arrest rates. *American Sociological Review* 44 (Oct. 1979): 843–50.

Hagen, John, Ilene H. Nagel (Bernstein), and **Celesta Albonetti** (1980). The differential sentencing of white-collar offenders in ten federal district courts. *American Sociological Review* 45 (Oct. 1980): 802–20.

Heath, R. G. (1960). A biochemical hypothesis on the etiology of schizophrenia. In *The Etiology of Schizophrenia,* ed. D. D. Jackson, pp. 145–56. New York: Basic Books.

Heston, Leonard L. (1970). The genetics of schizophrenia and schizoid disease. *Science* 167: 249–56.

Hornblower, Margot (1980). Hmongtana: Laotian tribe starts over in bewildering new world. *Washington Post,* July 5, 1980, pp. A1ff.

Klemesrud, Judy (1981). Gray Panther founder and a family of choice. *The New York Times,* June 22, 1981, p. G3.

Kluckhohn, Clyde C., and **Dorothea C. Leighton** (1962). *The Navaho,* rev. ed. Garden City, N.Y.: Doubleday.

Lemert, Edwin M. (1967). *Human Deviance, Social Problems, and Social Control.* Englewood Cliffs, N.J.: Prentice-Hall.

Lombroso, Cesare (1911). *Crime: Its Causes and Remedies.* Boston: Little, Brown.

Maccoby, Eleanor E., Joseph P. Johnson, and **Russell M. Church** (1958). Community and the social control of juvenile delinquency. *Journal of Social Issues* 14: 38–51.

Malcolm X (1966). *The Autobiography of Malcolm X.* New York: Random House, Inc.

Meislin, Richard J. (1981). The Crime-without-punishment crisis. *The New York Times,* Aug. 10, 1981, pp. B1ff.

Merton, Robert K. (1938). Social structure and anomie. *American Sociological Review* 3: 672–82.

Morris, Norval (1973). Crimes without victims: The law is a busybody. *The New York Times Magazine,* Apr. 1, 1973, pp 11ff.

The New York Times, Jury in "town bully" shooting returns a closed indictment. Aug. 22, 1981, p. 14.

Parker, Robert Nash, and **M. Dwayne Smith** (1979). Deterrence, poverty, and types of homicide. *American Journal of Sociology* 85, no. 3 (Nov. 1979): 614–24.

Parsons, Talcott (1954). *Essays in Sociological Theory.* New York: Free Press.

Plummer, Kenneth (1975). *Sexual Stigma.* London: Routledge and Kegan Paul.

Rosenhan, D. L. (1973). On being sane in insane places. *Science* 179: 250–58.

Schuessler, Karl F., and **Donald R. Cressey** (1959). Personality characteristics of criminals. *American Journal of Sociology* 55: 476–84.

Shaw, Clifford R., and **Henry D. McKay** (1931). Report on the Causes of Crime (vol. 12, no. 13). Washington, D.C.: National Commission on Law Observance and Enforcement.

Sheehan, Susan (1978). *A Prison and a Prisoner.* Boston: Houghton Mifflin.

Sheldon, William H. (1949). *Varieties of Delinquent Youth.* New York: Harper and Row.

Socolar, Milton J. (1981). *Income Maintenance Experiments: Need to Summarize Results and Communicate the Lessons Learned.* Washington, D.C.: U.S. Government Printing Office.

Srole, Leo, Thomas S. Langer, Stanley T. Michael, Marvin K. Opler, and **Thomas A. C. Rennie** (1962). *Mental Health in the Metropolis: The Midtown Manhattan Study.* New York: McGraw-Hill.

Sutherland, Edwin H., and **D. R. Cressey** (1966). *Principles of Criminology,* 7th ed. Philadelphia: J. B. Lippincott.

Thomas, W. I. (1928). *The Child in America.* New York: Alfred A. Knopf.

Vorenberg, James (1972). The war on crime: The first five years. *Atlantic Monthly* 229: 63–69.

Zimbardo, Philip G., W. Curtis Banks, Craig Haney, and **David Jaffee** (1973). A Pirandellian prison: The mind is a formidable jailer. *The New York Times Magazine,* Apr. 8, 1973, pp. 39–60.

8

SOCIAL STRATIFICATION

On Friday, March 12, 1982, residents witnessed an event unprecedented even in New York, a city used to the unexpected. In order to advertise a new continuing education program, its founders decided to throw $10,000 in one-dollar bills from an 86th floor window of the Empire State Building. Just as they were about to start, a bank robbery got underway on the first floor of the same building (*The New York Times*, March 13, 1982, p. 1ff). Needless to say, the police had some difficulty keeping track of which money was going where and why! The robbers ended up being arrested; the school-founders were taken into protective custody before they could be overwhelmed by onlookers who wanted their money!

However confusing it was for the police, this incident highlights an issue of enduring concern in sociology: Why do societies tend to distribute material and social resources so unequally? Social stratification is the area of sociology that looks at this question most directly.

SOCIAL STRATIFICATION AND SOCIAL CLASS

Americans, lay people and scholars alike, have tended to view American society as either "classless" or "middle class." Given the national creed of equality, to think of American society as a class society seemed inappropriate, or perhaps

Collective action is a way for workers to question society's definition of their importance. By demanding more pay and better working conditions, the blue-collar strikers here are asserting their importance in a stratification structure that holds their labor less significant than that of professionals, such as doctors.

un-American. Scholars also were preoccupied with equality. In the card catalogue of the main library of Cornell University Reisman (1973) found a listing of 102 publications under the subject of "equality," 69 on the subject of "equal opportunity," and 11 under the subject of "inequality."

Sociologists have argued that social classes are, at best, arbitrary in their boundaries, and difficult to define and to measure. In more traditional societies, the distinctions between classes have developed over many years and are clearly understood by everyone. In India, for example, the elaborate system of castes has been estimated to be 3500 years old. Although the caste system has now been outlawed, authorities are finding that it is nearly inseparable from that society's history and their Hindu tradition. On the other hand, life in modern industrial societies is subject to continuous fluctuations of social norms and economic pressures. Reliable class definitions are difficult to establish. Furthermore, in a rapidly changing, complex, and specialized society, is the chauffeur who earns $25,000 a year part of the working class (based on occupation) or middle class (based on income)?

In spite of these problems, the concept that a society can be separated into ranks does give the sociologist a framework for understanding the distribution of wealth and inequality. **Social stratification** is a system of ranking individuals and groups who share unequally in the distribution of scarce resources, wealth, prestige, and power. Groups who share the same characteristics of economic resources, prestige, and power and are aware of their common situation constitute a **social class.**

Sociologists do not agree on the issue of why there is inequality in wealth, power, and status. Functional school proponents claim that inequality is necessary to the survival of society. On the other hand, sociologists of the conflict school argue that inequality is the result of a struggle between the haves and the have nots; those who have the scarce resources—in order to maintain and increase their resources—must exploit and control those who have no resources. A third group of sociologists focuses on social class as the major dimension of social stratification. We will look at these three approaches in more detail.

THEORIES OF SOCIAL STRATIFICATION

The Functionalist Framework

The functionalist framework of social stratification (Davis and Moore, 1945) centers on the notion that some positions are more important for the survival of society than others. If all the necessary positions were equally pleasant, equally important, or equal in terms of required ability and talent, presumably there would be no need for a system of social stratification. This, however, is not the case. Some positions require greater talent than others, and some positions are functionally more important for the survival or effective functioning of society. Garbage collectors require no special talent to perform their tasks, but bank presidents do. To become a lawyer requires ability and a long period of schooling, during which the prospective lawyer earns little. Lawyers work hard, and they are always on call. The sacrifices they make during their education and training, the long hours they spend on their jobs, and the complexities associated with the practice of law make it necessary for society to have some rewards to induce people into these positions. The rewards for the most important positions take the form of material benefits, prestige, deference, and privilege. Or, as stated by Davis and Moore, things that contribute to sustenance and comfort, to humor and diversion, to self-respect and ego expansion. This ensures that the most talented will be motivated to seek these positions, and to perform them dutifully.

Many sociologists have questioned whether social positions can, in fact, be rated by their importance. Why, for example, are doctors more functionally important than garbage collectors? Others have criticized the assumption that there ever really was or is a match between talent and rank. The functionalist argument assumes that most individuals who are talented or ambitious will be able to achieve their chosen position in society. However, it is clear that not everyone has equal access to the training systems that lead to highly rewarding positions.

Some sociologists feel that stratification, rather than motivating persons to achieve difficult positions that require long training, is more likely to preserve the privilege of people who already occupy such positions. Although the functionalist theory may help to explain how stratification originated, it ignores the mechanisms that preserve inequality. Those in the most advantaged positions are usually reluctant to share or relinquish their power and privilege. Doctors, for example, have tried to limit entry into the field of medicine by requiring a long and hard training program in a restricted number of approved institutions. They also limit the activities of potential competitors (chiropractors and acupuncturists, for example), and they resist governmental attempts to set standardized fees. Once people have accumulated power, prestige, and wealth, they will naturally try to pass on these advantages to their children, in whose well-being they are interested. Such practices perpetuate the already existing inequalities. If stratification is functional for society, the critics ask, for whom is it functional? Is it functional for society in general or only for some privileged group?

Sociologist Herbert Gans (1972), in what appears to be a tongue-in-cheek application of the functionalist framework, argues that poverty persists in the United States not because less talented or less capable individuals fall to the bottom, but because it serves the interests of the well-to-do groups in society. Poverty ensures that there will be people to fill the physically dirty, dangerous, temporary, underpaid, undignified, and menial jobs that must be performed in every society. Indeed, this function is so important that

in some Southern states, welfare payments have been cut off during the summer months when the poor are needed in the fields. . . . The poor subsidize, directly and indirectly, many activities that benefit the rich. . . . For example, domestics subsidize the upper and middle classes, making life easier for their employers and freeing affluent women for a variety of professional, cultural, civic, and social activities. . . . (Gans, p. 280)

Gans uses the functionalist framework to show that the function of poverty is to maintain the economic privileges of those in power. And as is clear from his analysis, what is functional depends on whose point of view is used. Stratification may be functional for the rich but dysfunctional for the poor. Society, which has to accommodate the rich and the poor, may benefit from having prestigious *and* dirty (but necessary) tasks performed. However, the waste of human resources and the conflict between rich and poor that result from institutionalized disadvantage may be anything but functional in the long run. These issues have led other sociologists to question the functional approach and to generate alternatives; the most widely known is the conflict approach.

The Conflict Framework

The premier conflict theorist was Karl Marx. Although American sociologists largely ignored Marx in the first half of this century, in the past two decades sociologists have begun to reexamine his theories.

In the Communist Manifesto of 1848, Marx wrote: "The history of all hitherto existing societies is the history of class struggles." What Marx meant was that social change comes through conflict between two opposing or contradictory classes. Thus, for example, capitalism emerged from feudalism through a struggle between the land-owning class and the emergent class of traders and manufacturers (the bourgeoisie).

As we noted in Chapter 1, for Marx social class meant the relationship to the means of production, e.g., factories, tools, and capital. In a capitalistic society, there are two basic classes whose relationships to the means of production are distinct. The bourgeoisie, who own the means of production, and the propertyless workers (the proletariat), who must sell their labor to the bourgeoisie in order to survive. Those who own the means of production constitute the dominant or ruling class. By virtue of their ownership of the economic resources, they control everything else: the state, the legal system, and so forth (see Chapter 1). Marx did not ignore other classes, but he did not atribute much significance to them. Under conditions of capitalism, they could not survive, and would be absorbed into the mass of propertyless workers. Consequently, the struggle will be between the two antagonistic classes, the bourgeoisie and the proletariat.

Before a revolutionary confrontation could take place, several preconditions would be necessary. One was the development among the working class of a class awareness or consciousness that would make possible both class solidarity and political organization. Marx argued that the bourgeoisie and the proletariat constitute two objective classes because of their relationship to the means of production. But objective class, or a "class in itself," is not sufficient for the development of class awareness or class consciousness, a "class for itself." The process of production in modern capitalism creates unique opportunities for the development of class consciousness, for it places large numbers of workers in factories in which they share common experiences and problems of survival. Individual workers may blame their position on themselves, or attribute their condition to the will of the Lord, and hope for the better afterlife that the prevalent ideology describes as their reward. Large masses of workers are different. Through

communication and social interaction, they begin to recognize their common exploitation, and under the leadership of the most advanced workers they can organize into a political group for the overthrow of capitalism.

The capitalist system in the most developed industrial society of the mid-nineteenth century was indeed a society based on the exploitation of men, women, and children. They toiled long hours under the most primitive and appalling conditions, trying to eke out a bare subsistence. Based on the reality of life in the nineteenth century, Marx anticipated that the revolution would begin in the most industrialized countries of Western Europe. But as is well known, the first revolution took place under the leadership of Lenin in one of the least industrialized countries of Europe, Russia, followed by China, an agricultural society. In spite of significant economic problems, the highly industrial societies remained capitalist.

Some of the major criticism of the Marxist framework centers on the fact that it ignores the viability and adaptability of capitalism. The extension of social and political rights, the rise of the middle class, and welfare capitalism alleviated and corrected some of the major problems raised by Marx. Marx's motto, "workers of the world unite; you have nothing to lose but your chains," proved to be erroneous. He underestimated the degree of cohesion exerted by nationalism. In World War I, workers across Europe did not unite on a class basis to overthrow the bourgeoisie; instead, they gave almost unanimous support to their governments in waging war (Bottomore, 1966). In the United States, the working class sought not a revolution, but collective bargaining and a share of the social and material wealth.

However much Marx erred in his predictions and overlooked the importance of other stratification variables such as power and status, sociologists nevertheless recognize the significance of his work. While separating the two classes on the basis of ownership of the means of production is not a profitable means of analysis of the contemporary United States, it is true that those who occupy similar economic positions are likely to have similar life chances, values, and attitudes. While lacking the necessary "class consciousness," and thus constituting merely an objective class, working-class people, as numerous studies have shown, tend to vote more liberally on economic issues then members of the upper class.

Some sociologists see the Marxist theory as still valid today. Wright and Perrone (1977) argue that the ownership of the means of production (the capitalist employer) contains two distinct dimensions: legal rights to the product of labor, and control over the activities of labor. In the nineteenth century these two dimensions were merged. Today, however, these activities are differentiated in large corporations. The employer (owner of property or capital) continues to have legal rights to the product of labor, but control (authority) over the activities of labor is vested in the manager, particularly in large corporations. Separating ownership and control suggests a new transformation of capitalism "from individual forms of capitalist ownership to more collective forms of ownership" (Wright and Perrone, 1977:34).

Other critics of the Marxist framework argue that today conflict is based on authority relations, not on property relations: there is conflict between those who exercise authority and those who lack authority. Those who exercise authority in the government, corporations, or labor unions constitute the upper class, and those who lack authority, the lower class (Dahrendorf, 1959). Dahrendorf dismisses property relations as unimportant and substitutes authority as the one major variable which divides the upper from the lower class.

Many sociologists today have found Marxist concepts of class relations worthy of further exploration, although they vary in the way they approach this task. Others, however, have adopted yet a third approach to social stratification

based on the work of Max Weber. This view focuses on social class, and approaches it from a multidimensional perspective.

The Weberian Approach

Weber's approach to social stratification was multidimensional, including class, status, and power. Class for Weber meant a number of people who had similar life chances:

It is the most elemental economic fact that the way in which disposition over material property is distributed among a plurality of people meeting competitively in the market for the purpose of exchange in itself created specific life chances. The mode of distribution . . . excludes the nonwealthy from competing for highly valued goods; it favors owners and, in fact gives them a monopoly to acquire such goods . . . the mode of distribution monopolizes the opportunities for profitable deals . . . it increases . . . their power in the price struggle with those who being propertyless, have nothing to offer but their labor. Property and "lack of property" are therefore the basic categories of all class situations. (Weber, 1978: 927)

While Weber's formulation of class does not significantly differ from Marx's in the sense that economic factor is primary, Weber's addition of the status and power dimensions served to expand the concept of social stratification. According to Weber, *social status* was based on *"esteem"* or *"honor"* (prestige) and characterized by a unique life style of people or a group who belong to the same "circle." Thus, wealth alone is not sufficient for status and prestige. Weber notes that at first wealth may not bring honor or prestige; however, as one "learns," so to say, to use the wealth in the proper manner it will inevitably lead to the required credentials and inclusion in the proper circles.

"Power," the third dimension of social stratification, is "the chance of a man or a number

Sociological measurement techniques can easily verify the high standing of the Kennedy family within American society. Objective measures show family members to be wealthy, well-educated, and holders of prestigious jobs—including high government posts. Subjective measures would show that many Americans know of the family and respect the accomplishments of many of its members.

of men to realize their own will in a social action even against the resistance of others'' (1978: 926). Weber, as Reisman (1973) has noted, did not develop the power dimension sufficiently. He did, however, argue that people may strive for power to enrich themselves or as a means to attain status, or people may value power for its own sake. Power is also associated with political parties; these parties may represent class interests, status interests, or a combination of both class and status interest groups. Analytically, the dimensions of social stratification as conceptualized by Weber are distinct, but in reality the three dimensions of class, status, and power tend to coincide, as Weber himself acknowledged. Let's now look briefly at efforts of American sociologists to study these three dimensions, starting with occupational prestige as a measure of the status dimension.

Three Dimensions of Social Stratification

Occupational prestige. Studies of occupational prestige (Hodge et al., 1964) provide a generalized view of how a national cross section of people rank occupations in the United States (Table 8.1) These studies reveal that occupational prestige has remained highly stable through time. There was relatively little change over a period of years in the high rank given to professional and managerial occupations, or the high status accorded to a Supreme Court justice and physician. The ranking of occupations reflects a clus-

TABLE 8.1 / RANKING OCCUPATIONS IN TERMS OF PRESTIGE

The chart below shows the way occupations were ranked in terms of prestige in a classic study done in the 1960s. But times change, and on March 16, 1982, The New York Times *reported that many were concerned that young people were moving from prestigious, but lowly paid occupations like sociologist teaching in a college or university, to more highly paid jobs in industry, medicine, engineering, and computer science. This shows how the whole economic system has an impact on the decision making of individuals.*

Occupation	Score	Occupation	Score
U.S. Supreme Court Justice	94	Biologist	85
Nuclear physicist	92	Sociologist	83
Scientist	92	Instructor in public schools	82
Government scientist	91	Captain in the regular army	82
State governor	91	Accountant for a large business	81
U.S. representative in Congress	90	Owner of a factory that employs about 100 people	80
Chemist	89	Building contractor	80
Diplomat in the U.S. Foreign Service	89	Artist who paints pictures that are exhibited in galleries	78
Dentist	88	Musician in a symphony orchestra	78
Architect	88	Author of novels	78
County judge	88	Economist	78
Psychologist	87	Official of an international labor union	77
Minister	87	Railroad engineer	76
Member of the board of directors of a large corporation	87	Electrician	76
Mayor of a large city	87	County agricultural agent	76
Priest	86	Owner-operator of a printing shop	75
Head of a department in a state government	86	Trained machinist	75
Airline pilot	86	Farm owner and operator	74
Banker	85	Undertaker	74

Source: Robert W. Hodge *et. al.,* "Occupational Prestige in the United States, 1925–1963." Reprinted by permission of the University of Chicago Press from the *American Journal of Sociology* 70 (November 1964): 290–292. Copyright 1964 The University of Chicago.

tering of wealth, prestige, and power, although there are exceptions. The college professor is ranked higher than the plumber but the plumber is likely to earn more than the college professor, and the railroad conductor is likely to earn more than the elementary school teacher. Social status is also affected by other variables, such as race, religion, ethnicity, and style of life.

Status inconsistency. Differences in the dimensions of stratification have been conceptualized by Gerhard Lenski (1954) as **status inconsistency;** for example, some individuals are high on the power dimension, but low on the status dimension, or high in status, but low in wealth (e.g., a professor may have high occupational status, but a low income; racketeers may have a

TABLE 8.1 / (Continued)

Occupation	Score	Occupation	Score
Welfare worker for a city government	74	Streetcar motorman (bus driver)	56
Newspaper columnist	73	Lumberjack	55
Reporter on a daily newspaper	71	Restaurant cook	55
Radio announcer	70	Singer in a nightclub	54
Bookkeeper	70	Filling station attendant	51
Insurance agent	69	Dockworker	50
Manager of a small store in a city	67	Railroad section hand	50
A local official of a labor union	67	Night watchman	50
Mail carrier	66	Coal miner	50
Railroad conductor	66	Restaurant waiter	49
Traveling salesman for a wholesale concern	66	Taxi driver	49
Plumber	65	Farmhand	48
Automobile repairman	64	Janitor	48
Playground director	63	Bartender	48
Barber	63	Clothes presser in a laundry	45
Machine operator in a factory	63	Soda fountain clerk	44
Owner-operator of a lunch stand	63	Sharecropper—one who owns no livestock or equipment and does not manage farm	42
Corporal in the regular army	62	Garbage collector	39
Garage mechanic	62	Street sweeper	36
Truck driver	59	Shoe shiner	34
Fisherman who owns his own boat	58		
Clerk in a store	56		
Milk route man	56		

high income, but low status; or union leaders may have high political power, but little status or wealth). Numerous studies have found that status inconsistency has a variety of consequences ranging from psychological frustrations to dissatisfactions which lead to support of extremist political parties of the right or left (Lipset, 1960; Geschwender, 1967; Eitzen, 1970).

Social status in the American community. Nearly fifty years ago sociologist W. Lloyd Warner and his colleagues investigated the class structure of a New England town which they called Yankee City. Relying on the Weberian dimension of social status they defined it as ". . . two or more orders of people who are believed to be, and are accordingly ranked by members of the community, in socially superior or inferior positions" (Warner and Lunt, 1941: 71). Using the method of *evaluated participation,* which relies on the evaluation and observations of a group of "prestige judges," Warner conducted interviews with selected townspeople to determine how they measured status, how many classes or strata were recognized in the community, and where they ranked themselves and others in the stratification system of the community. In addition, Warner developed an "Index of Status Characteristics" based on occupation (related to level of occupation and income), source of income (inherited or earned), type of house, and area of residence. Warner determined that "Yankee City" had six social classes, or status groups. (1) The "upper-upper" was composed of "old families," business people and professionals living in the "best" part of town. (2) The "lower-upper" resembled the upper-upper, but were not "old family." (3) The "upper-middle" was predominantly white collar and small businessmen living in a clearly defined part of the town. (4) The "lower-middle" was composed of skilled and semiskilled workers and the lower levels of white-collar workers. (5) The "upper-lower" consisted of respectable working people, and (6) the "lower-lower" were the unemployed and people on welfare, characterized by irresponsibility and moral laxity to community norms. While "Yankee City" and other communities in the United States have established status groups based on criteria other than wealth, it is clear nevertheless that wealth remains one of the most important criteria of social status.

The power dimension. The third dimension of social stratification, power, as we noted previously, is not always a reflection of wealth. Who, then, holds power? Some researchers (Domhoff, 1967, 1980; Mills, 1956) provide considerable evidence of the existence of a "power elite" composed of the upper levels of the corporate, political, and military structures. These people exert control over the decisions affecting the distribution of scarce resources as well as the foreign policy of the United States. On the other hand, the pluralists argue that there is no elite, only interest groups which join forces to veto decisions they consider disadvantageous to their interests (Riesman, 1961). We will look at power in more detail in Chapter 17.

Criticism of the Weberian Framework

Most American sociologists have found little to criticize in the Weberian approach to social stratification. But there has been considerable criticism of the fact that while sociologists acknowledge the importance of the multidimensional framework, they focus primarily on the status dimension (Huber and Form, 1973; Reissman, 1973). Anderson (1974) argues that while we cannot question the need for more than one variable in a model of social class

. . . one must look first *and* always *at property classes or ownership, as Marx and as Weber himself did, if the operation of a society's structure of inequality is to be understood. From property we can explore more fruitfully the other dimensions of stratification such as occupation, status, power. . . . (1974:121)*

British sociologists have also been highly critical of the usage of the multidimensional framework. Parkin (1971) points out that the distinction between class and status is fruitful in the analysis of traditional types of societies, but it cannot be applied to modern societies without some modification. Parkin doubts the validity of such arguments as, for example, electricians and railway conductors rank high on the economic dimension, but low on the social status dimension, or that teachers and clergy rank high on the status dimension but low on the economic dimension. These inconsistencies, Parkin argues, "do not reveal discrepancies between *class* and status position at all, but merely between income and status position (1971: 32)." Income, however, is only one factor which determines class position. Such factors as employment, promotion opportunities, long-term income prospects, and other social and material advantages referred to by Weber as "life chances" are important, but ignored by those who use the multidimensional framework (Parkin, 1971).

Comparing the Theories

Although they differ in some significant respects, the theories of social stratification do share a core of concepts.

1. *Stratification in complex societies is inevitable and it affects our behavior.* The functionalists emphasize the necessity for unequal rewards; the Marxists emphasize conflict and exploitation of the workers by the upper classes; the Weberians emphasize the various orders of social life and the interrelationships of class, status, and power. But all agree that social behavior is directly affected by stratification and class membership.

2. *Stratification affects the distribution of societal resources.* All theories, whether they stress income, power, or prestige, recognize that these factors relate to each other. They also affect the ability of persons at different socioeconomic levels to obtain other societal resources: housing, medical care, education, recreation, appliances, automobiles, and so on.

3. *Stratification is related to both change and stability.* The functionalists see stratification as a way of maintaining social equilibrium, with the major societal tasks being accomplished in an orderly and efficient way. The Marxists, in contrast, see stratification as a source of change. And the Weberians suggest that stratification motivates people to act within the economic, political, and prestige systems of society. Consequently, stratification contributes at once to change and stability in

society. As in so many areas of social life, no one theory explains all of the behavior that sociologists observe.

Measuring Social Classes

Although sociologists have found that the concept of social class is the most useful means of observing and understanding the process and the effects of stratification, questions remain: How should sociologists go about measuring social class? What are the major social classes in American society? Sociologists face two basic issues in trying to measure social class. First, what criteria should be used in deciding who belongs in what social class? Second, is it correct to call a set of persons who share the same occupational, educational, or income level a social class, even if they do not interact or are not conscious that there are millions of others with whom they have much in common? (see Svalastoga, 1964) The methods for measuring social

"Treat people as equals and the first thing you know they believe they are."

Drawing by Mulligan; © 1982,
The New Yorker Magazine, Inc.

class which sociologists have developed attempt to respond to these issues.

The subjective approach. In the subjective approach to the measurement of social class, the investigator is usually concerned with an individual's perception of his or her position in the class structure. The subjective approach is based on a person's feelings of belonging to a group. In the 1940s, national polls showed that the overwhelming majority of Americans, when asked whether they consider themselves upper, middle, or lower class, identified themselves as "middle class." Centers (1949), noting that the survey limited the response to only three classes, introduced a fourth category, "working class." Based on a national survey, Centers showed that about 50 percent of the respondents identified themselves as working class; about 4 percent upper class; close to 40 percent middle class; and a small percentage lower class. Similarly, Hodge and Treiman (1968) found that three-quarters of all adults in a national sample identified themselves as "middle class." But when respondents were asked to identify with a given class—upper, upper middle, working, or lower class—the responses were more precise: upper class, 2.2 percent; upper middle class, 16.6 percent; middle class, 44 percent; working class, 34.3 percent; lower class, 2.3 percent. The decrease in the proportion of persons who identify themselves as working class may be a reflection of the changing labor force from blue-collar work to white-collar work, the relative affluence of post-World War II Americans, as well as images of people about the class structure.

One of the difficulties with self-rating methods is that they deal only with people's *awareness* of their social rank. This perception is sometimes vague and may or may not accurately reflect class position as indicated by criteria that can be measured more directly: income, education, and occupational ranking. Moreover, people may not always evaluate themselves or their neighbors in the same way that other members in the same community do. As a result, the subjective approach is usually used with methods that employ the perception of others and the measurement of things like income and occupation.

The reputational approach. We have noted in the previous section the study by Warner and his colleagues (Warner and Lunt, 1941) of "Yankee City," where they used the method of *evaluated participation*. This approach relies on the observation and evaluation of "prestige judges," who variously defined people as old wealth or aristocracy, poor but decent folk, and so on. Other sociologists followed the method in various small towns in the United States, e.g., Davis, Gardner, and Gardner (1941), and West (1945).

The reputational method has serious shortcomings. It is effective primarily in small towns where most of the residents know each other at least by reputation. Consequently, this method is difficult to use in studies of the class structure in more anonymous cities and suburbs. Even in small towns, it is likely to be supplemented by other approaches. You will recall that Warner used an "Index of Status Characteristics," for example, along with the reputational approach. His index was an attempt to use an objective approach, the third way to measure social class.

The objective approach. While the subjective and reputational approaches provide a measure of how individuals and groups see themselves and others in the stratification system, most sociologists prefer what is called the *objective approach*. It uses income, education, and occupation, and occasionally other factors, as indices of social class. This information is more accessible to researchers and can be applied more broadly and uniformly to society as a whole. Three major objective measures of social class are education (measured by the number of years of schooling completed), income, and occupation. Today most sociologists interested in social stratification rely

The fundamental characteristic of poverty is limitation. Because the poor lack access to resources, such as financial opportunities and adequate education, they have little control over their lives and survive in a day-to-day existence that offers few options and rewards.

on the data collected by the Bureau of the Census and other agencies (e.g., Department of Education). These data enable sociologists to measure income, education, occupation, type of housing, family size, and so on.

The methods sociologists use to study social stratification depend on the specific issue they are addressing. While the objective method may be more reliable in delineating social classes in a society, it will provide few answers for those who seek to tap class consciousness. As we saw in Chapter 2, data-gathering strategies have to be closely tied to the research question. Naturally, when sociologists seek to look at all the dimensions of social class—class-consciousness factors as well as status and economic elements—they are likely to develop research strategies which utilize all three methods of measuring social class.

INEQUALITY IN AMERICAN SOCIETY

Who Gets What?

The American creed of equality has not prevented a large segment of Americans from falling into poverty. As Robin Williams has pointed out, the dominant conception has been that of *equality of opportunity* rather than equality of condition (Williams, 1970). The upper and middle classes of the society continually have insisted that differences in wealth are acceptable because they reflect different ways in which opportunities are used. As in other societies, wealth and power in the United States are not distributed equally. The distribution of income has changed very little since the United States has become a highly industrial society. In personal income, the wealthiest tenth of the population received 34 percent of the income in 1910, and 29 percent in 1959. Indeed, in 1980, 6.2 percent of families had an income of less than $5,000, and 6.2 percent had less than $7,500. Families with incomes of $35,000 and above constituted 19.5 percent of the population. But an income of $35,000 per year or even $50,000 per year does not make for riches. Many of the families in the income bracket of $30,000 to $50,000 a year consisted of two earners, hardly the rich. The super rich, e.g., chief executives of corporations, receive annual salaries ranging from $200,000 to upwards of $800,000 per year.

The disparities between the rich and the poor have not declined (see Table 8.2). The graduated income tax has had little to no effect on the distribution of income or wealth. Personal in-come taxes have affected mostly middle-income groups. High-income groups have found various ways to avoid progressive taxation; expense accounts, company automobiles, free vacations, state bonds, and capital gains have been so effective "that the distribution of income after federal income taxes is practically the same as the distribution before taxes" (Williams, 1970: 119). New federal legislation of 1981 which lowered taxes provided further reduction on personal income taxes for those in the $50,000 and above income. In 1980, median family income for a family of four was $21,023, so the people most affected by the legislation will be the wealthy.

Contrary to popular belief, poverty has actually begun to *increase* in the United States after decades of decline. Table 8.3 documents this fact.

TABLE 8.2 / PERCENTAGE SHARE OF AGGREGATE INCOME RECEIVED BY EACH FIFTH AND TOP 5 PERCENT OF FAMILIES, 1958–1980

The distribution of income has remained almost unchanged since 1958. The wealthiest fifth of families in the United States has received a little above 40 percent of the income, while the poorest fifth has received 5 percent of the income.

Year	Lowest Fifth	Second Fifth	Third Fifth	Fourth Fifth	Highest Fifth	Top 5 Percent
1980	5.1	11.6	17.5	24.3	41.6	15.3
1978	5.2	11.6	17.5	24.1	41.5	15.6
1976	5.4	11.8	17.6	24.1	41.1	15.6
1974	5.4	12.0	17.6	24.1	41.0	15.3
1972	5.4	11.9	17.5	23.9	41.4	15.9
1970	5.4	12.2	17.6	23.8	40.9	15.6
1968	5.6	12.4	17.7	23.7	40.5	15.6
1966	5.6	12.4	17.8	23.8	40.5	15.6
1964	5.1	12.0	17.7	24.0	41.2	15.9
1962	5.0	12.1	17.6	24.0	41.3	15.7
1960	4.8	12.2	17.8	24.0	41.3	15.9
1958	5.0	12.5	18.0	23.9	40.6	15.4

Source: U.S. Bureau of the Census, *Statistical Abstract of the United States: 1980,* and *Current Population Reports,* Series P–60, no. 127 (August 1981).

TABLE 8.3 / POVERTY IN THE UNITED STATES, 1957–1980

This table shows the percentage of the total population below the poverty level for each year from 1957 to 1980. After decades of decline, the small increase from 1978 to 1979, and then the sharp jump from 1979 to 1980, are particularly noticeable.

Year	% at Poverty Level	Year	% at Poverty Level
1957	22.4%	1969	12.6%
1958	22.2	1970	12.5
1959	21.9	1971	11.9
1960	21.0	1972	11.1
1961	19.5	1973	11.6
1962	19.0	1974	11.2
1963	17.3	1975	12.3
1964	15.7	1976	11.8
1965	14.7	1977	11.6
1966	14.2	1978	11.4
1967	12.8	1979	11.6
1968	12.1	1980	13.0
		1981	14.0*

Source: The New York Times, February 20, 1982, p. 1ff; figures are from U.S. Census Bureau.
* Figure is from *The New York Times,* July 27, 1982, p. D22.

These figures are based on cash income adjusted for inflation. In 1981, the poverty-level figure was $9,287 for a nonfarm family of four (Herbers, 1982: 1). Below this figure, people cannot sustain themselves with proper nutrition, clothing, and housing. Blacks continue to compose the largest percentage of those in poverty: 34.2 percent, compared to 25.7 percent for Hispanics and 10.2 percent for whites. While the data speak for themselves, the way in which poverty is built into a social structure is not so obvious. Yet understanding the impact of social stratification and social class on people's lives requires us as sociologists to understand this process. There-fore, we will now look at the effects of social stratification and social class on people's life chances.

The Consequences of Inequality

According to Weber, people who belong to the same economic class share the same **life chances;** that is, the same access to "a supply of goods, external living conditions, and personal life experiences" (Warner, Meeker, and Ellis, 1960: 542). For example, income differences directly determine one's ability to afford a house, a college education, or a car. Income differences affect not only the "big" things mentioned above, but they also determine how much meat and bread are consumed, and the overall nutrition of a family. Income differences affect our view of the world and our place in it. Access to financial resources largely determines a person's chances even for "life, liberty, and the pursuit of happi-ness." The higher up the income scale we go, the greater are our chances of being healthy, living longer, staying married, getting a good education, and controlling our destiny. We will now examine several aspects of life chances in more detail: life expectancy, health, mental health, education, justice, life styles, and value systems.

Life expectancy. Although overall rates of infant mortality have declined in recent years, the upper-class baby still has a far better chance to survive than the lower-class baby. The infant mortality rate of families with incomes under $3,000 a year was almost three times greater than that of families with a high income (U.S. Department of Health, Education and Welfare, 1972). The national rate of infant mortality in 1980 was 13 per thousand, but in Washington, D.C. the infant mortality rate in 1980 was 24.6 per thousand. Washington has a relatively high per capita income, but it also has a large number of poor people. Blacks make up 70 percent of the population and infant mortality predominates among

Different social classes are associated with differences in life-styles and access to the means and experiences that perpetuate those life-styles.

blacks: 26.6 infants die per thousand. For white babies in Washington, D.C., the infant mortality rate was 13.1 per thousand. The largest proportion of births in the city were registered to the poor and the young, the group least likely to receive prenatal care (Newland, 1981).

Poor health affects the life expectancy of those in low-income groups. Kitagawa and Hauser (1968) found that people in the lower class were eight times more likely to die from tuberculosis than upper-class people.

It is well known that during the Vietnam War, poor Americans generally and poor black Americans specifically were more likely to be drafted than upper-class youth. Americans who died in Vietnam were more often from low-income groups, and more blacks than whites died in Vietnam (in proportion to their number in the population). In short there is a positive correlation between a person's class position and that person's chances of survival. Those who are more affluent live longer and their children's chances of survival are better.

Health. The rich live longer partly because they live healthier lives than the poor. The poor are more prone to contract all kinds of diseases. Cardiovascular disorders occur with greater frequency among the lower socioeconomic strata. Rheumatic fever, rare among the well-to-do, becomes more commonplace as family income declines. Heart disease, premature births, diabetes, and even cancer are all more prevalent among the poor (Krause, 1977; Luft, 1978; Ornati, 1966). Poor nutrition, overcrowded and unsanitary living conditions, and poor health care contribute to the high incidence of ill health among the lower classes.

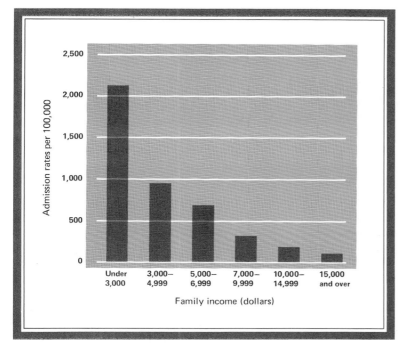

Fig. 8.1 / Social Class and Mental Health

The figure shows admission rates to outpatient psychiatric services by family income.

Source: *Statistical Note #47,* National Institute of Mental Health, Survey and Reports Section, Biometry Branch.

Mental health. Available studies indicate that mental illness is closely related to social class (Dohrenwend, 1975; Fried, 1975). Many in the lower income groups cannot afford private mental health care, and public care is often of poor quality. Frequently, there are hidden costs to the "free" care offered by public clinics: an individual may need to take a day off from work or have to hire a babysitter in order to go to the clinic to receive free treatment. In addition, individuals from the lower socioeconomic groups are far more likely to be committed to a state mental hospital. The same symptoms diagnosed in a middle-class patient and a lower-class patient will often place the middle-class individual in a psychiatrist's private office and the lower-class individual in a state hospital (Miller and Mishler, 1970). An examination of first admissions to mental hospitals in Washington, D.C., showed that the rate of hospitalization increased steadily with each drop in social class, and that the rate for lower-class males was much higher than for all others (Rushing, 1969). This is also true for admission to outpatient psychiatric services (see Fig. 8.1).

In the 1950s Yale University researchers August Hollingshead and Frederick Redlich (1958) found considerable cultural differences between the upper-class psychiatrist and the lower-class patient. Such differences may lead to poor communication and lack of rapport, and they may contribute to the higher incidence of hospitalization for lower-class persons. The higher rate of mental illness among the lower class may also reflect the pressures and difficulties they face in daily life. Possibly, too, the well-to-do have more alternatives, while the poor are locked into their situation. If, for example, job tension is a major aspect of a person's mental problem, more options for changing jobs are available to members of the upper-middle class than to the working- or lower-class person.

Education. Credentials are very important in our society. The amount of education individuals receive strongly affects their future occupation, income, and chance to find employment. A male college graduate can expect to earn $236,000 more in the course of his lifetime than can the man who goes to work directly after high school. In turn, the high school graduate will earn far more than will the man with only elementary schooling. An extra year of schooling is worth nearly a 6 percent increase in income (Jencks et al., 1972). Where one attended school also matters, especially at the college level.

Social class strongly affects the educational performance of children. Middle- and upper-class children are more likely to perform well in school than lower-class children. Educational achievement may be no less important to poor parents than to well-to-do parents, but by virtue of their own educational achievements, upper income groups provide considerably greater support for good school performance than lower income groups. Children from poor families, on the other hand, fall behind; at times their reading skills at grade six are no higher than at grade one. They lack the support of the family, the peer group, and not infrequently, the school system itself. Not surprisingly, lower income group children are more likely to drop out of school than more affluent children.

Justice. The United States does not have one set of laws for the poor and another set for the rich. Sleeping on a a park bench, as Anatole France noted, is against the law for the poor as well as the rich. The rich, however, are not likely to ever have to sleep on a park bench, whereas the poor might. And as the President's Commission on Law Enforcement and the Administration of Justice has noted, "a policeman in attempting to solve crimes employs, in the absence of concrete evidence, circumstantial indicators to link crimes with specific people" (President's Commission on Law Enforcement and the Administration of Justice, 1966). The President's Commission also noted, "the death sentence is disproportionately imposed and carried out on the poor, the Negro, and the members of unpopular groups."

Today, the key issue of inequality lies not in deliberate discrimination, but in the inability of the poor to have a good defense and inability to secure bail. The well-to-do are frequently able to avoid prosecution because they possess greater resources and status. Few cases of embezzlement, a white-collar crime, result in criminal action. White-collar criminals are rarely imprisoned because they are not seen as a threat to the community. As a result of these inequities, the poor are convicted more often and sentenced to longer jail sentences than the more advantaged members of society. Table 8.4 documents the direct rela-

TABLE 8.4 / CLASS AND INCARCERATION, 1974

Personal Income Year Prior to Arrest	Estimated Number of Inmates of State Correctional Facilities	Percent of Inmates
No income	7,600	5
Less than $2,000	32,400	19
$2,000 to $3,999	30,700	18
$4,000 to $5,999	30,400	18
$6,000 to $9,999	29,900	18
$10,000 or more	23,000	14
Amount not known	12,000	8
Not reported	1,800	1
Total	168,300	100

Source: Sourcebook of Criminal Justice Statistics 1980, p. 500 (Washington, D.C.: U.S. Department of Justice).

tionship between income and the likelihood of going to jail.

Life styles. People who share the same economic class and have access to the same life chances tend to develop life styles based on these shared experiences. **Life style** refers to the attitudes, values, and patterns of behavior that typify a particular social group. While Americans share the overall culture of television shows and movies, magazines and newspapers, the Fourth of July "cook-out" and fireworks, apple pie and hot dogs, the life style of Americans varies from one social class to another because their members have similar life chances and tend to interact primarily with members of their own social class. The life styles of the different social classes in the United States are distinguished by their consumption patterns and reflected in the type of housing they live in, their dress, and their social, cultural, and leisure activities.

In the United States, mass production has eliminated some of the telling signs of life styles. Designer clothing for the upper class is mass produced for the middle class. Mass production of cars has made the automobile available to the middle-class American, and at times to the lower-class American. The leisure industry has tried to duplicate some of the upper-class activities for the middle class, but the middle-class family with a median income of $21,023 can afford only a very modest life style (see Table 8.5). And, of course, those in lower income groups continue with their own life style of poor housing and few opportunities for leisure of any type.

Table 8.6 is only partially a tongue-in-cheek representation of life style differences among members of different social classes. It focuses on sex, marriage, and leisure as parts of the lives of people with different economic resources and social class backgrounds. The intent of the figure is to capture images that represent life style differences, rather than listing detailed data about them. Nevertheless, it is clear that there are important life style differences, a point supported

TABLE 8.5 / FAMILY INCOME IN 1980

Median income for a family of four in 1980 was $21,023.

Income Level	% of Population
Under $2,500	2.1
2,500— 4,999	4.1
5,000— 7,499	6.2
7,500— 9,999	6.5
10,000—12,499	7.3
12,500—14,999	6.9
15,000—19,999	14.0
20,000—24,999	13.7
25,000—34,999	19.8
35,000—49,999	12.8
50,000 and over	6.7

Source: Adapted from U.S. Bureau of the Census, *Current Population Reports,* Series P–60, no. 127 (August 1981).

by voluminous sociological data (Bernard, 1981; Duberman, 1976; Rubin, 1976).

Values, beliefs, and goals. In a cross-cultural study of men in Turin, Italy, Washington, D.C., and a national sample of men in the United States, sociologist Melvin Kohn (1977) demonstrated that the nature of their jobs, or where they are positioned in the occupational hierarchy, determines how men perceive themselves and the world. Middle- and upper-class men perform occupational roles that embody self-direction, or action based on their judgment. Working-class men, at the lower level of the hierarchy, are subject to direction of those above them. Opportunities for self-direction are not generally available to these men. Their work is routinized, ordered, and regulated. Men from different social classes have a variety of experiences in the work situation. For upper-class men these experiences are reflected in their image of themselves as competent members of a benign society. Men in

TABLE 8.6 / LIFE-STYLE DIFFERENCES AMONG SOCIAL CLASSES

	Highbrow	Upper middlebrow
How girl meets boy	He was an usher at her best friend's wedding	At college, in the psychology lab
The proposal	In his room during the Harvard-Princeton game	In the back seat of a Volkswagen
The wedding	In her living room, by a federal judge	College chapel (nondenominational)
The honeymoon	Mediterranean	Bahamas
Marriage manual	*Kama Sutra*	*Sexual Efficiency in Marriage*, volumes I and II
Sex novels she reads	Jane Austen	*Lady Chatterley's Lover*
Sleeping arrangements	Double bed	King-size bed or twin beds with one headboard
Sleeping attire	He: nothing. She: nothing.	He: red turtleneck nightshirt. She: gown with matching peignoir.
Turn-ons	Pot	Champagne and oysters
The schedule	Spontaneously, on an average of 2.5 weekly (that means 2 times one week and 3 times another)	Twice a week and when the kids go to the Sunday matinee
Number of children	1 each by a previous marriage, or as many as God provides	2.4
Anniversary celebrations	A weekend in Dublin	He gives her a new dishwasher. She gives him a power lawn mower.
Quarrels	"I don't care what your analyst says."	"I don't care if he is your brother."
If the marriage needs help	He consults her analyst. She consults his.	They go (a) to a marriage counselor; (b) to the minister.
The affair	"But I assumed you knew."	"It was basically a problem in communication."
Sex education	"Ask Doctor Grauber, dear, when you see him tomorrow."	"Well, you see, Daddy has something called a . . . etc. And Daddy and Mommy love each other very much."
Vacations	Europe in May. She takes the children to the Cape. He commutes.	Europe in July. Family camping in Yosemite.
Financial arrangements	Separate trust funds	Joint checking account
Who raises the children	English nanny, boarding school, and Dr. Grauber	Mommy and Daddy, Cub Scouts, and Dr. Freud

Source: "Sex, marriage, and social class." *McCall's* (October 1969): 31–32. Reprinted by permission of William Simon, Institute for Juvenile Research, Chicago, Illinois, and Professor John H. Gagnon, Department of Sociology, State University of New York at Stony Brook.

lower-class positions see themselves as less competent, as members of an indifferent and threatening society.

Class membership affects the socialization process. Upper-class parents socialize their children to value self-direction, while lower-class families socialize their children to value conformity. In essence, socialization reflects the opportunities and expectations available to each class.

Social class is consistently related to fathers' values for children: the higher their class position, the more highly they value self-direction and the less highly they value conformity to externally imposed standards. This is true regardless of the age and sex of the children—even though age and sex are related to fathers' values. Moreover, the relationship is much the same in all segments of the society— regardless of race, religion, national background, region. . . . In short, despite the heterogeneity of American society, the relationship of social class to fathers' values is remarkably pervasive and consistent.

The implications are impressive. In this exceptionally diverse society . . . social class stands out as more important for men's values than does any other line of demarcation, unaffected by all the rest of them, and apparently more important than all of them together. (Kohn, 1977: 71–72)

For working men, conforming means to have a job; lack of conformity is a threat to one's job, and consequently a threat to oneself and the livelihood of one's family. We can see, then, that the life styles of different social classes are a reflection of their values and behavior, which in turn expresses their condition in the social struc-

Poverty in the United States

In the post–World War II affluence of American society, little attention was given to the poor. Hidden in segregated housing and in rural regions, this inarticulate group was largely ignored. The work of Lewis Coser (1965), Michael Harrington (1962), and others called dramatic attention to the large number of Americans living in poverty, for whom the future held little promise of social and material well-being.

Poverty is relative; the poor in the United States, compared to the poor in India or other developing societies, are not poor. But as Americans, their standard of living is judged relative to other Americans. Compared to the general affluence of the majority of the population, the poor are deprived, unable to afford the standard measure of well-being in housing, consumption, health, and so on. Americans believe that the United States, more than any other society in the world, offers unique opportunities to those who are willing to work hard and strive for a better life. The rags-to-riches stories and the Horatio Alger myth in which hard work is always rewarded have dominated our thinking. They have led to the belief and conviction among vast segments of the American public that the poor deserve to be poor because they are lazy and indolent. Many believe that the poor would rather depend on public handouts than engage in useful work. Many people also believe that only the black are poor, and that vast sums of public funds, or "our taxes," are handed out to blacks and other minorities.

The available data, however, show that the beliefs about the poor are no less erroneous than the Horatio Alger myths. Poverty in the United States is structural, caused by the nature of our economic system. In some regions of the country, such as the South, it is a consequence of low levels of economic development. Indeed, in the South the likelihood of a family being poor is twice as high as in the remainder of the country (Williams, 1970). The poor are not indigenous to the South, however. The poor are to be found in Appalachia, California, Wisconsin, and Missouri. The poor are not people who reject work; the poor are the subsistence farm worker, the unskilled worker replaced by automation, the unemployed due to closed factories, the old, mothers with dependent children, and the young high school "dropout."

The Swedish social economist Gunnar Myrdal was the first in modern times to note that poor people can become so isolated from the social institutions of society that they become what he called an *underclass*. Myrdal wrote of a rural and urban underclass cut off from society, its members lacking "the education and the skills and other personality traits they need in order to become effectively in demand in the modern economy." They were, he feared, "superfluous" (cited in Auletta, 1981: 91). Estimates vary as to the size of the underclass, but one informed figure is about 45 percent of those below the government's poverty level. These are people who are unlikely ever to escape poverty because they lack the needed skills or motivation; because they are old or disabled; because they are mentally ill; because they are female heads of families who must care for children rather than work; or because there are simply no jobs for them (Auletta, 1981: 95). In a sense, the underclass represents the cumulative effect of structural factors—like racism, sexism, and economic policies—that create disadvantage year after year for certain groups.

Among the poor, as noted above, certain groups are especially visible. Female-headed households constitute one major group. In 1980, 32.7 percent of such households had an income below the poverty line; 50 percent of children in female-headed households were poor (Waite, 1981: 32). According to the Bureau of the Census (1981), 10 million children live in poverty, and the majority depend on welfare assistance. Minorities are overrepresented among the poor relative to their proportion in the population, but the majority of the poor are white. In 1980, 19.7 million people below the poverty line were white; 8.6 million were black, and 3.5 million were of Spanish origin (Bureau of the Census, 1981: 3–4). Thirteen percent of all people over the age of 65 are poor.

Much has been said about people on welfare: they are chiselers; they do not want to work; they could manage without assistance; and so on. But as the research by Goodwin (1972), sociologists Jennie McIntyre and Janet Schwartz (1973), and others has demonstrated, welfare mothers are as eager to work as other self-respecting Americans. The poor, and especially the underclass, suffer most from structural causes of poverty, not from lack of motivation. Americans tend to have contradictory views regarding entitlement to federal subsidies. Provisions made available to the affluent and very rich in the form of deductions from taxable income are considered a legitimate right. Americans seldom, if ever, question why the pleasure of home ownership should be rewarded by a subsidy from the Federal Government in the form of a tax deduction on mortgage payments. Few raise questions of why capital gains should be taxed only at 20 percent. It is worth noting that those with incomes of $1 million per year receive 82 percent of this income from capital gains (Turner, 1976: 142).

People who receive some form of public assistance are seen as unworthy, an example of undeserved support. Americans are appalled to find that a Ms. Dow has been given a few dollars more than she should receive in her welfare allotment; she is promptly branded a "cheat," and the photograph of Ms. Dow is displayed in the newspaper for all to see. But it is rare for Americans to be treated to a photograph in the newspaper of a tobacco farmer receiving a government subsidy (welfare) for a product labeled "dangerous to your health." Defense industries have "cost overruns" that are promptly taken care of in the name of national defense and never labeled government handouts.

The cumbersome procedures of checking and rechecking welfare recipients have not shaken the belief that they are cheating, and that they do not deserve assistance. Mrs. Paula Hawkins ran successfully for the U.S. Senate in 1980 on a platform of "weeding out" welfare chiselers. How many such chiselers there were in the state of Florida was apparently not important. On the other hand, might we not wonder whether she would have been equally successful in the quest for a Senate seat had she run on a platform of weeding out those who "chisel" or underreport on their income tax? Our ideology of equality is based on the belief that each individual has the opportunity to earn a livelihood, or even become rich. It is easy to assume that failure to support oneself or one's family is a personal failure. Indeed, research by sociologists Joan Huber and William Form (1973) has shown that the majority of (white) rich Americans, and 50 percent of middle-class Americans, believe that regardless of parental wealth, everyone has an equal opportunity to become rich. If this were true, it would have to be possible for persons born into poor families to move up in the social class structure. The next section will examine these opportunities.

SOCIAL MOBILITY

Every complex society has a stratification system that ranks its members and distributes money, power, and prestige among them. In a true **caste system,** a person's social rank is unchangeable. This is a type of **closed class system,** in which it is difficult or impossible to change one's social class. In an **open class system**—such as in the United States—social status is not rigid or permanent. People sometimes increase or decrease their share of socially valued resources. **Social mobility,** the movement of an individual from

Caste systems assign people to social class according to their birth, with little or no chance for changing their social position during their lives. This beggar is from the lowest or "untouchable" caste of India.

one social class to another, occurs in all societies in varying degrees. Every stratification system provides some channels that determine *how* people can move up or down and *how far* they can go. This is true even in most caste systems, although they offer very limited opportunities for mobility.

In most cases, if people move at all, they do not make great leaps up or down the class ladder. While it is true that a pauper may become a prince, or a millionaire a bum, such events are extremely rare. Usually movement proceeds only a step at a time, with one generation making opportunities available to the next that enable mobility to occur (called **intergenerational mobility**). For example, a factory worker who was a high school dropout may make sure his or her daughter completes college. When the daughter becomes an accountant, movement from the working to the middle class has occurred between the two generations. The factory worker who attends night school and becomes an accountant, however, experiences **intragenerational mobility** (movement between classes that occurs within one generation). In spite of societal values which emphasize dramatic stories of passing from rags to riches within one generation, most of us end up in the class system not too far from where we began, and the mobility that does occur is generally between generations.

Social mobility within a stratum is called **horizontal mobility,** and in essence means that no change in one's social status has taken place. Thus, for example, the faculty member who leaves the university to become a social analyst in a research organization, or the steel worker who becomes an assembly line worker has not changed his or her position. On the other hand, the faculty member who becomes an assembly line worker, and the steel worker who attends night school and becomes a teacher have changed their social status moving down and up, and this type of mobility is called **vertical mobility.**

Sociologists view social mobility as structural when, as a consequence of social change (e.g., industrialization), large masses of people respond or are forced to respond to new opportunities in factories and offices. Farm workers may become blue-collar workers, and blue-collar workers may move into white-collar jobs. New technology provides opportunities for urban groups with the proper education to move into professional and technical positions. Structural mobility does not, however, mean that a society has become more egalitarian, offering equal opportunities to all groups in society. Most mobility in industrial societies has been of a structural nature, and it has not occurred because opportunities have become more equalized.

Mobility Studies

Upward mobility. Studies in social mobility have generally focused on the movement or lack of movement from one class to another between generations or within a generation, i.e., from the working class to the middle class, or from unskilled and semi-skilled jobs to upper level positions. The general image of the social stratification system that emerges from studies done from early in the 1920s to the present is of a relatively stable system with only modest shifts from one class to another. Lynd and Lynd (1929), in their study of Muncie, Indiana, found that the chances of working-class persons moving into supervisory jobs were small at best. Lipset and Bendix (1964), Warner and Abegglan (1955), and Kahl (1961), found that the proportion of business leaders whose social origin was of skilled or unskilled work was small: only 10 percent among the business leaders in the Lipset and Bendix study came from the working class; 18 percent of business executives in the Kahl study came from the working class; about 15 percent of the business leaders in the Warner and Abegglan study were from working-class origins. As sociologist Melvin Tumin (1967) noted, there were few if any differences in how "open" or "closed" the system of social stratification in the United States was in 1940 or 1910. Social mobility in the United States has remained relatively unchanged; there were and continue to be opportunities to move up—or down—but the opportunities are generally small.

More recent studies examine social mobility and **status attainment.** Status attainment research, pioneered by sociologists Peter Blau and Otis Dudley Duncan (1967), focuses on the process through which individuals attain a specific position, i.e., the degree to which "the circumstances of birth . . . condition subsequent status," and the effect of attained status at a particular stage of the life cycle on subsequent status attainment (Blau and Duncan, 1967: 163). Based on a representative sample of 20,700 men between the ages of 18 and 64, Blau and Duncan tried to determine which factors were most important in the life cycle of an individual, and the degree of influence of each factor on subsequent status attainment. Some of their basic findings suggest that status attainment of males is a combination of ascribed and achieved factors. The education and occupation of the father exert an influence on the educational attainment of the son. The education achieved by the son determines the nature of his first job and subsequent jobs as well, although the influence of the father on the first job remains important.

Sons of self-employed fathers—independent professionals, proprietors, and farmers—show high levels of occupational inheritance. Other factors contributing to status attainment include race (white men achieved higher status than black men regardless of education); urban residence; and family size and birth order. Men from smaller families achieved higher socioeconomic status than men from large families, and the oldest and youngest child tend to have a higher socioeconomic status than middle children. Blau and Duncan show that social mobility in the United States is not of a Horatio Alger variety. Social mobility consists of small steps, generally within a specific category (i.e., white-collar, blue-collar, and farm work).

Other studies on status attainment were conducted by Hauser and Featherman (1978), and Jencks et al. (1979). Education, family background, cognitive skills, racial and ethnic background, social class origin, urban residence, and a number of other factors were examined. While a variety of factors contribute to status attainment, family background was by far the most important factor. As Jencks et al. point out:

If we define "equal opportunity" as a situation in which sons born into different families have the same chances of success, our data shows that America comes nowhere near achieving it. (1979: 82)

Compared to other industrial societies of the Western type, the United States offers neither less nor more opportunities for social mobility with one exception: men who originate in the lower social strata have greater opportunities to move into top positions in the occupational hierarchy (Blau and Duncan, 1967: 437). While the proportion of such men is small, the existence of such opportunities provide support for the ideology of equality in the United States. Nevertheless, research done in 1975 suggests that Americans have become more aware of barriers to social mobility, especially for minorities and the poor (see Table 8.7). Social mobility consists of moving up or down in the class structure. So far our discussion has centered on upward mobility. But how do people move down in the class structure?

Downward mobility. Although people do not normally choose to lower their status positions, it is always possible in an open society to move down as well as up. What of the downwardly mobile people in our society? Some are handicapped by physical, mental, or emotional disabilities that make it impossible to meet the demands of their socially assigned roles. Others, such as the investor who loses a fortune on the

TABLE 8.7 / PERCENTAGE DISTRIBUTIONS OF RESPONDENTS ACCORDING TO ITEMS COMPOSING THE INDEX OF PERCEIVED INEQUALITY, ENGLAND AND THE UNITED STATES, 1975

Items Composing the Index of Perceived Inequality	England (%)	United States (%)
1. "In America [Britain], people of higher social class are given much more respect than those of a lower social class"		
Strongly agree (perceives most inequality)	32	53
Somewhat agree	49	34
Undecided	3	5
Somewhat disagree	12	6
Strongly disagree (perceives least inequality)	4	2
Total	100	100
Cases (N)	101	113
Mean*	2.93	3.30
2. "Generally, people of higher social classes in this country get easier treatment by the police and the courts than people of lower classes do"		
Strongly agree (perceives most inequality)	25	51
Somewhat agree	31	22
Undecided	13	12
Somewhat disagree	14	9
Strongly disagree (perceives least inequality)	17	6
Total	100	100
Cases (N)	101	113
Mean	2.34	3.04
3. "In actual practice, people of lower social class background have the same chance to get good jobs as people of higher class backgrounds"		
Strongly disagree (perceives most inequality)	32	35
Somewhat disagree	25	27
Undecided	4	9
Somewhat agree	21	13
Strongly agree (perceives least inequality)	18	16
Total	100	100
Cases (N)	101	112
Mean	2.33	2.51
4. "These days blacks [colored people] have the same opportunity as whites to get good jobs in America [Britain]"		
Strongly disagree (perceives most inequality)	15	20
Somewhat disagree	23	20
Undecided	7	10
Somewhat agree	28	18
Strongly agree (perceives least inequality)	27	32
Total	100	100
Cases (N)	100	113
Mean	1.71	1.80

* The means of each item are based on scoring the responses from 0 to 4, with the perception of the most inequality receiving the highest score.

Source: Wendell Bell and Robert V. Robinson, Cognitive maps of class and racial inequalities in England and the United States. Reprinted by permission of the University of Chicago Press from the *American Journal of Sociology* 86, no. 2 (September 1980): 325–26. Copyright © 1980 The University of Chicago.

TABLE 8.7 / (Continued)

Items Composing the Index of Perceived Inequality	England (%)	United States (%)
5. "How about race?† Overall, whites get easier treatment by the police and the courts than blacks [colored people] do"		
Strongly agree (perceives most inequality)	4	28
Somewhat agree	22	13
Undecided	17	15
Somewhat disagree	27	25
Strongly disagree (perceives least inequality)	30	19
Total	100	100
Cases (N)	99	111
Mean	1.44	2.05
6. "In fact, in America [Britain] all persons, regardless of social class background, have an equal opportunity to get a college or university education"		
Strongly disagree (perceives most inequality)	15	23
Somewhat disagree	15	10
Undecided	4	3
Somewhat agree	19	27
Strongly agree (perceives least inequality)	47	37
Total	100	100
Cases (N)	101	113
Mean	1.31	1.54
7. "And what about different races?† Blacks [coloreds] have the same opportunity as whites to get a college or university education"		
Strongly disagree (perceives most inequality)	9	20
Somewhat disagree	15	13
Undecided	9	2
Somewhat agree	26	30
Strongly agree (perceives least inequality)	41	35
Total	100	100
Cases (N)	101	113
Mean	1.24	1.51
8. "In America [Britain], a white person usually makes more money than a black [colored] person for doing the same job"		
Strongly agree (perceives most inequality)	5	19
Somewhat agree	19	23
Undecided	9	12
Somewhat disagree	24	26
Strongly disagree (perceives least inequality)	43	20
Total	100	100
Cases (N)	99	112
Mean	1.20	1.94

† Because these items appeared in the interview schedule following question on class, they have a lead phrase added to maintain logical continuity.

(Continued)

TABLE 8.7 / (Continued)

Items Composing the Index of Perceived Inequality	England (%)	United States (%)
9. "Regardless of social class, anyone willing and able to work has an equal chance to earn a good income in this country"		
Strongly disagree (perceives most inequality)	5	18
Somewhat disagree	11	13
Undecided	3	3
Somewhat agree	27	28
Strongly agree (perceives least inequality)	54	38
Total	100	100
Cases (N)	100	112
Mean	.86	1.45

stock market, may be victims of bad luck. Research also shows that being born into a large family, failing to get an education, marrying young, and having a large number of children can all cause downward mobility.

Not everyone who is downwardly mobile ends up on skid row. But in her study of skid row alcoholics, University of California sociologist Jacqueline Wiseman (1970) explored some of the reasons why people slide down the socioeconomic scale. No one is born on skid row; you have to move down to get there. Some of these alcoholics seem driven by economic misfortunes: by unemployment, poor skills, or limited opportunities. They have gradually centered their lives around the consumption of alcohol. Others are driven by psychological problems and a pattern of failure that leads to alcoholism. Subsequently they lose their jobs and family ties and descend to skid row. Wiseman used the concept of **social margin** to explain how some people wind up on skid row. Social margin is the social "credit" that people extend to each other. Those of us who are surrounded by sympathetic family and friends, whose employers tolerate an occasional lateness or incompetence, and who have some money in the bank have a reasonable social margin which we can draw on when we are sick, tired, angry, or fed up with playing our roles and fulfilling our obligations. The higher we are on the social class scale, the greater our social margin. For example, behavior that is grounds for certification to a mental hospital in a lower-class person may be seen as a brief irrational outburst in a middle-class person or tolerated as an amusing eccentricity in a millionaire.

Wiseman's study illustrates that mobility, both upward and downward, is closely tied to the social and economic structures of society. People with opportunities can usually use them to obtain resources and improve their class standing. Those without opportunities—the sick, the uneducated, the poor, and the discriminated against—have few chances to obtain the resources they need and want. Once opportunities are removed or lost, it becomes increasingly difficult for people to find or make use of other opportunities. Upward and downward mobility are, therefore, tied to the same social processes, although the effects on people's lives are vastly different.

So far, our focus on social stratification has centered on the United States. In the next section

No one is born on skid row. The only route there is through downward social mobility, the less attractive side of our open class system that also allows individuals to rise from rags to riches.

we will look at the system of stratification in two other societies: India, a caste system, and the USSR, a socialist type of society.

THE CASTE SYSTEM OF INDIA

The principal difference between the caste system of India and the class system of an industrial society is the closed nature of the former and the relatively open nature of the latter.

The caste system of India has existed for thousands of years. Abolished by decree in 1949, and significantly affected by industrialization and urbanization, the centuries-old patterns of caste relations continue to exert a major influence on the social organization of Indian life. There are four major castes in India: Brahmins, or the priests; the Kshatriya, or the warriors; the Vaisya, or the merchants; the Suhdra, or the workers and peasants. The outcasts, or untouchables, are the group of people whose ancestors have been expelled from a caste for breaking caste rules.

Membership in a caste is hereditary and no social interaction is permitted between castes. Eating and drinking together by members of different castes is taboo, which of course means that marriage is endogamous (within each caste). Not only is contact with members of a lower caste proscribed, but a meal is polluted if looked at by a member of a lower caste, and requires purification before it can be eaten. Each caste is characterized by a specific occupation; e.g., the Brahmins are the traditional priests and the Suhdra, the workers. But each caste contains hundreds of subcastes that are hierarchically organized, with each subcaste performing a specific occupation such as weaving, hunting, hair cutting, and so on. As a hereditary system, each individual will follow the occupation of the father. When a change in occupation is made, it is the subcaste, and not the individual, who will initiate change (Simpson and Yinger, 1965: 242). Until fairly recently the American South was a caste society. What distinguished the caste system of the South from its Indian counterpart was the justification given for the nature of the social order.

The caste system of India is an integral part of Hindu religion, elaborated in the religious scriptures of Hinduism. The support for it is provided by the doctrines of Karma and transmigration of souls. After death an individual is judged on how well he or she observed the caste rules: the obedient member is reborn into a higher caste (Simpson and Yinger, 1965). The centuries-old religious beliefs constitute the major source of acceptance of subordination and social psychological deprivation as "right."

Comparing the caste systems of India and the United States, sociologists have argued that the distinguishing feature of the two caste systems is that in India people of subordinate castes accept their low status willingly. Higher castes do not need to rely on power, or on such forms of social control as lynching, to ensure segregation and subordination of lower castes.

We [the United States] lack a set of religious principles justifying a rigid system of social stratification and causing it to be willingly accepted by those at all levels. (Simpson and Yinger, 1965: 245)

Not all sociologists agree that the caste system in India is as willingly accepted as some suggest. Berreman (1960) has argued that there were few distinguishing characteristics between the caste system of India and the United States. Members of subordinate castes, not unlike the blacks in the United States, are merely "accommodating" to the system because they lack the power to change it.

The caste system today is in the process of disintegration, but it is at best a very slow process. In urban areas, industrialization leads to change. For example, people of different castes work side by side in factories, regardless of caste. In urban centers, marked by impersonality and anonymity, people are in a sense forced to ignore caste status. The untouchable who was forced to remain outside the village boundary lest his or her presence contaminate and defile the community may become a cook, and the high-caste Brahmin has no way of knowing who prepared the food. Moreover the government has been actively involved in ensuring that untouchables have access to higher education and government jobs. As Auerbach noted in a recent dispatch from India, the Indian government "runs the world's largest affirmative action program" (1982: A1).

But in the multitude of towns and villages the caste system has barely changed. As in the past, untouchables are segregated and forbidden to use the water from the common well, or to sit next to a caste Indian. Their status as untouchable continues to be a mark of inferiority, a means of denying their humanity, and justification for restricting their access to scarce goods (Berreman, 1973). Large numbers of untouchables (there are 100 million untouchables) have converted to other religions to escape humiliation and harassment. In 1956, one-half million people converted to Buddhism, and more recently there have been conversions to Islam (Auerbach, 1982).

Others, however, under the impact of rising literacy, and government support, have become more militant, and they are challenging the power of the caste system. As in other societies, such challenges are resisted. Caste Indians feel threatened socially and economically; the low-caste worker fears competition for jobs, and the high-caste member fears that the elimination of an outcast category will mean that they too will demand a minimum wage.

The militancy of the untouchables has brought conflict and, not unlike in the United States in the 1960s when blacks challenged the system of white supremacy, increasing attacks on the untouchables. In 1979, there were 15,000 attacks on untouchables; in 1981 ten people were massacred in the village of Sadhofur, and 24 in the village of Daoli (Auerbach, 1982). And as Auerbach reports, the police and local authorities support those with the vested interests in the status quo. Again the pattern of alignments resembles events in the United States. The police and town authorities in the South were most often in the forefront of white supremacy movements, using their power to punish, intimidate, and inflict physical violence on those who were, as in India today, demanding their right to share in the resources of the community and society.

SOCIAL STRATIFICATION IN THE U.S.S.R.

It may come as a surprise to many that while the Soviets make more than a few unsubstantiated claims about the achievements of their society, they do not claim that the U.S.S.R. is a communist society, nor do they claim that material inequality has been eliminated. In the early years of the Soviet state there were serious efforts to bring about wage equalization, but even then, considerable problems prevented the Soviets from attaining this goal. In 1931, however, all pretensions to equality came to an end. Stalin, in his quest for an industrial order, opposed wage equalization, claiming that it was detrimental to high productivity, discipline, and good performance. "Equality mongering," as Stalin called it, failed to motivate workers to work diligently and hard, to be productive, to study, and to take one's place in management or science. In essence, Stalin presented his own views of what is functional for a socialist society, and equality was neither functional nor desirable.

Stalin introduced incentives in the form of differential rewards—social and economic—cre-

These Russians are lined up waiting to purchase goods from a store. In spite of a national ideology supporting equality and the reduction of class divisions, Russian society—like our own—has class differences that unequally distribute desirable resources.

INTERVIEW/Joseph Schwartz

On social inequality in industrial societies: ". . . a white family which moves from an 'unskilled' position to a 'skilled' position is much more able to pass this status on to their children. The children in the white family retain the status of the father, but this is not the case among blacks."

Joseph Schwartz is Assistant Professor of Sociology at Columbia University. His research interests include social stratification, social inequality, and mathematical sociology.

■ **Q.** Is there more social inequality in American society than in other Western societies?

■ **A.** Well, yes, there is more social inequality in American society than in several Western European societies. In the past and in varying degrees today, race and sex were the main variables in the inequality structure of American society. Today, neither race nor sex is a legitimate criterion for the maintenance of differences in status and income. Today, we tend to say that the differences in status and income among social groups are based on education and this appears to be more acceptable, so to say.

■ **Q.** Would you say that the differences in income between whites and blacks are primarily a question of education?

■ **A.** There are some problems with the research of black-white income differences: The question we are asking is not whether blacks and whites get the same pay, but are the returns equal to. blacks and whites of similar years of education? In part this comes from the status attainment perspective. Thus we ask if one year of education is worth as much to a black as to a white. When the question is answered positively, namely, that each year of education produces the same increase of income for blacks as for whites, there is a tendency to assume that their incomes are equal. However, this of course is not what is being measured—what is measured is only the increment of one year of education; but of course the black and white started out at different levels. The black was at the lowest rung, and the white somewhere above

the black. Consequently, the added year of education constitutes an increment but not equal wages. The returns from education have to do with the increase of income per year of education, but not the actual level of income of blacks and whites.

■ **Q.** What about the income of black and white college graduates; are they not equal?

■ **A.** College-educated blacks are closer to whites in income than those with less education, and this is also true of women. But there is so far no dollar per dollar equality among college graduates, though there is increasingly greater consistency in such incomes.

■ **Q.** Does this mean that the significance of race is on the decline?

■ **A.** Overall, yes. But there is also a tendency to ignore the fact that a white family which moves from an "unskilled" position to a "skilled" position is much more able to pass this status on to their children. The children in the white family retain the status of the father, but this is not the case among blacks. Blacks who succeed are less able to pass on the gains to their children than whites are. Blacks do not establish the social networks that whites do; they are less able than whites to get their children to different or better school districts; they are unable to get away from some of the negative or debilitating difficulties of a neighborhood. Class is, of course, very important, but discrimination and the legacies of the past continue to exert an influence. And the proportion of blacks among the poor remains higher than whites.

■ **Q.** Do you think that poverty continues to be a significant issue in American society?

■ **A.** Yes . . . perhaps we should care less about how rich some people are and more about how poor some people are. Maybe what we need is an income base which should constitute a minimum necessary, and which should be adjusted with the changing median income in American society.

■ **Q.** How much of income would that be?

■ **A.** Some have suggested that at a minimum it should consist of 50 percent of the average family income in our society, which will supposedly ensure an adequate diet, physical and mental health care, and some of the other basic necessities.

■ **Q.** Is there a Western European society that comes close to having assumed such a responsibility?

■ **A.** Most European societies have assumed a greater burden for the well-being of their citizens than American society. Ours is the only society in the Western European fold which has no "child allowance" program, programs which were instituted years ago in Western Europe. The Swedes have certainly assumed a greater responsibility for the well-being of their citizens. In Sweden they believe that any person who works should earn a reasonable amount. Their policy is one of *How can the labor of a person be worth less than what is necessary for a reasonable life.* The Swedish "welfare" state protects people from poverty, not through what is called a "handout," but an effort to ensure that every person who wants to work has a job. Full employment is their primary goal.

The yearly labor management contract negotiations are labor solidaristic. The position of the workers in the lowest rungs of the hierarchy is improved more than the position of those on top of the hierarchy.

■ **Q.** Does that mean Sweden is an egalitarian society?

■ **A.** No, if you are thinking about some ideal type of equality, in which there are no social or material differences. This is not the aim of the Swedish government. There are social classes in Sweden, as in other societies. The aim of the Swedish government is the establishment of a society in which each person has the opportunity to develop his or her potential, which means the right to a job, a decent wage,

housing, health and welfare provisions, and education.

The Swedish government has developed these programs over a number of years, and today they constitute the right of citizenship. There are none of the stigmatizing aspects of "welfare" found in American society.

We might say that one of the major differences between the ideology of entitlement in Sweden and the United States is that the Swedes, contrary to Americans, view the various social programs as a right of the citizen and an obligation of society to ensure the well-being of all. The Swedes find it difficult to understand our ideology of blaming the poor for not working on one hand, and on the other hand, doing nothing about the very high rates of unemployment that have been so widespread in the last few years.

■ **Q.** What about unemployment in Sweden?

■ **A.** Sweden approaches unemployment from a policy of retraining. Their unemployment benefits consist of 85 to 90 percent of their old salary, plus a retraining program. The Swedish government will also supply special tax incentives to employers to create new jobs. The government also encourages relocation, and will pay half of the workers' relocation costs if a new job is made available in another town or city.

■ **Q.** Is there full employment in Sweden today?

■ **A.** No, in fact in the last two or three years, unemployment has nearly doubled and stands at 5 percent today. The Swedes consider this very high, and are encouraging employers to make greater investments and to develop more innovative approaches.

Sweden is a socially stratified society, but the distribution of resources is more equal, the well off pay a greater share in taxation than, for example, in the United States. The disparities are smaller between those on the top and those on the bottom. Residential segregation by class exists just as it does in the United States, but not quite to the same extent as in this country. There are no urban (or rural) slums in the cities of Sweden. What might be considered the very worst housing in Sweden would look like middle class when compared to the United States.

■ **Q.** What about access to higher education in Sweden?

■ **A.** The Swedes believe that their educational system ensures access to higher education for all those who are able to perform. As a meritocracy, it is the best that they can devise under existing conditions.

■ **Q.** Do cultural factors affect the meritocracy?

■ **A.** Sure. Sociocultural factors seem to have an impact on the performance of the young in all socie-ties, and Sweden is no exception. But the Swedes believe that if one is really good, he or she will invariably make it into the system of higher education.

■ **Q.** Do you think that is the case?

■ **A.** Probably yes, but at the moment I have no data to support it. I hope to have it soon. ■

ating considerable disparities between skilled and unskilled workers, between those in the professions and management, and those performing routine white-collar or unskilled jobs. Not unlike the functionalists in the United States, Stalin argued that inequality was necessary in order to motivate the most talented to enter positions necessary to create a new socialist society. By the time Stalin died in 1953, the Soviet rate of inequality, as measured by earnings and access to scarce goods, surpassed that of most capitalist societies.

Significant changes in the distribution of income were instituted by Khrushchev in the 1950s and by Brezhnev in the 1960s, but the opposition to wage leveling as necessary in a socialist society remained unchanged. Nevertheless, between 1956 and 1970, the income of those in the lowest decile (10 percent) increased 135 percent, and the average income increased 66 percent (McAuley, 1979). Western studies indicate that by 1969 the per capita difference between the income of those in the top decile and those in the lowest decile had declined considerably. This suggests that ". . . inequality in the U.S.S.R. is less than in the United Kingdom, and substantially less than in the U.S.A." (McAuley, 1979: 66).

While inequality in income has declined significantly, the official sources on which the data are based fail to show the earnings of the top elite. Sociological research based on reports of emigrés, however, shows that the highest ranking military officer earns about 2,000 rubles per month; the highly skilled coal miner earns around 200 rubles per month. Professionals who head research institutes earn 700 rubles per month, and a composer may earn as much as 8,000 rubles per month (Lane, 1979). Moreover, Soviet statistics say nothing about the access of high-level officials to special stores, vacation homes, medical facilities, cars, and a host of other resources not available to the average Soviet citizen. Housing

has been a perennial problem in the U.S.S.R., and while the government has made a special effort to increase the available units, almost one-third of the urban population continues to live in communal housing. But it is not likely that a high official will have to share an apartment. In fact, Soviet studies show that housing is not only more readily available to high-level professionals, but the latter receive larger apartments than working-class families.

One of the essential differences between capitalist societies and the U.S.S.R. is the fact that in the former, private property can be and is inherited. The privileges of the parent generation can be transmitted to their children, whether in the form of business or other capital. In the U.S.S.R. relatively little can be inherited by children. Regardless of how powerful politically the parent may be, neither the father nor the mother can transmit a position to children. But as Soviet studies have shown, children of the intelligentsia tend to enter institutions of higher education in larger numbers than children of the workers, and children of collective farmers constitute a poor third in gaining admission to higher educational institutions. Moreover, children of the intelligentsia are more likely to attend the elite higher educational institutions in Moscow or Leningrad than the children of workers and collective farmers. Soviet sociologists, not unlike their Western counterparts, attribute the higher rates of educational achievement of the intelligentsia children to the advantages provided by the higher educational achievements of their parents. This includes the supports that parents provide in the form of favorable home background, and the value that they place on education (Filippov, 1977; Shkaratan, 1970). Since education is the primary route to occupational attainment in the U.S.S.R., it is not surprising that there is a considerable degree of what might be called occupational inheritance.

Social mobility in the U.S.S.R. today is less

open than in the previous generation. For example, Western studies have shown that the elite positions today in the party, government, management, and the military are held by men whose social origin is "poor peasant" or "worker" (Hough, 1980). But these positions are held by old men. The emerging new generation of social, political, and managerial leadership are men and women born after World War II, whose social origin is intelligentsia rather than primarily peasant or worker. Thus, for example, 56.6 percent of scientists in the Eastern Coal Chemical Research Institute were from non-manual families. Among scientists below the age of 30, 23.4 percent were from the higher level intelligentsia, and 46.8 percent from the middle and lower intelligentsia (Lane, 1979).

Soviet sociologists, as we noted above, are well aware of these problems. Some have argued for some form of "affirmative action" program in the form of special preparatory courses at institutions of higher education to improve the chances of those in the working class and peasantry to compete with the more privileged in gaining entrance to institutions of higher education. While such preparatory courses were instituted nearly a decade ago, they have so far failed to significantly affect the distribution of students from the lower income groups in higher educational institutions.

Social stratification in the U.S.S.R. is not significantly different from that in capitalist societies. The Soviets, no less than those in the West, regard at least some measure of inequality as functional. And while the ratio between the richest and the poorest in the U.S.S.R. is significantly lower than in Western capitalist societies, this merely suggests that a considerable degree of inequality can be eliminated without undue consequences for society. The remaining differences, the Soviets seem to suggest, are necessary at least in the period of communist construction. But the final elimination of inequality, i.e., when communism is achieved, is problematic. For one

thing, the notion of communism is itself at best utopian. In addition the family, which the Soviets view as a basic and most important institution, will continue under communism, thus providing the younger generation with differential values. Moreover, according to Marx, equality requires an end to the division of labor, but the Soviets do not anticipate an end to the division of labor under communism. In fact, Soviet social scientists suggest that the notion that the division of labor could be eliminated under communism is utopian. To summarize, we can see that the systems of social stratification in the United States and the Soviet Union are, of course, not identical. Yet, given the highly significant social and political differences between the two societies, the similarities are striking.

MOBILITY AND FUTURE OPPORTUNITY

Mobility and the promise of mobility generate attitudes and behavior that encourage change. For one thing, mobility depends on equal opportunity to improve one's social standing. Consequently, a variety of disadvantaged groups are now demanding free and full access to the means of advancement. In traditional and peasant societies throughout the world, there has been a "revolution of rising expectations." As people in these societies become aware that they can improve their lives, they are demanding social changes and a more open opportunity structure. Social mobility does not necessarily mean that social inequality will eventually be eliminated. If everyone in a society were equal, there would be no class system, and movement up or down would be impossible. Mobility does mean, however, that opportunities are provided for people to change their socioeconomic position through their own efforts.

SUMMARY

1. The purposes of this chapter are to explore three major theories of social stratification; to discuss approaches to measuring social class; to examine the effects of social class on life chances and life style; and to examine the processes of social mobility and social stratification cross-culturally.

2. Social stratification is a system of ranking individuals and groups in terms of wealth, power, and prestige. Stratification systems can be closed or open. The concept that society is separated into classes gives the sociologist a framework for understanding both social behavior and the process of allocating social resources.

3. Three main theories are used to explain the unequal distribution of society's benefit and resources:

The Functionalist Approach: Every aspect of social organization contributes to the survival of society, and the class system ensures that the most important positions are filled by the most qualified people.

The Conflict (Marxist) Approach: Social classes form as a result of the struggle between owners of the means of production and workers, as both groups attempt to acquire scarce social resources.

The Weberian Approach: Three main forces operate together in social stratification; the social order, economic order, and legal order. All three theories share important points about social stratification: it is inevitable in complex societies; it affects our behavior and the distribution of societal resources; and it is related to both change and stability. Social class is measured through (1) *the subjective approach,* which is concerned with the individual's perception of his or her position in the class structure; and (2) *the objective approach,* which uses measurable characteristics like income, education, and occupation.

REVIEW

Key Terms

Social stratification	Life style	Social mobility	Horizontal mobility
Social class	Caste system	Intergenerational mobility	Vertical mobility
Status inconsistency	Closed class system		Status attainment
Life chances	Open class system	Intragenerational mobility	Social margin

Review and Discussion

1. Think of the socioeconomic (social class) environment in which you were raised. How has it affected your life? Do you think it has influenced the way you think about yourself and others?

2. To what social class does your family belong? On what criteria do you base your answer? Would other members of your family agree? Why or why not?

3. What are the mobility patterns in your family? Have your parents achieved a higher socioeconomic status than your grandparents? Do you expect to have a better paying or more prestigious occupation than your parents? Why or why not?

4. If you struck up a conversation with a person sitting next to you on a bus, how might you determine his or her social class? What clues would you look for? What questions would you ask?

5. Why do you think physicians are ranked high on the occupational prestige scale? Do you think they would be ranked as high if doctors earned less money? If most physicians were women?

6. Do you think most people in either the United States or Russia really want a classless society? Why or why not? Would you like one? For what reasons?

Experience with Sociology

This chapter has explored reasons why everyone is not equal in our society. We have seen that income is a very significant variable in determining where people are located in society's system of social stratification. Even though Americans have a belief system that supports equality, some people in our society have more money and better resources than others. This becomes the basis for unequal access to things like education, health care, decent housing, and so forth. Those who have the fewest economic resources are defined as living in poverty. They usually have the least of everything—money, and all that it can buy.

During the 1960s and the early 1970s, America mounted a "War on Poverty." Many social programs were developed to try to reduce the number of poor people and to improve the quality of life for all citizens. The Reaganomics of the 1980s approached the problem of poverty very differently. It asserted that poverty had already been reduced and that the best way to help the poor was to encourage business and industry. This, it was thought, would create more jobs and would enable the poor to find work and get money. Module 10 in *Experience With Sociology* presents data that enable you to assess whether any of these strategies have been successful. Has poverty been reduced, and have the minority groups that have traditionally been most affected by poverty been lifted out of poverty in any noticeable way?

References

Anderson, C. H. (1974). *The Political Economy of Social Class*. Englewood Cliffs, N.J.: Prentice-Hall.

Auerbach, S. (1982). Untouchables still India's outcastes. *The Washington Post,* Jan. 3, 1982, p. A1.

Auletta, K. (1981). The underclass. *The New Yorker,* November 16, 1982, pp. 63ff.

Beeghley, L. (1978). *Social Stratification in America: A Critical Analysis of Theory and Research*. Santa Monica: Goodyear Publishing.

Berle, A. A., and **G. Means** (1932). *The Modern Corporation and Private Property*. New York: Macmillan.

Bernard, J. (1981). *The Female World*. New York: Free Press.

Berreman, G. D. (1960). Caste in India and the United States. *American Journal of Sociology* 66: 120–27.

——— (1973). *Caste in the Modern World*. Morristown: General Learning Press.

Blau, P., and **O. D. Duncan** (1967). *The American Occupational Structure*. New York: John Wiley.

Bottomore, T. F. (1966). *Classes in Modern Society*. New York: Pantheon.

Bureau of the Census (1981). Money income and poverty status of families and persons in the United States: 1980. *Current Population Reports,* Series P–60, no. 127 (August 1981).

Centers, R. (1949). *The Psychology of Social Classes*. Princeton: Princeton University Press.

Coser, L. A. (1965). The sociology of poverty. *Social Problems* (Fall 1965): 140–48.

Dahrendorf, R. (1959). *Class and Class Conflict in Industrial Society*. Stanford: Stanford University Press.

Davis, A., B. B. Gardner, and **M. R. Gardner** (1941): *Deep South*. Chicago: Chicago University Press.

Davis, K., and **W. E. Moore** (1945). Some principles of stratification. *American Sociological Review* 10: 242–49.

Dohrenwend, B. P. (1975). Sociocultural and social psychological factors in the genesis of mental disorders. *Journal of Health and Social Behavior* 16 (1975): 365–392.

Domhoff, G. W. (1967). *Who Rules America?* Englewood Cliffs, N.J.: Prentice-Hall.

———, ed. (1980). *Power Structure Research*. Beverly Hills: Sage.

Duberman, L. (1976). *Social Inequality*. Philadelphia: J. B. Lippincott.

Eitzen, D. S. (1970). Status inconsistency and Wallace supporters in a midwestern city. *Social Forces* 48: 493–498.

Feagin, J. (1975). *Subordinating the Poor*. Englewood Cliffs, N.J.: Prentice-Hall.

Featherman, D. (1978). *Opportunity and Change*. New York: Academic Press.

Filippov, F. R. (1977). Social shifts in Soviet society. *Social Research* 4: 14–21 (in Russian).

Fried, M. (1975). Social differences in mental health. In *Poverty Research,* eds. J. Kosa and I. K. Zola. Cambridge: Harvard University Press.

Gans, H. J. (1972). The positive functions of poverty. *American Journal of Sociology* 78: 275–89.

Geschwender, J. A. (1967). Continuities in theories of status inconsistency and cognitive dissonance. *Social Forces* 46: 160–71.

Goodwin, L. (1972). *Do the Poor Want to Work?* Washington, D.C.: The Brookings Institution.

Harrington, M. (1962). *The Other America: Poverty in the United States*. New York: Macmillan.

Hauser, R. M., and D. Featherman (1978). *Opportunity and Change*. New York: Academic Press.

Herbers, J. (1982). Poverty rate, 14%, termed highest since '67. *The New York Times,* July 20, pp. 1ff.

Hodge, R. W., P. M. Siegal, and P. H. Rossi (1964). Occupational prestige in the United States, 1925–1963. *American Journal of Sociology* 70: 286–302.

Hodge, R. W., and D. Treiman (1968). Class identification in the United States. *American Journal of Sociology* 73: 535–547.

Hollingshead, A. B., and F. C. Redlich (1958). *Social Class and Mental Illness*. New York: Wiley.

Hough, J. (1980). *Soviet Leadership in Transition*. Washington, D.C.: The Brookings Institution.

Huber, J., and W. Form (1973). *Income and Ideology*. New York: Free Press.

Jencks, C. (1972). *Inequality*. New York: Harper & Row.

Jencks, C., S. Bartlett, M. Corcoran, J. Crouse, D. Eaglesfield, G. Jackson, K. McClelland, P. Muesser, M. Olneck, J. Schwartz, S. Ward, and J. Williams (1979). *Who Gets Ahead?* New York: Basic Books.

Kahl, J. (1961). *The American Class Structure*. New York: Holt, Rinehart.

Kitagawa, E., and P. M. Hauser (1968). Education differentials in mortality by cause of death, United States, 1960. *Demography* 5: 318–353.

Kohn, M. (1977). *Class and Conformity*. Chicago: University of Chicago Press.

Krause, E. A. (1977). *Power and Illness: The Political Sociology of Health and Medical Care*. New York: Elsevier.

Lane, D. (1979). *Politics and Society in the USSR*. New York: Random House.

Lane, R. E. (1965). The lower classes deserve no better than they get. In *Poverty and Affluence,* eds. R. Will and H. Vetter. New York: John Wiley.

Lenski, G. (1954). Status crystallization: A nonvertical dimension of social status. *American Sociological Review* 19: 405–13.

Lipset, S. M. (1960). *Political Man*. Garden City: Doubleday.

Lipset, S. M., and R. Bendix (1964). *Social Mobility in Industrial Society*. Berkeley: University of California Press.

Luft, H. S. (1978). *Poverty and Health: Economic Causes and Consequences*. Cambridge: Ballinger.

Lynd, R. S., and H. M. Lynd (1929). *Middletown: A Study in American Culture*. New York: Harcourt.

McAuley, A. (1979). *Economic Welfare in the Soviet Union: Poverty Living Standards and Inequality.* Madison: The University of Wisconsin Press.

McIntyre, J., and **J. S. Schwartz** (1973). Do poor women want to work? Paper presented at the Eastern Sociological Society, Boston, Mass.

Marx, K. (1848). *Selected Writings in Sociology and Social Psychology,* 1964 ed., eds. T. B. Bottomore and M. Rubel. Baltimore: Penguin.

Miller, S. M. (1960). Comparative social mobility. *Current Sociology* 9: 1–72.

Miller, S. M., and **G. Mishler** (1970). Social class and mental illness and psychiatry. In *Social Stratification Theory and Research,* ed. E. O. Laumann. Indianapolis: Bobbs Merrill.

Mills, C. W. (1956). *The Power Elite.* New York: Oxford University Press.

Newland, K. (1981). *Infant Mortality and the Health of Societies.* Washington, D.C.: Worldwatch Institute.

Ornati, O. (1966). *Poverty amid Affluence.* New York: Twentieth Century Fund.

Parkin, F. (1971). *Class Inequality and Political Order.* New York: Praeger.

Pear R. (1982). Study of budget finds poor get fewest benefits. *The New York Times,* February 28, 1982, pp. 1 and 22.

President's Commission on Law Enforcement and the Administration of Justice (1966). *The Challenge of Crime in a Free Society.* Washington, D.C.: U.S. Government Printing Office.

Reissman, L. (1973). Social stratification. In *Sociology,* ed. N.J. Smelser. New York: John Wiley.

Riesman, D. (1961). *The Lonely Crowd.* New York: Doubleday Anchor.

Rich, S. (1982). Welfare cuts boomerang, study finds. *The Washington Post,* March 9, 1982, p. A17.

Rubin, L. (1976). *Worlds of Pain.* New York: Basic Books.

Rushing, W. (1969). Two patterns in the relationship between class and mental hospitalization. *American Sociological Review* 34: 533–41.

Rytina, J. H., W. H. Form, and **J. Pease** (1970). Income and stratification ideology: Beliefs about the American opportunity structure. *American Journal of Sociology* 75: 702–16.

Shkaratan, O. I. (1970). *Problems of the Social Structure of the Working Class of the USSR.* Moscow: Mysl' (in Russian).

Shubkin, V. N. (1965). Youth starts out in life. *Soviet Sociology* 4: 3–15.

Simpson, G. E., and **M. Yinger** (1965). *Racial and Ethnic Minorities.* New York: Harper & Row.

Svalastoga, K. (1964). Social differentiation. In *Handbook of Modern Sociology,* ed. R. E. Faris. Chicago: Rand McNally.

Tucker, R. C., ed. (1972). *The Marx–Engels Reader.* New York: W. W. Norton.

Tumin, M. (1953). Some principles of stratification: A critical analysis. *American Sociological Review* 18: 378–86.

———— (1967). *Social Stratification.* Englewood Cliffs, N.J.: Prentice-Hall.

Turner, J. H. (1976). *American Society: Problems of Structure.* New York: Harper & Row.

United States Department of Health, Education and Welfare (1972). Infant mortality rates: Socioeconomic factors. Rockville, Md.: National Center for Health Statistics.

Useem, M. (1979). The social organization of the American business elite and participation of corporation directors in the government of American institutions. *American Sociological Review* 44: 533–72.

Waite, L. (1981). *U.S. Women at Work.* Population Reference Bureau, vol. 36, no. 2 (May).

Warner, W. L., and **J. C. Abegglan** (1955). *Big Business Leaders in America.* New York: Harper & Row.

Warner, W. L., and **P. S. Lunt** (1941). *The Social Life of a Modern Community.* New Haven: Yale University Press.

Warner, W. L., M. Meeker, and **K. Ellis** (1960). *Social Class in America.* New York: Harper & Row.

Weber, M. (1978). *Economy and Society,* eds. G. Ross and C. Wittlich. Berkeley: University of California Press.

West, J. (1945). *Plainville, U.S.A.* New York: Columbia University Press.

Williams, R. M., Jr. (1970). *American Society*. New York: Alfred A. Knopf.

Wiseman, J. (1970). *Stations of the Lost*. Englewood Cliffs, N.J. Prentice-Hall.

Wright, O. S, and **L. Perrone** (1977). Marxist class categories and income inequality. *American Sociological Review* 42: 32–55.

Yanowitch, M. (1977). *Social and Economic Inequality in the Soviet Union*. White Plains: M. E. Sharpe.

9

INTERACTIONS BETWEEN MAJORITIES AND MINORITIES

It is sometimes difficult to understand reports of bloodshed we read about and see graphically portrayed on television. Catholics and Protestants fight in Northern Ireland. Black leaders mysteriously die while in detention in South Africa. Bombs explode in the synagogues of Vienna and Paris. Nazi rallies lead to rioting and death in the United States. And in Central Africa, two tribes— the Tutsi and the Hutus—engage in widespread bloodshed. Indeed, the only readily apparent results of such conflicts are death and destruction, and we wonder why these various groups of people don't live together in harmony rather than in terror.

A common sociological concept underlies all of these examples. In all cases, a minority group is struggling with a majority group for power and control. What at first seems like senseless killing is revealed to be a very purposeful effort by those who lack power to get it so that they can preserve their own culture and way of life. In this chapter we will focus on the factors that create minority and majority groups, and the nature of their interactions. We will look in depth at minority groups defined on the basis of race, ethnicity, and old age. However, keep in mind that the basic sociological processes involved apply to any minority group in its interactions with majority groups. For example, women and homosexuals are minority groups addressed elsewhere in this book that have had experience with issues similar to the ones we will look at in this chapter.

MAJORITY AND MINORITY GROUPS

Sociological definitions of majority and minority groups do not center on the numerical ratio of the group. In South Africa black Africans are numerically in the majority, with a population of 11 million. Whites, who number $2\frac{1}{2}$ million, are clearly the numerical minority. Yet, sociologists define South African blacks as a minority and the whites as the majority. Majority and minority groups are sociologically understood to be dominant and subordinate groups respectively. According to the sociologist Louis Wirth,

*We may define a **minority** as a group of people who, because of their physical or cultural characteristics, are singled out from the others in society in which they live for differential and unequal treatment and who therefore regard themselves as objects of collective discrimination. The existence of a minority in society implies the existence of a corresponding dominant group with higher social status and greater privileges. Minority status carries with it the exclusion from full participation in the life of society. (1945: 347)*

Others have provided additional components to the definitions of minority groups, including hereditary membership, marriage mostly within the group (called endogamy), and political, economic, or social discrimination by the dominant group (Williams, 1964: 304).

Minorities are usually distinguished by their physical and cultural characteristics. The more differences there are among members of a population, the more likely it is that a minority situation will emerge. Conquest, territorial annexation, and immigration often result in coexistence of different types of groups, and this frequently leads to the creation of minority groups. Wagley and Harris note that primitive groups usually do not experience the conflicts of dominant-minority groups. To a large extent, this is because such societies are made up of people who have similar customs, language, and other characteristics. In primitive societies there are no socially recognized ways to incorporate diverse social and cultural groups. "Only with the development of the state did human societies become equipped with a form of social organization which could bind masses of culturally and physically heterogeneous 'strangers' into a single social entity . . ." (Wagley and Harris, 1958: 241).

Wagley and Harris further note that the dominant group ". . . tend(s) to act as if the state or society to which they belong ideally ought to consist of their own physical and cultural type . . ." (1958: 242). We have experienced or heard remarks which exhibit such an attitude. For example, a school should be limited to white children only; a neighborhood should exclude people who are not Protestant; or, "it is all right for these people to live in our neighborhood as long as they speak, sound, and act as we do."

Such individual views correspond to some of the forms which dominant groups use to deal with minorities. Simpson and Yinger (1966: 20–25) distinguish six types of dominant policies.

1. **Assimilation** occurs when the minority group relinquishes its cultural and social organization and its native language and takes on the sociocultural patterns of the dominant group. Assimilation can be either voluntary or forced. Forced assimilation occurs when the dominant group restricts or prohibits the minority group from continuing to practice its religion, language, or other cultural customs. In the United States the policy of assimilation has varied from group to group. Tsarist Russia often demanded complete assimilation when it conquered other lands. Thus, for example, in the nineteenth century when part of Poland was annexed by Russia, total assimilation was demanded. Polish schools were closed, Polish books and newspapers were banned, and the use of the Polish language was forbidden. The tsarist policies were not unlike the policies of the American government toward Native Americans. The passage of the General Allotment Act of 1887 aimed to destroy the tribal organization and the native culture. Language and dress were to conform to the pattern of the dominant group. Children of Native Americans were to be placed in boarding schools, their hair was to be cut, and the use of their native language was prohibited. Discipline was harsh, and those who ran away and were recaptured were jailed (Berry, 1965: 234–35). Mexican Americans, while not subjected to a national policy of forced assimilation, nevertheless experienced similar policies in some of the towns and cities where they lived.

2. **Cultural pluralism.** In principle, the United States has followed a policy of **cultural pluralism.** Members of different ethnic groups could practice and learn their language, attend schools in which their native tongue was used as a medium of instruction, worship in the church of their choice, and maintain their culture as they wished. The underlying assumption was, nevertheless, that eventually all ethnic groups would assimilate to the dominant Anglo-American model. Gordon (1964) points out that such assimilation has indeed been the pattern of ethnic groups in the United States. Other

societies provide clearer examples of cultural pluralism, with Switzerland being the most dramatic. Subdivided into three linguistic cultural groups of Germans, French, and Italians, Switzerland provides a model of cooperation and political unity of ethnically diverse groups.

3. **Legal protection of minorities.** Protection of minorities through legal means has occurred in various countries. In the United States efforts to protect the rights of blacks were exemplified in the constitutional amendments after the Civil War, though without success. More recent efforts, such as the Voting Rights Act of 1964, have been more successful.

4. **Population relocation.** While moving a population may sometimes reflect a humane effort to ease the condition of a minority group, most population relocations reflect the discriminatory policies of the dominant group. The forced relocation of the Volga Germans in the Soviet Union during World War II, driving Native Americans from area to area in this country, the forced relocation of Japanese Americans during World War II, and the notion of resettlement of blacks into one state are all examples of inhumane population policies toward minorities.

5. **Continued subjugation.** *Continued subjugation* means the acceptance of a minority but only to perform jobs which members of

The earliest and most enduring oppression of a minority group in America has been against Native Americans. Forced migration from tribal lands, portrayed here in Robert Lindneux's The Trail of Tears, *was followed by seizure of Indian hunting grounds and government policies designed to weaken tribal networks.*

the dominant group have rejected. Some minorities are welcomed by the dominant group not as fellow citizens but as a cheap labor force, e.g., the Mexican illegal immigrant. In South Africa, the dominant group would find it nearly impossible to manage without its "minority."

6. **Extermination.** History provides many examples of *genocide,* or the extermination of a minority group. Indians in colonial America were ruthlessly destroyed by the dominant group. A more recent example of genocide was the extermination of six million Jews by Nazi Germany. In 1972 the Tutsi killed close to 100,000 members of the Hutu tribe in Burundi in Central Africa.

The patterns of majority-minority relations are seldom limited to one form. In the United States, cultural pluralism, subjugation, and assimilation have coexisted side by side for much of our history. The "melting pot" notion implied that new immigrant groups were blending into the dominant culture, yet at the same time those in power were restricting their access to socioeconomic resources. We shall examine the nature and extent to which various racial and ethnic groups experienced these policies in our society, and the degree of prejudice and discrimination encountered in the process of cultural assimilation. But first let us examine the meaning of ethnicity, race, ethnocentrism, and racism.

RACE

Race is a biological concept. But social definitions do not always coincide with biological ones; a person can be genetically "white," yet be called "black." In everyday life, we usually differentiate between races on the basis of such visible variations as skin color, hair color and texture, and the shapes of nose, eyes, and lips. But to a social scientist the distinction between races is much more complex. Human beings differ physiolog-

ically from each other in an infinite number of ways. What should be the criteria for grouping them into races? Is the concept of "race" even biologically correct?

Confusion over Racial Characteristics

Evidence from comparative anatomy, fossils, blood studies, and genetic research points to the conclusion that all varieties of humans make up one single species and share the same prehistoric ancestry (Montagu, 1972). As far as we know, *Homo sapiens* emerged in North Africa about 2 million years ago. From there, humans spread to the Middle East and eventually to the far corners of the earth. Gradual biological changes took place as they migrated.

Some of the characteristics we associate with race evolved because they had survival value in certain geographical areas. For example, skin color controls the amount of sunlight the body absorbs. Dark pigment in the skin cells protects them from damage from ultraviolet light rays. (This is why light-skinned people tan after exposure to the sun. The skin is protecting itself). Furthermore, sunlight affects the production of Vitamin D, which is related to the body's use of calcium—too much or too little Vitamin D causes abnormalities in bone structure. As a result, racial classifications based on such superficial characteristics as skin color, nose structure, or hair texture reflect geographical settlement and inbreeding rather than evidence of racial differences.

A second classification problem is racial mixing. Although inbreeding has produced some racial similarities, breeding between populations has often blurred the biological boundaries between them. Throughout human history, people have wandered, conquered, and mingled with each other. There are no "pure" populations. Mexicans and Central Americans, for instance, are the descendants of Spanish settlers and the native inhabitants. Some Australian aborigines have dark skin, but blond hair inherited from early English inhabitants. And such major events as the Korean and Vietnamese wars mix inhabitants from opposite sides of the earth. On the basis of such mixings, biologists are reluctant to use the concept of race as a rational basis of classification, or an indicator of differential genetic abilities between groups.

Race in our society is in reality a social definition. The person who had one-sixteenth black ancestry was socially defined as black in parts of this nation at an earlier point in its history. The white author John Griffin, who "became" black to experience what it was like to be a black in the United States during the 1960s, was ostracized by his friends and neighbors in Texas. In essence, his experiences in being treated as a black person forced them to confront the fact that the attributes associated with being black were nothing more than social arrangements imposed by the dominant group.

The Myth of Racial Superiority

Each race seems to have its own definition of what constitutes racial superiority—namely, its own characteristics. According to a Chinese folktale, the "gold" race is the most perfect:

One day the master potter decided it might be amusing to make men. So he scooped up some clay, molded it into a man and put it into his kiln to bake. However, while it was baking something else attracted his attention, and he left it in the kiln too long. When he took it out, it had been blackened by the heat. Thus was born the black man. Realizing his mistake, the master potter fashioned another man and tried again. This time he took it out too soon, before it was fully baked, and thus was born the white man. Being a patient artisan, the master potter tried again. This time he was successful. There emerged from the kiln the perfectly formed, golden founder of the Chinese people.

To white supremacists, Caucasians are the most perfect people—the most highly evolved, the highest in cultural achievement, and the most intelligent. During the nineteenth century, some tried to prove their superiority with scientific theory. They cited Darwin's theory of the survival of the fittest, and argued that the *technological* superiority of Europeans proved that they were ahead of Asians, Indians, Polynesians, and Africans on the evolutionary ladder. This idea persisted well into the twentieth century before being discredited.

Yet another argument for white supremacy is the notion that white skin is genetically linked with superior intelligence. During World War I the army used IQ tests for sorting GIs into assignments requiring different levels of ability, and more recent IQ tests of children from Headstart programs (Jensen, 1969) show a 15-point gap between the average scores of whites and blacks. In spite of the fact that there is a greater IQ variation within groups of whites and blacks than between them, racists use these statistics as proof that whites are inherently smarter than blacks.

It has been demonstrated that these poor scores actually reflect such environmental factors as poor nutrition, substandard housing, inferior schools, and widespread prejudice and discrimination. They also reflect cultural bias in the test itself. The IQ test itself is not, as many people believe, an absolute measure of mental ability. It simply measures an individual's ability to perform certain tasks, and compares his or her ability with that of others of the same age. However, the questions used reflect behaviors and beliefs of the dominant group. Members of minorities are less likely to find that the questions relate to their life experiences; therefore, they may be less prepared to answer them "correctly." The recently released four-year study of the National Academy of Science (Adams, Smelser, Treiman, 1982) has once again demonstrated that standardized tests do not measure inherent ability or potential. The differences between blacks and whites in test performance reflect the differences in the background and opportunities of each group, not innate differences based on race.

ETHNICITY

While a race is genetically defined, an **ethnic group** is most commonly associated with a specific national, cultural, religious, or linguistic group (see Fig. 9.1). Schermerhorn (1970) defines an ethnic group as

. . . a collectivity within a larger society having real or putative common ancestry, memories of a shared historical past, and a cultural focus on one or more symbolic elements defined as the epitome of their peoplehood. (Schermerhorn, 1970: 12)

The unifying feature of an ethnic group is a sense of "peoplehood," from the Greek "ethnos"

Fig. 9.1 / Race or Ethnicity?

This map shows the distribution of 26 types of Homo sapiens. *The relationship of type to geographic area is striking, illustrating the importance of inbreeding as a factor in the transmission of both genetic and cultural traits.*

Source: Reprinted by permission of Macmillan Publishing Company, Inc. from *Race and Races* by Richard A. Goldsby. Copyright 1971 by Richard A. Goldsby.

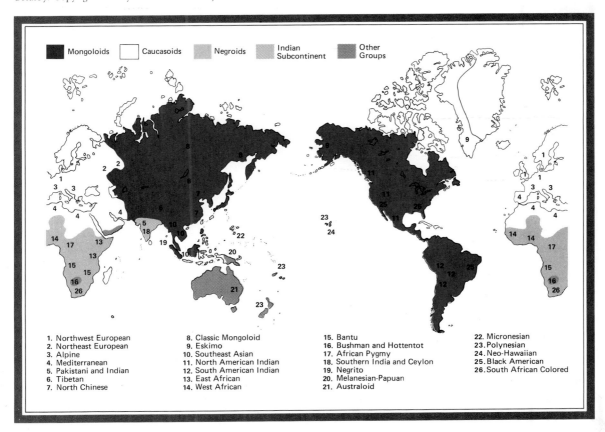

| Mongoloids | Caucasoids | Negroids | Indian Subcontinent | Other Groups |

1. Northwest European
2. Northeast European
3. Alpine
4. Mediterranean
5. Pakistani and Indian
6. Tibetan
7. North Chinese
8. Classic Mongoloid
9. Eskimo
10. Southeast Asian
11. North American Indian
12. South American Indian
13. East African
14. West African
15. Bantu
16. Bushman and Hottentot
17. African Pygmy
18. Southern India and Ceylon
19. Negrito
20. Melanesian-Papuan
21. Australoid
22. Micronesian
23. Polynesian
24. Neo-Hawaiian
25. Black American
26. South African Colored

meaning people and community. As Gordon (1964) points out, ethnic and racial groups have a common social psychological referent which creates this sense of identity or peoplehood. On the other hand this does not mean that the concepts of "race," nationality, or religion are the same. White ethnic groups were not subject—as a rule—to racist policies as were the blacks in the United States. And, as the following section shows, there are differences between ethnocentrism and racism, which in part explains the experiences of different racial and ethnic groups in American society.

ETHNOCENTRISM AND RACISM

Ethnocentrism is the belief that one's own group and its values are the best, and other groups are judged and evaluated relative to one's own group. The process of socialization generally ensures that people will accept the values and beliefs of their own group or society as right and desirable. The anthropologist George P. Murdock stated, "Always the 'we-group' and its codes are exalted, while 'other groups' and their ways are viewed with suspicion, hostility and contempt" (quoted by Williams, 1964: 22).

With a few exceptions, ethnocentrism is common to all societies. While all groups tend to be ethnocentric, not all groups are racist. The difference between ethnocentrism and racism, notes Noel, is the "assumption about the educatability of out-group members . . . [ethnocentrism] assumes that with the opportunity and training out-group members could be acculturated and become the equals of members of the in-group" (1971: 157). Racism makes no such assumption. On the contrary, it assumes "that members of the relevant out-groups are biogenetically incapable of ever achieving intellectual and moral equality with members of the in-group" (Noel, 1971: 157). **Racism** constitutes a belief system that justifies and rationalizes an existing social order in which one racial group oppresses another. The Nazis elevated the ideology of racism to supreme importance by portraying themselves as the defenders, and the Nazi state as the bulwark and protector of the pure Aryan state, threatened by the impure and polluting race, the Jews. "Judenrein," free of Jews, became the overriding goal of Nazi Germany.

The Amish, a small religious group, believe in a simple lifestyle and strong group control of its members. Like any tightly knit community, it is highly ethnocentric in its rejection of the values and behaviors of outsiders.

Racism is a concept of relatively recent origin. It is a product of European expansionism which began in the sixteenth century, but it did not emerge strongly until the eighteenth and nineteenth centuries, when it became embedded in the culture and institutions of American society (Noel, 1971). While ethnocentrism and racism differ in many ways, they are similar in that they often lead to a variety of attitudes and behaviors toward certain groups which take the form of prejudice and discrimination.

PREJUDICE

Prejudice is an attitude, a stereotyped prejudgment of people belonging to certain social groups. As sociologists George Simpson and Milton Yinger (1972) point out, the group which is the object of prejudice may exist only in the mind of the prejudiced person, and in reality the group may bear no similarity to what is imagined. Prejudiced people do not readily accept new information to alter their attitudes. When a prejudiced person states that no woman is capable of handling money, that no black person is intellectually the equal of a white person, or that all Poles are stupid, he or she does not want to hear evidence to the contrary. In the prejudiced person, opinion overrides evidence. Conflicting facts are reshaped or ignored to fit preconceptions.

Allport and Postman (1945) ran an experiment that demonstrated how prejudice can distort people's perceptions of other groups. They worked with groups of seven or eight subjects. The first subject was shown a slide while the others waited in a nearby room. The slide was then hidden. The second subject was brought into the room, and the first subject described the picture to the second. The second subject then described the picture to subject 3, who described it to subject 4, and so on. One of the slides showed a rather tall, conventionally dressed black man talking to a rough-looking white man who held an open razor in his hand. In over half the groups it was the black man rather than the white man who was said to be holding the razor by the time the story reached subject 4. In one group, the black man became four black men; in another, he became a "giant." The white subjects who participated in the experiments had unwittingly exaggerated, invented, and altered the observed facts to conform to the prejudicial stereotypes of the day.

Prejudice blinds people to the weaknesses of the groups they admire, to the strengths of the groups they look down on, and to others as individuals, distinct from any group affiliation. Prejudice is an attitude, but **discrimination** is overt social action. It is "the differential treatment of individuals considered to belong to a particular social group" (Williams, 1947: 39). Prejudice and discrimination are interrelated, but they are not the same phenomenon. While prejudice often leads to discrimination, it is erroneous to assume that one invariably accompanies the other. In the past, a white person may have refused to sell a house to a black person for fear of being ostracized by friends in the community. A white merchant may have refused to employ a black person, fearing that customers would refuse to patronize the store. A prejudiced person may be prevented from acting out the prejudice by simply not having the opportunity to discriminate. However, when men and women attempt to stop a bus with black children to prevent them from attending a "white" school, their action reflects both prejudice and discrimination.

Sociologist Robert Merton (1949) has developed a typology that takes account of the differences in people's attitudes, prejudices, and behavior-discriminations. He suggests four possible types of people:

1. The unprejudiced nondiscriminator, or all-weather liberal. This is a person who accepts the American ideal of equality of all people. Such an individual is not prejudiced, nor does he or she discriminate.

2. The unprejudiced discriminator, or fair-weather liberal. Such a person is not prejudiced, but supports discrimination because it is profitable, or because he or she is concerned with what others may think or do. The fair-weather liberal may refuse to hire a Jew or black person fearing that this action may lead to a loss of business or social status.

3. The prejudiced nondiscriminator, or fair-weather illiberal, is prejudiced but, fearing legal sanctions, conforms to the law. He or she is, as Merton notes, a "timid bigot." Thus, for example, when a law is passed outlawing discriminatory practices in hiring, the fair-weather illiberal fears the cost of discrimination and will abide by the rule of law. Therefore, while maintaining or even increasing his or her prejudice, this person is at the same time decreasing discrimination.

4. The prejudiced discriminator, or all-weather illiberal, is consistent in belief and action. Generally closely identified with a group whose values support his or her behavior patterns, such a person acts out prejudice by discriminating against one or another minority group. Such people occasionally rationalize their behavior as selective, rather than discriminatory.

Merton's typology illustrates the fact that prejudice and discrimination are not merely questions of individual feelings, but affect national policy. If the law penalizes discrimination, and if there are costs to the person who discriminates, such people are less eager to do so.

THE DIMENSIONS OF PREJUDICE AND DISCRIMINATION

Why people are prejudiced has been the subject of numerous studies. A variety of explanations have emerged to show that prejudice is not a simple attitude that can be explained solely on the basis of psychology or economics. The theories that exist show prejudice to be multidimensional. In the following section we will look at the economic, cultural, and psychological dimensions of prejudice and discrimination.

The Economic Factor of Prejudice

The economic explanation centers on prejudice as a rationalization in the struggle for scarce

Many types of discrimination in American society are not commonly known. For example, during the 1800s, Chinese immigrants were often subject to physical and social abuse. This 1880 illustration shows a mob in Denver harassing Chinese workers and ransacking their homes.

resources. Thus, for example, Cox (1948: 475) states that racial prejudice is a social attitude propagated by an exploiting class in order to stigmatize people of color and thus justify their exploitation. Klineberg (1954) acknowledges that the economic factor is not the sole factor underlying prejudice, but he argues that it is a powerful factor: prejudice is there because there is gain in it.

There is considerable evidence that economic factors do play a part in prejudice. The Chinese in California were accepted as good citizens as long as they did not compete with whites for jobs or in business. Once they emerged as competitors there was considerable prejudice and discrimination against them. White agitation against the Japanese led to their internment during World War II, and provided whites with considerable economic gains from Japanese property. Irish, Polish, and Italian immigrants encountered

far greater prejudice and discrimination in periods of economic difficulties. The attitude of whites toward Vietnamese refugees who settled in Louisiana in the 1970s was not marked by prejudice. But in 1980, when the Vietnamese were competing with whites in the fishing industry, prejudice, discrimination, and hostility reached such high levels that the situation verged on violence.

Cultural Factors

We learn prejudice as part of our cultural heritage the same way we learn what to like and what not to like. There is no need for special lessons advocating specific attitudes toward blacks or other minorities. Throughout the process of socialization we experience the overt and covert assumptions of what the proper attitude is toward this or that minority group. Stereotypes are fairly stable: some groups are said to be industrious;

Reminder Box / VALIDITY AND RELIABILITY

As we saw in Chapter 2, validity is the degree to which a research device actually measures the variable it has been designed to measure. Reliability refers to the degree to which a research device yields consistent results each time it is used. Both are important indicators of the accuracy with which data have been collected, and are critical to good social science research. If data are inaccurate, any resulting analysis will also be inaccurate.

Sociological research in the area of relationships between majority and minority groups can raise special problems of reliability and validity. For example, sometimes people are reluctant to admit to being prejudiced. As a result, they may deny being prejudiced if they are asked such a question directly. That is why sociologists will often ask several questions about a range of attitudes related to prejudice, rather than one direct question. The indirect questions may in fact produce more valid results.

When doing research among members of different racial and ethnic groups, researchers must be aware that similar language may refer to different things. For example, the expression "to raise a person" can mean to treat someone like a child in American black culture, whereas the average nonblack is likely to think it refers to upbringing. This, of course, creates problems of reliability—can the researcher be sure the same question means the same thing to each respondent? Issues of validity and reliability, then, help to sensitize sociologists to special concerns in doing research related to relationships among majorities and minorities.

others lazy; and still others stupid. The black person used to be thought lazy and musical; the German hard working and industrious; the Pole gullible and not too smart.

In 1925 sociologist Emory Bogardus devised a *social distance scale* to measure the degree of social distance, or how intimately people are willing to socially interact with racial, ethnic, or nationality groups. The scale measures the relationships to which people would admit members of different groups, e.g., English, Canadian, Scotch, blacks, Turks, Chinese, and others. Would they welcome them as fellow citizens, neighbors, members of their club, marriage partners, or would they exclude them from the country even as visitors? This very early study revealed that white Protestant Americans rejected some na-

tionality groups more than others. At the top of the list of acceptable groups were the English, Canadians, and Scotch. Less acceptable groups were blacks, Turks, and Chinese (see Fig. 9.2).

LeVine and Campbell (1972: 14) after reviewing some twenty more recent studies on social distance, concluded that there is support for a universal generalization: all in-groups manifest some social distance to out-groups. Cross-cultural studies do, however, show variations in factors associated with social distance. In the United States, race constitutes the most important variable in social distance. For Greeks, it is religion, followed by race and occupation, and for Germans the most important variable is occupation, followed by religion and race (Triandis and Triandis, 1962).

Fig. 9.2 / The Effects of Intermarriage on Races

Many people fear that intermarriage will radically alter the racial groups involved. The figure shows how unfounded such fears are in terms of changing skin color. Would you expect the cultural consequences to be more or less significant?

Source: Reprinted by permission of Macmillan Publishing Company, Inc. from *Race and Races* by Richard A. Goldsby. Copyright 1971 by Richard A. Goldsby.

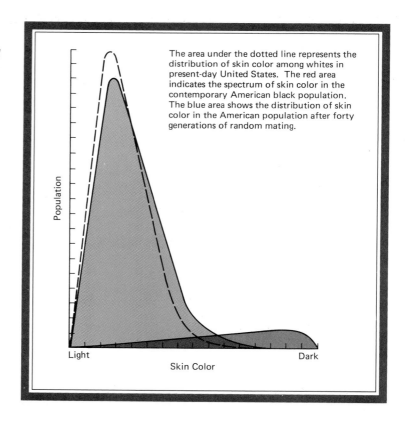

The area under the dotted line represents the distribution of skin color among whites in present-day United States. The red area indicates the spectrum of skin color in the contemporary American black population. The blue area shows the distribution of skin color in the American population after forty generations of random mating.

Psychological Factors

Psychology, largely based on the psychoanalytic theories of Freud, provides a variety of psychological explanations for prejudice and discrimination. The most common and widely utilized are scapegoating, frustration-aggression, and the authoritarian personality. Frustration-aggression theorists argue that the process of socialization imposes restraints and inhibitions which are experienced as frustrating, and which result in aggression. Dollard (1949) argued that the frustration and resulting hostility can be freely vented on a minority group. Since minority groups are usually relatively powerless, they often cannot fight back. Poor southern whites, for example, oppressed by bad economic conditions, often relieved their frustrations through hostility and aggression toward blacks. Similarly, using minority groups as "scapegoats" provides a release of frustrations when goals are blocked. For example, the inability to find a job, the loss of a business deal, or any number of things that prevent goal attainment may lead to frustration and aggressive action. Unable to vent the aggression against a frustrating object which may have enough power to be able to retaliate, the individual finds that the minority group serves as a convenient scapegoat.

The authoritarian personality theory argues that the prejudiced person is a product of a rigid and punitive socialization process. Characteristic of a prejudiced individual is a childhood experience marked by submission to parental authority and ambiguity in interpersonal relations. Such people are authoritarian, rigid, and conformist. They repress hostile and threatening traits of their personality and project them on others.

The authoritarian personality is not particularly discriminating in his or her prejudice; hostility to minority groups also extends to other groups. Hartley (1946) asked his subjects about their attitudes toward 35 groups, of which three were nonexistent: Damireans, Pireneans, and Wallonians. He found that those who showed prejudice toward one group were also hostile to other groups, including the three nonexistent ones.

All of the factors discussed above are important to an understanding of some aspects of prejudice; economic factors played an important part in the experiences of Polish, Italian, Irish, blacks, and other groups. Psychological and cultural factors are also important, and may become more important in the future. But neither psychology nor economics enables us to understand the experience of prejudice and discrimination directed to blacks in southern parts of the United States.

In the South, until fairly recently, prejudice and discrimination were sanctioned by law, which made them characteristic of good, moral, and law-abiding citizens in many states of the union. To discriminate, to deny access to jobs, education, and public facilities, and to shun and exclude black Americans as neighbors or coworkers constituted highly approved behavior. "When an individual's parents and peers are racially prejudiced . . . (and) when nondeviance means certain ostracism, then his anti-Negro attitudes reflect . . . social adjustment" (Pettigrew, 1964: 137). How and when did such behavior become part of the fabric of American society?

SLAVERY

Unlike European immigrants who came to America in search of religious or political freedom and economic opportunities, Africans were brought to America involuntarily and by force. Their early status was similar to that of white indentured servants, but by 1669 the social position of the black person was lowered to that of a slave. Some historians have argued that the ethnocentrism and prejudice of the English settlers were the basis of black enslavement. Their contact with the people of Africa in the sixteenth century showed evidence of considerable ethnocentrism, and even Elizabethan literature was marked by prejudice and ethnocentrism (Jordan, 1982).

Prejudice and ethnocentrism, however, do not produce slavery. The attitude of the English or Anglo-Americans toward the Indians was no less prejudicial than their feelings toward the Africans. Indians, however, were able to resist enslavement, because the social organization of the tribe was left intact. The cohesiveness of the tribe, the ability to organize "military" types of resistance, and their knowledge of the terrain made them more difficult targets of enslavement.

Brought to the new continent by force, having experienced the torture and debasement of the "Middle Passage," blacks arrived in the new world lacking social organization. The black man or woman was a stranger to the area. There was no place to run to, and slaves were easily identified by color. Escape—tried by many— offered no road to freedom. In essence, the black man or woman was defenseless.

Prejudice and ethnocentrism toward a people different culturally and physically are not rare, but ethnocentrism is not inherent to slavery. The "peculiar institution" as it developed in colonial America was helped by ethnocentrism, but the foundation of slavery rested on economic factors. The opportunities in the South to achieve wealth were considerable, but the scarcity of labor was severe. Slavery became the answer.

The Economic Factor of Slavery

The significance of the economic factor is apparent when North and South are compared. Slavery was present in the early colonies of New York, New Jersey, Pennsylvania, Delaware, and New England. But the commercial economy and subsistence agriculture of the region did not require an extensive labor force. By the end of the eighteenth century, slavery had largely ceased in the North (Franklin, 1948). However, the developing agricultural economic system in the South proved to be too strong a support for slavery in that region.

The cotton gin, invented in 1794, and other mechanical inventions had a clear impact on the profitability of slavery. In 1793, one-half million pounds of cotton were exported; by 1805 the quantity increased to 40 million pounds; by 1850 to over a billion pounds (Simpson and Yinger, 1965). The early rationale for enslavement of blacks was attributed to their heathen state and barbarism. It was the "burden" of the "white man" to temper the blacks' barbarism and make them into good Christians. Then, in the first decades of the nineteenth century, when slaves had in fact become Christians, an elaborate ideology developed which claimed the biological inferiority of blacks. The church, together with writers and statesmen of the South, defended slavery as a natural state for the "subhuman" blacks. Biological inequality became the major theme of the defenders of the "peculiar institution." Presbyterian ministers wrote tracts espousing these theories, and learned men provided pseudoscientific support.

In *Sociology of the South*, George Fitzhugh recognized the economic base of slavery:

Our Southern patriots, at the time of the Revolution, finding Negroes expensive and useless, became warm antislavery men. We, their wiser sons, having learned to make cotton and sugar, find slavery very useful and profitable and think it a most excellent institution. We of the South advocate slavery no doubt, from just as selfish motives as induce the Yankee and English to deprecate it. We have however, almost all human and divine authority on our side of government. (cited by Mydral, 1944: 1188)

The slave system was categorical: only a black could be a slave. Color became a sign of an inferior person and a subordinate role. While interpersonal relations between slave and master may have been warm at times (Genovese, 1974), as an institution slavery had "great clarity and consistency . . .—the maximization of profit. In the last analysis the slave was property, without personal rights, without family rights, without religious rights" (Simpson and Yinger, 1965: 88).

The antebellum South was a slave society, but the number of slaveowners was small. Out of a population of 8 million only 384,000 owned slaves; the majority—88 percent—owned fewer than 20 slaves, and most fewer than 5 (Franklin, 1948: 27). Thus, while the majority of whites had no economic stake in slavery, the values of the South were permeated by an ideology of slavery. Slavery provided every white, regardless of position, with a superior rank. No matter how lowly the whites were, they were always superior to the slaves.

Socialization of the Slave

Slaveholders gave considerable attention to instilling obedience and unconditional submission in their slaves. A consciousness of personal inferiority was imperative (Stampp, 1956).

They had to feel that African ancestry tainted them, that color was a badge of degeneration. In the country they were to show respect for even their master's non-slaveholding neighbors; in the towns they were to give way on the streets to the most wretched white man. . . . (Stampp, 1956: 145)

To recognize the enormity of the master's power and awe of whites was another goal in the training of the slave.

Frederick Douglass believed that most slaves stood in "awe" of white men; few could free themselves altogether from the notion that their masters were "invested with a sort of sacredness." Olmsted saw a small white girl stop a slave on the road and boldly order him to return to his plantation. The slave fearfully obeyed her command. (Stampp, 1956: 146)

To destroy any strivings for independence, the final step in the training of slaves was to impress on them their helplessness and total dependence on the master.

Whether slaves accommodated to the definition of subservience and their own inferiority or merely played a role expected of them by their masters has been the subject of much debate. Elkins (1959) has argued that slavery did in reality produce a "Sambo"-like personality, infantile and dependent. The total power of the master over the slave led to infantilization, specifically among slaves who were the field hands and for whom the only social model was the "plantation owner-father." Slaves who worked in the manor, or as artisans, had opportunities for other social interactions and different role models.

It has been argued that this dependence on the master and acceptance of one's own inferiority are not to be found in Latin American societies which have also been slave societies. What differentiated slavery in the United States from slavery in Brazil, for example, was the absence of institutions in colonial America that could create a buffer between the slave and the uncontrolled power of the slave owner.

Spain and Portugal were feudal societies, and the church and crown were dominant institutions. The crown as well as the Catholic church could thus provide some measure of relief, and control the raw pursuit of profit. In the colonies of Brazil and Cuba the church encouraged baptism of the slaves, and church attendance. In the sight of God, according to the Catholic church, there was no difference between slave and non-slave. Slaves could purchase their freedom, and emancipation was encouraged. The law provided some redress for the slave when the master overstepped the legal bounds. Slave families could not be separated. A freed slave became an "equal" member of the community. As a result, the absence of absolute power over the slave by the master enabled the slave in Brazil to escape total dependence and infantilism. In the United States the owner did have complete control over the slave, and it was often used to destroy any sign of initiative and spirit.

Although the history of American blacks has often been one of exploitation and exclusion, they have fought hard for opportunities to participate. Hiram R. Revels of Mississippi (left) was the first black to sit in the United States Senate. The other men in this engraving were Congressmen in 1872.

The End of Slavery and the Short-lived Freedom

The end of the "peculiar institution" came with the Emancipation Proclamation and the Civil War. But the abolition of slavery put an end to white supremacy for barely more than a decade. Disorganization and the physical destruction of the South following the Civil War affected both blacks and whites. Congress established the Bureau of Refugees, Freedmen and Abandoned Lands (the Freedmen's Bureau) in 1865, which was to aid freedmen and poor whites. It established schools, provided supplies and medical services, managed confiscated lands, and performed a host of other activities that were meant to improve the condition of both groups. In addition, many black men were elected to Congress and state assemblies.

The inadequate material support from the North, the return to political power of the leaders of the Confederacy, and the Compromise of 1877 turned the tide against black progress. The ruling of the Supreme Court that the Civil Rights Act of 1876 was unconstitutional and the 1896 *Plessy*

v. *Ferguson* case, in which the Supreme Court ruled that segregated facilities were not in violation of the Thirteenth and Fourteenth Amendments, provided the final touches of approval to the system of white supremacy. Between 1890 and 1910 the Jim Crow laws ensured once more the supremacy of whites in all spheres of life (Woodward, 1957). A series of local and state laws effectively disenfranchised blacks. These included the poll tax, the literacy test, the grandfather clause, and the white primary. Extralegal means, such as economic reprisals and physical violence, were used to ensure that blacks remained docile.

The efforts of whites to keep the blacks subordinate were not limited to the political sphere. A caste system separating blacks and whites was established based on segregation and etiquette. Segregation in all public facilities—or exclusion of blacks altogether—became the law. Hotels and restaurants, except for those owned by blacks, excluded blacks. Public transportation relegated the blacks to separate and less desirable seating areas. Separate schools for whites and blacks were established in 17 states. Economic segregation, specifically in the realm of employment, meant that no blacks were to work side by side with whites. Blacks generally were employed in the most menial and least paid jobs, which whites often turned down. Tenant farming was the only occupation in which both blacks and whites were employed, but they did not work together (Marden and Meyer, 1973).

The caste etiquette required blacks to demonstrate their low status. White people did not shake hands with blacks; the white person addressed the black by first name only, or as "boy" or "girl." Blacks, on the other hand, were to address whites always as "Mister" or "Missus." Black men were required to remove their hats when speaking to whites. Marriage between blacks and whites was forbidden in all Southern states, and the taboo against casual interpersonal relations between a black man and a white woman was one of the strictest, and most seriously observed by black men. The most innocent interaction could lead to a lynching (Marden and Meyer, 1973).

Blacks in the North

Slavery was abolished in the North almost a century before the Emancipation Proclamation. While prejudice, discrimination, and segregation were by no means absent in the North, a categorical caste system like the one in the South was never developed. The migration of the black population from the South to the North and West began in 1915, and continued throughout the century. Blacks migrated to urban centers in search of employment. Poverty relegated them to crowded and color-concentrated neighborhoods, a pattern exhibited by many ethnic groups. Contrary to the experiences of other ethnic groups, however, prejudice led to *restrictive covenants.* These were informal arrangements between homeowners and real estate agents to exclude blacks from white residential areas. Segregated urban housing patterns, in turn, created segregated schools. This *de facto* (informal) segrega-

tion, as opposed to *de jure* (legal) segregation in the South, became the norm for most cities of the North.

Occupational discrimination was widespread in the North, in part reflecting the low educational levels and lack of training of the southern migrants. Craft unions excluded blacks from membership, but industrial unions (which included workers in mass production industry regardless of skill) accepted blacks. While there was no formal segregation of workers in northern or midwestern plants, blacks nevertheless occupied most of the unskilled and semiskilled jobs in them (Simpson and Yinger, 1965).

Blacks were frequently denied employment because the employer feared that white workers would refuse to work with blacks, or that customers would resent the service of a black clerk or salesperson. There were no legal restrictions on black political participation. However, control of the political process by members of the majority group kept blacks from achieving their share of success. There were only occasional exceptions to this rule. In Chicago, for example, there were two black aldermen, one state senator, one state representative, a city judge and a congressman (Drake and Clayton, 1945). Prejudice and discrimination in the South were the norm, supported by an elaborate ideology of racism. They were a part of the process of socialization and education, to be experienced daily. The North did not promote an ideology which regarded the black as inferior, but there were numerous informal ways in which blacks were discriminated against.

THE CIVIL RIGHTS MOVEMENT

The system of white supremacy in the South remained unchanged until the mid-1950s. In 1954, the Supreme Court overturned the *Plessy* v. *Ferguson* decision of 1896 in *Brown* v. *Board of Education,* ruling that segregated schools were

Legal action to eradicate racial and cultural discrimination has been an important force for greater equality in American society. The historic integration of Little Rock (Arkansas) Central High School in 1957 was possible only under the protection of federal troops.

unequal. The court order to desegregate schools "with all deliberate speed" proved to be a long and painful process. Resistance by whites, with the support of duly elected white officials, took

TABLE 9.1 / MINORITY VOTING BEHAVIOR, 1978

In spite of the Voting Rights Act, minorities continue to be underrepresented in national elections. This reflects a legacy of institutional discrimination which has denied minorities the education and economic security that are positively associated with voting.

Voters	Percent of Persons Reporting They Voted
Male	46.6
Female	45.3
White	47.3
Black	37.2
Hispanic*	23.5

* Many Hispanics are not citizens, so they are not eligible to vote.
Source: U.S. Bureau of the Census, *Statistical Abstract of the United States: 1980*, Washington, D.C., p. 520.

a variety of forms. These ranged from closing schools and creating "private white academies," to violence. These events helped to stimulate the Civil Rights movement in the 1960s.

The protest expressed in the Civil Rights movement culminated in two major pieces of legislation. The Civil Rights Act of 1964 outlawed discrimination in public accommodations and employment, and the 1965 Voting Rights Act provided federal support to ensure the franchise to blacks in the South (see Table 9.1). Federal legislation did not, however, end the movement. Riots in Los Angeles, Detroit, New York, Newark, Washington, D.C., and numerous other cities shattered the belief that the South was the only region in the nation where blacks suffered the indignities brought by discrimination.

The assassination of the civil rights leader Dr. Martin Luther King, Jr., in April 1968 led to some of the most significant urban riots in the nation. The Kerner Commission appointed by President Johnson to investigate and explain the riots concluded "that our nation is moving toward two societies, one black, one white—separate and unequal . . ." (1968). The Commission warned of increasing polarization between blacks and whites, and "the destruction of basic democratic values."

The legislation of 1964 and 1965 addressed the issue of discrimination and the denial of the rights of citizenship to black Americans. The new laws enabled the black person in the South to ride in the front of the bus, to eat in a "white" restaurant, and to ask for a room in an expensive and prestigious hotel. Yet these newly gained rights, however immense their significance, did not address other aspects of institutional discrimination, as is illustrated in Table 9.2. A "War on Poverty" was declared and was directed under the auspices of the Office of Economic Opportunity (OEO). Such programs as the Job Corps, Community Action, Headstart, Neighborhood Youth Corps, Upward Bound, and Vista emerged to ensure and facilitate the well-being of all Americans, blacks and whites.

"Affirmative Action" programs were instituted in the late 1960s to cope with past discrim-inatory practices and to challenge institutional discrimination. These regulations required major government contractors and subcontractors to demonstrate that specific efforts had been made to ensure the employment of minority groups. Institutional discrimination need not mean that there is a specific policy of excluding blacks from jobs, decent housing, or an adequate education. Previous patterns can be perpetuated by continuing practices from the past. Thus for example, if a trade union has a policy to hire for apprentice jobs only those who have a relative who is a member of the union, obviously blacks who have been excluded from union membership are not going to have such relatives. Consequently no blacks will be found in the apprentice program, and no blacks in skilled jobs. If a company has traditionally directed blacks to unskilled jobs, or women to clerical jobs, it is not likely that the company will suddenly deem it proper to change this pattern. Affirmative action was designed to prevent such tracking by requiring the company

TABLE 9.2 / MINORITIES IN CONGRESS, 1969–1979

The impact of institutional discrimination continues to be felt in the political process. Despite the fact that women make up slightly more than half the total population, and blacks over twelve percent, both groups continue to be dramatically underrepresented in Congress. This, of course, continues to disadvantage these groups in the societal decision-making processes.

Chamber of Congress and Year	Number				
	Male	Female	White	Black	Other
Representatives					
1969	425	10	424	9	2
1973	419	14	416	15	2
1977	417	18	417	16	2
1979	417	16	414	16	2
Senators					
1969	99	1	97	1	2
1973	100	—	97	1	2
1977	100	—	96	1	3
1979	99	1	98	—	2

Source: U.S. Bureau of the Census, *Statistical Abstract of the United States: 1980*, Washington, D.C., p. 511.

or organization to demonstrate that if equally qualified blacks (or other minorities) and whites applied for such jobs, the minority person would be hired.

These programs created a great deal of controversy. Accusations of quota systems, something contrary to the American creed of equal opportunity, were common (Glazer, 1978). Complaints of government harassment of firms that had hired few or no minorities were widespread. In the case of *Weber* v. *Kaiser Aluminum*, Brian Weber, a white worker, challenged the company's Affirmative Action Plan. He contended that the training program which reserved half of its places for blacks constituted reverse discrimination. The Supreme Court ruled that there was no discrimination, and Weber was not entitled to enroll in the program which was set up voluntarily between the trade union and the company. Does the Weber case mean reverse discrimination? The Kaiser company began to hire unskilled blacks in 1969, but a decade later there were still no black workers in skilled jobs. Given the seniority system and past discrimination, a black worker could rarely, if ever, achieve skilled status. In essence, the existing system left black workers perpetually in low paid and unskilled occupations. The agreement was an attempt to alter that discriminatory system.

THE BLACK AMERICAN TODAY

Blacks no longer face obvious discriminatory policies of exclusion. The proportion of middle-class blacks has increased: close to 20 percent of black families in 1980 earned over $25,000 per year. The proportion of high school graduates in 1979 who entered college was almost the same for blacks and whites: 11.9 percent and 12.5 percent respectively. A shift of black middle-class families to the suburbs has occurred and a substantial increase in black workers in skilled jobs—a function of Affirmative Action Programs—has taken place.

The proportion of blacks in managerial and professional positions remains small, but there has been an increase between 1969 and 1979. Many of these jobs are in the public sector, but there has been some change in the private sector as well (Wilson, 1978: 171). According to Kanter and Steiner (1980), the proportion of blacks in managerial and professional positions has increased from 2 to 4 percent in management, and from 3.5 to 6.5 percent in the professions.

In spite of these improvements, however, blacks generally continue to suffer in the workplace. The national rate of unemployment in January 1982 was 8.9 percent, but for blacks the

Despite a shift of blacks to middle-class suburbs and an increase in the number of blacks holding skilled jobs, the majority of blacks continue to suffer in the workplace, with a higher national rate of unemployment and a lower median income than those of their white counterparts.

rate of unemployment was 17.4 percent. The unemployment rate for nonwhite teenagers was 39.6 percent, and for the nonwhite age group between 20 and 24 years the rate was 30.8 percent for men and 26 percent for women (Robbins, 1982). Black median income has declined from 61 percent of white income in 1970 to 59 percent in 1979. Whites under the age of 24 without a high school education are more likely to have a job than blacks with a high school education.

Many of the programs instituted in the past two decades that enabled blacks to change their status are in the process of being changed or eliminated (see Table 9.3 for an example in sociology). Busing as a means of integrating school systems has, under the pressure of some senators and with the support of the Reagan administration, been practically eliminated. A U.S. Assistant Attorney General for Civil Rights stated recently: "We are not going to compel children who don't choose to have an integrated

TABLE 9.3 / SOCIOLOGY AND MINORITY SUPPORT

Sociology has a commitment to increasing opportunities for minority scholars within the discipline. It has a minority fellows program to provide financial support for students in doctoral programs. Much of the funding for this program comes from government grants, which have recently been cut back due to a changing national climate regarding civil rights. The results show in the declining number of minority students able to be supported in sociology.

	Distribution of Fellows by Year of Appointment, Race/Ethnicity, and Sex									
	Black		Hispanic		Asian		Nat Am		Total	Total
Year	M	F	M	F	M	F	M	F	New	Supported*
1974–75	5	5	5	1	0	2	3	0	21	21
1975–76	4	12	6	3	2	0	2	0	29	49
1976–77	13	15	9	0	2	1	1	1	42	82
1977–78	7	9	5	6	3	4	0	0	34	80
1978–79	2	3	7	1	2	0	3	0	18	71
1979–80	1	5	3	2	0	3	0	0	14	67
1980–81	2	2	2	0	2	0	2	0	10	69
1981–82	2	3	3	0	1	1	0	1	11	62
TOTAL	36	54	40	13	12	11	11	2	179	

* New and old awardees minus withdrawals and terminations.
Source: American Sociological Association, *Footnotes* 10, no. 2 (February 1982): 3.

education to have one" (cited by Robert Pear, *The New York Times,* Dec. 14, 1981, p. 21). The extension of the 1964 Voting Rights Act has been endorsed by President Reagan, although with some modification. The President would like the act changed to focus on the "intent" to discriminate, not the physical denial of the right to vote. Legal professionals have argued that intent is extremely hard to prove, and the result would be to weaken the program. In January 1982, President Reagan revoked the 12-year-old policy of withholding federal tax-exempt status from private schools that discriminate against blacks. Only very strong criticism by blacks and whites led the president to state that he plans to ask for legislative action forbidding such discrimination.

The vast majority of blacks have relied on the federal government to right the wrongs imposed by the states and the private sector. This experience is reflected in the disparate views of blacks and whites on the role of the government. Blacks, more than whites, believe that the reduction of federal programs will affect them directly; they believe that unemployment is more important than inflation; and they think that food stamps should not be reduced (see Table 9.4).

Differences between black and white perceptions are evident in other areas as well. White Americans tend to place less importance on material things and "social recognition" than black Americans. Sixty-four percent of blacks and 32 percent of whites gave a high importance rating to high income; and a nice home and car were seen as important by 63 percent of blacks and 35 percent of whites. Thirty-four percent of blacks and 21 percent of whites rated social recognition as important (*The New York Times,* January 28, 1982). Of course whites, in significantly higher numbers than blacks, have achieved the nice home, car, and income. Consequently,

TABLE 9.4 / DIFFERENCES OF OPINION ON MAJOR ISSUES BETWEEN BLACKS AND WHITES

Percentage of respondents who . . .	Whites	Blacks
1977:		
Favored pardon for Vietnam draft evaders and deserters (Jan.)	30	51
1978:		
Favored curbing pornography sales to adults (Jan.)	44	24
Felt country was making "a lot" of progress in ending discrimination (Feb.)	66	45
Were generally satisfied with police protection (Feb.)	71	53
Were generally satisfied with housing (Feb.)	52	31
Favored federal loans to New York City (June)	38	61
Felt politicians were less trustworthy than other people (Sept.)	59	74
Favored death penalty (Nov.)	72	46
1979:		
Approved of U.S. negotiating a strategic arms limitation treaty with Russia (Jan.)	66	47
Believed the walk on the moon was worth it (July)	50	23
Felt youths should train for high pay, not study what they want (July)	45	73
Favored taking over oil companies to solve energy problem (Nov.)	19	42
1980:		
Listened to religious broadcasts frequently (June)	26	64
Believed programs of 1960s made things better (Nov.)	28	51
Believed unemployment to be more important than inflation (Nov.)	37	60
1981:		
Favored busing for school integration (Jan. and June)	13	41
Thought federal level most efficient of government (Jan.)	18	41
Believed laziness to be a major cause of black unemployment (Jan.)	43	7
Felt food stamp spending should be reduced (April)	55	17
Believed military spending should be increased (April)	57	33
Approved of Reagan's handling of his job (June)	66	13
Believed they would be hurt personally by budget cuts (June)	38	76
Believed the Social Security System to be short of money (June)	60	35
Felt Social Security should pay full, not partial, retirement costs (June)	33	63
Preferred staying out to taking diplomatic or military action if Russia invaded Poland (June)	37	52
Felt the players, not the owners, were more right in baseball strike (June)	24	54

Source: The New York Times/CBS News Poll, *The New York Times,* August 18, 1981. © 1981 by The New York Times Company. Reprinted by permission.

when they are confronted with a question about the importance of these things, it may be relatively easy to relegate them to secondary importance.

PROSPECTS FOR THE FUTURE

Wilson (1978) has argued that today economics is more important than race as a factor in discrimination. He did *not* say that race is no longer important, or that there are no significant differences in the economic bases of the white and black middle classes. But these factors obscure the distinction between the effect of race in the past and today. Wilson notes that gains have been made by those who are employed. But the poor, underemployed, and unemployed have become an "underclass." Sixty percent of the underclass live in the urban sector, where jobs are scarce and becoming scarcer. They are poorly educated and lack the skills to compete for jobs. They have little or no chance to move from their underclass position. The major focus of federal efforts, argues Wilson, should be the economic upgrading of all the poor. The reality is, however, that minorities are disproportionately represented among the poor. Black Americans are three times as likely to be poor as whites, and Hispanics more than twice as likely (Auletta, 1981: 118; also see the figures in Table 9.5). The Humphrey-Hawkins bill, whose goal was "full employment" by 1983, was passed in 1978. It stipulated that the private sector should be the main area of employment, although the original version of the bill which stipulated that the federal government should be "an employer of the last resort" was not incorporated in the law (Wilson, 1978: 177–78).

While President Reagan hopes that the private sector will help decrease unemployment, so far his own administration's policies have contributed to the rising rate of unemployment and dismantled many programs aimed to train young

TABLE 9.5 / PERSONS IN POVERTY BY RACE AND ETHNICITY, 1959–1980

Year	Numbers in Poverty	Poverty Rate
All races and ethnic groups		
1980	29,272,000	13.0
1973	22,973,000	11.1
1965	33,185,000	17.3
1959	39,490,000	22.4
Whites		
1980	19,699,000	10.2
1973	15,142,000	8.4
1965	22,496,000	13.3
1959	28,484,000	18.1
Blacks		
1980	8,579,000	32.5
1973	7,388,000	31.4
1965	8,867,000*	41.8*
1959	9,927,000	55.1
Hispanics		
1980	3,491,000	25.7
1973	2,366,000	21.9
1965	NA	NA
1959	NA	NA

* Figure is for 1966.
Source: U.S. Bureau of the Census, *Statistical Abstract of the United States: 1981,* Washington, D.C., p. 51.

people for jobs. Funding for CETA (the Comprehensive Employment and Training Act) was reduced in 1978 and further decreased in 1981 and succeeding years. The chief architect of Reagan's economic policies, David Stockman, has acknowledged that the new economic policies are not viable, and will only increase the wealth of the well-to-do (Getler, 1981). As jobs become scarcer, the moral and legal supports from the president for an integrated society become fewer and fewer, the gains in "mutual accommodation" (Williams, 1977) become tenuous, and the possibility of racial and class conflict increase. The large defense budget may, as Simpson and Yinger note, with reference to the Vietnam conflict, "reduce lines of separation within a country . . . but international tensions give the bigot an opportunity for attacking minority groups as somehow threatening to the nation" (1965: 541).

We have devoted considerable space to black Americans, because as a formerly enslaved minority their experiences in many respects differ from those of other minorities in American societies. However, the economic, cultural, and psychological factors that have led to prejudice and discrimination among blacks have also affected other minority groups. In the remainder of this chapter, we will look briefly at Hispanic Americans, Native Americans, Asian Americans, white ethnics, and the elderly. (Women were discussed in Chapter 5, and homosexuals in Chapter 7.)

HISPANIC AMERICANS

Mexican Americans (Chicanos)

There are over 13 million Spanish speaking people in the United States; 7 million are Mexican Americans, or Chicanos. Most of the Chicano population is concentrated in California, Arizona, New Mexico, Colorado, and Texas. Spanish-speaking people have inhabited the Southwest for close to 400 years. After the Mexican-American War in 1848, the Mexican territory north of the Rio Grande became part of the United States. What used to be a distinctive Spanish-American cultural group became defined as a minority group.

The Mexican-American population has grown rapidly in the past 50 years. The Quota Act of 1924 curtailed European immigration, and the ensuing labor shortages were promptly filled with Mexican immigrants, legal and illegal. Illegal migrant workers entered the United States to harvest the crops. They have been encouraged to enter until the harvest is completed, and they are often deported when their job is completed.

Mexican immigration, as noted by Simpson and Yinger nearly two decades ago, depends on a delicate balance of forces in American politics.

Some desire low-paid, tractable laborers; others try to keep out "undesirables" or workers who depress the wage scale. In either event, the migrant feels the full weight of discrimination and prejudice. (1965: 97)

Chicanos were not only employed at substandard wages as agricultural laborers but they were also among the laborers who built the railroads and industries of the Southwest. In the 1930s, when the Great Depression created a vast sea of unemployment, over half a million Mexicans were deported, many of whom were native-born Americans. As noted earlier in the chapter, economic factors very much influence what happens to members of minority groups.

The expanding defense industry during World War II made the Chicano population a mostly urban group. In 1978, 85 percent of the Chicano people in the United States lived in cities. There, as elsewhere, Chicanos did not experience formal legal restrictions, as did blacks, but they were subject to the informal employment discrimination that was common for blacks in the northern cities. In some cases, children were exposed to arbitrary segregation in public schools, and they were assigned poorly trained teachers. Not infrequently, Chicanos were refused service in public places, and some counties denied them the right to vote. In many cities, they were denied the right to rent or own real estate, and law enforcement officials engaged more often in acts of terrorism than in protection (Marden and Meyer, 1973: 314–15).

Following the model of successful black organizations, Chicano-Americans have become more organized and politically active in recent years. In the early 1950s they effectively challenged the conviction of a Mexican American in a county in which no Chicano had ever served on a jury. They have also been successful in challenging "overt segregation of Mexican chil-

On racial and ethnic inequality in America: "The expectations of the 1960s were that . . . we'd change society. The present expectations are that the government is not going to be responsive to anyone who wants to change things in the direction of greater social equality."

Robin M. Williams, Jr., is Henry Scarborough Professor of Social Sciences at Cornell University. His research interests include social organization, formal organizations, and majority-minority group relations.

■ **Q.** What would you say have been the major positive and/or negative consequences of school desegregation?

■ **A.** The best experiences have been where it has been done right; that is, it's been done cleanly, quickly, decisively, all at once, with adequately integrated staff, teachers, and administrators, and with clear planning and full information. Where it has been done in that way, the advantages have been that many black children who were going to separate and unequal schools, which by and large were never as good as white schools, were getting better education. Also, white children who would have otherwise only heard stereotypes about blacks got to know them for better or for worse, as it were, and vice versa. You got out of it a moral victory for those who believe that people should not be separate from each other. The disadvantages are those that come out of the frictions that are inevitable when people who have been separated come together. It takes a while for them to live together. And in many instances, the class composition was quite different. So you are getting middle-class whites confronting working-class blacks with different vocabularies, different patterns of play, aggression, and the like. And in some cases, it's been very, very rough. It's hard to say how much of that is due to desegregation. It's certain that a lot of it is due to suspicion and fear. But there have been real problems of vandalism and fighting and drug use, which many peo-

ple attribute to desegregation. Certainly part of it is due to that. But mostly, it's due to other factors that have nothing to do with race. Vandalism, drug use, and all the rest of it are in all-white suburban high schools on a large scale. So, what we're dealing with is something much larger than the issues that are usually talked about. The long-term advantages, if continued as they should be, will be greater equality of opportunity and more realistic understanding.

■ **Q.** Then you feel that one of the critical elements is that desegregation be done at one time?

■ **A.** If you say, look, parents and children, we're a little worried about this, so we're going to school X and we're going to try it this fall. What effects does this have? School X is likely to be in an area that has both blacks and whites nearby, which typically means a middle to low-income area. Those people already feel put upon. And the reaction of the parents is, "We're being used as an experiment. We're being used as guinea pigs." And the other schools say: well, they're just trying it out; if we resist it enough, we won't have to do it. And it allows for maximum mobilization of fear, anxiety, stereotype, and anticipatory anxiety, and it just produces the worst possible atmosphere. If it's done at once, it says, there's no moral ambiguity about this. This is the right thing to do and we're all doing it at once. We're all going to be in this together. There's not going to be any picking on any one group of the population. Fair is fair. And, where it's been done that way, it seems clear to me, from the case studies I know of, that conflict is minimized and the education objectives have been better achieved.

■ **Q.** To what extent do you see the issue in terms of race versus class?

■ **A.** It's both. Both clearly. And much of the argument about whether it's race or class is misplaced. The question is: How do these two aspects of living interact with one another? In many instances the racial stereotypes are encouraged because the two populations are of a different class, and they would have difficulties even if no racial factors were involved until they learned how to deal with one another. The class differences within the black population have become greater over time, so that in many instances now, you have fairly substantial black populations that are middle or upper middle class. They want to be in the mainstream. They want their children to do well. They have very little in common *except* for racial identification with people who are unemployed, excluded, low-income, living in the heart of the ghetto. When the two things interact at once, if you get class differences and so-called racial differences superimposed on one another at the same schools, then special care is required to deal with discipline problems, problems of pacing and timing, and all the rest of it.

■ **Q.** Do you see future conflict as revolving more around race or class?

■ **A.** I think it's going to revolve more around class in the long run. But, I think that maybe it will be a conflict about whether we are to have an effective public school system or not. As part of the general mood of the country in the last few years, you've had people talking more and more about private schools and the like. As you de-emphasize equality and emphasize getting ahead on your own, you have more and more people saying, "Well, let's send our kids to private school." The more middle-class people do that, the more difficult it becomes to have a good public school system. The more that happens, the more religious groups are encouraged to emphasize parochial schools, which further weakens the public school system and also increases resistance to school bond issues, taxes, and so forth. This makes it increasingly difficult to have the special services needed in the schools for children who need professional help, which in turn tends to encourage

more middle-class families to take their kids out of public schools. I don't expect the public school system to fail, but I do think that we'll have difficult times ahead and we'll also have an increasing political conflict over whether or not private schools should receive public support.

■ **Q.** So, just to make sure that I understand the relationship—you're saying that essentially there are class factors involved in parental decision making about the kind of education they want for their children, and race can be one of the elements that enters into that.

■ **A.** That's one of many, and I think the essential thing that goes into parents' reactions is their concern for where their children will have the best chance in the world. If they feel that the public schools are in difficulties and too much time is spent with slow learners, too much time is spent with discipline problems, then, instead of saying—this is something we should all get together and change—they run! . . . which makes it more difficult in the schools. Where effort is put into sustaining a high-quality public school system on the part of all the groups in the community, it can be done.

■ **Q.** Well, do you anticipate an increase in dissent or protest against established institutions?

■ **A.** In the immediate future, for the most part, no. The reason for this is that the political climate has changed from one in the 1960s in which the emphasis was on equality, social justice, building strong welfare systems—I mean that in the broad sense of welfare or well-being—to an atmosphere in which the emphasis is on getting ahead, economic productivity, military strength, and where the whole emphasis of the present political situation is on decreasing the role of the federal government in managing the affairs of the nation. And we know from past experience that when these responsibilities are handed back to the localities and the states, that local prejudices and class divisions play a much larger part than they do in the national government, which has to take into account all the people. The expectations of the 1960s were that if you spoke out, you would be listened to and the government would respond and eventually we'd change society. The present expectations are that the government is *not* going to be responsive to anyone who wants to change things in the direction of greater social equality; rather, it is emphasizing a traditional, individualistic, economic-oriented kind of society. If we discover the policies are not working, there still is not likely to be large-scale collective protest immediately, because most of the people who are being hurt are the poor, the weak, the sick, the elderly, and minorities, who have the least political clout under the circumstances, and are least able to articulate and organize to fight for their interests. They cannot organize and fight

for their interests the way a Chrysler or a Lockheed can do it, or the National Association of Manufacturers or the American Medical Association or the Bar Association or any other large, powerful, organized group. People are most likely to organize for protest when they have hope for the future, when they feel a sense of confidence and strength. The people who are being hurt the most now don't feel they have much strength, and don't feel they have much chance of being heard.

■ **Q.** Do you see a shift in the mood of America toward a re-emphasis on equality of opportunity rather than equality of conditions?

■ **A.** Yes. And I think that this has been the case—the emphasis on equality of opportunity has been deep in the system of American tradition over 200 years of national history. What you have been able to do is to say: Let's put a floor under the bottom so that people don't drop into starvation or abysmal miseries of a kind that no civilized country should tolerate. So you've been able in the past to justify this policy partly on humanitarian grounds, that you just shouldn't let people suffer that way, when there's this much wealth in the country. And partly on grounds of efficiency, because a labor supply of healthy, motivated workers is an enormous asset over undernourished, disease-ridden, apathetic, disgruntled masses of people. The third thing has been that, to put it crudely, we bought social peace by providing help for people who might have otherwise become mobs in the streets. So humanitarism, efficiency, and social peace are the three big arguments in addition to equality. As soon as you say everybody should not only start at the same point in a race, but they should all finish at the same point, you immediately get rejected by the voters.

■ **Q.** How do you view pluralism in the United States relative to other Western industrial societies?

■ **A.** You mean cultural, ethnic pluralism? This has always been a pluralistic society. But it has also been a society that had a commitment to a political philosophy and a broad, general way of life, which was supposed to cut across vast differences. I don't really believe, contrary to what some people say, that there were ever very many citizens, and certainly not very many social scientists, who really thought that we had a melting pot in which everybody would eventually be identical. What many people *meant* by the "melting pot" was that the strong ethnic divisions that lead to political separatism would be minimized . . . and to a very remarkable degree, that has happened. Now, ethnic differences are *not* going to disappear, religious differences are *not* going to disappear, regional differences are not going to disappear, ethnic heritages are not going to disappear. As long as parents and children need to talk to each other, you need continuity in society. As long as people need a sense of identity with some group that's more distinctive and smaller than the whole nation, you'll have a psychological and social need for pluralism. There's a big difference, I think, between pluralism in that sense and a plural society.

Pluralism means some mutual acceptance of differences and mutual toleration of differences, even though sometimes we don't like them, but a general commitment to the same political system and a general commitment to a kind of public life. That's a pluralistic society. A plural society is one in which these group identifications would become central, so that all your institutions are segmented by it—trade unions, neighborhoods, schools, newspapers, voluntary associations, lodges, clubs, everything. All your institutions would become identified with subsegments of this society. If *that* happens, the only thing that could hold a society together is the exercise of some central authority, and the central authority is *not* likely to have the same degree of legitimacy in the eyes of all. Such a society is probably going to have a lot of political conflict. And if it holds together at all it will probably be held together by force. That's been the history of many plural societies.

■ **Q.** Could you give an example of such a society?
■ **A.** Well, most colonial societies were plural societies. The situation in Belgium at the present moment is very close to that. Switzerland, on the other hand,

has contained in its whole history, five languages, separate regional and local cultures, but nevertheless a common Swiss sense of identity in a common society. So right there, in Europe, in two industrial, prosperous societies, you have very different situations. Belgium is managing it with a very complicated political solution, but it's having real problems. As you look around you at other countries, the United States, in spite of all its troubles, still probably is better off than a great many societies from the standpoint of being able to maintain a single society with considerable ethnic differences in it.

■ **Q.** What do you see as the state of intergroup relations today in the U.S., or do you just want to project what direction you think they're moving in?
■ **A.** The state of intergroup relations as of 1981 has worsened from what it was a few years ago for the various reasons I've given in earlier answers. There's less aid to disadvantaged segments of the population. The political climate is unfavorable. The national government is not committed to minorities, there are tensions among the minorities, and between minorities and the dominant political forces of the moment. I'm thinking of a lack of support nationally for busing, the lack of support for following through on much of the Civil Rights activities of the last 15 years, the cutbacks in programs for education, child welfare, family support, nutrition, special educational programs, job corps, a form of aid and training programs, and so on. All of these produce a sense of frustration, an alienation among people who feel disadvantaged. This is worsened by the influx of refugees in Florida and elsewhere, and the presence of substantial numbers of southeast Asians. There are increasingly bitter recriminations about illegal immigration, with many labor union people feeling that the country is permitting a large illegal immigration as a way of undercutting the power of labor unions. All of these things, to me, mean a worsening of the situation. In a way, it's far less hopeful than it was when the cities were burning, because there's less sense of movement. There's less sense of

opportunity. There's even less sense that there's a crisis that has to be coped with. So this crisis is diffuse, not highly visible.

People who say social science is just common sense always act surprised when they get riots and social conflicts as the result of having ignored the problems about which we are now talking. If I try to look toward the future, there are too many things about which we don't have adequate information because nobody's collecting it, so you cannot say that we have the data that would permit us to know what's going to happen. My guess is that we will never go back to the kind of crude discrimination and segregation that we had prior to 1954. But we're going to have to contend for a long time to come with this more subtle, more diffuse set of problems that are much harder to deal with because they're not obvious, they're not clear-cut, they are invisible. ■

The ability of minority groups to organize on their own behalf has been an important force in achieving greater equality. Activist leader César Chavez has been instrumental in helping Chicano farm workers in the West unite and negotiate for better pay and working conditions.

dren in public schools" (Marden and Meyer, 1973: 320–21). In the 1960s and 1970s, César Chavez led a successful struggle to organize Chicano agricultural workers, especially grape and lettuce pickers. They challenged the discrimination and exploitation they experienced when employed by large growers like Gallo and Del Monte. Because of these actions and others, the economic conditions of Chicanos as a group have improved. Relative to blacks, fewer live in poverty. Yet low levels of education and poor knowledge of the English language remain a barrier to better occupational opportunities.

Organizations such as MAPA (Mexican American Political Association) and PASSO (The Political Association of Spanish Speaking Organizations) aim to organize the Chicanos politically, although the large numbers of Mex-

icans who enter the country illegally complicate political organization. The widespread poverty in Mexico continues to make the United States attractive to millions of Mexicans. The continuing demand for menial and cheap seasonal labor is not likely to bring a solution to the problem of illegal immigration or to facilitate political organization.

Puerto Ricans

Puerto Ricans are the largest group of Spanish-speaking Americans. As citizens of the United States since 1917, they have migrated freely to the mainland since the 1920s, although large-scale migration did not begin until the late 1940s. Like other immigrant groups, Puerto Ricans came in search of better jobs and economic opportunities. They settled mostly in the states of New York, New Jersey, Illinois, California, Pennsylvania, and Connecticut. Puerto Ricans remain among the poorest of American ethnic groups. About 40 percent had an income below the poverty level in 1980, and in the 1970s large numbers returned to Puerto Rico after finding their efforts to improve their lives on the mainland unsuccessful.

But Puerto Ricans, like other minority groups, are becoming better organized. The Hispanic population in New York, estimated at 1.4 million in 1980, is predominantly Puerto Rican, and some of the elected officials of Hispanic origin have considerable political influence. The upcoming reapportionment will increase the number of people of Hispanic origin in the City Council and State Assembly of New York (Carroll, 1982: E7). This should provide a stronger voice for the Puerto Rican community in the political decision-making process.

Cubans

A significant number of Cubans are among the most recent immigrants to the United States. More than any other recent group, they provide an example of high achievement and a rapid rise in status.

Cubans fleeing Fidel Castro's revolution began to enter the United States in 1959. Unlike Puerto Ricans and Chicanos, the Cubans who arrived in the United States came in search of political freedom. As a group they were well educated, skilled workers, professionals, and business people who promptly adapted their skill, professional "know-how," and business experience to the United States. Within two decades, Cubans have become a potent economic and political force in Florida, where most of them settled. The immigrants of 1980 were younger and less skilled, so their integration into American society will probably be slower and less smooth.

NATIVE AMERICANS

It is estimated that in 1492 there were close to 1 million Native Americans in what is today the United States. In 1871 the population was less than half its original number, and by 1890 it had declined to 248,253 (Marden and Meyer, 1973: 278–79). The early contact between white colonial settlers and Indians was relatively peaceful, since the abundance of land enabled both groups to satisfy their requirements. As the number of colonists increased, and they began to move westward, conflict increased and genocide was not unknown. The treaties Native Americans negotiated with the federal government were rarely observed. As a result, the Native Americans fought continuous battles to protect their land from white encroachment. Many Native Americans were killed in these battles. Population was further reduced through illnesses, especially cholera, scarlet fever, smallpox, and measles. Unlike Europeans, Native Americans had not been exposed to these diseases, and they had no immunity to them.

The final solution to "the Native American problem" devised by the majority group was the "reservation." Established by the federal government in 1871, the Bureau of Indian Affairs was charged with administering the program of setting aside pieces of land where groups of tribes were to live, away from other settlers. But the bureau had little understanding of Indian tribal organization or culture. The primary goal of the bureau was to force the Indians to assimilate. Children were sent to boarding schools where they could not wear their native dress or use their native language. Since reservation land was often barren land unwanted by others, economic success was practically impossible. As a result Native Americans are the poorest group in the nation. Numbering about 800,000, more than half live on or near a reservation. Unemployment approaches the 50 percent mark. Housing—in or near the reservations—often consists of abandoned railroad cars, automobiles, tents, and chicken coops; 90 percent of it is below minimum living standards. Only 40 percent of the households have running water. Few have adequate waste disposal systems. Life expectancy is ten years lower than the national average; the infant mortality rate is three times that of the rest of the country; the suicide rate among teenagers is 100 times the national average (Josephy, 1971; Montagu, 1972).

Following the model of black and Hispanic Americans, Native Americans have become more militant and have begun to organize. The American Indian Movement (AIM) represents urban Native Americans, who comprise about 40 percent of the total group. The National Indian Youth Council represents the young on the reservation. Recently, Native Americans have instituted a series of claims against federal and state governments for lands that were seized illegally. In some cases the courts have ruled cash awards as restitution for lost property, while in others they have had their land claims validated. Whether or not successful in their legal efforts, Native Americans will continue to suffer the economic and cultural effects of the discrimination inflicted on them.

ASIAN AMERICANS
The Chinese

Americans of Asian descent constitute 1 percent of the population. The two major groups are the Chinese and Japanese. Chinese migration began in 1850 in response to work opportunities in mining and railroad construction in California. The overwhelming majority of the immigrants were male, and in 1910 there were 1,430 males to each 100 females. At first, the acceptance of Chinese immigrants was relatively uncomplicated. But in the 1860s, with the completion of the Central Pacific Railroad, unemployment and increased job competition led to much agitation against the Chinese. Whereas originally the Chinese man was viewed as "industrious," "sober," and "law abiding," with increasing general unemployment he became "deceitful," "unassimilable," "servile," and an "opium smuggler." Hostility and agitation toward the Chinese were so pervasive that Congress passed an act in 1887 suspending Chinese immigration for ten years. This legislation was continually renewed. The Immigration Act of 1924 drastically curtailed immigration from eastern and southern Europe, but barred immigration from Asia, reaffirming the Act of 1882, which remained unchanged until 1965.

The Chinese constitute one of the poorer groups in our society. Chinatown in New York, it has been said, is "a poverty ridden, overcrowded ethnic slum" (Marden and Meyer, 1973: 373). Not unlike other groups, the Chinese have begun to organize. The younger generation of Chinese Americans is challenging the traditional structure of power in their community, and more militant young Chinese are seeking a greater share of power within and outside the Chinese enclave. The closeknit nature of the Chinese culture has tended to reduce outsiders' knowledge about it. As a result, assumptions have been made that Chinese Americans have avoided the problems of economic insecurity and interpersonal tensions that are more visible in other groups. There is increasing evidence to show that this minority group, like the others, has been affected by prejudice and discrimination in the society in which it lives.

The Japanese

The early experiences of Japanese immigrants mirrored those of the Chinese. Welcomed at first, by 1906 Japanese children were barred from white schools. Prior to World War II, the federal government attempted to restrain the anti-Japanese agitation in California, where most Japanese Americans lived, because it was creating diplomatic difficulties. With the outbreak of World War II, the federal government capitulated to the racist sentiments operating in the state of California (Simpson and Yinger, 1965: 92). Seventy thousand American citizens—Japanese Americans—and forty thousand Japanese (permanent residents) were interned in camps in the United States during World War II. The "justification" for the internment of the Japanese was their possible disloyalty to the United States in the war with Japan. But Americans of German or Italian origin were not interned, in spite of the fact that the United States was at war with Germany and Italy as well. In addition to being interned, the Japanese were forced to sell many of their possessions at a fraction of their real worth.

The violent prejudice and discrimination exhibited in California prior to World War II spread throughout the nation. Neither the government nor the United States Supreme Court, which ruled that internment was constitutional, seemed to be aware of the fact that racist policies were being implemented. Following the war, 80 percent of the interned Japanese returned to the West Coast, and 20 percent settled in other cities. Among the various ethnic groups in our society today, Japanese Americans constitute a model of high achievement, in terms of material and ed-

Mealtime at a detention camp. During World War II, the federal government violated the civil rights of many Japanese Americans by crowding them into internment camps hundreds of miles from their homes.

ucational accomplishment (see Table 9.6). They have moved beyond their period of earlier mistreatment to become assimilated into the larger American culture, as indicated by their occupational and educational successes.

WHITE ETHNICS

Today's white ethnics are the second- and third-generation children of Italian, Russian, Polish, Czech, and other immigrants. Generally, they

TABLE 9.6 / ASSIMILATION OF JAPANESE AMERICANS

	Visit Relatives Infrequently*		Ethnicity of Favorite Organization is Non-Japanese		Ethnicity of One or Both of Two Closest Friends is Non-Japanese		Ethnicity of Spouse is Non-Japanese	
Occupation (males only)								
Professional	39%	(359)	70%	(278)	64%	(387)	16%	(289)
Proprietor	22	(195)	48	(146)	47	(203)	6	(182)
Clerical	24	(124)	44	(82)	47	(137)	9	(95)
Blue collar	21	(139)	43	(86)	45	(143)	10	(111)
Service	21	(100)	19	(83)	31	(109)	8	(89)
Farm	21	(132)	43	(122)	39	(153)	5	(131)
Education								
Postgraduate	45%	(280)	79%	(220)	73%	(299)	22%	(221)
College graduate	37	(281)	63	(214)	56	(312)	13	(234)
Some college	25	(635)	54	(407)	53	(678)	9	(511)
High school graduate	23	(864)	37	(579)	45	(945)	6	(797)

* Visiting relatives is derived from the question: "About how many times in the past month have you visited or been visited by relatives living in the same metropolitan area as you?" No visits that month was defined as infrequent.

Source: Darrel Montero, The Japanese Americans: Changing patterns of assimilation over three generations, *American Sociological Review* 46, no. 6 (December 1981): 833.

have acculturated to the dominant culture; their native tongue is English and their values and beliefs are those of the dominant group. There is relatively little difference between the overt behavioral or cultural patterns of ethnic Americans and Americans whose ancestors came on the Mayflower. The differences that exist are usually based on class, not culture.

Ethnic Americans have retained their ethnicity and their sense of peoplehood through the development of ethnic or religious subcommunities. These subcommunities were originally a source of stability and a means of adjustment to the uncertainties and hostility of the new environment. The church conducted services in the native tongue, and instruction in the native language was an effort to instill in the new generation a sense of past traditions. Native language newspapers and mutual aid societies provided further supports to the continuity of ethnicity.

The native language school or the church sermon in Polish or Czech is by and large a thing of the past among white ethnics. Nevertheless, ethnic subcommunities remain which have been modified through acculturation. The ethnic subcommunity can be identified in some of our major cities and their suburbs: the Poles in Buffalo or Chicago, the Italians in Boston. Until the late 1960s, ethnic Americans were engaged in the pursuit of middle-class status and the American dream. Ethnic consciousness was not discussed, although politicians were very much aware of ethnic and religious groups at election time. Cultural pluralism, in which different cultural groups coexisted and preserved their distinct identities in modified form, is thus not a new phenomenon. However, only since the 1970s, taking the cue from blacks, has it become respectable in the larger society to claim an identity as a Polish or Italian American.

The respectability of an ethnic identity and the apparent interest of such Americans in their "roots" seem to suggest that there has been a great resurgence of ethnicity. Based on a study of Italian Americans in Boston, sociologist Herbert Gans (1962), however, found little support for this notion. Still, if resurgence of heightened ethnicity means an interest in one's past, or the acknowledgment of one's origin as a Polish American or Italian American, then there is evidence to suggest a "resurgence." Pan-American Airlines ran a television commercial in 1980 calling on ethnic Americans to see the world and the country of their grandparents, to explore their "roots" in Poland or Italy. While Pan-Am tries to convert the resurgence of ethnicity into cash, its efforts should not lead us to conclude that any response also means a resurgence of separation of white ethnic groups from the larger society.

Gans (1979: 242) suggests that the ethnicity of the third generation is a "symbolic ethnicity," a nostalgic adherence to the culture of the immigrant generation without the need to incorporate it in daily behavior. This symbolic ethnicity is a sometime thing, which does not interfere with primary relations with other groups. The majority of third-generation Irish, Polish, or Italian Americans are also marrying outside their ethnic groups (Alba, 1976). For example, intermarriage rates of American Jews, who have had one of the lowest intermarriage rates among all ethnic-religious groups, reached 35 percent in 1980.

Subcommunities of white ethnics are not likely to disappear tomorrow, but their future is by no means certain. Research reveals considerable decline in ethnic cohesiveness among Polish Americans in Los Angeles; for fourth-generation Polish Americans, ethnicity has little significance (Sandberg, 1974). While the future directions which white ethnics will pursue in American society are uncertain, there is little evidence to suggest that we will all become like each other. The imposition of martial law in Poland and the conflict in Northern Ireland continue to generate considerable feeling among Americans with those ethnic backgrounds.

AGE

Age, like race and ethnicity, is commonly used to create minority groups. Age groups are given different rights and responsibilities based on the belief that social abilities change with age. As babies we are totally dependent; we cannot walk or talk or control our environment except by crying for help. Children are controlled by adults who are assumed to be more mature and knowledgeable. Even adolescents are restricted in the performance of such activities as drinking, voting, and sexual behavior. At the other end of the spectrum, old age, new restrictions are imposed. The elderly are often forced out of the workplace, and they may even be removed from their homes and placed in nursing homes which govern their daily activities.

When we define dominant groups in our society, we think first of white males of middle age and middle to upper socioeconomic status. For example, in Table 9.7 we can see that middle-aged men have higher incomes than women of any age, as well as men at the lower and upper age ranges. We saw earlier in this chapter that

whites have greater social and economic resources than do racial and ethnic minorities. It is middle-aged people who are most active in business, politics, and education. They make decisions which govern the lives of the old and the young. It is their needs which are considered especially important when need-meeting structures are created. As a result, children's needs and rights are frequently violated by adults (Billingsley and

The elderly are a minority group that has effectively organized to challenge the inaccurate stereotypes upon which discrimination feeds.

TABLE 9.7 / AGE, SEX, AND INCOME, 1976

Age	Median Income	
	Women	Men
14 to 19 years	$5,205	$ 5,617
20 to 24	6,966	8,949
25 to 34	8,939	13,240
35 to 44	9,120	15,693
45 to 54	8,546	15,889
55 to 64	8,451	14,718
65 yrs. and older	8,591	11,668
Total, 25 years old and over	$8,728	$14,732

Source: U.S. Bureau of the Census, *Current Population Reports*, Series P-60, nos. 37, 80, and 114.

SOCIAL ISSUE/The Elderly as a Minority Group

Robert J. Havighurst/*University of Chicago*

Within a modern society there are a number of visible subgroups. The differences between these subgroups may be due to sex, age, race, and other visible features. Some groups are very small in numbers, but very noticeable, generally because they have a highly unusual physical characteristic, such as blindness, deafness, loss of legs or arms, cerebral palsy, very short stature, or very tall stature. Other groups are universal, in the sense that every member of the society is seen as belonging to such a group at one time or another. The *age group* is the most universal, with three broad subgroups: young, mature, and old. While the dividing line or transition between any two varies according to the nature of the society, every society recognizes a stage of childhood or youth, a stage of adulthood, and a stage of old age.

The "old" or "elderly" subgroup is always a minority, as is the "child" or "youth" subgroup. Although these two "minority" groups do not experience prejudice or discrimination in the ways that a minority racial or ethnic group may do, they do experience certain disadvantages as well as certain advantages relative to the large adult or "middle" group. In general, it may be said with some caution that youth are favored because they will in due time be the group with most to contribute and most responsibility for the general welfare of the society. And the elderly, on the other hand, may be disfavored because they no longer contribute as much to the material welfare of the society as they did during their adult stage.

In this essay, we will examine the elderly age group in terms of a number of characteristics that are significant with respect to their own life satisfaction and with respect to the general welfare of the society.

AGE AND NUMBERS

Although certain stages of life—such as puberty and menopause—are biologically defined, "old age" is not. One does not become "elderly" as the result of any specific event. In agricultural societies men and women go on with their work in the field and the home, with gradual reductions as they grow older and as their adult children take on more responsibility. Only as they become physically or mentally feeble are they relegated to a status of "dependent old age." But in modern industrial societies, where much of agricultural production is industrialized, a certain age period marks the transition to old age. This period is roughly between ages 60 and 70, and the transition is generally located at age 65 for purposes of old-age pensions, Social Security benefit payments, and retirement from certain occupations.

In the United States, about 3.3 million or 13 percent of the population over 65 years of age were in the labor force in 1980. This number were either working or actively seeking work. The proportion of men over 65 who are employed has decreased steadily from about 67 percent in 1900 to 20 percent in 1980. On the other hand, the proportion of women over 65 in the labor force has been nearly constant at about 9 percent during this century.

The median age of the U.S. population in 1980 was 30 years. That is, half of the population were 30 years old or older. In 1970, the median age was 28. Americans are living longer. The 1980 census reported 9.3 million more people aged 50 and older than did the 1970 census. The 65 and over group numbered 25.5 million people, 11.3 percent of the total population. Table A shows the percentages of the total United States population age 65 and over, and age 75 and over from 1960 to 1980. Since about

TABLE A / RELATIVE SIZE OF THE ELDERLY POPULATION IN THE UNITED STATES

	Percent of Total Population					
	1900	*1960*	*1970*	*1980*	*1990**	*2000**
Age 65 and over	4.1	9.2	9.9	11.3	11.8	11.7
Age 75 and over	1.2	3.1	3.7	4.1	4.7	5.1
Dependency ratio						
65 plus/20–64	0.08	0.18	0.19	0.20	0.20	0.20

*Estimated figures.

1970, the relative size of the 65 and over population has been quite stable, and will increase only slightly between 1980 and 2000, if the birthrate remains stable at about the "replacement level," with the average woman bearing 2.1 children during her childbearing years. The increased proportion of the 65 plus population between 1900 and 1975 is due not so much to increased longevity of adults as to decreased infant and child mortality. Most of the contagious diseases that killed children in the early years of the century—diphtheria, scarlet fever, typhoid fever, tuberculosis, measles, and, later, infantile paralysis—were brought under control by inoculation and antibiotics, so that the principal causes of death shifted from acute and infectious diseases to chronic and degenerative diseases, which are the principal killers of people in adulthood and old age.

Extending Life

The average life expectancy of American women in 1980 was 78 years. This means that when the sum of ages of death of all females, from newborn babies to the oldest age of death on record for that year, is divided by the number of deaths, the result is 78 years. For males, the life expectancy was 70 years.

The "human life-span" is defined by demographers as the oldest age to which men or women survive, except for a very small two or three percent who may live to be 100 years or more. The concept of a life-span of about 100 years is useful to students of human aging. Their goal, if they are working on health problems, is to find ways of increasing the proportion of people who live out the human life-span.

Public health experts believe that life expectancy will increase another two years between now and the year 2000. This is based on the assumption that more people will cease inhaling tobacco smoke and that more adults will improve their diet, thus reducing the mortality due to cardiovascular disease.

As shown in Table A, the proportion of people over 75 years of age is expected to increase by 25 percent between now and the year 2000, while the proportion over 65 will increase by only 3 percent. This means that the so-called old-old, or 75 plus, age group will become more noticeable, and that there will be proportionally more of the elderly who are retired and who need a good deal of personal care than there are today.

THE STATUS OF THE ELDERS

Among the Hebrews of biblical time, from the traditional Chinese culture, and from what we know of a number of simple, relatively unchanging folk societies, the elders, and especially the old men, were thought to be wise because of their long experience.

Even the English language contains the noun *sage,* meaning a man venerated for his wisdom, and applied mainly to older men. Still, a changing society such as that of the United States does not expect increasing age to give persons practical wisdom. New technology changes the conditions of economic and political and social life, and the society tends to look to the middle-adult age group for wise leadership.

Health and Physical Vigor

Studies of the cost of health services report that approximately 30 percent of national health expenditures goes to pay for services to people over 65,

who are 10 percent of the population. There was a substantial increase in national health expenditures per capita, from $142 in 1960 to $334 in 1970 to $943 in 1979, which was 9 percent of the Gross National Product, compared to 5 percent in 1960. The per capita cost for people over 65 in 1980 was approximately $2,000.

The disparity is due partly to the increasing amount of illness for people as they grow older, and in a major degree to the creation of Medicare and Medicaid in the 1960s. These two government programs account for about two-thirds of health expenditures for people over 65. Some of the cost of Medicare is paid from a Social Security Fund for people over 65, while all of the cost of Medicaid is paid by the government for people who have incomes below the poverty level.

The perception elderly people have of their own health is decidedly positive. The national poll of 1981 (Aging in the Eighties) asked older people, "How would you rate your health at the present time—excellent, good, only fair, poor?" The 65 and over group reported their health as 17 percent *excellent* and 39 percent *good,* 30 percent *only fair* and 13 percent *poor.* The survey did not include residents of nursing homes, or people who were home-bound—a total of about 15 percent of the over-65 population.

As would be expected, among the elderly are a considerable number of persons who are physically or mentally impaired and therefore must be cared for by other people. A careful national survey made in 1975 found about 1 percent of the over-65 population living in "old people's homes" and about 4 percent living in "nursing homes," where they had as much skilled nursing as they needed. Another 5 percent, or about 1 million persons, are living in their own homes, but are either "bedfast" or need a great deal of assistance from someone in the home—an adult child or a housekeeper. Finally, another 2 or 3 percent cannot go out of their homes without special effort. They may have severe arthritis or rheumatism, or they may have high blood pressure, or a heart condition that prevents them from climbing stairs.

When these persons who need careful attention from helpers of one kind or another are set aside, there remain more than 85 percent of people over age 65 who are able to look after themselves physically, even though many of them have reduced hearing or senses of taste and smell, poor eyesight, and a growing amount of trouble from rheumatism.

Employment and Retirement

The question of when to retire from employment is a concern, of course, for the individual man or woman who is employed and earning a living. At the same time, employers are concerned with the problem of getting the best productivity from their employees. Some employers have set a particular age of mandatory retirement. Age 65 was often selected by employers, and also was often chosen by employees, but there has been much disagreement about this, especially since about 1960.

Congress passed the Age Discrimination in Employment Act in 1967, barring discrimination in the workplace for persons aged 40 to 65. But numbers of people in various kinds of work, from physical labor to business employment to college teaching, wanted employment beyond the age of 65, and may of them were clearly competent in their jobs. Consequently, Congress in 1978 passed amendments to the law, making age 70 the age when mandatory retirement is permissible and prohibiting mandatory retirement based on age for most employees of the federal government. This policy is now being worked out by various employee and employer groups. It comes at a time of high unemployment of young people aged 20 to 30, and thus creates a conflict of interest between young adults needing employment and a good start in their careers, and seniors who like their work, need the income, and have good work performance.

The elders have a good deal of economic and political power. Especially the group between 60 and 75 are very much involved in local community and civic activity. This group has been called the *young-old.* The young-old people vote more often than any other age group. Many of them belong to a national organization, the American Association of Retired Persons (AARP). Senior members of labor unions in fairly large numbers belong to the National Council of Senior Citizens (NCSC).

Approximately 75 percent of the elders in America are living in comfortable economic circumstances, and some of them are quite wealthy. They may own their homes, and they have made investments which bring them a substantial income. Most of them have annuities from insurance companies or pensions from private or government pension funds. In addition, most of them receive Social Security benefits. Even if monetary inflation continues to

308

raise the cost of living in contemporary dollars, their savings and property holdings will carry most of them through.

On the other hand, 25 percent of the elderly are on the margin of poverty, or below the poverty level. Fifteen percent of the people over age 65 are definitely below the poverty level as defined by the U.S. Department of Labor. With 1980 prices, the poverty level was about $4,000 for an elderly couple and about $3,200 for a single individual living alone. People with incomes below these levels are eligible for welfare payments from the federal government entitled Supplementary Security Income. The Social Security benefit payment for retired workers who have been receiving low wages for all their working lives was about $200 per month as of 1980, and this was below the poverty level.

In addition to the 15 percent who are definitely below the poverty level, another 10 percent are just above this level, and are vulnerable to rises in the cost of living which have clouded their lives during the 1970s and into the 1980s. The American system of Social Security benefits for retired people is not as good for the lowest half of retirees as is the North and West European system of Old Age Pensions which are carefully set at a level above the poverty line, and are supported financially by the regular government income from a variety of taxes. The U.S. payroll tax for support of the Social Security Trust Fund does not meet the needs for Social Security payments during periods of high unemployment or monetary inflation. Thus the Congress or the president and his advisers must find ways of meeting the Social Security costs. This is bothersome to all the groups involved, those who receive payments, and the government agencies responsible for finding the money to make these payments.

Living Arrangements

Older people who can afford a comfortable standard of living have a variety of choices about living arrangements. A substantial group migrate to the Sun Belt states. Florida has the nation's largest proportion of elderly residents. In 1980, Florida had 17.3 percent over 65, compared with 7.5 percent in Utah, which has the smallest proportion of elders. More than 12 percent of the population of the State of New York was aged 65 or older, compared to about 10 percent in California.

There is a large difference between older men and women in the extent to which they are living with a spouse. Since men have a shorter life expectancy and since men have generally married younger women, the result is that older men are much more likely to be living with their wives, while older women are much more likely to be widows. About 80 percent of men aged 65 and over are living with wives, while about 50 percent of women over 65 are widows. Also, about one-third of married men over 65 have wives under 65.

How the Elderly Are Perceived by the Adult Majority

There are two contrasting perceptions of the elderly by the general adult public. One image is that of a rather passive, dependent group who have little power or influence in the society, and are happy to be left alone as long as their material needs are met. The other image is that of a politically and economically active group with a desire to participate quite fully in contemporary civic and political life.

There are several national organizations of older people which are active politically and educationally. The Gray Panthers, founded and headed by Maggie Kuhn in her seventies; the National Council of Senior Citizens, consisting largely of retired labor union members; the American Association of Retired Persons; and the National Association of Retired Federal Employees have put their political clout behind the 1978 Amendments to the Age Discrimination in Employment Act, which raised the age of allowable mandatory retirement from 65 to 70. The vote for this bill in the United States House of Representatives was 359 to 4, indicating both the political effectiveness of these organizations and the general belief of the American public that nobody should be forced out of his or her job on account of age, if he or she is doing satisfactory work.

The Elders as a Resource for the Welfare of the Country

A considerable group of elders do volunteer work that is useful to the local community in various ways. They may help other older people who are ill or need companionship, by visiting and providing services. They may do volunteer work in their church. Those with automobiles can transport people to social affairs and to shopping centers.

The federal government maintains a Retired Senior Volunteer Program (RSVP) which places men and women with special abilities in a variety of programs and projects, and pays only their travel expenses. There are about 5000 Senior Centers in the United States, which offer social and educational programs for senior citizens, and use a substantial number of volunteer staff members.

The 1981 national survey of Aging in the Eighties asked the national sample of elderly men and women "Apart from any work you're paid for, do you do any volunteer work?" Among the 65 and over group, 24 percent of the men and 22 percent of the women reported that they were doing volunteer work, while another 11 percent of men and 10 percent of women said they were not doing volunteer work but would like to do it.

Jobs for Seniors

A substantial number of men and women who are over 55 and up to 70 or 75 are interested in part-time or full-time jobs that will give them some income and comfortable working conditions. They may need brief training and some assistance in finding a suitable kind of work.

A National Committee on Careers for Older Americans was created in 1979 with Arthur S. Flemming as Chairman. Flemming is Chairman of the

TABLE B / AGE STRUCTURE OF RACIAL AND ETHNIC GROUPS IN THE UNITED STATES, 1980

	Percentages		
	Under 15	65 and Over	Median Age (Years)
White	21.3	12.2	31.3
Black	28.7	7.9	23.2
Hispanic	32.0	4.9	23.2
Total, U.S.A.	22.6	11.3	30.0

United States Commission on Civil Rights, and formerly Commissioner of the United States Administration on Aging and Secretary of Health, Education and Welfare. The Committee on Careers for Older Americans has published an 87-page report, "Older Americans: An Untapped Resource." It urges the following:

Special employer review to identify jobs that can make use of older people's skills and experience.

Training programs to help older people update or learn skills that qualify them for job openings.

Employer-offered internships that allow older people to test their career interests and capacities for particular lines of work.

Community action to stimulate older people to engage in self-employment to meet business and service needs.

Thus, in contrast to the image of the elderly as an inactive and burdensome minority, there is ample evidence that old age may be perceived and experienced as an energetic and creative span of years.

References

Birren, James E., and **K. W. Schaie,** eds. (1977). *Handbook of the Psychology of Aging.* New York: Van Nostrand Reinhold.

Birren, James E., and **R. Bruce Sloane,** eds. (1980). *Handbook of Mental Health and Aging.* Englewood Cliffs, N.J.: Prentice-Hall.

National Center for Health Statistics (1978). *Health: United States, 1978.* Washington, D.C.: Dept. of Health, Education and Welfare: Public Health Service. DHEW Publication No. (PHS)78–1232.

National Council on the Aging (1981). *Aging in the Eighties.* Washington, D.C.

Poon, L. W., ed. (1980). *Aging in the 1980s: Psychological Issues.* Washington, D.C.: American Psychological Association.

Giovannoni, 1972; Goldstein et al., 1973). Similarly, the elderly are burdened with societal assumptions of their incompetence (Kalish, 1975).

Given existing legal structures, it is difficult for children and adolescents to organize in their own behalf. They lack voting power and access to financial resources, and they are subject to laws which discourage their independence from their families—that is, the middle-aged adults who control their lives. The elderly represent an age minority group that is in a position to challenge societal structures, however, and this group has followed the lead of racial and ethnic minority groups in organizing in their own behalf. They have challenged societal assumptions about their abilities (Kalish, 1975). They have fought legislation which denies them access to needed resources, or which tries to force them into an unnecessarily dependent position. The Social Issue section that appears earlier in this chapter explores the elderly as a minority group in more depth.

SUMMARY

1. The main purposes of this chapter are to explore and discuss relationships between minority and majority groups; to define the concept of majority and minority groups; to define and illustrate discrimination and prejudice; to discuss the major policies of dominant groups toward minorities; to show how the black experience differed from that of other ethnic groups; and to define and discuss acculturation and assimilation.

2. A minority group is differentiated from the majority and is subject to unequal treatment in political, economic, and social spheres. Minorities see themselves as objects of collective discrimination.

3. Race is a biological concept and is defined as a group of people distinguished by inherited physical traits.

4. Racism occurs when one racial group is regarded by other racial groups as inherently inferior. Racism is legitimized by a belief system supported by pseudoscientific theories.

5. Prejudice is an attitude, whereas discrimination is action, denying a minority access to some resource.

6. Prejudice may be rooted in economic, psychological, or cultural factors. It may also reflect the social and legal patterns of a society.

7. Acculturation, rather than assimilation of minority groups, has been the prevalent pattern in the United States. Acculturation is the acceptance by a minority of the language, values, and norms of the dominant group.

8. Assimilation involves acculturation as well as primary relations with the dominant group. The latter leads to other forms of assimilation.

9. Some maintain that there has been an increase in ethnic consciousness among white Americans. However, research in the 1970s and 1980s suggests a decline in cohesiveness among white ethnics.

10. The elderly represent a rapidly growing minority group in American society. Its increasing size and organization among its members may have profound effects on the entire society.

REVIEW ▬▬▬▬▬▬▬▬▬▬▬▬▬▬▬▬▬▬▬▬▬▬

Key Terms

Minority	Race	Racism
Assimilation	Ethnic group	Prejudice
Cultural pluralism	Ethnocentrism	Discrimination

Review and Discussion

1. Think of the racial and ethnic environment in which you were raised. How has it affected your life? Do you think it has influenced the way you think about yourself and others?

2. Have you ever been in a situation in which your racial or ethnic identity worked against you? How did it disadvantage you? What was the outcome of the situation? How might the outcome have been different if race or ethnicity had not been a factor?

3. In colleges and universities, students usually lack power. They cannot hire or fire faculty, decide curricula, or evaluate themselves. Are students therefore a minority group? Why or why not?

4. To what extent are you able to trace your ancestry? Are your racial or ethnic "roots" important to you? Give some examples of experiences that made you aware of the group to which you belong and that group's position in society.

5. Do you think the elderly are a minority group? What experiences have you had with the elderly that support your views?

6. To what extent do you feel that our society has eliminated racism? Interview someone of a different race than yourself, and ask them the same question. How similar are your views? Why?

Experience with Sociology

We all get old. The elderly represent a minority group that we will all confront in our own lives and, often, in the lives of those important to us—parents, relatives, lovers, and friends. As with any minority group, the experience of getting old is closely tied to the societal values and structures that create the life context of the elderly. We don't get old alone. Instead, we get old in a society that reacts to us differently as we age. Those reactions may help or hinder our efforts to adapt psychologically. They may also facilitate or block our getting the resources we need—income, housing, employment, health care, and so on.

Module 3, Social Issues in American Society, helps you to look at the elderly as an increasingly significant minority group in our society. It will show you how to use census data to examine the interaction between social and personal issues related to getting old. Both society and individual people—you and me—are affected by the aging process. The module will assist you in understanding what some of the important societal effects of an aging population may be. It will also focus your attention on the implications for yourself (and others important to you) of getting old in an aging society.

References

Adams, R. M., N. J. Smelser, and **D. Treiman,** eds. (1982). *Ability Testing*. Washington, D.C.: National Academy Press.

Adorno, T. W., *et al.* (1950). *The Authoritarian Personality*. New York: Harper & Row.

Alba, R. D. (1976). Social assimilation among American Catholics. *American Sociological Review* 41: 6, 1030–1046.

Allport, G. L., and **L. Postman** (1945). The basic psychology of rumor. *Transactions of the New York Academy of Sciences* 118: 61–81.

Auletta, Ken (1981). The underclass (III). *The New Yorker,* Nov. 30, 1981, p. 110ff.

Berry, B. (1965). *Race and Ethnic Relations.* Boston: Houghton Mifflin.

Billingsley, A., and **J. Giovannoni** (1972). *Children of the Storm.* New York: Harcourt, Brace, Jovanovich.

Bogardus, E. S. (1925). Measuring social distance. *Journal of Applied Sociology* 9: 299–308.

Carroll, M. (1982). Influence and numbers swell new wave in Hispanic politics. *The New York Times,* January 24: E7.

Clymer, A. (1981). Polls find black–white gaps on variety of issues. *The New York Times,* August 28, p. 37.

Cox, O. (1948). *Caste, Class and Race.* Garden City: Doubleday.

Dollard, J. (1949). *Caste and Class in a Southern Town.* New York: Harper & Row.

Drake, St. C., and **H. R. Clayton** (1945). *Black Metropolis.* New York: Harcourt.

Elkins, S. M. (1959). *Slavery: A Problem in American Institutions and Intellectual Life.* Chicago: University of Chicago Press.

Franklin, J. H. (1948). *From Slavery to Freedom.* New York: Knopf.

Gans, H. (1962). *The Urban Villagers.* New York: Free Press.

———— (1979). Symbolic ethnicity: The future of ethnic groups and cultures in America. In *On the Making of Americans,* eds. H. J. Gans, N. Glazer, J. R. Gusfield, and C. Jencks. Philadelphia: University of Pennsylvania Press.

Genovese, E. D. (1974). *Roll, Jordan Roll!* New York: Pantheon.

Getler, M. (1981). The education of David Stockman. *The Atlantic,* December 1981, pp. 27–54.

Glazer, N. (1978). *Affirmative Discrimination.* New York: Basic Books.

Goldstein, J., A. Freud, and **A. J. Solnit** (1973). *Beyond the Best Interests of the Child.* New York: Free Press.

Gordon, M. (1964). *Assimilation vs. American Life.* New York: Oxford University Press.

Hartley, E. L. (1946). *Problems in Prejudice.* New York: King's Crown.

Jensen, A. (1969). How much can we boost I.Q. and scholastic achievement. *Harvard Educational Review* 29: 1–23.

Josephy, A. M. (1971). *Red Power: The American Indian's Fight for Freedom.* New York: McGraw-Hill.

Kalish, R. A. (1975). *Late Adulthood.* Monterey, Ca.: Brooks-Cole.

Kanter, R. M., and **B. A. Steiner** (1980). *Value Change and the Public Work Force: Labor Force Trends, the Saliency of Opportunity and Power and Implications for Public Sector Management.* Cambridge, Mass.: Goodmeasure.

Kerner, Otto (Chairperson) (1968). *Report of the National Advisory Commission on Civil Disorders.* Washington, D.C.: U.S. Government Printing Office.

Klineberg, O. (1954). *Social Psychology.* New York: Holt.

LeVine, R. A., and **D. T. Campbell** (1972). *Ethnocentrism.* New York: John Wiley.

Marden, C. F., and **G. Meyer** (1973). *Minorities in American Society.* New York: Van Nostrand.

Merton, R. K. (1949). Discrimination and the American creed. In *Discrimination and National Welfare,* ed. R. M. MacIver. New York: Harper.

Montagu, A. (1972). *Statement on Race.* New York: Oxford University Press.

Moore, J. W. (1976). *Mexican Americans.* Englewood Cliffs, N.J.: Prentice-Hall.

Myrdal, G. (1944). *An American Dilemma.* New York: Harper and Brothers.

The New York Times. Rating the things Americans value. January 28, 1982, p. C3.

Noel, D., ed. (1971). *The Origin of American Slavery and Racism.* Columbus, Ohio: Charles Merrill.

Novak, M. (1971). *Politics: Realism and Imagination.* New York: Herder and Herder.

Pettigrew, T. F. (1958). Personality and sociocultural factors in intergroup attitudes: A cross-national comparison. *Journal of Conflict Resolution* 2(March): 29–42.

———— (1971). *Racially Separate or Together?* New York: McGraw-Hill.

Robbins, W. (1982). Job odds are against young Philadelphia blacks. *The New York Times,* February 1, p. A-8.

Sandberg, N. (1974). *Ethnic Identity and Assimilation: The Polish American Community.* New York: Praeger.

Schermerhorn, R. A. (1970). *Comparative Ethnic Relations.* New York: Random House.

Simpson, G. E., and **J. M. Yinger,** (1965; 1972). *Racial and Cultural Minorities.* New York: Harper & Row.

Stampp, K. M. (1956). *The Peculiar Institution: Slavery in the Ante-Bellum South.* New York: Alfred Knopf.

Triandis, H. C., and **X. Triandis** (1962). A cross-cultural study of social distance. *Psychological Monograph* 76: 1–21.

Turner, J. H. (1976). *American Society: Problems of Structure.* New York: Harper & Row.

Van denBerghe, P. (1967). *Race and Racism.* New York: John Wiley.

Wagley, C., and **M. Harris** (1958). *Minorities in the New World.* New York: Columbia University Press.

Waite, L. (1981). *U.S. Women at Work.* Population Reference Bureau, Vol. 36, no. 2 (May).

Williams, R. M., Jr. (1947). *The Reduction of Intergroup Tensions.* New York: Social Science Research Council.

———— (1964). *Strangers Next Door.* Englewood Cliffs, N.J.: Prentice-Hall.

———— (1977). *Mutual Accommodation.* Minneapolis: University of Minnesota Press.

Wilson, J. W. (1978). *The Declining Significance of Race.* Chicago: University of Chicago Press.

Wirth, L. (1945). The problem of minority groups. In *The Science of Man in the World Crisis,* ed. R. Linton. New York: Columbia University Press.

Woodward, C. V. (1957). *The Strange Career of Jim Crow.* New York: Oxford University Press.

PART THREE SOCIAL ORGANIZATIONS

10

GROUPS AND COLLECTIVE BEHAVIOR

Charlie Smith was born at 120 Elm Street, where he lived with his parents and three sisters for the first 17 years of his life. At age six, Charlie spent most of his time working on a clubhouse with other boys in the neighborhood. At age 14, he fell in love and began spending most of his time with his girl. A year later, when Charlie failed to make the football team and lost his girl, he stole a car and took the gang for a ride. He was not caught, but his parents found out and they urged him to join the army after graduation. Discharged two years later, he went to Berkeley and enrolled in the university. Today, Charlie plays lead guitar with the Revelation Bank, an up-and-coming rock group that spent last year touring the country. The band travels in its own bus with a manager and an assortment of "roadies" who handle equipment and luggage. In Des Moines, they were mobbed when they tried to leave the theater; police estimated the crowd in Madison at 10,000. What Charlie's fans do not know is that he is a Catholic who attends Mass every Sunday, a registered Republican, a member of Phi Beta Kappa, and a partner in a record company in San Francisco. And, of course, he belongs to the musicians' union.

In this brief biography, we focused on the groups to which Charlie Smith, a fictitious musician, had belonged. Like Charlie, all individuals belong to numerous groups in the course of their lifetime: families, friendship cliques, love triangles, student bodies, churches, armies, political parties, unions, and audiences. The list is endless. There are large groups (the army) and small groups (the family); voluntary groups (a bridge club) and involuntary groups (the first grade); groups anyone can join (environmental action groups) and groups restricted by age, sex, race, religion, income, or professional status (the Little League, the Black Muslims, the exclusive New York Athletic Club, the American Medical Association); friendship groups, work groups, and interest groups. Because groups provide their members with security, identity, and compan-ionship, they are basic to the social behaviors studied by sociologists.

THE IMPORTANCE OF GROUPS

In small premodern societies—our primary clue to our past—the only recognized social group is often the family or clan. If a person is not a relative, he or she is automatically an enemy and perhaps considered somewhat less than human. Describing a trip through Australia, anthropologist A. R. Radcliff-Brown told how at each village his Talainji guide would painstakingly trace his relationship to the men who lived there. On the one occasion when he could not discover any kin ties at all, he refused to sleep in the village out of fear for his life (Stephens, 1963).

Presumably, humans have always lived in groups: first, because the group protects the individual from human and nonhuman dangers; second, because members of a group can share responsibilities for acquiring food, clothing, and shelter. Children, women with infants, and old people cannot hunt, but they can gather food, make clothes, and perform other chores that require less physical strength. This frees the men to devote their time to hunting. In the end, all of the community's tasks are accomplished more efficiently, and everyone benefits. Groups make the division of labor possible—in primitive societies, where sex and age determine what jobs the individual performs, and in modern societies, which depend on specialization and extensive education and training.

The family is only one of the groups which individuals rely on for material and psychological support in modern societies. In Chapter 3, we cited studies that suggest the infant needs warmth and affection to *become* human; the adult, to *remain* human. Social isolation has been linked to suicide, to the mental problems of the aged, and to schizophrenia. In his book *Suicide* (1897),

Durkheim concluded that one reason for attempting or committing suicide was lack of involvement in groups. Excessively self-reliant individuals are more vulnerable during times of personal crisis: they have fewer attachments and responsibilities to restrain them. Sociologist Matilda Riley (1969) suggested that isolation is most acute for the aged in our society. Only rarely do old people live with their married children, and physical immobility makes it difficult for them to maintain friendships or to take advantage of programs for their age group. Other researchers have linked isolation to emotional disorders. For example, one of the earliest studies of mental patients from urban areas (Faris and Dunham, 1938) found that mental illness is most common in the rooming-house districts of big cities, where interpersonal contacts are few. In "Cultural Isolation and the Schizophrenic Personality" (1934), Robert E. L. Faris suggested why:

Our actions are conventional (that is, normal) because of our participation in the primary group life of our communities. What order we can detect in human minds is principally the result of the necessity to communicate with these friends and neighbors. As long as a person wishes to appear sensible, and fears gossip, ridicule, and the sneers of his fellows, he must accept the roles defined for him by his community, and must think and feel in harmony with the attitudes and sentiments of his neighbors. To most normal people this conformity is second nature. . . . When there is no longer any necessity or desire to communicate with others, or to appear sensible to them, there is nothing to preserve the order in the mental life of the person. (p. 157–58)

Families, friendship groups, work groups, professional associations, and the like are not only pleasant and convenient—they are necessary.

DEFINING GROUPS

In everyday conversation, we use the word "group" to describe any collection of people ranging in size from three to several million: our families, our classes, the people at a restaurant, the crowd at a football game. But sociologists

Sociologically speaking, there are many kinds of groups. Whatever the type, however, a group must by definition be composed of members who interact regularly and identify with one another.

use four different terms to make important distinctions among all of these. They distinguish among *groups, aggregates, collectivities,* and *social categories.*

A **group** is two or more people who interact regularly and identify with one another. That is, they perceive themselves as belonging to a group, distinguish between members and nonmembers, and expect certain kinds of behavior from one another that they do not expect from outsiders (Merton, 1957). This definition includes such diverse groups as a family and a corporation, a street gang and a symphony orchestra, a student body and a president's cabinet. The key elements are *recurrent interaction* and *consciousness of kind.* Five men who meet at their neighborhood bar for a drink every Friday night, always sit together, tell stories about their bosses, crack jokes about one another that outsiders might not understand, and leave expecting to meet again the next week are a group. The bartender calls them the "payday guys"; their wives know they are out with "the boys." Five men who go to the same bar just as regularly but drink their beer alone are not a group in the sociological sense. Nor are five men who meet, strike up a conversation, talk intensely for several hours, then go their separate ways. Groups are based on ongoing interaction.

An **aggregate** is a number of people who happen to be at the same place at the same time, but whose interaction is limited and unstructured; for example, the passengers on a train. Except for an occasional request for the time of day and muttered "excuse me's" brushing past one another in the aisle, they have nothing in common but their proximity. A few may start conversations, but most act as if they were alone. The difference between an aggregate and a group is the difference between the people on a busy street and on an assembly line. People on an assembly line are well organized and understand their relationship to one another. Spending a lot of time together in related tasks, they talk actively about themselves and each other. They distin-

guish clearly between themselves and others, sitting together for lunch, giving each other congratulations or sympathies as personal events occur, competing with other divisions of the company, seeing each other after work hours and on the weekends. They are united by their common activity and by their sense of being part of something larger than themselves. This is not so with people on a street or passengers on a train, who have their minds on their own lives.

Aggregates are potential collectivities. A **collectivity** is a temporary collection of people who are interacting in response to a specific stimulus. For example, if an auto accident occurs on a busy street, the people gathered around the scene would no longer be part of an aggregate but would be a collectivity. They would talk animatedly, sharing information and observations, and perhaps help the injured or call the police. Their interaction is limited to an immediate situation and ceases whenever the situation ends.

A **category** is a number of people who share the same characteristics but who do not necessarily interact with one another. Examples are women, teachers, musicians, cat lovers, consumers, redheads, and the elderly. Social scientists often use categories in research, for example, when they want to see if there is any correlation between income and political attitudes, mental health and urban residence. But categories are abstractions. The individuals involved neither interact with one another in any ongoing way, nor are they conscious of belonging to a group. Blue-collar workers complain about the difficulty of making ends meet, but most do not feel that they have anything in common with college instructors, who also earn relatively low wages.

Any collection of people, whether an aggregate, collectivity, or category, has the potential to become a group. A category represents a number of people who, while presently not a group, have a basis for becoming one by virtue of the characteristics they share. A collectivity is already in the process of developing group characteristics by virtue of having established interaction among its members. If the situation that has united its members continues, a group will most likely result. Even an aggregate, although usually unstructured, could become a collectivity and eventually a group. If the passengers on a train were to be involved in a lengthy delay, they might begin to discuss the situation and consider alternative ways to reach their destinations. At this point, the aggregate has become a collectivity. If the passengers were to decide to band together to work for improved train service, they would be functioning as a group.

THE CONTINUUM OF GROUPS

As we have seen above, when people come together the kind of behavior that results may be one of several kinds. Indeed, it can best be seen as a continuum ranging from random behavior at one extreme to highly organized behavior at the other. When a group is formed, it may take a variety of forms. Sociologists employ two especially useful criteria to categorize kinds of groups. One is on the basis of *size*. Here again we can think in terms of a continuum ranging from a minimum of two to an almost unlimited maximum number of group members. For the most part, sociologists focus on the two opposite ends of the size continuum: small primary groups and large secondary groups. Small groups may vary in size, but usually they have no more than 8 to 12 members. Large groups, on the other hand, may have hundreds or even thousands of members.

A second criterion sociologists use for categorizing groups is *function,* that is, the goals that a group helps its members to attain. Function can be analyzed in two ways. One includes the specific life tasks that are performed in the group. For example, there are recreational groups such as swim teams, self-help groups like Alcoholics Anonymous, educational groups such as opera study clubs, therapy groups like those formed as

part of the treatment of mental patients in hospitals, and friendship groups. Function can also be looked at more broadly in terms of the way the group affects the individual's sense of identity and social well-being. This latter sense of function will be used as the focus for the later discussion of in-groups, out-groups, and reference groups.

Before discussing how groups of different sizes and functions influence the behavior of their members, we need to analyze the common properties of groups. Every group, regardless of its size and function, has structural properties that influence the way it develops. These properties can influence size and function, which is why we will look at them before turning to considerations of group size and function later in the chapter. We have already indicated two common properties in our definition of a group; *recurrent interaction* and *consciousness of kind* are essential if a number of individuals are to begin to identify themselves as a group. In the next section we will describe several other common properties of groups.

COMMON PROPERTIES OF GROUPS

In order to understand how groups are formed and why they endure, the following common properties of groups have to be addressed: member similarity, spatial proximity of members, leadership, group communication, group cohesion, and conformity of members to group norms. In this section we will take each in turn.

Member Similarity

Things that people share with each other tend to draw them together. Similarity may be seen in two kinds of appeals: personal characteristics and goals desired. College students are comfortable with other college students by virtue of their shared dress patterns and recreational activities. In addition to these personal characteristics, they also share goals that create a need for similar activities like reading books, taking exams, and making sure their registrations are properly processed by the registrar's office. Similarly, when a woman has her first child, she suddenly finds that she is spending more time with friends and neighbors who also have small children than with those who are single and childless.

Changing patterns in higher education also illustrate the importance of member similarity on group formation. The rapidly increasing numbers of students who are older, married, working, and from various ethnic groups are changing the similarity among personal characteristics that used to be taken for granted. Older students with families have somewhat different interests than traditional college-age students. While the younger student may prefer extremely casual dress and bar-hopping, the older student is often more used to dressing for work and spending leisure time with the family and nonstudent peers. The result is a more fragmented student population composed of several groups, each reflecting its similarity in personal characteristics of particular importance to that group.

Spatial Proximity

Sharing space tends to give people a sense of common identity. Groups often form among people who work or live near each other because opportunities to meet, to share information and experiences, and to transform acquaintances into friends are multiplied. As noted earlier, this is why aggregates generally have good potential for developing into a group. Spatial proximity also relates to member similarity since people often share a particular spatial area because of shared interests and personal characteristics. Consider, for example, residential patterns of segregation in which people who share similar economic standing, education levels, occupational category, and ethnicity live together.

Modern communications technology has somewhat altered the impact of spatial proximity on group behavior. It is now possible for persons who are geographically separated to maintain close contact through media like the telephone, computers, television, and recordings. The sense of common identity which occurs from spatial proximity may now result from electronically created proximity. For example, through conference calls, closed circuit televison, and computerized message transmission, businesses can maintain a sense of group cohesion among employees who are geographically distant. The result can be improved productivity, job satisfaction, and organizational control.

Leadership

As group size increases, so do the problems of coordinating decisions and activities. Group leaders emerge to try to solve these problems. A **leader** is someone who has the potential, ability, and power to influence the way other people behave (Lewin, 1951). Leaders are able to bring individuals and cliques together by directing communication, coordinating activities, settling disputes, and making decisions.

Ideally, the leader performs two essential functions: directing activities and making group decisions **(instrumental leadership)**, and creating harmony and ensuring that all group members are relatively happy **(expressive leadership)**. Usually, one person cannot fill both roles at the same time. Making sure everyone performs his or her task may interfere with encouraging and creating harmonious relationships within the group. Therefore, there are usually two (or more) leaders in a group—the instrumental and the expressive (Heap, 1977).

While there is some evidence that leaders tend to direct groups toward activities in which the leaders themselves excel (Whyte, 1955), the *way* a leader directs a group's activities is often as important as *what* he or she influences the group to do. In studies with groups of boys,

Pope John Paul II, spiritual leader to the members of the Roman Catholic Church, has the power to make decisions for the group and to influence the way other people behave.

White and Lippit (1960) found that groups with permissive or laissez-faire leaders could not seem to get organized. Autocratic leaders were no more effective: their attempts to dominate the group created disruptive internal dissension. Democratic leaders, who involved all members in group decisions and activities, seemed best able to maintain harmony while directing the group toward its goal. Table 10.1 summarizes three common leadership styles.

Communication

A group's ability to meet its member's needs and hence to continue over time is strongly influenced by the communication patterns within it. One way sociologists study communication in groups is by observing meetings and recording who speaks to whom and how often. In one study, the Harvard sociologist Robert Bales (1951) observed 18 meetings of groups of six men. He ranked each individual in two areas: the number of one-to-one communications he ini-

TABLE 10.1 / EXAMPLES OF LEADERSHIP STYLES

Consensus	Conflict	Confrontation
1. Preliminary study of history and events in the environmental system	1. Infiltrate community and identify problem	1. Plan a scene
2. Determine the problem and meet with group members	2. Locate the indigenous leaders	2. Publicize and spread rumors
3. Discuss problem, possible solutions, and select course of action	3. Meet with leaders and discuss problem and means of solving it	3. Arrange for free items and props
4. Discuss and act upon the problem	4. Demonstrate to show how power can be used	4. Action—do anything but don't get caught
5. Discuss related problems and plan continuation of committee actions		5. Act in front of media cameras
		6. Plan another scene

Source: Edward A. Mabry and Richard E. Barnes, *The Dynamics of Small Group Communication.* Copyright 1980, p. 162. Reprinted by permission of Prentice-Hall, Inc., Englewood Cliffs, New Jersey.

tiated and received and the number of times he addressed the group as a whole. Bales found that the individuals who ranked high in one area ranked high in other areas as well. J. L. Moreno's sociogram, illustrated in Fig. 10.1, is another method commonly used to chart interaction and communication among members of a group.

In large groups especially, leaders tend to dominate communication. They not only do the most talking, they also do the most listening; that is, individuals are more likely to address them than other group members. There is much evidence, however, that when leaders dominate communication, individuals are not as motivated to work toward group goals as they are when they actively participate in discussions and decisions (McQuail, 1975: 103–06).

The amount of communication that takes place in a group depends on the nature of the group and the situation. In close-knit groups,

Fig. 10.1 / The Use of a Sociogram

J.L. Moreno, a psychiatrist, developed the **sociogram** *as a method for analyzing the relationships within a group. Each group member is asked which other members he or she prefers. For example, the researcher might ask the following questions: "Who are your closest friends? With whom do you like to spend your spare time? With whom would you like to share a room? Whom do you like the best?"*

The sociogram demonstrates how the collected responses of an imaginary group of eight people might be illustrated. Each circle represents one group member. The solid arrows show mutual preferences in the responses while the broken arrows show unreciprocated preferences. With the aid of such a pictorial representation, the researcher can easily identify the networks of communication, influence, and decision making within the group. In the sample, F is the most popular member of the group. The smaller group of G, F, and H is a clique whose members choose one another exclusively. A–D is an example of a dyad (two people who mutually prefer only each other). C, who neither chooses anyone nor is chosen by anyone, is an isolate.

Whom would you expect to be the group leader? Who is most likely to be able to influence that leader's decisions? Starting at any point, can you say along which routes information will pass? Who is most likely to receive the information? Who is least likely?

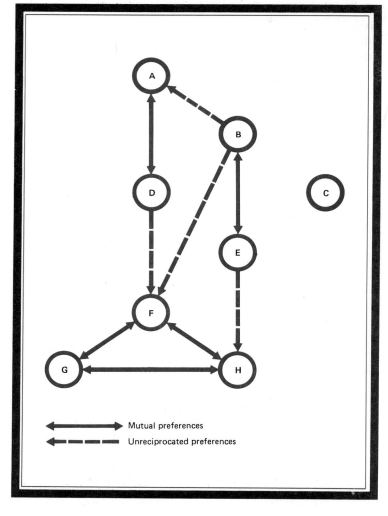

members tend to avoid dissension. When individuals disagree, the level of interaction drops until the dissenters are convinced to give in. In more loosely organized groups, the reverse is true: the level of conversation rises when members disagree on an issue that concerns the group. Usually interaction is directed at the dissenters until such time as the group realizes that they cannot be persuaded (McQuail, 1975: 99–101).

Cohesion

Group cohesion refers to the strength of the bond between group members (Heap, 1977: 64). Evidence of group cohesion includes such behaviors as members talking in terms of "we" rather than "I"; willingness to sacrifice personal satisfaction for the group; and quick defense of the group from external criticism.

When a group is together for a long time, its members establish set ways of dealing with one another. If too many new members are not familiar with these patterns, they threaten established relationships and reduce group cohesion.

In his study of soldiers in Vietnam, Moskos (1970) suggested that the policy of rotating soldiers every 12 months tended to make infantrymen "isolated and self-centered." Individuals concentrated on "making it through" to the end of their tour of duty, at which time their relationship to their combat unit ended. People need time and stability to learn how to function as a group.

Finally, the amount that individual members invest emotionally and otherwise in their membership also affects group cohesiveness. A student who must save and work hard for tuition is apt to be more dedicated to school than a student for whom raising tuition has not presented special problems. For this reason, many organizations, like college fraternities or the Marines, have deliberately used stiff initiation procedures to instill fierce group loyalty in their members.

Conformity

The more cohesive the group, the more likely the group is to require conformity from

---

Reminder Box / THE LABORATORY EXPERIMENT

The laboratory experiment, as we saw in Chapter 2, is one in which researchers can control every step of the study. Subjects' responses can be recorded exactly using a range of recording devices, and outside interferences are reduced. In the laboratory, very little is left to chance.

Small groups lend themselves very well to laboratory research since not too many people are involved. They can be formed readily, costs are minimal, and the researcher is better able to observe all the interactions that occur. As a result, many laboratory experiments have been done with small groups, especially in sociology and psychology.

You have already read about small-group laboratory research earlier in this chapter. J. L. Moreno's research utilizing the sociogram was primarily laboratory research. After forming a group, interactions were carefully observed and the various patterns such as cliques, dyads, and isolates were identified.

Laboratory research is limited by its somewhat artificial environment. On the other hand, it allows for the precise manipulation and recording of social behavior. In many cases, the behavior patterns observed in the laboratory can then be generalized to situations that are not reproducible in the laboratory. For example, the interaction patterns identified by Moreno apply to most groups, regardless of size or function.

Drawing by Lorenz; © 1976, *The New Yorker* Magazine, Inc.

members. People abide by group norms because they want acceptance and validation. Group norms give members something to believe in and give them a method for evaluating the events around them. Groups also influence the way individuals perceive themselves. At various points in *Street Corner Society,* Whyte (1955) showed the dramatic effect the Norton gang had on individuals' self-images.

For example, Alec was a good bowler when he bowled with other groups for fun during the week. In fact, he made the highest score of the season. But on Saturday nights, when the gang bowled together, Alec seemed to fall apart. The same was true of Frank, a semiprofessional base-ball player who performed poorly when he played with the gang. Why? Because both Alec and Frank ranked low in the group's esteem. For either of them to have defeated Doc or Mike or Danny, the leading clique, would have been inappropriate. With the Nortons, as with most groups, order depends on stable relationships. If the leadership and ranking in the gang had changed with every match, the gang would not have provided members with the security and stability they sought.

THE IMPORTANCE OF GROUP SIZE

Now that we have considered the basic charac-teristics of all groups, we can return to the two commonly used sociological criteria for distin-guishing between groups mentioned earlier: group size and group function. We will begin with group size analyzed in terms of primary and secondary groups. In the next chapter, the topic of large secondary groups will be further devel-oped by an in-depth examination of formal organizations and bureaucracies. These are large secondary groups of particular importance in our society.

In 1909, Charles Horton Cooley coined the term **primary group** to describe a small, inti-mate group of people who relate to one another in direct, personal ways: a family, a child's play group, peer groups, work groups, friends, neighbors (in the traditional sense), and lovers. Cooley wanted to distinguish these groups from **secondary groups** in which relationships are formal and impersonal: committees, business acquaintances, professional associations, and neighbors who are cordial but distant. The chief difference between the two kinds of groups lies in the quality of relationships between members and the degree of individual involvement. For example, a woman and her male doctor constitute a secondary group. When she undresses in his office, she assumes that he will keep a professional detachment. They discuss her anatomy dispassionately and objectively. A woman and her lover constitute a primary group. Undressing in his presence is altogether different.

Primary Groups

Primary groups are small for the simple reason that large numbers of people cannot relate to one another directly and personally. Two, four, even six or seven people can carry on a single conversation. Beyond that number, direct interaction personally involving every individual becomes impossible (Berelson and Steiner, 1967). The group may break into cliques of two or three, or one individual may take over, acting as a leader and directing group activities. In either case, some degree of distance and formality replaces spontaneous communication. But while all primary groups are small, not all small groups are primary, as the patient-doctor relationship indicates.

More important than size is the fact that primary groups are person-centered. Members of a committee, a secondary group, get together because they want to achieve a goal and consider cooperation expedient. New members are admitted because of their ability to contribute to the group's goal; conversation is limited to relevant, purposeful discussion. Usually interaction between members is impersonal and rational. In contrast, lovers or friends get together because

they want to talk, to share experiences, to discuss personal problems, to play ball or cards for fun—in short, because they want to be with each other. What they do does not matter as much as the fact that they are doing it together. Lovers, friends, and family members relate to one another as *whole* people not in their social roles as patient to doctor, Democrat to Democrat, cat owner to cat owner. Among friends, conversation ranges from gossip to political debate to reminiscence; there are few limits and certainly no "rules of order." In primary groups, people shed pretenses and reveal parts of themselves that they do not ordinarily show "in public." Communication is spontaneous, emotional, and expressive. Figure 10.2 outlines the major elements of this small-group process.

For the child, primary groups are an introduction to society. The care and nurturing of family members help the child to develop a healthy sense of self, which then makes it possible to learn social skills and adapt to the social environment. Later, groups of playmates and school friends support the child as he or she encounters the inevitable conflicts and disappointments of growing up. For adults, too, primary groups are islands of intimacy in an increasingly impersonal world. With so much of our daily activity organized around roles—as wage-earner, parent, spouse, neighbor—it is important that we have opportunities to relax and be recognized as *individuals* rather than as *role occupants*. Going to a favorite disco with friends, perhaps having a drink or two, and then dancing and laughing into the wee hours is an example of the way people shed their usual role-limited behavior in primary groups. This is an important source of continuing to feel good about ourselves which, in turn, makes it possible to carry out role responsibilities willingly and effectively.

Secondary Groups

A goal-oriented group of people who relate to one another in relatively formal and impersonal

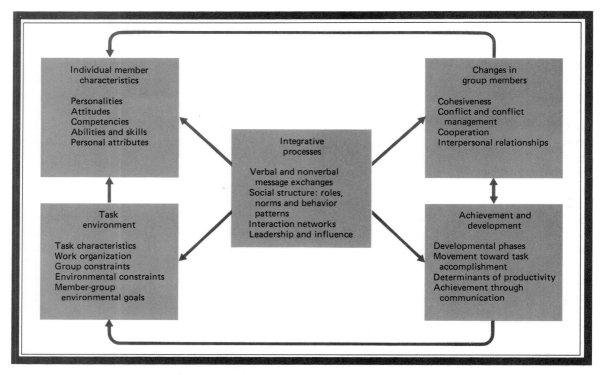

Fig. 10.2 / The Small-Group Process

This chart summarizes the major elements of the small-group process. At the left are characteristics of group members and the environment that affect a group. At the right are group activities, including ways members relate to each other. In the center is a summary of basic group processes that enable groups to function.

Source: Edward A. Mabry and Richard E. Barnes, *The Dynamics of Small Group Communications.* Copyright 1980, p. 246. Reprinted by permission of Prentice-Hall, Inc., Englewood Cliffs, New Jersey.

ways is called a secondary group. For example, when Mr. Smith speaks to Ms. Jones at a convention, he is usually focusing on her as a political science colleague, not as a woman who enjoys mountain climbing. Her likes and dislikes, her hopes and fears are irrelevant in the secondary setting, as are his. They are exclusively interested in each other's ideas about government. Interaction is formal in secondary groups in the sense that people limit themselves to narrowly defined roles. For Ms. Jones to begin discussing her childhood in Brooklyn or to comment on Mr. Smith's blue eyes in the middle of a public debate

on the future of democracy would be grossly inappropriate. Both know and accept these limits. They are together for a purpose, not because they necessarily like each other and other members of the group. For this reason, membership in secondary groups is transferable: if Ms. Jones cannot chair the meeting, another well-known political scientist will do just as well. Businesses, universities, and other secondary groups outlive individual members.

Secondary groups focus on skills and interests, not personality. As a result, secondary groups can be—and often are—larger than primary groups. Indeed, all large groups are of necessity secondary groups, although, as we will see shortly, it is possible to have small primary groups within larger secondary groups. Relationships between secondary-group members are impersonal; communication, rational and purposeful; role expectations, precisely defined; interaction, goal-oriented, not person-centered. Secondary groups are created to perform such functions as defending countries (the army), educating children (the school), making money (the corporation), or circumventing the law (the crime syndicate). As noted earlier, they are merely means to an end. In most cases, the individual's emotional attachment to secondary groups is minimal.

As you have probably experienced in your own life, "primariness" and "secondariness" are matters of degree. There are moments of intimacy in even large, impersonal, secondary groups. Sometimes, for example, we find ourselves discussing an intimate part of our lives with a stranger we happen to be seated next to at a professional meeting. It is precisely the anonymity of the situation that allows us to feel safe expressing feelings that we fear might be troublesome to members of our primary group. Similarly, we can become preoccupied with our own thoughts and interact minimally with members of primary groups. The important thing to remember, though, is that these are unusual events. For the most part primary groups involve us totally, whereas secondary groups limit the nature of our participation. Table 10.2 provides examples of types of primary and secondary groups.

Primary Groups within Secondary Groups

In addition, primary groups frequently develop within secondary organizations. For example, a college class starts out as a secondary group. Students and teacher assemble at a predetermined hour in order to study certain topics and to fulfill requirements for a degree. Membership in this group depends on objective qualifications (having satisfactorily completed prerequisite courses), not personal characteristics. At first, behavior during class is formal; the teacher lectures and the students listen, raising their hands if they want to speak. However, as

TABLE 10.2 / PRIMARY AND SECONDARY GROUPS

Primary and secondary groups are distinguished on the basis of group size and the intimacy of contact between group members.

	Primary	Secondary
Typical Group	Family Gang or clique Work group "Buddy" group Encounter group Village community	School Little League Factory Army PTA Urban area
Characteristics	Personal Informal Spontaneous General goals Small number	Impersonal Formal Utilitarian Specialized goals Large number

The ties of primary groups tend to reinforce the functional, but impersonal, bonds that link members of secondary groups.

time passes, class members learn each other's names; they begin talking about subjects other than the one they are studying, going to lunch together after class, asking the professor what he thought about Saturday's tennis match. Friendships develop that will last well beyond the semester. Most secondary associations—even in huge bureaucracies, such as the army—can give birth to close and enduring relationships.

One of the most important functions of primary groups is to protect individuals from impersonal social forces. In effect, the primary group *mediates* between the individual and society, between the individual and large organizations. Friends know how hard Michael worked on a term paper for English. If he gets a low grade nonetheless, they console him by suggest-

ing that the professor is biased or by pointing to his talent for acting. This is an example of how primary groups provide individuals with essential psychological support in their dealings with "the outside world."

This point is further illustrated by interviews with released prisoners of war (POWs) after the Korean War. The results confirmed earlier studies which suggested that soldiers depend heavily on primary group ties. Chinese prison officials in the camps systematically destroyed all attempts at social organization. Group activities were prohibited (except those arranged by the Chinese); officers and emergent leaders were segregated from other prisoners; interrogators made a point of telling men that their buddies were informers; written confessions of war crimes were printed in the camp newsletter; mail from home was delivered only if it contained bad news. Prisoners who asked for letters were told their families and country had forgotten them. Not knowing whom to trust, the typical prisoner withdrew emotionally from his comrades and concentrated on survival. Often he began to mistrust his own sense of judgment, simply because he had no opportunity to discuss his feelings and beliefs with others. For some, this emotional withdrawal lasted for weeks and months after their release (Schein, 1968). These studies illustrate the importance of the primary group in social life.

GROUP FUNCTIONS AND MEMBER IDENTITY

In addition to categories by size, groups can be differentiated on the basis of the effects they have on the identity of their members. As we noted in previous chapters, the interaction between people and those in their environment is a critical part of socialization and personality development. Since most social life occurs in groups, they obviously have a powerful impact on people's identity. In this section we will look at in-groups, out-groups, and reference groups in terms of their effects on their members.

In-groups and Out-groups

A young woman is far more likely to respond to a strange man who approaches her in a museum than to a man who attempts to strike up a conversation on a subway platform. Why? Because the very fact that he is in a museum tells her something about him: "He is interested in Renaissance art." The man's grammar and accent provide a clue to his social background. Turning around, she notes his age, clothes, haircut, and race. He decides to proceed and comments on the painting in front of them, a self-portrait by Rembrandt. If he says he knows it must be a

good painting or it would not be in the museum, but why did the painter use such dull colors, he is "out." The young woman gulps and walks away. If he praises Rembrandt's use of light and mentions that he recently visited Amsterdam, he is "in."

An **in-group** is any group or social category to which a person feels he or she belongs: family, members of the same sex, people of the same age, those who share the same religious or ethnic background, coworkers or graduate students or mothers, fellow citizens. Conversely, an **out-group** is any group or social category to which a person feels he or she does not belong: other families, the opposite sex, those higher (or lower) in the company, people from other nations. Out-groups include both those people an individual rejects or ignores and those who reject or ignore that individual. In-group and out-group, developed in the early part of the century by W. G. Sumner (1906), continue to be sociological concepts useful for understanding human behavior.

Rejecting members of another group is often perceived in a positive way because it serves to reaffirm one's own sense of identity and well-being. Even though we may feel pity for a so-called bag lady we pass on the street, seeing her helps us to feel better about our own position—we are not destitute like she is, we have friends and family who are concerned about our well-being. Conversely, being rejected by those in another group is sometimes a painful experience. When we walk into a restaurant that turns out to be unexpectedly fancy, and cannot enter because we are too informally dressed, we usually feel uncomfortable. We know we can go home, dress appropriately, and return. However, for the moment we are acutely aware that we don't measure up to the standards of that social category (people who dine in a certain restaurant).

Individuals usually belong to a number of overlapping in-groups, and loyalties vary depending upon the situation. The hospital volunteer, who is a young debutante, and the nurse's aide, who is a Puerto Rican mother of four, are comrades during working hours but strangers after five. At a company party, John and Mary exchange hidden jokes about the boss's tie. The next day finds John joking about wives with the boss and Mary expressing doubts about men at a women's meeting. People feel comfortable and secure with members of their in-groups.

Stereotyping and Hostility

Sometimes members of different groups get along quite peacefully. But often people are hostile toward out-groups. Because individuals rarely venture far beyond the boundaries of their in-groups, lack of contact can lead to misunderstanding and suspicion. For example, whites in this country seldom go to restaurants in black neighborhoods because they assume they would feel uncomfortable. They do not know what to expect or how others would react to them. The soldiers who went to Vietnam in the sixties and seventies knew little or nothing about Vietnamese culture and consequently misinterpreted much of what they saw. In some areas, Vietnamese women rejected new houses built by American GIs for small, crude huts of their own making. What the soldiers did not know was that the Vietnamese believe that it is improper for a married woman to live in a house with a one-piece roof, such as those the GIs had built. Many of the Americans who had believed they were going to war to help the Vietnamese people ended up stereotyping them as "gooks," "dinks," and worse (Hersh, 1970) because they never had the opportunity to learn about the Vietnamese culture.

Strangeness and ignorance of other people's ways set the stage for prejudice, avoidance, hostility, and outright aggression. Negative impressions harden into stereotypes: the in-group is glorified; the out-group, dehumanized. Contact with outsiders is viewed as disloyalty to one's fellows. The extreme example of this, of course, was the extermination of the Jews in Nazi Germany. As far as Hitler was concerned, Jews were not part of the human race. It is doubtful that ordinary citizens could have manned the concentration camps if they, too, had not viewed their captives as less than human. A Jewish survivor of the camp recounted an incident in which a dog did not attack him when he took some potatoes from a bucket the animal was guarding. "If it had been a Nazi, he would have shot me," he said. "The dog was better than a Nazi" (Shipler, 1981).*

Intense competition and frustration also promote hostility toward out-groups and the formation of negative stereotypes. In one of his experiments with boys at a summer camp, Muzafer Sherif, a social psychologist at the University of Oklahoma, divided a group of 24 average white Protestant twelve-year-olds into two teams—the Bull Dogs and the Red Devils. He then offered a prize of twelve camping knives to the team that earned the most points in competitive games and activities that required group cooperation. At first, relations between the two teams were friendly and sportsmanlike, but this peace did not last. As the Red Devils began to slip behind, they started accusing the Bull Dogs of cheating. Friendly relations came to a halt. Then Sherif and his colleagues invited both groups to a party, expressing the hope that they would "let bygones be bygones." Actually, the party was designed to increase intergroup hostility. Half of the refreshments were crushed and dirty. When the Red Devils arrived in advance, through carefully disguised planning, they naturally ate the good food. When the Bull Dogs came in and saw what was left, they exploded. By the next day, the staff was having difficulty preventing out-and-out war. Hostile feelings between the two teams continued until Sherif invited boys from another camp for a day of sports. On this occasion, the Red Devils and Bull Dogs formed an in-group in response to

---

* © 1981 by *The New York Times* Company. Reprinted by permission.

these outsiders and combined their efforts to defeat this out-group in the sporting events that took place (Sherif and Sherif, 1956).

Reference Groups

Both in-groups and out-groups influence the way an individual thinks and behaves. Take, for example, a high school entrant who makes his school's football team. Among his peers, his in-group, he laughs at the way senior boys swagger and brag about their sexual adventures. In this context, seniors are an out-group. Privately, however, he measures his own love life against theirs and longs to be part of the football clique. Sociologists use the term **reference group** to describe any group that individuals take into account when they evaluate their own behavior

A reference group is any group that individuals take into account when they evaluate their own self-worth.

or self-concept: the groups to which they belong, the groups to which they aspire, and negative reference groups with which they do not want to be associated.

People modify their attitudes and behavior to fit those of their reference groups because they want to be accepted. Recent research suggests that recruitment into religious cults and sects is strongly influenced by interpersonal bonds that make the cult or sect a reference group (Stark and Bainbridge, 1980). We can also see this process occurring with peer groups in school and other settings which have the power to isolate individuals. Most people prefer to be accepted rather than rejected by reference groups. Therefore, high school students exaggerate stories about their arguments with their parents, eager young executives carefully observe and imitate their superiors, and soldiers hold their ground in battle at the risk of their lives. In each case we can see reference groups exerting their influence on behavior.

In a study that spanned over 20 years, psychologist T. M. Newcomb found that reference groups can have a *lasting* effect on attitudes and beliefs (Newcomb, 1943, 1963). In 1935, Newcomb sent questionnaires to students at Bennington College who at that time were typically young women from wealthy northeastern families. He found that while first-year students tended to reflect their families' conservative political views, juniors and seniors were much closer in attitudes to their liberal professors. Did these women come from different backgrounds? When Newcomb followed the 1935 students through their college careers, he found that with each year their attitudes moved a little further to the political left. He concluded that conservatism was "out" at Bennington in that period: the woman who expressed liberal ideas was applauded by both faculty and prestigious older women, so many did. Interestingly, these women did not revert to their former views after they graduated. Even after 20 years, their attitudes and beliefs remained the same.

LESS STRUCTURED GROUPS: COLLECTIVE BEHAVIOR

So far, this chapter has focused on group behavior in forms that are relatively stable and orderly. However, there are also less structured forms of group behavior called **collective behavior**: group activity that is spontaneous, relatively unstructured, and focused on a particular stimulus. The following are examples of collective behavior, and they demonstrate how unpredictable it often is: an audience at a rock festival, panic-stricken people fleeing a fire in a theater, a mob rioting in an urban slum, and wild outbursts of financial speculation. Forms of collective behavior which will be studied in this section include crowds, the mass, and public opinion.

Collective behavior is at the fringes of the sociological definition of a group. It includes two or more people who interact regularly and identify with one another; however, the period of time during which interaction takes place can be fairly brief. Collective behavior is always temporary. Some forms—fads and fashions, for example—may last for months or years, while others are over in a matter of hours or even minutes.

Since goals and procedures are unplanned, emerging spontaneously during the course of events, collective behavior may take unexpected turns. Symbolic interaction theory best captures the way in which the emergent quality of collective behavior can be understood sociologically. It focuses on the way structure emerges as people interact with each other. When the context in which the interaction takes place is fairly stable, as at work, regular patterns of group life are likely to result. When the context is rapidly changing, such as during a fire, a riot, or a period of rapid financial fluctuations, then the patterns of interactions which develop are also likely to be relatively fluid and unpredictable.

Collective behavior is collective activity that is spontaneous, relatively unstructured, and focused on a particular stimulus.

The sociologist Neil Smelser (1963) identified six determinants of collective behavior that occur in regular order. He called his theory "value added" because each determinant follows the one before it in a specific sequence; each must be present before the next stage in the sequence can occur. With each added step, the final result becomes more specifically determined. Let us look briefly at each step.

1. *Structural conduciveness* refers to the general background and cultural preconditions necessary for a given form of collective behavior. The destructive 1980 riot in Miami could not have occurred without a large, residentially segregated black population. Conflicts and tensions between blacks and whites, the physical isolation of the black district from other areas of Miami, and the ongoing economic recession were all structurally conducive to the riot.

2. *Structural strain* refers to conflict between norms or values. The conflict in Miami and throughout the country between the traditional American belief in equality of opportunity for all and the less-than-equal opportunities given to blacks was a structural strain.

3. A *generalized belief* includes notions about who or what is causing the structural strain and what can be done to relieve it. In the Miami riot, the generalized belief was that white society was responsible for the exploitation of blacks and that this situation could be relieved by attacking whites and looting white-owned stores. Destruction was also a symbolic refusal to continue participating in a system that humiliates and exploits blacks.

4. *Precipitating factors* are those that trigger the event. In Miami, the precipitating factor appears to have been the brutal beating of a black businessman by police.

5. *Mobilization of the participants for action* includes development of a communication network and leadership. In Miami, rumors, unsubstantiated and exaggerated reports, spread quickly. Police brutality was especially emphasized. Organized groups in the community moved into the situation and asserted their claims to leadership. At this stage, overt collective action began.

6. *Operation of social control* refers to how society reacts to an impending or actual episode of collective behavior. At any point in the cycle just outlined, agencies of social control, such as the police, the courts, the legislature, and public opinion, can intervene to alter the course of collective behavior.

Each determinant can take a variety of forms. The final result, the kind of collective behavior that emerges at the end of the sequence, depends on the specific nature of each determinant and the interaction between the determinants. Thus, for example, if the agencies of social control intervene forcefully and effectively at an early stage of the process, potential violence might be averted. Yet, on the other hand, if these forces of control overreact to a peaceful situation, they may become precipitating factors leading to violence (Rattner, 1981).

THEORIES OF CROWD BEHAVIOR

Crowds are among the clearest examples of collective behavior. Crowds at a parade, at a sporting event, in front of a government building demanding social reform—all of these are common to our way of life. Sociologists define a **crowd** as a temporary, relatively unorganized group of people who interact in close physical proximity. Much of the study of crowds (especially in recent years) has focused on the behavior of crowd members. Why, for instance, did ordinary citizens form lynch mobs? Under crowd influence, people seem to behave in ways that are out of character and that would be inconceivable under normal circumstances.

Gustave Le Bon, one of the earliest social theorists to study the psychological impact of a crowd on its members, concluded that crowds developed a *"mental unity"* that transformed the behavior of individual participants:

Whoever be the individuals that compose it, however like or unlike be their mode of life, their occupations, their character, or their intelligence, the fact that they have been transformed into a crowd puts them in possession of a sort of collective mind which makes them feel, think, and act in a manner quite different from that in which each individual of them would feel, think, and act were he in a state of isolation. (Le Bon, 1969)

Most social scientists have abandoned the term "collective mind" but not the hypothesis that members of a crowd may share a common mood and that *collective excitement can profoundly alter the behavior of crowd members.* We still use many of the key concepts developed by Le Bon to explain collective behavior: anonymity, suggestibility, and social contagion.

Anonymity

Since crowds are large and temporary gatherings, it is easy for individual members to feel *anonymous.* Acting *en masse,* no single member feels singled out or responsible for the crowd's actions. As a result, inhibitions are reduced, and people are free to act out feelings they would normally keep in check. The Ku Klux Klan, for example, goes to great lengths to preserve the anonymity of members. Dressed in white robes and hoods, respected members of the community may feel free to participate in extreme violence. But, one does not always have to be intentionally anonymous. An individual can be anonymous by being part of a huge crowd, such as the one that celebrates New Year's Eve in Times Square.

Suggestibility

Heightened suggestibility means that people are apt to respond to rumors. A **rumor** is an unsubstantiated report that tends to spread rapidly. Rumors find fertile soil in situations where people are emotionally aroused and lack accurate information. A crowd will be more inclined to accept uncritically rumors that confirm their own attitudes or biases.

When people lose their sense of individuality and there are no established rules to guide behavior, they may respond readily to suggestions that they would not accept in standard group situations. If a few people begin throwing rocks at storefront windows, others may follow suit. An aroused crowd is particularly susceptible to suggestions and directions delivered in an authoritative manner. Whoever is able to grab a microphone, for example, may temporarily gain control of a mob. People may respond to suggestions without stopping to consider their own feelings or the consequences of their behavior.

Emotional Contagion

Collective excitement often builds as members of a crowd stimulate and respond to each other, communicating and reinforcing a mood by shouting, clapping, milling about, stomping, and so on. This sharing of feelings that stimulates crowd behavior is called **emotional contagion.**

On many television shows that are recorded live, studio audiences are "warmed up" before the show begins. Pep rallies and canned laughter also help to "tune up" crowds, stimulating people to respond and reinforcing natural applause, cheers, or laughter. Crowd members are unified not by group norms, shared goals, or group structure but by their common emotional responses. Once this psychological unit is developed, it runs its course, often taking unexpected turns. Thus, a crowd attending a political rally may be whipped to a frenzy by a demagogic speaker and become an angry mob bent on destruction.

Critics of the contagion theory of crowd behavior dispute the idea that crowd members "catch" something from each other, or that they are unanimous in their intentions. Ralph Turner (1964) argues that the behavior of crowds probably follows many well-known sociological principles. As the crowd members interact with each other, and by means of examples by a few highly visible leaders, new norms (such as chanting, holding hands, or throwing stones) emerge which determine correct behavior in the new situation. Many crowd members quickly adopt these norms and the direction of the crowd takes shape. The illusion that the crowd is unanimous comes about because those who do not agree with the new norms (and perhaps there are many who disagree) are unable or unwilling to oppose the emerging dominant behavior. Thus, the emergent norms theory explains seemingly irrational behavior in terms of the standard sociological principle that individual behavior is influenced by the norms that dominate in a particular social setting.

TYPES OF CROWDS

All crowds are not alike. We have mentioned many different types of collective gatherings, such as audiences, lynch mobs, and demonstrations. Sociologists have tried to classify collective phenomena on the basis of the different forms that crowd behavior can take. Roger Brown classified crowds as either active or passive. *Active crowds* include mobs and crowds of different kinds. A **mob** is one type of active crowd that is emotionally aroused and that may openly engage in destructive behavior. Other types of active crowds include aggressive, escape, acquisition, and expressive (Brown, 1965). *Passive crowds* he called audiences.

An **audience** is a passive crowd that assembles for a specific event and reacts to an external stimulus. The stimulus may be a ballet performance, a presidential nominee making an acceptance speech, a ball game, a movie. For the most part, each audience member is responding in an individual way and interacts little with other members. But if the audience is responding to a live performance of some kind, there will be interaction between the audience and the performers. Actors, for example, are quite aware of audience reactions. They speak of "good," or responsive, audiences and "bad," or unresponsive audiences. Political candidates who know that a cheering audience is "with" them will become more emotional and enthusiastic as they speak.

Active crowds may also be motivated by other factors. One is **panic,** which is likely to occur when a crowd is partially entrapped and

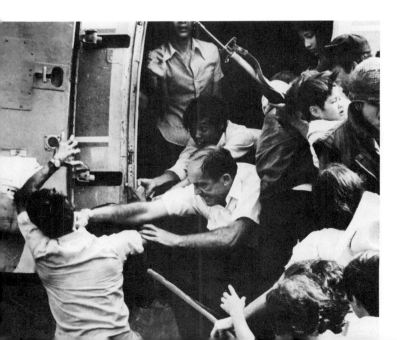

The people who fought for space on planes leaving Saigon in the advance of the North Vietnamese army were an example of a panic crowd.

perceives a threat, and if the means of escape are blocked and communication is poor. Although the mob's goal is to escape, the crowd defeats its own purpose because of its frenzied state (Turner and Killian, 1972). A classic example is the behavior that erupts following the cry of "fire" in a crowded theater.

A classic example of panic was provided by the departure of U.S. forces and the capitulation of South Vietnam to the North Vietnamese. People were desperate to leave the country fearing that there would be economic collapse and personal repression under the new regime. Planes and military helicopters leaving the country were mobbed by people trying to escape. Since each plane or helicopter could accommodate only a certain number of people before it would be too heavily loaded to fly, people fought with each other to control access. Those on the aircraft pushed away others trying to board, while those seeking refuge fought with each other to try to reach the planes. With limited transportation available, no means of crowd control, and an immediate threat at hand, those trying to escape became panic crowds.

A crowd bent on possession of economic goods or some scarce resource is an **acquisitive crowd.** Until federal legislation guaranteed all bank deposits, bank failures were not uncommon. Depositors who believed that a bank was about to fail would all rush to the bank and demand their money. Because banks never keep all of their depositors' money on hand, such a run could cause even a perfectly sound and stable bank to collapse. Such acquisitive panics involve competition for something that is in short supply. The object in demand may be almost anything, from gold to food. For example, during the earthquakes in Naples, Italy, in 1981, crowds of injured and destitute people gathered at clinics, hospitals, and emergency shelters to demand water, food, housing, and medical care.

Highly emotional crowds that focus on the subjective experiences of the members are called **expressive crowds.** At football rallies, at New Year's Eve festivities in New York's Times Square, at victory celebrations, orgies, and religious revival meetings, the behavior itself seems to be the mob's goal (Brown, 1965). These mobs are often motivated by a need to release tension in a manner that often goes beyond the restraints and inhibitions of our daily lives.

THE MASS

Not all forms of collective behavior take place in crowds. Some forms arise among scattered individuals. Clothing and grooming styles, for example, sweep across the United States almost yearly. And each Saturday afternoon, millions tune their televisions to the same sporting event and simultaneously drink beer and eat salty snacks. In the late 1950s the nation was swept by the hula hoop craze, and in 1981 we bought millions of dollars worth of jelly beans after President Reagan's election. In all of these situations, people are behaving collectively, although they are not necessarily gathered in the same place at the same time. Rather, they constitute what sociologists refer to as a mass. A **mass** is a large number of people whose members are physically dispersed and who react independently to a common stimulus.

Crowds and mobs are not unknown in premodern societies, but the mass is unique to urban, industrial society—or what sociologists sometimes call **mass society.** This refers to a large social system characterized by impersonality, anonymity, and functional interdependence. Technology is an important element in mass societies. It enables the aggregation of larger numbers of people in small areas—as in apartment houses—as well as the rapid spread of goods and information among them. This is made possible through things like television, the telephone, and the jet plane. Having a large population that is interdependent, and mechanisms to quickly spread information and goods among them, make mass behavior possible.

Fads, fashions, and crazes are all behaviors that gain sudden and widespread popularity and then decline abruptly (Brown, 1965). A **fad** is a behavior that enjoys short-lived popularity and usually involves rather trifling and superficial activities or expressions. Some examples are the phrases "far out" and "ya know," Farrah flips, skateboards, designer jeans, and so on. A **fashion** is a form of briefly popular collective behavior that involves not only variability in dress styles but also changing behavior patterns in almost any area of cultural activity. There are fashions in music, literature, art, architecture, and even in scientific theories: neoclassicism, expressionism, impressionism, and cubism in art; Freudianism and behaviorism in psychology; Roman, Gothic, and the Bauhaus schools of architecture; swing, folk, and disco music. All have enjoyed a heyday of public popularity, reflecting currents of social change. A **craze** is a form of collective behavior similar in nature to fads and fashions but usually involving larger sums of money and tending to be more obsessive. Often crazes involve economic speculation such as the Florida land boom of the 1920s. The typical craze follows a course of events comparable to the spread of a contagious disease: a period during which only a few seem concerned with an idea; a period in which many people suddenly adopt the idea; and a period during which interest tapers off (Brown, 1965).

Mass hysteria ia also a kind of contagion— the spread of irrational, compulsive beliefs or behavior. It may involve a brief episode limited to the members of a crowd, such as the screaming, jumping up and down, and fainting that often took place at Beatles' concerts. Or it may involve scattered individuals. The hysteria that followed Orson Welles's 1938 radio drama about an invasion from Mars is a classic example.

Welles's broadcast began with an announce-ment about the nature of the drama, then switched to what sounded like a program of ballroom music. The trouble that was to follow occurred because those who turned in late thought they *were* listening to a program of music. From time to time the music was interrupted with strange news reports. Finally, the music was stopped altogether as eyewitness reports and other news sources described the invasion of ugly and murderous Martians in a New Jersey farm field. It is estimated that over 1 million people mistook the dramatization for a news report and were terrified by the prospect of imminent destruction by

When Orson Welles broadcast "War of the Worlds," he created a state of mass hysteria. Many listeners missed the opening introduction identifying the show as fiction and, instead, believed that they were listening to an actual news report of an invasion from Mars.

Martians. People interviewed after the episode described their reactions to the broadcast:

. . . people started to rush out of the apartment house all undressed. We got into the car and listened some more. Suddenly, the announcer was gassed, the station went dead so we tried another station but nothing would come on. Then we went to a gas station and filled up our tank in preparation for just riding as far as we could . . . (Cantril, 1958)

Different explanations have been proposed to explain the phenomenon of mass hysteria. It has been suggested that the hysteria following Welles's broadcast was due in part to the general level of tension in the country produced by the Depression and the imminence of war in Europe. As we would expect, conditions in the social environment affected people's perceptions and behavior.

THE PUBLIC AND PUBLIC OPINION

In a mass society, new issues are arising all the time, capturing the interest and attention of large numbers of individuals. For example, public debate began as soon as there was a proposal made to build the Alaska pipeline as a way of reducing the dependence of the United States on foreign oil. Diverse interest groups began voicing conflicting interpretations and opinions about the proposal. Environmental groups were opposed, pointing to the destruction of the Alaskan environment and the wanton squandering of scarce natural resources. The petroleum industry was in favor, emphasizing the immense need for oil products in this country. Some Alaskan citizens regarded the proposal favorably as a way to bring revenue into the state, promoting the development of new industry and communities. Others feared being overrun and dominated by the large oil companies. In other words, a public emerged from the mass. A **public** is a scattered group of people who share some interest or concern over

a controversial issue where norms are shifting or uncertain. The members of a public have some way of registering their views and may exert some influence over the actions of others, particularly politicians.

As more and more people become involved in debate, discussion, and exchange, public opinion develops. It will be influenced by the psychological makeup of the members of the mass, by their special interests and social backgrounds, by networks of informal interaction, by spokespersons for diverse interest groups (opinion leaders), and by the mass media as they broadcast the news and publicize the controversy. Out of all this, a limited number of viewpoints emerge and become dominant. Public opinion may still be divided, but the members of each interest group have reached a consensus. **Public opinion,** then, refers to the newly formulated and shared viewpoint held by the members of a public.

Public opinion may be *measured* by its direction—how many people are for and how many against an issue; by its intensity—how strongly people feel about the issue; and by its integration—how closely the opinion fits a person's general value system and outlook on life. For example, one person might oppose keeping United States troops in the Middle East because he is a pacifist and is against military activity of any kind. Someone else opposes the policy because she regards it as an expression of imperialist expansion. Another might be against the idea because she believes that the money spent on out its own problems. A fourth might be opposed because she believes that the money spent on military activities abroad should be used for social needs at home. While these people all vehemently agree on the issue, their opinions are quite different, springing from distinct sets of beliefs and values. The more closely an opinion is integrated with a person's total outlook, the more lasting and the less easily changed it will be.

Researchers have devised sophisticated methods to measure these dimensions of public

TABLE 10.3 / PUBLIC EXPOSED TO LEADING MEDIA

Newspapers	Average Weekday Circulation	Time Period
Washington Post	510,688	Six month period, ending September 30, 1971
Chicago Tribune	745,210	
New York Times	814,290	
Los Angeles Times	981,661	
Magazines		
Newsweek	2,631,442	Period ending March or June 1971
Time	4,262,625	
Networks		
ABC	13,708,400	Two-week period, ending February 25, 1973
NBC	15,767,700	
CBS	17,695,800	

Source: Ayer Directory of Publications (Fort Washington, Penn.: IMS Press, 1972), and Nielsen Television Index, two weeks ending February 25, 1973.

opinion through sample surveys of various kinds to determine people's attitudes. Public opinion research has become extremely important to political observers, businesses, and government. In addition to predicting election results, politicians use polls to guide their election campaigns; governments use them to determine how people feel about official policies and to discover the felt needs and interests of the citizenry; businesses use polls to determine what kinds of products the public will buy and how those products can be sold most effectively.

Public opinion research also has tremendous manipulative potential. The information gleaned from an opinion survey can be used to change or mold public opinion. **Propaganda** is the deliberate attempt to persuade people to adopt a particular point of view, whether to buy a certain brand of soap or a particular government policy. Typically, propaganda is based on an emotional appeal and gives a one-sided interpretation of a situation. Often it plays on people's fears and anxieties: the fear of communism, subversion, bad breath, or body odor. Another technique is to associate the partisan cause with existing values, people, organizations, or symbols. For example, a cigarette may be advertised as one that is smoked by liberated females; a brand of coffee presented as the one preferred by discriminating people; or, conversely, a politician might try to discredit the opposing candidates by associating them with "subversive" elements. Finally, propaganda portrays its cause as a strong or popular view, representing "what everybody is thinking" or "the wave of the future."

There are, of course, limits to the effectiveness of propaganda. If the propaganda goes contrary to a group's basic values or norms, most people will probably reject it as they will if they have adequate factual knowledge or counterpropaganda from the other side. Right now, for example, in the United States, the debate on the right of abortion is tightly locked with neither side able to sway the other (Ryan, 1976: 87–116). Those who believe that women should control their own bodies are not swayed by charges that they are "baby killers." Those who believe that abortion is wrong are not swayed by reports of desperate abortions performed under dangerous conditions. If propaganda is to be successful, it must not conflict too strongly with a person's existing norms, values, and viewpoints.

SOCIAL ISSUE/The Mass Media

Muriel G. Cantor/*The American University*

The mass media of communications are an integral part of modern, industrial society. Without mass media, society as we know it would not exist. Social communication among members is necessary in any society. What distinguishes mass communication from other forms of communications is that theoretically one person is able to reach an entire population simultaneously through print, radio, film, or television with an identical message. Because of this ability, some critics and scholars have attributed great power to the mass media, especially as the means to sway public opinion and attitudes and even to control behavior. Some are so concerned about the power of the media that they claim the media are the perfect tools for organizing a revolution and establishing a totalitarian regime (Bramson, 1961: 121–39). Others defend the media, insisting they reflect the tastes and opinions of the majority and thus function to integrate otherwise diverse groups by providing a national source of information and entertainment (Hirsch, 1978).

This debate concerning the power of mass media has been ongoing since the advent of the penny press in the nineteenth century. Essentially, the very factors that make the mass media unique in various societies have generated much of this criticism. The mass media in the United States are criticized because they are organized for profit (Gans, 1974: 19–64; Tuchman, 1974: 1–40); the mass media in the Soviet Union are criticized because they are state-controlled; and the mass media in developing countries are criticized because they are dependent on the United States and Great Britain for much of their content (Tunstall, 1977). The common element in all the critiques is that one group, either the state or entrepreneurs, is believed to control the communications received by the masses who are perceived as having little or no input into what is seen, heard or printed. These criticisms should alert people that the mass media of communications cannot be examined in isolation, but rather, must be examined within the context of the society in which they occur. This essay examines the media in the United States. The media operate differently in other societies, and therefore may be more or less powerful (Lee, 1980; Wright, 1975: 23–59).

In all societies, the mass media have at least one element in common; they could not exist without advanced technology. Yet, although mass media depend on advanced technology, they are not synonymous with it. Mass media of communications are different from other forms of communications that also depend on advanced technology. Obvious examples of technological apparatuses that are not mass media are the telephone, home-movie camera, and home videotape equipment. It is not the equipment that makes the communication process a form of mass communication, but rather how the content is used, developed, and transmitted. Mass media differ from other forms of communications because they are directed toward a relatively large, heterogeneous audience, because they are rapid, transient, and public, and because the media messages are produced in an organizational context (see Wright, 1975: 7). To understand the power of the media, the audience, the content, and the communicators and their organizational context must be understood. Because television in the United States is closer to the "ideal" of a mass medium, much of what is said applies most accurately to it rather than to radio, movies, or the press. Commercial television has become the major national mass medium, supplanting radio and the movies which were national media before World War II (Charters, 1933; Halloran, 1964: 13–17). While movies, radio, and magazines are becoming specialized in content and distribution, network television is watched by huge numbers of Americans who are inoculated simultaneously with the same message. Although network television may be changing because of the adoption of new technologies, such as videotape recorders, videodiscs, and pay television transmitted by cable, it remains the only medium available to advertisers and power-holders to reach all of the people.

CREATING THE MESSAGE

Most research on mass media has focused on the audience. Descriptions of the audience for various messages and the effects of the communications on the audience have been researched extensively for several decades (Holz and Wright, 1979). This research has resulted in an extensive and growing body of literature (see Murray, 1980). This does not mean, however, that there is a common understanding of how people are affected by the media. As indicated earlier, there is no clear agreement on how media affect human behavior, opinions, and attitudes. Several researchers who have been concerned with the effects of mass communications on people's lives, culture, and personalities have repeatedly suggested that research is necessary first to understand the communicator, the decision makers, the process of producing media messages, and the structure of the entertainment and information industries (Cantor, 1982).

Regardless of who is in control of the means of communication (whether the government, as in many of the socialist and Third World countries, or those who own the various media, as in Western democracies) the structure of the communication process is similar in one respect: mass communications are organized. All mass communicators, whether they are part of a government or commercial medium, work in a formal, complex structure with an extensive division of labor organized bureaucratically. This means that the power to decide what is broadcast or printed rests with very few people, and the creative people working in these settings do not necessarily express their own values but rather the values of those in control of the bureaucratic structures (Cantor, 1971, 1980; Mills,

1953; Johnstone et al., 1976). Moreover, several of the mass media of communications in the United States depend on more than one bureaucratically controlled organization (Tunstall, 1977). For example, a large city newspaper is organized as a complex bureaucracy with ultimate control over content resting with the publisher. The function or purpose of the organization is to produce a profit-making newspaper each day. Part of the organizational tasks include gathering, editing and printing of news, features, and entertainment. To do these tasks properly not only are journalists, editors, and copywriters needed within the organization but usually the services of others in large bureaucratic organizations are also required. Most city newspapers depend on the wire services (Associated Press and United Press International), which are also large, complex, bureaucratically organized enterprises. The actual processes of newsgathering within these complicated structures have been investigated by several social scientists in the last decade. Gaye Tuchman (1978) and Herbert Gans (1979) provide descriptions of how journalists work and how organizational and professional constraints shape the selection, content, and presentation of the news.

Television and movie production are even more complicated. Television stations are more dependent than newspapers on many varied kinds of outside organizations to provide information and entertainment programs. If a television station is affiliated with one of the three major television networks [The National Broadcasting Corporation (NBC), The American Broadcasting Corporation (ABC), and The Columbia Broadcasting System (CBS)], as 85 percent of the commercial stations are, then a large percentage of entertainment, news, and information programs are provided by the networks, which in turn depend on Hollywood production companies for dramatic programs, other production companies for game and variety shows, and the wire services for news. If a station is independent and not affiliated with a network, it must buy programs from distribution or syndication companies. The

The information and images carried by the mass media are the product of choices made by those who control the media.

above is a brief sketch of the complexities of media production. Besides the controls already mentioned, radio and television are regulated by the Federal Communications Commission, and the press and the electronic media also must take into consideration the advertisers who finance their enterprises.

The bureaucratic and organizational complexities of mass media production have important social consequences which can be discerned. The writers, journalists, artists, actors, and other creators are often stages away from their final product (Cantor, 1980; Johnstone et al., 1976). Power over what is

shown rests with those who own or control the means of communication rather than with the individual creators. Actors, for example, cannot choose the roles they play and how to interpret them unless they are stars. And even then, the stars are viewed as products to be marketed. Also, the audience has little direct impact on the creation of content. A dramatic production is usually filmed or videotaped weeks before it is broadcast or seen by an audience. An exception is the soap operas which are taped daily, but even their scripts are written several weeks before they are taped. Theater films, too, are often made months, sometimes even years ahead of time. Although audiences are able to show their displeasure by not buying tickets or by turning off the programs, the audience has only eventual veto power but little direct control over creativity during the immediate production process.

In a free enterprise system, as it exists in the United States, those who control the means of communication (newspapers, radio stations, television stations) and the means of distribution (networks, distributors) depend on advertisers and other financiers as well as on the creators. However, controllers and owners are in effect the most powerful force in the selection of what is seen, read, and heard. There are several reasons why power rests with the controllers rather than creators. One is that there are more people able to create content than there are jobs available. Unless journalists, actors, writers, or other creators are stars, they must satisfy the producers, editors or officials, or they are replaced. Also the popularity of a medium with an audience gives more power to the owners and distributors than to the advertisers or entrepreneurs. In this sense, the audience does have power. The owners and selectors in harmony with the largest part of the heterogeneous, mass audience are able to attract the financial support they need. If one advertiser of a very popular TV program protests the content, other advertisers are waiting in the wings to buy space on that show. The same would apply to high-circulation newspapers and magazines much of the time although advertisers have more direct influence over those media than over television because those media are usually more specialized and therefore advertisers more scarce.

THE EFFECTS AND THE NATURE OF THE MASS MEDIA EXPERIENCES

Because the most successful communicators are those ideologically in tune with the largest portion of the audience, the content would appear to follow social change rather than lead it (Gans, 1979). Does this mean that the power of the mass media as a source of influence on opinions and attitudes is overestimated? As mentioned earlier, this subject has been debated for decades. What does seem to be clear is that as a source of information and as an influence in agenda setting, the power of the mass media cannot be denied.

Media function to define problems and alert people to the issues. In that sense, they are powerful, and in recent years television has become the most powerful of the mass media. Roughly 75 percent of the people in the United States get most of their news from television, and half the population gets all of its news from the home screen (Schram, 1973). Television at this time is truly a national medium, because it does reach millions of people simultaneously with an identical message. Thus the topics broadcasters select to present on the air become those topics immediately important and salient to viewers. When broadcasters choose to ignore events, it is possible that otherwise important happenings never reach the attention of the public.

There are many examples of events becoming important because of media attention. Frank Mankiewicz and Joel Swerdlow (1978) show that busing was propelled into a national issue by television news reports. Television news focused on the few cities where violence over busing occurred rather than on the majority of cities where school children were peacefully integrated. Another example was the wave of student protests over the late sixties and early seventies. The evidence suggests that student protests persisted for several years after they received media attention, but because they occurred in the smaller, less prestigious colleges (rather than at Berkeley, Columbia, and Chicago), they were no longer considered news worthy of national media attention. The events that led to the resignation of President Nixon provide still another example. The Watergate "break-in" was not presented as a major news event by the national media until months after its occurrence. If Katharine Graham, then publisher of the *Washington Post,* had not supported the investigation by reporters Robert Woodward and Carl Bernstein, which forced the national media to publicize the event many months later, it is possible that Nixon might have been able to finish his term in office (Paletz and Entman, 1981).

Tuchman (1978) and Gitlin (1980) believe that some social movements, interest groups, and political figures have more access to news media than do others. Elites are a main source of news, and according to Paletz and Entman, their access to (and control over) the content translates into actual political power. The evidence they cite is indisputable and overwhelming. The media confer political power on individuals and help these individuals maintain their power, because of both what does and does not get reported. Power holders are insulated from public accountability and scrutiny when events and decisions are withheld from the media.

THE AUDIENCE—PUBLIC OPINION AND BEHAVIOR

Space limitations make it difficult to do more than advise people of the complexity, questions, and problems involved in attempting to assess the impact of the media on public opinion and behavior. It is clear that news and entertainment should not be considered mutually exclusive categories. To understand mass communications, both must be examined, for each is important as an influence on opinions and attitudes. Those who have studied political campaigns and the influence of the media on voting behavior have discovered that audiences are not passive recipients of propaganda but are selective in what they read and view. Sociologists and other social scientists have found that audiences are part of a social milieu and that the effects of the mass media are tempered by a number of factors, such as the context in which people receive the communication, the social characteristics of the viewers, and the

viewers' values, beliefs, and attitudes (see Katz and Lazarsfeld, 1964; McQuail, 1969). In contrast, some social scientists who have examined the effects of television entertainment on adults and children consider television the primary socialization agent in American society. For these critics, television has become more important than the family and the school system for educating the young, and it continues to define values and reality for adults (for example, see Gerbner and Gross, 1976).

One of the ongoing problems of media research is to try to integrate these disparate findings. Dennis McQuail points out that, despite frequent comments about the power of the press, movies, and television to change opinions and influence behavior, attempts to measure the effects of mass communications by scientific means have lagged behind conjecture (1969: 44). Also, there is a problem with the interpretation of research results. The popular press frequently gives the impression that there is clear agreement on what effect viewing violence on television has on the behavior of children. For example, *Reader's Digest* (Steinfeldt, 1973: 37–45) reports that (1) most children are exposed to many violent acts on television and (2) heavy viewing of these acts of violence leads to crime in the streets on a societal level, and to increased "antisocial" behavior (mostly aggression) and mental health problems on the individual level. During the 1970s there were numerous reviews on the subject of televised violence and its influence on viewers' behavior. In 1982, still another review was published (Pearl et al.), and the controversy has not been settled. Thus, the issues concerning the relationship of television violence and aggressive behavior continue to be debated by social scientists, political leaders, and journalists. There is probably no other question concerning television's impact that has generated as much public interest and professional study as this question. Various people examining the same literature on the subject continue to come to very different conclusions (Murray, 1980: 29). This issue can be considered the problem that will not go away.

CONCLUSION

The newest issue to emerge in the relationship of the mass media to society is no longer how the audience might be affected by television content (e.g., sex and violence, alcohol and drug use, sexism, etc.) but how the distribution of information and entertainment to home audiences will be affected by advances in transmission. Since the 1930s when radio became a mass medium, social scientists, policy makers, and citizens have been concerned over the limited range of programs offered. The newer concern will be over the future structure and public accountability of the even greater communications industry to be made possible by cable and satellites (*Business Week,* 1981). Will the now-few program suppliers and distributors continue their control, or will that power shift to industrial conglomerates that are still few in number (Cantor, 1982)? Also, no one can predict what the effects will be on those members of the audience who are offered an unlimited choice of opportunities for self-education and entertainment.

Innovations in cable and satellite transmission (especially those with interactive capability) raise another important issue for the future: these innovations offer the opportunity for direct surveillance of homes and offices. On-site capability to invade privacy could become the serious ethical and political issue of the twenty-first century. Will Big Brother be watching the audience while it watches Big Brother?

Researchers in the United States and other parts of the world, such as Great Britain (Tunstall, 1977) and in Third World countries (Katz and Wedell, 1977; Lee, 1980) are now considering the problems and questions reviewed in this essay, as well as others relating to the role of mass media in maintaining or changing societal relationships. However, there is one generalization that can be made: The media are part of the society in which they are generated or adopted. Both those who believe that media are very powerful in the formation of opinion and behavior and those who are not as certain make the same point: the mass media do play a role in influencing the young and old, particularly because they function to alert people to problems and issues, but the influence can be understood only within the social and cultural context of the society being considered.

REFERENCES

Bramson, Leon (1961). *The Political Context of Sociology.* Princeton, N.J.: Princeton University Press.

BusinessWeek (1981). Information processing: The home information revolution. June 29, 1981, pp. 74–83.

Cantor, Muriel G. (1971) *The Hollywood TV Producer: His Work and His Audience.* New York: Basic Books.

———— (1980). *Prime-Time Television: Content and Control.* Beverly Hills, Ca.: Sage Publications.

———— (1982). The television industry: The problems of responsibility and control. In *Television and Behavior: Ten Years of Scientific Progress and Implications for the Eighties,* eds. D. Pearl, L. Bouthilet, and J. Lazar. Washington, D.C.: United States Government Printing Office.

Charters, W. W. (1933). *Motion Pictures and Youth.* New York: Macmillan.

Gans, Herbert (1974). *Popular Culture and High Culture: An Analysis of Taste.* New York: Basic Books.

———— (1979). *Deciding What's News: A Study of CBS Evening News, NBC Nightly News, Newsweek and Time.* New York: Pantheon Books.

Gerbner, George, and **Larry Gross** (1976). The scary world of TV's heavy viewers. *Psychology Today* 9: 41–45, 89.

Gitlin, Todd (1980). *The Whole World Is Watching: Mass Media in the Making and Unmaking of the New Left.* Berkeley, Ca.: University of California Press.

Halloran, J. D. (1964). *The Effects of Mass Communication: With Special Reference to Television.* Leicester, U.K.: Leicester University Press.

Head, Sidney (1976). *Broadcasting in America: A Survey of Television and Radio,* 3rd ed. Boston: Houghton Mifflin.

Hirsch, Paul M. (1978). Television as a national medium: Its cultural and political role in American society. In *Handbook of Urban Life,* ed. D. Street. San Francisco: Josey Bass.

Holz, Josephine R., and **Charles R. Wright** (1979). Sociology of mass communications. In *Annual Review of Sociology,* vol. 5, eds. A. Inkeles, J. Coleman, and R. H. Turner. Palo Alto, Ca.: Annual Reviews, Inc.

Johnstone, John W. W., Edward J. Slawski, and **William W. Bowman** (1976). *The News People: A Sociological Portrait of American Journalists and Their Work.* Urbana, Ill.: University of Illinois Press.

Katz, Elihu, and **Paul E. Lazarsfeld** (1964). *Personal Influence,* paperback ed., New York: Free Press.

Katz, Elihu, and **G. Wedell** (1977). *Broadcasting in the Third World: Promise and Performance.* Cambridge, Mass.: Harvard University Press.

Lee, Chin-Chuan (1980). *Media Imperialism Reconsidered: The Homogenizing of Television Culture.* Beverly Hills, Ca.: Sage Publications.

Mankiewicz, Frank, and **Joel Swerdlow** (1978). *Remote Control: Television and the Manipulation of American Life.* New York: Times Books.

McQuail, Denis (1969). *Towards a Sociology of Mass Communications.* New York: Collier-Macmillan Publishers.

Mills, C. Wright (1953). *White Collar.* New York: Oxford University Press.

Murray, John P. (1980). *Television and Youth: 25 Years of Research and Controversy.* Stanford, Wash.: The Boys Town Center for Study of Youth Development.

Paletz, David L., and **Robert M. Entman** (1981). *Media • Power • Politics.* New York: Free Press.

Pearl, David, Lorraine Bouthilet, and **Joyce Lazar,** eds. (1982). *Television and Behavior: Ten Years of Scientific Progress and Implications for the Eighties.* Washington, D.C.: United States Government Printing Office.

Schram, Wilbur (1973). *Men, Messages, and Media: A Look at Human Communication.* New York: Harper & Row.

Steinfeldt, Jessie (1973). TV violence is harmful. *Reader's Digest* (April): 37–45.

Tuchman, Gaye (1974). *The TV Establishment: Programming for Power and Profit.* Englewood Cliffs, N.J.: Prentice-Hall.

———— (1978). *Making News: A Study in the Construction of Reality.* New York: Free Press.

Tunstall, Jeremy (1977). *The Media Are American: Anglo-American Media in the World.* New York: Columbia University Press.

Wright, Charles R. (1975). *Mass Communications: A Sociological Perspective,* 2nd ed. New York: Random House.

SUMMARY

1. The main purposes of this chapter are to define and discuss the importance and characteristics of various types of groups; to discuss the nature of collective behavior as a type of group activity; and to discuss types of collective behavior, including crowds, public opinion, and mass behavior.

2. Groups of all types are important to human development and society. Sociologists distinguish among groups, aggregates, collectivities, and social categories on the basis of the duration and the character of the interactions among their members.

3. Factors such as similarity, proximity, and common goals lead to the formation of groups. Once a group is formed, instrumental and expressive activities characterize the group's daily functioning. The types of interaction within a group are influenced by communication, cohesion, and conformity, each of which influences the maintenance of the group.

4. Groups can also be categorized according to size and function. Primary groups are small and are characterized by personal interactions. Secondary groups are usually larger and have more impersonal goal-oriented interaction. In-groups function to give their members a sense of belonging, and they may stereotype or be hostile to those in out-groups. In addition, people have any number of reference groups against which they evaluate themselves by either accepting or rejecting their values.

5. Collective behavior is relatively spontaneous, unstructured, and unpredictable group activity focused on a certain stimulus. Smelser's "value added" theory identifies six determinants that occur in sequence and which indicate whether an episode of collective behavior will occur and what its probable form will be.

6. Because crowds are the clearest examples of collective behavior, various theories try to explain the reasons for crowd behavior: the contagion theory (involves anonymity, rumors, and emotional contagion) and the emergent norms theory.

7. Sociologists try to classify collective phenomena on the basis of the different forms that crowd behavior can take: passive (audiences) or active (aggressive, panic, acquisitive, and expressive crowds).

8. Some forms of collective behavior arise among a scattered mass of individuals. A few of the significant types of mass behavior are fads, fashions, crazes, and mass hysteria.

9. Often a public that shares an interest or a concern will arise within a mass. Because public opinion (one aspect of public behavior) may exert influence over the actions of others, some people (especially politicians and business executives) are interested in measuring it. The information gained from such public opinion research can be used as propaganda to persuade people to adopt a certain viewpoint.

REVIEW

Key Terms

Group	Instrumental leadership	In-group	Rumor
Aggregate	Expressive leadership	Out-group	Emotional contagion
Collectivity	Sociogram	Reference group	Mob
Category	Primary groups	Collective behavior	Audience
Leader	Secondary groups	Crowd	Panic

Acquisitive crowds	**Fad**	**Public**
Expressive crowds	**Fashion**	**Public opinion**
Mass	**Craze**	**Propaganda**
Mass society	**Mass hysteria**	

Review and Discussion

1. Would you make a better instrumental or expressive leader? Why? Which leadership role would you prefer to have, regardless of the way you have evaluated your abilities?

2. From the student's point of view, the faculty is an out-group. Separate office buildings, faculty lounges and clubs, and the custom of calling professors by their last name emphasize this division. In your experience, do students stereotype faculty and vice versa? What kinds of events might bring students and faculty together in one in-group?

3. Name an in-group to which you belong, and an out-group to which you don't belong; name some of your reference groups; and name some secondary groups to which you belong.

4. Have you ever been a participant in any kind of crowd behavior? If so, what type of crowd was it? Which theory best explains your involvement?

5. Think of some propaganda that has been aimed at you. What was the purpose of the propaganda? What strategy was used? How did it affect your viewpoint?

6. Analyze your family as a small group. Who performs what leadership roles? What are the usual interaction patterns among family members? What is your role in the family group?

References

Bales, Robert F., Fred L. Strodtbeck, Theodore M. Mills, and **Mary E. Roseborough** (1951). Channels of communication in small groups. *American Sociological Review* 16: 461–68.

Berelson, Bernard, and **Gary A. Steiner** (1967). *Human Behavior: An Inventory of Scientific Findings.* New York: Harcourt, Brace, Jovanovich.

Brown, Roger (1965). *Social Psychology.* New York: Free Press.

Cantril, Hadley (1958). The invasion from Mars. In *Readings in Social Psychology,* eds. E. E. Maccoby, T. M. Newcomb, and E. L. Hartley. New York: Holt.

Durkheim, Emile (1951). *Suicide,* translated by John A. Spaulding and George Simpson. New York: Free Press. (Originally published in 1897.)

Faris, Robert E. L. (1934). Cultural isolation and the schizophrenic personality. *American Journal of Sociology* 29: 155–64.

Faris, Robert E. L., and **H. Dunham** (1938). *Mental Disorders in Urban Areas: An Ecological Study of Schizophrenia and Other Psychoses.* Chicago: University of Chicago Press.

Heap, Kenneth (1977). *Group Theory for Social Workers.* New York: Pergamon.

Hersh, Seymour M. (1970). My Lai 4. *Harpers Magazine,* May 1970.

LeBon, Gustave (1969). *The Crowd: A Study of the Popular Mind.* New York: Ballentine.

Lewin, K. (1951). *Field Theory in Social Science.* New York: Harper.

McQuail, Dennis (1975). *Communication.* New York: Longman.

Merton, Robert K. (1957). *Social Theory and Social Structure,* rev. ed. New York: Macmillan.

Moskos, Charles C., Jr. (1970). *The American Enlisted Man.* New York: Russell Sage Foundation.

Newcomb, T. M. (1943). *Personality and Social Change.* New York: Dryden.

——— (1963). Persistence and regression of changed attitudes: Long-range studies. *Journal of Social Issues* 19: 3–14.

Rattner, Steven (1981). British riots stem from deep resentment. *The New York Times,* July 15, 1981, pp. A1ff.

Riley, Matilda, *et al.,* eds. (1969). *Aging and Society: Aging and the Professions,* vol. 2. New York: Russell Sage Foundation.

Ryan, William (1976). *Blaming the Victim,* rev. ed. New York: Vintage.

Schein, Edgar (1968). Brainwashing. In *Interpersonal Dynamics,* rev. ed., ed. W. Bennis *et al.* Homewood, Ill.: Dorsey Press.

Sherif, Muzafer, and **Carolyn W. Sherif** (1956). *Outline of Social Psychology,* rev. ed. New York: Harper & Row.

Shipler, David K. (1981). Survivors of Hitler's camps tell of their resistance. *New York Times,* June 21, 1981, B-3.

Smelser, Neil J. (1963). *Theory of Collective Behavior.* New York: Free Press.

Stark, Rodney, and **William Sims Bainbridge** (1980). Networks of faith: Interpersonal bonds and recruitment to cults and sects. *American Journal of Sociology* 85 (May): 1376–95.

Stephens, William N. (1963). *The Family in Cross-Cultural Perspective.* New York: Holt, Rinehart, and Winston.

Summer, W. G. (1906). *Folkways.* Boston: Ginn.

Turner, Ralph H., and **Lewis M. Killian** (1972). *Collective Behavior.* Englewood Cliffs, N.J.: Prentice-Hall.

White, Ralph K., and **Ronald D. Lippitt** (1960). *Autocracy and Democracy.* New York: Harper & Row.

Whyte, William F. (1955). *Street Corner Society,* Chicago: University of Chicago Press.

11

FORMAL ORGANIZATIONS AND BUREAUCRACIES

355

We have all spent time in waiting rooms, been met by receptionists, been routed from one office to another, and filled out a variety of forms and applications in triplicate. Such experiences cause most of us to equate the term "bureaucracy" with buck-passing, red tape, runarounds, and frustration. To sociologists, however, bureaucracies are not necessarily evil or inefficient. They are merely one type of **formal organization,** a complex and deliberately constructed group that is organized to achieve certain specific and clearly stated goals. Whether it is to manufacture cars, to raise money for cancer research, to bring together people interested in collecting stamps or in losing weight, to educate the young, or to care for the sick, the objectives of an organization are usually well understood.

An organization sometimes has more than a single goal. A hospital, for example, not only provides medical care but might also conduct biomedical research and train young interns to become doctors. Unlike informal primary groups such as the family or the neighborhood gang, formal organizations are purposely structured so that specified goals can be accomplished with maximum speed and efficiency.

THE RANGE OF FORMAL ORGANIZATIONS

Sociologists have suggested various models for clarifying the differences and similarities among the wide range of formal organizations. Two of these classification systems are especially helpful. Sociologists Peter Blau and Richard Scott (1962) suggested that formal organizations can be usefully classified according to who benefits most from the goals of the group. They proposed four categories:

1. Mutual benefit associations, which are supposed to serve mainly the membership—for example, a veterans group.

2. Businesses, where benefits go mainly to the owners or stockholders.

3. Service organizations, such as the Red Cross or a school designed for the benefit of clients.

4. Commonweal organizations, such as Sing Sing or the Defense Department, which presumably benefit society as a whole (pp. 42–45).

Alternatively, Amitai Etzioni (1961) suggested that we might use a classification scheme based on how organizations obtain compliance from their members. He identified three categories:

1. The coercive organization, such as a prison or a concentration camp where force is used to obtain compliance.

2. Utilitarian organizations, which obtain compliance on practical grounds. People cooperate because it is in their interest. This category includes most businesses.

3. Shared-interest organizations, where most people participate because they share the norms and values of the organization. This group includes most schools, religious organizations, and other voluntary associations (pp. 66–67).

By using these two classification systems together, we can study formal organizations in terms of (1) their purpose and (2) the extent of their control over their members' lives. Observing organizations in this way, we can develop a continuum ranging from total institutions to voluntary organizations. Between these extreme types lie more familiar structures, most notably utilitarian organizations (such as businesses) to which people voluntarily belong in order to acquire needed economic resources, but from which they are able to resign at will. While they are members of these organizations, people allow their structures to exert significant influence over their lives.

Total Institutions

A highly structured formal organization that controls major portions of its members' lives is known as a **total institution.** Monasteries, military organizations, prisons, and mental hospitals are typical total institutions. They have more direct control over their members' lives than other types of organizations. They are usually of the *coercive* type identified above. Normally, compliance is not voluntary but is obtained through force or the threat of force. Members typically work, play, and sleep within the institution. Often there are barriers against contact with outsiders, and the members' privacy and personal affairs are regulated by the organization's staff—wardens, guards, or psychiatrists, for example. There is an extreme emphasis on rules, routines, and regulations. In terms of the members' lives, the scope of such structures is, in effect, "total."

Voluntary Associations

Organizations formed by persons who join freely to pursue mutual interests, **voluntary associations,** are far more limited in scope. The members are free to attend or withdraw at will. These organizations are built on a free expression of individual interest and commitment. Usually they occupy far less of a person's life than do the bureaucratic organizations in which we typically study or work. In our "nation of joiners," many people choose to participate in voluntary associations. These are clearly of the shared-interest type identified by Etzioni. Countless American parents are PTA members; their children may belong to the YMCA, the Girl Scouts, or the Young Zionists' League. Thousands of business people belong to the Masons, the Elks, and the Chamber of Commerce. Whatever the association, these structures all allow individuals to

The shared interests which can bring people together into a voluntary association are practically endless. Members of the Polar Bear Club, for example, share the "pleasure" of swimming in icy winter waters.

pursue their personal interests and activities with other like-minded people.

Many voluntary associations serve as channels for social and political action. The National Association for the Advancement of Colored People, the Women's Christian Temperance Union, and the National Organization for the Repeal of Marijuana Laws are just a few of the thousands of groups that band together to seek some change in social arrangements. Common Cause is an association founded to make politicians accountable to their constituencies which has promoted legislation for improving campaign practices and for guaranteeing equal rights for women. It is supported solely by voluntary public contributions.

Voluntary associations may also provide an opportunity for social experimentation and personal growth. Many established social welfare programs, labor unions, and reform movements began as voluntary associations staffed by volunteers and supported by private funds. Today many have become established bureaucratic organizations with large professional staffs, while many other voluntary associations have become bureaucratized but not professional (that is, their members still belong in order to pursue mutual interests).

BUREAUCRACY

The growth of large-scale formal organizations has occurred throughout our society in businesses, military organizations, religious groups, hospitals and welfare organizations, educational structures, and government agencies. The larger the organization, the more specialization is required of its members. The more specialization, the greater the need for coordination, and coordination in turn requires more specialization, especially in the coordination of positions. William Whyte provided an interesting demonstra-

tion of this principle by analyzing the changing social structure of a restaurant:

In the first stage, we have a small restaurant where the owner and several other employees dispense short orders over the counter. There is little division of labor. The owner and employees serve together as cooks, countermen, and dishwashers.

In the second stage, the business is still characterized by the informality and flexibility of its relationships. The boss knows most customers and all his employees on a personal basis. There is no need for formal controls and elaborate paperwork. Still, the organization has grown in complexity as it has grown in size. The volume of business is such that it becomes necessary to divide the work, and there are dishwashers and kitchen employees, as well as those who wait on the customers. Now the problems of coordination begin to grow also, but the organization is still small enough so that the owner-manager can observe directly a large part of its activities and step in to straighten out friction or inefficiency.

As the business continues to expand, it requires a still more complex organization as well as larger quarters. No longer able to supervise all activities directly, the owner-manager hires a service supervisor and a food production supervisor, and he places one of his employees in charge of the dishroom as a working supervisor. He also employs a checker to total checks for his waitresses and to see that the food is served in correct portions and style.

In time, the owner-manager finds that he can accommodate a larger number of customers if he takes one more step in the division of labor. Up to now the cooks have been serving the food to the waitresses. When these functions are divided, both cooking and serving can proceed more efficiently. Therefore, he sets up a service pantry apart from the kitchen.

The cooks now concentrate on cooking; the runners carry food from kitchen to pantry and carry orders from pantry to kitchen; the pantry girls serve the waitresses over the counter. This adds two more

© 1979 King Features Syndicate

groups (pantry girls and runners) to be supervised, and to cope with this and the larger scale of operation, the owner adds another level of supervision, so that there are two supervisors between him and the workers. Somewhere along the line of development, perhaps he begins serving drinks and adds bartenders to his organization. *

As long as a group remains relatively small, temporary, or without a specific purpose, there may be no need for a system of rules to assign and to coordinate positions. But as an organization becomes larger, the interlocking spiral of specialization and coordination tends to produce the elaborate social structure we call a **bureaucracy:** a formal organization with specialized functions, fixed rules, and a hierarchy of authority. Figure 11.1 provides an example of a bureaucracy.

Weber's Model of Bureaucracy

Power is an integral part of Weber's concept of bureaucracy. **Power** means the ability to

---

* From William Whyte, "The Social Structure of the Restaurant," reprinted by permission of the University of Chicago Press from the *American Journal of Sociology* 54 (January 1949): 302–10. Copyright 1949 by the University of Chicago.

impose one's will upon others, but Weber was not interested in the concept of power as brute force. He explored a power relationship which both the ruler and the ruled believe in: the former believes in the right to rule and the latter in the command as legitimate (when it is consistent with their beliefs), which gives authority to the superior to issue commands. **Authority,** then, is legitimate power, as opposed to power as brute force, which is significantly less stable. Weber described three "ideal types" of authority. An **ideal type** is a construct, based on empirical elements, which demonstrates a basic form. The construction of an ideal type enables the sociologist to show how many of the characteristics of the ideal type are to be found in real situations. The ideal type tells us what to look for in the study of organizations. Weber's three "ideal types" of authority are based on substantially different forms of legitimacy. We will review them in brief before looking at bureaucracies in more detail.

Traditional authority is based on custom. Acceptance by the ruled rests on the belief that the way things were done in the past continues to be the appropriate way of doing things today. Traditional authority may be based on the hereditary rights of the King or the feudal lord. Under traditional authority the rule may be arbitrary, but it has to remain within the bounds

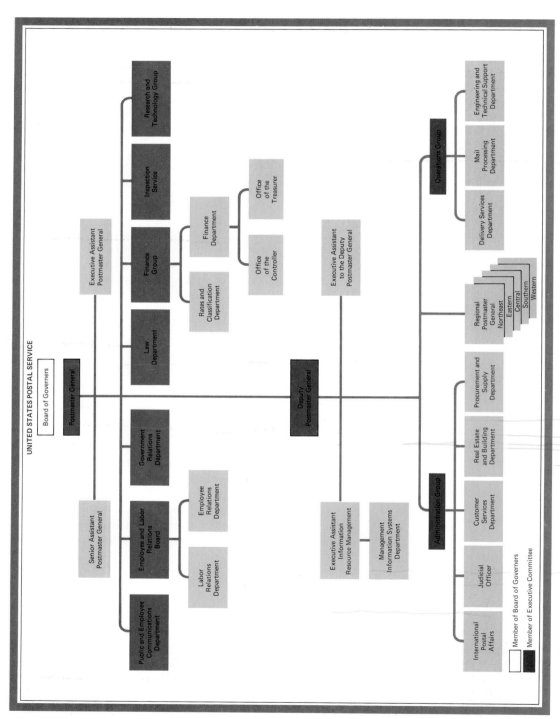

Fig. 11.1 / An Example of a Bureaucratic Structure

Source: U.S. Government Manual 1981–82 (May 1981), p. 861.

of traditional custom to be accepted as legitimate. Parental authority is based on tradition, although parents themselves need not be traditional.

Charismatic authority is based on the belief by the ruled or followers that the leader has a special quality—a personality considered extraordinary, endowed with special powers to lead, not usually present among ordinary mortals. These qualities are believed to be of divine origin and these characteristics legitimize the authority of the leader.

Such leaders emerge during periods when existing authority structures fail to meet the expectations of the ruled. Charismatic leaders are to be found in political, social, and religious realms. Germany in the 1920s and 1930s, with its high rate of unemployment, widespread dissatisfaction and alienation, seemed to be "ready" for a leader who promised the dispirited nation not only full employment, but greatness as be-

Charismatic leadership is based on the ability of a person to become the symbol of a people's faith.

hooves a "superior" Aryan race. Fidel Castro was the "extraordinary" leader accepted by the people as the savior of a Cuban society that was poor, unjust, and exploitative. Leading a small army of revolutionaries, and with wide support among Cubans, Castro fought a successful revolution against the old regime. He was perceived as the extraordinary man leading the people and the nation to justice and democracy. Gandhi, Muhammed, and Lenin were charismatic leaders in other societies.

Rational legal authority is based on the law. The legal rules accepted by the members of society as properly constituted legitimize the order of the ruler or official. Obedience is to the principle of the legal order. Rules are impersonal and specify in a rational manner the structure of the organization, i.e., the hierarchy, the rights, and duties of each role position.

Bureaucratic organizations were not unknown in the past. Large bureaucracies existed several centuries ago in China, Egypt, in the Catholic church, and in the Roman empire. What distinguishes bureaucracies of the past from contemporary bureaucratic organizations is the process of rationalization. Modern bureaucracy is characterized by coordination of activities in which every position serves the larger system. Rules are explicit and calculated to ensure maximum efficiency:

> Bureaucracy develops the more perfectly, the more it is "dehumanized," the more completely it succeeds in eliminating from official business love, hatred, and all purely personal, irrational, and emotional elements which escape calculation. (Weber, 1978: 975)

The process of rationalization is the reliance on rules and calculation. It is a means of eliminating affect and emotion to do away with elements that escape logical calculations.

Bureaucratic organizations have become the mainstay of life in modern societies. Craftspeople are replaced by giant factories in which the assembly line reigns; the neighborhood store is replaced by the giant supermarket; the village school gives way to the central high school; family counsel is replaced by the welfare agency; the hospital replaces the home as a place to care for the ill, and so forth.

The emergence of large-scale bureaucracies in all areas of social activity has had a variety of impacts, not all of which are negative. As noted by Etzioni:

Without well-run organizations our standard of living, our level of culture, and our democratic way of life could not be maintained. Thus, to a degree, organizational rationality and human happiness go hand-in-hand. But a point is reached where happiness and efficiency cease to support each other. Here we face a time dilemma. (1964: 2)

Before we examine the strengths and weaknesses of bureaucracy, or the point where happiness and efficiency no longer support each other, let us examine the characteristics of a bureaucracy.

The Components of Bureaucracy

To be identified as a bureaucracy, a structure needs certain essential characteristics.

Specialization. Every bureaucracy has a staff organized into subunits or bureaus that are given responsibility for specific portions of the workload. For instance, the Internal Revenue Service is divided into a collection division, which processes tax returns and charges taxpayers, and an intelligence division, which gathers information about delinquent taxpayers and turns cases over to the Justice Department for prosecution. By this principle of specialization, it is reasoned, each task will be performed by an expert in the most efficient way.

Hierarchy. A bureaucracy has clear-cut lines and levels of authority and responsibility. The structure resembles a pyramid with a small policy-making group at the top, a middle echelon of managers and supervisors who carry out policies, and a broad base of workers. General Motors, for example, is run by a small group of executives and directors who set company policy and prices to achieve the primary corporate goal of earning maximum profits. A clearly defined chain of command runs from those at the top through the middle managers, engineers, and administrators who coordinate the company's activities; then through the supervisor; and down to the workers on the assembly line, the people who actually put the cars together.

Merit-selection. Bureaucratic personnel are selected on the basis of standardized criteria, such as civil service examinations or educational background. Employees are expected to possess or to acquire specialized knowledge needed to perform their jobs. They are supposed to be hired on the basis of their knowledge or skills and not, for example, because they are related to the boss. This principle of impartiality is supposed to ensure the most efficient use of people to achieve the goals of the organization. In reality, however, this rule is frequently violated.

Objective rules and routine procedures. Job performance and responsibility are specified by objective rules and regulations. For example, welfare workers cannot accept only clients they like and reject those they dislike. There are clear-cut rules to determine eligibility, and the case-worker is expected to apply them uniformly.

Separation of private and official domains. The private (or personal) and official spheres are kept separate. Bureaucratic officials are not permitted to mix the properties of the office with personal possessions.

Career pattern. A clearly established career line within each bureaucracy outlines the route to the top. Promotions, raises, job security, and tenure are guaranteed at each level if employees do their jobs properly. Seniority is valued and rewarded. For example, army officers usually begin their careers as second lieutenants and, in time, may work their way through the ranks of first lieutenant, captain, major, lieutenant colonel, full colonel, and the various grades of general.

The six elements of a bureaucracy listed above compose the formal elements of the structure. Weber's work provided significant insight into the basics of bureaucracies. Subsequent work has extended his thinking, especially in the areas of informal relations.

Informal Relations

A company's organizational chart reveals the formal structure of the organization. But as sociological studies have found, the formal organization constitutes only one feature of the organization. There is also an **informal organization,** a network of personal relations that emerges spontaneously among the members of a formal organization. People modify their for-

mally assigned roles in response to their personal needs and interests. Informal cooperation among employees in organizations reflects their perception of what is desirable and "fair," which may not always conform to organizational rules and goals.

The earliest and best known study of informal relations was "discovered" through research at the Western Electric Company (Hawthorne plant) between 1927 and 1933 (Roethlisberger and Dickson, 1939). The purpose of the study was to determine the effects of such factors as lighting, rest periods, etc., on work-group productivity. What these early studies discovered was that whether the physical factor, e.g., lighting and rest periods, was increased or decreased had no impact on productivity. Productivity depended significantly more on social factors. Further insight came from the experimental Hawthorne studies in which work groups of 14 people were set up to wire switchboards. "The bank-wiring-room" experiments led to the observation that production was determined by informal norms

An important element of bureaucracies is their informal organization—networks of personal relationships that emerge between members of an organization. Such informal cooperation between employees reflects their perception of what is desirable and "fair," a view that may run contrary to formal rules and goals.

of how much to produce, or what might be called a "fair day's work." Workers who underproduced were censured by the group: they were called "chiselers." Contrary to organizational rules which mandated that each employee work unassisted, there was considerable cooperation and mutual help among employees, which, contrary to management's assumption, supported organizational goals.

Columbia University sociologist Peter Blau (1963) demonstrated how the informal structure plays a critical role in achieving organizational goals efficiently. He found a clear-cut difference, for example, between what interviewers and receptionists in the employment agency were *supposed* to do and what they actually *did* in day-to-day situations. While interviewers were instructed to process all clients at length, to get detailed background information on each, and to find the best qualified applicant for every job, employers usually needed workers so quickly

that this lengthy process was impractical. Receptionists also modified their assigned work roles to meet clients' needs. During periods when jobs were scarce, organizational rules called for 30- to 60-day delays in scheduling appointments for clients. Since many applicants were desperate for work, receptionists would often schedule appointments more quickly if they knew that job openings were actually available. While the office was often overcrowded and all applicants were not treated equally, the organizational goal of placing as many people as possible was achieved. Blau observed numerous other instances when personnel at all levels adapted bureaucratic rules and procedures in response to the needs of clients and to the pressures brought to bear by the state legislature. Through the informal structure, the agency adjusted itself continually to achieve organizational efficiency.

Studies of informal relations in military organizations during the Korean conflict demon-

Reminder Box / FIELD RESEARCH

Field research takes advantage of natural settings which allow observers to control the variables being studied. This is an important research strategy for sociologists seeking to study ongoing behavior with minimal disruption by the researcher. In that sense, field research is similar to participant observation. However, it also has elements of a laboratory study, since there may be a conscious manipulation of the environment (as in the Hawthorne experiments). Also, because field research can be used to study groups which the researcher is not a part of, it allows more potential behaviors to be studied than is the case with participant observation.

The workplace is an excellent site for field research, since behaviors are structured and subject to control by management. As a result, sociologists who have obtained the cooperation of management can have various elements of the work situation modified without the workers necessarily knowing that the changes are part of a study (although researchers must observe the ethical cautions noted in Chapter 2). Sociologists might wish to do such studies to focus on the processes within work groups, the relations between the management and the workers, or worker responses to changes in the work task or the work environment. All are important aspects of organizational functioning which are of interest to sociologists, and all would lend themselves to field research.

strated the importance of informal relations, or what was known as the "buddy system," among soldiers in combat. While such relations may have appeared to be contrary to military effectiveness (i.e., organizational goals), nevertheless, these relationships enabled the soldiers to endure the harsh conditions of combat (Little, 1970).

The emergence of informal groups suggests that while in principle a bureaucracy may be a highly effective organization, in reality it is not without problems. We shall return to these issues in the latter part of this chapter but first we will examine the strengths of bureaucratic organizations.

ASSESSING BUREAUCRACIES

Bureaucratic Strengths

Weber pointed out that the greatest strength of bureaucratic organizations and the most important reason why they have spread so widely is that they get things done with maximum speed and efficiency. Among other things they are probably the most effective way of coordinating large numbers of people to achieve large-scale goals. The magnitude of such a task is illustrated in Table 11.1.

Coordination. By specifying what each employee must do and where and when he or she should do it, bureaucracies facilitate complex events and activities. In a hospital, for example, the schedules of many people are coordinated so that the patient is tranquilized and wheeled into the operating room at the same time that the anesthesiologist, the surgeon, and the supporting nursing staff are present to perform the required surgery. All of these interlocking activities are coordinated and scheduled as part of a bureaucratic organization.

Bureaucracies also assure a continuous flow of goods and services. The worker who puts the

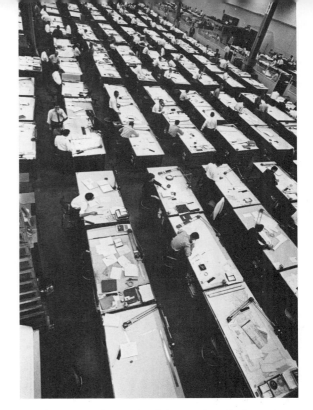

Coordination, order, predictability, and continuity are among the advantages of bureaucratic organization that Weber identified.

hinge on a door on an auto assembly line is part of a cast of thousands that includes the top executives who decided to produce such a model years ago because they thought it would be profitable, the purchasing agents who bought the steel and tin, the fabricators who cast the hinge and punched out the door, and the railroad personnel who carried the parts to the assembly plant. Each of these activities is directed toward a specific overall goal: making and selling large numbers of automobiles at a profit. The importance of the bureaucratic approach lies in its ability to mesh efficiently many specific activities into an overall pattern that realizes a broad goal. Ideally, bureaucracy promotes orderliness, predictability, impartiality, and continuity.

Order and stability. By assigning roles and by specifying procedures, bureaucracies mini-

TABLE 11.1 / BUREAUCRATIC SCALE

These data are for the Grumman Corporation, a manufacturer of major aircraft (commercial and military) and large vehicles like buses, fire engines, and ambulances. The huge scale of such a company makes it clear why a formal organization structure is needed. Data are for 1980.

Income Data (Million $)

Year Ended Dec. 31	Revs.	Oper. Inc.	% Oper. Inc. of Revs.	Cap. Exp.	Depr.	Int. Exp.	Net Bef. Taxes	Eff. Tax Rate	[2]Net Inc.	% Net Inc. of Revs.
1980	1,729	73.8	4.3%	34.3	22.9	27.8	54	42.9%	30.7	1.8%
1979	1,476	70.5	4.8%	25.9	22.6	26.5	34	41.9%	19.6	1.3%
[3]1978	1,455	64.3	4.4%	48.4	19.9	17.4	37	40.7%	21.9	1.5%
1977	1,553	78.8	5.1%	24.1	19.0	14.1	57	41.9%	32.4	2.1%
1976	1,502	55.6	3.7%	22.9	17.1	20.1	40	40.0%	23.6	1.6%
1975	1,329	56.0	4.2%	27.8	16.1	19.5	42	42.0%	23.6	1.8%
1974	1,113	48.3	4.3%	17.7	16.3	11.1	38	44.7%	20.0	1.8%
[1]1973	1,083	54.1	5.0%	16.1	17.2	8.0	34	46.6%	16.9	1.6%
1972	683	d88.4	NM	10.1	19.6	5.8	d111	NM	d70.0	NM
1971	799	d9.2	NM	16.7	21.9	6.8	d36	NM	d18.0	NM

Balance Sheet Data (Million $)

Dec. 31	Cash	Current Assets	Current Liab.	Ratio	Total Assets	Ret. on Assets	Long Term Debt	Common Equity	Total Cap.	% LT Debt of Cap.	Ret. on Equity
1980	55.6	712	210	3.4	906	3.4%	232	266	683	33.9%	9.5%
1979	44.0	603	303	2.0	798	2.8%	204	226	485	42.0%	7.9%
1978	36.7	418	202	2.1	607	3.6%	182	213	399	45.5%	10.4%
1977	33.0	421	235	1.8	569	5.7%	123	196	330	37.4%	17.6%
1976	31.5	417	214	1.9	551	4.3%	157	166	334	47.2%	14.9%
1975	36.7	397	154	2.6	522	4.8%	210	144	365	57.7%	17.4%
1974	19.8	330	156	2.1	445	5.0%	156	124	289	54.0%	18.2%
1973	43.8	238	138	1.7	353	4.6%	113	94	215	52.4%	21.0%
1972	24.5	261	165	1.6	377	NM	140	67	212	66.2%	NM
1971	9.8	238	134	1.8	365	NM	86	141	231	37.1%	NM

Data as orig. reptd. 1. Reflects merger or acquisition. 2. Bet. results of disc. opers. in 1978 & spec. item(s) in 1974, 1973. 3. Excludes dis. opers. and reflects merger of acquisition. d-Deficit. NM-Not Meaningful.

Business Summary

		Sales	Profits
Grumman Corp. designs and manufactures military aircraft and space systems and a diversified line of commercial products. Contributions in 1980 (profits in $ million):	Aircraft and space	71%	$106.3
	Special vehicles	15%	−11.0
	Energy	1%	−20.9
	Services and other	13%	7.2

About 70% of sales in 1980 were to the U.S. Government.

Source: Standard and Poor's Stock Report, January 1982, p. 1070 (Vol. D-K). Reprinted by permission of the publisher.

mize chaos and competition and keep them from interfering with attaining organizational goals.

Predictability and impartiality.   Bureaucratic rules and hierarchy make the operation of the organization predictable and ensure that everyone will be treated equally. The requirements imposed by most colleges as prerequisites for graduation, for example, are essentially arbitrary. It could be argued that the goal of a college to educate a student is still achieved if the student's overall average is a shade below the required C, or if he or she misses a required assembly, or if he or she fails to complete the physical education requirement. However, these formal rules are necessary so that students (and their parents), faculty, and administrators can know who is entitled to graduate and who is not, and to guarantee uniform treatment for everyone. Otherwise, persistent or persuasive students with a failing average might graduate, while more timid students with a better record might not. The rules and regulations may change, but the existence of some set of rules is vital. When there are no rules, there is likely to be endless argument. Nobody knows where he or she stands in relation to achieving the goals, and there is no clear-cut way to find out.

Continuity.   The bureaucratic system assumes that everyone is replaceable and that every task within an organization can be standardized. An individual may retire or be fired, but the position remains the same, and replacements are not free to alter the procedures or goals of the organization. Neither the assassination of President Kennedy nor the resignation of President Nixon created chaos in the bureaucratic structure of the federal government; the various departments and divisions continued to function in spite of the turmoil surrounding these events.

Our discussion of the strength of bureaucratic organizations is functionalist in nature, which is what Weber intended bureaucracies to be. But there are also dysfunctions to bureaucracy, and on the basis of the current literature the problems are having severe effects on the organization and the individual. Some of the problems are long-standing and have been noted by many observers. We will now look at some of the dysfunctions as well as the problems that have accompanied them.

Bureaucratic Weaknesses

Means-end inversion.   The most common of these bureaucratic "diseases" is the **means-end inversion,** the obsessive adherence to rules to the point of excluding the overriding objective. Ideally, the bureaucracy is set up to accomplish certain goals. The formal rules and procedures are designed to achieve these goals: they are means to achieve an end. But even though rules and routines are supposed to serve organizational purposes, and not vice versa, sometimes the means become ends in themselves and goals become secondary.

Overconformity to rules may actually interfere with organizational objectives. Blau (1956) quoted a file clerk's description of how a trivial ruling prevented him from doing his job:

> *You know how we tab the records of recent high-school graduates. We used red tabs for February graduates . . . and we decided to use black tabs for June graduates, because you can see that color well on the cards. The department head didn't know about that and sent around a memo saying they should be tabbed in yellow. Yellow you can't see at all. But since it had come down in writing, [the supervisor] refused to change it without permission from [the department head]. [The department head] had just arbitrarily chosen this color; it didn't make any difference. [The supervisor] could have changed it, but he didn't want to do it himself. [The department head] wasn't here, and we had to wait two days. (p. 250)*

In extreme cases, obsessive adherence to rules may lead to the conviction that conformity is valuable in and of itself, regardless of original purposes. For example, at the end of World War II when Berlin was being destroyed by Allied bombers and Soviet tanks were moving through the devastated city, German government officials could be observed figuring how many paper clips should be ordered for the following year. The government had collapsed and the city was burning, but the functionaries continued their now meaningless task (Bensman and Rosenberg, 1971). This is an example of bureaucratic pathology, a blind concern for following customary routines to the letter, whether or not they serve any useful purpose.

The Peter Principle. Another common inversion occurs when the members of the bureaucracy are evaluated not on how effectively they do their job, but solely on whether they possess formal qualifications for the position. In *The Peter Principle,* Peter and Hull (1969) expressed this phenomenon as an axiom: "In a bureaucracy everyone rises to his level of incompetence." For example, a good teacher is promoted to assistant principal. If she is an (incompetent) assistant principal, the position will be retained; if she is good, promotion to principal is likely. If she is incompetent as a principal, career progress will stop. If she is good, there will be promotion to the superintendent's staff, and so on.

The most significant consequence of such bureaucratic pathology is obvious; the organization's goals are not realized. But this is not the only consequence: Bureaucratic dysfunctions also affect the lives of the people who work in the bureaucracy.

The bureaucratic personality. Robert Merton (1957) suggested that a bureaucracy attracts people who value and need stability, continuity, and precise rules and routines. In turn, the environment reinforces their tendencies to become "ritualists," people for whom rules and routines become ends in themselves. These "bu-

TABLE 11.2 / SOME PRINCIPLES OF ORGANIZATIONAL BEHAVIOR

Murphy's Law: Nothing is as easy as it looks; everything takes longer than you expect; and if anything can go wrong, it will and at the worst possible moment.

Weiler's Law: Nothing is impossible for the person who doesn't have to do it.

Fanagle's Law: Once a job is fouled up, anything done to improve it makes it worse.

Chisolm's Law: Any time things appear to be going better, you have overlooked something.

Dunsen's Law: The specialist learns more and more about less and less until he knows everything about nothing, while the generalist learns less and less about more and more until he knows nothing about everything.

Gumperson's Law: The probability of anything happening is in inverse proportion to its desirability.

Douglass's Law: Clutter tends to expand to fill the space available for its retention.

Zimmerman's Law: Regardless of whether a mission expands or contracts, administrative overhead continues to grow at a steady rate.

Man's Law: No matter what happens, there is always somebody who knew it would.

Source: *Managers Magazine/78*, September issue, published by the Life Insurance Marketing and Research Association, Inc.

reaucratic personalities" are rewarded by a system that encourages conformity and punishes deviation and innovation (Mannheim, 1952).

Recent research, however, suggests that bureaucratic systems may also have the opposite effect. By providing stability and job security, bureaucracies free individuals to innovate and experiment. Sociologist Melvin Kohn (1971) suggested that people who work in bureaucracies tend to be more intellectually flexible, more open to new experiences, and more self-directed in their values than their peers in nonbureaucracies. Blau has also pointed out that a secure position in the bureaucratic structure does not necessarily lead to ritualism, but rather may stimulate bureaucrats "to seek new fields to conquer in order to revitalize their work so that new goals will succeed the old ones" (Blau, 1956). Anxieties and obsessive concern with rules are responses to bureaucratic pathology, but they are not typical or necessary responses to every bureaucratic system. But Blau and Scott (1962) also note that the possibility that free men and women become cogs in bureaucratic organizations is "one of the greatest threats to our liberty."

Organization and Oligarchy

Many sociologists have observed that formal organizations often drift into the hands of a small leadership elite. Examining this question over 70 years ago, Robert Michels concluded that in every formal organization—no matter how large and what its purpose—the pattern of membership participation makes oligarchy inevitable: "Who says organization says oligarchy" (1949: 41). Michels, a German socialist, observed that the socialist parties of Europe were no less dominated by their leadership than the presumably less democratic conservative parties. According to Michels, when an organization is loosely organized, there is no need for a professional leadership. But as organization develops, the tasks of administration become more complex, and a specialized leadership emerges. This leadership becomes an **oligarchy,** a small group that rules a much larger one. And while the actions of the leaders are subject to criticism and the control of the rank and file membership, in reality with increasing size of the organization the member-ship exerts less control. In large measure, this is because the work of the organization is highly specialized and the average member has little knowledge about administration. Consequently more and more of the decisions which presumably were to be made by the members become the domain of the administration and its special committees.

In principle, in democratic organizations the members can vote the leadership out of office, i.e., they can be changed. In reality those who reach positions of leadership and power also gain knowledge which they utilize effectively to remain in their positions. The rank-and-file member usually lacks the skills, knowledge, and access to files and other resources to challenge the leading incumbent effectively. While the history of American trade unions seems to validate Michels's theory—George Meany was elected president of the AFL–CIO in 1955, and remained in office until his death at the age of 82 in 1980—the International Typographical Union shows a different pattern (Lipset, Trow, and Coleman, 1956).

The Republican and Democratic parties demonstrate that organizations are subject to takeover by competing groups. The election of Jimmy Carter is a recent example: a segment of the Democratic party that was nonmainstream took control of the party bureaucracy by winning the presidency. But if the iron law of oligarchy is not quite as "iron" as Michels has suggested, can we conclude that members of formal organizations participate in decision making?

The Structure of Participation

By definition, formal organizations, especially bureaucracies, have a hierarchical arrangement of power and authority, with decision-making personnel centered at the top. To what extent do the people in middle and lower level positions participate in making policy? Is it possible to have a democratic bureaucracy?

INTERVIEW/Rosabeth Moss Kanter

On power in the workplace: *". . . it is increasingly important that a manager have real power. This means a power that his or her subordinates respect, which backs up formal authority."*

Rosabeth Moss Kanter is Professor of Sociology and Professor of Organization and Management at Yale University. Her research interests include formal organizations, the sociology of work, and social psychology.

■ **Q.** Why do you think power is important in the workplace?

■ **A.** Even though management attempts to structure organizations that would essentially eliminate personal issues and substitute depersonalized efficient, rational, universalistic organization, power issues intrude anyway because people are human. As long as resources are scarce, and as long as there's something to be gained by people jockeying for position and beating each other out, then there'll be power issues. In fact, most organizations are set up to be competitive anyway. And so power issues arise. The pyramidal shape means that not everybody can move ahead at the same rate to the same number of positions, so scarce resources always breed power issues. In addition, in today's corporation, given the kinds of shapes that it's starting to take on, power has become even more important. In many jobs, formal authority is loosened. Instead of automatically being able to command respect or deference, simply by virtue of position and formal title, it is increasingly important that a manager have real power. This means a power that his or her subordinates respect, which backs up formal authority. And the reasons why formal authority is loosening are several. One is simply a changing workforce that's much more concerned with having a voice in decisions, much more concerned with how democratic and fair things are. So people speak up. They don't sit still for the boss to tell them what to do, simply because the boss is the boss. Without power

backing up the formal position, the boss can't manage. We see this for people like women, minorities, and others who have a problem establishing themselves as powerful figures in organizations. It almost doesn't matter what their title is. If they're not connected to sources of real power—what really makes things happen as opposed to the official designation—they can't get respect and therefore they can't get any cooperation.

■ **Q.** Are there other reasons for changing views of authority?

■ **A.** Yes. The other reasons authority is loosening are because of the emergence of new organizational structures. The old-fashioned, traditional machine bureaucracy, with its unitary chain of command, clear mobility pathways, and directions largely issued from the "top," is losing ground. This is a surprisingly widespread trend. One interesting new form is called the matrix, where subordinates may report to several bosses along several dimensions. They may be in one function, such as sales, but work on a particular product, such as "BLUE WIDGETS." They'll report to a boss who manages sales, and they'll report to a boss for the "BLUE WIDGETS" product line. Whenever that happens, authority is very loose, because neither of those bosses alone can automatically command the respect, the kind of immediate response, that a boss could in the old-fashioned machine bureaucracy. That means that whichever boss can wield the most power and informal clout, and do the most for the subordinate's career, will get the time and the energy of a subordinate. Basically, the argument is that without power in my sense—the capacity to mobilize resources and get cooperation—it doesn't matter what the formal authority system of the organization looks like. Power is the ingredient that energizes the system. Authority is just the formal array of titles and positions.

■ **Q.** Is that essentially a change from the Weberian model?

■ **A.** Yes. It's a very interesting change, because it's not simply criticizing the Weberian model for not taking into account power differences, or the human side of organizations, or the inevitable conflict between specialized functions. It's saying that we've got another form that, in fact, works better under certain circumstances. Several of the companies in my recent research have a matrix organization. And several of the people we interviewed had up to four bosses or formal reporting relationships. That gives them a lot of freedom—a lot of freedom to maneuver in the organization. They have much more autonomy in that situation; consequently they're much more creative and enterprising. And so their organizations are also more effective. This is a real challenge to the Weberian model. It makes for a more efficient kind of organizaation under some circumstances. An organization that's flatter, that puts more control at lower levels, is more effective in a changing and competitive environment.

■ **Q.** So, in essence, the changes are not specifically coming from management. It's simply part of the organizational structure?

■ **A.** Well, some of the changes are deliberately introduced by management. I would say, obviously, that management has to be the initiators in any case, no matter what the source of the change is. [The environment] may put pressure on the organization, but the decision maker has to make the decision to reorient. So, management is always directing to some extent. Things generally do not happen because of grass roots activism inside large corporations; that's not the way they change. But there are many managements that are very concerned with

power sharing, participation, although it is not clear how far this is going to go. It's motivated in part by the new workforce issues. One company has a project they call "Managing Today's Workforce"; under that umbrella, they have a whole set of participative teams that are making many decisions about employee policy and reporting them back to a management team. At the same time, that company is also decentralizing as fast as it can, because it recognizes that it's more effective when decisions are pushed downward. Thus, the new management principle involves pushing decisions down, sharing power. This is the side of power that says more power in the hands of more people can get you more effective organization. There's also a personal impetus for power sharing in "new-style" companies. For example, in order to get done what I need to get done, I need you, and so I can't hurt you too badly because we're going to be here for a long time together and I'm going to need your support at some time in the future.

■ **Q.** How much of it do you think is the response to today's market conditions?

■ **A.** A great deal. I think most American companies would not be considering changing at all if it weren't for the competition from other countries, and also our own declining economy. Some of the new forms much predated the current crises, but they're being adopted at a much more rapid rate because of the crises. I date the changes to just after World War II and the introduction of new industries with more progressive policies. The time of founding has a great deal to do with the kind of structure an organization develops. This is the legacy of being a late nineteenth-century versus a seventeenth-century kind of organization. Today, many post-World War II, late twentieth-century organizations have become prominent. Indeed, many of the companies I'm studying weren't founded until the 1950s: aerospace and electronics firms, for example. IBM, of course, is a major company in electronics, and is a big exception. But their real growth spurt was in this new era.

The new era organizations are more empowering for several reasons. For example, in aerospace—really the origin of the matrix—they had very big projects to work on. And they used a high proportion of highly skilled technical people. The way you manage highly skilled technical people is not by dividing the job up into tiny pieces and giving them each a chunk and commanding them, in a beaureaucratic fashion.

■ **Q.** How is it best done then?

■ **A.** Well, they worked on big problems, requiring a lot of freedom, where a team of people from a number of functions needed to come together under the project. So they would both report to their project leader and back to their technical speciality leader. And that was the origin of a complex matrix. In electronics, and in all of the new industries, they also could learn from the labor-relations problems of their predecessors. So every new generation of organizations can put in more modern and more responsive policies because they can simply say, that's how we'll keep the union out, or this is how we'll attract good people.

The importance of post-World War II companies showed up in a recent study I did. We wanted a sample of what were considered the most progressive companies in their structure and personnel policies, so we surveyed 65 human resource vice presidents and had them nominate the best companies. Of the 47 nominated companies, the highest proportion were in electronics, a modern industry. They are simply considered the leaders; they're the models for everybody else.

■ **Q.** Do you see any kind of movement on the part of labor unions or the workers themselves in the direction of more decentralization?

■ **A.** Certainly the workers are concerned about their own future in this new world. Some of the unions are very much in favor of more participative management, such as joint labor-management committees that make more decisions about the workplace and set workplace policies. In some places it's working very well; for example, in many General Motors factories. We also have one example in this country of a union leader on the board at Chrysler. We could see more of that, though I doubt if we'll ever have much union partnership with management in guiding industry in general the way one does in Germany. I don't think that will happen in America. But I think we will see more employee participation in matters of immediate concern to them. I also think we'll get more team-oriented top management—that is, rather than single decision makers, we'll see coalitions of decision makers. But we'll *never* have a situation where employees have a say in absolutely everything about the workplace including the product, capital investment, and other things. I don't think that's realistic.

■ **Q.** How would you look at control on the one hand and participation on the other hand?

■ **A.** Obviously, to many people they look like opposites. And many neo-Marxist scholars argue that it's the drive for control that has made organizations consider such a minute division of labor and put a tall hierarchy in place. They say that hierarchy stems more from a desire for control than economic efficiency. In some of my own recent research, in contrast, control and participation look like they can be highly complementary in certain forms. Of course, I don't want to make these looser authority structures sound like a utopia or like an employee paradise. They constitute only some small steps and participation about local issues and job activities. Still, it's happening. In those situations, in fact, participation of a certain kind often substitutes for more formal controls to serve as a check on decisions. In most situations where middle-managers have more autonomy, they have to work by forming coalitions. Participation can even serve as one of the new forms of social control. This control is peer-based, rather than management-based, superior-based. I see that lateral relations can be a very potent form of control, as opposed to simply vertical relations.

A sociologist from Norway was studying three different publishing firms there. One was a collective, one was a traditional bureaucracy, and one was somewhere in between, more like a small, craft-based shop. He found that in the collective, which was highly participative, people complained about not having enough freedom. Everybody else had the right to poke their noses into their work; they had no autonomous area in which they could operate. So they had much lower job satisfaction than did people in the conventional bureaucracy. In short, social control is not absent; it's just that it is not a control by top management. What top management does is

set the boundary conditions and then choose among competing proposals or competing solutions. They do not provide minutely detailed job assignments the way they do in a rigid bureaucracy. I'm rethinking this issue of what *kinds* of social control exist, but I'm sure it always exists or an organization would fall apart.

■ **Q.** Does that imply that to some extent, however minute, we are moving in the direction that Japan is?

■ **A.** A qualified "yes." Some of the specific techniques they're using, they learned from us. Many of the ideas have been around in the U.S. since the turn of the century. And, it is the new industries in America, just like the new industries in Japan, that are bringing this about. The one difference that I think emerges from my acquaintance with Japanese companies versus U.S. companies is that their concern for people does seem to extend to the total person, and the importance of the person as a group member is somewhat greater. On the other hand, there are examples of American companies that have that same concern, that have long-term employment and so forth. We also, however, have a degree of entrepreneurial spirit in our organizations that we need to tap. But yes, participative management is a more effective form for the future. And so I do think that American firms will increasingly jump on the bandwagon and move in this direction. It's hard for some of them—and that's not due to ill will on management's part so much as the limits of certain kinds of technology. It's also very hard to do when you've had a certain kind of traditional structure, and all the good intentions in the world don't do any good if you can't make the rewards system and the structure promote participation.

■ **Q.** To what extent do you think the American worker is really interested in participation?

■ **A.** The American worker wants to be consulted. That doesn't necessarily mean spending a lot of time on a committee, but it does mean being asked for an opinion. That, I think, you can say universally about everybody. Some people are also very eager to get things done, to be in a position that, regardless of what their regular job is, they can really shape things, leave their mark, guide things. And we see a lot of that kind of interest. Then we also see a lot of people who simply want more autonomy.

Q. If you compare participation and autonomy, which would you consider more important?

A. I'd say they're both important. One has to do with the design of the job and whether there's real responsibility in the job for independent decision making and the use of judgment. The second has to do with the design of the decision-making structures of the organization and whether there's involvement and a voice. There are two ways people are linked to an organization. One way is through their job, their tasks that they are assigned to do. The other is via their ability or inability to participate in the decisions about the governance, the shape, and the style of the organizational role. So, they're both important. I don't want organizations to go overboard in either direction: toward participation, or simply having a lot of autonomous people working independently but with no say about how their tasks are put together. That's also not a useful direction. Both need to be worked on. ∎

Voluntary associations usually encourage active participation. Even the largest voluntary associations at least pay lip service to democratic values. After all, the organizations were founded by and for the membership. The American Legion and the American Medical Association are both run by centralized groups of decision makers who tend to be self-perpetuating, but the leaders are careful to preserve democratic values and to hold periodic elections. The membership takes a vocal and sometimes active part in the organization. But what happens in a mass organization —the world of blue- and white-collar workers? As Table 11.3 illustrates, this issue is further complicated by the distribution of men and women in different parts of the labor force, since men have traditionally been more accustomed to demanding some decision-making power. As a result, female service workers, such as secretaries, are likely to accept positions in large organizations

that give them little opportunity to participate in decision making. They are also less likely to develop unions in order to increase their power in the organization.

HUMAN RELATIONS AND WORKER PARTICIPATION

Worker participation in decision making was never part of our free enterprise ideology. The development of the American trade union movement primarily reflected a concern with the opportunity to earn a decent wage, not a desire for increased participation. Management assumed, and was supported in the assumption by "scientific management theories," that the worker was motivated only by economic factors and under the right conditions would produce as much as physically possible. But the Hawthorne studies (as noted previously) challenged these assumptions: the findings, supported by subsequent research, showed work to be significantly affected by noneconomic factors. Workers act less as individuals and more as members of a group. Leadership, assumed to be the function of the formally designated leader, is also provided by the informal group leader, a member of the group whom the workers respect and whose advice they seek.

The informal group became a central factor in the study of organizations. It is a key component in understanding the relationship between the formal organization, i.e., the highly structured rational hierarchy, and the fact that the informal group, through its social norms, has a significant impact on organizational goal attainment. The Hawthorne studies led to a new approach to labor-management relations: **human relations.** The central thesis of this approach was that the enterprise provides a major focus for the life of the workers. As long as management provides warm and understanding leadership, a supportive environment, and good and effective communication, the goals of management and

TABLE 11.3 / DIFFERENT ROLES FOR THE SEXES

Bureaucracies continue to use men and women very differently in their structures, and to involve them in various types of bureaucracies. For example, women are far more likely to have white-collar and service roles, while men do more "heavy," blue-collar and farm work.

Work by Sex	Percent of the Work Force in 1979
Male	
White collar	41.0
Blue collar	47.0
Service workers	6.7
Farmworkers	5.3
Female	
White collar	60.0
Blue collar	16.1
Service workers	21.7
Farmworkers	1.8

Source: U.S. Bureau of the Census, *Statistical Abstract of the United States: 1981,* Washington, D.C. p. 418.

While the toys made in this factory may bring children pleasure and excitement, the assembly lines on which they and other products are put together often call for monotonous labor that workers find boring and alienating.

the workers will coincide. As Etzioni noted, the human relations approach suggested that workers need more than a cold, formal, rational organization—that in fact such an organization did not lead to constructive and cooperative relationships between the workers and supervisors, but to conflict and loss of productivity. The role of management was to encourage "the development of social groups on the job and (to) provide them with democratic, participative, and communicative leadership. The way to make the organization fully rational was to increase by deliberate efforts the happiness of the workers" (1964: 38–39).

Many sociologists were skeptical about some of the human relations notions. They specifically questioned the emphasis on warmth and symbolic rewards and the tendency to ignore the fact that, while money may not be the sole factor motivating the workers, it nevertheless is vital—it constitutes the worker's livelihood. Sociologists also noted that the unity of management and labor is not automatically assured as the human relations approach suggests. The rationalization process has led to work fragmentation and made

the job boring and monotonous. Work which was to mean creativity and a means of self-expression became alienating under conditions of the division of labor and rationalization. In a workplace marked by **alienation** the worker has no control over the job; the work process is divided into minute tasks that prevent the workers from seeing the product of their labor. They feel powerless and alienated from their work and their social world.

The human relations approach did not become a panacea for the problems of industrial civilization as Mayo (1946) had hoped. But it did lead to further research, and considerable evidence emerged to show that democratic leadership, which enabled the worker to participate in some decision-making processes, increased productivity and made for a more satisfied labor force. This knowledge, however, did not lead to a significant change in the structure of organizations.

In the 1960s and 1970s national surveys showed that while workers were generally satisfied with their work there was a significant increase in work dissatisfaction over the period studied. In 1977, 54 percent of Americans stated "That they feel they have a right to take part in decisions affecting their jobs. Among younger workers, 62 percent expressed this view . . ." (Rosow, 1979: 176).

A HEW Report done in 1973 found considerable problems among blue- and white-collar workers, and suggested that widespread work dissatisfaction had led to alcoholism, absenteeism, mental health problems, and low productivity (see Fig. 11.2). On the other hand, companies which had instituted some form of "quality of work" program involving worker participation had seen increased productivity and a more satisfied labor force.

More recently, the notion of worker participation has diffused outside the sphere of academic research. Magazines such as *Business Week* and *Life,* television programs, and newspaper articles report approvingly of various programs which have been implemented in this or that company involving rank and file workers in some form of decision making. A changing image of the worker is emerging, a recognition, as Kanter (1978) has pointed out, that today's worker is less awed by management. Unlike the unskilled immigrant workers of the past, most of today's workers are native born and relatively well educated. Their expectations are higher: workers want jobs that are meaningful and over which they have a modicum of control.

Fig. 11.2 / Personal Problems in the Workplace

For many people, the workplace creates stresses that impede work performance. There is also, of course, interaction between personal problems and work-related problems. The International Paper Company has an Employee Assistance Program to help its workers deal with all life-stress problems. The pie chart depicts the breakdown of sources of problems coming to the program to date through self-referral as well as the result of deficiencies in job performance.

Source: International Paper Company, "Employee Assistance Program: Guidelines for Managers," undated and unpaginated. Used by permission.

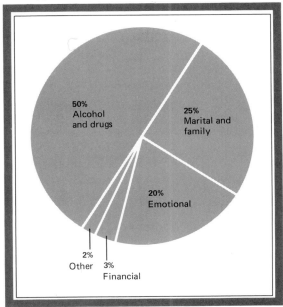

Theory Z

The declining productivity of American industry and the competition from a steadily rising productivity of Japanese industry, where the structure of the organization invites greater commitment by the worker to the organization, has led to a more serious examination in the United States of the worker as a participant.

The work of William Ouchi, *Theory Z,* and its immediate success as a "best seller" suggests that there is far greater interest and perhaps concern about the role of the worker than is generally assumed. Ouchi suggests that American industry adapt the Japanese model of the industrial organization and management-labor relations. While Ouchi recognizes that not all aspects of Japanese management can be adapted to the United States, he notes that trust and loyalty to one's employer, and more job commitment, can be successfully adapted in American industry. In fact, much of "Theory Z" incorporates the human relations approach and is built on the work of McGregor, Argyris, and others, which Ouchi acknowledges.

Some American firms do practice aspects of Theory Z today, e.g., IBM, Eastman Kodak, Hewlett Packard, and others (Ouchi, 1981). Ouchi differentiates type "Z" firms from "A" firms by noting that in the former the approach is holistic. There is:

a broad concern for the welfare of subordinates and of coworkers. . . . Relationships between people tend to be informal and to emphasize that whole people deal with one another at work, rather than just managers with workers and clerks with machinists. This holistic orientation, a central feature of the organization, inevitably maintains a strong egalitarian atmosphere that is a feature of all Type Z organizations . . . An organization that maintains a holistic approach and forces employees at all levels to deal with one another as complete human beings creates a condition in which depersonalization is impossible, autocracy is unlikely, and open communication, trust, and commitment are common. . . . Egalitarianism is a central feature of type Z organizations. Egalitarianism implies that each person can apply discretion and can work autonomously without close supervision because they can be trusted. (pp. 79–81)

Type "A" firms, on the other hand, are in essence today's bureaucracies, characterized by lack of trust in and absence of commitment to the organization, segmentation, hierarchy, and direct supervision. The development of American organization into "Z" type organizations will be at best a very slow process. But quality-of-work-life projects, which attempt to include the worker as a participant, have emerged in a variety of organizations.

American Experiments in Worker Participation

The General Foods plant in Topeka, Kansas, which manufactures pet food, is one of the most cited experiments of worker participation. Changes in the structure of the organization of the Topeka plant were motivated by high labor turnover and low productivity. The premise of the innovators was that workers will support the goals of the organization if the organization is aligned with their career goals and other human needs (Walton, 1975: 124).

The planners decided that workers in the Topeka plant would have a voice and power in areas that affected them directly: for example, pay and benefits, hiring and firing, training, promotion, job assignments, and a host of other things related to the job.

Employees hired for the plant were subject to long and thorough interviews and testing. The "team leaders" were subject to an intensive training program to ensure a smooth and cooperative organization. Work was organized on the basis of self-managing work teams, whose responsibilities included scheduling, solving production problems, and hiring new employees. While the team leaders had the final say on whom to hire, workers at Topeka voted on whether to hire a prospective worker, and the team's vote generally prevailed. Employment of a new worker was based not only on how well the employee could perform, or learn to perform the job, but on how well the employee would fit into the self-managing work group. The criterion of "would you want to have a beer with this guy," was important. Those who did not pass this test were considered "a bad system fit" (Zwerdling, 1980: 23). Work discipline and firing are in the domain of the work team. Members of a work team could learn the different jobs of team members, which permitted flexibility and allowed team group members to rotate from one job to another. Learning the other jobs was encouraged: those who do so earn 50 percent more than the base pay.

The Topeka plant became a highly productive organization. Seventy workers were producing what management engineers had thought would require 110 workers. Absenteeism was low—1.5 percent. In 1976, however, things began to change. Team decisions and worker perception of influence on plant policy began to crumble. Some of the problems are attributed to a lack of commitment to the project by corporate management. Success of the plant was apparently seen as of little importance by corporate management. Managers of the Topeka plant who were instrumental in organizing the project realized that the effective operation of the plant was no assurance of recognition—all were overlooked for promotion. According to *Business Week,* management felt that workers exercised too much power—e.g., decisions about hiring and firing were in the realm of workers' rights; quality control managers in the corporate structure thought that rank-and-file workers should not be controlling quality control; engineers resented the fact that rank-and-file workers were handling engineering tasks. Work that was performed productively and efficiently without much of a hierarchy is today subject to supervision and direction—new management positions were added to supervise and control the work groups.

The lesson from Topeka is that quality-of-work-life (QWL) projects do constitute a threat to middle-level management. And unless middle-level management is included, supported, and rewarded in such plans there is little incentive for them to support QWL projects. In essence, middle-managers view the projects as a threat to their jobs. As a result, they are likely to show little enthusiasm, and much hostility.

Another QWL project was initiated in 1971 at the General Motors plant in Tarrytown, N.Y. It is one of private industry's largest QWL projects, including 3,500 employees. This highly successful project—nurtured at a cost to management of 1.6 million dollars—had a modest objective: "to change old ways of dealing with the workers on the shop floor." Guest defines QWL as a:

process by which the organization attempts to unlock the creative potential of its people by involving them in decisions affecting their work lives. . . . The goals are not simply extrinsic. . . . They are also intrinsic, regarding what the worker feels as self-fulfilling and self-enhancing ends in themselves. (1979: 77)*

The Tarrytown effort was a ten-year process supported by corporate management and top union leaders. It directly involved middle-management, local union leaders, and workers. With the help of training personnel it greatly improved relations between management and labor, increased mutual trust, and legitimized worker involvement in problem solving. In a plant where warnings, disciplinary layoffs, and firings were commonplace, where the foreman ordered a worker to do a job or be fired, where workers perceived the company as a place where they number the parts and the people (Guest, 1979), the cooperative relationship that has emerged constitutes considerable progress. In preparation for the introduction of the new 1980 model car, "managers and hourly personnel together evaluated hundreds of anticipated assembly processes. Workers . . . talked directly with supervisors and technical people about the best ways of setting up various jobs on the line" (Guest, 1979: 84).

Tarrytown is one of the more effective projects in the QWL experiments. Preparation and training, the cooperation of management and labor, and particularly the inclusion of middle-management contributed to its success. In comparison to the Topeka project, however, it was a more modest program; it did not enlarge the occupational role of the GM worker to the same extent as the Topeka worker. Workers felt appreciated, trusted, and desirous of making a contribution, but their "contribution" did not threaten the supervisory personnel and engineers.

It should be clear by now that the problem of organizational change is not merely an idle concern of sociological theorists. Bureaucratic dysfunctions, impersonality, job segmentation,

---

*Reprinted by permission of the *Harvard Business Review.* Excerpt from "Quality of work life—learning from Tarrytown" by Robert H. Guest (July–August 1979). Copyright © 1979 by the President and Fellows of Harvard College; all rights reserved.

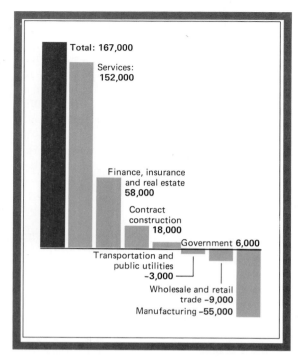

Total: 167,000

Services: 152,000

Finance, insurance and real estate 58,000

Contract construction 18,000

Government **6,000**

Transportation and public utilities **−3,000**

Wholesale and retail trade **−9,000**

Manufacturing **−55,000**

Fig. 11.3 / Employment Changes in New York City
This figure portrays the number of jobs added or subtracted in each general classification of employment between 1977 and 1981. It is a microcosm of the shifting national pattern in types of bureaucracies dominating the workplace, showing the especially rapid growth of service organizations at the expense of manufacturing.

Source: *The New York Times,* March 13, 1982, p. 29. Copyright © 1982 by The New York Times Company. Reprinted by permission.

compartmentalization, and rigidity and authoritarianism can frustrate clients and alienate personnel, and the consequences for the individual and society are not trifling. Another variable is changing patterns of types of organizations (see Fig. 11.3). It may turn out that quality-of-work-life issues may be different for white-collar and blue-collar workers. Should this be so, the rise of white-collar jobs will have a substantial impact on workplace issues.

Opposition to Change

Because positions and roles in a formal organization are so carefully meshed, a change in one element of the structure also requires corresponding changes in other elements. If changes are to be successful, careful planning and full cooperation are needed from people at all levels of the hierarchy.

As in any group, change is often disturbing and upsetting to members of an organization. Some may have vested interests in opposing change. Satisfaction and comfort are derived from the established routines and procedures, and the old ways of doing things are like well-worn grooves leading to a predictable outcome. The top executive, as well as the lowest functionary, may be committed to his or her familiar and time-tested routine.

While we might expect resistance to change from those who hold positions of power, opposition may also come from the lower levels or from the informal organization. For example, the top management in many large American corporations endorsed nondiscriminatory employment policies years ago, but implementation was delayed by foot dragging and informal opposition among middle and lower echelons who felt their status was threatened. Administrators have found that it is one thing to change employment policies on paper and quite another to see that they are carried out in practice. Informal clique structures make acceptance and advancement difficult for minority members of the workforce.

Informal obstacles to deliberate organizational changes are illustrated in Richard McCleery's case study of prison reform (1957). Originally the prison authority system had been based on the threat of force and the indirect manipulation of prisoners through frequent body counts, searches, and bribes. When a reform-oriented warden introduced a liberal manual of rules and regulations to replace the prevailing authoritarian "wake'em and work'em" philosophy, the staff resisted: "the [liberal] policy-making group . . . wrote new regulations and the guards continued to enforce the old."

The new manual emphasized two-way communication between the prisoners and the staff, encouraged consultation among all levels of the staff, and stressed treatment and rehabilitation as goals. Yet, "three years after its publication, few of the guards knew of its existence." Other guards, who saw their traditional prerogatives and authority threatened by a new emphasis on the individual prisoners and their rights, actively subverted the reforms: "Gaining access to the treatment office was made so complex and, for selected inmates, so humiliating that many who valued their self-respect in the yard abandoned the efforts. Requests sent through the custodial channels to the treatment office were often lost" (McCleery, 1957: 389, 392–93).

Thomas Scheff (1961) found a similar situation in a mental hospital where attendants successfully resisted efforts made by top administrators to set up therapeutic groups in each ward. The administrators introduced ward meetings for the staff, physicians, and patients to improve communication. By eliminating authoritarian ward discipline and the wide social distance between the patients and the staff, the innovators hoped to speed patient recovery. But the attendants felt threatened by this change and resisted it strongly, taking as their motto "Whitecoats stick together." Unlike the administration, attendants did not see the patients as people like themselves with perhaps a few more problems, but as irrational people to be controlled. They believed the proposed changes in the traditional authority structure would make their jobs impossible. By withholding cooperation and needed information from the physician, by manipulating the patients (for example, by encouraging dozens of them to surround the doctor and clamor for attention), and by outright disobedience (used selectively), the attendants successfully obstructed changes in the ward structure and operations despite their relatively subordinate position.

Bureaucratic organizations, as we noted previously, are not unique to the United States. But some societies have adapted or modified their organizations; in part these modifications reflect the cultural values of a society or their political goals. Let us then look at formal organizations cross-culturally.

The Japanese Factory: An Alternative

Weber's model of bureaucracy assumes that impersonality, fixed roles, clear-cut career lines, and technical qualifications for specialized positions are essential to organizational efficiency. But the Japanese factory raises the possibility that there may be successful alternatives to this model.

Can you imagine the reaction if the head of one of our corporations said to the employees,

Not only is there the fact that our life's work is our employment in our company, but I feel that as people in this situation we have two occasions that can be called a "birth." The first is when we are born into the world as infants. The second is when we all receive our commissions of adoption into the company. This is an event that has the same importance as our crying birth. (Abegglen, 1958: 569–70)

So spoke the president of a large Japanese steel company to his employees in 1952. He was not hooted and jeered off the stage as the president of a Western steel company probably would have been. The Japanese executive was describing what appears to be a feeling shared by many Japanese.

Lifetime employment. Contrary to organizations in the United States, Japanese organizations hire their personnel for life. To be sure, not all Japanese work in this system: about 35 percent of the labor force is so employed. Major firms will hire graduates from secondary schools or universities for the duration of their working lives, until age 55 when employees have to retire, unless they have reached a high managerial position.

The pattern of lifetime employment is common for men, but not for women. Women are employed until they have children, but they will return to the firm when they are free of child care responsibilities. Women are seldom employed as professionals or managers. Women are considered "temporary" employees, even if they have been employed for ten or twenty years. In periods when the company encounters economic difficulties, women will be laid off. As Ouchi noted ". . . women serve as a 'buffer' to protect the job stability of men" (1981: 24). The significance of lifetime employment is not simply a job for life. The significance lies in the differences in values and norms that permeate the labor force and the organization in Japan and the United States.

In the United States it is accepted that work relations between employers and employees are organized around self-interest. Japanese people generally tend to be collectivity oriented, and the place of work with its lifetime commitment reinforces solidarity with the group and the organization. Cooperation and cohesiveness are supported in principle because there are no major threats to job security, and because the value of cooperation is constantly emphasized. Supervisory personnel recognize the importance of the group and the value of group cohesiveness. The interdependence of the group and the supervisor is clear in the following statement: "The master can't make good sake by himself. Most important is that he gets good cooperation from all workers" (cited by Marsh and Mannari, 1976: 179). Work groups are highly integrated—workers engage in various group activities at work. "When a staff member . . . was being transferred to another section . . . the members . . . gave him a farewell party, even though they would see him at lunch and around the factory" (Marsh and Mannari, 1976: 181).

Paternalism is a cultural value in Japan, and it is reinforced in the workplace. When asked if they would prefer a department chief who "sticks

The typical Japanese factory seeks to develop in its workers a sense of loyalty and belonging. Exercise sessions like this are one way for workers to share in activities that help them feel they are part of a worthwhile and rewarding work group.

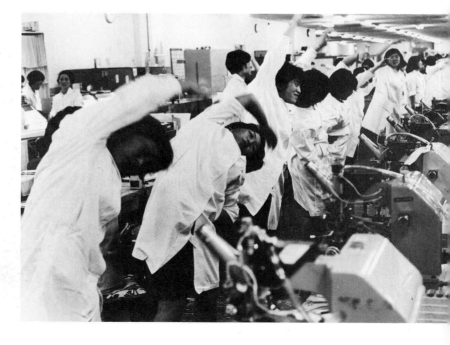

IN FOCUS/The Changing Workplace

During the mid–1800s, industrialization brought sweeping changes to our nation's cultural and social life. This photo essay examines the impact of technology on America's changing workplace.

(a)

(a) Prior to the Civil War, the United States was primarily an agricultural nation. Large landowners formed a rural aristocracy, while the typical worker was a farmer who labored long hours for low wages.

(b) During the 1850s, the invention of mechanized tools reduced the need for human labor but increased the cost of farming, establishing a trend toward large-scale agriculture geared to specialized markets. This modern harvester is an example of the advances, including new pesticides, fertilizers, and management skills, that have revolutionized farm work.

(b)

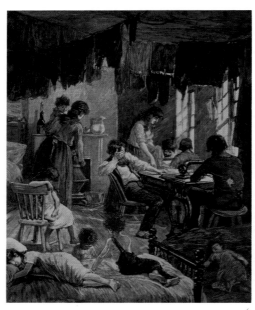

(c)

(d)

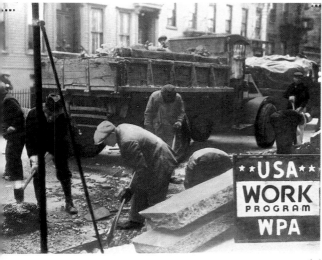

(e)

(f)

(c) During the nineteenth century, the average American worker faced a long work day at low pay, often in unsanitary buildings. Unskilled workers suffered the most; the drudgery of their lives in grimy, steaming sweatshops was a form of bondage. Furthermore, for decades any attempt to form labor unions was regarded as a criminal conspiracy.

(d) By the 1820s, half the workers in cotton-textile factories were children under sixteen. Often laboring twelve to thirteen hours a day, six days a week, many were physically stunted, emotionally deprived, and even punished in special whipping rooms.

(e) During the Great Depression of the 1930s, government spending to provide public relief became an integral part of the American economy. The Works Progress Administration employed millions on small-scale projects such as road building, dams, parks, and schools.

(f) The rise of labor unions gave American workers the power to protect their interests in the workplace. Until the 1960s the Hispanic ethnic group was a "sleeping giant." As their numbers swelled, they began to organize, like these grape pickers, to improve their position in American society.

(g) As more women enter the workforce, our society must confront the problem of caring for the children of dual-career and single-parent families. Several large corporations have set up quality daycare facilities to meet their workers' needs—a far cry from the abusive child labor practices of the early nineteenth century.

(h) Technology poses both future threats and benefits to the American worker: New equipment may soon render many jobs obsolete. On the other hand, new advances, such as computerized production methods, may result in new jobs and improved quality control.

(g)

(h)

(i) Before the industrial revolution, manufacturing was done in the home or in a small shop by a master artisan and apprentices. The Testing of the Liberty Bell *suggests the personal pride in one's work that was characteristic of the era.*

(j) The mass production process, consisting of assembly lines, standardized operating procedures, and the use of precision-made parts, permits factories to make more efficient use of labor and materials. On the dark side, assembly line production may require repetitive tasks that workers find alienating and monotonous.

to the work rules and never demands any unreasonable work, but . . . never does anything for you personally in matters not connected with work" or "A man who sometimes demands extra work in spite of rules against it, but on the other hand, looks after you personally in matters not connected with work," Japanese respondents overwhelmingly—84 percent—preferred the paternalistic chief (cited in Marsh and Mannari, 1976: 317). Furthermore, the paternalistic chief was seen by those who preferred him as warm, flexible, trusting his subordinates, a kind and human person, considerate, responsible, and possessing good leadership skills (Dore, 1973: 238).

The Japanese factory approximates a community in which role relationships are diffuse, affective, and collectivity oriented. Identification with the organization is reinforced through lifetime employment and paternalism. The attitude of management and the manner of communicating with employees on questions of importance are what might be considered typically paternalistic in nature. On being late to work: "The beginning is important, as in all things. Staying up late the night before, just taking the relaxed holiday mood too far on a Sunday and forgetting the next day is Monday—if we can lead more regular daily lives this kind of lateness is reduced to zero. We should all think about this, because it is our problem, the problem of every one of us" (Dore, 1973: 239–40).

Authority relations in the Japanese factory are no less important than in the American factory, but there are significant differences. Dore (1973) found in the Hitachi company a pyramidical structure organized into teams, sections and departments; responsibilities are given to groups and can be shifted or moved around from one individual to another. Cooperation between managers is important and supported; there is a tendency to share responsibility, as well as to make it more diffuse. As Ouchi (1981) pointed out, when a major decision is required, 60 to 80 people will be involved—consensus is the goal

and the sense of responsibility is collective. As leaders of their teams foremen are still part of the team, not simply supervisors. Their role is diffuse—they are concerned not only with the task at hand, but with the general well-being of team members. Discipline is based on rules, and reinforced by exhortations to bring the workers back to virtue. Workers express a pride in their work, and they accept the legitimacy of the enterprise; consequently, managerial authority is accepted readily (Ouchi, 1981: 261–62).

The Japanese cultural heritage facilitates the acceptance of authority. There is greater "submissiveness" among the Japanese as a society. The structure of the work team also inhibits the expression of hostility, because (1) the foreman is part of the team and the center of the network of personal relations, and (2) the trade union does not control the work situation (Dore, 1973: 262). While no authority relations are ever purely rational legal, or traditional, in the Japanese factory there is a far greater tendency to rely on a combination of authority structures, with considerable emphasis on traditionalism. The latter is more inclusive, extending to the sphere outside the work situation. In a sense, then, the factory approximates familial relations.

Yugoslavia represents a significantly different case from Japan as well as the United States. Let us then examine what is unique to work organizations in Yugoslavia.

Workers' Councils— the Yugoslav Case

Yugoslavia is a socialist country which broke with Stalin and Soviet-style socialism in 1948. Since 1950 the Yugoslavs have aimed at transforming every organization into a form of "self-management." In principle, self-management is the universal form in all organizations: factories, schools, higher educational institutions, hospitals, research organizations, mines, forestry, etc.

The essence of the Yugoslav organization is that the decisions affecting the factory are to be made by the employees. In each factory employees elect a workers' council and a management board. Depending on the size of the enterprise, workers' councils range from 15 to 20 members. The smaller the enterprise, the fewer members there are in the council. In enterprises which employ less than 29 people, the entire workforce constitutes the council. Employees are elected for two-year terms, and to prevent the creation of oligarchies, an employee can serve only two consecutive terms. A council member is subject to recall. Among the responsibilities of the council are the adoption of the economic plan, production volume, sales, and labor relations, e.g., recruitment of workers, job allocation, holidays, occupational safety, hiring, dismissals, discipline, etc. Basic guidelines on wages are set by the government, but within these guidelines the council determines the wages of the employees.

The management board membership is chosen from among the workers' council for a one-year period. The management board works in close cooperation with the director of the enterprise who is responsible for the day-to-day operation of the factory. The director, a professional, nonelected administrator, serves as the chief executive of the company. Since the mid-1960s other enterprise executives are appointed by the management board, rather than by the director, as was the practice in the early period of workers' councils.

The elected members of the council do not relinquish their jobs. Meetings take place after working hours, and their work on the council is unpaid. During their period of service they may not be fired or transferred to other jobs (Blumberg, 1968; Hunnius, *et al.*, 1973).

While the majority of representatives on the councils are workers, as in all organizations, those elected tend to be the better educated and more skilled male workers. It should be noted, however, that large segments of the Yugoslav labor force were for some time newly urbanized peasants, who were frequently illiterate and unlikely to seek representation on the councils. They were not likely to be perceived by fellow workers as capable of making decisions affecting the enterprise.

Workers' councils have been in existence for over 30 years. Throughout this period much has been learned about self-management. Among the lessons was the fact that large-scale enterprises allow less effective forms of self-management than small enterprises. Consequently, new laws were established aimed at decentralizing the decision-making process and empowering workers at lower levels of the plant (the working unit) to have a more direct say in decisions. Enterprises are divided into units with their own workers' councils, with each unit operating autonomously. Each unit acts almost as an independent entity ". . . managing its own affairs and calculating most of its finances on the basis of the activity of the unit itself" (Sachs, 1975, cited by Zwerdling, 1980: 161).

Self-management has not been a universal success in Yugoslavia. The rules empowering workers to "run" their factories nevertheless cannot make the manager or the workers' council share with the workforce all that is being done or why. Some reports suggest that unskilled and poorly educated workers are apathetic and show little interest or concern. At times management "manipulates" the council to make decisions desired by management. Technical decisions and complicated financial matters are poorly understood by the rank-and-file workers, and this leads to disinterest. Thus, while workers' councils were a dramatic innovation, which have worked well and effectively in many organizations, they can not be said to be universally successful. But as Blumberg has noted, mass production methods, the division of labor, and rationalization of tasks have led to fragmentation of the workers' consciousness. Workers have lost a perspective of the production process, as well as a sense of integration with the work environment.

. . . to the extent that worker's management is successful, it enables—or rather, compels—the

worker to see beyond the narrow horizons of his minute task and to take on a greater perspective which encompasses his economic unit, his department, his factory. . . . (1973: 233–34)

Worker management today is imperfect, but it is the law in Yugoslavia, and contrary to participatory types of projects in the United States it can not be discarded if it functions poorly. The more that is learned of what is required to make the workers' councils achieve their potential the more they may live up to the promise of industrial democracy.

THE FUTURE OF BUREAUCRACY

In each society examined, there are efforts to make the organization less alienating and more responsive to the individual. The case of Yugoslavia is unique, because private property has been eliminated. Consequently the state can mandate new types of organization that conform to the image of a socialist society. As a late industrializing state Japan has learned, as Dore (1973) has pointed out, from the experience of the "old" industrial societies how not to make the same mistakes. Thus, Japan has modified its bureaucratic organizations and made them into a community. In creating these work-like communities with diffuse and affective relationships, business has been significantly helped by the prevalent cultural values in Japan. But it is by no means

clear that the paternalistic model of the Japanese factory will remain the norm in the future. This, of course, does not mean that the model which might evolve will necessarily resemble the old bureaucratic organization; considerable modifications are possible.

The dysfunctions of bureaucracy are evident throughout the world, and in many other societies efforts are at hand to humanize the bureaucracy. In Sweden, the car manufacturers SAAB and Volvo have modified the assembly line. Teams of workers decide how the work is to be performed, and who is to do what. Even the Soviets have begun to realize that the structure of their organizations is conducive neither to work satisfaction (evident in high absenteeism, alcoholism, and truancy), nor to productivity. For the past decade efforts have been made to involve the worker in some form of participation. While so far, success has been minimal at best, labor shortages and a decline in productivity—from 6.8 percent in the 1970s to 3.4 percent in 1980—may yet lead to a more serious effort to involve the workers in "their" plant.

The American experience suggests that change in bureaucratic organizations is difficult and costly to implement. It is a slow process. Some scholars predict an end to bureaucracy in the next few decades (Bennis, 1970); they anticipate an organization based on skill and professional training, not on rank and role. While change is occurring, its rate of progress is not rapid enough for us to anticipate the demise of bureaucratic organizations in the near future.

SUMMARY ▬▬▬▬▬

1. The main purposes of this chapter are to define and discuss the characteristics of formal organizations; to discuss the structure of participation in organizations; to describe some of the changes in organizations; and to examine organizations cross culturally.

2. Formal organizations are groups that are organized to achieve specific goals. They may be classified in terms of their purposes (ranging from mutual benefit to commonweal organizations) and the extent of their control over members' lives. Using these classifications, we can arrange formal organizations on a continuum from total institutions (such as prisons) to voluntary associations (such as Girl Scouts).

3. As a formal organization becomes larger and more complex, it turns into a bureaucracy. Max Weber cited several characteristics of a bureaucracy: specialization, hierarchy of authority, merit selection, objective rules and routine procedures, and career pattern. Informal organizations based on personal relationships between members of a bureaucracy develop within the formal bureaucratic organization. These informal organizations can either support or undermine the workings and goals of the bureaucracy.

4. Bureaucracies have certain strengths: they establish coordination to get things done efficiently, minimize chaos, and promote impartiality. But they also have many dysfunctions such as means-ends inversion and the Peter Principle. The subdivision of tasks may also lead to worker dissatisfaction and alienation.

5. Modifications in some organizations through worker participation or Quality of Work Life projects have been instituted in some organizations, with some success.

6. The Japanese and Yugoslav organizations differ considerably from their Western counterparts. Each takes a distinctive approach to the involvement of workers in organizational planning. Japanese paternalism and work-life employment make the organization more humane. The workers' councils in Yugoslavia have at least in principle the authority to make decisions affecting workers and the enterprise.

REVIEW

Key Terms

Formal organization	Power authority	Informal organization	Human relations
Total institution	Traditional authority	Means-end-inversion	Alienation
Voluntary associations	Charismatic authority	Oligarchy	
Bureaucracy	Rational legal authority		

Review and Discussion

1. Make a chart of the organizational structures of your college or university. Be sure to include students in the structure. After making your chart, would you find it easier to navigate the structure of your school if you wanted to get something done—get exempted from a course, or petition to start a new student club, for example? Why or why not?

2. Would you be more inclined to buy an American car or a Japanese car? What considerations about the operation of bureaucratic structures could enter into your decision?

3. From your own experience, give an example of a bureaucratic dysfunction. Did it affect you personally? If so, how did you deal with the problem?

4. Think about a job you have had, or your work as a volunteer in a hospital or other structure. Was your supervisor a man or a woman? What kind of supervisor would you have preferred—a man or a woman? Why?

5. In Chapter 3, we talked about culture and the way it affects social structures. How has culture affected the growth of the bureaucracy in Japan and the United States? How much potential do you see for modifying bureaucracies in either nation in order to incorporate features used in the other?

References

Abegglen, J. S. (1958). *The Japanese Factory*. New York: Free Press.

Bennis, W. G., ed. (1970). *American Bureaucracy*. New York: Aldine Transaction Books.

Bensman, J., and **B. Rosenberg** (1971). The meaning of work in bureaucratic society. In *Society As It Is,* eds. Glen Gavuglio and David Rye. New York: Macmillan.

Blau, P. (1956). *Bureaucracy in Modern Society*. New York: Random House.

———— (1963). *The Dynamics of Bureaucracy*. Chicago: University of Chicago Press.

Blau, P., and **R. Scott** (1962). *Formal Organizations: A Comparative Approach*. San Francisco: Chandler.

Blumberg, P. (1973). *Industrial Democracy*. New York: Schocken Books.

Dore, R. P. (1973). *British Factory: Japanese Factory*. Berkeley: University of California Press.

Etzioni, A. (1961). *A Comparative Analysis of Complex Organizations*. New York: Free Press.

———— (1964). *Modern Organizations*. Englewood Cliffs, N. J.: Prentice-Hall.

Guest, R. (1979). Quality of work life: Learning from Tarrytown. *Harvard Business Review* 57 (July–August): 76–87.

HEW Report (1973). *Work in America*. Cambridge: MIT Press.

Hunnius, G., G. D. Garson, and **J. Case,** eds. (1973). *Worker's Control*. New York: Vintage Books.

Kanter, R. M. (1977). *Men and Women of the Corporation*. New York: Basic Books.

———— (1978). Work in a new America. *Daedalus* 107 (Winter): 47–78.

Kohn, M. (1971). Bureaucratic man: A portrait and interpretation. *American Sociological Review* 36: 461–474.

Lipset, S. M., M. Trow, and **J. Coleman** (1956). *Union Democracy*. New York: Free Press.

Little, R. (1970). Buddy relations and combat performance. In *The Sociology of Organizations,* eds. Oscar Grusky and G. A. Miller. New York: Free Press.

Mannheim, K. (1952). *Essays on the Sociology of Knowledge*. New York: Oxford University Press.

Marsh, R. M., and **Mannari, H.** (1976). *Modernization and the Japanese Factory*. Princeton: Princeton University Press.

Mayo, E. (1946). *The Social Problems of an Industrial Civilization*. Cambridge: Harvard University Press.

McCleery, R. (1957). *Policy Change in Prison Management*. East Lansing: Governmental Research Bureau, Michigan State University.

Merton, R. K. (1957). *Social Theory and Social Structure*. New York: Macmillan.

Michels, R. (1949). *Political Parties*. New York: Free Press.

Ouchi, W. G. (1981). *Theory Z*. Reading, Mass.: Addison-Wesley.

Peter, L. J., and **R. Hull** (1969). *The Peter Principle*. New York: Morrow.

Roethlisberger, F. J., and **W. J. Dickson** (1939). *Management and the Workers*. Cambridge: Harvard University Press.

Rosow, J. M. (1979). Quality of work life issues for the 1980s. In *Work in America,* eds. Clark Kerr and Jerome Rosow. New York: Van Nostrand.

Scheff, T. (1961). Control over policy by attendants in a mental hospital. *Journal of Health and Human Behavior* 2: 93–105.

Walton, R. E. (1975). From Hawthorne to Topeka and Kalmar. *Harvard Business Review* 53 (July–August): 88–97.

Zwerdling, D. (1980). *Workplace Democracy*. New York: Harper & Row.

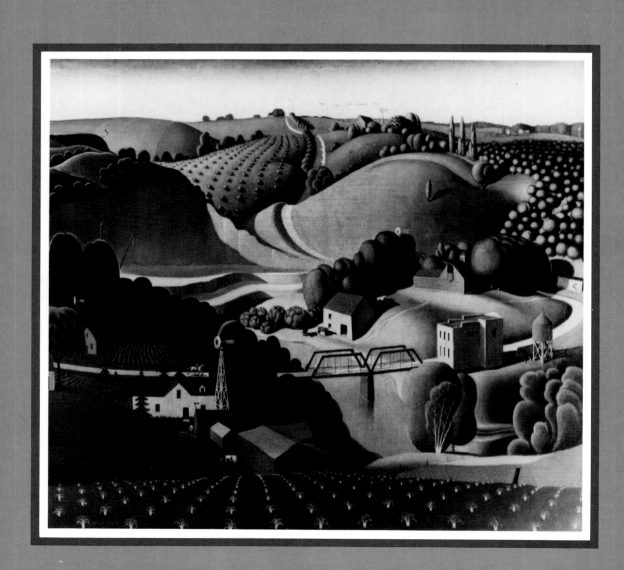

12

COMMUNITIES AND URBANIZATION

Where we live and who our neighbors are greatly influence the quality of our social relationships, the pattern of our daily activities, and even the attitudes we hold.

". . . There is wide diversity among communities . . . readily observable in external appearances, for example, in the contrast between a small fishing village with its wooden huts rising on stilts in a cluster above a lagoon and a large industrial city with its skyscrapers, factories, and church spires intermingled across its skyline. On one extreme, there are communities where it takes great expenditure of human energy to achieve even a precarious subsistence, where people live in personalized relationships with one another in accord with sacred traditions that have been handed down for generations. At the other extreme, there are affluent communities where highly specialized personnel using intricate mechanized processes achieve voluminous output of goods and services with little expenditure of human energy, where life is largely formalized and caught up in a network of worldwide interdependencies." (Edwards and Jones, 1976: 11)

Many of our social relationships, attitudes, and daily patterns of activity are based on *where* we live and on who lives next to us—that is, on the kind of community in which we live. For example, a man who lives in a bustling, urban center will not be on first-name terms with most of the people who live within a five-mile radius of his home. He will not spend his day outdoors actually producing the food that his family consumes, nor his evenings playing cards at the local firehouse with fellow volunteer firefighters, many of whom are his friends from childhood. His life will be shaped very differently from that of someone who was born and raised in a quiet, rural town, or whose family has lived for generations in an isolated and tradition-bound peasant village.

THE CONCEPT OF COMMUNITY

In studying the way people live together, how they organize themselves, and the consequences of these arrangements, sociologists often find it helpful to identify a group of people as a community. Clearly, there are many ways in which people live together. And each arrangement has different effects on the inhabitants' relationships with each other and their sense of togetherness. Therefore, community becomes an important topic for sociologists to study as they seek to understand human behavior.

When we use the term **community** we mean a group of people living within a specific geographic area who cooperate in all their life activities and who share a sense of belonging. As Edwards and Jones explain,

The people of a community do occupy a specific geographic space; they do have enough shared concern to see to it that the means exist for meeting their daily needs, and they do engage in enough collaborative endeavor to provide the order and continuity by which their community can endure, even as patterns of living change and as people come and go." (Edwards and Jones, 1976: 11)

Members of a community rely on one another to accomplish the social functions that are essential to organized human life. Teachers, plumbers, shopkeepers, doctors, mechanics, and lawyers each take care of some particular social need, and together they create a self-sufficient or autonomous social unit.

Clearly the sociological concept of community begins with reference to a geographical area. This is both similar to and different from the everyday use of the idea of community. While we commonly use this word in the way sociologists do, we also use it to refer to a group of people with a specific shared interest but without a specific shared geographical area. For example, we may talk about a "community of scholars" or "the gay/lesbian community." In these cases, we are referring to a group of people who share an interest in scholarly activities or life styles influenced by sexual orientation, respectively. In neither case is the sociological concept of community altogether appropriate since there is no specific geographical area involved. The sociological concepts of reference groups or in/out groups, discussed earlier in Chapter 10, would be applicable, however. Furthermore, communities have members who are scholars and gays or lesbians, and who are important contributors to the ongoing social life of their communities as sociologically defined. As we proceed in this chapter, it will be helpful to remember that we will be using the sociological meaning of community.

THE CONTINUUM OF COMMUNITIES

Communities range in size from small to large, with size having a powerful effect on the nature of community life. Size, however, must be calculated along two interrelated dimensions: by geography and population. We will look at each as they interrelate, focusing on the ways in which both affect the nature of community life.

The Geographic Dimension of Size

A community is usually partly identified by its location; some territory determined by generally recognized boundaries (rivers, mountain ranges, city blocks) contains the people in the community and separates them from noncommunity members.

Communities are also shaped by the geographic resources that are available to them. Looking at a community's relationships with its geographical environment is called an **ecological perspective.** It

. . . provides information about the relationships between the people and the geographic setting of the community as they are reflected in the particular uses the people make of particular segments of space, the processes by which the uses undergo change, and the effects that particular land uses have upon the natural environment in decreasing or increasing the community's viability. (Edwards and Jones, 1976: 97)

A community is made up of people living in a specific geographical area who cooperate in daily activities and share a sense of belonging.

It is not surprising that resources actually determine the location of communities and continue to attract large concentrations of people and activity. Most of our nation's largest cities, for example, developed commercially because they were located along major train or trucking routes, on large bodies of water, or near transportation breaks—places where goods had to be shifted from one form of transportation to another (Dentler, 1968). Chicago's enormous business traffic depends on its central location, its nearness to transportation lines, and its access to the Great Lakes. Similarly, San Francisco's location as a Pacific seaport largely accounts for its commercial success. Other communities have profited from the availability of certain natural resources that are essential to industrial or social development. Pittsburgh became a great mining and manufacturing center because of nearby coal and iron ore depostis. A desirable climate and a long stretch of oceanfront property enabled Miami Beach to develop a thriving tourist industry.

If geographic resources encourage certain types of community development, they also limit others. Clearly, Pittsburgh could never have become a seaport, and Chicago would make an unpopular resort. Certain of the harshest areas of the world are so limited by their geographic conditions that few major cities, or permanent communities of any kind, have ever developed there. In the Arctic, for example, Eskimos live in simple, highly flexible communities that they can expand, contract, or relocate as the people follow the seasonal migrations of seals and caribou, their main sources of food. Even in our own society, many communities, although not subject to such severe environmental limitations, follow a pattern of seasonal reorganization. Beach resort towns that may appear abandoned during the winter months often undergo a population explosion in the summer. And many New England ski areas spring to life only after the first snowfall.

Usually a community must organize necessary social functions within the limits of its environmental resources. In a few cases, however, enterprising developers have managed to overcome tremendous geographic obstacles. For example, Las Vegas planners have transformed a once sparsely populated, bleak, and isolated desert area into one of the nation's most popular entertainment centers. Few communities have been developed so purposefully and independently of natural living conditions, but as our technological ability has become more sophisticated, we have been able to change and manipulate the natural environment to suit our own needs and plans. Over the centuries, communities have changed as technological developments have opened up new ways of using the environment.

In addition to *the kind of space* occupied by a community, *the amount of space* in relation to the number of residents also influences community life. Whereas small-town and farm communities consist mainly of single-family houses, each with a separate plot of land, in urban areas people generally live and work closely in steel and concrete towers. This difference in the amount of available living space causes many of the differences between urban and rural life styles. Rural inhabitants must typically give up the cultural stimulation made possible by great numbers of people and organizations in return for quiet in their daily encounters; in return for bustling city life, urban dwellers must deal with such problems as increased noise, crime, and pollution.

Some cities are more spread out than others. The newer cities of the western United States have more land area per person than the older industrial cities of the East. The nearly 8 million residents of New York are packed into 365 square miles; close to the same number of people in Los Angeles are spread out over 450 square miles. This variation accounts for some of the differences in the way people live in the two cities. Whereas New York is a city of towering skyscrapers, much of downtown Los Angeles is without any buildings at all, given over to parking lots and giant multilaned expressways. Los Angeles is, nevertheless, far more congested than most rural communities.

The interplay of geographic and population dimensions of community size is most effectively depicted by viewing communities on a continuum. At one end are urban communities with large populations and comprised of several subparts: the central business district, wholesale trade and manufacturing areas, middle-income residential areas, upper-income residential areas, suburbs, and a rural-urban fringe (Edwards and Jones, 1976: 126–31). (The urban community will be explored in more detail in the latter part of the chapter.) At the other end of the continuum is the rural community with a small population which is geographically isolated and characterized by little differentiation in its social and geographic structure. In between are communities with medium-sized populations and ties linking them to relatively nearby urban areas as well as surrounding rural areas (Edwards and Jones, 1976: 126–31). In trying to understand and describe this continuum, sociologists have tended to focus on its rural and urban ends. We will now turn to these efforts.

The Rural and the Urban

Gemeinschaft and Gesellschaft. Relatively few people in the United States today live in small towns where everybody knows everybody else, or where children follow in their parents' footsteps, running the family farm or store. Most of us are accustomed to dealing with people we do not know personally. We expect to move more than once in our lives, and we see our future in terms of individual achievement, not in terms of carrying on a tradition.

Ferdinand Tönnies (1887), a German sociologist, predicted these changes nearly 100 years ago, when industrialization was just beginning to take hold. He called the small, rural villages of his boyhood *Gemeinschaft* (communities) and

Tönnies's description of a Gemeinschaft was modeled on the intimate primary communities of rural Germany.

the growing centers of activity *Gesellschaft* (associations).

A **Gemeinschaft** is a primary community that is rooted in tradition. Usually inhabitants were born in the community. The individuals' commitment to their village is based on shared values and traditions. Relationships between neighbors are intimate and personal, as if the village were a large extended family. People identify with their home and neighbors. In contrast, the term **Gesellschaft** refers to a voluntary association of people who live or work together for convenience. Relationships are impersonal and utilitarian. Individuals are committed only to the degree that their cooperation within the association serves their needs. Decisions are based on practical considerations, not emotional attachments. The *Gesellschaft* is characterized by individualism, impersonality, mobility, the rational pursuit of self-interest, and the substitution of efficiency and progress for tradition.

Contemporary sociologists have incorporated the basic ideas of Tönnies in their concepts of urban and rural communities. We will use these concepts in the remainder of the chapter. After a brief survey of rural communities, we will study urban communities in depth. As we will see, the great majority of people in the United States live in urban communities. Because America as a society is dominated by its urban areas, knowledge about the nature of urban life is fundamental to understanding the society as a whole.

RURAL COMMUNITIES

Sanders and Lewis (1976) define rural communities as follows:

By rural *we mean communities that are (a) relatively small in size . . . (The United States Census definition is 2,500 or less); (b) non-metropolitan, i.e. does not fall within the (shadow) of a metropolitan area . . ., and (c) of a clearly rural character, i.e. exists in the midst of an agricultural area, an area characterized by a "primacy economy," or one marked by other obvious nonurban cultural, social, and ecological characteristics. (p. 35)*

To summarize, a **rural community** is characterized by small population size, low population density, and primary relationships among its members. There are several kinds of rural communities. The *peasant village* exists in most under-

developed and developing nations. While usually very small, agricultural, and isolated, even these rural communities are becoming more dependent on outside sources for at least some essential farming and household tools and for some dietary staples that cannot be grown at home. These influences are being felt primarily because of increasingly sophisticated communication and transportation technology.

The *small town* is another type of rural community. It is larger, less isolated, and more complex than the peasant village, yet still small and remote by urban standards. Compared to the peasant village, a wider range of occupations is represented in the small town: business proprietors, farm owners, veterinarians, lawyers, clerks, salespeople, skilled and semi-skilled workers, and farm laborers. Moreover, unlike the homogeneous and classless peasant village, the small town may include a number of social classes. In Springdale, sociologists Arthur Vidich and Joseph Bensman (1960) found a middle class, an "old aristocracy," traditional farmers, and "shack people." The small town also has far less control over internal local matters than the traditional peasant village. County extension agents, land tax assessors, teachers, radio, television, newspapers, and the Sears catalog all bring the outside culture into the local community. In fact, most small towns are rather closely tied to urban areas, as we will see shortly.

Changes in traditional American rural life had already begun more than a century ago. As late as 1787 a farmer could write:

At this time my farm gave me and my whole family a good living on the produce of it, and left me one year with another 150 silver dollars, for I never spent more than 10 dollars a year, which was for salt, nails, and the like. Nothing to eat, drink, or wear was bought, as my farm provided all.

But by the nineteenth century, rural life was beginning to change under the influence of industry, railroads, and the growth of the city. Hundreds of mining, fishing, and lumber communities began to shrink in size and wealth as these industries became large-scale mechanized operations that required relatively few workers. Farming, too, became a complex and specialized industry, requiring less and less labor and more investment in heavy machinery, special feed, fertilizer, pesticides, and land. The huge specialized factories in the field—the large wheat and corn producers of the Great Plains and the fruit and vegetable growers of California and Texas—replaced the all-purpose family farm. Small farmers often cannot make the necessary capital investments to compete with these "agribusinesses." Fewer people are now needed to operate these larger concerns. Whereas in 1820 one American farmer could produce only enough to support four people, technological advances today enable a single farmer to supply food for 43 people (Weitz, 1971).

All of these changes in agriculture, while improving production, have been a mixed blessing for our rural population. As mechanization has left fewer jobs available, the farm population has shrunk drastically. In 1910, one in every three Americans was a farmer; today fewer than one in ten persons farms or merely lives on farms (Dentler, 1968). This sharp drop has led some people to propose half seriously that farmers should be declared an "endangered species." Moreover, as farming has become big business, many small towns that served as agricultural market centers have lost their original economic purpose and have become stagnant. Farm produce is often shipped directly to urban areas, and most marketing and processing activities—collecting produce, sorting, weighing, packing, and distributing—have been turned over to outside centralized agencies.

Not only does a farmer's income depend on market forces based far beyond the local community, but rural communities also depend on federal and state aid to help meet educational costs, build roads, and provide social services for the old, disabled, and unemployed, just as large cities do. They too are regulated by state and federal laws and agencies that regulate a variety of other "local" community matters: the health of their cows, the conditions of their schools, the construction of their sewage systems.

Most rural communities, then, have ceased to be isolated and self-sufficient. They have lost a good deal of control over their own local affairs as they have become part of mass society. They are influenced by mass communication, depend on mass marketing both for selling their own products and for buying needed goods, and are subject to outside political and economic controls. There seems little doubt that

. . . structural change is occurring at two levels and results in two kinds of (rural) community growth: differentiation of local institutions in the community and the location of regionally backed institutions in the community. . . ." (Sanders and Lewis, 1976: 44)

The entry of regional structures and services into rural communities, a process called **regional articulation,** is the most obvious sign of the impact of mass society on rural communities.

Despite these conditions, a village in northern Maine or central Idaho may still seem to represent an ideal way of life. The neighborliness and hospitality of most small towns provide a sense of security and belonging. In times of need, people are usually assured that someone will be available and willing to help out. Neighbors may drop in with a word of encouragement, friendly advice, or comfort. Yet along with the advantages of living in a friendly and peaceful community go certain problems. The interpersonal network that makes social support possible may also lead to strong social control. In a small town, it is difficult to escape the notice of neighbors, and privacy may become a yearned-for luxury. Gossip and the grapevine may prove to be stricter and more stringent social controls than the rules of law that operate in more impersonal settings, preventing people from doing things that they would not think twice about in a more anonymous urban environment. At times, even this may be an advantage. It is far less easy for someone to snatch a purse or rob a bank and get away with it on Main Street in Springdale than in downtown Chicago.

A rural resident may not have to worry about getting mugged on the way home from the movies or about coming home to an apartment that has been cleaned out by burglars. A country town has to cope with fewer people in need of medical care or welfare assistance. But there are also fewer, and often less adequate, programs and services to handle the problems that do arise. While mining, farming, and lumbering are three of the most dangerous occupations in the United States, many of these workers—particularly farmers—are not covered by compensation or unemployment insurance. As a result, incomes of 13 percent of the population in nonmetropolitan areas fell below the poverty level in 1978, compared with 10 percent of the population in metropolitan areas (*Social Indicators,* 1980: 495). Yet welfare assistance in rural areas is notoriously less adequate than in most cities, often in regions where poverty is greatest. For example, in 1977 the average monthly payments per family in the Aid to Families with Dependent Children Program (AFDC), a basic welfare program for financially needy families, varied greatly between states that are predominantly rural and urban. The three lowest payments in the country that year were $47, $84, and $104 for Mississippi, South Carolina, and Texas, respectively. In contrast, the three highest were $371, $302, and $300 for New York, California, and Massachusetts, respectively (*Social Indicators,* 1980: 404).

Rural areas, then, offer a way of life that is appealing to many even though rural life also has identifiable social and economic risks. Rural America is increasingly subject to external influences, however. The process of urbanization has been a worldwide phenomenon, closely tied to political, economic, and technological changes. We will now turn to the nature of urban communities, starting with a review of their historical development.

URBANIZATION
The Rise of the City

The patterns of life in rural communities remained essentially unchanged for thousands of years. Each new generation continued to work its land, using the same tools and methods as their parents and producing just enough food to support themselves and their families. Then, about 6,000 years ago, some communities located in the especially fertile river valleys of the Middle East, Pakistan, and northern China began to change. All of these regions had large areas of land that yielded abundant food surpluses needed to support a large population. The natural transportation system provided by slow-flowing rivers permitted these growing communities to bring additional supplies from outlying rural areas. Many people were consequently freed from the task of producing their own food and were able to become full-time specialists: artisans, traders, religious and government officials (Lenski, 1970).

As these settlements grew larger and the proportion of specialists increased, new systems were needed to preserve order and to coordinate social activities under these changing and more complex conditions of life. Gradually, the traditional social system was replaced by more formal social mechanisms and institutions—governments, written laws, and armies. This is the process of **urbanization,** in which rural and suburban communities increase in population size, population density, structural complexity, and reliance on advanced technology. This "urban revolution" altered many of the basic characteristics of community life and had far-reaching effects on the development of human society everywhere (Childe, 1952).

The Preindustrial City

The earliest cities were tiny by our standards and, in many respects, were more similar to the traditional folk community than to our modern

Abundant crops and easy access to trade routes encouraged urbanization of the fertile Nile Valley. Over the centuries, the simple farming communities of ancient Egypt evolved into a highly complex society. The accomplishments of its citizens have been memorialized in magnificent architectural structures, like this gateway to the temple, constructed during the age of the Pharoahs.

industrial centers. Despite a relatively dense and diverse population, the type of city that existed until the nineteenth century was still dominated by extended family and kinship networks. Industry was not mechanized or highly specialized. Craftsmen both produced and marketed their goods in their own homes. The population in these cities was limited by the absence of large-scale manufacturing needed to provide for a large work force. Large percentages of the population were periodically wiped out by plagues and epidemics that flourished in the unhealthy living conditions of these early cities (Sjoberg, 1960). It is only within the past 150 years that industrial cities have existed as we know them. The huge metropolitan areas and urban-dominated societies of today are products of the Industrial Revolution which began in England in the late eighteenth and early nineteenth centuries. In the non-Western world, however, where nations have begun to industrialize only recently, many cities have remained preindustrial.

The Impact of Urbanization

Urban communities in the Western world are both a cause and a consequence of industrialization. Cities were necessary because early factories could not have developed without the availability of a large work force. But a large number of workers could never have assembled in one place without certain technological advances. In the eighteenth century, competition for land had forced many small farmers off their properties. Factories provided employment for those who had been left without any other means of livelihood. People began to leave the countryside in droves to settle in communities that were springing up around new manufacturing centers.

Technology also made it possible, as well as necessary, for large groups of people to live in concentrated urban communities. Improved transportation systems enabled large numbers of people to migrate from isolated rural areas to relatively distant towns and cities, and helped to weld communities into a larger economic network. Food surpluses, produced by more efficient agricultural techniques, could also be transported to support larger urban populations. Advances in health care, such as the discovery of the smallpox vaccine in 1792, helped to lower the death rate; urban population growth began to spiral upward (Cook, 1970).

Even in the preindustrial age, people in urban areas depended on those in the countryside for food and raw materials. Often the city rulers simply took what they needed, collecting tithes

Fig. 12.1 / Urban population growth in the United States: 1840–1980

The figures for 1960 include people in unincorporated urban areas (areas that do not have a city government). Although many of these urban areas are suburbs on the outskirts of large cities, they were included in the figures for rural areas before 1950. In 1960 almost 10 million people lived in unincorporated urban areas. Thus, the figures for 1840–1940 probably show too many people in rural areas and not enough people in urban areas.

Source: From *Promise of America: Sidewalks, Gunboats, and Ballyhoo* by Larry Cuban and Philip Roden. Copyright © 1971 by Scott, Foresman and Company. Reprinted by permission.

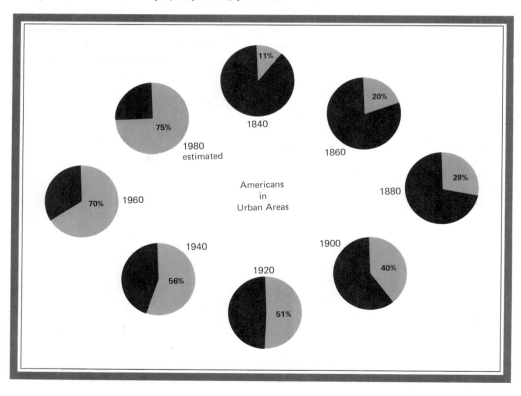

and taxes by threat of force. The early urban communities established political dominance over rural areas, but the Industrial Revolution drew the village world further into the orbit of the city. The Oaxacan villager who uses a steel plow instead of a wood digging stick has already taken the first step toward involvement in the industrial-urban economy.

Today, when virtually everyone in the United States has radios, cars, and television sets, the influence of urban areas is spreading throughout the country. Similarly, the physical reach of the cities themselves is increasing. Our cities are invading the rural areas both socially and spatially. In 1800, only 5 percent of our population lived in towns of more than 2,500 people. By 1960, over 65 percent lived in such towns; and by 1970, 73 percent of Americans lived in cities of more than 100,000 (Southwick, 1972). Seen another way, the population growth rate of metropolitan counties was 1.57 for the period from 1960 to 1970, but only .77 from 1970 to 1976. In contrast, nonmetropolitan counties adjacent to metropolitan areas grew .71 for the period from 1960 to 1970 but 1.37 for the 1970

to 1976 time span (*Social Indicators*, 1980: 45). These data make it clear how urban areas have grown and encompassed previously rural areas (see also Table 12.1). Later in the chapter we will look at some recent shifts in urban growth that seem to be establishing yet different relationships between rural and urban areas.

While industrialization in the West was a long, slow process, today many nations in Asia, Africa, and Latin America are confronted with a very different set of problems and conditions. In these largely agrarian countries, there has been no pronounced industrial revolution to generate the capital necessary to provide jobs for large numbers of unskilled workers. Urbanization in the Third World is occurring much more rapidly than it did in the West. A declining death rate and a high birth rate in many places have created an explosive population growth that has outstripped the development of commerce and industry. The vast numbers of people who migrate to the cities often settle in the slums or "shack towns" that are located along city fringes. Here they frequently encounter unemployment, hunger, squalor, and disease, conditions that may be

TABLE 12.1 / THE UNITED STATES AS AN URBAN SOCIETY

The following table documents the growth of urban areas in the United States. Between 1940 and 1976 the population living in metropolitan areas grew from 32.6 to 73.0 percent of the total population.

Metropolitan Area Population, 1940 to 1976

	1940	*1950*	*1960*	*1970*	*1976*
Metropolitan areas: Number of SMSAs	168	168	209	243	277
Population (×1,000)	69,270	84,501	112,885	155,021	156,754
Percent of total U.S. population	32.6	56.1	63.0	72.8	73.0
Percent U.S. land area	7.0	7.0	10.9	13.9	14.1
Nonmetropolitan areas population (×1,000)	62,390	66,196	66,438	63,793	58,114

Source: From Bureau of the Census, *Statistical Abstract of the United States:* Washington, D.C., 1978, p. 17.

worse than the rural miseries they are trying to escape (Baali and Vandiver, 1970). Generally they live without any of the facilities that we regard as basic: sewers, water, and electricity. "Houses" are often made of cardboard, discarded bricks, corrugated tin, or whatever else can be scavenged. For example, although Calcutta is a fast growing city and an important seaport and manufacturing center, inadequate technological and economic development has left millions without jobs and homes. More than three-fourths of the 3 million inner-city dwellers live in overcrowded tenements where families share a single water tap or latrine with as many as 30 other persons. Except for a few new high-priced residential districts, Calcutta is a city filled with hungry people, uncollected garbage in the streets, unsanitary water supplies, and traffic-choked roadways (Bose, 1965).

Despite very different urbanization experiences in Western and Third World nations, the growth of cities has led to certain very fundamental changes in culture and social structure everywhere. Life becomes more impersonal. Economic activities and relationships are separated from the web of family and kinship relations as new and specialized occupational roles replace the old agricultural activities. New jobs in different settings cause a rise in geographic and social mobility. Traditional social castes or class systems break down, and the individual's place in society is based more on wealth and occupation than on birth. Formalized law and centralized bureaucratic political agencies become primary mechanisms of social control as mobility undermines the informal system of extended kin networks and life becomes more complex (Lenski, 1970).

URBANISM AS A WAY OF LIFE

Urban communities are places where large numbers of very different kinds of people live together very closely. During the 1920s and 1930s, a group of sociologists at the University of Chicago began to investigate the rapid urbanization taking place in the United States. Using the city itself as their laboratory, this "Chicago School" of sociologists (especially Robert Park, Louis Wirth, and Ernest Burgess) elaborated upon the earlier work of Tönnies and others.

Wirth's essay, "Urbanism as a Way of Life" (1938), is the classic presentation of the Chicago School's analysis of urbanism. Wirth argued that urban life is not simply rural life in a different setting, but that it has its own distinct characteristics. He defined a city as "a relatively large, dense and permanent settlement of socially diverse individuals" (p. 8), and he showed how the three elements of this definition (largeness, population density, and social diversity) operate together to create a way of life that is uniquely characteristic of cities.

The individual has to cope with the size and density of the population in the city. A **city** is an urban community, but the term is often used to refer to the most densely populated center of an urban community. It would be impossible for each person to give even passing attention to everyone he or she encounters in a day's activity; therefore, interaction with many people is goal-directed and hence anonymous and impersonal. Primary-type relationships tend to be restricted to significant family and peer group members rather than being characteristic of most day-to-day interactions.

The nature of the city also tends to magnify social differentiations (see Chapter 8) as people relate to one another in relatively superficial ways. People can interact more comfortably and more efficiently with those who are most like themselves. Consequently, groups of those with similar occupations, social classes, races, and ethnic backgrounds can be observed to cluster together. Cities become segmented into such distinct areas as financial and theatre districts, ethnic neighborhoods, high-price shopping areas, and ghettos. But even though city life is more divided

Traffic jams are not new, as this scene of Chicago in 1905 illustrates. For decades, transportation problems have been one of the social ills accompanying rapid, large-scale urbanization.

than rural life, the combination of *physical closeness* with *social distance* gives city dwellers a higher tolerance for the social diversity that exists around them. Because urban life tends to be anonymous and goal oriented, diverse individual life styles usually are accepted by the general population.

It should be noted that the rapid growth of cities posed many new and tremendous problems for the United States in the early part of this century. Life had been largely rural in orientation and urban life was viewed as the source of disruption and social distress. The work of the Chicago School reflects some of this bias in favor of rural life styles. The more recent work of sociologists like Gans, Fischer, and others has helped to dispel some of this earlier view of urban life which tended to overemphasize its disruptive and impersonal aspects (Alexander, 1973; Fischer, 1981; Mirowsky and Ross, 1980). Later in this chapter we will return to the question of the quality of life in urban areas.

PATTERNS OF URBAN GROWTH

As urban communities change and grow, certain changes take place in the way that people, businesses, and neighborhoods are distributed throughout a city. New social and economic conditions lead to new patterns of cooperation and competition that are reflected in the way different sections of the city expand or shrink, in the way different social activities are organized, and in the way neighborhoods develop, change, or dissolve.

The SMSA

For purposes of measuring changes in population, the United States Bureau of the Census has identified a statistical unit called a **Standard Metropolitan Statistical Area (SMSA)** by which it identifies urban areas. An SMSA must have either a city of at least 50,000 residents, or an urbanized area of 50,000 or more, plus a total population of at least 100,000. In 1981, there were 323 SMSAs in the United States (Herbers, 1981), an increase of 35 between 1970 and 1980. These data provide ". . . further evidence that the American population is spreading to once remote, sparsely populated areas that earlier in the century were losing people to the big cities" (Herbers, 1981). An SMSA contains both rural and urban land, but most people live in urban places. For example, Jasper and Newton counties in Missouri form an SMSA with Joplin as its urban hub; Albemarle, Fluvanna, and Greene counties in Virginia have Charlottesville; and Thurston county in Washington has Olympia, which also happens to be the state capital (Herbers, 1981).

The growth of the SMSA reflects several societal trends (Herbers, 1981). One, already noted, is the desire of many people to live in environments which are less hectic than big cities usually are, yet allow access to major urban services. An important related factor is advances in technology and transportation which make some geographical dispersion possible. For example, industries like electronics, computer software, and research do not depend on access to bulk raw materials (like coal or iron ore, for example). They are freer to move away from rivers and the ocean which have traditionally been major shipping routes for such supplies. Similarly, their output is usually small and light. It is easily adaptable to trucks or even planes rather than being restricted to trains or ships whose routes are relatively fixed and unchangeable. Finally, these new industries often find it desirable to be near universities and colleges, since research is important to their growth and they often need large numbers of highly educated workers. It is, therefore, no surprise that six of the 35 most recently formed SMSAs have major state universities located in them; a number of others have smaller colleges as well (Herbers, 1981).

The SMSA is an important tool for identifying population shifts among communities, as well as for helping to identify the sociological reasons for these changes (such as new technology). Once these areas have been identified, sociologists have used other models to analyze the nature of the social interactions that take place within a certain locality (Fischer, 1975). We will now turn to some of these models.

Ecological Models of Urban Communities

Early in this century, sociologists began trying to understand the rapid urban growth taking place throughout the Western world. They studied particular cities in detail and developed models of how they were developing. These models were imperfect because they could not describe the growth of all cities, but they did call attention to some basic patterns of urban development that might otherwise have remained unnoticed. Like the concept of community, these models are tools for attacking a difficult subject.

Earlier in the chapter we saw that geographic factors influence the development of communities, and that the ecological perspective looks at the relationship between a community and its environment. Sociologists who study the relationships between people and their urban surroundings are called *urban ecologists,* and they have proposed a number of theories or models depicting how and why urban spatial patterns develop. While very few cities have been as deliberately planned and designed as Brasilia or Washington, D.C., neither have they grown randomly, entirely without rhyme or reason.

Using Chicago as a model, the University of Chicago sociologist Ernest Burgess suggested in the early part of this century that competition for land use led to the development of a series of **concentric zones** spreading outward from the city's center in a series of rings. The central business district lies at the heart of the city, surrounded by a ring of ethnic ghettos and slums. Around these are working people's homes, often second-generation immigrant families. This area is ringed by high-priced residences and the entertainment district, with single-family commuter homes in the outermost circle (Park, Burgess, McKenzie, and Wirth, 1925).

While many cities reflect this model to some extent, the circles are often neither symmetrical nor unified, since topography, transportation routes, and natural boundaries may disrupt the arrangement. Observing that types or grades of residences and specialized areas are often concentrated mainly on one side of a city, Hoyt proposed a **sector model** that depicts the city as a circle cut into V-shaped wedges. According to this model, the central city is first divided into business, industrial, and housing districts which expand outward in pie-shaped sectors until the pattern is interrupted by a river or some other physical barrier (Hoyt, 1939). This pattern can be seen roughly in Minneapolis, San Francisco, and Richmond, Virginia.

According to the third major growth model, most large cities are composed of several smaller cities that eventually grew together. Each of the smaller communities is already fully developed; when they merge, the new city is composed of **multiple nuclei**—several business districts, entertainment areas, ethnic and exclusive neighborhoods, each of equal importance. Boston is perhaps the major example of a multiple-nuclei city (Harris and Ullman, 1945).

While each of these models depicts significant tendencies and processes at work in cities, none of them offers a perfect explanation that accounts for all of the complex factors operating in an urban setting. Today urban ecologists are developing newer and more refined models that take into account many different geographic, economic, and environmental forces, as well as a wider range of psychological, social, and cultural factors that affect the organization of people in

Fig. 12.2 / Ecological Models of Urban Growth

Source: Concentric zone model adapted from Ernest W. Burgess, "The Growth of the City." In R.E. Park, E.W. Burgess, R.D. McKenzie, and L. Wirth (eds.), *The City* (Chicago: University of Chicago Press, 1925). Sector and multiple-nuclei models adapted from Chauncey D. Harris and Edward L. Ullman, "The Nature of Cities," *Annals of the American Academy of Political and Social Science*, 242, (November 1945): 13. Copyright, 1945, by The American Academy of Political and Social Science. Reprinted by permission. All rights reserved.

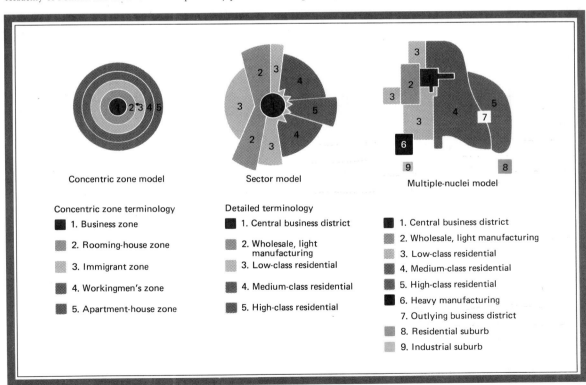

Concentric zone model

Sector model

Multiple-nuclei model

Concentric zone terminology
1. Business zone
2. Rooming-house zone
3. Immigrant zone
4. Workingmen's zone
5. Apartment-house zone

Detailed terminology
1. Central business district
2. Wholesale, light manufacturing
3. Low-class residential
4. Medium-class residential
5. High-class residential

1. Central business district
2. Wholesale, light manufacturing
3. Low-class residential
4. Medium-class residential
5. High-class residential
6. Heavy manufacturing
7. Outlying business district
8. Residential suburb
9. Industrial suburb

TABLE 12.2/ CHANGES IN POPULATION DISTRIBUTION IN URBAN AMERICA

These two tables describe shifts in population that have affected urban areas. Table A looks at the loss of white population in central cities between 1960 and 1970, and the concurrent growth of the black population. Table B documents the dramatic shift of population from the East and Midwest (here shown as North Central) to the South and West between 1960 and 1975.

A: Metropolitan Population by Race, 1960 – 1970 (in percentages)

	1960	1970
Blacks		
Metropolitan areas	67.5	74.3
Central cities	52.3	58.2
Outside central cities	15.2	16.1
Nonmetropolitan areas	32.5	25.7
Whites		
Metropolitan areas	66.7	67.8
Central cities	31.1	27.8
Outside central cities	35.6	40.0
Nonmetropolitan areas	33.4	32.2

B: Regional Metropolitan Population Changes, 1960–1975 (in thousands)

	1960	1970	1975
Northeast	44,678	49,061	49,454
Metropolitan	38,609	42,481	42,411
Nonmetropolitan	6,069	6,580	7,043
North Central	51,619	56,593	57,665
Metropolitan	34,859	39,408	39,902
Nonmetropolitan	16,760	17,185	17,763
South	54,961	62,812	63,101
Metropolitan	32,579	39,819	43,546
Nonmetropolitan	22,382	22,993	24,555
West	28,053	34,839	37,831
Metropolitan	21,891	28,119	30,238
Nonmetropolitan	6,162	6,720	7,593

Source: Bureau of the Census, *Statistical Abstract of the United States:* Washington, D.C., 1978, pp. 17 and 18.

urban space and the reasons why they move (Fischer, 1975). Examples of some of these factors and their effects on population composition in communities are shown in Table 12.2.

Centralization

We have already seen that urban communities are complex wholes made up of many subparts: the central business district, wholesale trade and manufacturing areas, middle-income residential areas, upper-income residential areas, suburbs, and a rural-urban fringe. These concentrated and specialized areas of work and play, residence and commerce, illustrate the processes of the development of natural areas and the centralization which results. **Natural areas** are the sections within the urban community where people engage in particular activities. **Centralization** is the clustering of certain economic and social activities within a particular part of the city. For example, all or most of a city's largest financial offices are usually located in the same section; theaters are in another area, and factories in still another.

Most natural areas develop more or less spontaneously. They are not planned or created by arbitrary political boundaries. Certain residential areas, for example, may develop "naturally" because city people with many of the same basic social needs and life styles will often group together to help solve the problems of living and working in a crowded urban environment. Although they were not required to, most of New York's Italian immigrants settled in the same part of the city, nicknamed "Little Italy." Natural areas may be located next to each other and still remain separate and relatively isolated. Chicago's "Gold Coast," a wealthy neighborhood, is within blocks of a rooming-house area, a bohemian settlement, and a skid row. Yet all of these natural areas are visibly distinct, and residents usually stay in their own socially separate worlds (Suttles, 1968). Elaborating on this process, Sut-

The garment district is one of New York's most colorful areas. Blocks of shops filled with fabric, buttons, beads, and other clothing accessories provide an example of the sociological phenomenon known as centralization in an urban area.

tles has said, "Complex urban societies seem to produce such great social distances that those at the extremes can do little more than build myths about one another" (Suttles, 1976: 5).

While these natural areas often result from intangible social pressures, in some cases more concrete factors, such as the availability of a natural resource, have provided the initial stimulus for the growth of a natural area. For example, a city's dockyards must be built along its waterfront; most of its large factories will locate near a river; and expensive residential areas generally develop in highland sections. As these natural areas become established, other industrial and social functions cluster around them: import-export offices settle near the dockyards; wholesale outlets locate close to the factories; and expensive shops open near posh residential areas. In the heart of New York City's huge garment district, for example, entire blocks are filled with wholesale shops selling hat trimmings—buttons, beads, and feathers. Along La Cienega Boulevard, a major tourist thoroughfare in Los Angeles, virtually all of the shops sell expensive antiques (Bernard, 1973).

This pattern of specialization not only divides the city into myriad sections, it also fragments the daily lives and personal contact of most urbanites. The central business district, alive with activity on weekdays between nine and five o'clock, appears desolate on weekends and in the evening when it is populated solely by a few cleaning people. Even the restaurants, geared to a lunchtime clientele, close down. To eat supper, everyone must go somewhere else—either to their homes in residential sections, or to the "bright lights" districts where the restaurants, theaters, and bars are just beginning to start their business hours. On the weekends, a city family may travel to a park where they can enjoy some greenery for a few hours and where the kids can ride their bikes. Shopping entails an expedition to still another area of the city.

Neighborhoods

Centralization occurs in residential areas as well as business areas. **Neighborhoods** are areas in which people live near each other and interact on a friendly, or at least a somewhat personal, basis. Neighborhoods vary tremendously in the degree to which they are characterized by personal interaction. In some city neighborhoods people may live next door to each other and still be worlds apart (Keller, 1968). In others, neighborhoods can be important support systems for their inhabitants (Kornblum, 1974).

Most early studies of urban neighborhood interaction were based on highly unstable residential areas in the inner city: rooming-house districts, skid rows, and slums where there was little family life and people moved frequently. Herbert Gans did much to dispel the dismal view of urban neighborhoods by showing that in some urban working- and middle-class neighborhoods, interactions are not at all impersonal (1959). Most recently, Carol Stack (1974) has demonstrated that the very forces that keep the poor in poverty also encourage them to develop highly organized systems of mutual support and sharing of resources. Another study by Hodges (1969) showed that extended family ties are extremely important among working- and lower-class San Francisco residents, and that almost half of the people interviewed had close relatives living within a four-block radius. Most of their social life is spent visiting with close neighbors or kin. These findings are reinforced by Suttles (1976) and Fischer (1981), and by Kornblum's study of a Chicago steel mill neighborhood (1974).

Types of Neighborhoods

Two very different types of neighborhoods have captured the attention of sociologists because of their social importance: the inner-city ghetto and the suburb. We will look at each in turn. The term **ghetto** has usually meant the oldest, least desirable residential areas of the city, generally in or near the central business district. Since the mid-nineteenth century, the urban ghetto has traditionally been inhabited by the most recent immigrants from other regions in the United States as well as those from other countries.

The ghettos served two functions, one economic and the other social. Economically, they were closest to the places where immigrants arrived, provided the city's cheapest housing, and were accessible to transportation and employment. Socially, they provided kinship and in-group ties that offered social support and emotional security for newcomers who often lacked money, language skills, and knowledge of United States urban customs.

As these immigrants began to acquire jobs and financial security, learn English, and become more *acculturated*, or used to ways in the new land, new neighborhood patterns developed. As ties to their parents' way of life grew weaker, many second-generation immigrants moved away from the central areas of the city, dispersing the old ethnic communities in an effort to find better housing, schools, and public services (Drake and Drake, 1962). Their places were usually taken by newer arrivals. However, some ethnic groups have continued to live in the inner-city ethnic areas even after several generations—for example, the Italians in Boston's North End and the Chinese in San Francisco. Finding life more comfortable among their own kind, they have stayed in the old neighborhoods by choice (Bensman and Vidich, 1975).

Blacks who moved to northern cities from the South have followed this pattern only up to a point. Most live in the inner city by necessity, not choice. In fact, a disturbingly large percentage of blacks have been unable to leave the ghetto. In virtually every city with a large black population, most blacks live in the inner-city area (Frey, 1980). Blacks have been prevented from leaving the ghetto by a number of obstacles that the earlier European immigrants never had to face. First, as industry has become more mechanized and automated, there is no longer a need for the large numbers of unskilled laborers who were so valuable in the late nineteenth and early twentieth centuries. Second, even highly educated and trained blacks face the problem of job discrimination. Finally, unlike Europeans who could literally disappear into the white middle-class population as they attained a certain level of income and shed their original accents and customs, blacks will always remain visibly black—no matter what kinds of jobs they get or how much money they make. And in this society, a dark skin still tends to impede upward social mobility (Frey, 1980; *The State of Black America,* 1981).

In contrast to ghettos, **suburbs** are areas which offer less crowded living conditions and, often, private ownership of land and a home. Most of the growth that is occurring in urban areas is attributable to a recent explosion of the suburban population. The 1970 census showed that for the first time more people lived in suburbs than in either central cities or nonmetropolitan areas. By 1980, the proportion of the population living in the suburbs had climbed to 44%; the figures for central cities and nonmetropolitan areas were 30 and 25 percent respectively (Fava and DeSena, 1981: 3).

There are many different kinds of suburbs, ranging from upper-class areas such as Darien, Connecticut, and Grosse Point, Michigan, to working-class Levittowns. The price of housing is one indicator of social differences between the ends of the suburban spectrum. Affluent suburbs had housing prices in the early 1980s of hundreds of thousands of dollars, while more modest working-class areas were more likely to have housing available for $50,000 or even less. The median price for a home in 1981 was $72,000. Sociologist Leo Schnore has distinguished between three different types of suburbs. The *residential suburb* comes closest to fitting the suburban stereotype; it has a larger population at night than during the day since residents commute to work. The *satellite* or *employing suburb,* in contrast, is a trade or manufacturing center and has a higher daytime population since other suburbanites and even some city dwellers commute to jobs in the satellite suburb. An inter-

From The Wall Street Journal,
Permission—Cartoon
Features Syndicate.

mediate type of suburb combines both residential and industrial sections (Schnore, 1965). Suburban communities are not composed exclusively of relatively affluent whites. In recent years many more blacks have become suburban homeowners, although their homes are very often in segregated, predominantly black suburbs. Table 12.3 presents data that look at this process in more detail. We will look at other aspects of suburban life later in this chapter.

How Neighborhoods Change

Like most other features of urban life, neighborhoods change. Yet neighborhood turnover is not necessarily rapid and may not be noticeable for several generations. When change does take place, however, it may occur through various processes. **Segregation** refers to the establishment of certain neighborhoods as residences for specific minority groups. This pattern may or may not be voluntary. Blacks and many ethnic

TABLE 12.3 / CHANGES IN RACIAL POPULATIONS IN WESTCHESTER COUNTY

Westchester County is adjacent to New York City's northern border. It is a perfect example of trends in suburban population growth around the country (McAdoo, 1982). Minorities have been moving to the suburbs, especially to those areas closest to the center city. This is clearly seen in Westchester if it is divided into 3 regions: south (closest to New York City), central, and north (farthest from New York City). In Westchester, as in many other areas, the Hispanic suburban population is the most rapidly growing.

Year	Total White Population			Total Non-White Population		
	South	*Central*	*North*	*South*	*Central*	*North*
1970	400,595	198,749	203,331	57,441	21,592	12,396
1975	382,000	193,000	211,000	66,000	24,000	14,000
1980	343,186	177,384	209,261	86,733	32,747	17,288

Source: Westchester's Population: Toward the Year 2000 (May 1981), p. 9. Westchester County (New York) Department of Planning, 432 COBI, White Plains, New York 10606.

groups often have little choice in the matter of where they live. On the other hand, the "beatniks" who lived in New York's Greenwich Village and the "hippies" who lived in San Francisco's Haight-Ashbury district freely chose to live apart from the rest of the community with people who shared their life styles.

Invasion refers to the process by which a new group of people or a new industry enters an area for the first time. Related to this concept is **succession,** the process by which a group that was previously dominant in an area is replaced by others. This process is well illustrated by the changes that have occurred over the years in New York's Harlem. Now considered the ultimate black urban ghetto, Harlem has not always been poverty stricken. In the late nineteenth century, in fact, it was considered the choicest residential district in New York City. In 1890, after the first elevated railroads, street lights, and telephones had been installed there, Harlem became an upper and upper-middle-class community, with prosperous restaurants, private schools, theaters, and even an opera house. However, in the first decade of the twentieth century, the area underwent a major change. In the early 1900s,

A view of Morningside Avenue and 145th Street in Harlem, 1911. At this time, low rental rates had already begun to attract low income families, many of whom were black, and the exodus of older, wealthier residents was underway.

Jews who had first settled on the lower East Side but had now become prosperous began moving into West Harlem. Older residents, who objected strongly to the influx of Jews, moved out, abandoning Harlem to the newcomers. By 1904, in order to fill their many vacancies, landlords offered extremely low rental rates, attracting the first influx of poor black people to Harlem (Osofsky, 1972). Since that time, as more poor blacks have moved in, virtually all the wealthier people and most of the whites have moved out, gradually turning Harlem into the urban ghetto that it is today.

Not all neighborhoods have experienced such a parade of groups or such a complete change of character. Older residents do not always leave their homes as new groups enter a neighborhood, and several groups may coexist within the same residential area. This pattern has occurred in parts of Chicago's South Side where the residents include Jewish families that have lived there for generations, faculty and students from the nearby University of Chicago, and many foreign professionals, mainly from India, China, and Japan.

AGGREGATING COMMUNITIES INTO REGIONS

Rural and urban communities have always co-existed, with each type of community exchanging important resources and services with the other. Rural areas provide food, for example, in return for banking and commercial services centralized in urban areas. This clustering of communities has created **regions,** large geographical areas characterized by distinctive ecological adaptation by the communities within the region. We are all familiar with the most commonly used regional labels: Northeast, Southwest, South, and so on.

Within some regions, a unique urban phenomenon is occurring: the rise of the megalopolis. A **megalopolis** is an almost unbroken urban region formed as metropolitan areas overlap and merge across municipal, county, and state bound-

aries. America's largest megalopolis now includes parts of eleven states and most of our major northeastern cities. Stretching from southern New Hampshire to northern Virginia and from the Atlantic Ocean to the Appalachian foothills, it includes New York City, Washington, D.C., Baltimore, New Haven, Boston, Newark, and Philadelphia.

Some analysts have predicted that by the year 2000, the United States will consist primarily of three enormous population centers nicknamed "Boswash," "Chipitts," and "Sansan." "Boswash" will be a 500-mile stretch of urban sprawl between Boston and Washington, D.C. It will include 80 million people, one-fourth of the country's total population. Our second major megalopolis, "Chipitts," from Chicago to Pittsburgh, will be concentrated around the Great Lakes and will probably include another 12 percent of our population. "Sansan" will extend from San Francisco to Santa Barbara and is expected to have a population of about 20 million. According to this projection, fully one-half of the nation's people will live in one of these three areas by the year 2000 (Eells and Walton, 1969).

Another type of regional phenomenon is the growth of what is commonly called the "Sun Belt." America's aging population began moving from northern to warmer climates, creating housing booms and the rapid growth of services for this new population. Florida, California, and the Southwest have been the primary beneficiaries of this regional shift. In addition, the South benefitted from relatively low labor costs due to low levels of unionization and generally lower living standards. As a result, many businesses moved south, abandoning older northern unionized industrial areas. The result has been a substantial regional redistribution of population from the Northeast, Midwest, and parts of the West, to Florida, parts of the South, and the Southwest (*Social Indicators,* 1980, xlviii; *Statistical Abstract,* 1978, 20–21).

Wayne County in Michigan, which includes Detroit, provides a microcosm of this process.

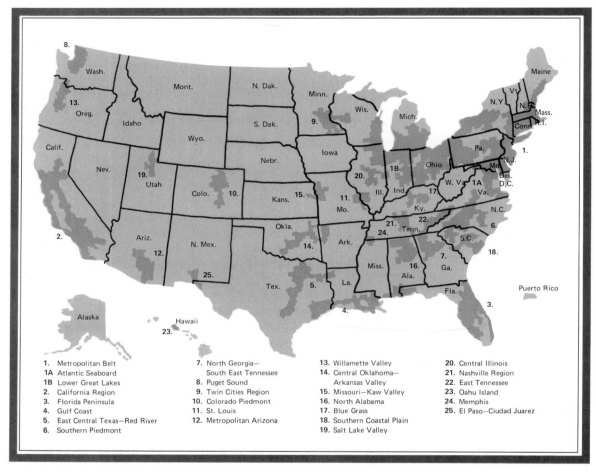

1. Metropolitan Belt
1A Atlantic Seaboard
1B Lower Great Lakes
2. California Region
3. Florida Peninsula
4. Gulf Coast
5. East Central Texas—Red River
6. Southern Piedmont

7. North Georgia—
   South East Tennessee
8. Puget Sound
9. Twin Cities Region
10. Colorado Piedmont
11. St. Louis
12. Metropolitan Arizona

13. Willamette Valley
14. Central Oklahoma—
    Arkansas Valley
15. Missouri—Kaw Valley
16. North Alabama
17. Blue Grass
18. Southern Coastal Plain
19. Salt Lake Valley

20. Central Illinois
21. Nashville Region
22. East Tennessee
23. Oahu Island
24. Memphis
25. El Paso—Ciudad Juarez

Fig. 12.3 / Megalopoli in the Year 2000

Source: Presidential Commission of Population Growth and the American Future, *Population Growth and the American Future* (Washington D.C.: United States Government Printing Office, 1972).

In the decade from 1970 to 1980, Wayne County lost almost 345,000 people. This is more than Kansas lost during the 1930s when it was ravaged by the Dust Bowl and the Depression. Wayne County's out-migration reflects the Midwest's generally depressed employment opportunities. Many of the migrants have moved south and southwest in response to job opportunities and more agreeable living conditions (*The New York Times,* June 13, 1981, p. 8). It is too soon to predict what the result of such migration patterns will be on the nation as a whole, but there is no doubt that regionalism will continue to be a significant force in America's future.

To meet the demand for new homes, developers of Sun City, Arizona, plan a 6,000 acre expansion that will add another 15,000 to the city's population.

Reminder Box / THE CASE STUDY

We saw in Chapter 2 that the case study is an attempt to look at a research problem in depth. Social phenomena which occurred in the past or behavior in progress over an extended period of time are often studied this way. As in participant observation, the focus is on the completeness of data; however, in the case study, data are also used to supplement behavior observed by the researcher. For example, historical data, interviews with relevant persons, and analysis of documents may be part of a case study. This would be less likely in participant observation.

Communities have often been researched through the use of the case study. This process enables the researcher to gather the many types of data necessary to understand a social unit as complex as a community. However, while the researcher may learn a great deal about the community studied, it is not clear how applicable his or her findings are to other communities.

As a result, case studies are often used as sources of data that provide the basis for developing hypotheses with more general applicability. For example, using a case study to identify the class structure in one community may then spawn survey research to see if similar results are obtained in a large number of other communities. This is a good example of the way research techniques may be used in combination to better understand the breadth, depth, and complexity of social behavior.

URBAN PROBLEMS

Beyond its natural loveliness, pollution serves the City . . . in so many ways. It helps keep the City from becoming overpopulated; it ensures that only the fittest survive and the rest move to the suburbs. It helps keep the City from becoming overgrown with foliage; it kills roses and tulips and other harmful weeds. It provides employment for window-washers and car-washers and eager little shoe-shine boys. And it saves money; it provides all the joys of cigarette smoking without any of the expenses.
(Eells and Walton, 1969)

Although Richard Eells's comment on pollution is humorous, it raises some of the most sobering issues of modern urban life. We are apt to forget sometimes that we, like all other animals, depend on air, water, land, and energy for survival. Daily, our air is filled with poisonous pollutants, we continue to discharge wastes into our waterways, and we are rapidly using up irreplaceable supplies of gas, oil, coal, and other essential resources without fully developed plans for continuing without them. The way in which we redistribute and regulate our industry and population will determine not only the future of our communities, but also our survival as a species. Other concerns of the future involve crime and conflict between urban residents.

In spite of these problems, urban areas have proven to be powerful magnets to people all over the world. Much of the urban appeal lies in the promise of economic opportunity, cultural diversity, and the richness of experience that are possible only when large numbers of different kinds of people live close together. Yet these aspects of urban life also have their disadvantages. The greater personal freedom and independence possible in the city can lead to impersonality and detachment. Cultural diversity provides excitement and enrichment, but it can be a source of social conflicts as well. And many who are lured to the city by the prospects of better economic conditions find themselves trapped in high-rent tenements in crime-ridden areas of the city where prices and unemployment are disproportionately high. Recent research indicates that Americans have a love-hate relationship with large cities. Only 13 percent of white Americans studied would choose a city of over 250,000 population as their first place to live, and most saw it as an overwhelmingly negative and problem-ridden environment (Fava and DeSena, 1981: 4). Yet these same people view the large city very positively as a center for economic, cultural-intellectual, and recreational services. What, in fact, are the realities of urban life?

On the whole, the experience that people have in cities depends on what part of the city they live in. Because of urban demographic shifts related to national economic and other trends mentioned earlier, there has been an increasing difference between the downtown, inner-city area and the outlying suburbs. **Demography** refers to such social variables as population size, the composition of population by age, sex, and race, birth and death rates, and migration into, out of, and within an area (Edwards and Jones, 1976: 97). These demographic factors help us to understand and describe urban changes that either are or threaten to be problematic.

The Interdependence of Inner Cities and Suburbs

It used to be thought that inner cities were places that bred alienation, disorganization, and apathy, but more recent sociological research has found this isn't necessarily so (Fischer, 1975, 72). Similarly, suburbs were once believed to be havens of tranquility, abundant resources and services, and low crime. Here, too, additional research has shown that there are in fact many types of suburbs, some which meet these criteria and others which do not (Logan and Schneider, 1981). Rather than seeing the inner city and suburbs as separate from each other, it is becoming clear that they are instead interrelated parts

INTERVIEW/Gerald D. Suttles

On the urban community in its social context: *"But its [public housing's] most important negative consequence is that of increasing segregation. It also diminishes the economic viability of the adjacent area."*

Gerald D. Suttles is Professor of Sociology at the University of Chicago. His research interests include the sociology of community, social disorganization, and the sociology of deviance.

■ **Q.** What, in your judgment, are some of the more notable successes and failures of urban renewal?
■ **A.** Probably the most notable failure has been public housing. The reason I say that is that there is no good argument for public housing. It resegregates the population using it, and it is a very expensive way to buy housing for the poor. Each unit, I think, now costs in the neighborhood of $60,000. With that much money, you ought to be able to buy lesser quality housing for a much larger number of people. But its most important negative consequence is that of increasing segregation. It also diminishes the economic viability of the adjacent area. You close off the area as a potentially mixed area, potentially one in which private housing might succeed. So in a way, public capital invested in housing chases out private capital.

I do believe that a number of the community organizations that got underway in the 1960s and early 1970s have shown greater lasting power than people thought they would. I don't think that's going to make a great deal of difference to a place like Chicago, or some of the older cities of the country which already had a kind of infrastructure community organization in them dating from an earlier era (e.g., Progressive Era). But it will make a difference in places like Los Angeles, Berkeley, and Oakland, places which had very little in the way of local community organization capacity. I don't mean to say that local communities solve all their problems through these organizations. They do provide

some vehicle, though, through which there could be some genuine representation in the local communities and begin to have some kind of orderly relationship with the wider society through the mayors' offices and various other institutions. That may be important to the future because I think the federal government will probably abandon a lot of programs, and communities will have to look for what they would call the "private sector" to carry out some projects. I suspect that these groups will have to be the ones that will carry the burdens of local mobilization and of enrolling the local population in some kind of political party system, so as to broaden participation in future American urban decision making. But it is hard to say what is going to happen.

■ **Q.** What do you see as some of the future problems in urban areas?

■ **A.** One of the main things down the road is the anticipation of some considerable division of opinion between the residents of a community—those who are relatively poor and those who are well off—and public employees of the cities. Public employees now constitute an enormous expense. Their numbers and their increased payrolls have rather substantially increased in the last 15 years. As a result, property taxes and the costs associated with central city living have risen considerably. New York is the tip of that iceberg. One sees it emerging in Boston with Proposition 2½ and in California with Proposition 13. One can expect to see something not too different in Chicago soon. The demands of public employee unions, schoolteachers, police, firemen, and so forth will not slacken. In a period of inflation, there is a real danger to their jobs and this will generate very considerable tension. This conflict will be at a very different level than what we have had in the past. In the past, we've always thought of labor unions, the poor, residents of urban communities, and so forth as being a collaborative sector, a single political constituency. I suspect that period is over and that there is going to be much more of a redefinition of people as being taxpayers and tax consumers. Again, community organizations can help to articulate some of these conflicts.

■ **Q.** What do you think will happen to minority populations presently living in center cities?

■ **A.** If you look at the recent suburban population data, I believe it shows that about 20 percent of the minority population now are in the suburbs. That is a large figure, when you think about it. I assume they will continue to move to the suburbs as the welfare benefits in central cities are reduced, making it more and more difficult for them to make it in the central city, or more and more difficult for landlords to make it. One of the areas that they seem to be moving into is some of the older suburbs that did not have a good housing stock to begin with. In places where you have just tract housing, built before World War II, then you get a lot of minority people moving in. My suspicion is that you have a more diversified pattern of settlement in the suburbs. Some of the suburbs will manage to segregate minorities by hook or crook. Some will adopt a policy of population balance, while others will become all black. Thus unlike most inner cities, where you had a block by block pattern of change, the suburbs seem to be spotty. Some expand, some are completely stabilized, and others have undergone complete population replacement.

■ **Q.** What do you think are the most significant issues facing most American communities, and what accounts for their significance?

■ **A.** I'd like to separate the question by region, because I think the Sun Belt, the suburbs, and the central city each has its own set of questions that one has to think of differently. For the old central cities in the Frost Belt, it seems to be a rehabilitative strategy, one that is aimed at retaining the physical plan of the city and making it livable and competitive as a place of residence. Suburbs, it seems to me, are going to face a population change over the next two decades. As many of the minorities and other groups get to move into the suburbs, we are going to see a replay to some extent of what happened in the central cities. I think population change is going to be occurring in the suburbs, and as the population ages, and as they perhaps begin to develop more services, then you're going to see some fiscal problems in those areas as well as some problems in social conflict. These may resemble the late 1950s and early 1960s, I suspect. And the suburbs may not have much capacity to deal with these problems, but as long as it's somebody else's community and across the jurisdictional line, you can't deal with it, even if you wanted to. You wait until it comes to your door, and then it may be too late.

■ **Q.** How about the issues facing the other regions you mention?

■ **A.** In the Sun Belt, the problems may be similar to those of the suburbs. Growth always generates a lot of problems. It seems to me that there are a number of natural resource problems: water shortage, pollution, and things of that kind. These are going to diminish the quality of life for a large number of people who went to the Sun Belt to get away from other problems. Of course, you already have population loss in many of the older cities of the South. And they are not really new cities; they are only old cities with new suburbs around them. California, Arizona, New Mexico, Texas, the Carolinas, and Georgia, these will be the interesting places to look at and see whether or not they're experiencing some of the problems that the old heartland is now facing. Frankly, I don't know what their capacity to deal with these problems will be like. As new populations come into the South, they are going to want more services than the southerners. They will start taking over the PTA . . . they may start raising taxes, but old timers don't want to pay them. There will be some friction as a result.

■ **Q.** We are interested in the relationship between community and crime. Can you speak at all about any of the major community variables that you think influence crime?

■ **A.** If people stay in a community for a long time, if they are not uprooted by new people moving in, and if they can develop a subculture in which mutual trust begins to grow, it is probably the most effective way to reduce the kind of crime in which the community is the victim of its own members. The general image that I have in mind is that of a network of coresidents whose members have common knowledge of each other. The children are related to one another, and they are restrained from victimization by this kind of common personal knowledge of one another. So are the adults. That, I think, is the most effective strategy for lower income populations. There are other communities, though, where that is not a possible strategy. For example, communities for the elderly, with their high concentration of Social Security recipients, are dumping grounds for mental hospitals and other institutions. These communities are your skid rows, and where you get your prostitutes, porno shops, and so forth. Those communities, I think, have very great difficulty in forming networks. The new skid rows are made up of ex-drug addicts, ex-mental patients, and ex-prisoners who are being quickly released, because we have discovered that it is expensive to keep them in institutions. Those are also going to be the places where the prostitutes and other predatory people will congregate. When it comes to the suburbs, I think you're going to find it increasingly difficult to avoid similar developments. This is going to disrupt many informal networks of residents. Working against that, of course, you do have a declining youth population, and youth is the main problem, both as victims and victimizers.

■ **Q.** So in a sense, it's almost like going back to where you began. Public housing and the failure of public housing, this breakdown or making much more difficult the creation of the networks of trust.

■ **A.** It's a terrible obstacle to building any kind of acquaintanceship because everybody knows that everybody else in public housing is someone who is desperately poor. But on top of that, it also means that individuals would have to leave public housing if they ever improved their social standing. So it selects out those various people who have made it, leaving those left there thinking that they are the dregs of society. It's going to be very difficult to get anyone in public housing to take much pride in the area. ■

of a community whole. The problems that affect one have an impact on the other.

In many ways, the crux of urban problems lies in the economic effects of changes in population groups.

The fiscal problems now being experienced by the nation's oldest and largest cities can be attributed, in large measure, to a steady redistribution of the population, employment, and industry to the expanding suburbs of their surrounding metropolitan units and to the new, fast-growing metropolitan areas in the Sun-Belt. (Frey, 1980: 1396)

It isn't just that many inner cities are losing population, it is that they are losing certain population groups. Whites have been moving to the suburbs—a process sometimes called *white flight*—and they are being replaced with blacks (Frey, 1980, Table 4). Unfortunately, because of the cumulative effects of racial discrimination in our society, blacks as a whole have lower incomes

and less earning potential than whites (*The State of Black America,* 1981). The result is that when whites are replaced by blacks, the economic base of the inner city declines.

Since urban services are paid for from tax revenues, a decline in the economic base inevitably means reduced urban services. This, in turn, reduces the quality of life in the inner city for most people. For example, in 1976 13.3 percent of owners and 24.1 percent of renters in central cities wanted to move because of inadequate transportation, school, shopping, police, fire, and health services. This compares with 6.9 percent of owners and 15.0 percent of renters in urban areas outside of central cities (*Social Indicators III,* 1980: 149). James Rouse, a well-known real-estate developer, said recently,

We have lived so long with grim, congested, worn-out inner cities and sprawling, cluttered outer cities, that we have subconsciously come to accept them as inevitable and unavoidable. Deep down in our

Suburbs are becoming more diversified. In addition to areas populated predominately by affluent and middle class whites, many suburbs have heavy concentrations of lower income or racial and ethnic groups.

national heart is a lack of conviction that cities can be . . . truly responsive to the needs and yearnings of our people. (quoted in Demarest, 1981: 44, 46).

One of the worst social and individual consequences of decayed central cities is the loss of human potential that results when people are unable to believe in a better future for themselves and unable to move out of the slum even when they manage to achieve some success in school or at their jobs. Of course, it should be kept in mind that there are affluent areas within the inner city as well as poor areas. Affluence makes possible a life style which is in large measure shielded from the urban problems experienced by the poor.

For those who can leave the central city, do the suburbs provide a more satisfying living environment? In spite of the rapid growth of suburbs the nature of suburban life varies greatly among suburbs. There are high-status and low-status suburbs, primarily residential suburbs and those with rapidly growing commercial and industrial areas (Logan and Schneider, 1981). In the suburbs as in the inner city, income makes a substantial difference in the quality of life. Just moving to a suburb doesn't guarantee escape from problems noted in the inner city. In fact, in 1977, 47.9 percent of owners living in places other than the central cities of urban areas complained of poor health facilities, 8.2 percent of inadequate police protection, and 5.3 percent of poor schools (*Social Indicators III,* 1980: 148).

Clearly, suburbanization will not solve urban problems by itself. Suburbs can be dilapidated and unsafe and, since suburbs are closely tied to services provided by central cities, their growth has tended to drain the central cities. The latter lose tax monies when people move to the suburbs but they are still expected to provide services for them. These urban phenomena have occurred in the context of a society characterized by substantial discrepancies between various racial and ethnic groups. Consequently, urban problems have to be seen in the context of the larger

society. Given this fact, solutions to urban problems have to be found at both the local and national levels.

We will now turn to efforts to find ways to make urban living more enjoyable and economically sound.

SOLVING URBAN PROBLEMS

A number of strategies have emerged for attempting to solve America's urban problems. In this section, we will look briefly at some of the most promising prospects.

Center City Revitalization

Revitalization has been defined as ". . . an upturn in the social and physical conditions of previously deteriorated neighborhoods" (Baldassare, 1981: 4). It has taken several forms, some concentrating on residential areas and others on business districts. Federal legislation in the form of Model Cities and Urban Renewal has spawned the demolition of deteriorated areas and construction of new residential and commercial property. These efforts have commonly been supported by city governments and, in some cases, by private real estate developers. There have been some spectacular successes, at least as measured commercially, in the joint attempts of government and private interests to revitalize urban cores. Harborplace, a revitalization of a 3.2-acre site in downtown Baltimore, is a $20 million creation of restaurants, shops, and entertainment sites. In its first year of operation, it attracted 18 million visitors (more than Disney World), earned $42 million, created 2,300 jobs, and generated $1.1 million in taxes (Demarest, 1981: 42). Boston's well-known Faneuil Hall and Quincy Market redevelopment are similar—and similarly successful—ventures.

While even commercial developments like Harborplace have been criticized on aesthetic

The revitalization of Faneuil Hall and the Quincy Market area preserved historic structures and opened Boston to the sea. At the same time, it created an attractive shopping mall that brought the city substantial revenue in the form of tourists' and shoppers' dollars.

grounds, revitalization of residential areas has had a far less successful record. Demolishing areas of deteriorated housing has been criticized by many as unnecessarily destructive of social relationships (Gans, 1962; Suttles, 1976). It has also created even more difficulties for the displaced who then had to find other affordable housing, often more expensive but no more desirable than what they left (Ryan, 1976). Low-cost housing itself has suffered from the image of Pruitt-Igoe, a housing development in St. Louis that was so unappealing to those who tried to live in it that they moved out. Vacant and the target of constant vandalism, it was ultimately torn down, a monument to the problems encountered by low-income housing which isolates the poor from larger community networks. Recent research in Manhattan suggests that ". . . neighborhood revitalization, in all probability, has occurred without an overall economic upturn or 'back to the city' movement" (Baldassare, 1981: 21). Nevertheless, revitalization efforts continue, and offer some promise of success if they can be integrated into coordinated, community-wide development efforts.

Homesteading

The basic concept in **homesteading** is allowing people to purchase deteriorated housing very cheaply—sometimes for as little as $1—in return for a commitment on their part to rehabilitate the property. Homesteading, of course, pertains to residential property, often in or near the center city. *Shopsteading* is a similar program whereby business people are encouraged to rehabilitate old stores (Demarest, 1981: 42). Both the programs have as their goal the preservation of basically sound buildings and bringing new populations as well as revived economic activity (including an improved tax base for the city) into badly deteriorated areas.

Unfortunately, homesteading (and other efforts to encourage people to buy and renovate deteriorated but basically sound inner-city housing) has been linked with a process called **gentrification.** Typical "gentrifiers" have been described as follows: ". . . young individuals or couples without children, who have recently purchased a home near their downtown workplace, and who have the financial resources and lifestyle associated with interest in restoration of historic or unique structures and with central city living" (Stephens et al., 1981: 4). Gentrification has been seen as a process through which the poor—many of whom are members of minority groups—are displaced by wealthy people. Those who are displaced have social ties broken and are forced into a housing market that offers them little in the way of decent, affordable living conditions. This can lead to community conflict and intergroup resentment, as has happened in areas of San Francisco and Washington, D.C. However, some researchers raise questions as to whether homesteading and similar rehabilitation efforts are always carried out by gentrifiers; many local residents may also participate in these activities (Stephens et al., 1981: 20).

New Towns

Columbia, Maryland is an unusual city. It has a population of close to 60,000 who live in five self-sufficient village centers, each made up of three or four neighborhoods. The population is 20 percent black; the school system is highly regarded; and businesses which have located in the city employ about 30,000 people (Demarest, 1981: 47). Columbia is what is called a **new town,** a community designed and built from scratch to create optimal living conditions for its residents. Although Columbia is relatively new, having been built in the 1960s and 1970s, the concept is an old one going back to utopian communes and the British garden cities of the nineteenth century. New towns continue to be built in this country, too. Las Colinas near Dallas and The Woodlands outside of Houston are currently under construction (Stevens, 1981). Reston, Virginia, is another well-known and relatively new example.

New towns explicitly try to mix residential, commercial, and business areas in order to create a total living environment. This is not to say they are isolated and totally self-sufficient: quite to the contrary, since new towns are usually built fairly close to large cities—Columbia is near Baltimore, and Reston is near Washington. It is

Columbia, Maryland is a new town in the Washington, D.C. area. Designed and built from scratch, it provides a planned community that combines residential, business, and recreational functions in ways designed to maximize the amenities of urban living.

assumed that the residents of new towns will utilize the specialized services of nearby cities, and that many of them will work there as well. Nevertheless, much of the inhabitants' day-to-day living will occur in the planned city, and interaction will occur with the diversity of people whom the new towns are planned to attract—note that Columbia's population is about 20 percent black, for example. For all the theory and the planning, however, critics of new towns point to their generally middle- and upper-class populations. With suburbs becoming increasingly diversified, many having commercial and business as well as residential areas, one could make the case that new towns are no more than planned suburbs. Even so, they represent a potential strategy for finding solutions to urban problems.

Urban Planning

James Rouse, the real-estate developer quoted earlier, made the following comments about urban planning:

. . . our cities grow by sheer chance, by accident, by whim of the private developer and public agencies. . . . In this way, bits and pieces of a city are splattered across the landscape. By this irrational process, non-communities are born, formless places without order, beauty or reason. . . . urban-suburban sprawl is intolerable not just because it is ugly, oppressive and dull but because it is inefficient. (Demarest, 1981: 46)

Few would argue with Rouse's assessment, but the strategies for developing more effective planning are not as apparent. We do know some places to begin, however.

Effective **urban planning** must address not only the need for new housing, but also the questions of water supply, clean air, waste disposal, transportation, education, medical and welfare services, and so on. These problems call not only for the skills of the specialist, but also for the involvement of metropolitan residents.

Too often planning efforts have failed because the people involved were not consulted about their needs and wishes.

In planning an urban community, human scale must also be considered. Many residents of multi-storied high-rise buildings feel dwarfed by their homes. Generally housing projects in which the number of units have been kept small enough so that the residents can become well-acquainted and develop a sense of community have been much more successful than mammoth projects that stretch for blocks (Suttles, 1976). Diversity is another essential consideration in urban planning. Jane Jacobs, a popular author writing about urban life, stressed that antiquated zoning laws requiring all buildings in an area to be of the same general type and purpose—all single-family houses, all commercial buildings, or all apartment dwellings—lead to monotony and can destroy a neighborhood. Such areas breed community apathy and indifference (Jacobs, 1961).

We must also pay greater attention to *where* we locate our urban areas. Urban areas make tremendous demands on the environment for natural resources such as fresh water. The persistent water problems and sink holes in South Florida are directly related to the rapid growth of cities like Orlando, Tampa, Ft. Lauderdale, and Miami. The burgeoning growth of cities like Dallas, Houston, Phoenix, and Tucson in the Southwest creates similar problems with water, energy, housing, and other forms of ecological disruption such as air pollution. In addition to environmental problems, planning must include the future of the older industrial cities in the Midwest and East from which people are moving. What is to happen to the people left in cities like Detroit which has lost so much population and industrial production that remaining residents voted a 50 percent increase in the city income tax in 1981 in order to keep the city solvent? The problem of those left behind is made more difficult by the fact that a disproportionately large share of them are old, disabled, or minorities. Clearly, planning for urban growth must be done in such a way that the society as a whole benefits.

That our booming cities are becoming greater sources of social problems in addition to becoming greater centers of human activity is one of our most urgent concerns (see Fig. 12.4). That we are greatly in need of imaginative and far-sighted urban planning is obvious. And that this

Fig. 12.4 / *Arrest Rates (per 100,000 inhabitants) for Property Crimes, by Offense Charged and Region, 1978*

Regional population shifts have been accompanied by shifting patterns of social problems, as exemplified in this figure showing property crime increase by region.

Source: Cited in *Sourcebook of Criminal Justice Statistics 1980*, U.S. Government Printing Office, Washington D.C. p. 366.

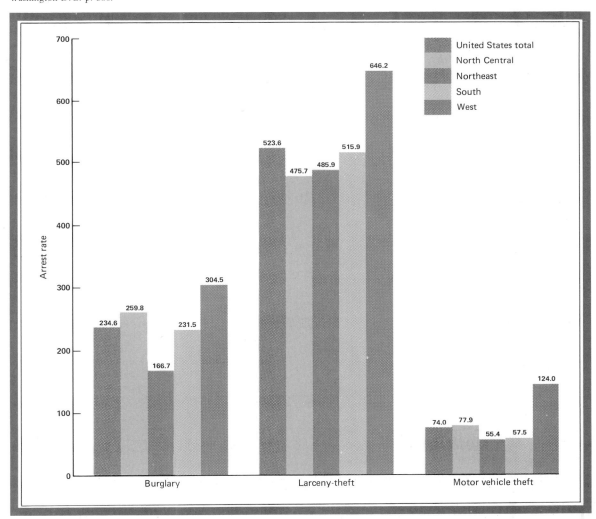

planning will be difficult is evident in all our cities. We should not expect to find any sweeping solutions that will solve all the problems and satisfy every human need. At best, urban planners will have to study each situation in detail, considering the city in all its dimensions: as a place of activity, as an ecological system, and as the home of thousands of diverse people.

SUMMARY

1. The main purposes of this chapter are to discuss the concept of community; to discuss the characteristics of rural and urban communities; to discuss the characteristics and impact of urbanization and the urban way of life; to illustrate the patterns and problems of urban growth; and to consider the possibilities and difficulties of urban planning.

2. Sociologists use the term community to identify a group of people who live in a specific geographic area, cooperate in activities, and share a sense of belonging. A community has at least four important dimensions: spatial (occupied space), geographic (available resources), psychological (sense of belonging), and demographic (size and characteristics of the population).

3. There are two basic theoretical models of communities: the folk (or rural) community and the urban (city) community. Tönnies distinguished communities as *Gemeinschaft* (intimate community, rooted in tradition) and *Gesellschaft* (impersonal, voluntary association of people for convenience). Because communities often present a mixture of folk and urban characteristics, it is helpful to arrange them along a rural-urban continuum.

   Peasant villages, small towns, and farming communities are located on the rural end of the spectrum. However, most rural communities are no longer as isolated and self-sufficient as they once were. Instead, they are part of the mass society, subject to outside political and economic controls and dependent on mass marketing for buying goods and selling their products.

4. Urbanization in the Western world is both a cause and an effect of industrialization: cities were necessary to provide a large work force for factories while at the same time technological advances made it possible for large numbers of people to work and live together. Whether urbanization benefits a population or causes problems, it leads to changes in culture and social structure: life is more impersonal, traditional class systems break down, and family and kinship networks become less important in economic relationships and social control.

   In the 1920s the "Chicago School" studied urbanism as a way of life. The study showed that a city's size, density of population, and social diversity determine certain characteristics of urban life: impersonal interaction occurs between individuals in terms of principal roles rather than complete personalities; social differentiations are magnified and divide cities into distinct areas; and city dwellers have more tolerance for social diversity than do rural dwellers. This study was somewhat biased in favor of rural communities, but more recent work has dispelled many of the earlier critical interpretations of urban life.

5. As urban communities grow, changes take place in different parts and components of the city—population, businesses, and neighborhoods, for example. Sociologists use many concepts to measure and study urban growth: the SMSA, centralization and natural areas, ecological models, neighborhoods, ghettos, and the megalopolis.

6. Urbanization has presented us with numerous social problems. Demographic shifts in population have created problems in the relationships between the center city and the suburbs, and between older urban areas in the Midwest and East and newly developing urban areas in the

South and Southwest. Some of these changes have had particularly serious consequences for the economic base of center cities and their ability to provide services for their residents.

7. A number of efforts are under way to find long-term solutions to urban problems. Center city revitalization, homesteading, and new towns are among the most recent promising possibilities. Whatever solutions are found, comprehensive urban planning will have to underlie the problem-solving process.

REVIEW ▬▬▬▬▬▬▬

Key Terms

Community	Urban communities	Natural areas	Regions
Ecological perspective	City	Centralization	Megalopolis
Gemeinschaft	Standard Metropolitan Statistical Area (SMSA)	Neighborhoods	Demography
Gesellschaft		Ghetto	Homesteading
Rural community	Concentric zones	Suburbs	Gentrification
Regional articulation	Sector model	Segregation	New town
Urbanization	Multiple nuclei	Invasion	Urban planning
		Succession	

Review and Discussion

1. Write a profile of your community, including its spatial, geographic, and psychological dimensions. Describe its rural and/or urban characteristics.

2. Review the section on *Gemeinschaft* and *Gesellschaft*. Was the neighborhood in which you grew up stable and friendly, or impersonal? Is your college more like a community or a goal-oriented, individualistic association? What are the advantages and disadvantages of each?

3. Have you (and/or your parents) lived in the same community for most of your life? If so, what changes (population, economic, and others) have you observed?

4. Identify and describe some of the natural areas around your home. Why do you think they developed as they did? What changes, if any, have occurred within them recently?

5. Which of the three primary "models" of urban development—concentric zone, sector, or multiple nuclei—best fits the city nearest your home?

6. If you were planning a city, what are some of the factors you would want to consider in order to provide for basic survival needs, the psychological well-being of residents, and the preservation of the environment? How would you decide what considerations deserve priority?

Experience with Sociology

Communities are complex social systems. In this chapter, we have looked at some of the geographic, population, social, and economic factors which help to define communities. We have also looked at how these interact to promote growth and change at the community level. Finally, it has been seen that any community is tied into a web of communities through regional, societal, and even international social processes. To understand a community—yours or any other of interest to you—entails looking at a wide range of data.

Module 1 in *Experience with Sociology: Social Issues in American Society* relates directly to this chapter. It will give you additional data about communities and help you to analyze them to better understand the many facets of a community. Of particular interest is the way the module will help you to apply the data to your own life. You will confront your own views on the type of community you find most attractive, and explore their significance for your own decision making about where you may wish to live.

References

Alexander, Theron (1973). *Human Development in an Urban Age.* Englewood Cliffs, N.J.: Prentice-Hall.

Baali, Faud, and **Joseph S. Vandiver** (1970). *Urban Sociology.* New York: Appleton-Century-Crofts.

Baldassare, Mark (1981). Evidence for neighborhood revitalization: Manhattan in the 1970s. Paper presented at the 76th Annual Meeting of the American Sociological Association, August 24–28, 1981.

Bensman, Joseph, and **Arthur Vidich** (1975). *Metropolitan Communities.* New York: New Viewpoints.

Bernard, Jessie (1973). *The Sociology of Community.* Introduction to Modern Society Series. Glenview, Ill.: Scott, Foresman.

Bose, Nirmal Kumar (1965). Calcutta: A premature metropolis. In *Cities,* Scientific American Series, New York: Alfred Knopf.

Childe, V. Gordon (1952). *Man Makes Himself.* New York: New American Library.

Cook, Robert C. (1970). The world's great cities; evolution or devolution. In *Urban Sociology,* eds. Faud Baali and Joseph S. Vandiver, pp. 5–22. New York: Appleton-Century-Crofts.

Demarest, Michael (1981). He digs downtown. *Time,* August 24, 1981, p. 44 ff.

Dentler, Robert A. (1968). *American Community Problems,* McGraw-Hill Social Series. New York: McGraw-Hill.

Drake, St. Clair, and **Horace R. Drake** (1962). *Black Metropolis,* vol. 1. New York: Harper & Row.

Edwards, Allan D., and **Dorothy G. Jones** (1976). *Community and Community Development.* The Hague: Mouton.

Eells, Richard, and **Clarence Walton,** eds. (1969). *Man in the City of the Future.* New York: Macmillan.

Farley, Reynolds (1970). The changing distribution of Negroes within metropolitan areas: The emergence of black suburbs. *American Journal of Sociology* 75:512–29.

Fava, Sylvia, and **Judith DeSena** (1981). The suburban generation: Young suburban migrants to New York City. Paper presented at the 76th Annual Meeting of the American Sociological Association, August 24–28, 1981.

Fischer, Claude (1975). The study of urban community and personality. In *Annual Review of Sociology,* eds. Alex Inkeles, James Coleman, and Neil Smelser, pp. 67–89. Palo Alto, Cal.: Annual Reviews, 1975.

———— (1981). The public and private worlds of city life. *American Sociological Review* 46: 306–16.

Frey, William (1980). Black in-migration, white flight, and the changing economic base of the central city. *American Journal of Sociology:* 85: 1396–1417.

Gans, Herbert (1959). Urbanism and suburbanism as ways of life. In *Sociology Today,* ed. Robert K. Merton, pp. 334–59. New York: Basic Books.

———— (1962). *The Urban Villagers.* New York: Free Press.

Harris, Chauncey D., and **Edward L. Ullman** (1945). The nature of cities. *Annals of the American Academy of Political and Social Science* 242 (November 1945).

Herbers, John (1981). College town turns into metropolis. *The New York Times,* July 22, 1981, p. A14.

Hodges, Harold M., Jr. (1969). Peninsula people: Social stratification in a metropolitan complex. In *Permanence and Change,* ed. Clayton Lane. Cambridge, Mass.: Schenkman.

Hoyt, Homer (1939). *The Structure and Growth of*

Residential Neighborhoods in American Cities. Washington, D.C.: Federal Housing Administration.

Jacobs, Jane (1961). *The Death and Life of Great American Cities.* New York: Random House.

Keller, Suzanne (1968). *The Urban Neighborhood.* New York: Random House.

Kornblum, W. (1974). *Blue Collar Community.* Chicago: University of Chicago Press.

Lenski, Gerhard (1970). *Human Societies.* New York: McGraw-Hill.

Logan, John R., and **Mark Schneider** (1981). The stratification of metropolitan suburbs, 1960–1970. *American Sociological Review* 46: 175–86.

McAdoo, Harriette P. (1982). Demographic trends for people of color. *Social Work* 27, no. 1 (January 1982): 15–23.

Mirowsky, John II, and **Catherine E. Ross** (1980). Minority status, ethnic culture, and distress: A comparison of Blacks, Whites, Mexicans, and Mexican-Americans. *American Journal of Sociology* 86: 479–95.

The New York Times (1981). 36 regions added to U.S. census list. November 30, 1981, p. B17.

Osofsky, Gilbert (1972). Harlem. In *The City in the Seventies,* ed. Robert K. Yin. Itasca, Ill.: Peacock.

Park, Robert E., E. W. Burgess, R. D. McKenzie, and **Louis Wirth** (1925). *The City.* Chicago: University of Chicago Press.

Peterson, Iver (1981). Michigan family chases American dream in Texas. *The New York Times,* June 13, 1981, p. A8.

Ryan, William (1976). *Blaming the Victim.* New York: Vintage.

Sanders, Irwin T., and **Gordon F. Lewis** (1976). Rural community studies in the United States: A decade in review. In *Annual Review of Sociology,* eds. Alex Inkeles, James Coleman, and Neil Smelser. Palo Alto, Cal.: Annual Reviews.

Schnore, Leo (1965). *The Urban Scene.* New York: Free Press.

Sjoberg, Gideon (1960). *The Preindustrial City.* New York: Free Press.

Social Indicators III (1980). Washington, D.C.: U.S. Government Printing Office, Department of Commerce.

Southwick, Charles H., ed. (1972). *Ecology and the Quality of our Environment.* New York: Van Nostrand Reinhold.

Stack, Carol B. (1974). *All Our Kin: Strategies for Survival in a Black Community.* New York: Harper & Row.

The State of Black America (1981). New York: Urban League.

Statistical Abstract (1978). Washington, D.C.: U.S. Government Printing Office, Bureau of the Census.

Stephens, Susan A., Cynthia W. Sayre, and **Lloyd Grooms** (1981). The social correlates of housing rehabilitation: Indianapolis, 1980. Paper presented at the 76th Annual Meeting of the American Sociological Association, August 24–28, 1981.

Stevens, William K. (1981). 2 planned towns flourish in laissez-faire Texas. *The New York Times,* September 15, 1981, p. A16.

Suttles, Gerald (1968). *The Social Order of the Slum.* Chicago: University of Chicago Press.

——— (1976). Urban ethnography: Situational and normative accounts. In *Annual Review of Sociology,* eds. Alex Inkeles, James Coleman, and Neil Smelser. Palo Alto, Cal.: Annual Reviews.

Tönnies, Ferdinand (1963). *Community and Society,* translated by C.P. Loomis. New York: Harper & Row (originally published in 1887).

Vidich, Arthur J., and **Joseph Bensman** (1960). *Small Town in Mass Society.* Garden City, N.Y.: Doubleday.

Weitz, Ranaan (1971). *From Peasant to Farmer.* New York: Columbia University Press.

Wirth, Louis (1938). Urbanism as a way of life. *American Journal of Sociology* 44:1–24.

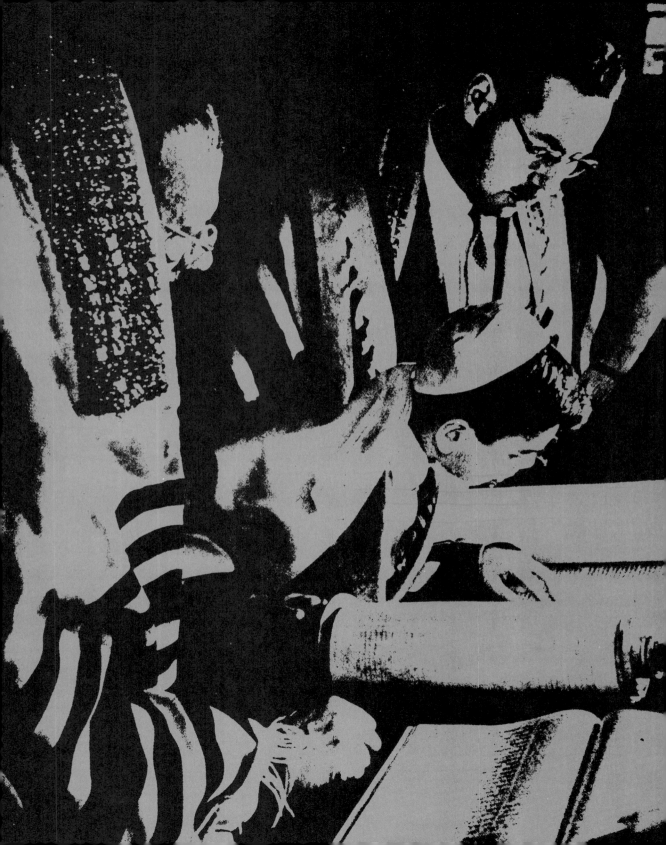

PART FOUR SOCIAL INSTITUTIONS

13

THE FAMILY

Most countries have a vision of the perfect family. England's, for instance, is best encapsulated in those big Victorian paintings of a father, mother, seven children, spinster sister, aged grandfather and, in the doorway's shadow, a maid with a tea cart. The American family's Golden Age came along about 50 years later, and its iconography involved a suburban house, backyard cookouts and a crowded table at Thanksgiving. To a generation raised in the Depression and separated by a world war, a house of one's own and "togetherness" were a promise of safety. Both images were rooted in a mixture of the real and the ideal. They have been so powerful they still linger in the fiction that is memory. . . . What we really long for is not the actuality of the American family circa 1952 but the illusion perpetuated by souvenirs. It is an illusion that cannot survive the test of statistics. (Editorial in The Washington Post, *November 9, 1981)*

What is a family, the institution that sociologists regard as the most important institution in society? What statistics are creating such concerns about the family in our society today?

The family, as Skolnick (1978) has noted, may be one institution about which we have some of our biggest misconceptions. In everyday speech we seem to understand what we mean by the word "family." But in everyday speech we are very likely speaking with people from our own culture, community, social class, and in-group—people, in other words, who share our values and expectations about how we relate to each other. However, sociologists need a definition that will include the families of more societies than we find within our limited experiences. The families of middle-class Americans differ from the families of the Trobrianders, the Toda, the Zuni, or the Eskimo, for instance. There are even many more versions of the middle-class American family than casual experience might suggest.

DEFINING THE FAMILY

Because there are so many variations in the social structure that various societies call a family, sociologists have had difficulties in agreeing on a proper definition of the **family.** Most tend to accept the definition of the anthropologist George P. Murdock (1949), based on a survey of family forms in over 200 societies, as a "social group characterized by common residence, economic cooperation, and reproduction, it includes adults of both sexes, at least two of whom maintain a socially approved sexual relationship, and one or

Fig. 13.1 / The Families of Orientation and Procreation

The emphasis in these definitions is on cooperation. Social scientists use the word "kin" to describe relatives with whom the individual neither lives nor shares his or her income. The family of orientation is also called the consanguine family; the family of procreation, the conjugal family.

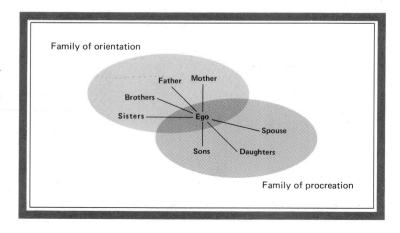

more children . . ." In the United States, most individuals belong to two families during a lifetime—the family into which one is born, the **family of orientation** (also called the consanguine family); and the family one creates through marriage, the **family of procreation** (also called the conjugal family). This is illustrated in Fig. 13.1.

On the basis of his research, Murdock has also postulated that all of the societies he studied recognize what sociologists call the **nuclear family:** a married couple and their children living together by themselves. He sees the nuclear family as a universal human social grouping. Either as the sole prevailing form of the family or as the basic unit from which more complex familial forms are compounded, it exists as a distinct and strongly functional group in every known society (Murdock, 1949: 2).

However, other sociologists and anthropologists have marshalled a considerable literature challenging the definition as well as the universality of the nuclear family. Critics point to the fact that the Trobrianders assign paternal responsibility for children to the mother's brother, not to the child's father. A Zuni husband and father works his mother's fields, not his wife's. The same was true in Nayar society, where women neither married nor lived with their mates: fatherhood did not exist for them. In these three cultures, the couple does not function as a cooperative unit. Moreover, in most **extended families,** in which family members representing three or more generations live together, an adult man or woman owes primary allegiance to parents and siblings, not to any spouse, who is often considered an outsider. Here the entire family is responsible for earning a living and rearing children. Other theorists have suggested that the mother-child pair is the basic family unit, but this idea has been questioned too. In societies where girls are encouraged to become pregnant before marriage to prove their fertility, the child is usually raised by an older, experienced woman, not by the mother (Stephens, 1963). The kibbutz

family in Israel is another example which fails to conform to the notion of the nuclear family as universal (Talmon, 1972).

We will return to the questions and issues of the nuclear family in the latter part of this chapter when we examine the family in other cultures. First, however, it is necessary to examine the nature of marriage and kinship in order to understand better the basic concept of the family.

MARRIAGE AND KINSHIP

All societies have standards and procedures for starting or expanding a family, but there is considerable variety in marital arrangements. Americans practice **monogamy:** marriage to one person at a time. According to Murdock's World Ethnographic Sample (1949), approximately 70 percent of the societies Murdock studied permitted **polygamy,** or marriage to more than one partner at a time. He found that **polygyny,** a man having more than one wife at a time, was practiced in 193 societies, but that **polyandry,** a woman having more than one husband at a time, was practiced in only two. In polygynous societies, a man may marry a group of sisters, as was common among the Crow Indians (Stephens, 1963), or several unrelated women.

Mate Selection

The routes to marriage are numerous. In different times and in different societies, spouses have been acquired by capture, elopement, interfamily contracts, for a bride price, or through free choice. But no society leaves the choice of a husband or wife entirely to the individual, not even those in which people believe "marriages are made in heaven" and consider love the greatest of mysteries. All societies take marriage seriously enough to set limits on free choice, because, in varying degrees, marriage joins two families in

An important function of marriage ceremonies is the public acknowledgment of newly formed alliances between families.

a web of reciprocal rights and obligations that affects their standing and their future.

For this reason, marriage is a family affair in almost all traditional societies. Sons and daughters represent an opportunity to form alliances with other families and to enhance each family's economic, political, and social standing. In nineteenth-century England, for example, wealthy merchants, whose social standing was low, married their daughters to sons of the aristocracy who had great prestige but no money, thereby combining status and wealth for both families. In some cultures marriages may be arranged by the couple's parents or by professional matchmakers when the couple themselves are mere children. Mahatma Gandhi was married at 13 to a bride contracted by his father and brothers after the first two fiancees they had chosen died. Arranged marriages were the norm in India, China, Japan, and much of southern and eastern Europe only a few generations ago.

In those societies personal compatibility was not considered as important as were obligations to the extended family. In some societies, a man was expected to marry his brother's widow (the levirate); a woman, her sister's widower (the sororate). This ensured that the death of one individual did not destroy the interfamily alliance.

In modern industrial societies, where the nuclear family predominates, marriage is generally seen as an alliance between two individuals, not as a family merger. Theoretically, the couple will live together by themselves for the rest of their lives, counting heavily on one another for emotional support (see Fig. 13.2). Their social status and that of their children depend more on what the husband achieves (and today on what the wife achieves as well), than on either his or her family name. In such societies, sexual attraction and personal compatibility—in a word, love—are the primary criteria for chosing a mate.

Our marriage system, like our economy, is based on "free enterprise." But just as the notion of free enterprise is less free than we assume, Americans usually "fall in love" and marry someone like themselves in race, religion, and socioeconomic background.

Exogamy—marriage outside a specific group of people—is not common in American society. Of course one does not marry within the family: parents, brothers and sisters, in-laws and first cousins. The incest taboo is nearly universal. Incest has been found in a legitimized form only in ancient royal families in Egypt and Hawaii, in which brothers and sisters married, probably to confine the royal line of descent to the family.

Rules of **endogamy**—marriage within the same clan or kinship group—are not an official

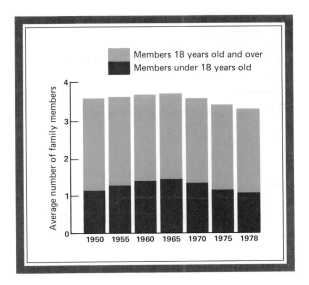

Members 18 years old and over

Members under 18 years old

Fig. 13.2 / Average Size of U.S. Families, 1950–1978

Source: Social Indicators III (1980), U.S. Government Printing Office, Washington D.C., p. 20.

part of our marriage system, but most of the marriages in the United States are endogamous, i.e., most marry people of the same social group, selecting as marriage partners those who resemble themselves in age, race, religion, social class and often geography.

Black and white marriages were legally forbidden in all of the southern states for many years, and breaking the law was fined by as much as ten years in prison. In 1967 the Supreme court declared laws against interracial marriage unconstitutional. The elimination of legal restrictions has not eliminated pressures against interracial marriage; nevertheless, there has been an increase in such marriages. Marriages between whites and others (i.e., blacks, Japanese, Chinese, Native Americans, and Filippinos) numbered 148,000 in 1960; 330,000 in 1970; and 421,000 in 1977. Among these there were 51,000 black-white marriages in 1960; 65,000 in 1970; and 125,000 in 1977 (Heer, 1974; Carter and Glick, 1976; Reiss, 1980). In the past, black man–white woman

marriages occurred more frequently than white man–black woman nuptials, and this pattern prevails today as well (Heer, 1974).

Jewish and Catholic religious leaders have been strongly opposed to interfaith marriages. Among Orthodox Jews, the offending family member who transgressed the rule would be mourned by a "shiva" or mourning reserved for a deceased family member. While the overwhelming majority of marriages are intrafaith marriages, changes in the last 20 or so years have led to a liberalization in the Catholic church, which has made interfaith marriage by its members more acceptable. The pre-1960 interfaith marriage ban has been dropped, but the requirement that the couple promise to rear the children in the Catholic faith remains.

The level of intermarriage is related to who is available to marry. Thus, for example, Jews living in a country in which there are few other Jews are likely to intermarry. In Washington, D.C., and its suburbs, with a large Jewish population, intermarriage was only 18 percent. In Iowa, where the Jewish population is significantly smaller, the rate of intermarriage between 1953 and 1959 was 42 percent. In 1980 intermarriage in the United States between Jews and others reached 35 percent.

The choice of a marriage partner requires social interaction. People of similar social class tend to reside in the same neighborhoods, attend the same school, engage in the same social activities, and attend similar institutions of higher education. Therefore, the likelihood of marriage within a specific social class is unusually high.

We are certainly not suggesting that Americans do not marry for love. But as sociologist Peter Berger (1963) pointed out, Cupid is curiously selective.

. . . In Western countries, and especially America, it is assumed that men and women marry because they are in love. There is a broadly based popular mythology about the character of love as a violent, irresistible emotion that strikes where it will, a

mystery that is the goal of most young people and often of the not-so-young as well. As soon as one investigates, however, which people actually marry each other, one finds that the lightning shaft of Cupid seems to be guided rather strongly within very definite channels of class, income, education, racial and religious background. If one then investigates a little further into . . . "courtship," one finds channels of interaction that are often rigid to the point of ritual. . . . Contemplating a couple that in its turn is contemplating the moon, the sociologist . . . will observe the machinery that went into the construction of the scene in its nonlunar aspects—the status index of the automobile from which the contemplation occurs, the canons of taste and tactics that determine the costume of the contemplators, the many ways in which language and demeanor place them socially, thus the social location and intentionality of the entire enterprise. (pp. 35, 36)

To be sure, we and other romantic people believe love necessary, and consider incompatibility, loss of affection, and sexual disinterest adequate grounds for dissolving a marriage. In a very real way, the expectation of love shapes marriage. However, as noted above sociologists have found that love is more likely to develop between people who share social and cultural characteristics than between people who are very different socially and culturally.

Residence, Descent, and Authority

In over half of the societies in Murdock's sample (1949), the bride moves in with her husband's family, or to an adjacent home (**patrilocal** residence). In a smaller number, the husband moves in with the bride's family of orientation (**matrilocal** residence). A few societies allow the couple to choose between living with the wife or husband's family (**bilocal** residence). Seventeen of the societies studied by Murdock practice **neolocal** residence: the mar-

ried couple move into a home of their own, apart from either spouse's kin. Murdock found that patrilocal residence was associated with hunting economies and polygyny; matrilocal residence, with agricultural economies where women are the landowners; bilocal residence, with small, migratory societies; neolocal residence, with monogamy, money economies, and individualism (Leslie, 1967).

Often, rules of descent follow rules of residence. In **patrilineal** cultures, descent is usually traced through the male line. Sons inherit from their fathers and pass this inheritance on to their sons. Daughters may also inherit from their fathers, but a daughter's children become part of her husband's family and inherit from him.

Our system of passing down family names has been patrilineal: sons use their father's family name for life; daughters, until recently, adopted their husband's family name. Today, however, women who marry often choose to keep their family name, but their children as a rule take on the name of the father. In **matrilineal** societies, descent is usually traced along the female line. In the United States, descent is **bilineal.** This means that no distinctions are made between the mother's and father's families, and children inherit from both sides.

In analyzing patterns of authority in the family, sociologists focus on the relative statuses of husband and wife and on who holds the power to make decisions for the family. The term **patriarchy** describes a family in which the male (usually the oldest male) dominates. His decisions on business, the home, and the children are law. **Matriarchy,** or female dominance, is rare. It occurs most often when males are regularly absent for long periods—for war, to hunt, or to find jobs.

In recent years much has been written about the female-centered or *matriarchal* family among poor urban blacks. Patrick Moynihan (1965) has argued that the deviant matriarchal family compounds the poverty and social disorganization of the family; that it is the "center of the tangle of

The absolute authority of the Hebrew patriarch is represented by the tale of Abraham, who was instructed by God to sacrifice his son Isaac. Here the angel of the Lord halts the sacrifice and brings a lamb to be slaughtered in Isaac's stead.

pathology" of the black family. While Moynihan did not ignore the poverty and disadvantages of race, he nevertheless argued that a stable family of father, mother, and children is imperative to break the tangle of pathology. Many of Moynihan's critics have argued that given the condition of blacks in American society, the matriarchal family was a positive adaptation ensuring survival of the family. Mother-centered families are not unique to blacks; they are to be found among oppressed ethnic groups, which are generally seen as strong and cohesive (see Fig. 13.3). Today, most social scientists believe that poverty, not the female-centered family, is the cause of the disorganized family.

The egalitarian family in which husbands and wives share authority and power is a relatively recent development. While most of the social science literature of the 1950s viewed the family as egalitarian, the degree of equality in decision making and power was highly skewed

Fig. 13.3 / Families, by Type and Race, 1960–1978
Source: Social Indicators III (1980), U.S. Government Printing Office, Washington D.C., p. 21.

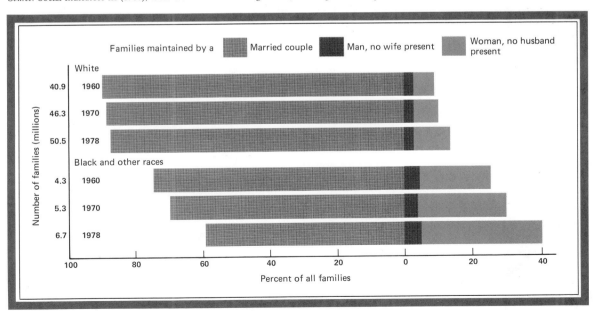

to the male. As a typical anecdote of the times revealed, the wife made the big decisions: How much aid should the United States give to other countries? Where should we stand on disarmament? Should we recognize China and admit China to the United Nations? The husband, on the other hand made the small decisions: the type of house to buy; where to go and how much to spend on vacations; what type of school the children should attend; how much money they should spend on furniture. With the increasing rates of female employment, women's material contribution to the family budget and the changes brought by feminism, the trend to egalitarian families appears solid in the United States and other industrial societies.

FUNCTIONS OF THE FAMILY

The family performs a variety of functions, but among the most important are the following: sexual regulation, reproduction and socialization, protection and intimacy, and social placement. Let's look at each in turn.

Sexual Regulation

Although there is no biological reason why people should not have sexual relations whenever, wherever, however, and with whomever they please, few people in any society take advantage of these possibilities. In this country, for example, norms governing sexual activity are changing, but restrictions on sexual activity are not disappearing completely. Sex may be natural, pleasurable, inevitable. But no society leaves decisions about sex entirely to individual discretion. Most people around the world limit their sex lives to activities their peers (if not their parents) approve. Norms governing sex are based on the belief that lack of restriction would lead to social chaos. Although these norms differ from culture to culture, each society attempts to ensure

that individuals will pursue their sex lives in predictable and socially acceptable ways.

Reproduction and Socialization

By regulating sexual activity, the family ensures that children will be born to replace the society's dying members at an appropriate rate, and that these children will be provided with adult care and socialization. Occasionally societies acquire new members by capturing them in battle, expanding their territory, or opening their borders to immigrants. More often they depend on the family to bear children and to teach them the values and mores of their culture. This is true even in complex societies, which include numerous specialized agencies of socialization.

Protection, Intimacy, and Affection

It is not surprising that the family institutionalizes close personal relationships. At various points, we have discussed studies of children in the care of hospitals or orphanages which indicate that babies need warmth and attention to develop normally. Trite as it sounds, lack of love is the most common cause of personality disorders. Children who grow up without affection are often unsure of their self-worth, unclear about their identity, and unable to participate easily in reciprocal relationships. Studies of adults confined in isolation show that they need warm human contact every bit as much as children do. In modern societies especially, relationships with neighbors, storekeepers, and business associates can be impersonal and transitory. Even friends sometimes move away to better jobs. Increasingly, children and adults depend on their family for emotional support.

Equally important, the family protects its members from social pressures. The child ridiculed on the playground, the heavily drinking husband, the son failing in college—all depend on the supports provided by the family. The family, then, acts as a sanctuary from social pressures and a source of personal attention in an increasingly impersonal world.

Social Identity

In nineteenth-century England, a person's status depended almost entirely on the family into which he or she was born. To lack parents was to lack a social identity, as Oscar Wilde showed in his play *The Importance of Being Earnest.*

The son of a farmer, John D. Rockefeller made a billion dollars and became one of our nation's most successful capitalists by eliminating his competitors in the oil industry. Concerned about his image as a heartless, greedy man, he began the practice of handing out a nickel to young boys to encourage them to become future businessmen.

Class lines have never been as clearly drawn in this country as they were in England, nor has family ever counted as much. In theory at least, an individual's social status in the United States depends on what he or she achieves in life. Nevertheless, the family into which we are born determines the kind of education we receive, the schools and colleges we attend, the people we meet in school and at home, job opportunities (in business and in government, "connections" help), even the people we marry.

THE CONFLICT VIEW OF THE FAMILY

Viewing the family as mostly functional for its members and for society is not universal. The socialist philosopher Friedrich Engels (1884) described the family in capitalist societies as the most exploitative institution. Engels argued that the first class antagonism in history is between men and women in the family; the monogamous family is nothing more than "disguised domestic slavery of women." Marriage in a capitalist society is simply legalized prostitution. The difference between a wife and a prostitute is that the prostitute sells her body by the hour, and the wife sells her body into slavery for life. Engels's view of marriage as an oppressive and subjugated relationship of husbands over wives was descriptive of highly patriarchal societies, and some of these practices could be found until recently in the United States (e.g., not unlike minor children women could not make contracts or receive credit on their own).

Some contemporary sociologists acknowledge some functions of the family as positive. Others see the family as obsolete, with its functions able to be carried on more effectively by other institutions. Barrington Moore (1958) regards the family as a repressive survivor of the past, and he asserts that if people knew about the difficulties and sufferings generated by raising a family "the birth rate would drop to zero."

In the past decade considerable research has emerged showing a high level of conflict in the family. Family violence (e.g., abused children, battered wives and family murder) is not a rare phenomenon (Gelles, 1974, 1978, 1980, Steinmetz, 1978, Strauss et al., 1980).

In 1975, there were over 3000 murders of a spouse by a spouse and 2000 children murdered by parents (Steinmetz, 1978). A recent national study on family violence (Strauss et al., 1980) shows that 3.8 percent of children aged 3 to 17 years are abused each year. When this ratio is projected to the 46 million children aged 3 to 17 years, who live with both parents, about 1.5 to 2 million children are abused. Twenty-eight percent of respondents reported marital violence at some time in their marriage, and 3.8 percent of women were subject to abusive violence (Gelles, 1980: 877). Sociologists have not found one specific factor to explain family violence. Many have suggested that those who have been abused as children are likely to be abusers as well (Gelles, 1974; Steinmetz, 1978; Strauss et al., 1980).

Socioeconomic factors are strongly involved in family violence, but this does not imply that there is no family violence among the affluent (Gelles, 1974; Steinmetz, 1978). Stress generated by unemployment, financial difficulties, single parenthood, alcoholism, and low job satisfaction are factors implicated in family violence.

Family violence is supported in many societies by cultural norms. It has long been taken for granted that spanking is a family prerogative. In the United States, the Supreme Court has ruled that a teacher has the right to use corporal punishment as a form of discipline; this legitimizes violence. Wife abuse has been an integral part of Russian culture, and while the Soviet government has instituted rules against such actions, wife abuse is no less common in the Soviet Union than in the United States.

While functional theorists have overstated the positive functions of the family and disre-garded the conflict, stress, and inequality do the problems mean that the institution of the family is on the way out?

The possibility that other institutions could perform the functions associated with the family are more plausible today than in the fifties. Test tube babies are no longer a figment of the imagination; the children, even infants, can be socialized in child care institutions, as for example in the kibbutz (Talmon, 1972). Yet there are few voices who advocate an end to the family or conceive the world as a better place without the family.

Jessie Bernard, the eminent sociologist and feminist, while critical of the traditional family, states that:

The future of marriage is as assured as any social form can be . . . men and women will continue to want intimacy, they will continue to want to celebrate their mutuality, to experience the mystic unity which once led the church to consider marriage a sacrament. . . . There is hardly any probability such commitments will disappear or that all relationships between them will become merely casual and transient. (1972: 301; edited by Skolnick, 1978)

To be sure, hardly a day passes without someone saying that the family is no longer what it used to be; that parents no longer provide the necessary care to their children; that the high rate of deviant behavior among the young is a sign of family disintegration; that contraception has liberated women and instead of being good mothers and wives they compete with men in the labor market; and so on. Community and religious leaders, welfare workers, psychologists and psychiatrists, congressmen and congresswomen, senators and presidents decry the changing family, or the "tragedy" of the family, and offer advice on how to salvage or strengthen it.

Sociologists also have commented on the changing structure of the family. In 1972, Zimmerman thought that the family was in a state of anarchy and that the church, school, and social welfare institution did not appear to care. Bronfenbrenner (1961, 1970) also sees threats to the family. The segregation of parents and children and the abdication of parental authority allow television and the peer group to become the major agents of socialization, setting standards of behavior contrary to adult models. The breakdown in parent-child relations has led to cheating, lying, and more serious forms of deviant behavior.

In the past, Bronfenbrenner notes, the extended family, the neighborhood, and the community provided firm social control over the behavior of young people. The anonymity of urban life has eliminated these social supports, and the young are left without adult influence and everyday adult models, relying on a code of behavior formed by the peer group which is generally contrary to adult norms. In Bronfenbrenner's view, the failure of the family and community to rear healthy and law-abiding citizens leads to a decline not only of the family but of society as well.

The family today indeed differs from its eighteenth- or nineteenth-century form. But whether the nuclear family is a recent development, the family is a dying institution, or the separation between parents and children is as great as some suggest is by no means clear. These are some of the questions that sociologists are studying and about which we can now examine available sociological theory and data.

THE FAMILY IN THE UNITED STATES

The Extended Family of the Past

Until about two decades ago the nuclear or conjugal family, composed of the married pair and their offspring, was believed to be unique to industrial societies. Preindustrial society was said to be characterized by an extended family, in which three or more generations lived together or nearby; all family members, young and old

alike, were engaged in a common economic endeavor. Industrialization made the economic functions of the family obsolete, and from the extended family a new nuclear family, or what sociologists Talcott Parsons and Robert Bales (1955) called an isolated nuclear family, emerged. But the notion of the nuclear family as an institution specific to industrial societies has been challenged by new research, which shows the nuclear family to have existed in Western Europe and the United States prior to industrialization (Demos, 1970; Laslett, 1973; Laslett, 1965). From a demographic standpoint there is support for this view, since in societies in which marriage is late and life expectancy short, the extended three- or four-generation family would necessarily be a rare phenomenon.

Using a special family research method, historians have examined church records, birth, and marriage certificates and have found that the typical family of the past was not an extended family but a nuclear one. Nuclear families existed over most of northern France before industrialization (Parish and Schwartz, 1972: 170). In a study of Rhode Island family structure, Pryor (1972), found that in 1875, 82 percent of the families were nuclear. Bloomberg et al. (1971), in their analysis of late nineteenth-century families in Southern Michigan in 1880, found that only 7.1 percent of rural households, 9.0 percent of village and town households, and 6.6 percent of Detroit households included parents of the household head (cited by Laslett, 1973: 99). Wells (1974) found that households in colonial Massachusetts averaged about 5.4 people in 1703 and 7.2 people in 1764. At the time of the first U.S. Census in 1790, the average household contained 5.8 people (Bane, 1976: 39).

The widespread belief that the extended family was the modal family prior to industrialization is generally an assumption not supported by data. In fact, based on the work of Nimkoff and Middleton who examined 500 societies, it appears that the modern independent family resembles the simpler hunting and gathering

Some theorists feel that the modern nuclear family, composed of only two generations, in many ways resembles the simple hunting and gathering family unit, exemplified by the San Bushmen of the Kalahari Desert.

societies. In part, this is because in both there is a "limited need for family labor and a need for physical mobility. The hunter is mobile because he pursues the game, the industrial worker the job" (1960: 225).

The idea of an extended family may have become part of the established social science literature because of a tendency to separate the family into types, relying on the notion that industrialization must produce unique families. Thus, for example, the isolated nuclear family as the model family of contemporary United States cities ignored other types of families, or considered the nonnuclear family as deviant.

Goode (1963) suggests that the image of the happy three-generation family is part of the romantic notion of what families were like in the past. Life on grandma's farm, notes Goode, was happy and orderly. Children and other kin lived in a big rambling house doing what was expected of them. The principle of economic self-sufficiency and the inclusion of education, vocational training, and religious instruction under the fam-

ilial roof produced an idyllic image of a hardworking but happy people. The stern and reserved father made the family decisions, accepted happily by all. The young married early, and the girls were virgins. Parents did not select the marriage partner but they had the right to reject a suitor. The happy couple moved in with the boy's parents, or built a house next door. Extramarital relations did not exist, and divorce was unknown (Goode, 1963: 6).

This image of what Goode calls the "classical family of Western nostalgia" is largely mythical, but this does not imply that the nuclear family of the past is the same nuclear family of today. One of the essential differences between the family of the past and the contemporary family is today's segregation of the family from the community. The traditional family as noted by Demos (1970), Laslett (1973), Skolnick (1978), and others was an integral part of the community. The integration of the family and community reflected the social organization of the preindustrial period, in which segregation of work activities and family activities did not exist. The home was not simply a familial abode, but a place of work, a domicile for servants, boarders, and apprentices for whom the nonkin "family" served—at least until industrialization—as a point of moral, educational, and physical well-being (B. Laslett, 1973). The preindustrial family, as sociologist Barbara Laslett argues, was more of a "public institution," in which familial and nonfamilial relations and activities coexisted side by side. The home life of preindustrial societies in seventeenth-century France, as well as at the end of the nineteenth century in New York tenements, was characterized by multiple activities which are relegated today to special institutions.

Shorter (1975) states that in traditional societies people are willing to put the demands of community above personal ambition. In modern societies individual freedom triumphs over demands of obedience. Community solidarity, preference for authority, and patriarchal rule over the family and its members are the marks of the traditional family. Skolnick asserts that the quintessential difference between the modern and traditional society is "the psychological quality of family life, and the relation between the family and the larger community . . . more intense emotionally (in the home), (while) ties between home and . . . community . . . (are) more tenuous" (1973: 106).

Clearly, the differences between the traditional and modern family are considerable, and the decline of patriarchal authority (noted by Zimmerman) and diminished social control over the young by the community (noted by Bronfenbrenner) are at least in part correct. But while the peer group and television exert considerable influence on the young today, it is by no means clear that current patterns of family relationships promote family disintegration. Patriarchal dominance may well have led to order in the family and the community, but it was often accompanied by lack of spontaneity and emotional closeness between the father as an authority figure and

those that he ruled. Exchanges between parents and children today are often closer, warmer, and more spontaneous, although they thereby allow for greater individual freedom and opportunities for acting out. Sociologists have been studying changes in the family, but recognize that change is different from disintegration. The interpretation of change can be that it is useful or destructive, depending on the point of view of the person viewing the change. Sociology's task is not to judge—it is to understand. With this in mind, let us look at some of the interpretations of what changes in the family may mean for society.

The Nuclear Family—Issues and Debates

One issue raised about the ability of the family to survive is its loss of functions. The varied and multifaceted activities performed by the family prior to industrialization have been assumed in modern societies by more specialized institutions. The family has changed from an economically productive unit to an economic consumption unit. Educational institutions have assumed the functions of education and much of the socialization of the younger generation. The courts, the legal system, and social welfare agencies have also impinged on the role of the family, further curtailing its functions. But the loss of functions has not made the family any less important than before, ". . . more specialized than before, but not in any general sense less important, because society is dependent more exclusively on it for performance of certain of its vital functions" (Parsons and Bales, 1955).

Another issue revolves around the isolation of the nuclear family. While many factors contributed to the isolation of the nuclear family, some sociologists thought that the degree of isolation was being exaggerated. Sociologist Eugene Litwak (1960) argued that the isolation was vastly overstated and that families relied on each other in time of need. He claimed that there was considerable interaction among close kin, marked by affection rather than obligation.

Yet another issue is whether all—or even most—American families are nuclear. Others questioned the notion of the nuclear family as the model American family, arguing that in the United States the Italian or Jewish family was closer to an extended family, relying on kin for various supports. The lower-class black family was also not infrequently a three-generation family, without a male head of household' (Gans, 1962). Because observers ignored the numbers of families that were not nuclear in structure, vast segments of American families were seen as deviant or problematic, rather than simply different.

The "ideal type" of the nuclear family, even though it was functional in industrial society, was not without problems and strains, thereby raising a number of issues. During the late 1940s and 1950s, a period referred to by sociologist Arlene Skolnick (1978) as "the golden age of the nuclear family," the division of labor mirrored the textbook model of the family. The husband performed the instrumental role of earning a living; the wife enacted the expressive role, rearing the children and providing emotional sustenance and support to the husband. Thus, for example, a typical text on marriage pointed out that:

. . . men and women—together . . . form a functioning unit. . . They are complementary. When men and women engage in the same occupations or perform common functions, the complementary relationship may break down. . . . One may say, 'Men can have careers because women make homes' . . . (Bowman, 1942: 23)

As Parsons (1955) noted, role segregation was functional for society, but it led to considerable strains. The domestic role of the wife declined in importance, leaving many women bored and feeling inadequately appreciated by their families. The various adaptations made by the wife lacked institutionalized status in society, so feelings of being second-class citizens remained. Skolnick (1978) stated the problem more strongly, pointing out that the nuclear family of the 1950s was experiencing strain from the con-

During the 1950s, the public image of the American family idealized the father as the wise patriarch. This still of the cast from the then-popular comedy series "Father Knows Best," starring Robert Young, captures the media's portrayal of father as the center of the family, looked up to by all.

tradictory ideologies which on one hand idealized the "democratic family," and on the other hand emphasized male domination. While few in the 1950s defined the problem of the family in terms of male domination, and not all families were male dominated, marriage and family life were often far removed from the idyllic portrayal of the movies or magazines. The disparity of power and authority between husband and wife emerged in the early 1960s, and centered on the middle-class family. Research by Komarovsky (1964) revealed that working-class families experienced similar problems, which were further compounded by low income.

These internal family problems were studied over twenty years ago by Bloode and Wolfe (1960), in a study of 731 urban wives and 178 farm wives. These sociologists found that in the first years of marriage and prior to the birth of children, the respondents saw marriage as romantic. In subsequent years, with the birth of the first child, satisfaction with the standard of living and companionship declined, followed by diminished love and understanding. "In the first years of marriage 52 percent are very satisfied with their marriages, and none notably dissatisfied. Twenty years later only 6 percent are still very satisfied, while 21 percent are conspicuously dissatisfied . . . corrosion is not too harsh a term for what happens to the average marriage in the course of time" (1960: 264).

Clearly, even in the 1950s the family was not a perfect institution in which love reigned supreme. But with the exception of a few observers, there was no widespread feeling that the family was a threatened institution. Why, then, in the last two decades has the demise of the family come to be feared by many Americans? High rates of divorce and efforts to develop alternative forms of family life are among the primary causes of the view that the family will soon become an endangered species. We will now explore how sociologists understand these social phenomena.

DIVORCE

Relative to several decades ago, the divorce rate in the United States is among the highest in the world (see Fig. 13.4). Most frequently we hear that for every two marriages, one will end in divorce. But statistics concerning divorce rates are not very accurate, and what is more, they may be calculated by a variety of methods that produce different results.

One simple method is to compare the numbers of marriages and divorces as recorded by local governments for any given year. For example, in 1976 there were 2,133,000 marriages and 1,077,000 divorces (*Statistical Abstract,* 1981:58). Based on these figures the divorce rate would be $1,077,000/2,133,000 \times 100 = 50$ percent. But this simple calculation contains a number of misleading factors. First, the population who is eligible for marriage is not the same population who is eligible for divorce. Those who marry come mostly from that part of the population that is between 18 and 30 years of age, and not already married. But those who divorce come from the population made up of all those who are already married with no other limitation, such as age. A simple comparison in any one year dramatically expands the divorce rate because the number of people who can be divorced is so much greater than the number of those who can be married.

Divorce can also be measured by the number of divorces per 1000 people. Thus, for example, in 1915 the rate was 1 divorce per 1000 people in the population. In 1966, it was 2.5 per 1000, and in 1977 it was 5.1 per 1000 (Glick and Norton, 1978).

The high rate of divorce does not, however, indicate that Americans reject marriage; there is a high rate of remarriage, which suggests that divorce results from disappointment with the marriage partner, rather than with the institution of marriage. As divorce rates increased, the remarriage rate increased as well, although the

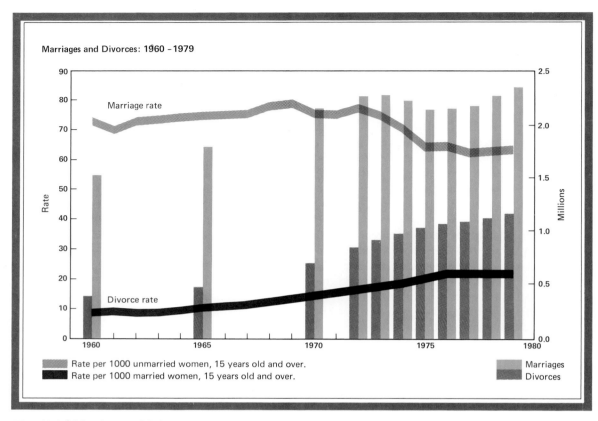

Fig. 13.4 / Marriage and Divorce Rates: United States 1960–1979

Source: *Statistical Abstracts 1981*, U.S. Government Printing Office, Washington D.C., p. 58.

rate of remarriage leveled off in the 1970s. More than four of every five divorced persons will remarry (Carter and Glick, 1976).

The fact that Americans continue to marry and remarry should not be taken to mean, notes Skolnick, that nothing has changed. There is a greater concern today with the quality of the relationship and the values and expectations that the partners bring to the marriage (1978: 236), factors that we will examine shortly. But it is clear from the data on divorce that an increase in the number of divorces does not automatically mean that the family as a social institution is being rejected.

Causes of Divorce

Although the cause for a divorce may be frequently attributed to a specific event—adultery, alcoholism, or incompatibility—it is rarely caused by one specific factor. Some attribute divorce and marital instability to a loss of family functions, economic problems, religious differences, unsatisfactory marital relations, and family disapproval (Goode, 1951; Reiss, 1980). Others suggest that the contemporary high divorce rate reflects changing values; we no longer consider marriage sacred.

In the not-too-distant past, family stability was of paramount importance. Divorce was a

impact on marital expectations. A marriage is expected to be a romantic and committed relationship, based on love, friendship, and honesty. Changing sexual mores and widespread premarital sexual relations have led to expectations of each marriage partner as a perfect lover. A "radical new romanticism" of marriage as the realm of new discoveries and growth has made long-lasting marriage a most difficult relationship.

. . . marriage was not designed as a mechanism for providing friendship, erotic experience, romantic love, personal fulfillment, continuous lay psychotherapy, or recreation. The Western European family was not designed to carry a life-long load of highly emotional romantic freight. (Cadwallader, 1966)

The monogamous family is supposed to be based on the fidelity of the spouses. But as the

Despite the increasing frequency of its occurrence, divorce remains a painful and divisive experience for most people.

sign of failure, immaturity, and poor adjustment. "Until death do us part," meant just that. Ladies' journals and newspaper columnists focused on "how this marriage can be saved." The wife was invariably advised to be patient, supportive, and understanding: communication was important. Today, the advice centers less on how the marriage can be saved, but on how each marriage partner can grow and develop as an individual. Growth, self-realization, and individual happiness have emerged as more important than the marriage itself.

Changing social norms of what is "right" or what "ought to be" have had a profound

"We're your new neighbors. I'm Steve Fitzpatrick. This is my wife, Martha Jorgenson, and our kids, Jason Connally and Beth Townsend."

From The Wall Street Journal, Permission—Cartoon Features Syndicate

well-known researcher of sexual behavior, Alfred Kinsey (1948), demonstrated in his research, men were involved in extramarital relations significantly more than women. Even before Kinsey reported this phenomenon, it was widely, if only covertly accepted, that men but not women had premarital sexual relations—perhaps not with "nice girls," but girls, nevertheless. The "double standard" was the norm. Whatever the origin of the double standard may have been, at least in part it was accepted because men did not fear pregnancy. The development of contraceptives and the legalization of abortion removed the fear of pregnancy for women, and the double standard, while still alive, is nevertheless changing. Women can engage in sexual relations not only with the marriage partner, but outside and before marriage as well. Sex for procreation and for recreation is available to and expected by women as well as men. Consequently, an inadequate sexual partner becomes a legitimate reason to dissolve the marriage.

The high rate of female employment has also changed the marital relationship. While women continue to earn significantly less than men, and married women consider the husband's career more important than their own (Paloma and Garland, 1971), the younger generation of women are less willing to subordinate their careers to those of their husbands. Research has shown that in 1960 and in 1975 women with 17 or more years of education had lower rates of "intact" marriages than women with fewer years of education, suggesting that highly trained women who are economically independent are less willing to accommodate to a husband's career and other demands imposed by marriage (see Table 13.1). On the other hand, men with 17 or more years of education have significantly higher rates of "intact" marriages. Given that there are fewer women with graduate training than men, men tend to marry women with lower levels of educational achievement, so their intact rate of marriage is higher.

As in the past, social class continues to exert an influence on divorce rates. People in lower socioeconomic status groups have higher divorce rates than those in higher socioeconomic status groups. The marriages of teenagers are more likely to end in divorce than those of older age groups, although the socioeconomic status of this age group exerts an influence on success or failure rates. As in the past teenage marriage is more frequent among low socioeconomic groups (Goode, 1956; Reiss, 1980). To be sure, divorce rates are significantly higher for young men and

TABLE 13.1 / PERCENT OF PERSONS AGED 35–54 IN INTACT MARRIAGES, BY LEVEL OF EDUCATION

Years of School Completed	Percent married once, spouse present			
	Men 35–54		Women 35–54	
	1960	*1975*	*1960*	*1975*
Total	72.8	72.5	67.4	66.0
0–11 years	67.6	64.6	62.5	57.1
12 years	74.6	72.2	69.8	66.4
13–15 years	75.5	72.1	70.8	69.1
16 years	81.3	78.6	73.0	77.3
17 or more years	80.2	81.8	54.8	63.4

Source: U.S. Bureau of Defense 1977. Series P–20 #312. Tables F and 3. U.S. Census of Populations 1960, Vol. 2, 4D, Marital Status Table 4, 1966, as reproduced and organized in Glick and Norton, 1977–79.

women generally. The median age of divorce for men is 29, and for women 27.

There is also evidence that interreligious and interracial marriages have higher divorce rates than racially and religiously homogamous marriages (Bumpass and Sweet, 1972; Reiss, 1980). Recent research by Jorgensen and Johnson (1980) on divorce "liberality" indicates that marriage partners who share the same religion have less liberal attitudes toward divorce.

Some feel that laws that permit divorce only for very specific and narrowly defined reasons—such as adultery—save marriages, even those with many problems. There is no evidence to support this view. Today's more liberal divorce laws, such as "no fault" divorces, do not contribute to divorce. They do, however, facilitate the process and reduce some of the interpersonal and economic damage that can result from divorce. As a result, fewer people are willing to stay in very unhappy marriages today. This raises the divorce rate, but may also decrease incidence of family violence and other forms of abuse.

Finally, we should note that among the results of divorce has been the creation of what are called **blended families.** These are families composed of previously married adults and their children from earlier marriages, plus whatever children the couple may have in the new marriage (leading to descriptions of children being "yours, mine, and ours"). Blended families require adequate flexibility to allow adults and children to establish roles that accommodate relationships already existing between parents and children, as well as among children themselves. On the other hand, the new mix of family members can lead to happy and satisfying new opportunities, as, for example, when a previously single child gains a long wished for brother or sister. The blending of families, then, may raise interpersonal and legal concerns, as well as affecting relationships with larger family networks. However, they are inevitable consequences of a society that accepts the value of widespread divorce and remarriage.

ALTERNATIVE FAMILY STRUCTURES

The increasing economic independence of women, changing social and sexual norms, emphasis and concern with individualism, and utopian expectations of marriage and the family have contributed to the high divorce rate. They have also led to a search for alternative family structures, such as communes, cohabitation, single-parent families and single life. We will look at these alternatives and at some of their ramifications.

Communes

Communes are formed by a group of people who want to dissociate themselves from society, break down the walls that separate family members from "outsiders," achieve group self-sufficiency, and create a new way of life. As a conception the communal family is a utopian one.

Communes are not a modern idea. Many experiments with communal living have marked American history. The current movement is an outgrowth of the 1960s, which brought together large numbers of people who were discontented with bureaucracies, sexual repressiveness, materialism, and the isolation that characterizes the nuclear family. Fairfield (1972), who spent the latter part of the sixties visiting communes, found several distinct types: religious collectives, ideological communes, hip families, group marriages, service collectives, and youth communes. With the exception of some religious communes, most were small and loosely organized. Sexual arrangements varied from nuclear families to group "marriages." Based on her research in urban communes, Yale University sociologist Rosabeth Moss Kanter (1979) finds them to be highly fluid arrangements, with considerable movement; old members move out and new ones move in. Life in these communes tends to be more public; there is a blurring of boundaries between nuclear families and other members of the communes, and conscious attempts to develop a family feeling among all members. Support of commune members resembles familial obligations in part. Financial resources are not shared, but a member in need will receive help. The structure of the urban commune is nonauthoritarian; role structures of men and women tend to be equal; everybody takes turns doing household chores. The decision-making process is "negotiated," and all members participate. Children tend to be looked upon as people, capable of making their own decisions; the overall tendency is toward greater equality.

Communes are not immune to problems and conflicts. Spontaneity—sought initially by all—gives way to order. Group living imposes pressures to conform. Communes tend to be highly transient; membership turnover is usually high. Of the 63 communes in the Boston area studied by Kanter only seven were over one year old. Kanter concludes that the chances of urban communes becoming a permanent alternative for large numbers of people are highly unlikely.

Cohabitation

The trend toward more liberal attitudes about sexual activity is reflected in the increasing interest in cohabitation before, or as an alternative to marriage. According to the U.S. Census Bureau, in 1978 there were 1,137,000 unmarried couples living together, and in 1980 the number increased to 1.5 million.

Middleton and Roark's (1981) survey of student personnel administrators on 150 campuses shows a significant increase in cohabitation. Over 30 percent reported an increase in cohabitation, and 7 percent a decrease in the last five years. College counsellors suggest that the relationships of cohabiting students are not unlike that of a traditional marriage, and many do indeed get married eventually. Macklin (1978) estimates that 25 percent of undergraduate students in the

Urban communes, such as this one, seek to reduce the anonymity of urban areas and change the stereotypical roles associated with most families.

United States have cohabited, and 50 percent would do so if they found the right relationship. Cohabitation is not limited to college students; it is also found among noncollege and older age groups.

Reiss (1980), reviewing several studies on cohabitation and legally married couples, found the latter to be more committed to the relationship, with a lower rate of dissolution. A comparison of cohabitors and noncohabitators shows more similarities than differences: those cohabiting tend to be less religious; cohabitating women are more assertive; and cohabitating males are more supportive emotionally. Individual freedom is more important to those cohabitating than to the noncohabitating. The expectation that cohabitating couples will show a less traditional division of labor than the legally married is not borne out. Stafford et al. (1977) suggest that the division of labor into male and female roles has been so firmly internalized that they remain unchanged in the new relationship. One study suggests that cohabitation does not appear to offer much as a school for marriage (Jacques and Chason, 1979). While there are cohabitating couples with children—272,000 in 1978—whether the children were from a previous relationship or the cohabitating relationship is not known. Macklin (1978) found that cohabitating students had no plans for children, and in case of pregnancy planned to get married or have an abortion. Surveys in Germany and other countries in the West in 1979–1980 found that there was a high degree of acceptance of cohabitation, but relatively little approval for children in a cohabitating relationship (DeBoer, 1981).

The apparent perception by some cohabitators that children do not belong in the relationship is probably one of the major differences between a legally sanctioned marriage and cohabitation. To be sure the increase in the number of married childless couples suggests that the desire for children is decreasing. Among cohabitators, however, the norm of "no" children is far more widespread. Reiss (1980) suggests that the exclu-sion of children among cohabitating men and women means that the participants do not regard cohabitation as a marital type relationship. But whether it is regarded as a marital or courtship type of relationship, cohabitation is part of the social fabric of our society today.

ONE-PARENT FAMILIES: FEMALE AND MALE

The rising divorce rate has led to an increase in the number of one-parent families, and changing social norms have led increasing numbers of unmarried women to keep their children, rather than to release them for adoption. In 1980, over 90 percent of the children born to unmarried white mothers were kept by the mother. The number of never-married, one-parent families increased from 83,000 in 1960 to 836,000 in 1978, and rose higher in 1980 (Reiss, 1980: 368). The total number of one-parent families in the United States grew from 1,891,000 in 1960 to 5,206,000 in 1978.

While the overwhelming majority of such families continue to be female-headed, changing sex roles and no-fault divorce have brought about a new phenomenon. Increasing numbers of male fathers are assuming custody of their children. In 1980 10 percent of single-parent families were male headed; in some cases single males have adopted a child. One recent study suggests that fathers are coping with their new responsibilities not unlike mothers: some find it relatively easy, others more difficult. While male parents face some difficulties in coping with situations for which they are not prepared—e.g., "what constitutes normal development" or "female sexuality"—generally they appear to be adjusting to their roles. Parenting provides these men with the opportunity to experience the nurturing role, a relatively new job for the male caretaker. Because they are usually perceived as less capable in the nurturing role, male parents tend to receive more help, as well as unsolicited advice (Parker,

1981: 96). Single fathers are not likely to become the majority of one-parent families. But as more women seek careers and more men seek custody of their children, this life style may become an alternative to more traditional arrangements.

FAMILIES IN OTHER SOCIETIES

In the past two or so decades, the American family has experienced considerable change, and analogous changes have taken place in other societies in the West. The Soviet and Israeli kibbutz families have changed as well. The USSR has retreated from its initial goal of the socialist-communist family, in which children were to be reared in child care institutions, and most, if not all of the functions of the family were to be assumed by public institutions.

The egalitarian ideology of the kibbutz, in which the mother and father were both fully participating members and the children resided in separate houses, appears to have changed as well. It is frequently suggested that both of these cases "prove" that no society can survive without a family. The Soviets tried to eliminate the family, but the resulting problems were so overwhelming that they were forced to return to the nuclear family. We will look at each case in turn in order to determine the validity of these assertions.

The Soviet Family

In Chapter 5 we noted that after the Soviets achieved power in the U.S.S.R., women gained legal rights to full equality in social, political, and economic realms. Following Engels and Marx, the Communists believed that public ownership of the means of production would lead to the elimination of the family as an economic unit: socialization of children would be assumed by the state, and housekeeping was to become a public industry, thus ensuring the economic independence of women.

Engels believed that monogamy would achieve its true meaning in a society in which private property does not exist, and the only reason for marriage would be love—"mutual inclination"—contrary to bourgeois marriage where economic factors exert a powerful influence on the choice of a marriage partner. Recognizing that love may not last forever, the marriage pair will be free to divorce.

The changes promulgated in the Family Codes closely followed Engels's notions, ensuring the right to divorce, abortion, and economic independence. Wives did not need to follow their husbands, and they could keep their own surnames. What we call cohabitation today entailed no penalties—children born of these unions were not penalized by the label "illegitimate," and there were no legal differences between an in or out of wedlock child. Personal freedom was supreme.

During the 1920s, following war, revolution, and civil war, social disorganization was high, poverty widespread, and resources few. Child care institutions failed to appear, and the new personal freedoms added to the chaos and disorganization. Divorce and freedom between men and women provided men with the opportunity to change their relationship at will; "post card" divorce, as it was called, enabled the man or the woman simply to send a post card declaring the end of marriage. But while both the man and the woman could divorce, it was the woman who was left pregnant or with the children. What was to be liberation and independence for women turned out to be increased freedom without responsibility for men.

Children were commonly abandoned, and the plight of homeless orphaned children was severe. The state lacked facilities to accommodate them and had to utilize foster homes. Those without adult care roamed the streets and became a public menace. The poor facilities and inade-

The extended family, composed of three or more generations living together, is illustrated by this Soviet family unit that includes the grandmother, parents, and their children.

quate resources of state orphanages led to high mortality rates (Geiger, 1968). The high abortion rate gave rise to concern about the future Soviet population. The plan to liberate men and women, to ensure women's independence, and provide a healthy and supportive environment for children came to an end.

In the early 1930s, faced with a variety of problems, some of which were seen as a direct result of family disorganization, divorce became more difficult; to stem the tide of juvenile delinquency, parents were made responsible for their children. Abortion was outlawed. By the mid-1930s, the family once more became the "indispensable primary cell of society," and in 1944, the new family law "to strengthen the family" absolved the family from the consequences of an extramarital liaison of the husband. No woman could sue for paternity for her out-of-wedlock child. Only those marriages that were registered created the legal rights and obligations of fatherhood (Lapidus, 1977).

The rocky history of the Soviet family, however, does not provide data to support the statement that the Soviets tried to do away with the family and discovered that without it there is social disorganization bringing on chaos. It hardly needs to be said that someone has to assume the responsibility for the care and socialization of the young; the failure to provide the necessary institutions, for whatever reason, made it necessary to turn to the family, in order to ensure that there would be a next generation of Soviets. Thus, at best, we might say, *not* that the Soviet case provides empirical data that the family is necessary, but that children require care.

In the post-Stalin era, divorce was made easier, abortion once more became legal, and the family continues to be glorified as the basic cell of society. In principle the Soviet family is nuclear, although the housing shortage has led to what might be called the extended family, i.e., two generations living together under very crowded conditions. The personal goal of each family, however, is to have its own living quarters, which the state supports.

It is difficult to classify the Soviet family as being of one specific type. The highly diverse population of the U.S.S.R. has generated a variety of families. In the Central Asian Republics, the family retains many of its traditional patriarchal forms, as is evident in occasional articles in the Soviet press criticizing communist party officials for permitting an arranged marriage. As a study of World War II emigres revealed, rural families followed the traditional patterns of life prior to the revolution. Geiger (1968) quotes a peasant commenting on the proper position of husband and wife in marriage as follows: "In the majority of good families the wife subordinates herself to the husband. . . . when my son comes home my daughter-in-law takes off his boots, cleans them for him, and you see how it is. She is obedient and devoted to her husband. There is no other way" (1968: 217). No doubt the pattern of husband-wife relations has changed in rural areas in the past several decades. Women collective farmers are better educated and more independent than their mothers and grandmothers; nevertheless, deferential behavior toward their husbands has not ceased.

The most significant changes in marital relations have occurred in urban areas, among the intelligentsia families, in which marital relations approximate those of the middle-class family in the West. To be sure, the burden of two roles—wife-mother and paid worker—is greater for the Soviet woman than for her counterpart in the West. This is partly because the Soviet wife is more likely to have a full-time job, but more important, because they lack the consumer goods and other supportive facilities available to Western women. But judging by the low birth rate and high divorce rate of urban women, not unlike women in the West, contemporary Soviet women are less likely to tolerate a subordinate position in the family than previous generations.

The Israeli Kibbutz

While the Soviet experience neither proves nor disproves the case for the functional requirement of the nuclear family, the kibbutz family constitutes a different case.

The Kibbutzim were established in the early 1900s by men and women who were committed not only to sexual equality, but to a change in the family structure in order to liberate children from patriarchal authority (Spiro, 1970). Another major principle of the kibbutz was espoused by the Zionist socialist ideology of the early settlers who rejected private property; the kibbutz community collectively owned all the resources.

Marriage and the family ceased to exist in the kibbutz in the traditional sense. Marriage itself was not formalized; a man and woman who decided to "marry" merely asked for a joint room. But they did not establish a separate household—such households did not exist. They continued to eat their meals in the community dining hall, and their roles as members of the kibbutz or as workers remained unchanged.

The birth of a child did not significantly affect the role of the mother or the father; they were not the economic providers for the child, not were they responsible for child-rearing and socialization. When a child was born, it was taken to the children's house, where it was cared for, together with other children, by a special nurse(s). The mother nursed the child during the early months, but all other necessary care was provided by the staff of the children's house. The parents visited the child daily, and the child visited with the family. Holidays were frequently spent together.

As the kibbutz became economically more affluent, changes emerged. Increased interaction of parents and children, greater involvement of parents in how the child should be socialized, and a fairly widespread pattern of children spending the night with their parents became commonplace.

Despite the more recent changes, the kibbutz experience suggests that the nuclear family is not imperative to the well-being of children. Other arrangements can be equally effective in developing healthy and well-adjusted persons, as studies of the children of the kibbutz have demonstrated (Bettelheim, 1969). The theory of the small nuclear family as indispensable to the well-being of society and the individual is not borne out by the kibbutz. To be sure, each kibbutz is only a small group, ranging from 200 to 600 people. Whether an equally effective system could be developed for a whole society is difficult to answer.

THE FUTURE
OF THE FAMILY

Industrialization brought a variety of changes to the family, decreasing its functions, and making it dependent on other institutions. Today's family relies more on supporting institutions than in the past; there is greater cooperation and role sharing between the spouses; and role differentiation has declined. While the government has been reluctant to provide the required supports to the family in the past and is even more reluctant to do so today, eventually we might anticipate increased support through publicly supported day care and other options.

In the private sector, the number of preschool institutions linked to workplaces is extremely low, but not completely unknown. Such preschool child care institutions are likely to increase, providing industry with a more stable labor force. Flexitime, a system enabling parents to accommodate to their dual roles, is increasing in popularity as well.

Major changes have taken place in the American family, but it would be premature either to

Illinois State Representative Susan Catania is shown here tending to her infant daughter during a meeting of the House. Similar new child-rearing patterns have accompanied the growth of dual-career families.

mourn or celebrate the death of the family. The structure of the family is changing, because as individuals we have outgrown the past and are seeking more distinct and different ways to live together and to rear future generations. The structure of the nuclear family, with its specialized division of labor, instrumental and expressive roles, and superordination and subordination, has not been the perfect solution for either husbands or wives. Consequently, society will continue to seek new and more effective family structures and processes, but there is little reason to believe that we will do away with the family in the foreseeable future.

INTERVIEW/Jacqueline P. Wiseman

On marriage and the family in a changing world:
". . . . I think there's an awareness that actually the family is the fabric that holds society together. That without family, you'd have neglected children, juvenile delinquents, unhappy adults, more people on welfare and few people supporting families."

Jacqueline P. Wiseman is Professor of Sociology at the University of California at San Diego. Her research interests include social psychology, marriage and the family, and social mobility.

■ **Q.** First, we would be interested in what you consider the major changes in the United States family in the last couple of decades.

■ **A.** I think the most obvious changes in the family have come about in response to and in interaction with the sexual revolution of the 1960s, the hippie movement, the women's liberation movement, and gay liberation. These totally unforeseen factors have changed the structure, if not the nature, of the family in America. For example, we are now more accepting of couples divorcing and men and women living together without marrying. Our attitudes toward gay relationships are undergoing reexamination. These modifications of the traditional norms have, as a consequence, resulted in changed relationships among family members. Additionally, some very, very complicated family memberships and arrangements have emerged. Art Buchwald, writing recently in his humorous/serious column, described the numerous permutations of couple relationships these days and the many kinds of arrangements that are made for children of either or both partners; who works and who stays home, how they handle the fact that one or both may have a lover in another town, and so on. It was a delicious bit of humor, but at the same time, the underlying thesis was true. The face of the traditional family has changed on several axes—legality, duration, division of labor, sexual liaisons, sexual orientation, and

child-bearing and socialization. However, change does not necessarily mean diminution, because deep down, people want some kind of family. It is how this family can be structured and changed that has broadened considerably.

■ **Q.** Do you feel that people want a structure in the family, but they want a more flexible or looser structure?

■ **A.** That's an interesting question to which the answers are complex and still in formation. Back in the sixties, many people said, "Oh, the traditional family is so confining! We're going out and starting a commune where everyone can do his or her 'thing.' " Or they said, "We're going to have relationships that allow the individual more freedom, unconfined by unnecessary responsibilities and loyalties."

However, what actually occurred, more often than not, was that after much trial and error these "revolutionaries" simply recreated the family. In some cases, the structure was even more confining and more rigid than the family they had turned their backs on! Commune members found that communes could not survive without close primary relationships. (Hardly anyone can survive with just secondary relationships—nor do they want to because there is no satisfactory emotional bond in them.) However, real primary relationships create the expectations and obligations of *continuity*. You can't have a primary relationship today and tomorrow go off and have another one with someone else. You have to stick to the people you love when they are sick or in need—often at the expense of your freedom.

Commune leaders also found that communes couldn't survive without rules. Certain dynamic aspects of any relationship, as they create rights and responsibilities, also forge some kind of an authority structure to enforce these expectations, and lo and behold—a family-like entity emerges like the phoenix! In many rural communes, even equality between the sexes reverted to traditional male dominance. However, this return to tradition does not mean that another structure for the family could not evolve that would allow for *both* continuity of caring and responsibility and equality of personal freedom (if not *complete* freedom). It merely means that the young people revolting against the "establishment" in the sixties were too inexperienced, too self-centered, too underfinanced, and probably too unrealistic in their expectations to work out anything truly revolutionary in family living forms.

■ **Q.** Have there been any other changes in the family?

■ **A.** There's another factor, one that I touched on before but that could use some expansion. I am referring to the far-reaching effects of the women's liberation movement. If the goals of this movement were to be completely achieved, the results would be greater changes in family structure than those caused by any of the other forces for change that I've mentioned. More particularly, there is the goal of a change in women's role in marriage. Women have traditionally been expected to play such a central part in family formation and maintenance that a shift in their role is bound to have momentous consequences. We're only just beginning to feel some of the effects of this force for change. For instance, increasing numbers of women are in the labor force, not just to add to the family income but to develop careers in their own right. We no longer have the traditional family composed of momma/poppa/children, with the mother at home and the father working. Projections are that by the year 1990, over two-thirds of all women will be in the labor force. That will mean a different kind of family life, with different arrangements for child care, household maintenance, plus a change in the power relationships in families.

Additionally, birth control and abortion on demand, both of which reflect the movement's belief that a woman has a right to control her own body, have changed family expectations. Childlessness is no longer seen as unthinkable or a stigma. Women are not having children as early in life, and the birth rate appears to be declining. Eventually, I think we're going to find that women are not going to have as many children as they used to have, nor are they going to be so eager to marry. Furthermore, they are going to expect their male partners to assume equal responsibility for home and children. However, the positive trade-off will be that men will no longer have to shoulder the burden of family support alone, and they will have a more interesting and exciting companion for a partner. Less certain is

455

the effect on the children, although it should be mentioned that middle-class America is one of the few places where such a premium is put on the mother's taking a primary role in child care. In underdeveloped countries, older relatives (grandmothers, aunts) and older siblings do a great deal of the child care. Among the wealthy in all countries, child care has been one of the tasks of trusted servants.

■ **Q.** How important have economic changes been insofar as their effect on the family?

■ **A.** The economy has always had a major effect on the family and will continue to do so in the future. Some of the changes to be expected in the upcoming years should be profound. For example, the cost of living will increasingly make the two-career or two-job family an absolute necessity rather than an option. Furthermore, various studies indicate that whenever women have a choice between work or having another child, they limit their fertility. In country after country, when economic opportunities are opened up to women, the birth rate drops. This fall in the birth rate will have its own economic repercussions: an older population and changes in buying, selling, investing, and housing patterns are just a few. There will be less job mobility for the young. These changes can be further accelerated by recession. We are beginning to see two generations living together again because of the cost of housing or job loss. Two couples or even unrelated persons are buying as a small corporation because they cannot afford to handle a downpayment or monthly costs of housing by themselves. Social security may be in danger now, but it will be in even graver peril when we become a nation top-heavy with elderly persons.

■ **Q.** Earlier, you discussed the effect of the women's movement—and you qualified it by saying, "*If it's ever successful . . .*"

■ **A.** Good point! The women's movement is not as successful as it might be. First of all, economically, it still has had only limited impact. For example, the gap between male salaries and female salaries is larg-er now than when the movement began. Second, even in countries where women are allowed and even encouraged to have employment outside the home, they are expected to put in an eight-hour day at work and then go home to do the housework and cooking. Thus, many women work close to an eighteen-hour day. Furthermore, under the present legal system and employment picture, women have less protection and financial security if they are deserted or get a divorce than do men. And since women often have custody of the children, the one-parent, female-headed household with children is one of the family forms most likely to be found below the poverty line.

So the major effect of the women's movement has been more in the area of consciousness raising, at least so far. Although there has been an undeniable shift toward equality of the sexes, women have to make a great deal more progress to consider their challenge to traditional society a success. Unfortunately, the economy is undoing some of the gains women have made. For instance, in employment, where they have been the beneficiaries of affirmative-action hiring, the lagging economy has resulted in a freeze in hiring. Furthermore, there have been layoffs of low-seniority people, with the result that individuals recently hired by affirmative actions are often first to get the boot.

■ **Q.** Have the moral majority and other conservative groups influenced the family?

■ **A.** The moral majority says the women's movement is out to destroy the family. In a sense they are right. It's certainly hoping to destroy the traditional family as such and replace it with a more flexible family. The women's movement would like to see a family oriented to the modern needs of *each* of its members—instead of the traditional form with the wife as a sort of live-in servant who takes care of housework, children, and all those other little details that provide peace and harmony for the male when he comes home. Women in the movement *are* very definitely out to destroy the male-dominated family structure. Have no doubt about that. They are *not,* however, trying to destroy love, concern, and socialization for children, cooperation, and other vital emotional feelings that are such important parts of the family. They're not out to destroy what I consider to be the only important aspects of the male/female relationship. But they certainly don't want Phyllis Schlaffly's antediluvian model, the put-on-your-negligee-and-be-a-cute-little-girl and the put-your-finger-in-your-mouth-and-pout-when-he-won't-let-you-have-your-own-way type of wife. Women want full, adult partnership in all areas of marriage—economic, sexual, parenting, and opportunity for personal development.

■ **Q.** Why do you think we are so concerned today that the family might disappear?

■ **A.** I don't think it's just a concern of today. I can remember in 1958 or 1959 when I went to several special symposiums entitled, "Is the family obsolete?" I have a feeling that every five years or so people get worried about changes they see happening around them; it's natural because the family is so important to everyone. The family provides the glue that holds society together. People fear that without the family, there will be neglected and deprived children, juvenile delinquency, maladjusted and alienated adults, more criminals and crime, fewer people supporting families, more families on welfare, and so on. The resulting societal breakdown could ultimately result in fewer citizens to fulfill needed economic, social, and political roles. Families, in taking care of their members, are the first line of defense for a healthy, producing society. Inasmuch as the traditional family has worked well as a primary structure in maintaining society, many people fear family forms that diverge from the orthodox pattern. What they don't consider, however, is that when a woman was limited to housework and motherhood, her potential creativity in other areas was lost to the nation. What is needed is a family form that manages *both* responsibility and understanding of individual needs and development.

■ **Q.** If I understand you correctly, you're going back to the point you made earlier that the family

can perform the various functions that you have summarized, in many different ways, and in many different forms.

■ **A.** Right!

■ **Q.** So perhaps we're not concerned so much about whether we're going to lose the family as what kind of family we want.

■ **A.** This is true, but I also worry about who is meant by "we." Because that's who the moral majority assume they are. They think they are the "we." I don't see moral decay and family break-up on such a huge scale that I would wonder what we're all coming to. So I am concerned about who the "we" is. We can see that there are bound to be special-interest groups in the pluralized society that exists today. I guess the kind of family you want, are willing to tolerate, or fear, depends on where your special interests lie. My special interest obviously lies with seeing that women are at last treated with full citizenship on every level. I think that the economic level is probably most important. But it's only the beginning: sexual, social, reproductive—all other decisional realms should be reconsidered.

I don't think that these particular changes will result in the termination of the family as an institution in society. Most women like men too well not to make permanent liaisons with them and enjoy the relationship. At professional meetings, when I meet other women friends, if they're not married, at least fifty to sixty percent of the time the main topic is who they're going with and how the relationship is progressing. If they are married, the conversation centers around who their husbands are, how the children are doing, and so on. And these are professional women, with lots of freedom. So, all things considered, I can't see individuals losing interest in what is basic to the family: a male/female relationship, love, compassion, graciousness, and interest in caring for the next generation. But, more and more, women want an equal part in the setting of the terms. ■

SUMMARY

1. The main purposes of this chapter are to discuss the structure of the family; to describe types of marriage and kinship arrangements and the functions of the family; to give a perspective on the family in the United States; and to examine alternatives to the nuclear family.

2. The family is the most basic social institution of society. The most prevalent family unit in the United States is the nuclear family, as it is in most industrial societies.

3. Marriage is a universal custom which includes a variety of arrangements for sexual and economic cooperation (monogamy, polygamy, polygyny, polyandry).

4. Contrary to widespread belief, the large, three-generation family did not constitute the norm in the nineteenth century. Low life expectancy precluded three- or four-generation families.

5. In the United States many internal and external pressures influence the family structure. Changing norms affect the structure of the family in other societies as well. The increasing number of women in the labor force, birth control, and the changing beliefs about the appropriateness of divorce and cohabitation have introduced a variety of alternatives to traditional family structures.

6. As the family institution changes, many people are experimenting with alternative forms of marriage and the family. Communes, single life, and cohabitation are some of these options.

7. The nuclear family was assumed to be the only form functional to modern industrial societies. So far there is no evidence that this is the family structure necessary to ensure the well-being of the individual or society.

REVIEW

Key Terms

Family	Polygamy	Matrilocal	Patriarchy
Family of orientation	Polygyny	Bilocal	Matriarchy
Family of procreation	Polyandry	Neolocal	Blended families
Nuclear family	Exogamy	Patrilineal	
Extended families	Endogamy	Matrilineal	
Monogamy	Patrilocal	Bilineal	

Review and Discussion

1. Describe your ideal mate in detail, either from imagination, or from reality. What qualities did you mention first? What influences affected your choice of qualities?

2. Give examples of how your family has fulfilled its societal functions or failed to do so.

3. Evaluate Urie Bronfenbrenner's description of the way children are prevented from seeing and participating in adult life in terms of your own experiences while growing up. Were you "segregated" as a child? Are you segregated now? Can you see advantages as well as disadvantages to age segregation?

4. If you are a woman, consider the possibility that you will have to leave your home, five days a week, for the rest of your life, to earn a living for your husband and children. If you are a man, consider a lifetime of cleaning, cooking, washing dishes, and asking your wife for money for a new suit. How would being "on the other side" influence your feelings?

5. Do you think the nuclear family is still the best arrangement for our society? Why? Which of the alternatives, if any, do you feel would be better? Worse? Why?

6. Today many people trace mental illness, juvenile delinquency, and other forms of deviance to childhood experiences in the family. Others argue that the family has become the scapegoat for problems in society. Which side of this debate is closest to your own feelings? Why?

Experience with Sociology

Most of us live in at least one family—the family into which we were born, or the one we have formed as an adult. Many of us live in both. Yet for all of our pleasant experience with the family, the sum total is often the most perplexing part of our lives. Maintaining satisfactory relationships with parents, siblings, relatives, and lovers requires a lot of time and energy, and sometimes even seems beyond our grasp. In this chapter, we have tried to present basic aspects of family structure and functioning which can help us understand better this fascinating, complex, and sometimes elusive social institution.

Module 2 in *Experience with Sociology: Social Issues in American Society* is organized to help you assess some issues about the family which are important to you. You will be helped to think through what the family means to you, which may be useful as you consider the type of family you may wish to form in your adult life. It will also assist you in putting your family experiences in perspective—have your experiences been uncommon, given processes going on in society as a whole? As you confront these issues, your understanding of the family as a part of your life will grow.

References

Bane, M. J. (1976). *Here to Stay: American Families in the Twentieth Century*. New York: Basic Books.

Berger, P. L. (1963). *Invitation to Sociology*. New York: Anchor Books.

Bernard, J. (1972). *The Future of Marriage*. New York: World.

Bettelheim, B. (1969). *The Children of the Dream*. New York: Macmillan.

Bloode, R., and **D. M. Wolfe** (1960). *Husbands and Wives: The Dynamics of Married Living*. New York: Free Press.

Bloomberg, S. E., M. F. Fox, R. M. Warner, and **S. M. Warner, Jr.** (1971). A census probe into nineteenth-century family history: Southern Michigan 1850–1880. *Journal of Social History* 5: 26–45.

Bowman, H. A. (1942). *Marriage for Moderns*. New York: McGraw-Hill.

Bronfenbrenner, U. (1961). The changing American child. *Journal of Social Issues* 17, no. 1: 6–18.

——— (1970). *Two Worlds of Childhood: U.S. and U.S.S.R.* New York: Sage.

Bumpass, L. L., and **J. A. Sweet** (1972). Differentials in marital instability. *American Sociological Review* 37 (December): 754–67.

Cadwallader, M. (1966). Marriage as a wretched institution. *Atlantic* 218 (November): 62–66.

Carter, H., and **P. C. Glick** (1976). *Marriage and Divorce: A Social and Economic Study*. Cambridge: Harvard University Press.

DeBoer, C. (1981). The polls: marriage. *Public Opinion Quarterly* 45: 265–275.

Demos, J. (1970). *A Little Commonwealth*. New York: Oxford University Press.

Duberman, L. (1976). *Social Inequality*. Philadelphia: J. B. Lippincott.

Engels, F. (1884, 1902). *The Origin of the Family, Private Property, and the State*. Chicago: A. H. Kerr.

Fairfield, R. (1972). *Communes U.S.A.: A Personal Tour*. Baltimore: Penguin.

Gans, H. J. (1962). *The Urban Villagers*. New York: The Free Press.

Geiger, K. (1968). *The Family in Soviet Russia*. Cambridge: Harvard University Press.

Gelles, R. J. (1974). *The Violent Home*. Beverly Hills, Cal.: Sage.

——— (1978). Violence towards children in the United States. *Journal of Orthopsychiatry* 48 (October): 580–92.

——— (1980). Violence in the family: A review of research in the seventies. *Journal of Marriage and the Family* (November): 873–85.

Glick, P. C. (1979). The future of the American family. *Current Population Reports*. Bureau of the Census, Series P-23.

Glick, P. C., and **A. J. Norton** (1978). Marrying, divorcing, and living together in the U. S. today. *Population Bulletin* 32 (October): 1–39.

Goode, W. J. (1951). Economic factors and marital stability. *American Sociological Review* 16 (December): 802–812.

——— (1956). *Women in Divorce*. New York: Free Press.

——— (1963). *World Revolution and Family Patterns*. New York: Free Press.

Heer, D. M. (1974). The prevalence of black-white marriage in the U.S., 1960 and 1970. *Journal of Marriage and the Family* 36 (May): 246–58.

Jacques, J. M., and **K. J. Chason** (1979). Cohabitation: Its impact on marital success. *The Family Coordinator* 28 (January): 35–39.

Jorgensen, S. R., and **A. C. Johnson** (1980). Correlates of divorce liberality. *Journal of Marriage and the Family* 40 (August): 617–626.

Kanter, R. M. (1979). Communes in cities. In *Co-Ops, Communes and Collectivities,* eds. J. Case and R. C. R. Taylor. New York: Pantheon.

Kanter, R. M., and **B. Stein** (1977). *Work and Family in the United States*. New York: Sage.

Kinsey, C., W. B. Pomeroy, and **C. E. Martin** (1948). *Sexual Behavior in the Human Male*. Philadelphia: Saunders.

Komarovsky, M. (1964). *Blue Collar Marriage*. New York: Random House.

Lapidus, G. W. (1977). Sexual equality in Soviet policy: A developmental perspective. In *Women in Russia,* eds. D. Atkinson, A. Dallin, and G. W. Lapidus. Stanford: Stanford University Press.

Laslett, B. (1973). The family as a public and private institution. *Journal of Marriage and the Family* 35 (August): 480–492.

Laslett, P. (1965). *The World We Have Lost*. New York: Scribners.

Leslie, G. R. (1967). *The Family in Social Context*. New York: Oxford University Press.

Litwak, E. (1960). Occupational mobility and extended family cohesion. *American Sociological Review* 25 (February): 9–21.

Macklin, E. (1978). Nonmarital heterosexual cohabitation. *Marriage and Family Review* 1 (March/April): 1–12.

Mendes, H. A. (1976). Single fathers. *The Family Coordinator* 25 (October): 439–44.

Middleton, L., and **A. C. Roark** (1981). Living together is widely accepted today. *Chronicle of Higher Education* (July 6): 3–4.

Moore, B. M., Jr. (1958). Thoughts on the future of the family. In *Political Power and Social Theory*. Cambridge: Harvard University Press.

Moynihan, D. P. (1965). *The Negro Family: The Case for National Action*. Washington, D.C.: U.S. Government Printing Office.

Murdock, G. P. (1949). *Social Structure*. New York: Macmillan.

Nimkoff, M. F., and **R. Middleton** (1960). Types of families and types of economy. *American Journal of Sociology* 66. (November): 215–225.

Paloma, M., and **N. Garland** (1971). The myth of the egalitarian family: Familial roles and the professionally employed wife. In *The Professional Woman,* ed. A. Theodore. Cambridge: Schenkman.

Parish, W. L., and **M. Schwartz** (1972). Household complexity in nineteenth-century France. *American Sociological Review* 37 (April): 154–73.

Parker, R. D. (1981). *Fathers*. Cambridge: Harvard University Press.

Parsons, T., and **R. F. Bales,** eds. (1955). *Family Socialization and Interaction Process*. New York: Free Press.

Peterman, D. J., C. Ridley, and **S. Anderson** (1974). A comparison of cohabiting and noncohabiting college students. *Journal of Marriage and the Family* 37: 344–54.

Pryor, E. T., Jr. (1972). Rhode Island family structure: 1887–1960, cited by B. Laslett (1973). The family as a public and private institution. *Journal of Marriage and the Family* (August): 480–492.

Reiss, I. L. (1980). *Family Systems in America.* New York: Holt.

Ridley, A., J. Peterman, and **A. W. Avery** (1978). Cohabitation: Does it make for a better marriage? *The Family Coordinator* 27 (April): 129–36.

Shorter, E. (1975). *The Making of the Modern Family.* New York: Basic Books.

Skolnick, A. (1978). *The Intimate Environment.* 2nd ed. Boston: Little, Brown.

Spiro, M. E. (1970). *Kibbutz: Venture in Utopia.* New York: Schocken.

Stafford, R., E. Backman, and **P. V. Debona** (1977). The division of labor among cohabiting couples. *Journal of Marriage and the Family* 39 (February): 43–57.

Statistical Abstract of the United States (1981). Bureau of the Census, Washington, D.C.: Government Printing Office: 58.

Steinmetz, S. K. (1978). Violence between family members. *Marriage and Family Review* 1 (May): 1–16.

Stephens, W. N. (1963). *The Family in Cross Cultural Perspective.* New York: Holt.

Strauss, M. A., R. J. Gelles, and **S. K. Steinmetz** (1980). *Behind Closed Doors: Violence in the American Family.* Garden City, L.I.: Doubleday.

Talmon, Y. (1972). *Family and Community in the Kibbutz.* Cambridge: Harvard University Press.

Wells, R. V. (1974). Household size and composition in the British colonies in America 1675–1775. *Journal of Interdisciplinary History* 4: 543–570.

Williams, R. M., Jr. (1970). *American Society.* New York: Knopf.

Zimmerman, C. (1972). The 1971 Burgess award address: The future of the family in America. *Journal of Marriage and the Family* 34: 2–20.

14

RELIGION AS A SOCIAL INSTITUTION

463

Through history, humanity has come together to bow heads, to sing special songs, to burn incense, to offer sacrifices, to chant, to meditate, to dance. What is it that we feel the need to worship? Some suggest that we are really worshiping society itself. As far as sociologists and anthropologists can tell, religion has been a part of every society throughout history. Relics of religious practices in the form of simple carvings and bunches of flowers have been found in ancient cave dwellings and buried with the bones of creatures we would consider more ape-like than human. Throughout the world religious beliefs and practices vary from our familiar **monotheism,** the worship of one god, to **polytheism,** the worship of many gods; from quiet church services to wild and dizzying dances; from the worship of ancient leaders to the worship of tree spirits; from the worship of good to the worship of evil within the same society.

When sociologists study religion, they do not challenge these varied beliefs, customs, or ethics. That is the interest of theologians and moralists. Sociologists attempt to look at all religions with objectivity. They want to know what meaning religion has for the people of a particular society. What functions does it serve? How does it affect individual and group behavior? How are religions organized? How is religion related to other social institutions? Does religion still serve vital functions in a modern technological world? Is religion changing or are new religions forming to meet the needs of modern life? (Demerath and Roof, 1976)

This does not mean that a sociologist cannot be a religious person. In personal life, he or she might be a devout member of any church. But in researching society, the sociologist hopes to put personal faith aside and to apply the "cooler" approach of scientific reasoning.

For the time being, you will find it helpful to set your own religious beliefs aside. Just as you have tried to avoid ethnocentrism (see Chapter 9) in other sociological topics, you will want to realize that your own religious faith is, to a

large extent, the product of your socialization. If you had been raised in another culture—perhaps as a Samoan or a New Guinea tribesman—your religious faith might be completely different, though you might hold to it just as strongly. Religion often stirs deep-seated emotions, and attention to measurable fact is not always easy to maintain.

RELIGION DEFINED

Whatever form it takes, **religion** is a system of beliefs and practices related to matters that are held to be sacred and supernatural. "Every known culture includes an institutional system of religious beliefs that provides an explanation of things that cannot be directly verified or explained otherwise" (Dressler and Carns, 1973: 504). Even the most technologically advanced society cannot prevent earthquakes and droughts, sickness and death, loneliness and fear. Religion cannot overcome all earthly suffering, but it does provide answers to people's concerns about pain, despair, death, and life after death. Its answers transcend reason and go beyond the "here and now" (O'Dea, 1970: 206–07) to answer the fundamental question, What is the meaning of life?

THEORIES OF RELIGION
The Functionalist Approach

The fact that every known culture includes some form of religious orientation suggests that religion is necessary to human groups—that it serves some fundamental purpose in human social life. Such, at least, is the view of the functionalists.

Impressed by the universality of religion, Emile Durkheim set about to identify the functions it fulfilled for society. These functions, he reasoned, should be easiest to identify in the simplest of the world's religions. Once identified, they might then be generalized to more complex and elaborate religious systems. For his study, he chose the totemism of the Australian aborigines.

A **totem** is usually a common object to which symbolic and sacred meaning has been given. Totems may be animals, plants, or some nonliving object. The aborigine clan holds some totem as the central symbol of its group identity and usually takes its name from the name of the totem. Durkheim argued that when clans gathered to worship their totem, they were, in fact, worshipping their own society. As he wrote in his study *The Elementary Forms of the Religious Life* (first published in 1912), "divinity is merely society transformed and symbolically conceived." One of the major functions of religion, in his view, is that it promotes "solidarity" within the society. Through its rituals and shared beliefs, it gives people the feeling that they are a part of something larger than themselves. People feel themselves moved although they cannot name what it is that has affected them. Though they may focus their feelings on some totem, it is the group which they unknowingly celebrate.

The Functions of Religion

Developing from Durkheim's pioneering work, the functionalist approach identifies several manifest functions of religion. We will look at each of them in brief.

The Egyptians believed that life after death was a continuation of the most important features of life on earth. In this frieze, the man at center left watches as his heart is weighed against a feather—the symbol of truth. If the scales do not balance, it is a sign that he has not lived righteously, and the monster on the right will eat the heart.

Provision for worship. The idea of all-powerful but unknowable forces that control human destiny can be frightening. Religious structures provide access to these forces through **worship,** the traditional channel for communication with the supernatural. "Through worship the religious group is related to God—to the realm of sacred and holy" (O'Dea, 1970: 263). Individuals who follow their religion faithfully—and individuals who recognize their errors and repent—improve their relationship with the supernatural.

In general, worship is directed toward the **sacred**—that is, the objects, places, people, and ideas that believers associate with special power.

Gods and spirits, of course, hold this extraordinary importance. And so do totems—many animals (such as the lion) and many plants (such as corn)—which may be held sacred by people whose lives bring them into intimate contact with the natural environment. Finally, as exemplified by many Eastern religions, a certain philosophy or principle of conduct may become the focus of ultimate devotion. In fact, the variety of things that have been considered sacred is enormous. Surveying religions, we may conclude with Durkheim that the objects of worship are not sacred in and of themselves. Instead, sacredness seems to lie in the meaning which groups of people have given to these objects.

TABLE 14.1 / MEMBERSHIPS OF SELECTED RELIGIOUS GROUPS: 1978–1979

Religious Body	Churches Reported	Membership (in thousands)
American Lutheran Church	4,837	2,377
Assemblies of God	9,410	1,293
Church of Jesus Christ of Latter-day Saints (Mormons)	6,272	2,952
Churches of Christ	17,550	3,000
Episcopal Church	7,009	2,815
Greek Orthodox Archdiocese of North and South America	535*	1,950*
Jehovah's Witnesses	7,526	519
Jewish Congregation	3,500	5,781
Lutheran Church in America	5,778	2,942
Lutheran Church-Missouri Synod	5,669	2,631
Mennonite Church	1,081	97
Presbyterian Church in the U.S.A.	4,007	862
Roman Catholic Church	25,542	49,602
Salvation Army	1,117	414
Seventh-Day Adventists	3,591	536
Southern Baptist Convention	35,357	13,391
United Church of Christ	6,491	1,769
United Methodist Church	36,682	9,732
United Presbyterian Church in the U.S.A.	8,567	2,520

* Data are for 1977.

Source: U.S. Bureau of the Census, *Statistical Abstract of the United States: 1981.* Washington, D.C., pp. 55–56.

Religious rituals provide a channel for communication with the unknown but all-powerful forces believed to control human destiny.

Instruction. In the United States religious instruction takes place during worship (as in the sermon), in Sunday schools or their equivalents, and in parochial schools. But in other cultures, religious education may play a larger part in one's life. In India, for example, boys of the higher castes have gurus, or teachers who instruct them in the intricacies of the Hindu religion. Many Buddhist youths live in monasteries as monks for as long as several years to gain instruction in their religion from the lifelong monks. And, more generally, some form of religious instruction is part of the public school

curriculum in most nations other than the United States and the Communist countries.

Religious education in all cultures includes instruction, not only in beliefs and rituals, but in ethical codes that provide moral guidance as well. Children learn what behavior is considered right and what is wrong—and in absolute terms—not just because their parents or teachers say so. Even for adults, one's religious leader has greater moral authority than one's mayor. Religion provides the moral guidelines that apply to all other aspects of social life.

Support and consolation. Religion offers support and consolation to individuals at what O'Dea calls the "breaking points of human experience" (p. 207). Religious individuals reconcile themselves to loss, failure, natural disasters, and injustices with the idea that there is a greater explanation beyond their immediate comprehension. Religious beliefs give people psychological support that sustains them in the most trying situations. For example, the death of a loved one might be the greatest "breaking point" we face in life. Most religions provide support and consolation to the survivors. Beliefs and rituals surrounding death may make the prospect less terrifying for the living and the emotional injustice of losing a "significant other" more tolerable.

Religion also provides support to individuals at points in their lives when they must reassert or redefine their self-identity, such as puberty, marriage, and parenthood. These changes in status are marked by time-honored religious ceremonies called *rites of passage*. These rites of passage formalize the changes and bestow social recognition on them, giving the participants approval in their new roles.

A religious wedding ceremony joins the couple not only for life before the law, but also before the community. Among many Protestant groups, individuals, at any time in their adult lives, have the opportunity, in a religious sense, to be "born again" through baptism or reconfirmation of their acceptance of Christ. Such a "rebirth" often follows a crisis in one's life and is itself an important turning point.

The attainment of puberty is acknowledged in religion by the admission of young people into full adult status within the community of believers. This is the intent of Christian confirmation. Similarly, a Jewish boy near his thirteenth birthday becomes Bar Mitzvah (a "son of the commandment") and is admitted to the privileges and responsibilities of an adult member of the congregation. And a Hindu youth knows he has attained adult religious status when his guru rewards him with his own sacred thread.

Community of believers.

Religion creates a community for its group of believers. In collective worship, families, friends, and strangers lose their sense of separateness and gain a sense of belonging to something larger. The individual's beliefs are reinforced by the group and glorified by the ritual. Collective worship thus makes use of the principle of social contagion and fosters social integration.

Belonging to a distinctive community of believers has helped subjugated or minority people keep their ethnic identity from disappearing into the larger culture all around them. The majority of Irish accepted the language of their English rulers, but in religion they steadfastly clung to their Catholicism rather then accept Anglicanism. The church became a rallying point of Irish nationalism. Jews scattered throughout the world retained their religious identity for 2000 years and in 1948 reestablished the Biblical nation of Israel.

The Conflict Approach

While religious structure may provide a rallying point for a group's identity, it simultaneously provides the means for social differentiations and group conflicts (as with the Irish Catholics and the Jews just mentioned above). Because religions institutionalize social values, they often provide one of the stoutest roadblocks to social change.

Karl Marx—Support of the status quo.

Marx pointed out that the dominant religion in a society was always the religion of the ruling class, and that religion always justified the power of the ruling class and taught a set of values that prevented the lower classes from rising to the top. He called religion the "opiate of the masses," claiming that it drugged the common people into submission by offering them consolation for their harsh lives (the meek shall inherit the earth) and by promising them rewards in heaven for their self-control. In this way they were discouraged from any attempt to create a better life on earth, and instead they meekly submitted to the oppression of the exploiting classes. Religion legitimized the power of the ruling classes and supported their privileged position. Marx saw it as a sophisticated tool employed to defend economic and political power.

In fact, religion often supports the status quo even when such support seems to contradict its teachings. Christianity stresses the doctrine of brotherly love, yet in times of war, church leaders rally to the support of the state. Special prayers for victory and blessings of the troops are offered. Jerold M. Starr examined the attitudes of a representative group of college freshmen toward war. He categorized the students by religious preference: Protestant, Catholic, Jewish, and none. His research led to the conclusion that

. . . religious preference is significantly correlated with opposition to war. Even when controls are applied for frequency of religious attendance, sex, father's education, and family income, those with no religious preference are most opposed to war, followed somewhat closely by Jews. Protestants and Catholics are very close in their degree of opposition to war, but rank well below Jews and those with no religious preference. (1975: 332)

William Eckhardt's studies over several years led him to conclude:

TABLE 14.2 / PERCENTAGE OF PEOPLE WITH VARIOUS RELIGIOUS BELIEFS (BY CHURCH AND SECT)

Belief in fundamental Christian doctrine differs widely among the members of various denominations and sects. This survey demonstrates that members of sects are far more apt to accept these doctrines.

	Congregationalists	Methodists	Episcopalians	Disciples of Christ	Presbyterians	American Lutherans	American Baptists	Missouri Lutherans	Southern Baptists	Sects	Total Protestants	Catholics
"Jesus was born of a virgin." Percentage who said, "Completely true."	21	34	39	62	57	66	69	92	99	96	57	81
"Jesus walked on water." Percentage who said, "Completely true."	19	26	30	62	51	58	62	83	99	94	50	71
"Do you believe Jesus will actually return to the earth some day?" Percentage who answered, "Definitely."	13	21	24	36	43	54	57	75	94	89	44	47
"Miracles actually happened just as the Bible says they did." Percentage who answered, "Completely true."	28	37	41	62	58	69	62	89	92	92	57	74
"There is a life beyond death." Percentage who answered, "Completely true."	36	49	53	64	69	70	72	84	97	94	65	75
"The Devil actually exists." Percentage who answered, "Completely true."	6	13	17	18	31	49	49	77	92	90	38	66
"Man can not help doing evil." Percentage who answered, "Completely true."	21	22	30	24	35	52	36	63	62	37	34	22
"A child is born into the world already guilty of sin." Percentage who answered, "Completely true."	2	7	18	6	21	49	23	86	43	47	26	68

Source: Rodney Stark and Charles Y. Glock. *American Piety: The Nature of Religious Commitment.* (Berkeley: University of California Press, 1968.) Reprinted by permission of the University of California Press.

Religion may serve as a means for promoting change—for example, when Dr. Martin Luther King led a social movement based on the values of human freedom and dignity.

Western religion contributes to wars . . . by way of fostering bureaucratic, conformist, and conservative attitudes, and by contributing toward conventional moral development with its emphasis on law and order. (1974: 468)

Too often in times of war religion has compromised its own best values by speaking out for "God and Country" instead of just for God.

We should note, however, that not all religion has the effect of supporting the status quo. Because religion can create a strong sense of community identity, such a community may gather the power to push for social change on the basis of their moral principles. Mohandas Gandhi, a devout Hindu, led the people of India in their struggle to gain national independence from Great Britain. Martin Luther King, Jr., a Baptist minister, led American blacks in their efforts to gain racial equality. Both men appealed to basic religious values—love of all people, nonviolence, moral righteousness—and inspired their followers to overturn the status quo.

Yet religion usually does teach values that promote social control. People are taught to respect authority (the priesthood, their parents), to refrain from murder, not to covet their neighbor's goods, and so forth. It they break these religious rules, they can expect punishment (here on earth or in an afterlife). Such religious rules and the acceptance of punishment for breaking them reinforce the acceptance of human laws designed to promote social order and control.

Religion sets the norm for what is "right and proper" and thus for what is legitimate in the political sphere (O'Dea, 1970). As long as government pursues what religious leaders view as a moral course, people are expected to support and obey the government. The law is based on *moral* law, which in turn reflects *divine* order.

Symbolic Interaction and Exchange Theories

Most of us learn our religion in the same way we learn about the rest of our social world—through socialization. By observing the behaviors of others, and by gradually interacting with them, we come to understand and accept our religious affiliation. However, many people at some time in their lives choose to change their religious identification. Symbolic interaction theory also helps us to understand how this happens. Essentially, this change seems to emerge from patterns of interaction in a way that is similar to other social behavior. For example, a couple planning to marry but not sharing the same religion interacts with friends and relatives in a variety of ways. Among them are planning for the wedding, thinking about children, and so on. Issues of religious compatibility are identified within a context of strong social support for one member of the couple to adopt the religion of the other. Recent research supports earlier findings that social networks are important for recruiting people to sects and cults as well as to more traditional religions (Stark and Bainbridge, 1980). Like other aspects of social behavior, symbolic interaction theory helps us understand better how interpersonal relations influence socialization and commitment to particular belief and behavior systems.

Religion is built on a basic exchange between the individual and his or her religious group. In return for the rewards of a sense of security in the afterlife, and a sense of order and well-being in life on earth, members of religious groups agree to obey religious teachings. Rewards may also take more concrete forms. For example, Stark noted that the group led by Reverend Moon helped members manage their interpersonal relations better and raise their self-esteem, and that the Hare Krishnas clothe, feed, and shelter adherents (Stark and Bainbridge, 1980: 1393). For traditional religions as well as sects and cults, then, exchange theory helps to explain why religion plays an important part in the lives of many people.

THE ORGANIZATION OF RELIGION

The history of religious organizations is one of increasing specialization. In small, premodern societies, religion is a family or clan activity, centering around the family's home, fields, and burial grounds. The Buryat of Mongolia, for example, worship household hearth spirits. And the East African Amba build shrines to their ancestors. In such societies, the head of the family often directs religious ceremonies just as he (or she, in some societies) directs economic activities—not because he is holier than others, but simply because he is the head of the family. There is little or no distinction between the sacred and the secular realms; praying to the gods for a good harvest is as integral a part of growing crops as is planting the field.

As life becomes more complex, religious organizations and practices become more specialized. Some individuals devote themselves to religion full time, freeing others to concentrate on political and economic activities. This priesthood class separates itself from other members of the society, often living apart and dressing differently. Temples are built, rituals become more complex, and the priesthood develops a hierarchy of authority. Gradually, people begin to distinguish between sacred and secular activities. This separation of the holy and the profane has two effects. First, participation in religious ceremonies becomes increasingly voluntary. Religion is no longer intertwined with daily activities. Second, the priestly class has a vested interest in maintaining its position and authority.

Sociologists find it useful to categorize religious groups on the basis of their size and their power. The most common of these categories are the *church* (either an ecclesia or a denomination), the *sect*, and the *cult*.

Church

Sociologists use the term **church** to describe any established religious organization with a stable membership and relatively fixed beliefs and practices.

In the United States, there are some 100 churches with memberships over 50,000. Of these, one-fourth have over 1 million members each. There are countless churches with a few hundred or a few thousand members. More than 90 percent of the people in the United States who belong to churches are members of Christian churches. More than 70 percent of the Christians are Protestants. Yet the single largest church in the United States is the Roman Catholic church with some 49.6 million members. The Mormons with 2.9 million members and the Greek Orthodox church with 1.9 million members are other large non-Protestant Christian churches. Jews, with 5 percent of the religious population, make up the largest non-Christian church. (All statistics from Table 14.1).

Ecclesia. Sociologists use the term **ecclesia** to describe a church that includes all or most of the members of a society and is recognized as the official religion of the state. In the Middle Ages, the Roman Catholic church was the ecclesia of Western Europe. The Reformation split Western Europe into Catholic and Protestant camps. The Pope's sovereignty was no longer acknowledged in Protestant countries. Instead, each ruling monarch became the head of a national church. This established church received financial support from the state, and it often administered the educational system. Even today, in such modern, democratic states as England and Sweden, there are established churches headed by the monarch. The United States does not have a state church.

Denomination. Obviously, most religious groups are not ecclesia, and sociologists use the term **denomination** to describe a large, well-established church that is neither officially nor unofficially linked to the government. In England, for example, the Church of England is an ecclesia, wheras the Methodist, Baptist, Presbyterian, and Roman Catholic churches are major denominations. As you might expect, no nation has more denominations than does the United States.

Sect

A **sect** is a small and separatist religious group that usually emphasizes fundamentalist teachings and strict ethical codes. Paul Sites has drawn some clear distinctions between a church and a sect:

A church is a well-established and highly institutionalized group that is integrated into the society of which it is a part. A sect tends to be smaller, less well-established, and often in opposition to the basic values or practices of the society of which it is a part. (1975: 379)*

Sects tend to be intolerant of other religions; they are right, others are wrong. Many sects believe that the kingdom of God is at hand and that they are the chosen people. Their primary concern is with the afterlife, not this transitory, sinful world. Their interpretations of Scripture—the Bible for Christian sects or the Koran for Islamic sects—are literal and open only to their "correct" readings. Members must adhere to strict ethical codes that affect all aspects of their lives or be expelled (see Table 14.3).

In the past, people have tended to join sects rather than being born into them. However, sects sometimes recruit whole families, and many sects are especially effective in convincing children of

---

* Reprinted by permission of the publisher.

TABLE 14.3 / DIFFERENCES BETWEEN CHURCH AND SECT

Characteristic	Sect	Church
Size	Small	Large
Relationship with other religious groups	Rejects—feels that the sect alone has the "truth"	Accepts other denominations and is able to work in harmony with them
Wealth (church property, buildings, salary of clergy, income of members)	Limited	Extensive
Religious services	Emotional emphasis—try to recapture conversion thrill; informal; extensive congregational participation	Intellectual emphasis; concern with teaching; formal; limited congregational participation
Clergy	Unspecialized; little if any professional training; frequently part-time	Specialized; professionally trained; full-time
Doctrines	Literal interpretation of scriptures; emphasis upon otherworldly rewards	Liberal interpretations of scriptures; emphasis upon this-worldly rewards
Membership requirements	Conversion experience; emotional commitment	Born into group or ritualistic requirements; intellectual commitment
Relationship with secular world	"At war" with the secular world which is defined as being "evil"	Endorses prevailing culture and social organization
Social class of members	Mainly lower class	Mainly middle class

Source: From *Sociology of Religion* by Glenn M. Vernon. Copyright © 1962. Used with the permission of McGraw-Hill Book Company.

members to remain in the group (Demerath and Roof, 1976: 28). For example, a recent account of The Community of Jesus, a sect composed of mostly wealthy people, describes very specific procedures to socialize children. While some would consider them brainwashing and abusive, they are generally effective in keeping young people in the group (Hartman, 1981). Some sects zealously seek converts; an example is Reverend Moon's Unification Church. Others, like the Mennonites, attempt to retain their exclusiveness. Often any member can become a minister if he or she feels the calling; there is little professional training for the clergy. Worship is intensely emotional and personal.

Sects are often offshoots of established churches. Christianity itself, which is the religion of one-third of the world, began as a sect of ancient Judaism. As noted earlier, the Christian Old Testament is based on the Jewish Bible. The Ten Commandments are part of the Mosaic Code, and Jesus himself was a Jew. His last supper, which is remembered in the service of communion, was a Passover *seder*. Like early Christianity, sects can gain momentum and become churches themselves. Many of the denominations in the United States were sects which in turn broke away from established churches.

The least formalized type of religious group is the **cult** (Johnstone, 1975). It is made up of people who share beliefs, and its emphasis is on these shared beliefs rather than on formalized rituals and doctrines that persist over time. Cults may follow astrology, biorhythms, transcendental meditation, the occult, and other quasi-mystical and/or quasi-scientific belief systems. As one set of sociologists points out, a cult is more akin to an audience than a group (see Chapter 10) (Stark and Bainbridge, 1980: 1390). Aside from the popularity of certain cults, one hears a lot about them because of the common confusion of cult and sect. A cult has very little to do with organized religion, yet such sects as the Hare Krishnas or The Unification Church (followers of Reverend Moon) are often referred to as cults. We will maintain the proper sociological terms and focus on sects rather than cults.

Modern sects. Few groups have stirred up more controversy on the modern religious scene than the Reverend Sun Myung Moon's Unification Church. This sect claims that it seeks to "mobilize the ideological army of young people to unite the world in a new age of faith" (Rice, 1976). Moon founded his movement in Korea in 1954 but moved his headquarters to the United States in 1973. Formerly a Presbyterian minister trained in the tradition of evangelical Protestantism, Moon claims that he has communicated with Moses, Buddha, and Jesus and that his mission is to complete the work begun by Jesus by establishing God's kingdom on earth. He proclaims himself the new Messiah and his followers regard him as such. He demands and receives complete allegiance from them.

Moon's Unification Church is a good example of how a sect works. Observers believe that sects appeal to people who feel vulnerable and in some way deprived. While these people are potential recruits, the variable that most directly relates to whether or not they will actually join a sect is the nature of the interpersonal bonds between sect members and the potential recruits (Stark and Bainbridge, 1980: 1378). Each group has a different strategy for developing

The Reverend Sun Myung Moon.

strong interpersonal bonds. In Moon's Unification Church, would-be converts are approached casually and invited to dinner or some other event. This is followed by invitations to retreats of increasingly longer duration, during which friendship and personal support are liberally mixed with intensive exposure to the sect's doctrines.

Many converts to the Unification Church are youths who had recently left home to attend college or to work outside their communities. On their own, they understandably may have been having difficulty adjusting to their new and independent existence. Perhaps they began to have self-doubts and to seek answers to their growing uneasiness. In the friendly embrace of the Unification Church they may have found great comfort. This conversion and acceptance into the church is what Paul Sites (1975) would identify as a salvation ritual:

Salvation rituals are useful as control strategies for individuals when their self-identity has been damaged or destroyed and their need for self-esteem goes unrecognized. Under these conditions, salvation can provide the individual with a new identity by transforming him into a new and "better" kind of person. (p. 400)

Not all sects appeal to the young or to those who are economically deprived. The Community of Jesus, a sect located on Cape Cod in Massachusetts, was founded by two women—Mother Cay and Mother Judy—who had been "called" by God. In an interesting twist, the sect seeks to meet ". . . the crying need for the Lord among the upper classes today." Or, as another member put it, "It's not just the 'down and outers' who need Christ. What about the 'up and outers'? They need Christ, too" (Hartman, 1981: 143). Unlike the Hare Krishnas, who can be found selling flowers in airports and other public places, the members of The Community of Jesus bring wealth to their group. Life is luxurious, especially for Mother Cay and Mother Judy, the spiritual leaders. Men in the sect work at high paying jobs in the surrounding area, commuting from their homes in the Community. As with other sects, exmembers talk of physical and psychological abuse, as well as the use of brainwashing techniques. Nevertheless, the sect is growing. Although small in comparison to sects like the Mormons or the Unification Church, The Community of Jesus has members spread across 19 states and five foreign countries. It is clear that sects take many forms, although they share characterisitics pertaining to recruitment and organizational structure.

RELATIONSHIPS WITH OTHER SOCIAL INSTITUTIONS

There is a great deal of interplay between religion and the other major social institutions. Religion has a profound effect on the family: often the clergy will refuse to perform an interfaith marriage unless the dissenting individual agrees to convert or to raise the children within the faith. The relationship between religion and education is tense: education may subvert fundamentalist beliefs in the miracles of the Bible; and the institutions of religion may strike back, as when a church condemns Darwin's theory of evolution. Religious principles have been the foundations of legal restrictions on gambling, prostitution, the sale of liquor, and other "vices." Catholics oppose the legalization of birth-control devices and abortions. Quakers are excused from active military duty, and Jehovah's Witnesses and Black Muslims seek the same exemption. Religious beliefs can influence family size and stability, attitudes toward education, political participation, work habits, and career choices.

Before looking at the relationships between religion and other social institutions in more detail, a word of caution is appropriate. Much of the research done by sociologists has used the categories "Catholic," "Protestant," and "Jewish" to measure religious affiliation. Recent research suggests that these categories mask important differences. For example, Abramson notes that ". . . ethnic diversity in Catholic America is considerable and significant in realms such as family patterns, life styles, and personal values" (cited in Demerath and Roof, 1976: 24). Differences between Irish, Italian, Polish, Puerto Rican, and Mexican Catholics are so great as to minimize their common label as Catholics. Similarly, Demerath and Roof note that ". . . the differences among Protestants are consistently greater than the differences between Protestants and virtually any other American religious group" (p. 24). Much of the data in the sections which follow are reported in these three categories. Until more research breaks each down into its component groups, what follows represents the best thinking we have. However, you will want to be aware that it probably describes broad relationships that will vary among specific denominations and subgroups.

Categorization by religious affiliation may mask significant differences in other aspects of a group's life style and value system. The wealthy Kennedy family, for example, leads a life that is quite different from that of this poor Puerto Rican family, despite their common label as Catholics.

The Family

The majority of people marry someone who was brought up in the same religion as they were—partly because many churches discourage interfaith marriages; partly because the church functions as a gathering place where couples meet; partly because there is a high correlation between religious affiliation, education, and in-come, and people tend to marry people from a similar socioeconomic background.

Researchers have also found differences in marital stability among religious groups. According to Gerhard Lenski's survey of Detroit (1961), Protestant couples are more likely to move away from their families than are Catholic or Jewish couples. Jews tend to visit relatives

TABLE 14.4 / SELF-CONCEPT AND RELIGION

The less students think of themselves as intellectuals, the more likely they will be highly involved in religion.

		"Do you think of yourself as an 'intellectual'":			
		"Definitely"	"In many ways"	"In some ways"	"Definitely not"
Religious involvement	High	26%	38%	49%	55%
	Low	28	32	34	31
	None	46	30	20	14

Source: Charles Y. Glock and Rodney Stark, *Religion and Society in Tension* (Chicago: Rand McNally, 1973), p. 282. Reprinted by permission.

every week; Protestants and Catholics, less often. Divorce rates are highest among Protestants (16 percent), lowest among Jews (4 percent), with Catholics (9 percent) in between. Thus, it appears that religious affiliation influences the choice of a marriage partner and also has an effect on family stability. This is not to say that religious beliefs alone discourage intermarriage or encourage divorce or juvenile delinquency. Income and educational level, occupation, and ethnic affiliation are also contributory factors.

Education

As we shall discuss in Chapter 15, education performs the function of changing people's attitudes. It appears that education exercises this influence even in matters of religion, an area often considered to be based on faith rather than on intellect. As indicated in Table 14.5, the education institution seems to be a place where many people reexamine their religious beliefs.

For instance, there is a correlation between the amount of schooling people have had and how often they attend church. Among Catholics and Protestants, people with a high school education are least likely to attend church, while those with only a grade school education and those who have been to college were slightly more likely to go to church. Among Jews, however, the tendency is sharply reversed—high school graduates are almost twice as likely to

TABLE 14.5 / EXPERIMENTING WITH RELIGION

The data in this table show the current religious identifications among a sample of freshmen at the University of California at Berkeley compared to the religion in which they were raised. These changes often reflect a period of intellectual and spiritual experimentation, rather than a lifelong change in religious affiliation; nevertheless, it is interesting to note that Catholics show the least change. (Data are in percentages.)

Present Religion	Religious Background*		
	Jewish	*Protestant*	*Catholic*
Jewish	32	†	0
Protestant	0	36	0
Roman Catholic	0	†	53
No religion	14	13	8
Agnostic	23	26	16
Atheist	11	6	3
Humanist	1	0	1
Eastern or mystical	2	1	4
"My own"	6	4	5
Christian—unspecified	1	3	4
Polytheist	0	†	0
Deist	0	†	0
Other—unspecified	9	8	8
Undecided, No answer	2	2	1
(Number)	(139)	(373)	(200)

* Percentages are rounded and do not add exactly to 100 percent.
† Less than 0.5 percent.
Source: Thomas Piazza, "Jewish Identity and the Counterculture," in Charles Y. Glock and Robert N. Bellah, eds., *The New Religious Consciousness* (Berkeley: University of California Press, 1976), p. 248. Reprinted by permission of the University of California Press.

attend church as grade school or college graduates are.

Researchers have also found evidence of correlations between religious affiliation and educational achievement. Of the major denominations in the United States, Baptists are the least likely to have attended college; Episcopalians and Jews, the most likely. The largest group of those with no religious preference at all, 10 percent, were those with college education (Gallup Opinion Index, July 29, 1976). Even the drop-out rate correlates with religion. Forty-eight percent of Catholics drop out of school before completing the highest grade they enter, as opposed to 39 percent of white Protestants and 25 percent of Jews (Lenski, 1961).

Civil Religion

There is no ecclesia, or national church, in the United States. What does exist is a strong Judeo-Christian ethic, an amalgam of principles loosely adapted from several religions combined with values generated by our economic and political systems (Bellah, 1975). This ethic, celebrated within most church settings, embodies such values as self-determination, community spirit, good will, honest work, and individualism. Mention of God is made in connection with all these values, but, ultimately, our religions seem to focus not so much on the supernatural as on our way of life.

In fact, our attitude toward religion has been termed a "civil religion" (Bellah, 1970). In other words, elements of sacred life are employed in our civic life. By including religious elements, public matters are given qualities of integrity and moral uprightness. For example, the President is sworn in with his right hand on the Bible; the Pledge of Allegiance proclaims us to be "one nation, under God"; our coins state "In God we trust"; and Congress convenes and adjourns with a prayer.

Questions of conscience. Because religion influences many matters of conscience and personal conduct, it can become a political issue. When John F. Kennedy was seeking the presidency in 1960, several prominent Southern Baptist ministers confronted him with their concern about whether a Catholic president could operate independently from the Pope. In 1976, the tables were turned when the bishops of the Roman Catholic church issued a statement that strongly implied that they supported the candidacy of Gerald Ford over that of Jimmy Carter. They were not cool to Carter because he was a Southern Baptist (although they could not forget the Southern Baptist tradition of anti-Catholicism) but because of his stands on such issues as abortion

When Ronald Reagan was sworn into office, he raised his right hand and placed his left on a Bible. This act is an example of civil religion, the influence of religion on governmental affairs, even though the United States has no state religion.

and aid to parochial schools. In both these cases, a religious group was concerned that the religious beliefs of a politician might adversely affect his decisions.

As well might be expected, people whose religious preference is traditional and conservative have the same preference in social issues. But sociologists have also found some correlations between people's religions and their choice of political parties. For instance, the Gallup Poll of 1971 revealed that 63 percent of the Jews in America were Democrats, while only 6 percent were Republicans. Similarly, 52 percent of the Catholics were Democrats, while only 19 percent were Republicans. Protestants, on the other hand, were nearly equally mixed in their politics.

The Economic System

Class correlations. Religious affiliation, income, and social status seem to have general correlations. In 1976, approximately 64 percent of Jews earned more than $10,000 a year, in contrast with 58 percent of Catholics and 49 percent of Protestants. Among Protestants, Presbyterians ranked highest with 71 percent; Baptists were lowest with 47 percent (Gallup Opinion Index, July 1976).

One contributing factor is that Jews and Presbyterians are more concentrated in urban areas; Baptists, in rural communities where incomes are generally lower. Catholics, who once were primarily recent immigrants or first- or second-generation Americans, have steadily increased their earnings as their roots have become more established in this country. Jews historically have emphasized the importance of education—a practice that encourages upward economic mobility. Parents with successful businesses often send their children to professional schools. In 1976 46 percent of American Jews were engaged in professional or business occupations compared with 20 percent for Catholics and 20 percent for Protestants. Episcopalians were highest among Protestants, with 37 percent in professional and business occupations, while Baptists were lowest with 13 percent (Gallup Opinion Index, July 1976).

Max Weber—The Protestant ethic. As we discussed earlier, Karl Marx believed that religion supports the status quo by turning economic circumstances (especially the class system) into divine laws. Weber suggested that was not always true and that religious beliefs have sometimes influenced economic systems and thus been the cause of social change. He focused particular attention on a connection between early Calvinist Protestantism and the rise of capitalism in sixteenth-century Europe and America. According to Calvinist teachings, God had predetermined who would go to heaven and who would go to hell. Thus, Weber argued, frightened for their souls, early Protestants looked everywhere for signs that they were among God's favored few and they interpreted good fortune and worldly success as signs of this predestination. At the same time, however, Calvinism taught that extravagant living and indulgence in pleasure did not please God.

The combined effect of these two teachings was that the Calvinists worked hard and lived simply. And this life style naturally led to economic success, which they regarded as a sign of God's blessing. Yet because they were prevented from spending their wealth on pleasure, they had to put their money back into their businesses. And this, in turn, led to still greater success and more investment. Weber argued that this practice of repeated investments of capital, encouraged by their religious eagerness for salvation, led earlier Protestants into a firmly established and self-perpetuating capitalistic economy.

Attempts to verify the idea that Protestants have developed a stronger work ethic than Catholics have not yielded clear-cut results. In Lenski's 1961 survey of Detroit he found that significantly more Protestants than Catholics had improved their social status—partly because they had fewer family ties and partly because they were committed to their jobs. In addition, 52 percent of Protestants, as opposed to 48 percent of Jews and 44 percent of Catholics, considered their jobs important and derived a sense of accomplishment from their work. Yet, when Lenski conducted a second survey in 1971, he found that differences between Protestants and Catholics were slight. Apparently, the work ethic has spread across denominational lines.

RELIGION IN MODERN SOCIETY

Much is written today about the decline of religion in American society. Some associate this apparent trend with lack of respect for authority, governmental and corporate corruption, sexual permissiveness, and other phenomena that are viewed as signs of decadence. Others see it as a consequence of the growth of science and a pragmatic, rational world view. In technological societies, writes Thomas O'Dea (1970), "Mysteries are replaced by problems" (p. 86)—and, by extension, priests by psychiatrists; prophets by pollsters. (We are prompted to recall Auguste Comte's prediction in the 1800s that in the industrial age, the world would look to science to explain the universe and to guide individual decisions. See Chapter 1.)

Even value instruction, once an important function of religion, is being carried out without the aid of religion: "In modern society, obligations associated with age, sex, and class roles can be fulfilled without serious attention to religious norms" (Roof, 1976, p. 196). *Functional integration,* which emphasizes how people are different and how we each perform different roles, appears to have become more important than *normative integration,* which emphasizes how people are alike in their values and traditions. There is increasing emphasis on individual decision making and life styles rather than on following codified community standards. In such a "highly differentiated society . . . religious norms are

increasingly segregated from other institutional sectors" (Roof, 1976: 196). Religion, once at the center of Western society, "has no direct influence over the large corporate structures which have emerged in the last 400 years. Big government, big business, big labor, big military, and big education are not directly influenced either by religion or by church" (Greeley, 1972: 14).

But Jacob Needleman, like many others, believes that the new gods of science have failed us:

The scientific world view, recently so full of hope, has left men stranded in a flood of forces and events they do not understand, far less control. Psychiatry has lost its messianic aura, and the therapists themselves are among the most tormented by the times. In the social sciences, there exists a brilliant gloom of unconnected theories and shattered predictions. Biology and medicine promise revolutionary discoveries and procedures but meanwhile we suffer and die as before; and our doctors are as frightened as we. (1970:9)

And recent data support Needleman's view. A study conducted for the National Science Foundation found that a 6 to 1 ratio of respondents felt that the benefits of scientific research outweighed the problems (Kristof, 1981). Eighty-one percent believed that it made life easier, more comfortable, and healthier. Yet 53 percent felt scientific discoveries were making life change too quickly, and 37 percent agreed that they tended to break down people's ideas of right and wrong. This ambivalence about science, progress, and basic values has spawned a variety of religious responses. Let us look at some of them.

The Return to Religious Conservatism

In 1979, the Rev. Jerry Falwell, a television evangelist, formed the Christian fundamentalist political movement called The Moral Majority. It has become the most visible and vocal proponent of a combination of religious and political beliefs that are generally referred to as the doctrine of the "New Right." "It espouses conservative views on a wide range of social, religious and political issues and has lobbied against the proposed equal rights amendment, abortion and civil rights for homosexuals" (McFadden, 1981). The Moral Majority has worked in conjunction with a number of prominent right-wing conservatives. These include Phyllis Schlaffly, a foe of the equal rights amendment, and Jesse Helms, the North Carolina senator who has fought against integration and many welfare programs. Even President Reagan's social and economic policies have been seen as supportive of the positions taken by Falwell and his group.

A number of actions have been attributed to the Moral Majority, although it is probably more accurate to say that this group is the visible expression of feelings held by a number of

This Mormon temple is an example of the enduring structures of worship often built by large, organized religions.

Americans which lead them to act in certain ways. Among the activities undertaken by The Moral Majority or its supporters are censoring library and textbooks, censoring television programs and commercials, and condemning abortion. They also seek to establish a rigid code of right and wrong which is based on a nuclear family model, as well as traditional sex-role behavior and child-rearing practices. The movement is, in some ways, an attempt to "stop the world" by returning to the values of the past and rejecting ideas and practices spawned by modern science and technology. Apparently it is a doctrine that appeals to the people discussed above who feel the world is changing too fast.

This same type of conservative retreat has characterized the development of a number of religious sects. Although research indicates that any of these groups are relatively short-lived (Bibby and Brinkerhoff, 1974), some have developed within large established religions like the Catholic Church (Fichter, 1975). Others, like the Mormons, have become large, wealthy, established religions with well-developed organizational structures (Stark and Bainbridge, 1980). Yet other sects, among them the most visible and controversial, fall somewhere in between. Reverend Moon's Unification Church and the Hare Krishnas, for example, have grown, but they have also remained secretive and encountered substantial public resistance. And still others, such as Jim Jones' tragic group, have experienced upheavals that have partially or completely destroyed them. As a whole, however, there is little doubt that conservative religious groups have brought to the public eye a number of moral issues, and that they have had an impact on America's religious, political, and family life.

The anticonservative response. In a recent Associated Press–NBC News poll, 66 percent of the respondents felt that there should be a separation of church and state (Harper, 1981). It was also found that the majority had not heard enough about The Moral Majority to have an opinion

SOCIAL ISSUE/Death and Dying

Robert Fulton/*University of Minnesota*

Experience with death in modern urban societies has changed significantly over the past few decades. At the turn of the century 53 percent of all deaths in the United States occurred among children under 15 years of age. They died of diphtheria, pneumonia, scarlet fever, and other infectious and contagious diseases. Today death is increasingly an experience of the aged. Of the 2 million persons who will die in the United States this year, two-thirds will be 65 years of age or older. Children under the age of 15, on the other hand, will account for less than 6 percent of the deaths. The majority of deaths today are due to heart disease, cancer, and stroke or other degenerative diseases typically associated with the aging process (U.S. Bureau of the Census, 1980).

The changes in mortality reflect a general increase in life expectancy. Whereas a child born in the United States in 1978 can be expected to live 73 years, a child born at the turn of the century had a life expectancy of 47 years (U.S. Bureau of the Census, 1980: 72, Table 106).

Twenty-four and a half million persons in the United States are now over 65 years of age. It is estimated that by the year 2000 the number will increase to 32 million, of whom 14.5 million will be over 75 years of age (U.S. Bureau of the Census, 1980: 338, Table 542).

To compare today's life expectancy with that of the past two millennia permits us to see more clearly the full extent of the mortality revolution that has occurred. In Julius Caesar's time, life expectancy was 27 years. In Shakespeare's time, it was 35 years. At the time of the American Civil War, one could have expected to live approximately 41 years (Peterson, 1975). And as already noted, life expectancy in the United States was 47 years during the life of our grandparents, while it is over 70 years for children today.

What is important to observe is that 2000 years passed before life expectancy increased 23 years in the rural, agriculturally based civilization of Western Europe, yet it has taken less than 80 years for life expectancy to increase 26 years in our urban, scientific, industrially based society. By way of contrast, life expectancy in rural India is still less than 30 years, a statistic that has remained essentially the same since the time of Alexander the Great.

What has made these changes in our mortality rates possible are the many and varied factors that have caused North American society to differ in certain important respects from all preceding societies. In slightly over seven decades we have shifted from a predominantly rural, agricultural society to a primarily urban, industrial society. Over the same period of time, we have, to a considerable extent, become removed from such experiences as the death of relatives in the home, the killing of domesticated farm animals, and other direct and immediate encounters with life: birth, aging, illness, and human death.

The contemporary family in the United States now lives under different auspices and circumstances than formerly and has responded to the change in its environment by an appreciable change in its character and structure. To a significant degree, the family has transformed itself from an extended family system to a nuclear family system. The extended family generally embraced more than two generations, while the nuclear family typically embraces only two.

One change that was brought about by the impact of industrialization upon the family involved the care of the dead. That task was taken over half a century ago by a paid functionary—the undertaker. This is not meant to imply that undertakers or funeral directors did not exist before the time of the First World War. The burial of the dead goes back 60,000 years. Over the millennia in Egypt, Europe, and America persons have always been available to assist in laying out the dead and disposing of the corpse. But the general extension of this service in the United States occurred following World War I. (A recent study shows that the average funeral home in the United States has been established for sixty years; Fulton, 1977.) The point is that the personal and time-honored practice of family members being directly responsible for the laying out of their dead—a practice that is probably as old as human-kind itself—changed in the United States. The principle of specialization is reflected by the undertaker who, in effect, said, "Let me take the deceased's body out of your home and place it in my establishment. I will relieve you of the responsibility of laying it out and of being concerned by its presence." When people, singly or in families, moved to the cities in great numbers at the time of World War I, traditional funeral practices changed. The absence of relatives, neighbors, and community, as well as the rush of city life and the time-oriented character of factory life all converged to cause the family to turn to the funeral director's public rooms to lay out their private dead.

By the Second World War, the general principle of American industrial enterprise—specialization—had also been adopted by medical science. The demands of the war and the scarcity of medical resources required the establishment of the all-inclusive public hospital. It was no longer practical or efficient for the physician to make house calls. The health-care adminstrator said, in effect, "Come to our hospital where you will have the counsel of many physicians and the latest medical equipment and other resources unavailable at home: x-ray machines, clean beds, blood banks, facilities and service, efficiency, and convenience." People went to the hospital. In 1925, hospital-bed occupancy totaled 7 million patients; by 1970, this figure was more than 32 million—a five-fold increase during a period of time when the population increase of the United States was two-fold (Hospital Statistics, 1977).

Today more than two-thirds of the deaths that will take place will do so in a hospital or a setting other than the deceased's home (projected from Public Health Service, 1958, last data statistic compiled).

The extension and continual enhancement of public-health services has not only reduced the mortality rate, but it has also changed the time and place of death.

With the development of nursing-home care for the elderly, the process of specialized human care has extended even further. Briefly, what is important to observe is that in less than 50 years, the care of the dead has been shifted away from the home and from the direct responsibility of the family, the seriously and chronically ill are hospitalized, and the dependent elderly are increasingly removed to health-care centers. The long-term implications of these isolating and segregating developments can be better understood, however, if we look at other changes that have concurrently taken place in our society.

First, the definition of death itself has undergone a change, and has acquired a different meaning from what it had only a decade ago. Until quite recently death was something that you could put your finger on, so to speak. You could check the person's eye for a light reaction, feel the person's pulse, test for respiration, prick the skin, and failing a response, you could reasonably conclude that the person was dead. Today, however, there are transplant programs and other medical procedures that make it frequently necessary to run an EEG to be certain that a patient is "brain" dead.

In addition to the clinical redefinition of death, the conception of death or—more correctly—the conception of life, has also changed. In other words, the conception of life has contracted. What is considered "alive" and what is considered "dead" are not the same as before. Viability has been foreshortened. Formerly, life began with conception, but with the Supreme Court's recent ruling that a fetus isn't "alive" until after 21 weeks of gestation, "life," in a manner of speaking, has had to pull in its belt. With birth as well as death, our attitudes have experienced a profound change.

Family relations have also been directly affected by contemporary mortality and the new social patterns that have emerged. The elderly, for example, are typically retired from gainful employment, less active socially, and frequently less central to the lives of their children and grandchildren. Prolonged separation due to hospitalization or residential change also serves to reduce familial and friendship contacts as it weakens social and emotional commitments. With a sense of having "lived out one's life," the death of an elderly person today need not affect the emotional life of his or her family to the same degree it once might have. This does not mean, of course, that when an elderly parent or relative dies grief is absent. Rather, the degree or extent of a survivor's grief appears to depend upon many factors, not the least of which is the nature and intensity of the social bond itself.

Observed variations in the response to loss by death permit us to make a distinction between what can be termed a "high-grief" death and a "low-grief" death. If the expression "low-grief" is allowed to decribe the reaction to the death of many elderly persons today, "high-grief" describes the impact of a death brought about suddenly or unexpectedly of a person on whom others depend heavily for their social and psychological well-being. This latter death usually precipitates a series of intense emotional and physical reactions that have been described in the literature as a "normal-grief" syndrome (Lindemann, 1944).

It is important also to note that the contemporary setting within which the majority of people die has brought changes not only in the level of emotional reaction to loss, but also in those who, in fact, share in the loss. Research has shown that frequently professional care-givers experience grief at the loss of a patient and in many other ways react as bereaved survivors themselves (Vachon, 1977). As the traditional kinship network falters or as family members disengage from their relationship with the dying patient, the attending nurse and other care-givers frequently find themselves participating in the social and emotional support of patients under their care. Such involvement, albeit at times inadvertent, brings with it a new responsibility as it involves new emotional risks. In fact, the data suggest that the stress levels of critical-care nurses are often as high as the stress levels of the patients for whom they care (Vachon, 1977).

That this could occur is made possible not only by the evolution of health-care programs for the care of the elderly, but also because of a phenomenon called "anticipatory grief." The term refers to the fact that the patient's death is anticipated prior to the event and there is an accommodation that goes on among the survivors and health-care personnel in expectation of what is to happen. Studies have shown that in instances where family members were observed withdrawing physically and emotionally from a patient, health-care members became caught up in that patient's life. New emotional bonds were established, giving rise to the potential for role discrepancy and role reversal on the part of the care-givers when the patient died (Binger et al., 1969; Natterson and Knudsen, 1965). Health-care personnel increasingly find themselves grieved when a patient dies. This phenomenon turns professional care-givers into grievers, or what might be termed "surrogate grievers" (Fulton, 1979).

The problems and issues associated with the surviving spouse have also received increased attention in recent years. Although many of the problems of the survivor are associated with old age *per se* in the United States, such problems are frequently aggravated to an intolerable degree with the death of the spouse. Financial difficulties, health, transportation, personal insecurity, and loneliness are the concern of the elderly widow or widower in our vigorously youth-oriented society. The problem is not a negligible one—particularly for widows. There are approximately 12.4 million widows in the United States (U.S. Bureau of the Census, 1980: 41, Table 50). In other words, almost one out of every seven adult women (18 years and above) in the United States is a widow (U.S. Bureau of the Census, 1980; Tables 33 and 50). The problems of widowhood do not end with the difficulties of surviving on a greatly reduced income or with the absence of the comfort and care provided by a husband. Research indicates that widows are at a mortal risk six times greater than their married counterparts (Rees and Lutkins, 1967). This is the result, presumably, of the stress associated with their bereavement. As it has been observed, it is indeed the fate of many widows to die prematurely of a "broken heart."

Changes in the experience with death have led also to a decline in traditional mourning practices. Although the length of time that these customs were practiced suggests a certain timeliness about them, this is not so. Ideas concerning death and the treatment of the dead are in a state of ferment. Since the Second World War, there has been an accelerated change in response to death at both the personal and the community level. The black tie, hat, armband, and funeral wreath, for example, have virtually disappeared in North America. These changes parallel a growing collective dissatisfaction with contemporary funeral practices. This was made evident in the early 1960s with the publication of Jessica Mitford's bestselling *The American Way of Death*. Her critical broadside at funeral customs in the United States brought into question the value of embalming, viewing a cosmeticized corpse, air-tight caskets, metal vaults, and elaborate and expensive caskets.

While rites for the dead have been criticized for their lavishness and display since the time of the visit of the Greek historian Herodotus to Egypt (300 B.C.), it has only been in the present century that we have seen concerted efforts to rid society not only of the funeral, but also of evidence of death itself by the immediate disposition of the corpse.

It would appear, however, that forces other than theology, aesthetics, or economics are at work. The decline of traditional religious beliefs, secular education, and the accomplishments and technologies of medical science have not only diminished our fear and awe of death, but have also challenged our belief in the existence of a world of the dead. Modern society, moreover, with its emphasis on efficiency, economy, and practicality, casts in a poor light those among us who are dependent or nonproductive. The death and subsequent disposition of a dead human being, like the conditions of his or her dying, thus become both problematical and contentious.

Our society is experiencing rapid social change with regard to death and death customs. We are currently in a process of defining and redefining grief, bereavement, and loss, to say nothing of death itself. The push toward the diminishment of the funeral and the abandonment of mourning customs are manifestations of this social upheaval. These movements have not gone unchallenged, however. There are those who argue that there are important aspects of the funeral and mourning rites besides the expression of a belief in immortality or the spiritual incorporation of the dead into an afterlife. Mourning rites and funeral practices can fill important emotional needs for the living. They do so by focusing attention on the grief of the survivors and by providing a public rite of separation.

Medical and behavioral science personnel have argued in recent years that loss through death provokes powerful emotions that need to be given adequate expression. It is believed that mourning and funerary rituals can aid in the ventilation of profound emotions and facilitate the dissolution of grief when they are responsive to the needs of the survivors and consistent with the social customs and values of the community.

A further development that is at once an expression of the social and demographic changes that have occurred over the last few decades, as well as a stimulus to the problems associated with contemporary death and dying, is the fact that American youth are death-insulated. They grow up in an environment in which, at the immediate personal level, direct contact with dying or death is rare. That is to say, the probability that a death will occur within any specific family (a family composed of parents and children) is only 1 in 25 prior to a child's achieving adulthood (U.S. Bureau of the Census, 1980: 45, Table 45).

The intermediary functions of the physician, the nurse, the ambulance driver, the police officer, and the mortician, however, serve to put death at a distance. Even the local butcher frees us of the responsibility of direct contact with the slaughter and preparation of our food, while the veterinarian offers us the service of putting our injured or aged pet to "sleep."

At the same time, however, news about and exposure to violence, dying, death or the prospects of a nuclear holocaust are everywhere made real and immediate by the mass media. In contemporary varieties of rock music explicit themes of death and violence enjoy an ever-widening audience, while such contemporary films as "Night of the Living Dead" vividly portray scenes of matricide, patricide, fratricide, and cannabalism. Significantly, the film, like so many of its genre, is devoid of any sympathy or concern for the victims.

In a past issue of the *National Lampoon,* for example, a mock interview is reported with the late Dan Blocker, formerly a star of television's "Bonanza." In the same issue are also pornographic displays of nude female suicides and cartoons that allude to necrophilia, while in a feature article the reader is callously instructed in how to tell a child his or her parents are dead (*National Lampoon,* 1973). The film "Night of the Living Dead" is a cinematic counterpart to the *National Lampoon.* The dramatization of violent death in a hostile world, as presented in this film and others like it, without the acknowledgment or depiction of humane responses or expressions of grief, portends serious problems for our youth in the area of loss and separation, as it possesses the potential to aggravate intergenerational relationships.

For youth to be insulated from direct experience with death while being innundated with images of death and violence has larger implications as well. Death insulation takes place in a social context in which the potential for unprecedented mass death and destruction is an unremitting reality. The twentieth century, and especially the post-World War II era, has been characterized by the proliferation of nuclear materials. Technological developments in weaponry and delivery systems have created a potential annihilation that threatens the cultural as well as the physical survival of humankind. The implications of new generations being death-insulated at the personal level while being threatened by the specter of extinction at the societal level have only now begun to receive the attention and study they merit.

The contemporary change in our attitudes toward death is reflected also in the number of young and old who kill themselves each year in the United States. While typically it is the elderly white, Anglo male over the age of 55 who kills himself, the picture is changing, as more and more young men and women successfully attempt suicide (U.S. Department of Commerce, 1980).

During the past decade suicide among the young has become increasingly common even though it must be pointed out that the rate of suicide for the young has remained relatively stable over the years. Since 1960, however, the suicide rate for young women has increased more than for young men, although the suicide rate for young women remains substantially below the rate for young men (U.S. Bureau of the Census, 1980). It is important, also, to point out that young women who attempt suicide do so increasingly in a manner that will assure success. This is in contrast to the past when a young woman might take an overdose of sleeping pills and then notify a friend. Today young women utilize more certain means of self-destruction, such as a gun or razor. Ready acceptance of suicide in the United States, moreover, parallels a burgeoning interest in the euthanasia movement, and the promotion of such programs as the "Right-to-Die."

It is a paradox in a country that has a tremendous commitment to life, as the United States has, and in a society that provides more material goods and other benefits than possibly any other society in the history of humankind, that so many people, both young and old, are embracing the idea of death. For the elderly, it is more readily understandable. Given what has been observed, many see in chronic illness and age dependency an intolerable indignity. For them it is preferable to "jump rather than be pushed" to their deaths. But for the young, we must examine the entire *zeitgeist* of our society if we are to find a satisfactory explanation for their suicides.

Concomitantly, interest in suicide parallels a revival of interest in life after death. The information market today is aflood with books, articles, and films purporting to give accounts of clinical death and revival, contact and communication with the dead, visions of the nether world, levitation, and out-of-body experiences. It is again paradoxical that we should have so many members of our society rushing to leave life on the one hand, while on the other hand a comparable number enthusiastically search for it, albeit somewhere else.

REFERENCES

Binger, C. M. et al. (1969). Childhood leukemia: Emotional impact on patient and family. *New England Journal of Medicine* 208: 414–18.

Fulton, Robert (1977). A compilation of studies of attitudes toward death, funerals and funeral directors. Minneapolis: Center for Death Education and Research, University of Minnesota.

———— (1979). Anticipatory grief, stress, and the surrogate griever. In *Cancer, Stress, and Death,* ed. J. Tache et al. New York: Plenum Publishing Co.

Hospital Statistics (1977). Chicago: American Hospital Association.

Lindemann, Erich (1944). Symptomatology and management of acute grief. *American Journal of Psychiatry* 101: 141–48.

Metropolitan Life Insurance Company (1977). *Statistical Bulletin* 58 (September): 9.

National Center for Health Statistics (1964). *Suicide in the United States, 1950–1964,* Series 20, no. 5, Table 1.

National Lampoon, January 1973.

Natterson, J. M., and **A. G. Knudsen** (1965). Observations concerning fear of death in fatally ill children and their mothers. *Psychosomatic Medicine* 22: 903–06.

Petersen, William (1975). *Population.* New York: Macmillan.

Rees, W. Dewi, and **Sylvia G. Lutkins** (1967). Mortality of bereavement. *British Medical Journal* 4 (Oct. 7): 13–16.

U.S. Department of Commerce, Bureau of the Census (1980). *Statistical Abstract of the United States.* Washington, D.C.: U.S. Government Printing Office.

Vachon, M. L. S. (1977). Measurement and management of stress of health professionals working with advanced cancer patients. Paper presented at the University of Chicago conference on "Developing New Services for Patients with Advanced Cancer." April 28, 1977, pp. 1–4.

about it, but of those who did know about it, most had an unfavorable opinion. These data suggest that most Americans do not favor religious conservatism that mixes religion with politics. Not unexpectedly, the public attack on the views of extreme religious conservatives has come from liberal academics. A. Bartlett Giamatti, the president of Yale University, attacked The Moral Majority and other conservative groups in ringing terms:

"Angry at change, rigid in the application of chauvinistic slogans, absolutist in morality, they threaten through political pressure or public denunciation whoever dares to disagree with their authoritarian positions" . . . . *Mr. Giamatti said that the values espoused by The Moral Majority— love of country, a regard for the sanctity of life, the importance of the family and high standards of personal conduct—were obviously not evil or pernicious and were held by millions of Americans. "The point is, the rest of us hold to ideas of family, country, belief in God, in different ways. The right to differ, and to see things differently, is our concern." (McFadden, 1981)**

Those who point to the dangers of the conservative views of groups like The Moral Majority highlight their attacks on humanist thought. Humanism developed from the eighteenth-century Enlightenment period; it emphasizes free thought, human reason, and the scientific method (Chandler, 1981). It is, of course, in direct opposition to the thinking of religious conservatives who believe in a literal interpretation of the Bible as the basis of human thought and history. The disagreement really does narrow down to fundamentally different views of human progress and human purpose. Liberal academics point out that scientific and technological development are compatible with respect for human life and basic moral values. They note that human freedom and improved living conditions for the

majority of the population are also important values. Without science and technology these are not possible, and a return to the past means a return to sexual, racial, and ethnic discrimination, reduced opportunities for people to achieve their intellectual potential, and greater chances for the rise of politically totalitarian regimes (such as the one which developed in Iran under the Ayatollah Khomeini).

Finding a Balance

The issues raised by groups like The Moral Majority serve to underline what a powerful force the religious institution is in society. In spite of changes people continue to hold religious beliefs. A 1975 Gallup Poll found only 11 percent of respondents identifying themselves as not religious. The same poll found that people with stronger religious beliefs identified themselves as happier than those with less of a religious identification. There are even more preliminary data to suggest that people who attend church or synagogue services on a weekly basis are more healthy than those who do not (*Washington Post*, 1981). Of course, knowing that there is a correlation between religiosity and happiness or health does not tell us that one is the cause of the other.

The most dramatic point of these surveys is that religion continues to be an important part of social life. Worries by The Moral Majority and other conservatives that morality will disappear seem to have no foundation in fact, although these groups may well feel that the moral beliefs which prevail are not the specific ones they want. Glock and Stark (1973) note that "What contributes to social integration is not necessarily institutionalized religion, but what society defines as 'sacred,' that is, a value orientation" (p. 180). Perhaps the influence of religious values will outlive religious institutions. This would be preferable to maintaining institutions that no longer perform meaningful services. Religious institutions may change, or even

---

* © 1981 by the New York Times Company. Reprinted by permission.

be swept away, in some contemporary societies, but "sacred" values will still serve a vital integrative function. "Society is not capable of maintaining itself when it lacks a high degree of consensus as to what it is ultimately committed to" (Glock and Stark, 1973: 180).

Andrew M. Greeley concedes that religion is in a crisis stage. But he believes that the problems confronting religion may ultimately strengthen it.

Religion is a more explicit and individual matter now than it has ever been in the past. While the *individual is by no means free from the power of the group, he still has a good deal more elbowroom for making religious decisions than he ever did in the past. . . Insofar as an ever-increasing number of people must, in some fashion or the other, face the religious issues as explicit and central, it is legitimate . . . to argue that the present era is more religious than any one of the past. (1972: 14–15)**

---

* Reprinted by permission of Schocken Books Inc. from *Unsecular Man* by Andrew M. Greeley. Copyright © 1972, by Schocken Books Inc.

SUMMARY

1. The main purposes of this chapter are to define religion and to discuss the major sociological approaches to religion; to outline the organization of religion; to explore the relationships between religion and the other major social institutions; and to evaluate religion in modern society.

2. Every society throughout history has had a religion, a system of beliefs and practices related to sacred and supernatural matters. The functionalists, building on Durkheim's work, believe religion fulfills certain functions for society: providing for worship directed toward the sacred; instructing in moral and ethical guidelines; giving psychological support and consolation in trying situations and/or turning points of one's life, and creating a community for its group of believers.

The conflict theorists (such as Karl Marx) believe that while religion may provide group identity, most religions also support the status quo, discourage social change, and provide the means for social differentiation and group conflicts.

Symbolic interaction and exchange theories help us understand the importance of interpersonal networks in religious affiliations, as well as the exchanges that take place between a person and his or her faith.

3. As societies become more complex, religious organizations and practices become more specialized. Sociologists categorize religious groups in terms of size and power. The most common organizations are churches (can be an ecclesia or a denomination) and sects (such as the Unification Church).

4. There is much interplay between religion and the other major social institutions. Religious beliefs can influence family size and stability, attitudes toward education, political participation, work habits, and career choices.

5. During the 1980s, American society has encoun-

tered an increase in religious conservatism. Through groups like The Moral Majority, this view has spilled over into the political arena. Other groups have identified the effects which extreme political conservatism can have on civil rights, intellectual freedom, and political totalitarianism.

6. The 1970s and 1980s also saw a rise in the number of sects. Many of these reflected the same fears that change was happening too fast, which led to an increase in religious conservatism. As a result, many sects also espouse values of obedience, literal interpretations of the scriptures, and resistance to social change.

7. In spite of changes in the structure of religious organizations in America, data indicate that religious moral values continue to be important to most people. While their participation in organized religion may change, there is little reason to believe that most people see religious values as declining in importance.

REVIEW

Key Terms

Monotheism	Worship	Denomination
Polytheism	Sacred	Sect
Religion	Church	
Totem	Ecclesia	

Review and Discussion

1. Which theoretical perspective on religion corresponds most closely with your own ideas? Why?

2. If you have a strong religious belief, why is it important to you? How does it help you function in society? If you don't have a strong religious belief, do you feel either at a disadvantage or superior to those who do? Why?

3. Would you like to (or could you) become a member of a sect like the Unification Church? Why or why not?

4. How has your religion affected or failed to affect your functions and/or your family's function in the other major social institutions?

5. Which view of the future of religion is closest to your own? Why do you feel as you do?

6. If your family is very religious and you are not (or vice versa), what factors influenced you to depart from your upbringing? If this situation does not apply to you, do you know someone to whom it might apply? If so, try to account for their departure from their upbringing.

References

Bellah, Robert N. (1970). *Beyond Belief.* New York: Harper & Row.

———— (1975). *The Broken Covenant.* New York: Seabury Press.

Bibby, R. W., and **M. B. Brinkerhoff** (1974). When proselytizing fails: An organizational analysis. *Sociological Analysis* 35: 189–200.

Chandler, Russell (1981). Humanism under heavy attack from ministries of new right. *The Washington Post,* Aug. 21, 1981, p. B14.

Demerath, N. J. III, and **W. C. Roof** (1976). Religion—Recent strands in research. In *Annual Review of Sociology,* eds. Alex Inkeles, James Coleman, and Neil Smelser. Palo Alto, Cal.: Annual Reviews.

Dressler, David, and **Donald Carns** (1973). *Sociology: The Study of Human Interaction.* New York: Alfred A. Knopf.

Durkheim, Emile (1954). *The Elementary Forms of the Religious Life,* translated by Joseph W. Swain. New York: Free Press.

Eckhardt, William (1974). Religious beliefs and practices in relation to peace and justice. *Social Compass* 21: 4.

Fichter, J. (1975). *The Catholic Cult of the Paraclete.* New York: Sheed and Ward.

Gallup Opinion Index (1975). Report #14. Religion in America. February 1975.

———— (1976). Report #130. Religion in America. July 1976.

Glock, Charles Y., and **Rodney Stark** (1973). *Religion and Society in Tension.* Chicago: Rand McNally.

Greeley, Andrew M. (1972). *Unsecular Man: The Persistence of Religion.* New York: Schocken Books.

Harper, Timothy (1981). Poll backs separation of church, politics. *The Washington Post,* Aug. 21, 1981, p. B14.

Hartman, Curtis (1981). God for the "up and out." *Boston Magazine,* May 1981, pp. 142ff.

Johnstone, Ronald (1975). *Religion and Society in Interaction.* Englewood Cliffs, N.J.: Prentice-Hall.

Kristof, Nicholas (1981). Public backing science, worries about change. *The Washington Post,* Aug. 21, 1981.

Lenski, Gerhard (1961). *The Religious Factor.* Garden City, N.Y.: Doubleday.

McFadden, Robert D. (1981). Head of Yale calls Moral Majority "peddlers of coercion" on "values." *The New York Times,* Sept. 1, 1981, pp. 1ff.

Needleman, Jacob (1970). *The New Religions.* Garden City, N.Y.: Doubleday.

O'Dea, Thomas F. (1970). *Sociology and the Study of Religion.* New York: Basic Books.

Rice, Berkeley (1976). The pull of Sun Myung Moon. *The New York Times Magazine,* May 30, 1976, pp. 8ff.

Roof, Wade Clark (1976). Traditional religion in contemporary society. *American Sociology Review* 41: 195–208.

Sites, Paul (1975). *Control and Constraint: An Introduction to Sociology.* New York: Macmillan.

Stark, Rodney, and **William Sims Bainbridge** (1980). Networks of faith: Interpersonal bonds and recruitment to cults and sects. *American Journal of Sociology* 85, no. 6 (May 1980): 1376–95.

Starr, Jerold M. (1975). Religious preference, religiosity, and opposition to war. *Sociological Analysis* 36 (Winter).

The Washington Post (1981). Going to church may be good for health. August 21, 1981.

Yearbook of American Churches (1975). Lebanon, Pa.: Sowers Printing Co.

15

EDUCATION

If a society is to continue, it must preserve and pass on its accumulated knowledge to future generations. But education is more than readin', 'ritin', and 'rithmatic. It is also the informal socialization that occurs through daily interactions. "How important are schools to one's future success—extremely important, fairly important, not too important?" This question was posed to a cross section of United States citizens. Seventy-six percent of the respondents felt that schools were extremely important to future success. Another 19 percent thought that they were at least fairly important. Only 4 percent thought that they were not too important. One percent of those questioned had no opinion (Gallup Survey, 1975). We in the United States regard education as a vital institution. No wonder it remains the center of varied and continuous debates.

EDUCATION DEFINED

Education is the social institution providing for the transmission and the generation of knowledge. For the most part, the study of education as a social institution concentrates on formal instruction. But any discussion of education must recall everything we have said about the process of socialization. Sociologists readily acknowledge that much human learning is the result of the informal training we receive through our families and through interaction with our peers. Children learn the unspoken norms and values of their society by observing the way adults and their own peers react to their actions.

Formal, institutionalized education as we know it is not necessary in nonliterate societies. In those societies, children learn to hunt or to weave first by observing their parents, then by assisting them, and finally by working on their own. But children in industrial societies cannot simply follow their parents to the office, shop, or factory to observe or to assist. Cultural knowl-

edge and occupational training in industrial societies are too complex to be transmitted only in such informal methods of learning. Computer programming requires a sophisticated understanding of mathematics; the average person cannot repair and maintain his or her own car without more training than is possible in a few days of observation. In complex societies, a formal social structure is needed to teach people what they need to know.

Of course, innumerable norms and values contribute to making education in industrial societies different from what it is in nonliterate settings. The belief in organization and achievement tends to place knowledge acquisition on a timetable. A high value placed on authorities and specialists leads us to set up teacher-student units. And a strong belief in scientific measurement motivates us to construct a battery of tests and measurements so that we may know the degree to which the student and the institution have been successful.

Furthermore, we also value a certain degree of choice and personal fulfillment in picking a career. If we were to learn only what our parents could teach, each of us would remain unaware of much of the possibility for our own growth and expression of talent. In an industrial society, it is not essential for everyone to be able to perform the same tasks (like hunting and weaving). One can make a life either in housebuilding or in music without so much as an elementary knowledge of the other. The individual will not suffer and society will be the richer for the diversity of its members. In fact, industrial societies require diversity for their success.

THE FUNCTIONS OF EDUCATION

Manifest Functions

From the individual's point of view, education may be a prerequisite for employment and

Education is not limited to the formal setting of school and classroom. The family serves as one of the most effective and influential sources of informal instruction.

a route to self-improvement. From society's point of view, education performs several essential functions: the transmission of general knowledge and specialized skills, cultural integration, and the generation of new knowledge and technology.

Transmission of knowledge and skills. The major manifest function of educational structures is the transmission of knowledge and skills. This process is one of handing down, from one generation to the next, the body of information accumulated by a culture. Clearly, such a process is necessary for the survival and the perpetuation of the culture. No generation can begin again from scratch. Therefore, students are encour-

aged, and even forced, to learn how the government works, why the sun rises and the rain falls, how people live in other countries, and how to speak other languages. While this information may not be of immediate use to the individual student, the general perpetuation of it is useful to the society. Most importantly, students are supposed to learn how to read and to write in their own language and to perform basic arithmetic operations. These last skills are considered minimal for survival in a modern industrial society. Without them, of course, many social interactions would be difficult, if not impossible.

The volume of information possessed by a modern industrial society is overwhelming. In primitive societies, a person could reasonably have an understanding, if not a complete mastery, of all the knowledge, arts, and traditions held by that society. But a person living in the United States in the 1980s could never master even a fraction of modern society's know-how.

Cultural integration. The United States always has been a culturally heterogeneous nation. Education provides our varied population with common experiences and ties. In school children from diverse backgrounds learn to be "Americans." They recite the Pledge of Allegiance, study this country's history and government, read *Tom Sawyer,* learn to play baseball, and celebrate Thanksgiving. These lessons—and the shared experience of spending ten or more years in classrooms, lunchrooms, and playgrounds—give young people a certain amount of shared identity, regardless of their family or neighborhood background. In other words, they get a "feel" for their culture and their society.

In the past, the schools paid little attention to ethnic identity. Assimilation was considered to be one of the primary goals of education. It was reasoned that to become more like the majority was to share in the best that life in the modern United States had to offer. Many practices we now consider thoughtless and even cruel

TABLE 15.1 / ILLITERACY IN THE UNITED STATES, 1900 TO 1970

These figures represent the percentages of state populations who could neither read nor write in any language.

State	1900	1920	1930	1950	1960	1970	State	1900	1920	1930	1950	1960	1970
United States	**11.3**	**6.5**	**4.8**	**3.3**	**2.4**	**1.2**	Virginia	24.3	12.2	9.7	4.9	3.4	1.4
New England:							West Virginia	12.6	7.2	5.5	3.5	2.7	1.4
Maine	5.5	3.6	3.0	2.0	1.3	0.7	North Carolina	30.1	15.0	11.5	5.5	4.0	1.8
New Hampshire	6.7	4.9	3.0	2.0	1.4	0.7	South Carolina	37.4	20.9	16.7	7.9	5.5	2.3
Vermont	6.4	3.3	2.4	1.7	1.1	0.6	Georgia	32.1	16.7	10.4	6.9	4.5	2.0
Massachusetts	6.5	5.3	4.0	2.8	2.2	1.1	Florida	23.4	10.2	7.7	3.9	2.6	1.3
Rhode Island	9.2	7.2	5.5	3.1	2.4	1.3	**East South Central:**						
Connecticut	6.5	6.9	5.1	3.1	2.2	1.1	Kentucky	18.1	9.4	7.3	4.3	3.3	1.6
Middle Atlantic:							Tennessee	21.9	11.3	8.0	4.7	3.5	1.7
New York	6.1	5.6	4.1	3.5	2.9	1.4	Alabama	35.1	17.8	14.0	6.2	4.2	2.1
New Jersey	6.5	5.8	4.3	2.9	2.2	1.1	Mississippi	34.1	18.8	14.8	7.1	4.9	2.4
Pennsylvania	6.9	5.7	3.5	2.7	2.0	1.0	**West South Central:**						
East North Central:							Arkansas	21.3	10.2	7.6	5.0	3.6	1.9
Ohio	4.5	3.2	2.5	1.9	1.5	0.8	Louisiana	39.6	23.4	15.1	9.8	6.3	2.8
Indiana	5.2	2.5	1.8	1.7	1.2	0.7	Oklahoma	11.7	4.1	3.1	2.5	1.9	1.1
Illinois	4.8	3.8	2.7	2.3	1.8	0.9	Texas	15.6	8.9	7.3	5.4	4.1	2.2
Michigan	4.8	3.4	2.2	2.0	1.6	0.9	**Mountain:**						
Wisconsin	5.4	2.8	2.1	1.7	1.2	0.7	Montana	6.6	2.5	1.9	1.8	1.0	0.6
West North Central:							Idaho	5.1	1.7	1.2	1.3	0.8	0.6
Minnesota	4.6	2.1	1.4	1.5	1.0	0.6	Wyoming	4.4	2.3	1.8	1.7	0.9	0.6
Iowa	2.7	1.2	0.9	0.9	0.7	0.5	Colorado	4.5	3.6	3.1	2.0	1.3	0.7
Missouri	7.0	3.4	2.5	2.1	1.7	0.8	New Mexico	35.7	17.4	14.9	6.6	4.0	2.2
North Dakota	6.1	2.5	1.7	2.3	1.4	0.8	Arizona	30.0	15.9	11.0	6.2	3.8	1.8
South Dakota	5.8	1.9	1.4	1.5	0.9	0.5	Utah	3.6	2.2	1.4	1.4	0.9	0.6
Nebraska	2.6	1.5	1.3	1.2	0.9	0.6	Nevada	13.8	6.4	4.8	2.2	1.1	0.5
Kansas	3.3	1.8	1.4	1.3	0.9	0.6	**Pacific:**						
South Atlantic:							Washington	3.4	1.9	1.1	1.3	0.9	0.6
Delaware	13.2	6.6	4.4	2.7	1.9	0.9	Oregon	3.7	1.6	1.1	1.2	0.8	0.6
Maryland	12.1	6.1	4.2	2.7	1.9	0.9	California	5.3	3.6	2.8	2.2	1.8	1.1
District of Columbia	9.4	3.0	1.7	1.8	1.9	1.1	Alaska	40.6	24.6	20.5	6.3	3.0	1.5
							Hawaii	35.2	21.2	17.5	8.4	5.0	1.9

Source: U.S. Bureau of the Census, *Statistical Abstract of the United States: 1977* (98th edition), Washington, D.C., 1977.

were rationalized as being good for the ethnic minority. For example, in the late nineteenth and early twentieth centuries (and to some extent even today), Native American children were taken from their homes and placed in boarding schools:

[These schools were] designed to separate a child from his reservation and family, strip him of his tribal lore and mores, force the complete abandonment of his native language, and prepare him in such a way that he could never return to his people. (United States Senate Committee on Labor and Public Welfare, 1969)

Today, however, Native Americans, blacks, Hispanics, other ethnic groups, and, most recently, women and homosexuals are demanding the right to learn about their roles in our history and culture. It is now realized that ethnic studies and women's studies also promote cultural integration by pointing up the roles diverse groups have played in our national heritage.

Generation of knowledge.

One of the most frequently overlooked functions of education is the generation of new knowledge and technology. Colleges and universities are research institutes as well as schools. Many professors devote much of their time to such studies as filling in the blanks of history, unraveling the mysteries of genes and of outer space, developing new ways to build cities, and analyzing the way people behave during riots. The atom bomb—to choose an example with obvious social consequences—was invented not on a secret army base in the Arizona desert but in a laboratory under the stadium of the University of Chicago.

The ideal of learning generated on college campuses is "knowledge for knowledge's sake." But the reality of obtaining funds for costly, long-term projects makes the actual case quite different. The schools themselves weigh the prestige value and the income that will be derived from research projects. Foundations and government bodies that give grants generally expect that the research will lead to visible social or cultural progress. Corporation grants are awarded to projects that support company goals (Crittenden, 1981). Oil companies, for example, will contribute funds to find ways to increase fuel efficiency in automobiles, but they are unlikely to fund research to develop non-oil based fuels. The issue of corporate support for research at colleges and universities is becoming increasingly important. As Fig. 15.1 shows, corporate support for higher education has been increasing rapidly. Its importance has been underscored by the decrease in governmental funds to support higher education. These changes inevitably raise questions about the future impact of big business or higher education.

Nowhere is this concern more apparent than in the area of **biotechnology,** the industrial use of biological processes, including genetic engineering. Biotechnology is widely believed to be an important source of discoveries that will improve human health and the quality of life—increasing food and fuel production and genetic engineering, for example (Cocking, 1981). Naturally these developments have tremendous economic potential, and corporations are willing to invest large sums for research if they can control the use of the results (Crittenden, 1981). Universities are struggling with the question of just how much control they can give up and still

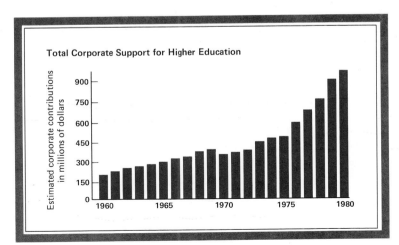

Fig. 15.1 / Corporate Support for Higher Edcuation

Source: *The New York Times*, July 22, 1981. p. D-1. © 1981 by The New York Times Company. Reprinted by permission.

Total Corporate Support for Higher Education

Estimated corporate contributions in millions of dollars

900
750
600
450
300
150
0

1960   1965   1970   1975   1980

maintain academic freedom, while at the same time they are faced with the need to bolster finances hard hit by fewer government dollars and, in some cases, declining student enrollments. At a conference in Toronto, Canadian universities were urged by a government official to forge links with existing corporations or to create their own companies to develop commercial applications of biotechnology (Cocking, 1981a). The outcome of this debate will have significant effects on the future role of higher education in the generation of knowledge.

Latent Functions

Besides these manifest functions, education also has consequences that may be less obvious but are no less important and real. Several of the latent functions of education are channeling students, caring for children, promoting a youth subculture, and changing attitudes.

Channeling students. In a 1969 article in the *Harvard Educational Review,* Arthur Jensen unleashed a thunderbolt that touched off a debate about an educational issue of profound importance: What causes the observed differences in the educational achievements of black and white youths? Jensen asserted that genetics were an important determinant of IQ, a position that seemed to infer that blacks were genetically inferior to whites. In the ensuing debate, many challenged Jensen's conclusions as well as his methodology. Sociologist Christopher Jencks (1972) was one of these critics. He took the problem beyond genetics, pointing out that inequality in educational attainment was part of social structural processes that supported a whole system of inequality. To solve the larger problem of inequality required a focus on changes well beyond the school: "As long as egalitarians assume that public policy cannot contribute to economic equality directly but must proceed by ingenious manipulations of marginal institutions

like the schools, progress will remain glacial" (Jencks et al., 1972: 265).

In the continuing debate over the way in which education relates to social inequality, the point that education is part of a larger institutional structure of inequality has been made repeatedly. Ogbu represents this position clearly in the following:

I do not think that differences between blacks and whites in cognitive and other skills can be explained in terms of black-white differences in "intelligence." I do not think that differences between blacks and whites in cognitive and other skills can be explained in terms of black resistance to acculturation, the failure of black parents to train their children as white middle-class parents do, or to biological differences between the two races. . . . What evidence there is suggests . . . that blacks would have developed their potentials for linguistic, cognitive, motivational, and other school-related skills to the same extent . . . if they had enjoyed the same opportunities as whites to be educated, to qualify for more desirable social and occupational positions, to occupy such positions when they qualified for them, to derive adequate financial and other rewards from their educations and jobs, to live where they desired and could afford, and to be evaluated as individuals on the basis of training and ability. (Ogbu, 1978: 4–5)

He supports his position with data comparing the educational experiences and outcomes of minority and majority groups in six other societies, three in which both groups are of the same race and three in which they are of different races (as in the United States). In all cases, Ogbu finds that educational disadvantage relates to similarly disadvantaged positions throughout the social structure.

Education, because it is tied to other social structures, becomes a mechanism through which students are **channeled**—guided into learning experiences that will prepare them for roles they will be expected to play as adults in society

Schools reflect the diverse educational needs of complex, industrial societies like our own. They range from private schools for the wealthy to vocational schools geared to preparing students directly for employment.

(Bowles and Gintis, 1976). Theoretically, this channeling proceeds on the basis of ability and effort alone; however, in most cases, middle-class children proceed through academic, college-preparatory programs, while lower-class children move into general studies and vocational programs. There are several reasons for this unofficial discrimination. First, aptitude and achievement tests are designed by middle-class professionals who more or less assume that all children play with blocks and puzzles, look at books, and visit zoos and national monuments. Children from poor families may have difficulty answering a question about buffaloes because they have never seen or heard of them, not because they are "slow learners." Similarly, elementary reading books, which focus on middle-class life experiences, may seem foreign to ghetto children.

The burden of low expectations falls heaviest on minority children—blacks, Hispanics, Native Americans—and the poor in general. With relatively few opportunities to achieve self-esteem in school, lower-class children are more likely to drop out before obtaining a diploma than are their middle-class counterparts. Indeed, sociologist Robert Mare (1981) points out that the increasing availability of schooling to all persons has not altered the fact that continuing in school is directly related to the socioeconomic origins of the student—the wealthier the family background of the student the greater the number of years of schooling that will be completed.

Unintentionally, then, our educational institution supports the class structure, channeling students from different backgrounds into different careers and different ways of life, preparing them for the places they will occupy on the social scale later in life. The inequality in the educational system "is a reflex of the inequality in the social structure. Schools are now, and they have always been, reflections of class structure, which they have reflected rather than altered" (Katz, 1973).

But the educational system tends to put students into categories on the basis of more than just economic advantage. Robert Rosenthal and Lenore Jacobson (1968) demonstrated that teacher expectations alone can influence student achievement. They chose a group of elementary school students entirely at random, but told the teachers that tests showed that these pupils were "late bloomers" who could be expected to advance rapidly during the coming school year. At the end of the year, the children were tested, and Rosenthal and Jacobson found that 47 percent of those labeled "late bloomers" had gained 20 or more points on the IQ test, as compared with 19 percent of the children who had not been singled out (Rosenthal and Jacobson, 1968). Apparently, through subtle encouragements and an optimistic attitude, the teachers had positively influenced the "special" students. Rosenthal and Jacobson reported their work in a book entitled *Pygmalion in the Classroom.* In Greek mythology, Pygmalion was a sculptor who carved his ideal woman out of marble. His statue was so beautiful that he fell blindly in love with his own creation. At last Venus took pity on Pygmalion, gave the statue life and Pygmalion's imagination became reality. Like Pygmalion, perhaps teachers mold students according to their imaginations, making them into what they want or expect them to be.

Unfortunately, the educational system is full of such cases in which students for one reason or another are presumed to be capable or incapable. If teacher (and peer) treatment reflects these assumptions, and if a student is encouraged to have a particular self-concept, the student is very apt to behave exactly as teachers and friends have come to expect. In other words, everyone—including the student—cooperates to bring about the result they all have come to expect. Such self-fulfilling prophecies are obviously harmful to those whose backgrounds or manners suggest they are somehow different, unwilling, or unable to perform. Those from middle-class or prestigious backgrounds are subtly aided by the favorable assumptions teachers make of them. In this way too, then, the educational system acts conservatively to route students into familiar channels or to return them to the same social status as their parents.

Caring for children. Schools also perform the latent function of providing custodial care for youth. The average student spends 1000 hours a year in school; only watching television takes up more time. The most obvious custodial service schools provide is keeping young people off the streets (where they could add to delinquency and crime) and out of the labor market (where they would have an impact on the unemployment level). When public school parents were asked if a problem student should be permitted to quit school, 82 percent answered "no" (Gallup Opinion Index, 1975). Schools are expected to "straighten out" problem students, not to turn them loose in the community at large. Schools also care for younger children whose mothers must or choose to work outside the home.

The amount of physical and psychological care a child receives in school depends on the wealth and priorities of the school district and its involvement in state or federally funded programs. Many schools provide medical screening of their students. They give physical examinations and tests for vision and hearing. Children with problems are referred to their private physicians or to public agencies. In times of epidemics, children may receive their inoculations or oral vaccines in the school itself. Some schools hire dental hygienists to clean and check the children's teeth. Children also receive psychological testing and may be seen regularly by a school psychologist or be referred to an outside agency. Even the feeding of children, once completely a function of the family, has to an extent been taken over by the schools. Some school districts now provide not only hot lunches, but also breakfasts.

Promoting youth subculture. The separation of people between the ages of six and 16 in peer groups has the latent consequence of promoting distinct, sometimes deviant, subcultures. In school, children are socialized by their peers as well as by their teachers. The protest movement of the 1960s and 1970s, for example, was in part the product of a youth subculture that developed on college campuses. In that period, students began to demand that the government be held accountable for the war in Vietnam and for civil rights at home. Of course, the activists were a minority, and only the most visible of many campus subcultures. They were distinguished from members of the vocational college subculture (composed mainly of ambitious working-class students) by both their relatively affluent backgrounds and their apparent lack of concern about future careers; from the "collegiates" (a set of students whose lives centered around

fraternities, dating, and football) by their commitment to social problems and their nonconforming appearance and life style; and from the "academics" by their preference for ideology over facts and scholarship (Clark and Trow, 1966).

While college and university campuses continue to reflect a range of students, some trends have emerged for the 1980s. Fraternities and sororities have regained the popularity they lost during the socially conscious 1960s and 1970s. This rebirth is associated with a rise in conservatism among students and less energy being devoted to campus social and political activities (Middleton and Roark, 1981). On the other hand, students are devoting more time to their studies, and in general have shown themselves able to deal maturely with greater personal freedom—in the area of sex and coed living on campus, for example. The pressures of late adolescence and early adulthood continue to challenge students, however, as is evidenced in such problems as high alcohol consumption and drug use on many campuses.

The educational institution reflects, as well as shapes, societal trends. The recent rise in popularity of fraternities and sororities mirrors the increasingly conservative attitude characteristic of college campuses during the 1980s.

TABLE 15.2 / SOCIAL CHANGE ON AMERICAN CAMPUSES

Type Activity	All Colleges/ Universities (percent)	Public Colleges/ Universities (percent)	Private Colleges/ Universities (percent)
Do provide student housing	92.7	90.0	94.0
Rules on visiting between men and women in dormitory rooms			
Permitted with restrictions	58.7	64.0	56.0
Prohibited	10.7	6.0	13.0
No rules	24.7	20.0	27.0
Rules on unmarried student couples sharing rooms			
Permitted on campus with restrictions	0.7	0.0	1.0
Permitted off-campus with restrictions	0.0	0.0	0.0
Prohibited on campus	84.0	82.0	85.0
Prohibited off-campus	12.0	0.0	18.0
No rules	87.3	100.0	81.0
Number of unmarried couples living together			
More than five years ago	30.7	40.0	26.0
61 Fewer than five years ago	6.7	6.0	7.0
No change	42.0	40.0	43.0
Amount of interracial dating			
More than five years ago	33.3	36.0	32.0
Less than five years ago	4.7	4.0	5.0
No change	54.7	52.0	56.0
Popularity of social fraternities and sororities			
More popular than five years ago	43.3	58.0	36.0
Less popular than five years ago	7.3	6.0	8.0
No change	18.7*	22.0	17.0
Provide counseling on sex problems	96.0	98.0	95.0
Provide gynecological services	67.3	84.0	59.0
Use of women's health services			
More than five years ago	41.3	56.0	34.0
Less than five years ago	0.0	0.0	0.0
No change	23.3	30.0	29.0
Homosexual-student organizations			
Present on campus	28.0	48.0	18.0
Prohibited	2.7	0.0	4.0
Officially recognized or supported	26.0	46.0	16.0
Campus attitude toward homosexual-student organizations			
More tolerant than five years ago	46.7	44.0	48.0
Less tolerant than five years ago	4.7	2.0	6.0
No change	46.7	52.0	44.0

* 32.7 percent of the colleges/universities did not have social fraternities or sororities.

Note: Percentages do not add up to 100 in all cases because of rounding, multiple responses, or nonresponses to inapplicable questions.

Source: The Chronicle of Higher Education, June 29, 1981, p. 4. Survey conducted for *The Chronicle of Higher Education* by John Minter Associates. Reprinted with permission of *The Chronicle of Higher Education.* Copyright 1981 by the Chronicle of Higher Education, Inc.

Changing attitudes. Finally, education seems to have a significant impact on people's attitudes. Numerous studies have shown that college graduates are far more tolerant of political and social nonconformity than are high school graduates, and that high school graduates are more tolerant than people who completed only grade school (Clark, 1962; Selznick and Steinberg, 1969). Education also seems to dispel stereotypes. A 1970 Harris Poll indicated that high school graduates tend to be suspicious of agreements with communist nations, uncomfortable with minorities, and hostile toward the youth subculture; college graduates are more open-minded (*New York Post,* April 30, 1970).

One reason higher education is so closely tied to attitude changes and increased social tolerance may be because campus life is itself a microcosm of social change. Recent research on sex on campus provides a case in point (Middleton and Roark, 1981). After a decade of increasing sexual freedom and coed living options, students have come to understand and respect sex as a part of relationships viewed in their totality. Rather than sexual freedom leading to promiscuous gymnastics, it has helped students to explore sex as only part of their relationships with other people. And, while sex may be important, it does not substitute for other types of human interaction. As a result of these changes, several trends are evident. Cohabitation is a common living alternative for many students. Second, interracial dating is accepted on many campuses. And third, homosexual students are "coming out" and forming officially-recognized social and educational groups (see Table 15.2).

These experiences cannot help but affect the way students view themselves and their world. As campus life exposes students to the human issues they will face when they graduate, they have the opportunity to better understand them and to grapple with them at first hand. The student subculture has always affected students' attitudes and behaviors. Now it appears that the student subculture is incorporating current changes in societal values and behaviors so that college students are better able to understand and accept them. We can therefore expect education to continue to be related to attitude changes and increased social tolerance.

THE ORGANIZATION OF EDUCATION

As we mentioned earlier, the need for education in complex industrial societies has given rise to a vast organizational structure to provide it. First, a person must devote several years to the occupation of *student* if he or she hopes to acquire a useful quantity of our culture's knowledge. "Student," of course, is a status and a role (Chapter 3) which is important to a society to help ensure its future. Second, the students are guided by teachers, whose role is to oversee their acquisition of knowledge. Teachers, of course, must be specialists in at least one field, and there must be many of them so that all general branches of knowledge are available to the students. Third, schools and school buildings must be specially designed places to organize teachers, students, and enormous quantities of books and special facilities such as comfortable classrooms, laboratories, theaters, and athletic equipment. And finally, the government oversees the entire organization, influencing funds and programs to fit the transmission of the knowledge and skills that it has identified as important for society. For example, certain books or subjects are considered unfit for official use in the classroom, while certain programs are initiated and heavily funded to encourage knowledge and training in various necessary subjects.

In the United States, formal educational structures come in many varieties and forms. The government maintains public education for the years of kindergarten through high school (K-12) (see Fig. 15.2). The public school system

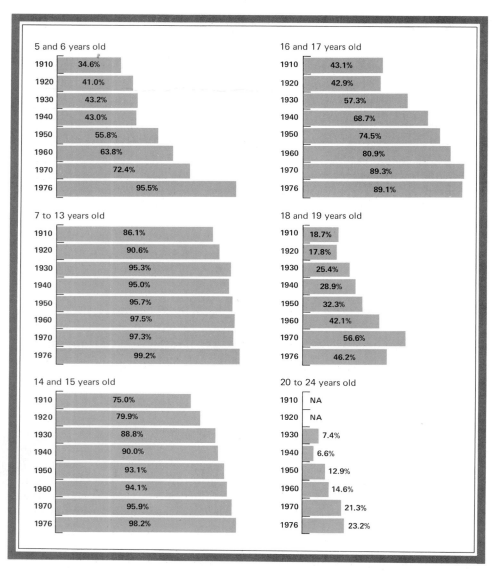

Fig. 15.2 / Percentage Enrolled in School by Age: 1910–1976

The greatest increases in enrollment in this century have been in the earliest years of schooling. The 1970s have experienced the first drop in enrollment among 16- to 19-year-olds since the 1920s.

Source: U.S. Bureau of the Census,
1970 Census of Population updated from
*Statistical Abstract of the United States:
1977* (98th edition), Washington D.C.,
1977.

TABLE 15.3 / EDUCATION IN AMERICA: A CONTINUING PRIORITY

The following two tables show that education is a major part of the society's expenditures, reflecting its importance in the social structure.

A. Expenditures for Education, Health, and Defense as a Percent of the Gross National Product: 1939–1976

Year	Gross National Product (in billions)	Expenditures for Education		Expenditures for Health		Expenditures for Defense	
		Total	*Percent of GNP*	*Total*	*Percent of GNP*	*Total*	*Percent of GNP*
1939	90.5	3.2	3.5	NA	NA	1.2	1.3
1945	212.0	4.2	2.0	NA	NA	73.5	34.7
1955	399.3	16.8	4.2	17.7	4.4	38.4	9.6
1965	688.1	45.4	6.6	40.5	5.9	49.4	7.2
1976	1,692.4	131.1	7.7	148.9	8.8	88.2	5.2

NA = Data not available.

B. State and Local Expenditures for Education and Other Needs: 1948–1977

Year	Expenditures for Education		Expenditures for Health*		Expenditures for Highways		Other Expenditures
	Millions of dollars	*Percent*	*Millions of dollars*	*Percent*	*Millions of dollars*	*Percent*	*Percent*
1948	5,379	30.4	3,328	18.8	3,036	17.2	33.6
1957	14,134	35.0	6,604	16.3	7,816	19.4	29.3
1967	37,919	40.6	14,858	15.9	13,932	14.9	28.6
1975	87,858	38.1	47,002	20.4	22,528	9.8	31.7
1977	102,780	37.5	58,946	21.5	23,058	8.4	32.6

* Includes expenditures for welfare.
Source: Social Indicators III, Washington, D.C.: U.S. Government Printing Office, 1980, p. 290.

is a complex network of independent organizations that attempt to coordinate the activities of some 45 million students, 2.3 million teachers, and 138,000 administrators. Expenditures for primary and secondary schools reached $64.8 billion in 1975. Education is big business (see Table 15.3).

In most nations of the world, the schools are run by one central agency, but in the United States, the public schools are run by local districts. Teachers, licensed by the state, report to principals and their administrative assistants (usually former teachers promoted through the ranks). These administrators are generally responsible for the daily activities of the students and teachers, hiring teachers, determining curriculum, communicating with students' families, and dealing with outside agencies. Principals report to the superintendents and boards of education that hired them. "Ninety-five percent of the school boards in the United States are elected, usually in a nonpartisan special election. Appointed school boards, however, are found in two of the largest school districts, those of New York city and Chicago" (Rich, 1974: 200). The functions of the school board include "the selection of the super-intendent, establishing educational policy, de-veloping the school budget, determining salary schedules, allocating funds for buildings and equipment" (Rich, 1974). Teachers' organiza-tions and unions also play a role in running the schools. Only rarely do parents' organizations have an appreciable influence. Student govern-ments are rarely given power; they are basically exercises in governing which serve as additional educational experiences.

The main source of funds for elementary and secondary education has traditionally been local property taxes. However, the share of costs contributed by the state and federal governments has been increasing, and in 1978–1979, for the first time state contributions exceeded total local contribution, although individual states vary widely in the proportion of the school dollars they provide to local school districts (Washington Social Legislation Bulletin, 1981: 59). Federal and state support is given in the form of indirect assistance: money for breakfasts and hot lunches; supplies and equipment, including state-ap-proved textbooks; building construction; and programs such as Headstart and special education.

Even though federal aid to education is indirect and small compared to state and local contributions and the federal government has no jurisdiction over public schools, its influence is strong. The government enforces legislative acts (such as laws against discrimination) and court decisions (such as orders to integrate schools) by threatening to withhold funds from recalcitrant districts.

In addition to public education, private schools have always existed as an alternative educational system. In 1980, over 20 percent of elementary and secondary school students attended private schools in some communities (Washington Social Legislation Bulletin, 1981: 59). Most people are aware of private colleges and universities, many of which are church-affiliated; however, private schools exist at all other levels as well. Montessori schools, private college preparatory schools ("prep

Like other private schools, parochial schools provide an alternative educational system serving the needs of special groups. Through private education, parents have greater control over the academic standards and social skills their children will receive.

schools''), and parochial schools are three examples of private schools that may encompass grades from kindergarten through high school. Private schools have also had periods of popularity to serve the needs and wishes of special groups. During school integration in the South in the 1960s, and during the busing controversies all over the country in the 1970s, private schools sprang up in areas where people wanted to avoid integration and busing. In the 1980s, fundamentalist religious groups have developed their own private "Christian" schools (including universities like Oral Roberts University in Oklahoma).

Private education has always been a way to give parents greater control over the type of education their children receive. Those wanting more rigorous academic standards and/or the teaching of social skills have usually selected preparatory schools. Strict discipline has traditionally characterized parochial schools, while fundamentalist schools emphasize particular "Christian" interpretations of human life. Private schools are subject to state licensing, but they have considerably greater freedom in most areas than do public schools. Ideally, public and private schools exist in a complementary fashion to give parents and students optimal choices in educational opportunities; however, there may be reason for societal concern if private schools attract so many students from the public sector that it is economically weakened. Problems can also arise when private schools are used to undermine societal efforts to achieve social justice and to ensure personal freedom.

ORGANIZATIONAL PROBLEMS: THE DILEMMA OF BUREAUCRACY

In the past quarter century, the United States has consolidated small rural districts into larger central districts intended to provide their students with a broader educational experience. It had been found, for instance, "that high schools with less than 100 students in the graduating class could not provide a curriculum with sufficient depth and range of course offerings" (Rich, 1974: 208). In 1960 there were 40,520 separate school districts in the United States, Their number dropped drastically to 15,781 by 1972 due to the continuing consolidation of small, rural districts into large, centralized ones. As further evidence of the changing structure of the school districts, in 1950 there were still nearly 60,000 functioning one-room schoolhouses. By 1970 their number had dropped to a mere 1800. But the problem at the other extreme—urban districts that are too large and unwieldy to run under the existing organization—remains with us.

In colleges and universities, the situation is different. The faculty nearly always has considerable autonomy in hiring instructors, in designing the curriculum, and in assigning courses and texts. The administration sets the overall policy for the school, approves faculty recommendations, raises and distributes funds, plans the construction of new buildings, and admits and processes students. The administration is responsible to its board of trustees; in state universities, to the state government. Most universities depend on government funds, particularly in the physical and social sciences. Government agencies tend to see the university as a public service institution whose main function is to train individuals for skilled jobs and to conduct research for the public good. Faculty members, on the other hand, consider the university as a place where individuals can pursue knowledge for its own sake, free from government and public scrutiny, wherever that knowledge may lead. Often faculty members are caught in a conflict between their roles as researchers and their roles as teachers. Students usually view the university as being at once a school and a community—*their* community. Colleges and universities thus serve the needs of several groups whose goals sometimes coincide and sometimes conflict.

RELATIONSHIPS WITH OTHER SOCIAL INSTITUTIONS

Education both influences and is influenced by the family, religion, and the political and economic systems. The school is one of the first social institutions outside of the family with which children come into contact, and the balance of their formative years is spent in a formal educational environment. Much of the educational process in the United States was once sponsored by religious denominations. Now, religion is not allowed in our public schools. Political awareness and participation are influenced by a student's level of educational achievement. Although most people want to keep educational issues out of politics, the increasing influence of the federal government on education has raised unavoidable political issues. The correlations between education and economic status are readily apparent. They are thought of as positive when it is pointed out that all people who attain a good education are apt to improve their economic standing, no matter what their background. But the correlations are looked upon with disapproval when it is pointed out that the poor have far less of an opportunity to receive a quality education than do the middle class or the wealthy.

I don't get it. When I was your age I'd made a million five. You can't even make your bed.

Reprinted by permission of Chronicle Features, San Francisco.

The Family

In studies of British children, Northwestern University sociologist Remi Clignet observed many connections between family structure and the student's achievement in school. For example, the relationship between family size and educational achievement may be negative.

Regardless of their position in the social structure, large families are characterized by a system of relationships between adults and children which discourages the explorative behavior demanded of pupils. The more children in a family, the less interaction develops between adult actors and each child and the less exposed is each child to adult vocabulary, syntax, and systems of logic. (Clignet, 1974: 50)

Furthermore, Clignet noted relationships between the position of a child in the family (oldest, intermediate, or youngest) and that child's scholastic performance. Although the oldest enjoys special contact with the parents, he or she has no immediate help in learning the rules of growing up. A middle child tends to identify strongly with the family as a group, and joins in by imitating brothers and sisters. The youngest child must try not to be thought of as inferior and may work harder to establish his or her place. Overall, Clignet found that "only" children and youngest children are most likely to succeed in school.

Viernstein and Hogan (1975) have shown that the achievement motivation of parents affects the educational aspirations of their offspring. Their research demonstrated that boys with high aspirations are most apt to have fathers and mothers with high aspirations. Girls with high aspirations also have fathers with high aspirations, but their mothers are most apt to have low aspirations. The boys are evidencing the "effective socialization of the norms of achievement" expected of them (p. 189). The girls, however, find themselves in role conflict, modeling themselves after the parent of the opposite sex. Their high aspirations may cause them anxieties that boys with similar aspirations do not experience.

There are innumerable, subtle ways that the family may function to support or discourage educational aspirations and opportunities for children. Making sure that children are prepared for school is important for successful performance; children require necessary supplies, clothing, and emotional support, for example. Being well fed boosts a child's energy level and his or her biological readiness to learn. Helping with homework provides encouragement, reduces frustration, and allows parents to make sure children follow through on completing assignments. Being interested in and rewarding good grades enables parents to reinforce the learning efforts of their children, although too much emphasis on grades can impede the learning process. Adult participation in the affairs of the schools—the PTA, fund raising activites, field trips, and so on— gives children the sense that school does have priority in the lives of those they love. This, of course, increases its importance in their own eyes. The family, then, is an important partner with the schools in achieving the educational goals of society.

Religion

A 1975 Gallup Poll asked if there should be an amendment to the Constitution that would permit prayers once again to be said in the public schools. An overwhelming 77 percent of the respondents answered that they were in favor of such an amendment. But despite such strong public sentiment, the Supreme Court continues to uphold the Constitution's separation of church and state as it applies to public education. For example, in a 1977 decision the Court disallowed the use of a textbook that presented only the Biblical interpretation of creation.

On the other hand, religion may greatly shape the content of education. Approximately one-third of the Catholic children in the United States attend parochial schools. There are also Yeshiva schools for Jewish children and church-related Protestant schools. Many schools founded by Protestant denominations, however, no longer stress religious education. Although parochial schools are run by religious groups, they are licensed by the state. In general, the main difference between parochial schools and public schools is one of focus: the former promote instruction in religious beliefs and practices and ethics; the latter are not allowed to include any religious instruction in their curricula. Since a 1962 Supreme Court decision, not even morning prayer is allowed in public schools.

The fact that some states provide funds for nonreligious activities in parochial schools has long been a source of controversy. Many people feel that even this is a violation of the principle of separation of church and state, of religious and political institutions. Others point to the fact that the church assumes much of the cost of educating a significant number of children, thus relieving the public education system of considerable expenses and responsibilities. Parents of children in parochial schools claim that they are doubly burdened; they pay taxes to support public education and tuition to support parochial education.

The resurgence of religion in the 1980s in the form of Far Eastern and fundamentalist Protestant sects revived the debate about the relationship of church, state, and schools. Members of these groups have pressed for curriculum content including Biblical interpretations of creation and for the elimination of sex education in the schools. They have sought greater control over school curricula so that what is taught more closely reflects their own religious beliefs. As noted earlier, in some cases these groups have formed their own private schools. These schools have sometimes been accused of providing indoctrination rather than education, and the massacre of Jim Jones' followers in Guyana was a chilling example of what can happen when people are taught to follow rather than to think. While public education continues to set standards which ensure that all licensed schools meet the basic educational needs of their pupils, there is little doubt that private schools can sometimes veer into areas that reflect ideology and indoctrination rather than fact and education.

The Political System

In 1957, the Soviet Union startled the United States by launching Sputnik, the first successful man-made space satellite. How had the Soviets been able to beat us? Why hadn't we developed the technical know-how first? Much of the blame was placed on the American educational system which, it was claimed, had not given enough emphasis to the teaching of the hard sciences and mathematics. To remedy this shortcoming, Congress in 1958 passed the National Defense Education Act, which provided massive funding for education in the sciences, mathematics, and modern languages (notably, Russian). The word "Defense" in the title of the act emphasized the direct role education was supposed to play in Cold War politics.

The relationship between education and the political system is usually more subtle, but it nevertheless is pervasive. Clignet (1974) summarized the findings of a number of studies on the relationship between educational achievement and political awareness and participation:

The political aspects of education are illustrated in this picture of a kindergarten playground in China. Before the recent "thaw" in Sino-American relations, children were using toy guns to shoot at a portrait of a hostile American.

. . . the scope of interaction developed by an individual varies as a direct function of his level of formal schooling. As this level becomes higher, the spectrum of political topics in which the individual is involved becomes broader. The higher this level, the wider is also the range of persons with whom this individual is willing to discuss political matters. Finally, the higher the level, the more the individual is likely to entertain optimistic feelings about the control he seems to be able to exact on his immediate surroundings. (p. 91)

Voter participation in elections also increases with educational level. In the 1972 presidential election, only about 51 percent of the eligible voters from households headed by someone with an elementary school education cast their ballots. For families headed by a high school graduate, the participation was closer to 62 percent. For families headed by a college graduate, voter participation approached 80 percent (National Center for Education Statistics, 1975). Although college graduates make up little more than 10 percent of the adult population, they comprise one-fourth of the electorate.

Since the government contributes heavily to education (see Table 15.3), it can subtly influence what is taught. This is most easily seen at the college and university level, where content is more specialized. When the Reagan Administration took office in 1981, it translated its pro-business and pro-defense policies into educational budgeting. Funds to support research and education in the arts and the social sciences were drastically reduced, but budgets were boosted in the areas of engineering and the "hard" sciences (American Sociological Association, 1981). Such budgeting shifts affect the number of faculty in various teaching areas, as well as available resources like books and classroom space. This, of course, has a direct influence on courses available to students and ultimately affects what they can study (and what they perceive they ought to study). While the government officially supports academic freedom, it can be a powerful force in

shaping the direction of education in the United States.

The Economic System

On the average, an individual with only an elementary school education will have lifetime earnings totaling less than half those of an individual with a college education, even though he or she will be in the work force for as much as ten years longer than the college graduate.

Success in school is directly related to the economic status of one's family. Robert J. Havighurst and Bernice Neugarten followed the academic careers of youths in the upper quarter of their classes. All these gifted youths from upper and upper-middle income households completed high school. Ten percent of their working-class counterparts failed to complete high school, despite their recognized ability. Ninety percent of the high-income youths entered college, whereas 76 percent of the low-income youths who had completed high school went on to college. But it was in college that the most striking difference occurred. A full 80 percent of the high-income youths who entered college completed at least a four-year program; but only 29 percent of the low-income youths completed their program (Havighurst and Neugarten, 1968).

Despite the inequities in educational success based on economic status, the educational system in the United States is still far more equitable than that in almost any other nation in the world (see Table 15.4). For instance, a black youth growing up in the South is more likely to attend college than is a young person growing up in Great Britain (Wattenberg and Scammon, 1967). And a 1973 study showed that:

. . . the academic elite among high school seniors (the top 9 percent) in the United States contained the largest percentage of children from lower-class (unskilled and semiskilled workers') homes of any of

TABLE 15.4 / FULL-TIME SCHOOL ENROLLMENT OF PERSONS 15 TO 24 YEARS OLD, SELECTED COUNTRIES: 1960 AND 1975

Country	15- to 19-year-olds		20- to 24-year-olds	
	1960	1975	1960	1975
Canada	49.2	66.4	7.0	14.5
France	32.5	51.3	7.3	9.9
Germany (Fed. Republic)	34.7	51.3	6.9	11.1
Italy	18.7	40.8	4.9	10.8
Japan	39.4	76.3	4.8	14.5
United Kingdom	16.6	43.9	4.9	7.5
United States	64.1	72.0	12.1	21.6

All figures are in percentages.
Source: Social Indicators III, Washington, D.C.: U.S. Government Printing Office, 1980, p. 303.

the nations surveyed. Specifically, the American lower-class segment constituted 14 percent of the entire group, compared with only 1 percent in West Germany. (Hechinger and Hechinger, 1975: p. 157)

EDUCATION IN MODERN SOCIETY

The Question of Control

There are several controversies over who should control educational organizations in the United States. Should the groups who use the school—students and community residents—have more control? Should the teachers have more influence? Or should our public system be completely discarded and replaced by a wide and varied choice of competing private schools?

The students. Often the last people who are asked what needs to be changed or improved in the educational system are the people most directly affected by it—the students and their community, parents, and employers who hope

that an educated youth population will strengthen the community's future.

When asked by the Gallup Poll "What would make school more interesting and useful to you?" the most frequent response of high school juniors and seniors was "wider variety of subjects" (35 percent), followed by "better or more interested teachers" (14 percent) (Gallup Opinion Index, 1975). These complaints are certainly worthy of attention. But how will the answers be found? It is difficult to foretell the future of a fast-paced modern industrial society. What subjects will be most useful to the students? And who can best decide such an issue? Society's leaders, who have the larger view of the most important social needs? Or the students themselves, who are able to identify their pressing personal needs? Students cannot be expected to run schools, but to what extent should their participation in decision making be encouraged and appreciated?

Everett Reimer has observed that schools are overcredited for the teaching of even such a basic skill as reading:

Literacy has . . . always run well ahead of schooling. According to census data, there are always more literate members of a society than persons who have gone to school. Furthermore, where schooling is universal, there are always children attending school who do not learn to read. (Reimer, 1971: 46)

Although many schools provide classes in specific vocational skills—from auto mechanics to typing—failure to build a foundation in "academic" skills still leaves the students unprepared for a successful career. If they are unable to read and to understand the manuals or the pamphlets or the instructions that make up part of their future jobs, they will certainly be handicapped in performing their chosen vocations.

The community. Many minority and community groups that had felt left out of the power structure found strength and solidarity in the civil rights struggles and the antipoverty programs of the 1960s, which encouraged community participation in decision making. With the rising sense of black pride and of *la raza* (pride among Hispanics) came a questioning of a faceless, impersonal educational bureaucracy that was unresponsive, if not outright hostile to them and their needs. Why, they asked, should they allow people from outside their community—people of different color and/or language, of different cultural experiences—try to make their children fit an alien model? Education, it was felt, must *serve* the community, not attempt to change it.

No doubt the proponents of community control recognize a real problem. Large, bureaucratically controlled school districts have failed to reach their educational goals with many students. But is community control an effective answer or only one element of a solution? Community control is indeed a radical answer, calling for no less than a "redistribution of power from the interests represented by central city governments to the poor" (Katz, 1971: 127).

The teachers. When parents are dissatisfied with their child's education, they usually blame the teacher because he or she may be the only member of the educational community with whom they come into contact. But parents are frequently unaware that it is not teachers, but politicians, bureaucrats, and school administrators who determine what books will be used, what teaching methods will be practiced, and what subjects will be emphasized or neglected. Many principals even tell their teachers how the classroom is to be structured and at what time of day particular lessons are to be taught.

Because of the size and complexity of the American educational institution, a certain amount of standardization of curriculum and of teaching procedures is necessary and desirable. But too much can be an obstacle to effective education. Teachers are professionals. Most have mastered the facts and figures of their subjects and they are also proficient in educational theory and many

teaching methods. They have the training and the experience to make decisions about basic classroom procedures and curriculum content. If they are not allowed to excercise these professional skills, they may become frustrated, unable to feel comfortable with someone else's decisions about their work. Many may lose their motivation to teach at all.

Furthermore, the teacher is the only person who has daily contact with the students. He or she is in the best position to decide what teaching methods will be most effective and how each lesson should be presented. Rigid teaching schedules and techniques cannot possibly be equally effective for a highly diversified student population.

For these reasons, there is a strong argument for teachers to have greater influence in educational decisions. As one critic of the present system has said, "Bright, creative, and well-educated people want to function as professionals, to make the decisions about how they will do their job. Education . . . has suffered from the suffocating atmosphere in which teachers have had to work" (Katz, 1971: 131).

The voucher system. A radical suggestion for improving the quality of education is to dismantle the public school system in favor of independent, competing systems. Parents would be given vouchers (financed as public schools are now, by taxes) that would be redeemable at whatever school they selected. A parent could choose a school where the three Rs were stressed or one that encouraged individual development. The environment could be rigidly disciplinarian or completely free and open. Proponents of the voucher system believe that this free-choice system would eventually level out. Poor schools would close because they could not attract students; good schools would flourish. But how long would this leveling out process take? Children remain in the educational system for between ten and twenty years. What could be done if it were realized that a student struggling in college was the victim of a poor choice in primary school? How many of these schools would feel compelled to alter or at least to dress up their records to make themselves look good in order to stay in competition? Some groups of parents would be better equipped to select the correct schools for their children than would others. What happens to the children of disinterested or misguided parents? What remains attractive in the voucher system idea is the possibility of alternatives and the great flexibility.

The Question of Goals

Besides the question of who should control the educational system, another major concern of education in modern society is what should be the goals of education. From a historical perspective, the disagreement over the goals of education is understandable. Our educational institutions have changed course several times. During the colonial period, the primary function of higher education was to train ministers to serve the established church. In the early republic, state-supported primary schools taught children

The founding of Harvard College in 1636 demonstrated the importance placed on education by the Puritans.

to read and to write and to perform a little arithmetic. Few children went on to higher education. With the massive influx of immigrants into the country in the nineteenth century, a major responsibility of the schools became the acculturization of foreign-born children. As industry required more and more skilled workers, diplomas became a prerequisite for employment. Education has become a big business with the primary goal of providing every child with the knowledge and skills needed to become a self-supporting citizen.

Career education versus general knowledge.
Economic pressures, worker dissatisfaction, student aimlessness, and any number of other social problems have led some observers to suggest that students be given not so much general education as specific training in a career of their choice.

Sidney P. Marland, Jr., former United States Commissioner of Education, proposed:

. . . a new orientation of education—starting at the earliest grades and continuing through high school—that would expose the student to the range of career opportunities, help him narrow down the choices in terms of his own aptitudes and interests, and provide him with the education and training appropriate to his ambition. (Marland, 1971: 25)

In the primary grades, the student would begin learning about the major career clusters—business and office, manufacturing, fine arts, and so forth. As his or her education progressed, the scope would narrow to one cluster, then to one specific career. In the end, ideally, "every student leaving school will possess the skills necessary to give him a start in making a livelihood for himself and his family" (Marland, 1971: 25).

Opponents object that such a program would necessitate even more rigid channeling of students than is now the case. Long before obtaining a degree, a student in a professional career track would be aware of his or her social superiority to a student in a service career track. Student groupings would have to be shifted as employment needs changed. The student population would exist to feed the needs of the economy, not necessarily the needs of the student. Besides, many employers are looking less for new employees trained in specific skills than they are for people with good work attitudes and basic knowledge. It is a commonplace that the first year or so on a first job is often spent forgetting much of the general knowledge taught in school and learning the special requirements of the job and the working world. Collins discovered that:

some employers indicated that they required high school degrees for manual workers, as one of them put it, "as an indication of character (perseverance, self-discipline, drive, etc.) rather than of knowledge." Several employers stated that high school degrees were now required of janitors and other low-ranking positions "in order that they may be able to read instructions." (1974: 440).

Compulsory versus optional education. For ten or more years students are compelled to attend schools. They must take and pass required courses in order not to be considered failures. The student must fit the program; relatively little effort is made to fit the program to the student. "The schools' failures to respond to the different needs of individual children, and even of specific groups of children, are not difficult to identify. . . . They spring in large measure from the mass education system's still heavy reliance on 'the one best.' " (Hechinger and Hechinger, 1975: 156).

Those in favor of giving students greater options ask why they should not be allowed to develop their own interests rather than be made to fit a predetermined set of standards. They argue that standardized programs may interrupt students' genuine interest in one class to make them change to another in which they are bored and consequently unproductive. They propose such alternatives as the open classroom, student contracts, and resource centers instead of classes.

In an attempt to raise the academic standards of their students 31 states have adopted standards of minimum competency for graduation from high school. The questions below are similar to those that appear on the literacy test administered by the state of Florida.

Mathematics

1. The Army had a special thirty-month recruitment program. Pat joined the Army on Oct. 1, 1977. When will Pat be discharged?
   A. April 30, 1979
   B. February 28, 1980
   C. March 31, 1980
   D. April 30, 1980

2. Mr. Jones maps out a route from Miami to Pensacola. The distance is about 685 miles. If Mr. Jones drives this distance in about fourteen hours, his average driving speed was about how many miles per hour?
   A. 40   B. 45
   C. 50   D. 55

3. A package of eight hamburger buns costs 65 cents. A package of twelve buns costs 95 cents. You need to buy four dozen buns. What would you save if you bought packages of twelve instead of packages of eight?
   A. $0.10   B. $0.30   C. Nothing. Cost is the same.   D. Nothing. You would lose money.

4. You are baking brownies in a nine-inch by twelve-inch pan. How many brownies will you have if you cut them into three-inch squares?
   A. 9   B. 12
   C. 27   D. 36

Communications

Two tourists to the Miami area, Bob Greene and Victor Hayes of New Jersey, suffered serious injury when their Ford van, driven by Greene, collided with a Chevrolet driven by Miami resident May Herndon. The accident occurred at 11 A.M. Saturday at West Dixie Highway and 25th Street.

The cause of the accident is under investigation and neither has been charged as of this report. Witnesses have stated that the van was out of control. At least one witness believes the driver of the van was "on something." Mechanical failure is another possibility.

Greene is listed in critical condition at Jackson Hospital. Hayes is listed as serious but stable. Herndon was treated for injuries and released last night. The investigation will continue.

5. Which of the following sentences is fact?

   A. Bob Greene was charged with reckless driving.
   B. Mechanical failure caused the accident.
   C. The investigation has been completed.
   D. Three people were injured.

6. Which of the following sentences is opinion?

   A. Bob Greene and Victor Hayes are visitors.
   B. The accident happened in the morning.
   C. The driver of the van was "on something."
   D. There are witnesses to the accident.

Fig. 15.3 / Raising Academic Standards
Source: *The Washington Post*, April 2, 1978. Reprinted by permission.

Opponents to these suggestions argue that students do not have the experience to make their own best decisions for a future of adult responsibility. They also point to plummeting scores of the Scholastic Aptitude Tests, which fell 49 points in math and 32 points in verbal scores between 1963 and 1978 (see also Fig. 15.3). These scores have traditionally been one of the strongest factors in college admissions. Furthermore, the opponents point to schools which have maintained rigorous academic standards and which have avoided the recent fads in education. These schools have generally shown little or no drop in S.A.T. scores.

Proponents of optional education claim that this line of argument is faulty. Traditional measures cannot be used for nontraditional students. Perhaps ultimately, the argument remains one of preference between conflicting cultural values. However, in the current trend of less radical social action, school practices seem to be returning to more traditional standards, and the phrase "back to basics" has already become a cliché.

The Question of Strategy

A higher percentage of the United States population attends school than is the case in any other nation. Despite our concern over the high school dropout rate—about one in every four who enter—it is lower than in almost any other nation. Education remains one of our leading priorities. We still heatedly debate questions of who should control the schools, what should be the goals of education, and, finally, how our schools can effectively serve more of the population.

Integration. The 1954 Supreme Court *Brown* v. *Board of Education* decision struck down the long-held doctrine of "separate but equal" educational facilities for blacks and whites. The Court concluded that segregation is inherently unequal and must cease as the policy of states and local school districts. Desegregation has been most pronounced in the South where *de jure* (recognized by law) segregation could be immediately attacked as unconstitutional. But where *de facto* (by circumstance) segregation prevailed, especially in large northern cities, desegregation is taking much longer.

The results of desegregation with regard to educational achievement are still inconclusive. We do know that standards have not been lowered, as some segregationists predicted. But neither has an upsurge in black achievement occurred, as many liberals had hoped. Desegregation may eventually break down racial barriers, but it is not having a strong immediate impact on educational achievement.

Desegregation has found new opponents from the black community. Blacks calling for community control of their schools realize that these schools will be more segregated than ever, with blacks also dominant in the teaching staff and administration. But they feel that they are best qualified to identify and serve their own needs. Overcoming their educational handicaps (due, they believe, to white neglect) in their own way in their own community is, they feel, better than trying to cope with a school system geared to and controlled by the white middle class.

Who gets bused? When many people in the 1960s said that they were for law and order, they really meant that they favored the repression of dissenters—be they political (antiwar) or civil rights activists, hippies, or rioting slum dwellers. Similarly, many people who say that they are opposed to busing are really voicing their opposition to school integration. Busing had been with us long before it became controversial. "Nearly 20 million children had been going to school by bus (not counting those who used regular public transportation) before it was proposed that busing be turned into a desegregation device'' (Hechinger and Hechinger, 1975: 272). Whites, with the means to do so, willingly leave their urban neighborhood schools behind them and move to the suburbs where their children must be bused to centralized schools. It is the poor whites who cannot afford to move to the suburbs and their black counterparts, who are blocked by racial barriers as well, who are compelled to take part in busing as a tool for integration. Affluent whites and a scattering of black elites have fled the problems of inner-city schools. Poor whites and poor blacks are left to share inferior urban schools. The class overtones of busing cannot be denied. Until it can be shown that the children—black and white—are being bused to better schools, the value of busing as an educational tool is open to question. It is little wonder, then, that busing as an effective way to achieve integration is being attacked. Still, other means have yet to be developed, leaving many

to wonder whether busing, for all its flaws, isn't better than nothing at all.

THE FUTURE OF EDUCATION

Everyone in the United States is involved in education. Unlike religion, it is not an elective institution. Individuals may choose to take no part in religion. And individuals can decide to avoid all but passive involvement in our political system: they need not vote or support political candidates or parties. But we all must attend school for ten of our childhood years, and every parent must then in turn send his or her children to school. Furthermore, even people without children must support education through taxes.

The concept of basic education has expanded from six to eight to twelve years. One needs a high school diploma to qualify for even some

In an earlier day, a break from classroom routine might have meant a visit and demonstration from the local iceman. Modern education regularly supplements traditional classroom work with specialized equipment intended to be highly motivational and individualized.

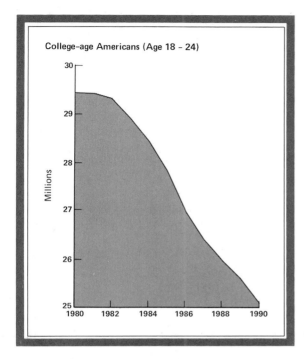

College-age Americans (Age 18 - 24)

Fig. 15.4 / The Decline in College-age Americans.

to close some, class sizes have declined. In extreme cases, greatly reduced student enrollments have meant that students are being bused to more populated districts so smaller boards of education can save money by closing whatever schools existed in the district. The problem of fewer students is, of course, financial. The cost of educating each student rises when the full range of services have to be provided for fewer students. In communities already struggling with inflation and high taxes, providing quality public education for fewer students at higher cost represents a serious issue.

At the college and university level, the decline in the number of traditional college age students (18–22) (see Fig. 15.4) has so far been balanced by the influx of what are often called **nontraditional students:** older students returning to school after years of work, women seeking new life opportunities after raising families, minority students who were previously financially unable to continue in school, and students who go to school while working full time (Washington Social Legislation Bulletin, 1981: 59). These students have distinctive educational strengths and needs. They are usually highly motivated and bring a rich fund of life experience on which to build their educational programs. On the other hand, they often have other life responsibilities that make it difficult for them to attend classes during traditional hours. As a result, classes must be scheduled for evenings, on weekends, or at other times which accommodate the demands of work and family responsibilities. These students sometimes have had poor academic preparation prior to college, and they may lack sound study skills. As a result, remedial and support services are important for them. And finally, the ability to spend many hours studying in the library is often limited. Instructors have to be creative in finding supplemental learning assignments that are more manageable for the nontraditional student.

The nontraditional student is often more interested in career-oriented programs than in

unskilled or semiskilled jobs. Besides expanding in length of time, education has expanded in breadth of content. Moral development, once the responsibility of religion and the family; health care, once a family responsibility; and vocational training, once gained in the economic sphere on the job, have in many ways been co-opted by education.

The 1980s have brought two new concerns to the fore in American education. In the primary and secondary grades there has been a steadily declining student population, the result of the end of the baby boom (Washington Social Legislation Bulletin, 1981: 59). In larger school districts selected schools have been closed. In smaller districts, which have too few schools to be able

regular liberal arts degrees. This change in goals has pressured liberal arts colleges to introduce new programs to supplement their traditional offerings, a process which has been fraught with turmoil and change. Some schools have tried unsuccessfully to make this shift; others have elected not to do so—and they have closed as a result. Others have had difficulty maintaining academic standards in the process of change and redirection. Since nontraditional students are usually local people, they do not board on campus. In order to tap this population, especially in the face of declining enrollments among traditional students, some schools that were previously sex-segregated have begun accepting men and women. And schools that attract many older students find that they often have to be helped to adjust to

academia (Gilinsky, 1981). While some bemoan the changes in higher education precipitated by its changing student population, others believe that colleges and universities are now more vital, responsive organizations than they have been in recent years. This greater responsiveness to student needs will no doubt be further encouraged by the fact that many big corporations are offering remedial and advanced education for their employees, even to the point of offering to finance degrees (Maeroff, 1981). This competition will probably touch off further efforts by colleges and universities to appeal to students. Whatever one's perspective may be, there is little doubt that higher education is experiencing a period of substantial change which is expected to continue at least through the 1980s.

SUMMARY

1. The main purposes of this chapter are to define education as a social institution; to explain the manifest and latent functions of education; to outline educational organization; to describe the relationship between education and the other major social institutions; and to explore the problems of education in modern society.

2. Education is the social institution that provides for the transmission and generation of knowledge. Institutionalized education is not necessary in societies where children learn by observing and assisting their parents. In industrial societies, however, cultural knowledge and occupational training are too complex for such informal methods of learning.

3. Education performs several manifest functions that are essential to society: the transmission of knowledge and skills, cultural integration, and generation of knowledge. In addition to these functions, education has less obvious (but still important) latent functions including channeling students into social positions, caring for children, promoting a youth subculture, and changing people's attitudes.

4. Complex industrial societies have developed a vast organizational structure to handle the need for education. This structure involves students, teachers, schools (public and private), and usually some governmental units to oversee the whole organization. In the United States, public schools are run by local districts and are funded primarily from property taxes with some state and federal aid.

5. Education both influences and is influenced by other major social institutions; the school is one of the first social institutions outside of the *family* with which children come in contact; in the past, *religion* sponsored much of the educational process, while today it is not allowed in public schools; *political* awareness and participation are influenced by the level of education; and there is a correlation between the level of education and *economic* status.

6. Education currently faces many difficult problems in the United States. One problem involves the question of who should control the educational organizations—students? the community? teachers?

   A second question involves the goals of education. Should it provide specific career education or general knowledge? Should the curriculum be compulsory or optional in design?

A third area of concern involves the strategy of how to make education accessible to more of the population. Can this be accomplished through integration and busing?

7. The future of education will be heavily influenced by changes in the size and composition of the student population. These changes are expected to continue throughout the 1980s.

REVIEW

Key Terms

Education   Biotechnology   Channeling   Nontraditional students

Review and Discussion

1. Have you been channeled by your education? Why do you feel as you do? What factors influenced the direction you have taken? If you feel you were channeled toward one path when you preferred another, how has this conflict affected your educational career and attitude? How could this problem be corrected for future students?

2. How has education affected your experiences in the other major social institutions?

3. Remembering that social institutions include organizational structures as well as values and norms, list as many factors as you can which make it difficult for the education institution to respond to the following social changes: (1) a sharp decline in the number of young people between the ages of 6 and 12; (2) an increase in the number of older and part-time students; and (3) the development of new knowledge areas, such as computer science.

4. On many college campuses, students are demanding a role in setting requirements and designing curricula. Construct arguments for and against this idea. (Remember the goals of education, preserving traditions and sparking innovation, and the college professor's dual role as teacher and researcher.)

5. Government cutbacks in funds for college students have forced many people to reassess whether they can afford to attend college. Do you think the government should help students to go to college? What can you see as the advantages and disadvantages to the individual and society of whatever position you take?

Experience with Sociology

Education serves many important functions for society, as we have seen. For the individual, it allows for cognitive growth and intellectual enjoyment, as well as preparation for social roles. For society, education is an important socialization mechanism and ensures that people will be ready to perform the wide range of tasks important for society's survival. The operational structure of education has still other functions: it provides employment for many people and channels young people into constructive activities. This helps to reduce their participation in destructive activities and delays their entry into the labor market. For both individuals and society, then, education is a very significant social institution.

Unfortunately, education is also increasing in cost. Education through age 16 is required by law, but beyond that, options are available. Although most people consider the completion of high school highly desirable, going on to college is often judged to be less essential. As the cost of college has increased, the question of whether or not to go has become a more serious one. In Module 9 of *Experience with Sociology,* you will have the opportunity to use data to examine the advantages and disadvantages of a college education. This module is a good example of how sociological data are useful in day-to-day decision making.

References

American Sociological Association (1981). *Footnotes* 9, no. 5 (May 1981): 1ff.

Bowles, Samuel, and **Herbert Gintes** (1976). *Schooling in Capitalist America.* New York: Basic Books.

Clark, Burton H. (1962). *Educating the Expert Society.* San Francisco: Chandler.

Clark, Burton H., and **Martin Trow** (1966). *College Peer Groups: Problems and Prospects for Research.* Chicago: Aldine.

Clignet, Remi (1974). *Liberty and Equality in the Educational Process.* New York: John Wiley.

Cocking, Clive (1981a). Biotechnology: Too risky for universities? *The Chronicle of Higher Education,* June 29, 1981, p. 9.

——— (1981b). Canadian universities urged to bolster corporate science ties. *The Chronicle of Higher Education,* June 29, 1981, p. 9.

Collins, Randall (1974). Where are educational requirements for employment highest? *Sociology of Education* 47: 419–42.

Crittenden, Ann (1981). Industry's role in academia. *The New York Times,* July 22, 1981, p. D1.

Gallup Opinion Index (1975). Report #115. January 1975. Princeton, N.J.: The American Institute of Public Opinion.

Gilinsky, Rhoda M. (1981). Easing the problems of college reentry. *The New York Times,* August 30, 1981, Sec. 12, pp. 9ff.

Havighurst, Robert J., and **Bernice Neugarten** (1968). *Society and Education.* Boston, Mass.: Allyn and Bacon.

Heap, Ken (1977). *Group Theory for Social Workers.* New York: Pergamon Press.

Hechinger, Fred M., and **Grace Hechinger** (1975). *Growing Up in America.* New York: McGraw-Hill.

Jencks, Christopher, Marshall Smith, Henry Acland, Mary Jo Bane, David Cohen, Herbert Gintis, Barbara Heyns, and **Stephen Michelson** (1972). *Inequality: A Reassessment of the Effect of Family and Schooling in America.* New York: Basic Books.

Jensen, Arthur (1969). How much can we boost IQ and scholastic achievement? *Harvard Educational Review* 29: 1–123.

Katz, Michael B. (1971). *Class, Bureaucracy, and Schools.* New York: Praeger.

——— (1973). On crisis in the classroom. In *Education in American History,* ed. Michael B. Katz. New York: Praeger.

Maeroff, Gene (1981). Business is cutting into the market. *The New York Times,* August 30, 1981, Section 12, pp. 1ff.

Mare, Robert (1981). Change and stability in educational stratification. *American Sociological Review* 46 (February 1981): 72–87.

Marland, Sidney P. (1971). *American Education* VII: 25–26.

McQuail, Denis (1975). *Communication.* New York: Longman.

Middleton, Lorenzo, and **Anne C. Roark** (1981). After the sexual revolution: Campus life without old rules. *The Chronicle of Higher Education,* June 29, 1981, p. 3ff.

Ogbu, John (1978). *Minority Education and Caste.* New York: Academic Press.

Reimer, Everett (1971). *School is Dead.* Garden City, N.Y.: Doubleday.

Rich, John Martin (1974). *Challenge and Responsibility.* New York: John Wiley.

Rogers, David (1968). *110 Livingston Street.* New York: Random House.

Rosenthal, Robert, and Lenore Jacobson (1968). *Pygmalion in the Classroom.* New York: Holt, Rinehart & Winston.

Ryan, William (1976). *Blaming the Victim,* rev. ed. New York: Vintage Books.

Selznick, Gertrude Jaeger, and Stephen Steinberg (1969). *Tenacity of Prejudice.* New York: Harper and Row.

U.S. Department of Health, Education and Welfare (1975). Washington, D.C.: National Center for Educational Statistics.

U.S. Senate Committee on Labor and Public Welfare (1969). Indian education: A national tragedy—A national challenge. Report no. 91-501. 91-501. Washington, D.C.: U.S. Government Printing Office.

Viernstein, Mary Cowan, and Robert Hogan (1975). Parental personality factors and achievement motivation in talented adolescents. *Journal of Youth and Adolescence* 4:183–89.

Washington Social Legislation Bulletin (1981). Washington, D.C.: Social Legislation Information Service, Aug. 10. 1981 (Vol. 27, Issue 15).

Wattenburg, Ben J., and Richard M. Scammon (1967). *This USA.* New York: Pocket Books.

16

THE ECONOMIC INSTITUTION

Few of us could adequately provide ourselves with a steady supply of life's essentials. Instead, we require goods and services others can make available to us. The economic institution provides for the regular exchange of such necessities. In the harsh Kalahari desert of southern Africa, hunters stalk a giraffe for days with hand-fashioned spears. When the hunt is over, they share their kill with all the members of their band, as they have always done. On our frontier, farmers who built their own houses and grew their own food traded livestock for cloth, tools, and guns at the town store. Sometimes they paid for medical care in the same way; money was scarce. On Madison Avenue today, advertising executives sell the creative talents of their firm's copywriters and artists to companies in search of markets, sometimes earning six-figure salaries for their work. They spend this money on houses and cars, books and restaurant meals, the services of doctors and tailors, and private schools. They invest in other companies through the stock market. Although there is a world of difference between the Kalahari hunter, the nineteenth-century frontiersman, and the successful ad executive, all are satisfying basic needs and desires according to the customs of their society. All are participating in the **economic institution:** the social structure which provides for the production, distribution, and consumption of goods and services.

THE IMPACT OF INDUSTRIALIZATION

Not since the emergence of agriculture some 9000 years ago has a change in the means of economic production had such a major impact on human life as has industrialization. **Industrialization** is the shift from human and animal power to the widespread use of mechanical power in the production process. Since the middle of the last century, one society after another around the world has experienced a transition from an economy based on limited agriculture or trade to one based on mechanical mass production of goods and services. Typically, mass production first affects a society's agricultural output, creating surplus food and labor to support other economic activities.

Industrialization did not occur all at once, but the shift was pronounced enough in eighteenth-century England to be identified as the Industrial Revolution. From England, industrialization first spread to western and northern Europe and then to the United States at the beginning of the nineteenth century. The process continues today in many areas of Asia, Africa, and Latin America.

Preindustrial societies were characterized by a subsistence economy. Each family produced most of what it needed and obtained what it could not produce through barter. There was virtually no surplus of food or goods to sell and no surplus time to supply services to others. This hand-to-mouth existence provided no opportunity to amass the means of improving one's situation. Because it was the source of badly needed food, land was of prime importance. The landowners dominated society, becoming its aristocracy. The more land, the more food, and food was power over those who owned nothing and had to live by farming large estates in return for such necessities.

A complex interrelationship of conditions made industrialization possible and was in turn affected by industrialization. Industrialization could not emerge until power had shifted from isolated feudal lords to a centralized nation state. The central government required a sophisticated transportation and communications system to maintain control and to collect taxes. This system also encouraged trade and the flow of raw materials and finished products. The capital of the nation also became, in most cases, the center for banking and commerce (the United States is an exception). Banks and other financial institutions such as stock markets and investment firms developed to bring together and to distribute the

During the early part of the nineteenth century, the labor force in the United States was primarily agricultural. Agriculture has traditionally been a family occupation, with all family members contributing to the overall effort. Only with the rise of industrialism did home and family separate from the work place.

vast sums of money required for large-scale capital investment. Major cities developed around these administrative and commercial centers.

The increase in the percentage of industrial workers was at the expense of the agricultural workers. In 1820, 72 percent of the employed United States labor force worked in agriculture. By 1870, those engaged in agriculture had dropped to 52 percent. In 1920, they comprised 29 percent; in 1978, only 3.0 percent. Agriculture itself had become industrialized. Mechanized farms could be operated with far fewer manual workers. Not all farm workers were attracted to the city, but they had no choice except to move there if they hoped to find work. Dislocated farm workers, together with immigrants (the majority of whom had been farm workers), provided the large, cheap labor pool required by fledgling industry.

The economic labor unit became the individual worker, not the farm family. Large families, once needed to work the farm, became a burden to the urban worker. Family members too young or too old to work in industry were just more mouths to feed. And every morsel of food had to be bought with money. Workers no longer owned what they produced. They were wage-dependent and needed money for goods. Before unions became effective and governments instituted such programs as unemployment insurance, workers were completely dependent on their employers.

Initially, industrialization required primarily unskilled labor. But as industry became more sophisticated, trained and specialized workers, managers, and executives were needed. Also needed were technicians and scientists to improve production capabilities and to develop new products. "Brain" power became even more important than "brawn" power. In this century, a large, powerful managerial class and a smaller, but influential, "technocrat" class has developed.

The wealth accumulated from profits and investments has replaced land holdings as the badge of success and power. Through monopolies, interlocking directorates, and special consideration gained through campaign contributions and lobbying, a few individuals and their corporations wield considerable influence over political institutions. Labor unions have also gained considerable political influence through their ability to disseminate views they favor, organized campaign workers, and encourage whole blocs of the electorate to vote "labor." In many industries, unions now work together with management in setting work policies.

The net effect of industrialization has been to drastically change the economic institution and related social values. In so doing, it has also had an impact on the other major social institutions—the family, education, the political system, and even religion.

MANIFEST FUNCTIONS

Living as we do amid seemingly endless supplies of items designed for our comfort and convenience, we easily forget that, at its most basic level, the economic institution deals with our elementary needs—food, clothing, and shelter. Not only must we have these things for our very survival, but, to make matters more pressing, they are scarce or difficult to obtain. This essential problem of supply and demand becomes more apparent when we consider all the things upon which modern life depends daily—such commodities as petroleum, electricity, and medical care. To ensure that all the things a society wants or needs are generally made available to its members, the economic institution organizes the manner in which these things are produced, distributed, and consumed (Moore, 1973).

Production

The production of goods involves the use of land, labor, and capital (Moore, 1973: 360). In preindustrial and agricultural societies, land was the primary source of production. From it came food, as well as the elements used to make the other necessities of life: wood for fuel, housing, and boat-making; cotton for clothing; reeds for making baskets; stone for tools and weapons. The land also supported animal life which was itself a source of food and items made from animal skins, bone, and so forth. Industrialization

reduced the need for and value of land, substituting technology as the primary source of productive capacity. Land, of course, continues to be a basic source of raw materials; however, synthetic goods (such as clothing fabrics like polyester or nylon) have replaced many goods that were previously only available from natural sources. Even the land's ability to produce has been greatly affected by technology. The troublesome outbreak of a Mediterranean fruit fly infestation in agricultural areas of California in 1981 is an example. Without aerial spraying of insecticides, crops would have been destroyed.

Industrialization shifted the basis of production from land to **capital,** or goods accumulated for the production of other goods. Money invested in the stock market (with the hope that it will make more money) is capital. So is a carpenter's collection of tools, with which he or she hopes to earn money in order to buy better tools and expand business. Land is *labor intensive,* meaning that many people are needed to carry out the tasks necessary to make it productive. This is true even in an era of sophisticated agricultural technology—tractors have to be driven and animals cared for. Industry, in contrast, is *capital intensive,* requiring heavy investments of money to obtain needed buildings, equipment, supplies, and workers or labor (see Fig. 16.1). While many industrial processes are performed mechanically, labor is needed to operate machines, program computers, inspect output, sell products, and so on. Workers, in turn, need jobs to earn money since most people no longer are able to support themselves from land that they own. This, of course, is the situation described by Marx: the means of production (factories and the capital to run them) are owned by one group, while the labor is provided by another.

Industrialization involves the organization of large numbers of people into complex, specialized work structures. It is built on the division of labor, enabling people to perform efficiently those work activities for which they have been trained either through schooling or experience. In Chapter 11 various aspects of the bureaucracy as a

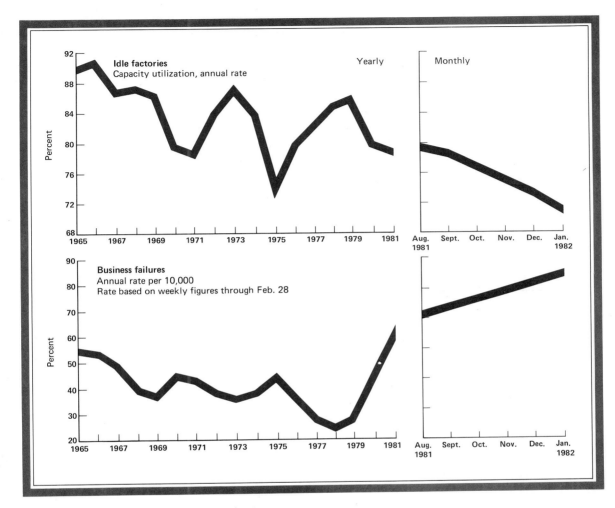

Fig. 16.1 / Indicators of Depressed Production

Production depends on active factories and healthy businesses. Inactive factories and business failures depress production and contribute to an economic recession.
Source: *The New York Times,* March 14, 1982, Section 3, p. 1. © 1982 by The New York Times Company. Reprinted by permission.

work structure were explored at length. Here we can simply refer back to the importance of worker motivation for the efficient functioning of large-scale formal organizations. Later in this chapter we will look at labor unions as a critical force mediating the interaction of workers and the whole industrial structure of production.

Distribution

Once clothing, food, shelter, and other goods are produced, society faces the problem of distribution. Some societies favor the ceremonial exchange of goods, as in the Kalahari desert. Others rely on bartering, where people with different goods exchange them for those they need in proportions that assure relatively equal value. While barter has not been a common part of the United States economic system, part of the airline deregulation that took place in the early 1980s allowed airlines to barter by exchanging transportation for needed services. For example, an airline could offer tickets with a set value to a newspaper in exchange for an amount of advertising space in that newspaper. In industrialized societies, however, distribution occurs primarily through the **market,** a system of distribution which uses money as a generalized means of exchange (Moore, 1973: 375).

In order for markets to operate, a number of other structures are critical. *Advertising* is needed so that consumers are aware of products. *Banking* and *credit* are used to manage the flow of money in the market, and to make money available both to producers (to pay for production costs) and to consumers (to facilitate expensive purchases). *Transportation* is critical for the movement of goods so that they can be made available to consumer groups. Transportation is also part of the movement of goods in the production process.

In addition to the distribution of goods and services, an industrialized economic system distributes money in the form of income from wages, interest, and returns on investments. In all industrial societies, there are considerable differences in the income received by members of different groups. Let us take wages as an example. In 1981, the salary of the president of the Rouse Company, a major real estate development firm, was reported as $427,500 a year (Demarest, 1981: 53). Even before the baseball strike in 1981, the average salary of players for the New York Yankees was $242,937; for the Oakland As it was $54,994 (Eskenazi, 1981: 65). In contrast, the average salary for a full professor at colleges and universities in the United States during 1980–1981 was $33,450 (Hansen, 1981: 215). In the country as a whole, the median income for white families in 1980 was $21,900, while it was $14,720 for Hispanic families and

Bartering is the oldest and most direct means of distribution.

$12,670 for black families (*The New York Times,* August 21, 1981: A12). In a market economy, such differences in income inevitably result in similar disparities in the ability to purchase goods and services.

Consumption

Consumption is the use of goods and services produced in an economic system. Four major units of society are consumers: private households (individuals and families); agencies of government at the federal, state, and local levels; manufacturing or business establishments; and nonprofit organizations (such as schools and churches) (Moore, 1973: 382). Each of these units makes decisions about what will be consumed. These decisions are influenced by the strength of the need for the product, the price, and knowledge as well as availability of options (see Fig. 16.2). In some areas, there may be little discretionary power over what will be consumed. The Reagan administration, for example, was reluctant to cut defense expenditures because it feared that doing so would make the United States appear to be vulnerable militarily. In other instances, there may be more choices. When car shopping, we can choose between imports or several brands of domestic models. Indeed, it is usually even possible to decide to keep the old car and fix it up, rather than buying a new one.

As noted above, consumers have to be aware of products in order to purchase them. Advertising takes on tremendous importance since it serves this function; however, it can also be used in misleading ways to manipulate consumers. We have all seen laundry detergent ads on TV that promise whiter clothes—but we are not told whiter than what. Advertising is also used to create perceived needs. We are told that only the latest styles enhance our image, even though last year's clothes still serve our needs for warmth and protection. Almost the reverse case is true of government expenditures. There the effort may be to reduce consumption in order to reduce taxes (thereby increasing the consuming power of private households). This, of course, simply shifts the type of consumption. Rather than governmental expenditures for the common good (public transportation, social services, education, and the like), there is more emphasis on personal expenditures for things like clothes, entertainment, vacations, and so forth. The Reagan Administration's tax cuts in 1981 moved very strongly in the direction of encouraging personal consumption and reducing governmental consumption (*U.S. News and World Report*, 1981).

Part of our belief in encouraging consumption by individuals comes from our capitalist economic system. We believe in free markets

Fig. 16.2 / *Unemployment and Consumption*

In Western, industrialized societies, consumption depends on income from employment. Rising unemployment in the 1980s has been a significant factor in the depressed consumption characteristic of the economic recession of the period.
Source: *The New York Times*, March 14, 1982, Section 3, p. 1. © 1982 by The New York Times Company. Reprinted by permission.

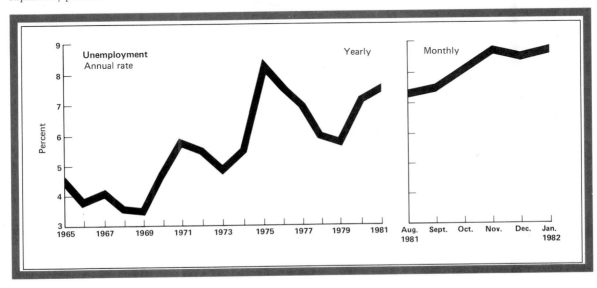

determined by consumer choice. When, for example, the gasoline shortages of the 1970s shifted consumer preferences to smaller, more fuel efficient cars, people felt free to buy such cars even though most of them were foreign-made. Our free market ideology combines with a societal value on self-reliance to generate some resistance to providing services and goods collectively. The famous Proposition 13 in California and the similar Proposition 2½ in Massachusetts restricted the taxing power of those two states. This legislation was passed because people felt government was controlling too many goods and services; and that it had become inefficient in the process. Similar feelings at the national level may have been an ingredient in Ronald Reagan's presidential victory in 1980—"big government" was seen as bad. Limiting collective funds means, of course, that services have to be cut back. In Boston, for example, subway stations were closed, park maintenance was cut back, and fire protection was reduced. It may be that voters are choosing to cut back on these services as an alternative to gradual loss of control over personal income—and hence consumption decisions—through escalating taxes.

LATENT FUNCTIONS

Industrialization has also had profound, unintended consequences for society. Most obviously, ties to the land were broken when individuals began to leave the towns in which they were born for jobs in the city. Industrialization made physical and social mobility possible and mass education necessary. Urbanization is primarily a product of industrialization. So is mass communication. Progress and efficiency have largely replaced tradition in the value system. More and more, people are future-oriented. These are only some of the latent functions of industrial economic institutions.

While teaching is a well-respected, white-collar profession whose members enjoy more social status than truck drivers, the blue-collar workers, nevertheless, earn more than most teachers.

Creation of Social Classes

Another of the latent functions of the economic institution is the creation and maintenance of social classes. The rise of capitalism in Europe and the United States created a new class of merchants and entrepreneurs who gradually acquired the power and prestige that once had belonged exclusively to the landed aristocracy. The Russian Revolution had a similar effect: it created a new class of party officials who enjoyed the power and prestige—if not the wealth—of their feudal predecessors. Except in societies where people live at a subsistence level, the distribution of goods and services is always unequal.

One's job often determines where one falls in the social hierarchy. Thus it is not income alone that determines prestige, but also one's position in the production process. Among laborers, there are clear distinctions between unskilled, semiskilled, and skilled workers. Then there is a vast and sometimes illogical chasm between blue-collar and white-collar workers. Many young people will train for a low-paying white-collar job rather than learn a better paying blue-collar trade. They prefer the prestige of wearing a suit and not doing manual labor to earning several thousand dollars more a year as a plumber or an electrician.

Enforcement of Social Differentiation

The economic institution also tends to maintain the status quo in defining differentiation. For example, it is often assumed that all young men applying for jobs plan to work until their retirement and that most young women applying for jobs will remain employed only until they are married or begin having children. Thus women have been and continue to be discriminated against by companies that consider a new employee to be a long-range investment. Many companies are also reluctant to employ women in jobs that they have traditionally reserved for men. Often they don't want their male staff members—or themselves—to feel threatened. Blacks have suffered even more severely from similar reasoning in terms of race.

In the past, minorities were often hired for particular jobs because their services could be acquired for less pay. They were also hired for lower echelon jobs without hope for advancement. A minority member hired as a bank teller might be expected to remain a teller for as long as he or she worked. A middle-class white male might be hired as a teller with the understanding that the job was the first step in learning the banking business.

CAPITALISM, SOCIALISM, AND COMMUNISM

In subsistence cultures, the central issue is survival. For societies with little industrialization, economic institutions are directly woven into the fabric of families and tribes. Obligations between kin govern the sharing of goods, the giving of gifts, and the exchange of services. Usually the only division of labor is on the basis of sex and age. Goods are shared freely or are obtained through barter.

So long as societies do not produce a surplus, the profit motive is practically nonexistent. In many preindustrial societies, giving goods away—not accumulating them—is a source of prestige. The Trobriand Islanders of the South Pacific, for example, collect yarn (a highly valued material) for the sole purpose of giving it away. A person's social standing depends in part on how much yarn he or she can give away. Individuals and families also exchange services, keeping strict account of precisely defined reciprocal obligations. Only in this sense do the Trobrianders assign a value to goods and services.

In industrial societies, the family or local community no longer functions as a self-sufficient economic unit, and relationships between employer and employee and between buyer and seller are depersonalized. People are more interdependent than ever before, and relatively few workers produce a complete product by themselves. Organizations that regulate the flow of money and coordinate the activities of numerous specialized workers are correspondingly complex. Throughout history, several theories and methods have been tried in an attempt to regulate the production, distribution, and consumption within societies. This section examines the organization and principal goals of three of the most influential economic theories: capitalism, socialism, and communism.

Capitalism

Capitalism is based on the ideas of private ownership and competition for profits. In theory, the freedom to succeed or to fail motivates individuals to work hard, compete, save, and invest—activities that ultimately benefit the entire society.

Briefly, capitalism works like this: capital and labor supply goods and services in return for money. Some of this money pays wages to the workers for their labor, some of the money is used as more capital, and some of the money is kept as profits. The system clearly depends on this circular relationship of capital investments and worker's labor to produce more and more goods and services. Increase in production leads to increase in profits if wages and capital investments are wisely controlled.

Economist Adam Smith, the founder of capitalist theory, believed that people are motivated primarily by self-interest, and that their interests coincide with national interests. He argued that a system of open competition, free from government controls, would lead to the greatest happiness for the greatest number. In pursuit of wealth, producers would seek better and less expensive methods of production. Consumers would naturally buy the better and cheaper product. Inefficient methods of production and unwanted products would fall by the wayside. Thus, Smith saw an open market as a self-

regulating mechanism. He believed that individualism and freedom from government interference were key elements for economic progress.

The economic system in the United States today is not true capitalism in spite of the fact that it is often called such. It is a modified capitalism which is the result of widespread reforms in the unregulated (laissez-faire) capitalism of more than a hundred years ago. There are many reasons laissez-faire capitalism did not work. First, powerful industrialists of the nineteenth century, pursuing their self-interest, as Adam Smith had predicted they would, cornered important segments of their markets. Through these monopolies, they were able to charge whatever they liked for goods. They had the power to cut off essential services and to keep wages low. In other words, laissez-faire competition actually led to a disruption of the "self-regulating forces" of the free market.

Labor was also exploited. In the United States in the late nineteenth and early twentieth centuries, men, women, and children labored ten to twelve hours a day, six or seven days a week for poor wages that could be cut or ended without notice. Employers were powerful enough to suppress unionization efforts.

With the Great Depression that began in 1929, the government had to step in with regulations protecting workers and investors alike, feeling especially obligated to assist those who were unable to work or to find meaningful work. If classical capitalism had ever existed, these increased government regulations put it decidedly into the realm of theory only.

Today, monopolies and price fixing are against the law (except for regulated monopolies such as public utilities). Public stock companies have largely replaced privately owned industry. Individual and corporate investors, banks, and the government share the financial risks of experimentation and expansion. Thus, individual liability is limited. Owners have largely left their companies in the hands of experts in organization and production—the managers. Government regulations attempt to protect the public from harmful goods and false advertising. Workers are

TABLE 16.1 / THE FIFTY LARGEST INDUSTRIAL CORPORATIONS

Rank '77	'76	Company	Sales ($000)	Rank '77	'76	Company	Sales ($000)
1	2	General Motors (Detroit)	54,961,300	26	22	Westinghouse Electric (Pittsburgh)	6,137,661
2	1	Exxon (New York)	54,126,219	27	26	Occidental Petroleum (Los Angeles)	6,006,019
3	3	Ford Motor (Dearborn, Mich.)	37,841,500	28	27	International Harvester (Chicago)	5,975,061
4	5	Mobil (New York)	32,125,828	29	28	Eastman Kodak (Rochester, N.Y.)	5,966,986
5	4	Texaco (White Plains, N.Y.)	27,920,499	30	31	RCA (New York)	5,880,900
6	6	Standard Oil of California (San Francisco)	20,917,331	31	34	Rockwell International (Pittsburgh)	5,858,700
7	8	International Business Machines (Armonk, N.Y.)	18,133,184	32	36	Caterpillar Tractor (Peoria, Ill.)	5,848,900
8	7	Gulf Oil (Pittsburgh)	17,840,000	33	30	Union Oil of California (Los Angeles)	5,668,520
9	9	General Electric (Fairfield, Conn.)	17,518,600	34	35	United Technologies (Hartford)	5,550,670
10	10	Chrysler (Highland Park, Mich.)	16,708,300	35	33	Bethlehem Steel (Bethlehem, Pa.)	5,370,000
11	11	International Tel. & Tel. (New York)	13,145,664	36	38	Beatrice Foods (Chicago)	5,288,578
12	12	Standard Oil (Ind.) (Chicago)	13,019,939	37	32	Esmark (Chicago)	5,280,160
13	15	Atlantic Richfield (Los Angeles)	10,969,091	38	37	Kraft (Glenview, Ill.)	5,238,807
14	13	Shell Oil (Houston)	10,112,062	39	40	Xerox (Stamford, Conn.)	5,076,900
15	14	U.S. Steel (Pittsburgh)	9,609,900	40	44	General Foods (White Plains, N.Y.)	4,909,737
16	16	E. I. du Pont de Nemours (Wilmington, Del.)	9,434,800	41	41	R. J. Reynolds Industries (Winston-Salem, N.C.)	4,816,022
17	17	Continental Oil (Stamford, Conn.)	8,700,317	42	43	Ashland Oil (Russell, Ky.)	4,785,578
18	18	Western Electric (New York)	8,134,604	43	39	LTV (Dallas)	4,703,296
19	20	Tenneco (Houston)	7,440,300	44	42	Monsanto (St. Louis)	4,594,500
20	19	Procter & Gamble (Cincinnati)	7,284,255	45	48	Amerada Hess (New York)	4,591,253
21	21	Union Carbide (New York)	7,036,100	46	46	Firestone Tire & Rubber (Akron, Ohio)	4,426,900
22	23	Goodyear Tire & Rubber (Akron, Ohio)	6,627,818	47	45	Cities Service (Tulsa)	4,388,200
23	29	Sun (Radnor, Pa.)	6,418,117	48	55	Marathon Oil (Findlay, Ohio)	4,252,028
24	24	Phillips Petroleum (Bartlesville, Okla.)	6,284,185	49	47	Boeing (Seattle)	4,018,800
25	25	Dow Chemical (Midland, Mich.)	6,234,255	50	53	Minnesota Mining & Manufacturing (St. Paul)	3,980,326

Source: Reprinted from FORTUNE Magazine's listing of "The 500 Largest Industrial Companies in the U.S.," (May 4, 1981 issue), © 1981, *Time,* Inc.

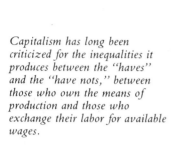

Capitalism has long been criticized for the inequalities it produces between the "haves" and the "have nots," between those who own the means of production and those who exchange their labor for available wages.

guaranteed the right to collective bargaining through unions (except for certain government workers). Government programs also provide some help for those in need through such social welfare as unemployment insurance, Social Security, and some health care.

Perhaps the best summary of the current level of capitalism in the United States is contained in the following excerpt from the work of the Cornell University sociologist Robin Williams (1970: 178, 188–189):

The fact that in the United States the great majority of decisions concerning investment and production, as well as consumption, are made by individuals and officers of nongovernmental corporations marks the American economy as basically capitalistic. The growth of giant corporations has centralized the making of economic decisions, but it has not socialized it . . . today competition in a free market has been partly replaced by a highly tangible web of financial and organizational controls. There are nodes or foci of concentrated production and centers of control in many crucial parts of the economic web, from which lines of control gradually fade out into areas of relatively free markets and independent production.*

---

* Reprinted by permission of Alfred A. Knopf, Inc.

Socialism

The goal of socialist economic systems is to free workers from dependence on the wealthy few, and to provide a decent standard of living for *all* members of society. Socialism is the economic institution most prevalent in the western European democracies. Great Britain is the most familiar example, while Sweden is the oldest and most fully successful. In **socialism,** profit is reinvested in the economy, not accumulated as wealth. As in capitalism, "Consumers are free to spend their income as they please and workers are free to choose their jobs. The prices of consumption goods and the wages of labor are established in genuine markets in response to the forces of supply and demand" (Leeman, 1963: 18). But where socialism differs from capitalism is in who obtains profits and how they are used. Because socialism retains some capitalistic elements, it does not attempt to do away with profits altogether. But instead of seeking the maximum profit (charging the highest price the market will bear) socialist industries seek the minimum profit (the lowest price that will cover costs and make some return to the economy as a whole).

Private industry, whose profits are heavily taxed, is allowed to operate as long as it does not interfere with the public good. Essential industries, such as coal mining in Great Britain, are run by the state. The directors of such nationalized industries are appointed by and are answerable to the government. The profits of nationalized industries are reinvested in plant expansion and product improvement or are turned over to the state, along with the income from taxes on the profits earned by private industry, to be reallocated to less profitable essential industries. The state also operates banks, transportation facilities, utilities, and communication facilities.

Socialist states often provide many social services for their citizens. Health care is free in Sweden; so are day-care centers and college tuition. The government grants housing subsidies and, in some cases, interest-free loans to low-income families and young people. As a result, poverty and slums are greatly reduced. Swedish economists become concerned if their nation's unemployment level rises to one-fifth of what is considered normal in the United States.

In Sweden, for example, socialism has eliminated the widest extremes of economic classes. There are no poverty-stricken people unable to find work, barely existing on government handouts. Wealth is so heavily taxed (there are no loopholes) that there are few people who could be called rich. The large working class, which includes many small farmers, need not fear unemployment or crippling medical or educational expenses. Sweden is not, nor does it want to be, a classless society. People still work hard to purchase a large house, a place in the country, and a finer car. The government provides the basic necessities, hard work and talent provide luxuries.

The 1980s have been years of questioning in several socialist countries like Great Britain and Sweden. The former, staggering under rapid inflation, high unemployment, frequent strikes, and reduced industrial productivity, has been slowly denationalizing major industries and trying to reduce the dependence of industry on government money. Sweden has been reexamining its extensive system of social welfare services, questioning whether the society can in the long run afford them all. These two examples briefly illustrate two potential problems with socialistic economic systems: industrial reinvestment and worker motivation. With profits in a system kept low, there may be less money available to reinvest in modernizing plants and equipment. In England, this has been a serious problem in industries like automotives, steel, and shipbuilding. Worker motivation can also suffer, reducing the amount and quality of output. At the management level, this can be a response to controlled profits which reduce some of the incentive to find more efficient work processes. At the other levels of work, less profit can also mean lower wages and less motivation. In addition, there is more of a feeling that the government "owes" workers jobs since part of the profits generated go to the government.

Leaving aside issues of societal beliefs and values for a moment, from a sociological point of view we can see that both capitalism and socialism are experiencing changes. Capitalism has been moving away from a "pure" model toward one with some government control. In the United States this form begins to incorporate aspects of socialism as an economic system, although under the Reagan Administration there has been some effort to return to less government control. In other nations socialism has begun exploring the limits of the services it can afford to provide to its citizens. Some socialistic societies, such as Great Britain, have also been moving toward reduced government control. All of these changes have had profound economic effects, among the most obvious being gradual reductions in social welfare services and benefits, social unrest (such as the rioting in England in 1981), increased unemployment, and high inflation with a resultant lowering of the standard of living of many people. It is too soon to predict the ultimate directions which these two economic systems will take: perhaps they will become more alike, or perhaps they will move more toward "pure" forms (as France seems to be doing under its new socialist government). It is clear, however, that whatever happens in the economic institution will have repercussions throughout the societal structure.

Communism

Communism, like capitalism, is an economic theory which does not truly exist in practice at the national level. The Soviet Union is not truly communist any more than the United States is truly capitalist. Still, communism continues to be an influential theory and an ideal goal for many governments, most notably mainland China.

The goal of communistic systems is to motivate individuals to think and to work for the people as a whole, with each individual sharing equally in the economic rewards. In other words, communism seeks an even distribution of wealth—a classless society. Both the means of production (capital) and the goods and services produced belong to all the people. The government is the sole producer, distributor, and employer. Karl Marx, who first set forth the prin-

ciples of modern communism, described it in this classic statement: "From each according to his ability, to each according to his needs."

Communist economies are thoroughly planned economies. Major decisions—the annual, five-, and seven-year plans; the creation of farming cooperatives; the rationing of consumer goods—are made in the upper echelons of the government. The central government directly controls and allocates all major raw materials and such manufactured products as heavy machinery. It also determines what industries will receive what materials and equipment to produce what products.

In addition, the government assumes responsibility for all the people, providing nurseries and day-care centers for working mothers, education, housing, and extensive social services. The government attempts to maintain full employment, considering a job to be everyone's right and duty.

A recent report described conditions in some of the rural Chinese communes today:

The creation of farming cooperatives is one economic method employed by Communist governments to achieve an even distribution of wealth. In China, agricultural communes rely on manual labor, rather than mechanization. For example, these workers are digging trenches in which their cabbages will be buried and preserved during the winter, instead of relying on refrigeration.

Household income averaged Y70 ($30.80) at the Ma Lu commune in the Yangtze Delta; Y65 ($28.60) at the Red Star commune near Peking. Under the work-point system, wages depend upon work done (and since the Cultural Revolution, on "attitude"). At Red Star, the highest household income was 80 percent more than the lowest. Education and health care are fairly good and extremely cheap. At the Ma Lu commune, each person pays Y2 ($.88) per year as a medical fee, and gets free service in return. At the commune schools, Y4 ($1.76) each year for each child covers all fees and books. (Terrill, 1972: 101)

Although the ultimate goal of communism is a classless, stateless society, no "communist" nation exists that even approximates the ideal stage that Marx had predicted, when the state would "wither away" and the motto "From each according to his ability, to each according to his needs" would become a reality. While the basic needs of every citizen are taken care of in communist states, above the lowest common denominator there exists a wide disparity in who gets what. Workers are still paid according to their skill and productivity. But it is not the workers, the proletariat, who receive the most benefits; government and party administrators and technocrats enjoy them instead. Those in the government and the party are the first to receive new apartments and scarce consumer goods, while ordinary citizens may have to remain on waiting lists for years. So important are government and party positions to economic and social success that it is doubtful that anyone in these privileged positions would want to see them disappear.

LABOR IN THE UNITED STATES

Labor is one of the basic elements in any economic institution, as we saw at the beginning of the chapter. In industrial societies, labor depends on those who own and manage businesses for jobs and income. This relationship can be a complex and sensitive one. Business needs a labor force that is skillful, dependable, and committed if it is to operate with the predictability needed by formal organizations (described in Chapter 11). It also attempts to minimize labor costs in order to maximize profitability. Workers, on the other hand, seek stable, gratifying, stimulating work at the highest feasible salary level. The fit between the needs of labor and capital is poor in several ways: workers seek maximum income while business tries to minimize cost; workers want jobs that are meaningful and interesting while business seeks a labor pool that will do exactly what it is instructed to do; workers want job security while business needs a flexible supply of labor that can expand or contract in response to changes in business conditions.

The nationwide strike of U.S. air traffic controllers which occurred in 1981 provides a dramatic example of some of these variables. The controllers—the people who control flight patterns of the planes landing at, taking off from, and passing by airports—struck over issues of pay and working conditions. They claimed that their work involved a great deal of stress resulting from having to direct the actions of thousands of moving aircraft in crowded airspace, a job made even more difficult in bad weather. They felt that they deserved higher pay, more time off, and earlier retirement as compensation for the stress and the skill needed to do the job. The Federal Aeronautics Administration (FAA), which runs the airports and employs the air traffic controllers, disagreed. Furthermore, as federal employees, the controllers were forbidden by law from striking. When the controllers nevertheless struck after a breakdown in negotiations between their union and the FAA, they were fired.

This confrontation represents a classical labor-capital dilemma. Workers try to obtain working conditions which give them a sense of participation and control over their own destinies, as well as the highest feasible income. Capital tries to maintain control over labor so that it can be assured that its business will not be disrupted, and so that its costs can be kept low. In this case, airline schedules were disrupted by the air traffic controllers' strike, and increased labor costs would have had to be borne by the airlines in the form of higher landing fees.

The air traffic controllers strike exemplifies the value of unions to workers. If one controller had decided to strike, he or she would have been quickly replaced. When the great majority of controllers struck as an organized whole, air traffic was snarled and the whole society got involved. A **labor union** makes such organized action possible. It is an organization of workers formed for the purpose of protecting their own interests in the workplace, especially with regard to income and working conditions. Organized labor is not a new concept. It dates at least as far back as organized slave rebellions in Roman times, and includes the well-known guilds of medieval times.

The rise of unions has provided increased power for workers in the form of support for wage increases and improved work conditions.

Characteristics of U.S. Unions

In 1980, only 25 percent of the U.S. workforce was unionized (Hooks and Haven, 1981: 17), with the membership distributed among almost 200 unions. Unions have been described in the following way:

Although a few represent professionals . . . most unions are comprised of workers who fall into what is customarily viewed as the working class by virtue of their occupation, income, or housing location. Organized labor represents almost half of all such workers. In terms of the present total population in the labor force, trade union members are more likely to be men rather than women, black rather than white, and old rather than young. . . . There are more northerners than southeners, more urban dwellers than rural inhabitants, more blue-collar workers than clerical workers, and more employees in manufacturing than in nonmanufacturing industries. (Akabas, 1977: 739)*

Labor unions are of many different kinds and the rate of unionization varies among different types of work.

Unions were slow to develop in the United States, and they have not had a strong emphasis on "class consciousness" or political power—for example, there has never been a general strike in the United States (Williams, 1970: 213). A significant reason for this is the ethnic diversity in this society. Any factor which makes it more difficult to get a consensus militates against unions, and the cultural differences in values and communication patterns among ethnic groups can create discord. However, as more awareness develops of the common economic needs of workers regardless of their ethnic background, union organizing is more likely to occur. Increasing numbers of women in the workforce can impede the development of unions if they see their economic security tied to the employment

* Copyright 1977, National Association of Social Workers, Inc. Reprinted with permission, from the *Encyclopedia of Social Work,* 17th edition.

of a spouse rather than resulting from their own employment. Women can contribute to the growth of unions if they see organizing as a way to improve their economic and career status.

Ultimately, the goal of unions is to increase worker security: "The worker, personally free but propertyless, . . . (is) fully exposed to the insecurities of a fluctuating job market" (Williams, 1970: 211). Unions attack this problem by focusing on improving concrete rewards such as salary and fringe benefits, increasing respect for workers and creating conditions under which their self-respect is supported, and increasing control over working conditions (disciplinary procedures, how jobs are assigned, and so forth). The popular movie "Nine to Five" illustrates the problems many workers face. They work in highly impersonal environments that are strictly hierarchical. It is difficult to feel that their work is recognized, and even more difficult to avoid feeling easily expendible. On top of these problems, even programs for long-term security like Social Security appear to be increasingly insecure. A 1981 study showed that 54 percent of the American people no longer believed that the Social Security system will have enough money available to pay them the full benefits they will be entitled to at retirement (Weaver, 1981). Under these conditions, it is little wonder that unions are appealing as a way to deal with these problems in an organized manner.

Technology is also seen as a further threat to worker security. Although it has been instrumental in improving working conditions (safety, less noise, and so on), it has also raised frightening new concerns. In the early days of industrialization in France and the Lowlands, workers who had been accustomed to performing piecework by hand felt threatened by the introduction of high-speed machinery. Machines were attacked and destroyed, quite often by hurling a wooden shoe, called a sabot, into the movements (the origin of the word sabotage). Today, again, improvements in machinery are outpacing workers' ability to adjust. Trained for one particular job, workers may find their skills useless when new equipment is introduced. Unions realize that they cannot forever prevent the introduction of new equipment or continue to insist that employers retain employees whose skills are no longer needed. Some unions have been working with employers to provide on-the-job retraining for workers whose jobs have become obsolete, but this solution only works when there are new jobs to be filled. Fully automatic machines may require little more than someone to press the button and watch over the operation. Machine operators, the backbone of industrialization, may become obsolete as we move into a postindustrial, automated age.

Unions are in a very difficult position when trying to deal with the need to protect the interests of their members. On August 24, 1981, more than 400 workers at a plant of Celanese Canada, Inc., found themselves out of work when the company decided to close the plant rather than meet union wage demands (Malarek, 1981). Should the union have dropped its wage demands in order to keep workers' jobs? (see Fig. 16.3). If it had, what kind of bargaining position would the workers have been put in for the future? The issue is obviously a sensitive one. It has been complicated by the fact that the U.S. has no factory closing legislation, as do many West European nations (Hooks and Haven, 1981: 1). Such legislation was defeated in Congress and both workers and communities are left to fend for themselves when a factory is closed. Yet research has shown that workers and their communities can be protected from the most severe aspects of plant closings if the departing employer provides severance pay, extended medical payments, job search training, retraining of laid-off workers, longer warnings to communities and workers, and a community assistance fund (Hooks and Haven, 1981: 5, 9). Unions have supported factory closing legislation, but so far the societal belief in free enterprise has been stronger than the desire to legislate a sense of social responsibility by industry.

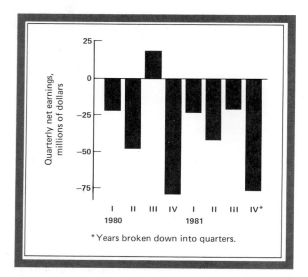

*Years broken down into quarters.

Fig. 16.3 / Business Woes, Union Woes

Braniff International Airlines was hard hit by airline deregulation, and it began experiencing serious losses in 1980. The chart shows just how serious the economic effects were. Braniff asked its employees to help: Many workers accepted layoffs, a 10 percent pay cut was implemented voluntarily, and one paycheck was deferred. The International Brotherhood of Teamsters did not fight these actions, arguing that the employees as well as management had an interest in the airline's survival. This new style of union activities, in which employees are asked to help bail out unsuccessful managements, has spread to other industries as well, notably the automobile industry. There employees have agreed to cut time off and defer increases in exchange for job security. In Braniff's case, the strategy failed, and the airline ceased operating in May 1982. However, in other industries the strategy seems to be helping.

Source: *The New York Times*, March 6, 1982, p. 31. © 1982 by The New York Times Company. Reprinted by permission.

The Future of Unions

While unions have undoubtedly improved the economic and working conditions of many of their members, they have also been accused of a number of abuses. Some of these practices have involved management cooperation; for example, requiring the employment of more workers than needed to do a job, commonly called **featherbedding,** is well known. Long apprenticeships have been used in some craft unions to limit opportunities for young workers to enter the union and move into the highest paid jobs. A third criticism centers on fringe benefits and retirement plans which are excessively costly. For example, some municipal and federal employees can retire at full pension after 20 years of service, regardless of age. Wage levels themselves have been criticized as too high in some cases. During the air traffic controllers' strike, many people felt the wage demands—which would have put most controllers in the $40,000 annual wage range—were simply too high. Finally, there is sometimes resentment among the public when unions go on strike. People are inconvenienced; business is disrupted; and money is lost. Even when there is sympathy for the grounds for the strike, many dislike the process.

The air traffic controllers' strike seemed to herald a new climate for unions in the United States. The willingness of the government to fire the controllers and to try to break the union suggested that the whole union movement was being questioned, especially since the actions of the government received considerable public support. The traditionally liberal stance of unions toward issues of economic equality and affirmative action were also at odds with the Reagan Administration's probusiness stance, as well as its desire to reduce federal government regulation of business and civil rights. All of these trends have been appearing during a period of weak union leadership and low levels of militancy, leading some observers to assert that unions have become rigid bureaucracies more concerned with the status quo than with change. As the union movement faces the future, it is clear how closely it is tied to the whole structure of the economic institution.

Disbelief on Wall Street: Under Reaganomics, wild swings and devastating losses

Auth in the *Philadelphia Inquirer*.

When President Reagan fired striking air traffic controllers, he clearly indicated his administration's tough stance toward union issues.

THE FUTURE OF THE ECONOMIC INSTITUTION

The Reagan Administration came to power in 1981 during a period of economic uncertainty and widespread dissatisfaction with high inflation and soaring interest rates. The decision to strengthen the productive capacity of the economy by bolstering the business climate was chosen as the best way to increase employment. Combined with a reduction in taxes, this policy was viewed as likely to increase the disposable income of individuals and business which, in turn, would further stimulate production and consumption (Weiner and Morse, 1981). The hitch has been that cutting taxes and government spending and reducing federal regulation of business and civil rights has meant cutting badly needed programs for the needy: the poor, the elderly, minorities, and so on (*The Boston Globe,* 1981).

Whatever the ultimate results of the economics of the Reagan Administration, the 1980s are clearly a period of change in the economic institution. All of the Western industrialized nations

SOCIAL ISSUE/Work and Leisure

Janet S. Schwartz/*American University*

From the economic viewpoint, work is continuous activity involving the production of goods and provision of services for which one receives pay (Dubin, 1958: 4). Work done by housewives or househusbands is generally overlooked by economists but is recognized in some definitions of leisure. Dumazedier defines leisure as that activity

apart from the obligations of work, family and society to which the individual turns at will for relaxation, diversion or for broadening his knowledge and his spontaneous social participation, the free exercise of his creative capacity (1967: 16)

In preindustrial societies, work and leisure were interdependent. There were no specified periods of time designated as leisure. Activities such as going to the market or hunting had leisure or recreational aspects; the nature of leisure was determined by the nature of work (Anderson, 1974). In the rural communities of America, leisure activities blended into family and community; the work–leisure relationship was holistic. Industrialization changed the structure of work and leisure—home industries gave way to centralized places of work such as factories; work and leisure became separate spheres. Those who view leisure from a holistic perspective (e.g., Marcuse, 1964) are pessimistic about leisure in a society in which work is fragmented and bureaucratized. According to the segmental perspective of work and leisure (i.e., work and leisure as separate spheres), as presented by Parker (1971) and Dumazedier (1967), for example, leisure time is seen as providing the individual with opportunities for self-development and growth. The holistic perspective, it is suggested by some, fails to recognize that work and leisure were never quite as unified as they are assumed to be today. Although jobs often allow for pauses to eat or to indulge in conversations, in the evening or holidays one generally ceases to think about work (Anderson, 1974: 11).

Work has been with us throughout the ages, though the meaning of work has differed. In Athenian society, where work was performed by slaves, work was a curse; it prevented the individual from seeking truth and virtue. For the Jews and early Christians, work was no less a curse, but it was gradually accepted as a means of atonement for original sin. With the Reformation, a new meaning was given to work. For Luther, work was a vocation, a calling through which one glorified and served God. Calvinism provided an additional dimension—work became a means of salvation for the rich, as well as for the poor. Work was to be disciplined and conscientious, and the fruits of one's labor were to be saved and reinvested.

The ideology and values of the Reformation and Calvinism gave us the Protestant ethic and, as Weber argued, contributed to the development of capitalism. However, in the nineteenth century new ideas about work as distinct from religion and capital accumulation were discussed and argued about by the socialists. Karl Marx denounced the evils of capitalism and the exploitation of the individual. Marx felt that work, which for him was a means of self-expression and creativity, had lost its meaning under capitalist exploitation. The individual had become a mere appendage of the machine, alienated from work and co-workers. According to Marx, with the elimination of private property and the division of labor called for by communism, a society would be brought to the fore ". . . where no one has one exclusive sphere of activity . . . where it is possible . . . to hunt in the morning, fish in the afternoon . . . criticize after dinner without ever becoming a hunter, fisherman, shepherd or critic. . . ." Marx clearly anticipated a society in which men and women could change their activities without having to assume one specific role. In his later work, Marx was less certain about the possibility of eliminating the division of labor even in a communist society.

But he assumed that the abundant leisure time that a communist society would provide would create vast opportunities for the development of the individual, enabling him or her to participate in all spheres of life.

In nineteenth-century America the Calvinist notion of work as a means of salvation had lost its significance, but diligence and thrift remained focal values in American society. Hard work and perseverance were not only the path to achievement, but the mark of a good and moral person. Idleness was condemned, for it was thought that an idle hand led to gambling, drinking, and shirking of one's obligations. And, in fact, some of the opposition to the proposed reduction of the 14-hour work day was framed in just such terms.

At the turn of the century, the 12-hour work day and seven-day work week were not unusual. Not until the mid-1930s did the 40-hour work week emerge as a reality for the industrial worker. By the mid-1970s, 24 percent of full-time nonfarm wage-and-salary employees worked slightly more than 40 hours per week; only nine percent worked less than 40 hours per week (Maklan, 1977: 42). The reduced work week was now accompanied by a paid vacation—40 percent of the labor force had gained a three-week vacation by the end of the 1970s, and paid legal holidays added an additional six to eight days per year to the workers' free time. Clearly, in 1980 employed American workers had improved their working conditions relative to their counterparts in the early 1900s. The quality of working life had changed immensely, yet despite the vast improvements not all was well.

Throughout the 1970s there were numerous commentaries about the erosion of the work ethic, a casual attitude toward work, a search for leisure comfort, and a lack of interest and commitment to work among American workers (*The Washington Post,* 1973; *Business Week,* May 10, 1976, cited by Katzell, 1979). Although there were indeed changes in attitudes toward work, there were little data to suggest that Americans were rejecting their work ethic. Morse and Weiss (1955) found that eight out of ten workers would continue to work even if they inherited enough money to live comfortably without work. In 1971, the response to this question did show a decline in the percentage of workers who would continue working if they inherited enough money to live comfortably without working: It decreased to 74 percent (Kanter, 1978). However, a decline of six percent does not constitute a major shift in values or an erosion of the work ethic.

Changes in the 1970s centered on the nature of work and the importance attributed to various aspects of the job. Americans, particularly young, well-educated Americans, wanted jobs that were interesting, meaningful, and challenging. They sought jobs that would allow them to make a contribution and that offered intrinsic job satisfaction (Kanter, 1978; Katzell, 1979; Yankelovitch, 1979). For example, from a 1976 survey of college students, Kerr (1979: xii) found little evidence to suggest that young people avoid work. Seventy-nine percent agreed that "hard work always pays off." Data have shown that 60 percent of college students take vocational courses and that interest in apprenticeship programs is high. Nearly half of college students work—some full time—while attending college.

Past studies have shown that work for most Americans is not, as Dubin (1958) argued, a central life interest. The same studies that showed high commitment to work even if there were resources to forego a job also showed that for a large segment of the work force, work was a means to use up time and to keep busy, even if there was little interest in the job itself. Blauner (1964) argued that work is alienating that does not involve workers as a means of personal self-expression, or that does not develop in them a sense of purpose and function which connects jobs to the overall organization of production. In the 1970s young workers sought jobs that provided economic well-being, but also responsibility, autonomy, and self-fulfillment. What is problematic is the fact that the structure of work organizations often fails to meet these expectations.

It remains to be seen whether these interests are long-term and will continue into the 1980s and whether the increasing rate of unemployment—10.4 percent in October 1982—will lead to a resurgence of concern with job security and advancement. Indeed, a recent international survey reported that Americans ranked "good pay" and "pleasant people to work with" as the most important characteristics of a job (CARA, 1982).

Although work and its meaning remain problematic, leisure is not without its problems. Changes in working conditions influence all spheres of life, not the least of which is free time. The five-day, 40-hour work week, along with paid holidays and vacation time provide Americans with an estimated one month of free time out of every 12 months. The substantial hours of free time available to Americans are accompanied by vast expenditures for radios, television, records, muscial instruments, games, sports equipment, travel, and so on.

Limited flexibility and choice have surfaced in the work place in the form of "flextime," which has had a beneficial impact on individuals and families. Flextime, introduced in the United States in 1972, is practiced widely in Germany and other West European countries; in the Soviet Union it has even reached the discussion stage. In Switzerland about 40 percent of the labor force is said to be on flextime (Nollen, 1979).

Flextime is a plan agreed upon by employer and employee that permits the employee to change the working hours in a manner most suitable for the employee. Many flextime programs permit a daily variation in schedule, while the actual working hours remain unchanged. In 1977, between 13 and 15 percent of work organizations, including the federal government, had flextime plans (Nollen, 1979). A review of about 40 reports and studies of flextime indicates that there are substantial benefits in such programs for both the employee and the employer, among them improved morale and a reduction of stress. An important advantage for families is the opportunity to coordinate family and work life more effectively. For the employer, benefits include increased productivity and reduced absenteeism (Nollen, 1979). Similarly, the four-day, 40-hour work week that some companies in the United States have experimented with suggests that flexibility in the work place and increased control over one's free time and the manner in which it is utilized can have benefits for all concerned.

Yet the vast changes in how long Americans work, how and when they work, and how much they spend on leisure pursuits are not issue-free. Not infrequently, these concerns are regarded as social problems, as exemplifed by a 1963 book entitled *Work and Leisure: A Contemporary Social Problem* (Smigel, 1963).

Work is usually seen as instrumental and leisure as expressive, and often in American society the instrumental endeavor is utilized to purchase the means for the expressive endeavor, thus making leisure an object to be consumed. But leisure, as has been argued by many, means spontaneity, flexibility, and the development of the self, rather than purchasing articles as one would in buying an article of clothing.

Weiss and Riesman (cited in Smigel, 1961: 173) have noted that in American society working time has not led workers to pursue leisure to "prepare themselves for higher vocational tasks." Few show an interest in participating in union meetings, in education programs, or in reading. Although some industrial workers attend art classes or amateur musical groups and although many have expensive hobbies such as hunting, the free time of most industrial workers is often spent in comparatively aimless ways.

Leisure is highly commercialized. It is big business, and Americans, who are used to being directed by others, often follow the prescriptions of organizations. We buy not only skis but also the leisure attire for after-skiing. Although tens of millions of Americans are involved in sports activities such as basketball, baseball, skiing, tennis, and golf, the majority of Americans are primarily passive spectators of sports. Viewing televised football games on Sunday has become a national pastime. Sports, which in a simpler America were conducted with spontaneity and free choice, are a highly organized endeavor, controlled by corporations employing professional athletes who are "bought and sold" or traded from one corporation to another. For the professional athlete, sports is a job, as it is for other segments of the population employed in the leisure industry.

As noted previously, the problems of leisure can also be the same problems faced at work. Dull and monotonous jobs—for example, jobs that permit little or no autonomy—lead to uses of free time different from those pursued by people with jobs that are creative and that permit a high degree of autonomy. The "spillover" hypothesis suggests that the worker on the assembly line, tired and bored at work, is also tired and bored away from work. Such a person's free time might be spent eating, sleeping, and watching television. Uninvolved at work, this worker is uninvolved away from work: He or she neither reads nor votes; alienated at work, the worker remains alienated from life (Wilensky, 1969: 112).

Even the choice of leisure activity is not unaffected by one's job, as noted by Etzkorn (1964). For example, Etzkorn found that persons with routine jobs often chose public campground activities, while persons with more creative and challenging occupations frequently chose wilderness camping. It should be noted that analogous patterns of work and leisure have emerged in other industrial societies, including the Soviet Union, suggesting that the problem of work and leisure is a universal one and not the domain of a particular society.

Although the issues surrounding leisure are numerous and are likely to remain with us for some time, some sociologists have suggested that America's overwhelming emphasis on work and achievement, nurtured by a deep-seated Protestant ethic, is at least partly to blame for the lack of creativity and self-expression found in our leisure time. The assumption that work alone is important has denigrated creative leisure, and to be truly at leisure in American society requires courage (Wilson, 1981). Still others have argued that true leisure has to be "taught" and nurtured, no less than other behavior patterns. If this is indeed the case, many of us in America have much to learn.

REFERENCES

Anderson, N. (1974) *Man's Work and Leisure.* Leiden: E.J. Brill.

Blauner, R. (1964). *Alienation and Freedom.* Chicago: University of Chicago Press.

CARA (1982). Press release of May 18. Washington, D.C.: The Center for Applied Research in the Apostolate.

Dubin, R. (1958). *The World of Work.* Englewood Cliffs, N.J.: Prentice-Hall.

Dumazedier, J. (1967). *Toward a Society of Leisure.* New York: Free Press.

Etzkorn, K. P. (1964). Leisure and camping: The social meaning of a form of public recreation. *Sociology and Social Research* 48: 4–12.

Kanter, R. M. (1978). Work in a new America. *Daedalus* 107: 47–78.

Katzell, R. A. (1979). Changing attitudes toward work. In *Work in America,* eds. Clark Kerr and J. M. Rosow. New York: Van Nostrand.

Kerr, C. (1979). Introduction. In *Work in America,* eds. Clark Kerr and J. M. Rosow. New York: Van Nostrand.

Maklan, D. M. (1977). *The Four Day Workweek.* New York: Praeger.

Marcuse, H. (1964). *One-Dimensional Man.* London: Routledge.

Morse, N. C., and **R. S. Weiss** (1955). The function and meaning of work and the job. *American Sociological Review* 20: 191–198.

Nollen, S. (1979). *New Patterns of Work.* Scarsdale: Work in America Institute.

Parker, S. (1971) *The Future of Work and Leisure.* New York: Praeger.

Smigel, E. O., ed. (1963). *Work and Leisure: A Contemporary Social Problem.* New Haven, Conn.: College and University Press.

Tilgher, A. (1930). *Work: What It Has Meant to Man Through the Ages.* New York: Harcourt Brace.

Weiss, R. S., and **D. Riesman** (1963). Some issues in the future of leisure. In *Work and Leisure,* ed. E. O. Smigel. New Haven Conn.: College and University Press.

Wilensky, H. L. (1969). Work, careers and social integration. In *Industrial Man,* ed. T. Burns. Baltimore: Penguin.

Wilson, R. N. (1981). The courage to be leisured. *Social Forces* 60: 282–304.

Yankelovitch, D. (1979). Work values and the new breed. In *Work in America,* ed. Clark Kerr and J. Rosow. New York: Van Nostrand.

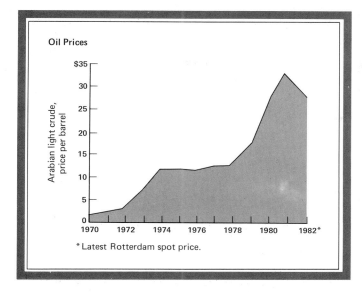

Oil Prices

* Latest Rotterdam spot price.

Fig. 16.4 / The World Economy

The management of a national economy is increasingly subject to international events. Rising oil prices provide a case in point, since this energy source is so basic to our production and distribution systems. When oil prices rise, the costs of production rise in a whole range of industries that rely on oil for energy. This raises consumer prices and may decrease consumption. When oil prices fall, other prices may fall too, leading to a rise in consumption.

Source: *The New York Times,* March 14, 1982, p. 17. © 1982 by The New York Times Company. Reprinted by permission.

are struggling to find new and more effective relationships between production, distribution, and consumption (see Fig. 16.4). Recent riots in England, a socialist economic system, and the widespread strikes in Poland, a communist-influenced economic system, show that every type of economy is being shaken. This certainly is true in our own capitalistic system, where polit-

ical battles have been fierce, as well as in Canada, which underwent a six-week national postal strike in 1981. These events, along with the dramatic air traffic controllers' strike, demonstrate how critical the economic institution is to the whole societal structure. As it changes in the future, all of society will be affected.

SUMMARY

1. The main purposes of this chapter are to define the economic institution; to explore the impact of industrialization on society; to discuss the manifest and latent functions of the economic institution; to outline the three most influential economic theories (capitalism, socialism, and communism); to discuss various aspects of work in the United States; and to consider the future of the economic institution.

2. The economic institution provides for the production, distribution, and consumption of goods

and services. Industrialization, which began in eighteenth-century England, drastically transformed economies based on agriculture and trade into economies based on mechanical mass production of goods and services. The shift from an agricultural society to an industrialized one had (and continues to have) an impact on social values and on the other major economic structures.

3. The workings of the economic institution are designed to ensure that things a society wants or needs are generally made available to its members.

This goal is accomplished by organizing the manner in which goods and services are produced, distributed, and consumed (a manifest function). Production involves the use of land, labor, and capital. Distribution occurs primarily through the marketplace; it is heavily influenced by advertising, banking, credit, and transportation. The major consuming units in a society are private households, agencies of the government, manufacturing or business establishments, and nonprofit organizations. Advertising is also a significant factor in consumption.

4. The latent functions of the industrial economic institution include the creation and maintenance of social classes and the enforcement of social differentiation.

5. Several economic theories and methods have been tried in an attempt to regulate production, distribution, and consumption. Three of the most influential are:

Capitalism: Based on private ownership of the means of production and on competition for profits, it depends on the circular relationship of capital investments and workers' labor to produce more goods and services.

Socialism: Aims to free workers from dependence on a few wealthy owners of the means of production and to provide a decent standard of living for all members of society; profits are reinvested in the economy rather than accumulated as wealth.

Communism: Aims to motivate individuals to think and work for the people as a whole with all sharing equally in economic rewards (a classless society); the means of production and the goods and the services produced belong to all the people with the government as the sole producer, distributor, and employer.

6. Unions are an important part of the labor component of the economic institution. They are organizations of workers formed to protect their own interests in the workplace; their major goal is increasing worker security. Their strategies usually include bargaining for higher salaries, more extensive fringe benefits, and greater control by workers over their own activities in the workplace. Their ultimate bargaining weapon is a strike, but there are risks in taking this action. As industrial technology develops, more and more workers may be faced with the loss of their jobs. This presents a sensitive issue for unions which must balance workers' needs against the ability of corporations to close plants they find to be unprofitable.

REVIEW

Key Terms

Economic institution	Market	Socialism	Featherbedding
Industrialization	Consumption	Communism	
Capital	Capitalism	Labor union	

Review and Discussion

1. To what extent are you or your family involved in the *production* of goods and services for the rest of society? To what extent are you involved in *distribution?* Beyond the "necessities," of what goods and services are you most regularly a *consumer?*

2. With which of the three economic systems do you most agree? Why? Would you like to see the economic institution in the United States changed? In what ways? How would you implement these changes? (Be sure to consider what opposition you would face.)

3. How do you feel about unions? Do you think they perform important functions? Do you think they create problems? Do you think they should be subject to greater or lesser government control than at present? Justify your answers.

4. Do you think that our economic system has gotten too greedy? It sometimes seems as if everyone wants more money, that the price of everything keeps rising. What strategies might society use to address these issues? Which would you favor?

5. As a consumer, what factors most influence your decisions? Do you feel as if you control your own decision making? Why or why not?

References

Akabas, Sheila (1977). Labor: Social policy and human services. In *Encyclopedia of Social Work,* 17th ed. Washington, D.C.: National Association of Social Workers, pp. 737–44.

The Boston Globe (1981). The $365b in cuts OK'd by Congress. August 3, 1981, p. 8.

Demarest, Michael (1981). He digs downtown. *Time,* August 24, 1981, pp. 42–53.

Eskenazi, Gerald (1981). Athletes' salaries: How high will the bidding go? *The New York Times,* August 16, 1981, pp. 15ff.

Hansen, W. Lee (1981). The rocky road through the 1980s. *Academe* 67, no. 4 (August 1981): 210–21.

Hooks, Greg, and **A. Eugene Haven** (1981). Factory closings and the viability of factory closing legislation in the U.S. Paper presented at the Annual Meetings of the American Sociological Association, August 1981.

Leeman, Wayne A., ed. (1963). *Capitalism, Market Socialism, and Central Planning.* Boston: Houghton Mifflin.

Malarek, Victor (1981). Sorel carpet plant is closed: Labor dispute cut sales: Firm. *The Toronto Glove and Mail,* August 25, 1981, p. 11.

Moore, Wilbert (1973). Economic and professional institutions. In *Sociology,* 2nd ed., ed. Neil J. Smelser. New York: John Wiley.

The New York Times (1981). Real income down 5.5% in 1980 in a record drop. August 21, 1981, p. A12.

Terrill, Ross (1972). *800,000,000: The Real China.* New York: Delta.

U.S. News and World Report (1981). Those budget cuts—Who'll be hit hardest. August 10, 1981, pp. 45–48.

Weaver, Warren (1981). Poll shows Americans losing faith in future of Social Security system. *The New York Times,* July 17, 1981, p. A12.

Weiner, Leonard, and **Robert Morse** (1981). Tax cuts: How you will be better off. *U.S. News and World Report,* August 10, 1981, pp. 20–24.

Williams, Robin M., Jr. (1970). *American Society,* 3rd ed. New York: Alfred A. Knopf.

17

POWER
AND
POLITICS

During the month of October 1981, newspaper headlines in two major American dailies, *The New York Times* and the *Washington Post,* were calling attention to the conflict between President Ronald Reagan and the U.S. Senate over the sale of AWACS (Airborne Warning and Command Systems planes) to Saudi Arabia. They also reported debates on how much the federal budget should be cut and which programs should be the subject of these cuts, social welfare or defense. Human interest stories centered on sample families and their suffering as a consequence of such cuts. Questions were raised about the president's claim of a "window of vulnerability" (i.e., the need to keep the defense budget high in order not to be vulnerable to the threat posed by the Soviets); the importance of the black vote; the assassination of President Anwar el-Sadat of Egypt; and the future of Camp David agreements.

During the same time period, the major Soviet dailies, *Pravda* (Truth) and *Izvestia* (News), carried headlines about the "warmongering" policies of the United States; the threat to world peace that these policies posed; and the steadfastness of the Soviet Union to remain a bulwark of peace (but if necessary the Soviets too promised to increase their defense spending). Their domestic policies were extolled as "good" and proper. The social and material well-being of the Soviet people was proclaimed; the need to increase work incentives was thought to be necessary. No one was arguing with Brezhnev on how much should be allocated to defense, or about the hardships that increased defense spending would impose on the Russian family.

The difference between Soviet and American newspapers in what they report is not simply a difference between Soviet socialism and American capitalism. The difference lies in the nature of the political systems; in the difference between an authoritarian and democratic society; in the differences between the rights and obligations of their respective citizens. We will return to these issues later in the chapter, but first we will look at the forces that underlie them: power, politics, and the structures of government.

POLITICS AS A SOCIAL INSTITUTION

Power

Politics is the realm of power: Who gets what, when, and how. **Power** is the ability to control collective decisions and actions. This includes affecting people's behavior and the ability to mobilize and allocate society's resources in order to achieve specific goals. Power ultimately rests on the ability to make people comply, through force, influence, or sanctions (see Fig. 17.1).

The **state** is the structure that claims a monopoly over the legitimate use of force within a territory (Weber, 1958). Legitimate power (as we noted in Chapter 11) rests on the acceptance

Fig. 17.1 / The Types of Power

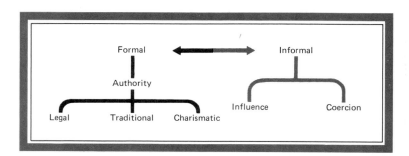

President Reagan addresses a joint session of Congress. Through such formalized procedures, a government exercises the legitimate power that it holds in a society.

by the governed that those who use the power have the right to issue commands or orders. Power is then transformed into **authority**. The power of the police officer who asks you to "pull over" rests on authority; the power of the person who enters your home, threatens you with a gun, and demands your silver, rests on **coercion**, which is illegitimate power based on force.

The state is a relatively recent phenomenon. In hunting and gathering societies people are "relatives" and formal political institutions are not used. Only with the development of agricultural societies, in which there is a surplus of food and the possibility (and reality) of accumulating wealth, does a central political authority emerge to maintain social order and organization. Authority is based on tradition in these societies. In industrial societies, technology leads to greater accumulation of wealth and education becomes a necessary ingredient of industrial management. Traditional authority becomes less valued as specialized education increases in importance. A rational legal order emerges as the "best" system for regulating the distribution of resources and ensuring the well-being of the nation-state.

The state is the structure that defines and regulates the society's activities, and the **government** is a particular group of people who hold legitimate decision-making power within that structure. Neither the assassination of President Kennedy nor the forced resignation of President Nixon changed the *structure* of the state. In spite of these changes, the democratic structure of the political system remained unchanged.

Democracy

The United States, France, England and some other countries are defined as democracies. **Democracy,** from the Greek "rule of the people," means that the people make the rules on how to govern. In large, complex societies, individuals cannot make the many rules needed. Democracy is thus *representative democracy;* people choose individuals from among contending candidates as their representatives in the affairs of government.

A central prerequisite of democracy is a two (or more) party system, representing the goals and wishes of the people. The institutionalization of parties contending for political office makes freedom of speech and of the press a central requirement for a democratic society. These rights enable the contending parties to express and debate positions on issues and thereby provide options to voters. The difference between reporting in the Soviet and American press reflects the one-party system in the U.S.S.R. and the multiparty system in the United States.

One-party states cannot permit the press to report the shortcomings of the party or to raise issues that would prove embarrassing to the leadership. A one-party state, such as the U.S.S.R., is always portrayed as cohesive in its decision-making process, and the activities of government are always depicted as "right." The squabbling between the Secretary of State, Alexander Haig, and other members of the Reagan Administration in the United States reflects the openness of the democratic decision-making process. It reflects the belief that every citizen has the right to know what is happening in the structures of the government.

Many authors (beginning with Aristotle) have suggested that democracy is only possible in a relatively affluent society, where a large proportion of the people are well housed and well fed. A study by Seymour Lipset (1959) confirmed this view. Lipset compared 48 countries in terms of their economies, education levels, urbanization, industrialization, political stability, and government organization. He found that nations in which most people enjoyed a high standard of living were likely to be more democratic and politically stable than others. Why? Because in less developed countries there are vast numbers of poor and discontented people who are "ripe" for coups d'etat or revolutions. In countries with a large middle class which feels it has a stake in existing political institutions, relatively few people are inspired by the thought of radical change or by the rhetoric of charismatic leaders.

An educated populace constitutes a major prerequisite for democracy. Education broadens people's outlook, creates tolerance for opposing views, and encourages tolerance of dissent. It also enables them to use the media to understand issues and the positions held by various political parties and candidates. Furthermore, a democracy can not function unless there is a value system that permits power to be shared and exchanged. Democracy is not possible unless those who are out of power adhere to the rules set by those in power. In other words, effective political channels to oppose the group in power are imperative to democracy.

Another prerequisite for a stable democracy seems to be the existence of a "secular political culture." In many European countries, party leaders are ideological absolutists—absolute monarchists or absolute communists, as the case may be. They approach political opponents as missionaries approach "savages," for the express purpose of converting them. Politics takes on religious overtones. In the United States and Great Britain, in contrast, people tend to view the political system as a market where they can exchange favors, work out compromises, and strike bargains (Almond, 1956). Of the two, the latter approach seems more stable. This is not to say that democracy is impossible in developing nations or in cultures where people are devoted to political ideologies, but that democracy may be more difficult to achieve in such societies.

THE SOVIET CASE: WHY IT IS NOT A DEMOCRACY

The U.S.S.R. clearly lacks much of what Lipset calls the prerequisite for democracy. To be sure, the educational levels of the Soviet population have dramatically risen in the last half-century; illiteracy has been eliminated and the educational achievements of the population approximate levels in the United States. On the other hand, the

U.S.S.R. lacks what might be called one of the major necessary components of democracy: tolerance of dissent. Few countries have institutionalized dissent to the same extent as the United States and England, although there are varying degrees of tolerance of dissent in the other Western democracies. The U.S.S.R., however, lacks a tradition of dissent. During centuries of tsarist rule dissent was never permitted; the people of Russia were considered the flock, led by the absolute ruler, the tsar. While there were efforts to curb the autocracy of the tsars at different periods of Russian history, none was successful.

V. I. Lenin and his small group of followers originally perceived a society in which freedom was to be universal, but even before the revolution was achieved, the principle of dissent was outlawed. What used to be the rule of an autocratic tsar became the rule of a Communist Party, which during some periods ruled far more ruthlessly than the last tsar. The terror of the Stalin era has been eliminated. It was described by Solzhenitsyn in *One Day in the Life of Ivan Denisovitch* (published during the Khrushchev era in the U.S.S.R.) and in the *Gulag Archipelago* (which in part earned him forced exile to the West). But individuals who question the role of the party, who write or paint outside of the party prescribed mode, or who try to assert their religious freedoms—purportedly assured by the Soviet Constitution of 1977—are imprisoned or sent to psychiatric hospitals. Like the all-powerful tsars, the Communist Party is the "guiding" force in Soviet society; it decides what is "best" for the people.

Western political scientists argue that the Communist Party today is no longer the sole decision-making body affecting the domestic and international policies of the U.S.S.R.; other groups such as the managers, the military, and scientists have an input into the policy process (Bialer, 1980; Hough, 1979; Skilling and Griffith, 1973). While a one-man dictator such as Stalin no longer rules the Soviet Union, the institutionalized restraints present in Western democracies are absent. The rights of free speech, of the press, and of assembly in mass meetings and demonstrations are guaranteed only for ". . . the purpose of strengthening and developing the socialist system . . ." (Article 50, the new *Soviet Constitution of 1977*). The development and strengthening of the state are the primary goals, and individual rights are secondary.

Contrary to the practice of Western democracies, there is no institutionalized succession process in the U.S.S.R. and in many other countries of the world. In the United States we may speculate about who will run for the presidency in 1984 or 1988, and who will be elected, but we do not speculate about whether there will be an election. We do not imagine that an incumbent president who fails to be reelected will refuse to relinquish the presidency. But this is hardly an unusual experience in other countries of the world, where "coups" are common, and the elected president is blocked from assuming power by a military junta. In the U.S.S.R., as the aging members of the Politburo—the ruling oligarchy—lose their influence due to the infirmity of old age and death, the struggle for power is likely to be considerable. Few analysts (within the U.S. or the U.S.S.R.) were willing to predict who would emerge as successor to Leonid Brezhnev. Yuri Andropov was just a good guess.

The Soviet political system relies on power to hold the system together more than any Western democratic society. But power is not the only factor. All societies ensure through political socialization that their people will understand and accept their system at a relatively early age (Greenstein, 1965; Hyman, 1969; Renshon, 1977). The U.S.S.R. devotes considerably greater efforts and more resources to formal and informal political socialization than other societies. From preschool through adolescence and adulthood, Soviet children are constantly exposed to a formal process of political socialization: they are socialized in the Oktiabrist (Octoberists)

Several months before his death, the camera captured a weary Brezhnev leaning upon his armchair, adding fuel to rumors that the Russian leader's health was poor. Although the Soviet system of government does not provide clearly for a successor, Yuri Andropov's selection caught few outside analysts by total surprise.

from age 6–8, the Pioneers from age 9–14, and the Young Communist League (YCL) from 15–28; then, of course, the Communist Party. Lenin and the Communist Party become part of the child's vocabulary as revered institutions at kindergarten age. The radio, television, newspapers, books, and the vast propaganda machinery ensure conformity and a belief system that the Soviet socialist system is superior to Western capitalist societies. While many in the West believe that the ultimate meaning of society centers on freedom and civil liberties, the average Soviet man or woman believes that freedom means to be assured of a job, of health and medical service, and a place to live.

This difference in belief patterns does not mean that each family is provided with decent housing, or that medical facilities are always adequate. What it does mean is that the state tries to ensure such housing whenever possible and the citizen has a right to expect it. At the same time the Soviet citizen has no right to demand freedom to write or say what he or she pleases.

THE CITIZEN AND THE STATE IN THE UNITED STATES

Contrary to life in the Soviet Union, the primary responsibility of the citizen in the United States is to ensure his or her own well-being. Private property is the basis of the American system. Industrialization was not achieved through central planning; there was freedom for ambitious individuals to pursue and develop the vast resources of the United States. This does not imply that the American citizen is ignored by the state. But the help we are currently accustomed to (such as Social Security) is a relatively new phenomenon.

Until the "New Deal" of the Roosevelt administration, the citizen who experienced poverty and want relied on private charity. The Depression of the 1930s ushered in a series of government measures meant to rescue huge segments of the population from unemployment and hunger. A variety of welfare provisions were instituted, including programs for the elderly, the disabled, the unemployed, and needy children. In the 1960s, the War on Poverty increased the involvement of the Federal Government, which financed additional measures such as Headstart and training programs that were meant to equalize opportunities for disadvantaged groups in the race for the "good life." Because many states were unable or unwilling to respond to various societal needs such as worker safety, antipollution controls, auto safety, voting rights,

TABLE 17.1 / THE PUBLIC V. THE GOVERNMENT

A 1982 poll conducted by the New York Times *and CBS indicated that most of those polled disagreed with the Reagan Administration's plans to reduce the federal deficit. Whether the representative structure of the political institution will enable popular opinion to affect government policy remains to be seen at this time.*

Unpopular Measures To Reduce Deficit*			More Popular Measures To Reduce Deficit†	
... to reduce proposed spending on programs for the poor	... to postpone cost-of-living increases in Social Security		... to reduce proposed spending on military and defense	... to reduce the size of income tax cut planned for July
		National total		
29%	37%		49%	59%
		Race		
30	38	White	48	60
25	27	Black	62	52
		Income		
33	45	Over $40,000	51	68
39	42	$30–40,000	51	67
31	39	$20–30,000	54	65
26	36	$10–20,000	47	55
20	28	Under $10,000	46	47
		Political philosophy		
41	43	Conservative	45	57
24	35	Moderate	52	62
23	34	Liberal	55	63
		Party identification		
43	47	Republican	46	61
31	40	Independent	49	62
19	29	Democrat	53	57
		Those seeing economy:		
39	48	Getting better	39	67
25	33	Getting worse	55	57
		Those saying Reagan economic program:		
37	45	Has helped them	41	68
25	32	Has hurt them	54	54
		Region		
31	45	West	49	63
31	35	South	44	56
33	35	Midwest	54	55
24	34	East	52	65

Poll of 1,545 adults conducted March 11–15

* Strategies favored by the Reagan Administration.
† Strategies rejected by the Reagan Administration.
Source: The New York Times, March 19, 1982, p. A20. © 1982 by The New York Times Company. Reprinted by permission.

and medical care, the solutions became the domain of the federal Government, or what is generally called "welfare capitalism."

Unemployment, inflation, and high interest rates created considerable strains in the 1970s, and in the 1980 presidential election, candidate Ronald Reagan ran on a platform calling for a decrease in power of the federal government. The goal was to return some of the prerogatives of decision making to the states, to reduce federal expenditures on programs for the poor, to decrease taxes for the well-to-do and for corporations, and to eliminate regulations established by previous administrations. Ronald Reagan was elected to the presidency in November of 1980, and he set out immediately to limit the role of the federal government. Reagan and his economic advisors believe that by decreasing the role of the government through the reduction or elimination of a variety of rules that interfere with business, and by reducing taxes, they will be providing American business leaders with the required incentives and motivations to explore new opportunities and to invest in new projects. As in the past, they assert, this independence will increase the wealth and well-being of all Americans (see Table 17.1 for polling data about responses to this approach).

Such policies are not without problems. Decreasing regulations, providing vast areas of land and water for exploration, encouraging strip mining, reducing regulations for worker safety in factories, and budget cuts have significant consequences for the individual and the environment. For example, there has been an increase in coal mine fatalities (Feaver, 1982: A21); relaxation of federal stripmining regulations might affect as much as one million acres of national forests and wildlife (Rusakoff, 1982: A 1ff.); and the cuts made in welfare programs, such as Food Stamps and Aid to Families with Dependent Children, have had a devastating impact on children (Perl, 1982: A 1ff.). The changes in these and other programs may affect the well-being of the individual and harm the environment.

Reducing social programs which have been established over a 40-year period—Social Security, unemployment insurance, Medicaid and Medicare, training programs for the unemployed, Headstart programs for the disadvantaged—in the hope that business and private charity will take up the burden is a highly speculative risk.

These changes raise the question of what the role of the government should be. In other words, what is the function of political institutions?

FUNCTIONS OF THE POLITICAL INSTITUTION

A society evolves a political institution as soon as it recognizes a "highest power," a source of authority to which all societal members will be subject. As we have already seen, the **political institution** is the social structure that legitimates certain ways of acquiring and exercising power and that defines the relationship between government and the people. Presumably, almost every society in the world recognizes a need to surrender a certain degree of individual freedom in return for a social structure that is empowered to maintain order, to protect the citizenry, and to coordinate the activities of the society's members. Through government the political institution performs these functions.

Maintaining Order

Many institutions play a role in maintaining order: families and schools socialize children; religious organizations teach ethical principles. But the ultimate responsibility for maintaining order falls on the government and the law, which take over when socialization and informal social pressure fail. Maintaining order has two aspects: enforcing norms and resolving conflicts.

Enforcement of norms. In one way or another, all governments enforce behavioral norms that are considered vital. In less complex societies, such enforcement may come from peer pressures. More often, however, these vital norms are formalized as laws, which are enforced by specific people empowered to apply specific punishments.

In this country, for example, there are prohibitions against violent and harmful acts such as murder, rape, and theft. However, there are also laws against such nonviolent acts as prostitution, gambling, and appearing naked in public. In these cases, the laws do not protect the safety of the citizenry. There are, in fact, no victims. Instead, the laws punish behaviors that do not meet the common standards of proper conduct. We might say that the victim, in these instances, is the social sensibility, the normative texture of the society.

Conflict resolution. The governing order also resolves conflicts that might otherwise cause internal strife. It arbitrates between conflicting groups such as, for example, environmentalists and business and labor and management by devising rules for settling disputes and conflict.

The government acts as the ultimate "umpire" in resolving conflict between and among contending groups and interests. Ideally, the state acts as a neutral force, with its overriding concern the welfare of the nation.

Managing External Relations and Protecting the Citizenry

The state is the only institution to form political, economic, and military relations with other nation states. When diplomacy fails it is the state that invokes the military resources of the nation. In the conduct of trade the state decides what products are available for trading. For example, President Reagan decided that the wheat embargo to the U.S.S.R. imposed by President Carter in 1980 should be discontinued; consequently, American farmers can sell their wheat to the Soviet Union. But highly complex computers are still not an item of trade with the U.S.S.R., because such computers can be used by the Soviets for military purposes.

One of our government's many functions is the managing of external relations with other nations. Here President Reagan represents the United States at the 1982 Versailles summit meeting in France.

Planning, Services, and Public Facilities

Finally, governments plan and fund facilities and activities that concern all members of society. The fact that our economy is based on private ownership does not mean that governmental policies do not affect how the economy functions. For example, the degree and nature of taxation, the tariffs imposed on imports, and the minimum wage all affect employment and unemployment. Highways and national parks must be planned and built. Welfare and medical services are provided; public health is monitored; the elderly must be ensured a modicum of services. Schools must be built and research carried out.

While few dispute whether these functions are appropriately carried out by the political institution, the extent to which the government should provide the various services and facilities or how the cost should be borne by different groups is open to considerable debate. Some advocate the dismantling of all welfare programs, except for private charitable efforts. They assert that there should be little government support for higher education and research, and that people should rely on their own resources and only in very extreme cases should the government become involved. Others believe that political institutions should plan and coordinate many aspects of social life to ensure that everyone shares equitably in its rewards. Some favor such programs as free medical care for all citizens, public ownership of natural resources, and governmental planning of economic distribution and growth.

VIEWS OF THE POLITICAL INSTITUTION

If so many divergent opinions exist, how are decisions made? We all know that the American form of government consists of three independent branches. These are the legislative, or Congress; the executive, or the presidency; and the judiciary, or the Supreme Court. The separation of powers is designed to prevent domination by a small elite, and it provides checks and balances on the conduct of government.

The principle of separation of powers has not, however, prevented widespread claims that the decision-making power of "who gets what and when" is less fairly distributed than it should be. Some feel that the power of the presidency is considerably greater than it was ever meant to be, or that some groups have a significantly greater impact on the decision-making process than others. Let us, then, examine the theoretical approaches used to study how the political institution actually works.

Karl Marx—A Conflict View

From previous chapters you know that Marx did not view the democratic order of a capitalist society as a system in which the people had much to say about the distribution of power. Marx perceived power as always under the control of those who owned the means of production. In a feudal order, power was in the hands of the social class that owned the land; in a capitalist society, power is under control of the class that owns the factories, technology, and other capital. In the Marxist framework political institutions are never independent of those who own the economic resources, and the state always reflects the interest of the property-owning class. For Marx, the state was not a neutral institution, an umpire in judgment of values. The state, as well as prevailing values and norms, literature, and religion, invariably served the dominant class.

The ideas of the ruling class are in every epoch the ruling ideas, i.e., the class which is the ruling material force of society, is at the same time its ruling intellectual force. The class which has the means of material production at its disposal, has control at the same time over the means of mental production, so that thereby, generally speaking, the ideas of those who lack the means of mental production are subject to it. (Marx, 1972: 136)

People become subject to the ideas of the dominant class through the control that the class exerts over all spheres of life. From a Marxist perspective, for example, educational institutions in the United States socialize each generation of students to accept the value of private enterprise as the best possible system. Furthermore, educational institutions socialize each generation to perform and behave according to the values that are most conducive to the continuity of such a system. Thus, our society values free speech, but the public school system would not tolerate a teacher who "advocates" a socialist system or an end to private property. And although each person, whether rich or poor, has a vote, resources available to the property-owning class enable them to manipulate the electorate. The main function of all institutions is to support the status quo. Marx believed that only when classes have ceased to exist and a communist system has emerged does the state cease to function. Since the primary role of the state is to preserve the dominance of the capitalist class, once the class system has been abolished there is no need for the state and it "withers" away.

Although the Soviet Union does not claim to have achieved its goal of a communist society yet, there is no evidence to suggest that the state has even begun to decline. During the Khrushchev leadership, it was sometimes said that communism was just around the corner, and the role of the state was said to be declining. Thus, for example, the Soviets claimed that many of the functions of the state were being assumed by voluntary groups, e.g., some parts of welfare administration were already performed by the trade union. Some functions of the police were performed by volunteer citizen groups. But these were minor things, and even these functions have reverted to state agencies since Khrushchev's fall in 1964. Today, the power of the party-state is rivaled by no other group in society.

But if Marx erred about the dominance of the economic factor, does it follow that power is "equally" distributed in a democracy? Do the welfare poor have as much power or influence as the leaders of corporations? Are they listened to? Are their interests as well represented as the interests of business? Who exerts power and influence in American society?

The Elites

Gaetano Mosca (1939) and Vilfredo Pareto (1916) have argued that all societies are ruled by elites. Members of the elite groups have superior intelligence, talent, and skill. Pareto argued that there is a continuous "circulation of elites," a movement of "lions," those superior individuals arising to challenge the "foxes," the old governing elite. The governing class is revived by the vigor brought by those entering it from the lower classes, who then have the capacity to remain in power until they are displaced by a new elite. For Pareto, rule by the few "superior" ones over the masses is inevitable. Pareto thought that the masses not only are incapable of being a governing class, but that their lack of capacity and intelligence prevent them from thinking about such possibilities.

The ideas expressed by Mosca and Pareto were accepted as applying to some societies, but it was long assumed that the structure of political power in American society was of a pluralist nature. There might be a ruling elite in some societies, but not in American society. Given this belief, we can understand how C. Wright Mills jolted the sociological community with the publication of *The Power Elite* in 1956. Mills centered his argument on the thesis that changes in American society in the last century have ushered in a new alignment of power: a **power elite**, composed of the upper levels of the military, government, and business executives, who shape the policies of the country at the expense of Congress, which has been relegated to a secondary place of middle-level decision makers.

According to Mills, the increasing dominance of the corporation, the federal government (especially the Office of Management and Budget, the president, and the cabinet), and the military have led to the development of a powerful elite. These leaders have neither seized power, nor do they constitute a conspiracy. But as modern armies and corporations have grown larger and more complex, and as the decision-making process has become more bureaucratized and centralized, the power of economic, political, and military leaders has increased vastly. These leaders now form an interlocking triangle of power (see Table 17.2). The increase in power of the political directorate, the military, and the corporation has been at the expense of the people and Congress.

The elite are simply those who have the most of what there is to have, which is generally held to include money, power, and prestige—as well as all the ways of life to which these lead. But the elite are not simply those who have the most, for they could not "have the most" were it not for their positions in the great institutions. For such institutions are the necessary bases of power, of wealth, and of prestige . . . No one, accordingly, can be truly powerful unless he has access to the command of major institutions, for it is over these institutional means of power that the truly powerful are, in the first instance, powerful. *(Mills, 1956: 361; emphasis added)*

Following Mills, Domhoff (1967, 1980) has provided considerable data to demonstrate the existence of a "governing class," composed of 0.5 percent of the population, who are businesspeople and their families. This group is closely knit through stock ownership, trust funds, intermarriage, private schools, exclusive clubs, and corporation boards. Members of this class hold

TABLE 17.2 / LOCKHEED AND THE GOVERNMENT

The Lockheed Corporation gained some notoriety when the government stepped in to save it from bankruptcy. The data below show why the government was so concerned. The whole relationship between Lockheed, the government, and the military addresses the issue of a military-industrial complex.

Business Summary

Lockheed Corp. is primarily engaged in the research, design, and production of military aircraft, missiles, and electronics systems. The L-1011 TriStar commercial jet program was discontinued in late 1981.

1980	Sales	Profits ($000)
Military and other aircraft	33%	$168
TriStar	18%	−199
Missiles, space, and electronics	39%	122
Aerospace support	8%	39
Shipbuilding and other	2%	14

Sales to the U.S. Government totaled 59% of 1980 sales, to foreign customers 30%, and to domestic commercial buyers 11%.

Important military aircraft programs include the C-130 Hercules transport, the CP-140 Aurora long-range patrol aircraft, the C-141 StarLifter transport modification program, the P-3 Orion antisubmarine warfare aircraft, the TR-1 Reconnaissance Aircraft, and the C-5 Galaxy Wing Modification.

LK is prime contractor for the Navy's fleet ballistic missile system; development is underway on the Trident II. Space contracts include NASA and DOD programs. The company is involved in Navy shipbuilding and repair.

Source: Standard and Poor's Stock Reports, January 1982, Vol. L-Q, p. 1364. Reprinted by permission.

positions in the major corporations, banks, the National Security Council, government departments, the Council on Foreign Relations, and boards of trustees of higher educational institutions. Other studies (Allen, 1974; Dye, 1976;

Useem, 1979) support Domhoff's work, though there is some question about the extent of interlocking positions and the amount of government recruitment from corporations.

Following the publication of *The Power Elite,* pluralists have argued that Mills and others were in error. Pluralists neither claim that power is distributed equally, nor do they see power controlled by a central elite. They see power as being dispersed among different groups, who balance each other out. Leadership changes from issue to issue, and diverse groups participate and make their voices heard. Pluralists argue that powerful groups are not uniformly committed on all issues. Auto manufacturers, for example, are interested in limiting imports of foreign cars, and they are likely to gain considerable support in this area from labor unions. On the other hand, the issue of a minimum wage is likely to find labor and business at opposite poles of the issue.

Kornhauser (1961), in his criticism of Mills' model of the power elite, notes that Mills appears to be concerned with foreign policy ". . . where only a few people finally make the big decisions . . ." (1961: 264). Kornhauser argues instead that the decisions made are for the general interests of the community. While Kornhauser agrees that there has been extensive centralization and bureaucratization, he feels that "centralization cannot be equated with a power elite" (p. 265).

While the critics of the concept of a power elite acknowledge that there is considerable interlocking in the corporate and government structure, they nevertheless argue that there is no evidence that those who wield power have a "common purpose," or that decision makers in large corporations and the government share a common set of values and goals (Orum, 1976). Conflict rather than unity is also possible among powerful business interests as a result of regional shifts of power. Sale (1975) points out that changing concentrations of economic power and influence from the Northeast and Midwest to the Sunbelt states are likely to continue and increase (cited by Orum, 1976). As a result, traditional power alignments will probably change, and competition among groups seeking power will no doubt increase.

The issue, then, is not whether there is an upper class with a disproportionate amount of wealth deeply involved in governmental decisions—clearly there is such a group—but it is whether this group constitutes a *ruling* class. The subject will remain a continuing issue of debate among sociologists.

THE POLITICAL PROCESS IN THE UNITED STATES

Political Parties

The Constitution of the United States makes no reference to political parties, and in fact no parties existed in the early years of the nation. The gentry ruled not because they engaged in electioneering, but by a right associated with their status. The rudiments of a party system came with the Jeffersonians who created a political organization to displace the Federalists from power (Key, 1964).

The Federalists looked upon the party system warily, regarding the party as a threat to the Republic. Washington warned about a "combination of men" as inherently threatening to the state. Washington's warnings against the spirit of the party reflected only in part the "fears of the upper orders against those who would rouse rabble. He was also speaking for an era that had not yet seen the possibility of routinely conducting government in an environment of continuous partisan attack by a minority seeking to gain power" (Key, 1964: 203). The development and institutionalization of a two-party system channelled discontent into an opposing party, and helped prevent major strife or revolution by providing for the orderly expression of disagreements.

Today political parties are generally seen as instruments of democracy.

Chicago's late mayor Richard Daley was one of the last powerful, big-city party bosses who acquired considerable control over party machinery and the patronage system.

". . . parties, in fact have played a major role as makers of governments, more especially they have been the makers of democratic government . . . modern democracy is unthinkable save in terms of the parties. . . . The parties are not . . . merely appendages of modern government; they are in the center of it and play a determinative and creative role in it." (Schnatschneider, 1942: 6–7, cited by Keefe 1980: 20–21).

Political parties play a major role in the recruitment, election, and appointment of officeholders; they play a role in political socialization, by educating the citizen about how and whom to support; and they translate the needs and interests of the electorate into demands on the government. Strong party machines such as Tammany Hall in New York, and others in Philadelphia and Chicago, provided individuals and groups with patronage, minor jobs, and legal aid. They also helped to "fix" things in the courts and with neighborhood police officers. They created a party identification, and these bonds of allegiance translated into votes on election day.

Old types of machine politics have all but disappeared. Civil service and social welfare have decreased or eliminated patronage and handouts. Young, educated city dwellers have banded together to eliminate "machine politics," reform the city, and introduce a more rational and openly democratic structure. On the state level, the power of the political party was challenged in the early 1900s by the Progressive Party, which argued that state and federal officeholders should reflect the will of the people more directly. Progressives felt that a direct **primary** would be more democratic and would simultaneously decrease some of the power and influence of the political party. A primary is an election in which party members choose among candidates within their own party for a particular office. Candidates selected in the primary then run in the general election. Presidential primaries were introduced as early as 1904, and within a decade the primary was adopted by nearly half of the states. The lack of support for primaries in subsequent years reversed the process, and by 1968 only 16 states had a presidential primary.

Each of the major political parties has a particular public image. Since the election of President Franklin D. Roosevelt the **Democratic Party** has been identified as the party more responsive to working-class people and the poor. The **Republican Party** is linked to higher income groups and is generally viewed as more conservative (see Fig. 17.2).

In the 1940s and 1950s, studies of the American voter revealed that Americans formed an early identification with a party, and this identification remained fairly stable throughout adulthood (Campbell et al., 1966). Today, Americans have ceased to identify themselves in large numbers as Republicans or Democrats (see Table 17.3). The proportion of voters who identify themselves as Independents has increased from about 20 percent in 1950 to close to 35 percent in 1970, and about 40 percent in 1980. Only 37 percent identified themselves as Democrats, and 24 percent as Republicans (Ladd, 1981: 3). The decline of the political party has led to stronger television influence and more reliance on effective "packaging" in the quest for office. A vast industry has emerged to advise and direct those seeking office: themes to be developed, issues to emphasize, and special groups to be appealed to. Advertising methods promote the candidate; leadership-like demeanor and effective communication—regardless of the merit and at times the truth of the statements—have become of overriding importance. Some have even suggested

Fig. 17.2 / Republican or Democrat?

Source: Lou Erickson, *Atlantic Journal*, reprinted in *The News and Courier*, Charlotte, North Carolina, March 27, 1978. Reprinted by permission.

American political lore has created stereotypes about our two major political parties. The following is a North Carolina columnist's tongue-in-cheek version of these stereotypes.

Republicans follow plans their grandfathers made. Democrats make their own plans, and they do something else.

Democrats raise Airedales, taxes, and children. Republicans raise dahlias, dalmations, and eyebrows.

Republican boys date Democratic girls. They plan to marry Republicans girls but they figure they're entitled to a little fun first.

Republicans think Santa Claus is a Democrat. So do Democrats.

Republicans fish from the sterns of chartered boats. Democrats sit on the dock and let the fish come to them. Democrats eat the fish they catch. Republicans hang them on the wall.

Democrats name their children after currently popular movie and TV stars and sports heroes. Republicans name their children after parents or grandparents, wherever the most money is.

When a Republican makes a highball he uses a jigger and carefully measures out the whiskey. A Democrat just pours.

Republicans tack up signs everywhere saying "No Trespassing," and "Private Property," and things like that. Democrats, with their picnic baskets full of beer, start fires with the signs.

Republicans tend to pull down their shades though there is seldom a reason why they should. Democrats ought to but don't.

Republicans sleep in twin beds. Maybe that's why there are more Democrats than Republicans.

Republicans like Democrats. So do Democrats.

Democrats consume three-fourths of all the turnip greens grown in our country. The rest are thrown away.

TABLE 17.3 / PERCENTAGE OF VOTING AGE POPULATION VOTING FOR PRESIDENT, 1932–1980

Year	Percentage Voting	Percentage Voting Democratic	Percentage Voting Republican
1932	52.4	57.0	40.0
1936	56.9	61.0	37.0
1940	58.9	55.0	45.0
1944	56.0	53.0	46.0
1948	51.1	50.0	45.0
1952	61.6	44.0	55.0
1956	59.3	42.0	57.0
1960	63.1	50.0	50.0
1964	61.8	61.0	39.0
1968	60.7	43.0	43.0
1972	55.4	38.0	61.0
1976	54.4	50.0	48.0
1980	53.9	41.0	51.0

Source: Adapted from M. Plissner and W. Mitofsky, "What if They Held an Election and Nobody Came?" *Public Opinion* 4 (February–March, 1981), p. 50. Reprinted by permission.

that in the future the party organization will play no role in the electoral function of national campaigns (Keefe, 1980).

Television has been instrumental in the emergence of the phenomenon of self-nomination. Jimmy Carter was unknown before television carried the story of his candidacy. The Democratic Party provided little support for Carter prior to the convention, but by creating an effective organization and through skillful use of the media Carter was able to defeat his rival, Hubert Humphrey, for the Democratic nomination, even though he was a well-known and respected former senator and vice president and

Politicians are increasingly using the mass media to develop images that will garner votes during election campaigns. Here President Jimmy Carter appeals to the Mexican-American community in San Antonio during a campaign stop.

a long-time supporter of labor and minorities. And Ronald Reagan almost defeated an incumbent president for the 1976 nomination.

The expense of running for office has increased; the cost of the 1980 election was 900 million dollars, a three-fold increase from 1968 (Congressional Quarterly, 1982). This exorbitant cost has made financial contributions more important, and groups with greater resources are thus likely to exert a greater influence.

Members of Congress are not immune to the spiralling trend in electoral expenses. Senator Jesse Helms of North Carolina, for example, spent close to 7 million dollars on his reelection campaign to the Senate in 1978, or 12 dollars per voter. His losing opponent spent 26 cents per voter. Money appears to be one of the primary ingredients of a successful campaign, but so far

not the sole one. Former Texas governor John Connolly spent over 9 million dollars in the 1979 presidential primaries—more than any other candidate during that same period—only to suffer defeat. It might be said that money will not ensure an election, but lack of it will surely point toward defeat.

The decline of the political party has made the individual office seeker more indepedent and less reliant on resources from the party. He or she can seek and receive financial contributions directly, and is thus relieved of the obligation to party discipline. But independence from a political party does not invariably mean that the candidate or elected official is free from influence. Numerous lobbies representing vast resources—the oil industry, the American Medical Association, the National Rifle Association, bankers and corporations, as well as the NAACP, and trade unions—expend vast sums each year to influence the vote. A **lobby** is a group that organizes to influence the political structure in order to advance specific identified interests that its members share. Since 1974, corporations have been allowed to establish PACs (Political Action Committees) with contributions from stockholders and company employees. In 1980, 25 percent of money spent on congressional elections consisted of contributions from PACs—almost double what it had been in 1972. As Senator Edward Kennedy noted, "We have the best Congress money can buy. Congress is awash in contributions from special interest groups that expect something in return" (*U.S. News and World Report,* January 29, 1979, p. 24, cited by Keefe, 1980: 175). To be sure, the decline of the political party has made the work of interest groups and lobbies easier. Officeholders are subject to more direct lobbying efforts; they are crowded and pressured by groups intent on getting their way (Keefe, 1980). Of course, in the past, as well as today, political parties engaged in "brokering" among interest groups, and they were not immune to lobbying efforts. The essential difference is that the political party made compromises in order to ensure a more equitable distribution of support among different groups; the political party was responding to the needs of a variety of groups, not simply to one group. It is important to remember that American political parties were never highly structured organizations intent on enforcing party discipline among their members under the threat of expulsion. While the Democratic Party has been regarded as the party of the less affluent and the Republican Party the more affluent, in reality both parties relied on a constituency composed of citizens of both groups, and accommodated their interests to varying degrees.

Interest groups have always been part of the American political landscape and, as sociologist Seymour Lipset (1959) has noted, the diversity of interests cross cutting and overlapping each other ensure a stable political system. Whether this balance will continue in the future is difficult to ascertain. The 1980 election brought to full force a series of single-issue groups such as "The Moral Majority," which profoundly affected the outcome of numerous congressional races. The long-range implications of single-interest groups and massive spending are difficult to predict, but they are likely to affect the electoral system for some years to come.

POLITICAL PARTICIPATION IN THE UNITED STATES

It is a commonly accepted axiom that voting constitutes a political act. But political participation ranges from such activities as wearing a button and expressing a preference for a candidate to attending a political rally, contributing time or money to a campaign, or holding political office.

Political participation runs the gamut from indifference to active work on a candidate's campaign. These enthusiastic convention delegates are obviously engaged in the latter.

Milbrath (1965) devised a hierarchy of political behavior that he classified as "gladiatorial activities, transitional activities, and spectator activities." Gladiatorial-type activities include holding political office, being a candidate for office, soliciting funds, and active membership in a political party. Transitional activities include attendance at a rally, monetary contribution, and contacting a political leader. And finally, spectator activities include such actions as wearing a button and initiating political discussions and voting (1965: 18).

Americans are not known to become widely involved in gladiatorial activities. Only 4 to 5 percent are active in campaign type activities; about 10 percent contribute funds, 13 percent contact a public official, and about 15 percent display a button or sticker (Milbrath, 1965: 19). Verba and Nie (1972) report somewhat higher percentages of political participation, but not sufficiently higher to suggest that more than a small segment of Americans are politically active.

Voting

Despite the considerable emphasis on the importance of the vote, and efforts to mobilize the voters through television ads, presidential elections have only rarely brought more than 60 percent of eligible voters to the polls. In non-presidential elections, fewer than 50 percent of eligible voters cast a vote. Between 1932 and 1980 only five presidential elections had a voter turnout of 60 percent or slightly more. President Ronald Reagan was elected to office by the lowest percentage of eligible voters since 1948, 53.9 percent (Table 17.2).

Historically there has been considerable variation in voting patterns by states. Thus, for example, in 1964, 77 percent of eligible voters in Utah cast their vote, but only 33 percent in Mississippi (Williams, 1970). The low voting rate in Mississippi reflected the disenfranchisement of the black voter, but whites did not vote in high

numbers in the South either (Key, 1964). Changes in voting rights implemented in the 1960s enabled blacks to participate in the political process, but current black voting patterns do not exceed white voter participation (see Fig. 17.3).

In the past, studies showed that high socio-economic status citizens are more likely to vote than the poor; males vote more often than females; older people vote more often than younger people; and the better educated are more likely to vote than the poorly educated. The "typical" voter is more likely to be a middle class, relatively well educated, middle aged, urban person living in the suburbs (Lipset, 1960; Verba and Nie, 1972; Williams, 1970). More recent studies, however, show that women vote no less frequently than men; that there has been a decline among middle-aged voters; and that rural residents vote in larger percentages than urban dwellers (Monroe 1977, cited by Keefe 1980).

The generally low level of involvement of Americans in the political process and the particularly low voter turnout in the 1980 election cast considerable doubt on the claim of a "mandate for change" so often reiterated by President Ronald Reagan and the Republican Party. Victory in an election does not invariably mean the voters support all of the winner's policies; the electorate includes people who care little about some issues and people who are poorly informed on other issues. The pro-Reagan vote included the sympathies of many groups which opposed specific Democratic platform principles. For example, those who oppose the Equal Rights Amendment or support a constitutional amendment to outlaw abortion do not compose the majority of the electorate. For nearly half a century the Republican Party has supported the ERA, so the shift in voter commitment suggests that people voted for Reagan despite his opposition to the ERA, not because of it.

A recent analysis by Ladd (1981) showed a highly disgruntled electorate. In the last three months of the 1980 presidential campaign voter

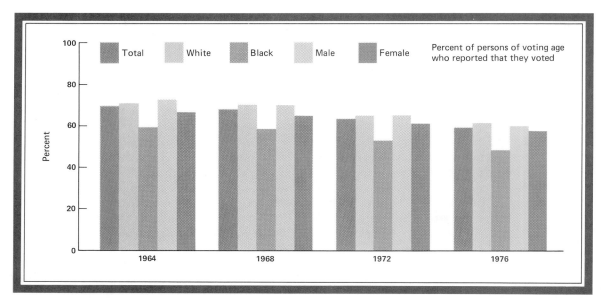

Fig. 17.3 / Voter Participation in Presidential Elections: 1964–1976

Participation in the democratic process of voting for a national leader has declined in recent years. Whereas about 70 percent of the eligible voters cast ballots in the 1964 election (Johnson vs. Goldwater), less than 60 percent voted in 1976 (Carter vs. Ford).

Source: United States Bureau of the Census, *Statistical Abstract of the United States: 1977* (98th edition): Washington, D.C., 1977.

indecisiveness was striking: 52 percent of the respondents stated in August of 1980 that they had not decided whom to vote for. In October, one month prior to the election, the ratings of Carter and Reagan were the lowest of any presidential candidates since 1952 (when candidates were first rated in a Gallup poll). In the last week prior to the election, 28 percent of the voters had not decided who would get their vote (Ladd, 1981).

The theory that Americans in 1980 were dissatisfied with the government may not be as clear-cut as Ladd has noted. At best, their position shows considerable ambivalence.

Americans of all classes and most social positions had come to accept that there is no alternative to a major role by government in regulating the economy, providing social services and assuring economic progress, and secondly, that these generally desired interventions by the state frequently cause problems. (Ladd, 1981: 21)

While Americans expect and want the government to do much, their confidence in the government has "dropped sharply." The 1980 election reflected voters' dissatisfaction with high inflation and their ambivalence about government and politicians. The claim of a presidential mandate when so few eligible voters turned out to vote is more indicative of an alienated electorate than a convinced and supportive one.

Political Alienation

Political analysts have often pointed to the low voter turnout in American elections; for example, only 53.9 percent of eligible voters voted in the 1980 general elections. In the democracies of Canada, France, and England the numbers of voters exceeds the United States average by over 20 percent.

Gilmour and Lamb (1975) argue that the level of cynicism and distrust in government rose considerably in the 1960s. Voters tended to feel that their votes did not affect the policy process; that politicians ignore "people like me"; that government is essentially run for the benefit of "big business." In 1977, 60 percent of the people (twice as many as in 1966) believed that "people running the country don't really care what happens to you," and "what you think does not count anymore" (Keefe, 1980: 177).

Low voter turnout reflects at least in part alienation and the feeling of powerlessness. Voters feel they are unable to exert any influence; consequently, the need to vote appears to be superfluous and meaningless. Verba and Nie suggest that the fact that lower-class persons participate less frequently than upper-class persons makes the political leadership less responsive to the lower class than the upper classes.

The 1983 budget proposal submitted by President Reagan to the Congress leaves little doubt that his government is less responsive and concerned about the poor and the less affluent. The president proposed reducing nondefense programs from $232.8 billion in 1982 to $194.3 billion in 1983, a cut of 16.5 percent; when the factor of inflation is taken into account the cuts reach almost 22 percent. Specifically, the cuts are to come from reducing Medicaid costs by $2.1 billion; Medicare by $3 billion; and education, labor training, and social services by $6.2 billion (Kaiser and Rich, 1982: 7). These actions seem to confirm the views of voters who feel that they are ignored and powerless. On the other hand, the Reagan administration has advocated a **new federalism** to return more decision making and fiscal control to the states where, supposedly, voters have more control. Let's look at this program in more detail.

The New Federalism

The president proposes that 43 programs instituted in the past decades and including a variety of political, educational, and welfare measures be turned over to the states, and partly, it would seem, to private charity. The federal government will assist the states in the first few years in funding these programs, but such funding would be phased out within the next few years.

If on principle such a program appears to be reasonable, in reality it creates not only major problems—where will the states get the funds?— but also major inequities, which the federal government had tried to alleviate by assuming the responsibilities in the first place. For example, the federal government assumed responsibility for the Aid to Families with Dependent Children program (commonly called "welfare") precisely because the states did not. Existing regional differences in this program can mean the difference between eating and not eating; for example, the state-funded welfare and food stamps for a family of three in Mississippi total about $279, and in New York, $577. The presidential proposal could also lead to efforts by states to reduce their number of members of vulnerable groups.

Private charity can not assume a major responsibility for health and welfare, either: the funds required are too large. It is not feasible that the welfare of a large segment of American people depends on the good will of charity, individual or corporate. Individual and collective generosity are inspiring to all Americans, but could we depend on good will to rescue people from fires, floods, famine, or other disasters?

Reducing the role of the federal government to ensure political equity may seem to be what the founders of this country had in mind. But there is considerable evidence that state legislatures act less equitably with respect to different interest groups than the federal government. The political columnist David Broder noted recently that the principle of "one person, one vote,"

Welfare mothers express concern over the effects of government cutbacks diminishing the funds available for federally subsidized programs.

mandated by the Supreme Court nearly 20 years ago, required the state of Tennessee to redraw its unfairly apportioned districts: the decision has not been widely implemented.

The claim that the state legislatures are sensitive to the interests or needs of the powerless—whether those minorities are political or racial—is hard to prove from the redistricting record. . . . The Arkansas legislature . . . passed a districting plan that the federal court threw out for failing to meet the 20-year-old population equality standards. (1982: A23)

Many black organizations have complained that the districting plans of Alabama, Mississippi, and other states will reduce the chance of electing blacks to Congress.

The policies that President Reagan is asking Congress to approve suggest a relatively small role for the government of the United States in all realms of society except one: defense. The military budget is scheduled to increase rapidly to a projected $364.2 billion by 1987, from $159.8 billion in 1981. This military growth returns us to an examination of another power sector of society: the military-industrial complex.

THE MILITARY-INDUSTRIAL COMPLEX

The military-industrial complex was not a term invented by a radical group. On the eve of leaving the presidency, President Dwight Eisenhower warned the people of the need to "guard against the unwarranted influence . . . by the military-industrial complex." Eisenhower referred to "grave implications" to the structure of American society through a "disastrous rise of misplaced power"

IN FOCUS / Contrasts in Power

This photo essay examines the interrelationship between power—the ability to control others and to compel obedience, even without consent—and politics, the game of power—how to achieve it, how to wield it, and what to do with it. In particular, we will focus on the different types of power and the contrasting ways in which power may be exercised.

(a)

Legal Power

The political system most common today is one based on legal authority, in which power is legitimized by specific laws and procedures. Democracies like our own elect public officials by popular vote, an occasion celebrated in (a) John Caleb Bingham's Verdict of the People *(1854–55). Such informal scenes have been replaced in modern times by massive national conventions (b), where factions vie for power within a highly structured set of procedures.*

(b)

(c)

Since public officials derive their power from the office they hold, they may be called to task for exceeding the authority of their office. For example, the police derive their power from legal authority; however, on occasion the courts have ruled that they have exceeded the limits of their authority—as in (c) the arrest of some twelve thousand anti-war demonstrators during the massive peace rally held in Washington, D.C., in May, 1971.

(d)

(e)

(f)

(g)

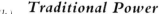

Traditional Power

In political systems based on traditional authority, power is legitimized by historical custom, and a claim to power is generally determined by one's birthright. Many modern monarchies, such as the popular British royal family (d), do not actually exercise significant power in the governing of their country.

By contrast, Ivan IV (1530–1584) ruled Russia with an iron hand (e). "Ivan the Terrible" seized power from both the church and the aristocracy, and his secret police spread terror throughout the country. Tales of his cruelty abound, including throwing dogs from rooftops and casting children from a captured city into an icy river, as well as killing his own favorite son and heir in a fit of rage. Although such traditional power may seem unlimited, in fact, it is usually held in check by informal social norms.

Influence vs. Coercion

The goal of interest groups is to sway decision-makers in positions of power, and their tactics are called lobbying. The influence of bloated trusts on Congress during the late 1800s was satirized by political cartoonist Joseph Keppler in (f) The Bosses of the Senate. Today, many substantial interest groups maintain well-paid, professional lobbyists in Washington (g), who meet regularly with legislators and government officials.

One function of political institutions is managing external relations with other nations. A government may use its authority persuasively by engaging in acts of diplomacy, such as (h) Richard Nixon's historic visit to China in 1972. On the other hand, it may resort to coercion, as in (i) the Israeli attack on West Beirut during the summer of 1982.

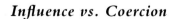

(k)

(j)

Charismatic Power

*In political systems based on charismatic authority, power
is legitimized by a leader's extraordinary ability to
command the allegiance of many followers. Of course, a
charismatic leader's power may be legitimized from other
sources as well, such as the holding of government office.
John F. Kennedy (j), who possessed both charismatic and
legal power, was elected to office by democratic means.
His inaugural address inspired Americans to a new
optimism and feelings of involvement in their government.*

*Because of his charismatic qualities, Fidel Castro (k)
emerged as head of the revolution that seized power in
Cuba in 1959. However, charisma does not guarantee
absolute power. Not all Cubans accepted Castro's
authority and many dissidents were imprisoned or fled to
the United States.*

*Adolph Hitler (l) achieved dictatorial powers through a
reign of terror and suppression of civil liberties. His
charismatic qualities helped him to appeal to the emotions
and fears of the German people and to glorify the myth of
the proud Aryan warrior. Ultimately, he was able to
persuade many of his followers to commit unspeakable
atrocities in the name of "The Führer and the
Fatherland."*

(l)

by a combination of military and industrial influence.

The military-industrial complex is a relatively recent phenomenon. Prior to World War II, the military were a relatively powerless group in the United States (Huntington, 1957), exerting little or no influence in the civilian industrial sector. World War II, followed by the "Cold War," changed the past pattern in several ways. Defense requirements made the production of arms a continuing necessity. Whereas in the past, industrial concerns manufacturing armaments returned to making civilian products at the end of hostilities, the end of World War II brought no such respite. The cold war seemed to make arms production a primary requirement; Korea, Vietnam, and other battles solidified the arms industry.

The Soviet increase in armament spending created a spiral of competition between the two nations, leading to increased allocation of funds for military hardware. The United States government does not manufacture aircraft, helicopters, and tanks. All of these products are built by the private corporate sector (see Table 17.2 earlier in the chapter). Since many large companies produce primarily products for defense, they have become supporters and lobbyists for increased military spending. The military, who invariably see a larger defense budget as best for the security of the nation, and military industrialists, who have a vested interest in producing the armaments, act in concert to protect the nation's and their "best" interests.

A wide variety of industrial organizations do business with the Department of Defense: they manufacture uniforms and shoes, tanks and missiles; they sell orange juice, meat, and building supplies to the government. The relationship is not one-sided; in times of conflict, the Defense Department may help out its suppliers. Thus, for example, during a widespread national boycott of grapes caused by a labor dispute in the 1970s, the Department of Defense became the major purchaser of grapes. But the largest allocation of resources is to military hardware. In this sphere many organizations become the beneficiaries of a defense contract, but only a few receive the very large contracts. In 1975, for example, six companies had a contract with the Department of Defense for over $1 billion.

These good relationships between the military and private sectors extend to employment and other practices. Defense companies commonly hire former military officers. Retired military professionals, having been part of the defense establishment, are sought by companies who produce armaments. The network of relationships established by former military officers facilitates access to the Department of Defense and contract procurement. As sociologist David Segal has noted,

One hundred eighty military contractors in the civilian sector employed 993 former military officers with the rank of major and above, as well as 240 former Department of Defense civilian employees or consultants who had been employed at or above the GS13 minimum salary. The largest single supplier of such personnel was the Air Force, which "recycled" 525 retired senior officers. The aerospace industry, in turn, was the major employer of retired officers. Six major aerospace contractors, for example, employed among them 234 retired senior officers. (1974: 160)

This protection of one party by another is manifested in other ways as well. Frequently, companies have cost "overruns" that the Department of Defense covers. And when Lockheed, one of the Department of Defense's major suppliers, was in danger of going bankrupt, the company was provided with a $250 million loan.

Public support for military spending has increased. In 1968, 8 percent thought we spent too little on defense; in 1980, 49 percent thought so. Whereas in 1969, 52 percent of the public thought that we spent too much on the military, by 1980, the percentage dropped to 14. In 1976, 21 percent of the American public thought the United States was militarily stronger than the

The production of sophisticated military hardware by private industry makes possible the ris[e] *military-industrial complex. The range of such hardware is illustrated by this international [show]* *of weaponry for sale.*

Soviet Union; 27 percent thought the United States weaker than the Soviet Union; and 43 percent thought the United States was about as strong as the Soviet Union. In 1980, the respective percentages have shifted to 16, 41, and 37 percent (Gallup Poll as reported by DeBoer, 1981: 133 and 129).

But public perception of the threat of war is not one gained through some personal experience, as is, for example, the experience of being one of nearly 10 million unemployed. The threat of war as perceived by the public is a consequence of world events as interpreted by government leaders, the military, professional analysts in various organizations, and many others. The mass media report what leaders are saying and

make further interpretations, and what follows becomes the public perception. To be sure, in the 1970s, efforts toward detente were not helped by Congressional refusal to ratify SALT II, the second U.S.-Soviet attempt to limit arms that was negotiated over a period of several years. Public perception of defense needs was also affected by the Soviet invasion of Afghanistan and events in Iran and Poland.

There is no doubt that Soviet defenses have improved vastly from what they were when President John Kennedy forced the Soviets to remove their missiles from Cuba in 1962. In some areas Soviet defense capabilities equal those of the United States; in others, such as conventional military capabilities, the Soviet Union surpasses the United States. But this is not a development of the past two to three years, nor is there evidence indicating that when all Soviet and American defense capabilities are measured the Soviets are stronger.

The All-Volunteer Force

Surprisingly, the major inequity between the United States and the Soviet Union's defenses is in personnel. Soviet armed forces are significantly larger, and conscription is part of their national policy. We, on the other hand, have a volunteer military force, and problems with it are considerable.

The Gates Commission Report of 1970 served as the basis of the All–Volunteer Force (AVF), and it was based on supply and demand variables of the labor force (Moskos, 1981). Military service was no longer to reflect an obligation of the citizen to serve the nation, but was to be looked upon as a "job." Remuneration comparable to the civilian sector for analogous jobs was to induce young men and women (though the proportion of women is not to exceed 12 percent) to volunteer, or take a "job" in the armed forces. The problem arose when insufficient numbers of young men volunteered; moreover, those who did volunteer were frequently high school dropouts who had difficulties mastering the tasks of servicing and using complex machinery. Half of the Army recruits in 1980 failed to complete high school.

An additional problem is posed by the racial and ethnic composition of the AVF. In the Army, blacks constituted 11.8 percent in 1964; 17.5 percent in 1972; and 32.9 percent in 1981. Total minority enlistment in the Army is 41.2 percent. Black enlisted youth have higher educational achievements than white youth: 64 percent of blacks and 53 percent of whites have completed high school (Moskos, 1981). Thus, as sociologist Charles Moskos points out, black enlisted servicemen are representative of the black community in education and social background, but whites come from the least privileged and least educated sectors.

To foster polices that accentuate the tracking of lower class youth into the military, especially the ground combat arms is perverse . . . (it) is to ask what kind of society excuses its privileged from serving in its military. (1981: 20)

Moskos does not suggest a return to the draft. He feels that such a policy lacks "national consensus" and is not likely to be embraced despite anxieties aroused by Afghanistan and Iran. Ironically, however, the brunt of the task of defending the nation is falling on the less privileged and the underclass. Moskos suggests instead a program of national service to include military reserve duty or civilian work; introduction of the "G.I. Bill" for the AVF; a link between federal aid to education and national service; and a differentiating system of compensation for the volunteer who serves two years and those who make the military a career. "The AVF . . . must attract middle class and upwardly mobile youth . . . this can be accomplished only if the AVF is placed in a new social and moral context, one which reconciles citizen rights with citizen duties" (Moskos, 1981: 34).

Moskos is not the only military sociologist to suggest a national service for all youth. Segal also suggests a national service to equalize the cost among all social groups. But he does not regard the problem of the AVF as the root of inefficiency of the Armed Forces: ". . . had we not abolished conscription in 1973, I suspect our armed forces would be no more effective than they are today" (1983: 15). Among the problems of the military, Segal suggests insufficient preparation of management personnel, overlapping management jurisdictions, ineffective coordination, and absence of some basic organizational functions in planning and personnel policies (1983: 16). Moreover, military procurement is "gadget happiness"; things that go "bang" are popular (hence planes and tanks), but not so

SOCIAL ISSUE/Social Welfare as a Social Institution

Ronald C. Federico/*Iona College*

THE DEVELOPMENT OF SOCIAL WELFARE

Individually and collectively, people need many resources in order to live happy and productive lives. We have already seen that the major institutions of society serve to organize social life so that people can grow and function in ways which more adequately meet their needs as well as the needs of society.

No social structure, however, meets all of the needs of its members all of the time. To a greater or lesser extent, every part of society generates some problems at the same time that it solves other problems. For example, the social institution of education both transmits knowledge which prepares people to better understand themselves and the world in which they live and prepares them for gainful employment. Yet at the same time the educational system serves to restrict aspirations and opportunities by tracking some students into early termination of their academic careers.

In relatively small, homogeneous, stable societies, problems tended to be dealt with very informally when they arose. The family and the church were major sources of problem solving that could be relied upon to take in an orphaned child or provide a sympathetic ear to an unhappy relative. With the advent of the Industrial Revolution, and the development of large, complex, heterogeneous societies, opportunities for problems multiplied at the same time that the family and the church were themselves beleaguered by social problems, such as rising divorce rates and declining church attendance.

As a result, specialized structures were gradually developed to meet those needs that were not being met in the existing social institutions. At first these helping efforts depended heavily on private charity, the willingness of people to share voluntarily with others. Private charity was often insufficient to meet existing needs, however, so helping became more formal: special taxes were levied to obtain funds for the needy; people were trained especially to provide help to others; and organizational structures were developed whose major purpose was to organize helping efforts.

The Social Welfare Institution

In sociological terms, efforts to help others gradually became organized into a social institution called social welfare. Like any social institution, social welfare has the following characteristics:

A value base. Social welfare activities exist because they are legitimated by societal values. In the United States, for example, we believe that we should help those in need, and that everyone is entitled to certain basic rights and opportunities. Because our society is a multicultural one, certain values are contradictory. While we believe that we should help those in need, we also believe that people are responsible for themselves. These value conflicts and inconsistencies get translated into social welfare structures which are sometimes similarly inconsistent. Nevertheless, there is a basic societal commitment to helping which serves to legitimate the social welfare institution.

A societal need. As has already been discussed, industrial societies have spawned a staggering assortment of human needs even as they have helped solve other problems of living. Poverty, mental illness, drug-related birth defects, divorce-adjustment problems, child-rearing difficulties, consumer-credit traps, widespread crime, employment problems, and the generation gap are only a few of the human difficulties of our time. As we have come to understand more about human behavior and the functioning of social structures, we have also come to understand that solving many contemporary problems requires resources and a level of expertise which are beyond the reach of informal helping networks like the family priest (although informal networks are still effective and commonly used for dealing with some problems).

A formal structure.   Helping activities have become organized into jobs with roles defined according to societal norms. Doctors, nurses, social workers, and lawyers are all occupants of such positions. Each job has roles associated with it: for example, doctors write prescriptions; nurses dispense medication in hospitals; social workers obtain financial, housing, and employment resources people need; and lawyers help people prepare wills. In carrying out these role behaviors, professionals operate within norms which dictate that clients and patients should be treated with dignity and respect. Social welfare positions and roles have been organized into formal organizations that manage and coordinate these activities. They also provide financial and other resources which make service delivery possible. A hospital, for example, provides housing and meals for patients, as well as operating rooms, a pharmacy, and other facilities health professionals need. Hospitals also collect fees from patients which then help support the operation of the organization.

THE STRUCTURE OF SOCIAL WELFARE SERVICES

Social welfare services may be available to all members of society when needed (called, in confusing but widely accepted terminology, an *institutionalized social welfare system*), or they may be available only to certain people under certain conditions (called a *residual social welfare system*). Social Security payments are an example of an institutionalized service. Most employed people are covered by Social Security benefits. Aid to Families with Dependent Children (abbreviated as AFDC and generally referred to as "welfare") is an example of a residual service. In

order to get the financial aid the program provides, applicants have to meet certain standards, called *eligibility criteria*. For example, they must prove that they have children under a certain age and that they lack financial resources. If these (and other) criteria cannot be met, applicants cannot receive AFDC payments. A further complication is that unlike Social Security, which is a uniform national program, AFDC varies by state (all states have the program, but eligibility criteria and payment levels vary from state to state).

These examples illustrate that a social welfare system can have some services that are residual and others that are institutionalized. A major reason for having both kinds of services is the conflicting societal values referred to earlier. Because our society values self-sufficiency, we have tried to emphasize social welfare programs that encourage people to plan for their own needs. Social Security exemplifies this effort. It is a program that is tied to employment, and while people are employed deductions are made from their wages and put into a fund used to provide retirement, health, and disability benefits. The concept is similar to buying a life insurance policy, except in this case people "insure" their retirement or disability income. This is why Social Security is called a *social insurance*. Since people are receiving benefits from a fund to which they have already made contributions, we look at Social Security not as a gift, but as getting back one's own money. This is altogether consistent with a societal value of self-sufficiency.

AFDC confronts societal values in quite a different way. Here, the societal value of self-sufficiency is superseded by the value that we should help those who cannot help themselves. Problems arise, however, when we seek to define those who can or cannot help themselves. Children are uniformly thought to need help from others, and it is the intent of the AFDC program to provide financial assistance to needy families that have dependent children (single adults and childless couples are not included). While it is obvious that a needy family has needy adults as well as children, the AFDC program focuses only on the children. The adults benefit by the money brought into the family, but this is only because of a grudging recognition that there have to be adults to care for the children. Here we see two societal values in direct contradiction. Children deserve help because they are helpless, but their parents do not because they should be self-sufficient. The fact that many adults cannot be self-sufficient due to illness, disability, discrimination, lack of training, child-care responsibilities, and other reasons is a reality sometimes ignored by societal values.

The result of this value conflict is an AFDC program that is fragmented and inadequate. AFDC monies come from general government funds whose primary funding source is taxes. AFDC is therefore considered an *income transfer program,* since it transfers money from one group (taxpayers) to another group (those in financial need). However, unlike social insurances which have no stigma because people are thought to be getting their own money back, the cash *grants* that AFDC recipients receive are stigmatized as "welfare." This occurs because AFDC recipients are considered not to have earned their grants. By accepting such funds, many believe they demonstrate their inability to care for themselves, in spite of the fact that studies have repeatedly shown that most people who need help need it for reasons that are beyond their control. This stigma, even though unfairly applied in most cases, results in payment levels that are inadequate to meet needs, and that make it extremely difficult for families to solve the problems that have generated their dependency (in most states, AFDC payments are well below the official United States poverty level). In a sense, then, our social welfare system is a curious hybrid of institutionalized and residual services. It gives help with one hand, but takes away social respectability and feelings of self-worth for many groups with the other.

Since the focus in the preceding examples has been on financial assistance, the point should be made that social welfare services do not only attempt to help people meet their financial needs. Those that do are called *income maintenance programs,* and they are an important source of basic financial

security for their recipients. However, an equally important part of the social welfare system is the nonfinancial services called *social services.* Social services include personal counseling, living arrangements for children and adults who cannot remain in their own homes due to neglect, abuse, or other reasons, employment counseling and training, family planning, and a variety of other nonfinancial services.

There have been many attempts over the years to reduce the conflicts inherent in the present social welfare system and to reduce the resulting inconsistencies, duplications, and gaps. While it is impossible to foresee with accuracy the specific characteristics of the social welfare system of the future, several general observations can be made on the basis of a sociological understanding of the social welfare institution.

THE FUTURE OF THE SOCIAL WELFARE INSTITUTION

The most fundamental point is that the social welfare institution fulfills a major societal need, and one which is increasing in importance. For example, in 1977 the United States spent approximately 27.5 percent of its Gross National Product on social welfare purposes, including education, health, Social Security, public assistance, and social services. Public assistance expenditures per capita increased from $41 in 1960 to $224 in 1976, an increase of 446 percent (*The Socioeconomic Newsletter,* 1978, p. 6). As other social institutions change, more and more of their functions are left for the social welfare institution. The stress to which the family as an institution has been increasingly subjected has reduced its ability to nurture, socialize, and emotionally support its members. The result is increasingly visible battered children and spouses, teenage runaways, and abandoned elderly people. Social welfare services have grown in response to these needs, all the while trying to strengthen the family's ability to function in other areas. Similar social welfare responses have resulted from changes in the educational institution (meeting the needs of children unable to learn because of home problems, for example), the economic institution (unemployment and technological obsolescence are illustrative), the political institution (violations of people's civil rights, for instance), and the religious institution (problems of alienation and despair).

In spite of these changes, the advent of the Reagan administration in 1980 signaled major redirections in government spending. For the period 1980–1983, Reagan's budget proposals sought to significantly reduce government expenditures for social welfare programs. For example, Reagan proposed to completely eliminate legal services for the poor; to reduce housing assistance by 84 percent; to cut food stamps by 16 percent; to drop funds for adult and vocational education by 45 percent; and to cut bilingual education funding 74 percent (*Human Services Insider*, 1982: 3). These cuts would be accompanied by an increase in defense expenditures from approximately one-fourth of the federal budget in 1978 to nearly one-third in 1983. Clearly, these changes would represent a major change in societal support for social welfare.

Part of the Reagan strategy is to shift funding for social welfare from the government to the private sector. Historically, this has not proven to be a viable strategy. Indeed, it was during the Great Depression of the 1930s that the federal government got so heavily involved in social welfare: the private sector was simply unable to meet large-scale social welfare needs. There is little reason to believe conditions are different today, especially since corporate profits fell from $163.2 billion in 1980 to $154.5 billion in 1981 (*The New York Times*, 1982). And, of course, there is no assurance that private firms would want to support social welfare programs even if profits were high. These events make it difficult to foresee how the social welfare institution will develop in the future.

Nevertheless, social welfare as a social institution is a complex but important part of the societal structure, and it has been receiving more and more attention from sociologists. Its interrelationships with other social institutions, its expression of societal values, its occupational structure, and its organizational characteristics are all of major importance to sociologists as they seek to better understand United States society.

REFERENCES

Dolgoff, Ralph, and **Donald Feldstein** (1980). *Understanding Social Welfare*. New York: Harper & Row.

Federico, Ronald (1980). *The Social Welfare Institution*, 3rd ed. Lexington, Mass.: D.C. Heath.

Human Services Insider 1, no. 3 (February 12, 1982).

The Institute for Socioeconomic Studies (1978). *The Socioeconomic Newsletter*, III, no. 1 (January 1978).

Kamerman, Sheila, and **Alfred J. Kahn** (1976). *Social Services in the United States*. Philadelphia: Temple University Press.

National Association of Social Workers (1977). *Encyclopedia of Social Work*, 17th ed. Washington, D.C.: National Association of Social Workers, especially pp. 1443–1528 in Vol. II.

The New York Times (1982). Plunging profits. March 14, 1982, section 3, p. 1.

Robson, William (1976). *Welfare State and Welfare Society*. London: George Allen and Unwin.

Trattner, Walter (1979). *From Poor Law to Welfare State,* 2nd ed. New York: Free Press.

spare parts. Parts from one plane are taken to service another plane, or what are euphemistically called "irregular logistical procedures," are widespread. Concern with gadgets has led to redundancy. The fancy planes bought by the Air Force are not appropriate for air mobility and close support of ground combat personnel.

The problems of the military are manyfold. Observers question the purchase of complicated planes and similar types of materiel. Indeed, the question might be raised whether more and more is not only redundant, but an extravagant waste of resources that do not contribute to the defense of the nation. In answering this question, as well as the multitude of others our complex society confronts routinely, issues of power become very significant.

POLITICS AND FUTURE DECISION MAKING

The political institution is essential to society's ability to make decisions basic to its well-being and survival. Decision making is power, and government and politics inevitably have to address issues of who will participate in decisions that will affect who gets what. Democratic, socialistic, and communistic political systems take rather different approaches to distributing power. Nevertheless, competing priorities always make decision making difficult, and questions of whether we should have more "guns" (military expenditures) or "butter" (more social-welfare expenditures) are not easily answered.

SUMMARY ▆▆▆▆▆▆▆▆▆▆▆

1. The main purposes of this chapter are to define political institutions; to discuss the differences between an authoritarian state and a democracy; and to describe the functions of political institutions.

2. The Soviet system is a one-party state; the Communist Party is the dominant group which defines and decides the rules and goals of the system. The Soviet system lacks a tradition of dissent, and it has failed to institutionalize the succession process.

3. The state in the Soviet Union has wider and greater powers than the state in a democratic society. Americans and Soviets perceive the rights of government differently. In the American case "the less government the better"; in the Soviet case, the state has widespread obligations to provide jobs, health and welfare, housing, etc.

4. Karl Marx argued that the state reflects the interests of the ruling class. In a communist system the state will eventually "wither" away.

5. The functions of political institutions include maintaining order, managing external relations, providing plans and funds for public facilities and services, and resolving conflicts.

6. Mills and Kornhauser perceived power in the United States in different terms. Mills argued that there is a power elite. Kornhauser argued that power is distributed among different groups, who act as "veto groups."

7. While there is no definitive study on the distribution of power in the United States, there is clear evidence that power is centralized, and that decisions are made by powerful interest groups, often acting together.

REVIEW

Key Terms

Power	Democracy	Democratic Party
State	Political institution	Republican Party
Authority	Power elite	Lobby
Coercion	Political parties	New Federalism
Government	Primary	

Review and Discussion

1. Everyone has had some encounters with legitimate authority—in school, at home, and in other everyday situations. Recount some of your own experiences. What were your rewards for compliance? What would the penalties have been if you had failed to comply?

2. Using a current newspaper as a source, cite several examples of the use of coercion—either real or threatened—to enforce legitimate authority. Find some examples also of coercion used to gain illegitimate power.

3. Wealth, prestige, and charisma are strong elements in determining how much power an individual has. Can you name some currently prominent person whose power depends on one of these elements?

4. Did you vote in the last national election? Did you follow the campaigns of the major contenders for office? What does your voting behavior indicate to you about the way you view the political process in our society?

5. Do you believe there is a so-called military-industrial complex? Cite the evidence you are using to support your beliefs.

6. What organizations have great decision-making power in your community?. How did these organizations acquire their power and how do they maintain it? Under what circumstances might these organizations lose their power?

Experience with Sociology

The opposites of power are apathy and alienation. Many people don't realize the access to power which they have, so they miss opportunities to gain and use it. Others believe that the structure of power (as described in this chapter) is too big or too complicated for them to understand and use. As a result, they retreat. They don't even try to participate in arenas of power where they could in fact function effectively. The only response to power many people have is to complain about it—their exclusion, and the way it is used by others.

Module 5 of *Experience with Sociology: Social Issues in American Society* asks you to confront these issues for yourself. It presents data about voting behavior in the United States, and asks you to compare your own behavior with the data. The module also relates other variables, especially social class variables, to voting behavior. This relates to the societal context in which voting occurs, a topic addressed in this chapter. Voting is only one type of power, although an important one in a democracy. However, examining what one's response is to this type of power may be a useful way to start thinking about participating in other societal arenas of power.

References

Allen, M. P. (1974). The structure of interorganizational elite cooptation: Interlocking corporate directors. *American Sociological Review* 39: 393–406.

Almond, G. (1956). Comparative political systems. *Journal of Politics* 18: 391–409.

Bialer, S. (1980). *Stalin's Successors*. New York: Cambridge University Press.

Broder, D. (1982). The states drop the ball. *Washington Post,* February 17, p. A23.

Campbell, A., P. E. Converse, W. E. Miller, and **D. E. Stokes** (1966). *Elections and the Political Order.* New York: Wiley.

Congressional Quarterly, (1982). *Dollar politics.* 3rd ed. Washington, D.C.: Congressional Quarterly, Inc.

DeBoer, C. (1981). The polls: Our commitment to World War III. *Public Opinion Quarterly* 45: 126–134.

Domhoff, G. W. (1967). *Who Rules America?* Englewood Cliffs, N.J.: Prentice-Hall.

———— (1980)., ed. *Power Structure Research.* Beverly Hills, Cal.: Sage.

Dye, T. R. (1976). *Who's Running America?* Englewood Cliffs, N.J.: Prentice-Hall.

Feaver, D. (1982). Accidents up, citations down in coal fields. *The Washington Post,* February 3, p. A21.

Gilmour, R. S., and **R. B. Lamb** (1975). *Political Alienation in Contemporary America.* New York: St. Martin's.

Greenstein, F. (1965). *Children and Politics.* New Haven: Yale University Press.

Hough, J. (1979). *The Soviet Union and Social Science Theory.* Cambridge: Harvard University Press.

Huber, J., and **W. Form** (1973). *Income and Ideology.* New York: Free Press.

Huntington, S. (1957). *The Soldier and the State.* Cambridge: Harvard University Press.

Hyman, H. H. (1969). *Political Socialization.* New York: Free Press.

Kaiser, R. G., and **J. Rich** (1982). Reagan plan shrinks domestic spending. *The Washington Post,* February 7, p. A1 and p. A10.

Keefe, W. J. (1980). *Parties, Politics and Public Policy in America.* New York: Holt.

Key, V. O. (1964). *Politics, Parties and Pressure Groups.* New York: T. Y. Crowell.

Kornhauser, W. (1961). "Power elite" or "veto groups"? In *Culture and Social Character,* eds. S. M. Lipset and L. Lowenthal. New York: Free Press.

Ladd, C. (1981). The brittle mandate: Electoral dealignment and the 1980 presidential election. *Political Science Quarterly* 96 (Spring): 1–25.

Lipset, S. M. (1959). Some social requisites of democracy: Economic development and political legitimacy. *American Political Science Review* 53 (March): 69–106.

Marx, K. (1972). The German ideology. In *The Marx-Engels Reader,* ed. R. L. Tucker. New York: Norton.

Milbrath, L. W. (1965). *Political Participation.* Chicago: Rand McNally.

Mills, C. W. (1956). *The Power Elite.* New York: Oxford University Press.

Mosca, G. (1939). *The Ruling Class.* New York: McGraw-Hill.

Moskos, C. C. (1981). Making the all-volunteer force work: A national service approach. *Foreign Affairs* 60 (Fall): 17–34.

Orum, A. M. (1976). *Introduction to Political Sociology.* Englewood Cliffs, N.J.: Prentice-Hall.

Pareto, V. (1916, 1935). *The Mind and Society.* New York: McGraw-Hill.

Perl, P. (1982). Devastating impact on children of needy. *The Washington Post,* June 23, p. 1ff.

Plissner, M., and **W. Mitofsky** (1981). What if they held an election and nobody came? *Public Opinion* 4 (February–March): 50–59.

Pomper, G. M. (1975). *Voter's Choice.* New York: Dodd, Mead.

Renshon, S. A., ed. (1977). *Handbook of Political Socialization: Theory and Research.* New York: Free Press.

Rusakoff, D. (1982). Interior concedes eased rules could threaten forests, wildlife. *The Washington Post,* June 21, pp. A1ff.

Segal, D. (1974). *Society and Politics.* Glenview, Il.: Scott, Foresman.

——— (1983). Military organization and personnel accession: What changed and what did not. In *Morality and Military Service,* ed. R. K. Fullinwider. Rowan Littlefield.

Skilling, H. A., and **F. Griffith,** eds. (1973). *Interest Groups in Soviet Politics.* Princeton: Princeton University Press.

Useem, M. (1979). The social organization of the American business elite and participation of corporation directors in the governance of American institutions. *American Sociological Review* 44: 553–572.

U.S. News and World Report, January 29, 1979, p. 24, cited by W. J. Keefe (1980). *Parties, Politics and Public Policy in America.* New York: Holt.

Verba, S., and **N. H. Nie** (1972). *Participation in America: Political Democracy and Social Equality.* New York: Harper.

Weber, M. (1958). *From Max Weber: Essays in Sociology,* eds. H. H. Gerth and C. Wright Mills. New York: Oxford University Press.

Williams, R. M., Jr. (1970). *American Society.* New York: Knopf.

PART FIVE SOCIAL CHANGE

18

POPULATION AND THE QUALITY OF LIFE

Every society experiences the arrivals and departures of members. The result of these pluses and minuses is a population that requires space to live and resources to support life.

The world population is swelling faster than ever before in history; moreover, as the number of world inhabitants increases, the time it takes for a population to double becomes shorter and shorter. In other words, our rate of growth is increasing. In the year 1 A.D., the world population probably stood at about 250 million. By 1650, the population had doubled to half a billion. But only two hundred years later (1850) it had doubled again to 1 billion. After another 80 years (1930) it had doubled to 2 billion. The next doubling took less than 50 years, so that by 1980 the world population stood at 4,414,000,000 (1980 World Population Data Sheet). In that same year, the United States population was 226,504,825 (see Tables 18.1 and 18.2).

DEMOGRAPHY

Demography is a branch of sociology which measures, describes, and analyzes populations and the ways they change. More specifically, demographers are concerned not only with determining specified numbers of people or measuring rates of population growth, but also with how people are dispersed over a varied land area and with their characteristics as a people (the proportion who are old or young, male or female, rich or poor, urban or rural, and so on). However, demographers do not stop with analyzing conditions in the present. Since populations are never static, demographers are also interested in seeing how the size, composition, and distribution of a population are changing. Is the number of people increasing, decreasing, or remaining relatively stable? Is the trend toward an older population, or is the average age declining? Are proportion-

TABLE 18.1 / THE COMPONENTS OF POPULATION

The size of the United States population is determined by the interplay of the birth rate, the death rate, and immigration. Births and immigration add to population, while death reduces it. This table shows how the death rate has been falling, reflecting medical technology and societal concern for the quality of life. The birth rate has also been falling since the 1960s, reflecting societal values and sex-role changes. The immigration rate has been rising, reflecting worldwide unrest.

Year	Total U.S. Population	Net Growth Rate	Birth Rate	Death Rate	Net Civilian Immigration Rate
1930	122,487,000	9.2	21.3	11.5	0.9
1940	132,054,000	9.2	19.4	10.8	0.6
1950*	151,135,000	16.3	23.9	9.6	2.0
1960*	179,386,000	16.1	23.8	9.5	1.8
1970	203,849,000	10.9	18.2	9.4	2.1
1980	226,504,825	11.4	15.7†	8.7†	2.1†

* The "Baby Boom" period after World War II.
† Figures are for 1979.
Source: U.S. Bureau of the Census, *Statistical Abstract of the United States: 1980* (81st edition), Washington, D.C., p. 6; 1980 Census of Population (PC80-51-1), p. 3; and the 1981 United States Population Data Sheet, Population Reference Bureau, Washington, D.C.

ately fewer people living in rural areas? Finally, what factors are producing these changes? If the population in a rural area is becoming younger, is it because old people are moving out or because more babies are being born there?

To investigate these questions, demographers must collect vast amounts of data and make careful statistical analyses. They need reasonably accurate measures of current populations—their composition, trends, and distribution. Demography relies mainly on government records of vital statistics (births, deaths, marriages, and migrations) and on data collected through the *census*.

The Census

The **census** is a periodic population survey. It is more than a simple head count, and it reveals more about a population than its size. Usually questionnaires are filled out by door-to-door census takers who ask standardized questions about age, sex, marital status, race, and income of each household member. Smaller samples are selected for more detailed questioning. From these data we may learn how many more men there are than women (or vice versa) in any given region, the percentages of rural residents and city dwellers, children and adults, and so forth. The United States census, for example, delves into areas such as ethnic affiliation, social class, and income and education levels. It can reveal highly specific information—that there are X number of families of Puerto Rican descent living in Brooklyn, New York, who earn over $50,000 per year, for example.

Problems of measurement. Although since 1933 each state has required official registration of all births and deaths, many, in fact, go unre-

TABLE 18.2 / WORLD POPULATION DATA, 1980

Population size and growth rates vary greatly between different areas of the world. In general, industrial countries have lower birth and death rates. Less developed countries generally have high birth and high death rates, although often birth rates are higher than death rates so that the population increase is substantial. The following data illustrate these points.

Region	Estimated Population (in millions)	Birth Rate	Death Rate	Percent of Annual Natural Increase
World	4,414	28	11	1.7
More developed countries	1,131	16	9	0.6
Less developed countries	3,283	32	12	2.0
Africa	472	46	17	2.9
Asia	2,563	28	11	1.8
North America	247	16	8	0.7
Latin America	360	34	8	2.6
Caribbean	30	28	8	1.9
Europe	484	14	10	0.4
U.S.S.R.	266	18	10	0.8
Oceania	23	20	9	1.1

Source: 1980 World Population Data Sheet, Population Reference Bureau, Washington, D.C.

corded. Collected statistics may not always be comprehensive or entirely accurate. Typically, a census undercounts the population somewhat. And at the international level, many gaps make it difficult to estimate world population. Since a census is an enormous and costly undertaking, many poorer countries have not been able to gather adequate census data at all. Even with modern methods, the United Nations has estimated that its own world population count could be roughly 55 million higher or lower—an error of 110 million, or roughly the population of Japan.

Even the United States census, conducted with painstaking care and the most advanced technology, is not foolproof. One major difficulty arises because certain segments of the population are often left out of the survey entirely. The census is taken on the basis of interviews and questionnaires administered to people in their homes; if a person has no home for some reason, he or she is less likely to be counted. Thus, homeless, unemployed people are often effectively "hidden" from census takers. Respondents may also provide inaccurate information—either intentionally or unintentionally.

The 1980 U.S. census highlighted another reason that census data may not be altogether accurate. During the 1970s and into the 1980s, a number of refugee groups sought a haven in the United States. Because of complex immigration quotas and regulations, many people from these groups could not qualify as legal immigrants. As a result, they entered the country illegally, a practice encouraged by business people who then employed them at substandard wages. Illegal immigration from Mexico has gone on for some time, but recently so-called boat people from Haiti and the Mariel flotilla from Cuba have swelled the tide of illegal immigrants. These immigrants fear that speaking to a census-taker will expose them and result in deportation. Their fears are accentuated by the fact that many of them cannot speak English well, hence they have little opportunity to learn about U.S. procedures.

Oppressive political and economic conditions are powerful incentives for many to seek refuge in the United States. However, those who cannot obtain legal admission, like these Haitians landing in Miami, are often jailed and then deported back to their homeland.

The undercounting of cultural minorities, especially people from Hispanic cultures, has been alleged to be substantial. Some cities, like New York, have filed suit to prevent the census count from being used to determine such things as the number of representatives in Congress and the receipt of federal aid, both of which are proportionate to population size.

Accurate demographic measurements are needed not only to make decisions for the benefit of people living now, but also to make public policy that will fashion and prepare society for conditions in the years ahead. In order to plan for the future, we must have some idea of how many people the future is likely to involve. Projections of future population size come directly from current data gathered by demographers. Analysts take the data and make specific forecasts about the population trends that will probably occur, based on similar trends recorded in the past. Because not every future development is foreseeable, demographers usually offer a low and a high estimate for every projection they make. Estimating world population for the year 2000, they predict that we can expect 5 billion, 400 million at the least, 7 billion at the most. Projections are not meant to predict exactly how many people will actually be living in a given year, but to estimate what the population *might* be if current trends continue.

Calculating population trends requires considerable effort and skill to be accurate. Since measures of fertility and mortality are essential to all population analysis, demographers have developed a number of very specific measures and techniques to analyze birth, death, and growth rates.

Growth rates. From a demographic point of view, there are only three ways by which a population can change: through fertility—people can be born into a population; through mortality—people can leave a population by dying; and through migration—people can move into or out of an area.

Demographers most frequently use three benchmarks when measuring societal birth and death rates: the crude birth rate, the fertility rate, and the crude death rate. We will look at each in turn.

The **crude birth rate** is the number of births per year per 1,000 people of all ages and both sexes in the population. It can be mathematically expressed as follows:

$$\frac{Births \times 1000}{Midyear\ population} = Crude\ birth\ rate.$$

A 3 percent birth rate means that each year a population of 1000 people will produce 30 babies. In 1980, the worldwide birth rate was 28, but it was only 16 in North America (the United States and Canada) (see Table 18.2). The **fertility rate** further specifies the crude birth rate. It is the number of birth per year per 1,000 women of

childbearing age (usually defined as those between 15 and 45 years of age). The mathematical formula is:

$$\frac{Births \times 1000}{Women,\ 15\ to\ 45} = Fertility\ rate.$$

Turning to death rates, the **crude death rate** is the total number of deaths per year per 1,000 in the population. Its mathematical formula is:

$$\frac{Deaths \times 1000}{Midyear\ population} = Crude\ death\ rate.$$

A death rate of 2 percent, for example, means that for every 1000 people, 20 died during a particular year. In 1980, the world death rate was 11, but it was only 8 for North America (see Table 18.2).

Most of us probably think that the current population boom is the result of a rising birth rate. In reality, the situation is far more complicated. A population will continue to grow as long as its crude birth rate exceeds its crude death rate. The rate of population growth is also affected by migrations into and out of a particular area. For example, if 30 people are added by birth and immigration during one year to a population of 1000 people, and 20 are removed by death and emigration (out-migration), the total population at the end of the year will be 1010—a 1 percent rate of growth. Table 18.2 contains illustrative data on world population growth.

Differential fertility and mortality. Fertility and mortality rates are not the same for all populations or for all groups within a population. For one thing, they vary greatly from one age group to another. A society that has a large number of old people will probably have a relatively low birth rate and a high crude death rate, for example. And where there are large numbers of women between the ages of 15 and 45, we can expect a relatively high crude birth rate. Because of these differences, demographers have developed a series of population measurements that focus on specific groups. Two commonly used specific measurements are the infant mortality rate and age-specific death rate.

The **infant mortality rate** reports the number of infants who died in their first year, per 1000 live births. This rate reflects the health and welfare conditions in a country. Despite our advanced medical facilities and innovative techniques, in 1978 the United States had a relatively high infant mortality rate of 13.8, placing us thirteenth among the world's highly developed nations. This figure reflects the disproportionately high incidence of infant mortality among blacks, Native Americans, and other disadvantaged groups in the United States population.

The **age-specific death rate** measures the number of people who die at a given age per 1000 people in that age category. Age-specific death rates can tell us things the crude death rate cannot. For example, the crude death rate tells very little about the quality of life in a society because it does not indicate who is dying. The crude death rate in England is 11.8, but in Venezuela it is only 7.2. This difference does not mean that the standard of living and health conditions are better in Venezuela than in England, but that the population of England is older than that of Venezuela. This conclusion results from the use of age-specific data which can be used to isolate trends. Age-specific rates can be used to measure any sort of population change—birth, fertility, death, or migration.

The age composition of a population is not the only factor that affects fertility and death rates. Demographers have found that reproduction and mortality patterns also vary in terms of sex, race or ethnicity, social class, and place of residence (see Table 18.3). In general, fertility is higher for rural residents than for city dwellers, for Catholics than for Protestants, for blacks than for whites, and for manual workers than for professional or white-collar workers. In many

TABLE 18.3 / WORLD POPULATION CHARACTERISTICS, 1980

The circumstances and quality of life are related strongly to geography. The inhabitants of more developed countries tend to have longer life expectancies and thus are older populations than less developed countries. The data below also show that as societies develop industrially and economically, they also urbanize.

Region	Percent of Population under Age 15	Percent of Population over 64	Life Expectancy	Percent of Population in Urban Areas
World	35	6	61	39
More developed countries	24	11	72	69
Less developed countries	39	4	57	29
Africa	45	3	49	26
Asia	37	4	58	27
North America	23	11	73	74
Latin America	42	4	64	61
Caribbean	40	5	65	50
Europe	24	12	72	69
U.S.S.R.	24	10	70	62
Oceania	31	8	69	71

Source: 1980 World Population Data Sheet, Population Reference Bureau, Washington, D.C.

industrialized nations in recent decades, groups with lower incomes and education levels have usually shown higher birth rates than the middle and upper classes. But in such places as England, Sweden, and the United States, the very highest income groups have higher fertility than middle-income groups.

All of these categories overlap, however, and some factors overshadow others. For example, a black woman with four years of college will probably have fewer children than a white woman who dropped out of high school. A Catholic career woman living in San Francisco will probably produce a smaller family than her Protestant counterpart who lives on an Iowa farm. These subcultural differences in fertility levels are sometimes greater than international differences, and they often cross national boundaries. For example, upper-class fertility rates in Sweden may be closer to upper-class rates in the United States than to lower-class rates in Sweden.

Death rates reflect sex differences as well as socioeconomic factors. Males and females do not die at the same rate. Although more males than females are born in the United States every year, males begin to die at an earlier age. From the fifth year of life on, the male death rate is at least 50 percent higher. By the 25-year age level, females begin to outnumber males in the population. This pattern has not always been the rule. In the past, many women died during childbirth, and a man often outlived several wives. Today a high maternal mortality rate persists in many countries including India, Pakistan, Cambodia, Malaya, Guatemala, Ceylon, and the Soviet Union.

POPULATION COMPOSITION

Of the many features we could describe within a population, the two most basic to societal makeup are age and sex. The distribution of these two traits influences not only birth and death rates, but also the marriage rate, the number

of people in the labor force, the proportion who are in school or retired, and a variety of other factors that determine the nature of our society and must be considered in planning for present and future social needs.

The Sex Ratio

Demographers refer to the number of males per 100 females in a population as the **sex ratio.** Where the number of males and females is the same, the sex ratio is 100. Where there are more males than females, it is over 100. Where there are more females than males, it is less than 100.

The sex ratio for the United States as a whole is 97: there are 97 men for every 100 women. However, the sex ratio is not the same at every age level—it drops from 106 at birth (106 males are born for every 100 females) to 74 for those who are 65 years old. Our low sex ratio reflects the generally higher death rates among men.

The sex ratio may become unbalanced for a variety of reasons. A low sex ratio may reflect the toll taken by war or other physically dangerous activities on the males in a population. Throughout most of our history, we have had a relatively high sex ratio that fluctuated between 102 and 106. This ratio reflects the large influx of males during our heaviest periods of immigration. During frontier days, the sex ratio in our western states was often extremely high. For example, after the Gold Rush, California's sex ratio was 1,200. Today the sex ratios of Alaska and Hawaii, in a sense our last frontiers, stand at 132 and 121. On the other hand, most urban areas—perhaps reflecting the need for a large number of clerical workers—tend to attract slightly more women and have a low sex ratio.

An unbalanced sex ratio may have a number of social consequences. Where there is an excess of either males or females, the rate of marriage will be lowered. Birth rates may sometimes be affected as a result. Because we are a monogamous society, we are concerned with maintaining a balanced sex ratio. However, in a polygynous society (where one man has several wives), an unbalanced sex ratio would not have the same consequences and would not be considered much of a problem.

Age

The age composition of a population is a major factor in determining a nation's economic productivity and consumer patterns—the goods and services that will be produced and needed. When a society has a large number of old and young people, much of the population will not be economically productive and will need economic support. Schools are needed for the young; pensions and health insurance for the old. While every member of the population is a consumer, only some will be producers. Particularly in an industrial society, where there are often laws against child labor and where retirement may be compulsory at age 65 or 70, the very young and the very old will not be able to participate in the labor force and will be dependent on the productivity of others. Demographers express the number of dependent individuals that must be supported by 100 working people as the de-

pendency ratio:

$$\frac{\text{Population under 15 and over 65}}{\text{Population 15 to 64 years old}} \times 1000$$

$$= \text{Dependency ratio.}$$

The dependency ratio of the United States is 54.2; that is, it takes 100 working people to support themselves plus 54.2 dependents. This ratio enables us to compare the dependency loads for different nations. Third World nations often have dependency loads that are roughly 40 percent higher than those in the United States, the Soviet Union, and Europe.

Due to a high birth rate and a shorter life expectancy, the population of developing nations is often very young, making it difficult to achieve economic growth and improve living conditions. With a large number of children to raise and a small number of people to support them, most economic activity will be used simply to maintain present living standards; there will be little if any excess profit to invest in economic development.

The United States was once a country of young people. At present, with a median age of 30, we are a nation of relatively "old people" in comparison with many Asian, African, and Latin

Boom times often result in an unbalanced sex ratio. Such was the case during the nineteenth and early twentieth century, when westward expansion and the lure of gold enticed many men to set out alone in search of new opportunities.

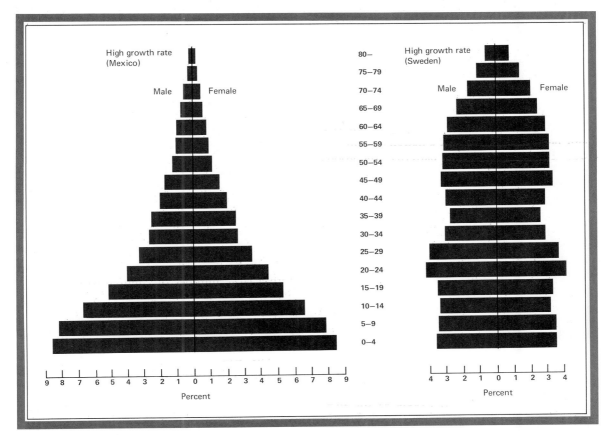

Fig. 18.1 / Population Pyramids

The population pyramid is a convenient method for studying the composition of a given population at a glance. Each level of the pyramid represents the percent of people within a certain age range. Each side of the pyramid represents the percent of males or females.

From the pyramids here, we see that Mexico is experiencing a rapid rate of growth. This young majority in Mexico's population can be expected to continue as a significant "bulge" in the shape of the pyramid. In contrast, Sweden's steady growth rate is illustrated by the relatively straight sides of its pyramid.

Notice how the left sides of these pyramids slope more sharply at the top than the right sides, as males on the average die younger than females. What effect would a war have on the shape of a population pyramid?

Source: 1972 Demographic Yearbook, United Nations (1972 data).

American countries where the median age is less than 20. Demographers often use the **average life expectancy** as a measure of the age of a society's population. It is the number of years lived, on the average, by each member of a given population. After computing the probability of a person's dying at each age, a demographer may develop a **life table,** a schedule of death rates by age, which in turn is a measure of chances of surviving to that age.

Table 18.3 demonstrates how widely life expectancy varies by area of the world. Whereas life expectancy in 1980 was 73 years in North America, it was only 49 in Africa and 58 in Asia. As average life expectancy in the United States has increased, the proportion of old people in our society has also increased. As a result, a smaller number of people are working and paying taxes, but a larger number need health and welfare services. We have a relatively smaller percentage of young dependents in comparison with many Third World areas; on the other hand, we have a larger proportion of older dependents. Nonetheless, our overall dependency ratio is still lower than that of most of the developing countries, and it is not such a serious obstacle to economic growth and well-being.

MIGRATION

The size and composition of a population are affected not only by patterns of fertility and mortality, but also by **migration**—the movement of people within and between countries. Few societies have been untouched by migration at some point in time. Since the beginning of human history, groups of people have moved from one geographic area to another. Before the development of agriculture, probably most of the human race migrated seasonally, following changes in vegetation and the movements of food animals. The entire North American continent was first populated by nomadic people who probably migrated from Asia across the Bering land bridge, gradually working their way to the tip of Tierra del Fuego in South America. Several thousand years later, the continent was again transformed as Europeans began migrating to the New World. Since 1800, about 75 million people have entered the Americas, making this migration the largest international population movement in history. In the decade of 1900 to 1910 alone, over 8.8 million immigrants arrived

in the United States (*Statistical Abstracts,* 1978: 86). The rich ethnic mix resulting from immigration is summarized in Table 18.4.

Push and Pull

People may be *pushed* to leave their homes by such factors as economic hardship, unemployment, crowded living conditions, food shortages, racial or religious discrimination, or political persecution. At the same time, they may be attracted or *pulled* to a new area by the availability of cheap land, wider economic opportunity, or the promise of political and religious freedom. Immigrants to the New World have responded to both push forces and pull forces (see Fig. 18.2).

By the seventeenth century, Europe had become crowded, and competition for land had forced many people off their farms. America, with its vast supply of cheap land, held almost unlimited economic promise. Other immigrants, pushed by political or religious persecution, sought new freedoms here—the Puritans, Europeans escaping political repression following the 1848 revolutions, eastern European Jews fleeing discrimination and pogroms, and later those escaping the Nazi regime.

Push forces are often associated with situations in which migration is forced or involuntary—African slaves, for example, were forced to migrate, as were many European Jews during World War II. The Korean and Vietnam Wars left many with little choice about whether to leave their homes or stay. On the other hand, people migrate voluntarily in response to positive pull forces. They move because they want to achieve a better life in a new home.

In the past, sparsely populated countries such as Canada, Brazil, and Australia needed people and laborers, and often welcomed large numbers of immigrants with very few restrictions. But in recent decades many nations—including our own—have begun to restrict immigration by establishing more selective policies. And although new methods of transportation have made

TABLE 18.4 / AMERICA'S ETHNICITY

America has a long history of ethnic diversity. Whereas earlier immigrants came primarily from Europe, more recent immigrants are more likely to be from Spanish cultures of South America and the Caribbean, and from Asian nations. These changes are reflected in this table, which shows how the older ethnic groups are better integrated into the educational and economic structures of this society. More recent immigrants are more likely to be younger; their movement reflects their search for opportunity and employment.

Ethnic Group	Total Population in U.S. in 1978	Median Age	Percentage Who Are High School Graduates	Median Family Income (1977)
English	10,892,000	42.5	76.0	$18,037
French	2,914,000	39.2	61.9	15,698
German	15,234,000	39.4	69.2	17,850
Irish	8,357,000	41.9	68.5	17,686
Italian	6,778,000	41.5	59.4	18,211
Polish	3,459,000	47.1	60.4	18,867
Russian	1,475,000	48.8	75.9	22,882
Spanish (except Mexican and Puerto Rican)	12,046,000	22.1	40.8	11,421
Mexican	7,151,000	21.3	34.3	11,742
Puerto Rican	1,823,000	20.3	36.0	7,972

Source: U.S. Bureau of the Census, *Statistical Abstract of the United States: 1980* (81st edition), Washington, D.C., p. 35.

travel easier than ever, more new social and political barriers have tended to reduce international migration levels everywhere. In the nineteenth century, for example, even passports were seldom required in most places. Today most governments limit the number and types of immigrants to people who can be easily absorbed into the society and economy.

As a country becomes more populated and highly urbanized, the costs increase for providing new schools, housing, and public services to support an expanded population and to maintain a high standard of living. These costs may outweigh the advantages of a new work force and expanded markets—particularly if job opportunities are becoming more limited. Responding to these pressures, Canada, for example, has recently tightened its immigration policies. Traditionally, Canada has been an "open-door"

country, and until 1972 almost anyone could become a permanent resident merely by moving there. However, now that unemployment is high and newcomers are competing with Canadians for scarce jobs, the government has enacted new rules requiring immigrants to obtain satisfactory scores on a rating scale that assesses education and training, age, employment opportunities, and similar factors.

Immigration and Emigration

In the broadest sense, the United States would not exist at all if it were not for migration. Since colonial times, the United States has attracted and been shaped by an enormous and varied group of immigrants—not only Europe's "tired, hungry, and poor," but also entrepreneurs seeking new investments and sources of wealth,

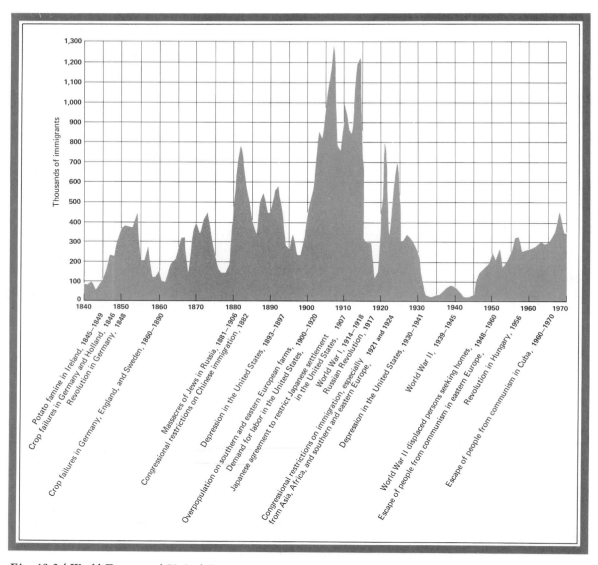

Fig. 18.2 / World Events and United States Immigration: 1840–1970

From *Promise of America: Sidewalks, Gunboats and Ballyhoo* by Larry Cuban and Philip Roden. Copyright © 1971 by Scott, Foresman and Company. Reprinted by permission of the publisher.

religious and political dissenters, single young men looking for adventure or whole families seeking land or jobs, prostitutes, debtors, and prisoners from penal colonies. All were admitted without restriction. All added to our human resources, providing the workforce necessary to develop our industries and farmlands and a domestic consumer market that stimulated further economic development.

Despite our reputation as a great "melting pot," however, continuous, successive waves of immigrants from countries with different languages and cultures created certain stresses and strains. As population pressures increased, as competition for jobs increased, and as nationalism became more fervent, the United States began to restrict immigration. After 1921, our immigration policy became extremely selective. Annual quotas, based on our population composition in 1920, in effect reduced immigration from Asia and Africa to a trickle while favoring immigrants from northwestern Europe. In 1968, new immigration laws were passed, relaxing the stringent and discriminatory provisions and again changing immigration patterns. The new system gives priority to those with occupational skills needed in this country and to those with families already living here.

Immigration to the United States has always been strongly affected by world events (see Fig. 18.2). Recent events in other nations have had a profound effect on the number of foreign-born people entering the United States. The number of foreign-born people in our society had been decreasing sharply. Between 1860 and 1920, 13 to 15 percent of the population was foreign-born; however, by 1970 this proportion had been reduced to 5 percent. Since 1970, this trend has reversed: immigration has increased rapidly (*Social Indicators,* 1980: 43). Indeed, in 1980 about 808,000 legal immigrants come to this country, the largest number of immigrants entering the U.S. in any single year (Lindsey, 1981). This rapid growth occurred in spite of immigration quotas because of allowances made for certain groups due to unusual need. America's involvement in Vietnam led to some feeling of responsibility for the Vietnamese, Cambodians, and Thais fleeing the armed conflict and political repression in their nations. Cubans have also been granted special status because of political repression, as have lesser numbers of Haitians and refugees from some war-torn South American countries. So many Mexicans have entered illegally and found jobs that many of them have also been allowed to stay. These changing patterns of immigration are summarized in Table 18.5.

Illegal immigration has always been part of the migration process, and each year a sizable number of people enter the United States this way. Many of these illegal immigrants are people who lack job skills or fail to meet other requirements, and would not normally be admitted to

During the 1920s, America's immigration policy became more selective, favoring groups that came from northwestern Europe. These newcomers, tagged with free railway passes, await release from the immigrant processing station on New York's Ellis Island.

TABLE 18.5 / ORIGINS OF RECENT U.S. IMMIGRANTS

The following data confirm that primary immigration to the U.S. has shifted from European immigrants to those whose last permanent residence was in Asian or Hispanic nations. (Figures are in percentages.)

Geographical Area or Country	1961–1970	1971–1978
Europe	33.8	19.0
Asia	12.9	33.4
Americas (total)	51.7	45.1
Canada	12.4	3.9
Cuba	6.3	6.7
Mexico	13.7	15.2
West Indies	4.0	5.8
Africa	0.9	1.6

Source: U.S. Bureau of the Census, *Statistical Abstract of the United States: 1980* (81st edition), Washington, D.C., p. 93.

the country. They are responding to the same push and pull forces that have motivated most immigrants. Most come from overcrowded areas where economic opportunities are limited—from the Caribbean, Mexico, and Latin America—and most come to find work.

Internal Migration

The same push and pull forces behind international migrations may also operate within a country. For the most part, people move from one region of a country to another in search of better economic opportunities or a different life style. In fact, the entire western portion of our country was settled largely by people who sought better farmlands and less crowding and competition. Today Alaska continues to provide a social and economic frontier for a hardy few. In the early half of the 1970s that state experienced a boom because of the labor opportunities provided by construction of the Alaska pipeline. But despite the promise of a rich economic potential,

migration to such relatively unsettled areas is often limited until social conditions become more comfortable. People are deterred by the isolation and hardships of life in a place that lacks abundant schools, towns, roads, and social services.

Similarly, earlier in this century, millions of people left the rural areas of the South and Midwest and moved to the urban areas of the Northeast and West. In recent years, however, a countermigration toward the Sun Belt has begun, with Arizona, Florida, and Nevada experiencing the greatest percentages of growth and Florida, California, and Texas receiving the greatest actual numbers of people (see Fig. 18.3).

The energy crisis, policies of the Carter and Reagan administrations favoring Sun Belt areas, and the growing scarcity of jobs in the Midwest and Northeast have all played a part in people's decisions to move south and west. However, increasing numbers of Americans are moving because of life-style preferences (especially those related to retirement, recreation, and climate), as well as family breakup or reunification and the impact of two-career marriages (Population Reference Bureau, 1980: 2). To some extent, the movement south and west reinforces another significant migration pattern that has developed since 1970: the movement from metropolitan areas to nonmetropolitan areas. From 1970 to 1980, almost 3 million more people moved to nonmetropolitan areas than left them (Population Reference Bureau, 1980: 2). Of further interest is the fact that these migrations have racial correlates. The flow from the South to the North was predominantly composed of blacks. The recent moves out of metropolitan areas as well as to the West and South are largely migrations of whites who are well-educated and earning above-average incomes.

In general, however, there is a substantial minority who move frequently in response to changing job opportunities. College-educated white-collar workers, for example, operating in a national labor market, tend to move over long distances; blacks move more often than whites but tend to stay closer to home; and, despite a considerable exodus to retirement homes in Florida and the Southwest, old people move less frequently than the young.

While internal migration, unlike international migration, does not change the size of a population, it does obviously change its distribution. The population composition of regions, cities, and towns will be affected by internal shifts. An area's population may become younger or older as a result of internal migrations, the sex ratio may become unbalanced, and income and educational levels may rise or fall. We have already looked at some of these effects in Chapter 12.

Such changes will obviously have an impact on society. Some demographers believe that distribution is one of the major population problems, and it could be solved by breaking up overly dense concentrations of people. In any case, the misery and despair of the poor who live in the densely populated inner cities of the

Fig. 18.3 / Net Population Change From Migration, 1970–1979

This map graphically illustrates the significance of population shifts from the Midwest and Northeast to the Sun Belt areas of the South and West.

Source: "The Impact of Internal Migration in the U.S.," Population Reference Bureau, Washington, D.C. 1981, p. 1.

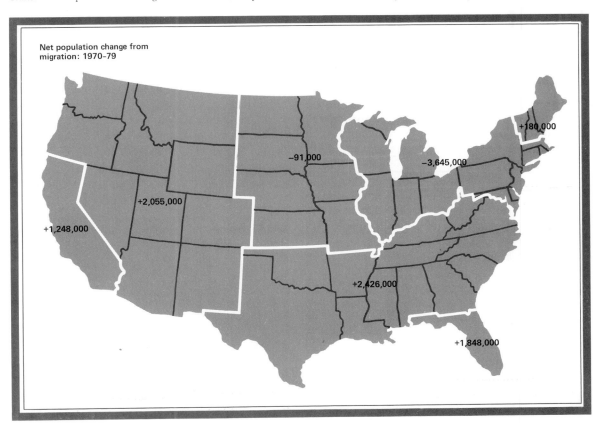

Net population change from migration: 1970-79

+180,000

−91,000

−3,645,000

+2,055,000

+1,248,000

+2,426,000

+1,848,000

United States or in the mushrooming shanty-towns of the Third World are one more aspect of rapid, worldwide population growth.

POPULATION AND THE QUALITY OF LIFE

Population data both *describe* the level of and partially *explain* the quality of life in a society. Birth and death rates, for example, indicate the ability of a society to encourage and support life. Migration data further indicate what societies, and what areas within a particular society, are considered safe and desirable. But population data can also explain the reasons for the quality of life in a society. Knowing that a population is aging indicates an eventual need for services to care for the elderly. These services may or may not be available, depending on a society's wealth, technology, and family structure. Populations which are highly concentrated geographically, or which inhabit geographical areas with few resources and many physical obstacles (such as severe cold, little water, or rugged mountains) can be expected to have to struggle to improve their standard of living.

When sociologists talk about the **quality of life,** they are talking about a population's perception of its own state of well-being. People's perceptions are commonly supplemented by data describing significant aspects of life: death rates, incidence of various types of illnesses, quality of housing, mean educational level attained, median income levels, and so forth. Well-being is a relative concept which varies between societies and even among groups in the same society. An American woman would usually not expect several of her children to die during infancy and childhood; a poor woman in a developing Third World country might view such infant mortality as inevitable. An urban resident of the United States may value anonymity and personal freedom, while a rural resident would probably expect more personal relationships.

The quality of life, then, covers both concrete, life-sustaining resources like the availability of food as well as more intangible factors like feeling valued and respected. The nature of an individual's life is closely tied to demography: race, age, where we live, and so on. These factors are, in turn, affected by population characteristics. As we have seen, people often migrate to improve their quality of life, yet they may end up in situations that are equally bad. Blacks, moving to escape rural poverty and discrimination, have often been forced into urban ghettos. Mexicans, seeking employment in the United States, are sometimes both physically and financially abused and exploited. As more and more people live longer, many are experiencing social isolation and financial need rather than "golden years." Even declining birth rates affect the quality of life in multiple ways. On one hand, women are freer not to marry and to work outside the home. On the other hand, they are subjected to higher risks of poverty, illness, and social isolation.

Recent data indicate that blacks in the United States feel that their quality of life is deteriorating (Clymer, 1981). In part, this is a perception, a feeling, that is well expressed by Alvin Poussaint,

Eskimo children in Greenland fish in the hazardous ice.

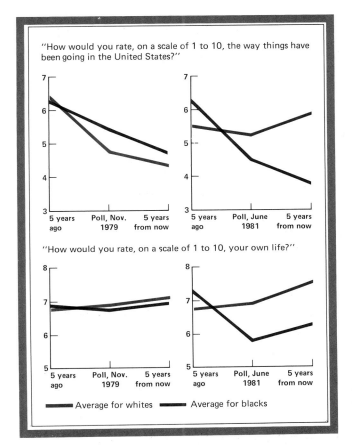

"How would you rate, on a scale of 1 to 10, the way things have been going in the United States?"

"How would you rate, on a scale of 1 to 10, your own life?"

— Average for whites   — Average for blacks

Fig. 18.4 / The Quality of Life: Changing Perspectives between Whites and Blacks
Source: *The New York Times*, August 24, 1981, p. B11. © 1981 by The New York Times Company. Reprinted by permission.

a professor of psychiatry at the Harvard Medical School. He said ". . . blacks saw (President) Reagan as 'no friend of black people' and fear the 'country is going to turn its back on them' " (Clymer, 1981: A1). However, there are also concrete indicators that life opportunities for blacks are indeed decreasing. For example, the income gap between blacks and whites has widened; there has been no improvement in black employment (as there has been for whites); and there has been a decrease in the number of blacks in professional graduate school programs like medicine and social work (Clymer, 1981: B11). It is significant that whites are more optimistic about their quality of life than are blacks—the above data would suggest they have reason to be! Figure 18.4 summarizes the results of a study comparing the perceptions of blacks and whites regarding the quality of their lives.

Population Factors

Population factors are clearly related to the quality of life, yet they do not totally determine it. Let us now look at some of the relationships between population, demography, and the quality of life.

Population size.   The number of people who inhabit an area affects the quality of life possible there. The higher the population density the greater the probability that social interaction will tend toward the impersonal, as we saw when looking at the nature of urban communities. High population density also places special demands on natural resources—the need for water and air pure enough to support life, for example. It also tends to require more highly developed technology to cope with needs like sewage disposal, hygiene and disease control, safe housing, and transportation to bring food and other goods from less densely population areas where they can be more readily produced. It is still unclear whether population density is in itself a factor in mental illness or aggressive behavior, but there is increasing evidence that it is not (Fischer, 1981; Mazur and Robertson, 1972).

While many variables associated with the quality of life can become problematic in a large, densely aggregated population, other effects are likely to enhance life. Large populations provide markets that make the production of many types of goods and services economically feasible. Entertainment is a good example. Producing a multimillion dollar movie like any of the "Superman" films is not warranted without a potential audience large enough to cover the massive costs. Similarly, many art forms are best developed where a large total audience can be divided into specialized groups interested in such things as ballet or chamber music. If the total population is large enough, even relatively small percentages of it will be large enough to support a particular art form—or, indeed, other specialized products such as ethnic restaurants, expensive perfumes, or Concorde supersonic aircraft.

It is again important to emphasize that what is considered a contribution to the quality of life will vary between groups and over time. The state of Oregon, for example, has taken the position that planning population growth by controlling immigration will enhance the quality of life by preserving the natural environment. A country like China has worked to restrict population growth by controlling the birth rate in order to maximize economic development, the Chinese definition of enhancing the quality of life (*Population Reports,* 1977). Yet other countries refuse to adopt policies restricting population growth, believing that child rearing is a fundamental part of the quality of life even if it creates financial hardship or material deprivation. However a society chooses to act, however, there is no doubt that population size and the quality of life affect each other.

Population distribution. As we have already seen, population can be distributed in two ways: demographically and geographically. Both can affect the quality of life. Let us take age as an example of demographic distribution. As was noted earlier in this chapter, the very young and the very old depend on others for their care. The dependency ratio (which we discussed earlier) is a measure of how many dependents 100 working people have to support. The lower the ratio, the less drain there is on the working population and the higher the level of care the dependent are likely to receive. In societies with low dependency ratios, it is more likely that norms and laws will exist to keep the very young and very old out of the labor market. This enables the young to go to school, and the old to have reduced pressure associated with work and child rearing. The result is that both groups may have a higher quality of life. The young can prepare themselves for careers that bring substantial financial rewards and personal satisfaction. The elderly can have more time to engage in pleasurable activities without the need to earn an income (although we have seen that this is actually not a reality for many elderly people).

Geographic distribution of population is also related to the quality of life. This is in part a reflection of ecological factors. A desert or the arctic can only support certain patterns of human life, even given the application of sophisticated technology. However, we have already noted that far less drastic environments exert an influence on human behavior and the quality of life.

The composition of Florida's population has been noticeably affected by an influx of senior citizens. Drawn by the warm climate, the elderly continue to move south in search of an improved quality of life.

When the elderly in the United States move from northern winters to year-round warm climates, they do so because they believe the quality of their lives will be enhanced through better health, better recreational facilities, and easier mobility. On the other hand, they may perceive separation from children who continue to live in the north as a decrease in the quality of life. As discussed above, the geographic distribution of population is also related to ecology with respect to basic life-sustaining resources like water. When Sun Belt communities experience water shortages because of their exploding populations and impose water rationing as a solution, the quality of life is affected.

Population distribution also relates to non-ecological variables affecting the quality of life. To the degree that densely populated urban areas experience problems with crime or substandard housing, the quality of life deteriorates. Rural areas having little population and hence few services like commercial entertainment, a hospital, or paid fire protection have a lower quality of life as measured by access to these services. Regions experiencing high outmigration and a declining industrial and economic base can no longer provide services that enhanced the quality

of life. These are all examples of the many ways that the quality of life can be affected by population distribution.

Population changes. Whenever populations change, the quality of life is affected for some people. An increasing birth rate may strain ecological resources. A declining death rate may reflect better health services and low rates of debilitating illness. Outmigration may sap a society or region of its most capable, highly trained, and productive people. Immigration often increases competition for jobs and other resources. A society is a social structure built by and through people. As people change in number or in kind, the relationships that are resources within the society will also change.

Overpopulation is a change that has serious social and ecological consequences wherever it occurs. But the pressures in the underfed, overcrowded nations of the developing world will differ from those felt by relatively affluent industrialized nations. Clearly the United States is not facing the prospect of famine. Some social scientists feel that there is really no population crisis in the United States because we could probably support twice our present population.

But even moderate growth will increase the problems of densely packed urban areas, crowded housing, air and water pollution, and natural resource shortages. In terms of the quality of life, many feel that we are already overcrowded. The underdeveloped nations, however, are concerned with basic survival—with staving off hunger and simply maintaining a precarious standard of living.

The Malthusian Prophecy

The controversy about unchecked population growth began as far back as 1798 when Thomas Malthus, an English clergyman and economist, published *An Essay on the Principle of Population*. In this work he challenged the popular eighteenth-century optimism that foresaw a rosy future for humanity without war, poverty, crime, or human suffering. Malthus asserted that human populations increased geometrically (1, 2, 4, 8, 16, 32, 64), while food production can only increase arithmetically (1, 2, 3, 4, 5, 6). Humanity was doomed by this tyranny of numbers since any increase in food supplies would be immediately wiped out by further population growth, making any efforts to improve the standard of living useless. Population could only be checked by disease, warfare, and hunger or possibly by

deferred marriage and celibacy. But Malthus did not really believe that human beings could curb their sexual drives sufficiently to contain population growth and avert disaster.

Of course, Malthus did not foresee, nor would he likely have condoned, the widespread use of artificial contraceptives. Moreover, his theory did not anticipate the revolutionary changes in agriculture that have occurred over the past century. Partly as a result of crop rotation, chemical fertilizers, irrigation, hybridization of seeds, mechanized tools, and so on, agricultural yields have increased tenfold.

As the standard of living began to rise in nineteenth-century Europe and the birth rate declined, Malthus's predictions seemed unnecessarily gloomy. But some demographers contend that his theory still applies in the underdeveloped areas of the world where agricultural production does lag behind population growth, and the balance between starvation and human increase is precarious.

The Theory of Demographic Transition

It is not difficult to see that a society's rate of population growth is intimately related to that society's economic development. As its technol-

Fig. 18.5 / The Demographic Transition

The theory of demographic transition predicts a sharp rise in population growth as a developing society first overcomes many earlier causes of death. However, the theory holds that this phenomenon should only be temporary. With the coming of industrialization, changing family patterns will cause an equal drop in birth rates.

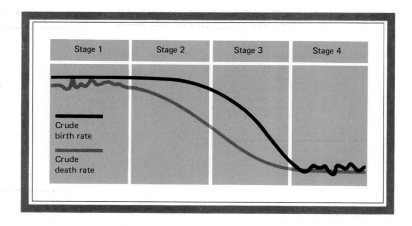

ogy becomes more advanced, the society is able to improve its general quality of life. Where before, the birth and death rates balanced each other, improved living conditions now cause a drop in the death rate. The result of this imbalance of birth and death rates is a rapidly expanding population.

The theory of *demographic transition* offers a more hopeful alternative to the analysis of population growth. Studying the history of industrialization, demographers noted that improved living conditions did indeed cause an initial growth in population, but that this growth was followed by a corresponding drop in birth rates as conditions improved still further. According to the theory of **demographic transition,** population growth will stabilize when economic growth reaches a certain level. In preindustrial societies, children are an economic advantage, laboring in fields to directly produce food. But with industrialization, children become an economic hardship, contributing little to family well-being, while requiring food, clothing, and extensive education. Therefore, the theory holds, parents will limit their families, causing a drop in birth rates and a stabilizing of population growth.

The "transition," then, can be broken down into four stages:

1. Stability, as found in all traditional, preindustrial societies. Death rates, especially for infants, are high and are subject to rapid fluctuations caused by epidemic, famine, or natural disaster. To compensate, the birth rate is also high.

2. The transitional conditions found in societies in the early stages of industrialization. Population growth is rapid as improved conditions reduce the death rate, but the birth rate remains high.

3. A marked decline in the birth rate as the changing nature of the economy discourages large families.

4. Stability as found in advanced industrial societies. The death rate is at a constant low.

The birth rate has fallen to a corresponding low, fluctuating slightly with the economy.

The theory, however, has its critics. First, they point out that it is, after all, only a hypothesis. They remind us that the balance of any society is so complex and specific to that society that we cannot predict its future on the basis of another society's experience.

Second, the historical transitions of Western industrialization may not be applicable to the non-Western nations that are currently experiencing the various stages of development. Japan is most often cited by these critics. Many of the values of ancient Japanese culture have persisted into modern society and are influencing social practices today. Among these is a sense of loyalty to the strongly established central government—something many other developing nations have lacked. Following World War II, the government began a program of limiting population growth. The main method of control was abortion, a practice not regarded as profoundly immoral among the Japanese. The program produced a drop in the birth rate from 34 per thousand in 1947 to a surprising 17 per thousand by 1957. Such a program instituted in most Western nations would meet with staunch resistance because it contradicts the principles of self-determination and Christian morality which are strongly valued in Western culture.

Optimistic as it is, therefore, the theory of demographic transition is fundamentally a description of historical trends. But its use as a tool for demographic projection is rather limited.

Prospects for Control

Most proposed solutions to the population crisis entail either voluntary or compulsory birth control. Proposals range from family planning programs promoting sex education and the use of birth-control pills, intrauterine devices (IUDs), condoms, and sterilization, to tax incentives for small families, to such bizarre schemes as dumping sterilizing drugs into food or water supplies

Population control has become a priority in many societies where overcrowding and depleted resources threaten the quality of life. Urban areas that attract people with opportunities for employment and high standards of living are the first to feel the pressures of overpopulation.

and requiring a license to have a baby. Because technical breakthroughs are useless unless people use them, motivation and attitude are crucial.

In all societies, industrial or underdeveloped, the prerequisites for successful population control are the same: first, people must want smaller families; second, effective means of contraception must be available (as yet there is no safe, easy, inexpensive universal birth control device); and third, people must be aware that these methods exist and must accept them.

In Asia, Africa, and Latin America, where most of the world's population lives, population-control programs have, for the most part, only begun. Most Third World governments now recognize that a population problem exists. Every

country in Asia now has some kind of voluntary family-planning program. But few have been successful in cutting population increases to desired levels. Despite the recent liberalization of abortion laws and the creation of a special Presidential Commission on Population Growth, birth control is by no means universally accepted in our society. It is opposed on many grounds—religious, nationalistic, economic, and emotional. Official Roman Catholic doctrine has discouraged any use of artificial contraceptives as a violation of divine will. For different reasons, various disadvantaged groups have opposed birth control as a tactic designed to keep them in a minority. Politicians have opposed any governmental efforts to promote population control on the grounds that it interferes with personal and religious convictions.

Yet, historically, it seems that neither governments nor churches have much effect on shaping birth-control policies. An increasing number of Catholics, for example, are apparently using birth control methods despite the church's prohibition (Westoff and Ryder, 1969). By the same token, Protestants and Jews seem to have been relatively unaffected by endorsement of birth control by their religious leaders. In fact, members of all religious groups seem to be more influenced by their general social milieu than by religious teachings. Catholics who live in areas where the birth rate tends to be low likewise have lower birth rates (Potvin, Westoff, and Ryder, 1968). Protestants who belong to social groups favoring large families tend to have more children.

Opponents of population control see it as a moral or tactical wrong. Some raise the question, "Who has the wisdom to regulate life?" They fear that controls may be exercised by the state, and that a new government bureaucracy will arise with the power to regulate human life. In addition, some biologists have pointed out that interfering with natural reproductive behavior may have unknown effects on human gene pools.

Proponents of population control see the issue as a matter of survival or of social justice. They point to the large number of unwanted children born in our society. Most of these were born to mothers in low socioeconomic groups— those who had least access to birth-control methods and information, and those for whom the economic burden is greatest (Commission on Population Growth and the American Future, 1972). Supporters of population-control programs argue that these people should be provided with the knowledge and means to limit their families. Other advocates point out that despite our relatively low birth rate and our ability to sustain a high standard of living, Americans are using up a disproportionate amount of the world's resources.

Part of the disagreement over control programs stems from disagreement about the consequences of population growth. There is little consensus, for example, on the ideal population size. The United States had a population density in 1976 of 23 persons per square kilometer—a low figure in comparison to England's 227 or Japan's 303 (*Social Indicators*, 1980: 54). But our high concentration in urban areas, our high standard of living, and our disproportionate impact on the environment may, in effect, make us overpopulated already. The issue is not just the quantity but the quality of life.

THE FUTURE OF POPULATION: DREAM OR NIGHTMARE?

We are entering an era where population control may encompass more than size. **Genetic engineering** is the ability to modify the genetic composition of fetuses in order to achieve socially desired ends. This means that we can not only influence whether a fetus will be conceived, but also what kind and under what circumstances (Rensberger, 1981). In other words, we are ap-

proaching the point where technology may make it possible for the society to affect both the size and the demographic characteristics of the population.

Before discussing some of the developing technological possibilities, we feel it is important to point out that social norms are changing and that these, too, affect a population. The growth of the women's liberation movement has given women more control over their own bodies. This is reflected in such ways as more women not marrying or marrying later in life; women having fewer children or having children later in life (*The New York Times,* 1981); or women deciding not to have children at all (see Tables 18.6 and 18.7). Other changes in societal values have affected women's behavior regarding childbearing. For example, it is now more common for women to have children without being married (*The New York Times,* 1981). New opportunities exist to conceive by using sperm banks and surrogate fathers. A **sperm bank** preserves donated male sperm (usually through freezing)

"Somehow I was hoping genetic engineering would take a different turn."

© 1977 by Sidney Harris/American Scientist Magazine

TABLE 18.6 / AMERICA'S SINGLE, MARRIED, AND DIVORCED POPULATION

This table supports common perceptions that more men and women are currently remaining single than was the case 10 years ago; more are also getting divorced. However, the number of divorced people is still a very small percentage of the population.

	1960	1970	1979
Total Populations			
Single	27,700,000	21,400,000	30,600,000
Married	84,400,000	95,000,000	101,500,000
Divorced	2,900,000	4,300,000	8,800,000
Males			
Single	25.3%	18.9%	23.3%
Married	69.1	75.3	69.2
Divorced	1.9	2.5	4.8
Females			
Single	19.0	13.7	16.9
Married	65.6	68.5	63.5
Divorced	2.6	3.9	6.6

Source: U.S. Bureau of the Census, *Statistical Abstract of the United States: 1980* (81st edition), Washington, D.C., p. 41.

so that it maintains the ability to fertilize a female egg; the sperm are made available to women who wish to be impregnated artificially (called **artificial insemination**). A **surrogate father** is a man who agrees to impregnate a woman who wishes to have a child, even though the man and woman are not married and come together solely for the purpose of reproduction.

The use of artifical insemination and surrogate fathers raises a number of issues. Although these techniques can be used by married women whose husbands are infertile, they are also used by unmarried women who wish to have children but who do not want to marry. Lesbians, for example, can readily have children while maintaining their usual life styles. The link between marriage, child-bearing, and child-rearing is no longer a necessary and automatic one (Zemel, 1981). As a result, the whole conception of the family is broadened to include parenting by people who were never married and who never aspire to marry. It should be noted in passing that men also have additional parenting options. Just as there are surrogate fathers, so there are **surrogate mothers:** women who agree to bear a child for an unrelated man.

These social and technological influences on population size have numerous implications. Increased opportunities for child-bearing and child-rearing among single people mean that birth rates can be maintained during periods of decreasing fertility in two-parent families. For example, during periods of high inflation the costs of child-rearing may serve to discourage families from having more than one or two children. However, if more family units, including one-parent families, have at least one child, the birth rate could potentially remain steady. On the other hand, changes in child-bearing and child-rearing patterns alter any number of other areas of social life. Male and female sex roles are called into question since procreation and child-care tasks are subject to much more personal control and interpersonal negotiation. The traditional patterns of husband-wife interaction in marriage are also subject to reexamination, since women are no longer as dependent on a husband for child-bearing. Nor, for that matter, are men so dependent on their wives for this purpose. And as noted above, the definition of the family is likely to be expanded to include single-parent units of many kinds. Some of these changes may raise value-related concerns, as well as insecurities among people used to and comfortable with traditional social patterns. Sociologically they can be seen as adaptations to social and technological changes.

In addition to population size, population composition is also on the brink of being dramatically affected by medical and biochemical technology. Steady progress in the ability to monitor development in the womb now enables doctors to detect various types of disease, de-

velopmental disorders, multiple births, and even the sex of the fetus. While these improvements have been of primary utility in protecting the life of the fetus and the mother, they also make it possible for parents to decide whether or not they wish to keep the fetus. Exercising this option can be especially important for parents faced with the agonizing decision of whether to allow the birth of a child they know will be severely handicapped.

Techniques of gene splicing and artificial insemination can also affect population composition. **Gene splicing** permits scientists to alter genetic material in order to "custom tailor" life (Golden, 1981). Indeed, it is now apparently possible to artificially create human life. Artificial insemination also allows manipulation of genetic matter to the degree that sperm can be stored and used to impregnate particular women. So, for example, one could mix or match the racial or intellectual characteristics of the man and woman as desired. All of these techniques permit conscious decision making about the type of human life desired. Obviously, a society must question who has the right to make such deci-

TABLE 18.7 / CHANGING DECISIONS ABOUT CHILD-BEARING

The figures below document the decline in the number of children born in the United States. Birth rates shown are per 1000 women 15 to 44 years old.

Live Births	1960 White	1960 Black and Other	1970 White	1970 Black and Other	1978 White	1978 Black and Other
First Birth	30.8	33.6	32.9	42.4	27.0	35.9
Second Birth	29.2	29.3	23.7	26.9	20.5	26.5
Third Birth	22.7	24.0	13.3	15.9	9.3	14.1
Fourth to Seventh	27.7	51.1	12.9	22.5	5.6	11.7
Eight and Over	2.8	15.6	1.2	5.3	0.3	1.1
Total	113.2	153.6	84.1	113.0	62.7	89.3

Source: U.S. Bureau of the Census, *Statistical Abstract of the United States: 1980* (81st edition), Washington, D.C., p. 62.

INTERVIEW/Kurt Finsterbusch

On scarcity and social organization: *"You can't have laissez faire, because you have to manage the allocation of resources. You can't just let the market mechanism work, because you have to make sure there are resources left for future generations."*

Kurt Finsterbusch is Associate Professor of Sociology at the University of Maryland. His research interests include the sociology of world conflicts, comparative sociology, and social ecology.

■ **Q.** Why are you as a sociologist interested in scarcity?

■ **A.** The world might be entering a period of scarcity until technology can produce a sufficient supply of safe and relatively cheap energy. Such a period of relative scarcity of resources would probably have a major effect on most of our institutions. There are people who believe very strongly that scarcity will lead to the demise of democracy. In other words, very few democratic countries will retain their democratic form of government under conditions of prolonged scarcity or under conditions of prolonged periods of no growth.

There are many analysts who believe that scarcity will bring about much more intense social conflict between groups. When the pie no longer grows, various groups will fight more intensely over their portion of the pie. Economic growth has facilitated social integration because the demands of lower groups and middle groups have been granted to a degree without jeopardizing the affluence of the upper groups. Now, however, demands can no longer be met without some sacrifice by upper groups, which they are not likely to accept. Fewer concessions will be made and many people feel that there will be a lot more social conflict and disruptions in society, which will lead to an emphasis on "law and order," higher levels of oppression, and greater levels of surveillance.

■ **Q.** What further effects will scarcity have on our society?

■ **A.** Scarcity is likely to require much greater control of an individual's actions. In this country we enjoy a great deal of personal freedom. This will change. I'm not saying that the Bill of Rights will be amended, but I am saying that there will be much more restraint on people than was required earlier. Certainly China, in order to deal with scarcity in that country, has instituted a great deal of restraint. As I understand it, the Chinese have to have permission to marry and permission from the community to have children. If they have children without permission, the child is often aborted. These kinds of steps are taken in order to deal with the problem of scarcity in the society. We will not go to that extent, but the government will have to intervene in people's lives or design policies to affect people's choices and behaviors in a way that's much more symbiotic with conditions of scarcity. Scarcity will affect the style of life very extensively, and it will probably lead to a different set of values. Material wealth has been an important form of status in our society . . . it is possible that we might shift away from an emphasis on materialism, or material values to an emphasis, say, on personal growth and communalism. The communal emphasis is more compatible with personal growth values and with conditions of scarcity than materialist ambitions.

■ **Q.** How does scarcity affect the world?

■ **A.** Let me review the problem on a worldwide scale. There are four basic biosystems upon which humankind depends. One is cultivated land, the second are the forests, the third are the grasslands, and the fourth are the oceans as a source of fish. The fact of the matter is that right now all of these four systems are in decline. The world's forests are seriously depleted, more than any of the other biosystems. Remember in Third World countries, they depend on wood for fuel, and they are already short. Many forests are gone, there's been a 40 percent reduction. Some of that is to remove the forest to put the land into cultivation, but a lot of it is just the use of wood for fuel. Denuding of the mountainside or hillside in the search for fuel results in much greater erosion, and all sorts of other problems arising out of this. Clearly, the world's grasslands are in decline. The deserts are advancing at an alarming pace. Grasslands have been in decline in many parts of the world. We have our dustbowl in the southwest. The Soviet Union tried to cultivate land that was previously grassland, but the cultivation didn't work out, and the land was seriously damaged before it could be returned to grasses. Throughout the world there has been a decline in grasslands. The ocean cache has remained stable since 1970, and has remained stable at the same time that the technology for taking fish out of the ocean has improved. So we have to consider the ocean as in decline. Although the tonnage of fish is about the same, the quality of fish has declined. Finally, the world's cultivated land probably is in decline. There has been a slight increase in the total amount of land under cultivation each year. However, so many adverse things are happening to the world's cultivated land. One is that some of the best land is taken out of cultivation and turned over to suburban development, housing, shopping centers, that sort of thing. And the quality of land that is added is much lower than the quality of lands taken out. Another problem is erosion and the thinning of topsoils. So, on the whole, the land itself in its natural productivity is in decline. That's overcome by increased fertilizer application and pesticides so that increased productivity can be continued even though the land is deteriorating. One of the problems of pesticides has been that they cause some damage to the organic matter in the soil. Another overall problem is that the structure of the soil is worsening year by year. So, you take a look at the four biosystems upon which humankind depends and they are all in decline. Now, technological developments have offset these trends and increased the production from these

biosystems. Nevertheless, we must be very concerned. We're more and more dependent on—well, what I would say are unnatural additions to the natural biosystems to make them more productive. Their natural productivity has declined.

■ Q. How much malnutrition is there in the world?

■ A. Well, there is disagreement on the extent of malnutrition and starvation. The U.N. statistics, which are not completely unbiased, paint a gloomy picture and one wonders whether that is in order to stimulate a humanitarian response and raise more money. Julian Simon analyzes a lot of these statistics and he successfully shoots holes in many of them. The number of half a billion, or 500 million, is the number that is kind of bandied about as the number of people who are seriously malnourished. Simon demonstrates that this number is too high, but no one has produced an alternative guess that carries weight.

■ Q. Will we in the United States remain the bread basket of the world?

■ A. We've been one of the largest producers of world food and will continue to be. The scarcity of food for the rest of the world is going to substantially affect our economy. We may need to exchange the food we produce for raw materials we need. Studies show that by the year 2000, we will have become very heavily dependent on Third World countries to supply us with raw materials, even though technological improvements will enable us to mine lower and lower grades of ores in the United States. But in general, we'll become very dependent on Third World countries for our basic metals. The point of all this is that our society and the standard of living that we are used to and the kind of society we've developed will become increasingly dependent upon imports from Third World countries. However, Third World countries are less and less inclined to be reliable sources for our raw materials, and are more and more interested in making various demands. These demands are not simply demands for higher prices for their raw materials. They may also make political demands that are hard to grant for the use of their raw materials as the Arab world did with oil.

■ Q. So you see the United States as vulnerable to being cut off from certain resources?

■ A. Yes. A lot of these countries are not terribly stable, and there's a possibility that this may jeopardize our access to these resources. Now, if you take a look at where these resources are, the major areas are in southern and middle Africa, Australia, New Caledonia and New Zealand . . . and well, of course the Middle East for oil. The Soviet Union also has designs on these areas. So, we're faced with a possibility of being cut off from raw materials. And we have to deal with that.

Let me go into the social effects of all these things, and how they will affect our own society. People have noted that the institutions of our society were developed in a period of abundance, a period of economic growth, a period in which one was not concerned about environmental limits. Ideas like laissez faire, the free-market economy, democracy, the value of individualism, the legitimacy of self-interests, the primacy of the individual, and individual rights are all basic to our philosophy. All of those institutions and ideas are maladapted to conditions of no growth. You can't have laissez faire, because you have to manage the allocation of resources. You can't just let the market mechanism work, because you have to make sure that there will be resources left for future generations. And you have to see to it that society values their preservation. There's a question as to whether democracy can survive, because what's required is restraints on individual consumption, and democracy has difficulty bringing about those restraints. We will not vote into office politicians who would vote for those kinds of restraints, because the restraints mean a lower standard of living for us now. It means we can't drive as much as we want to drive. We can't do the things we want to do.

■ Q. So, you feel that scarcity might alter the structure of our society?

■ A. Yes. Scarcity tends to increase the centralization of society. The need for planning and the need for the government to direct the economy in a way that most advantageously utilizes resources will bring about greater centralization and, in some areas, government control of the economy through regulations. Scarcity will, very likely, also bring about increased social conflict. We might see evidence of this in terms of strikes, possibly riots and demonstrations, and possibly even terrorist tactics. The latter are likely to bring about, as I said earlier, more repressive policies. So scarcity threatens democracy, threatens the integration of society, and is likely to bring about more repression. It is also likely to increase inequality. In our society, or any society, certain groups have more central control over resources. They will benefit from scarcity at the same time that the average person will lose out. So, it's likely to increase inequality. Increased centralization, increased inequality, decreased integration, increased disturbances, increased repression, decreased democracy. This is not a very attractive set of developments.

■ **Q.** What needs to be done to deal with these issues?

■ **A.** There are two fronts on which developments need to take place. One is in the technical field. We need technology to enable us to get more use out of the same amount of resources, or of less resources. On the other side would be changes in styles of living so that they are more conducive to conditions of scarcity. Ideally, we would move from a society that maximizes production to a society that minimizes production, but maximizes use. Right now much of our production is wasteful, because we produce many goods that break down and have to be replaced or many goods that go out of fashion and have to be replaced because they are no longer fashionable. So, there's a lot of buying that is simply to replace what breaks or what you no longer want any more—perfectly good, but you don't want it anymore. If you have a car that lasts 40 years, you get everywhere you want to go so you get much use out of little production. One such car could replace maybe 10 cars that you keep only four years before they start breaking down. Now if the automobile industry built a car that would last 40 years, they would go out of business. So, our economy requires obsolescence. Under conditions of scarcity, however, we need to change our economy to one that has incentives to produce durable goods instead of goods that break down and become obsolete. Then we could get as much "use" and the same quality of life at much lower levels of consumption of resources. As a result, there would be much less pollution of the environment and disruption of the environment. Some people advocate socialism as the best way to accommodate the economy to scarcity. The way we produce goods, however, is only one half of the picture. The other half is how we consume. We also consume wastefully. We consume conspicuously to attain status. We consume carelessly because our attitudes were formed over three decades of abundance. And we highly value convenience. In these areas our values need to change and I believe they will. We will come to respect the conserver more than the conspicuous consumer.

Facilities for genetic research, like this molecular research lab at MIT in Cambridge, Massachusetts, hold as yet unknown potential for affecting our nation's population size and composition.

We have already looked at some of the sociological implications of changes in population size and composition. If we were to decide to use our developing technology to drastically increase or decrease the size of the population, everything from community structures to the functions of the family would be affected. Were we to systematically shape the genetic characteristics of future generations, there would be consequences for health care, retirement policies, majority-minority group relations, the quality of life, and countless other sociological variables.

Author Boyce Rensberger poses the basic dilemma cogently: "Rarely in the history of science have new discoveries posed such a keen irony: The more molecular biologists learn about the ultimate nature of life, about the nuts and bolts, the cogs and wheels of our genetic apparatus, the more we reduce living organisms to machines. And yet the acquisition of this knowledge confers upon us the creative power of the gods" (1981: 45). Part of the concern about genetic technology grows out of the fact that business firms are eager to exploit it for their own uses (Demain and Solomon, 1981; Rensberger, 1981). This raises fears that decisions will be made on the basis of marketing and profit rather than to deal with the larger issues of societal needs and significant population variables. What our society ultimately decides to do will emerge through the social processes discussed throughout this book. Any actions will influence our population and hence the basic structure of the social system.

sions—if anyone does. The question is a highly charged value dilemma with no easy answer, but the possibility of tailoring a future population to meet the wishes of a particular social group raises both exciting and frightening visions.

SUMMARY ▰▰▰▰▰▰▰▰▰▰▰▰▰▰▰▰▰▰▰▰▰▰▰▰▰▰▰

1. The main purposes of this chapter are to discuss the methods and uses of demography; to describe the two basic features of population composition—age and sex; to explore the causes and effects of migration; to consider future population issues; and to outline the relationship that exists between population variables and the quality of life.

2. Demographers measure, describe, and analyze populations and the ways they change. To investigate a population, demographers make statistical analyses of data collected from government records and from the census. This demographic information (including growth, fertility, and mortality rates) can then be used to plan both current and future public policy.

3. Age and sex distributions within a population influence many aspects of the population's life, such as marriage rates and the number of people in the labor force. When making age- and sex-based evaluations and predictions for a population, demographers are especially interested in the sex ratio and the dependency ratio.

4. Along with fertility and mortality, migration affects the size and composition of a population. People may leave their homes because of push forces (usually forced or involuntary migration) or pull forces (usually voluntary migration). In the past, countries accepted immigrants without restriction, but today most countries have some restrictions on immigration because of the scarcity of jobs and the high costs of providing public services.

   Migration can occur within a country (internal migration) as well as between countries. Internal migration is influenced by the same push and pull forces that influence international migration, although it does not change the size of a population. It does, however, change population distribution and composition.

5. The quality of life refers to the objectively measured and subjectively perceived elements in the environment that are considered desirable or undesirable. This is affected by population size and density, as well as by the demographic characteristics of a population.

6. The serious consequences of overpopulation are different for underdeveloped nations (which are concerned with the basics of survival) and industrialized nations (which are concerned with overcrowding, resource shortages, and pollution). Two approaches to predicting population growth and its consequences, the Malthusian Prophecy and the theory of demographic transition, have many limitations, but nevertheless offer insights into the history and future of population growth.

   Most solutions to the population crisis involve either voluntary or compulsory birth control. But there are many problems in planning and/or implementing such programs. For example, birth control is not universally accepted, nor has a safe, effective, and inexpensive birth-control method been developed.

7. Developing technology and changing norms are both influencing the nation's population. People can choose whether to have children or not and, increasingly, what genetic characteristics they want their children to have. The implications of these changes for society as a whole are just beginning to be studied and understood.

REVIEW

Key Terms

Demography	Age-specific death rate	Life table	Sperm bank
Census	Sex ratio	Migration	Artificial insemination
Crude birth rate	Dependency ratio	Quality of life	Surrogate father
Fertility rate	Average life expectancy	Demographic transition	Surrogate mother
Crude death rate		Genetic engineering	Gene splicing
Infant mortality rate			

Review and Discussion

1. What factors account for the relatively high rate of infant mortality in the United States? What kind of programs could be instituted to decrease the rate of infant mortality?

2. Did you or any of your ancestors (parents, grandparents, great-grandparents, or further back) migrate to the United States? If so, what pull or push forces influenced the migration?

3. Have you or any of your ancestors migrated within the United States? If so, what pull or push forces influenced this internal migration?

4. Some countries feel they need a larger population to stimulate economic growth. Do you believe that these countries should encourage high rates of reproduction? What alternative measures might be taken?

5. Do you believe that a couple has a right to bear as many children as they want? Should we limit reproduction by law? If so, should quotas be based on financial ability to provide for children, parental IQ, or some other criteria? What are the moral implications of such a program?

6. Would you participate in artificial insemination, or surrogate parenthood programs? What conditions in your own life would influence your decision? Do you think you should have such options available to you, in case you choose to use them?

References

Clymer, Adam (1981). Blacks in U.S. are becoming more pessimistic, polls hint. *The New York Times,* August 24, 1981, p. 1ff.

Commission on Population Growth and the American Future (1972). *Population and the American Future.* New York: New American Library.

Demain, Arnold L., and **Nadine A. Solomon** (1981). Industrial microbiology. *Scientific American* 245, no. 3 (September 1981): 67–75.

Dullea, Georgia (1981). When motherhood doesn't mean marriage. *The New York Times,* November 30, 1981, p. B16.

Fischer, Claude (1981). The public and private worlds of city life. *American Sociological Review* 46 (June 1981): 306–16.

Golden, Frederic (1981). Shaping life in the lab. *Time Magazine,* March 9, 1981, pp. 50ff.

Jones, Landon (1981). *Great Expectations: America and the Baby-Boom Generation.* New York: Ballentine Books.

Lindsey, Robert (1981). 9,700 granted U.S. citizenship in Los Angeles. *The New York Times,* June 23, 1981, p. A14.

Mazur, Allen, and **Leon Robertson** (1972). *Biology and Social Behavior.* New York: Free Press.

The New York Times (1981). Births to the unwed found to have risen by 50% in 10 years. October 26, 1981, pp. A1ff.

Population Reference Bureau (1980). The impact of internal migration in the U.S. Washington, D.C., July 22, 1980.

Population Reports (1977). Department of Medical and Public Affairs, The George Washington University Medical Center, Washington, D.C. Series J, No. 13, January 1977.

Potvin, Raymond, Charles H. Westoff, and **Norman B. Ryder** (1968). Factors affecting Catholic wives' conformity to their church magisterium's position on birth control. *Journal of Marriage and the Family* 30: 263–72.

Rensberger, Boyce (1981). Tinkering with life. *Science* (November 1981): 45–49.

Social Indicators 1980. Washington, D.C.: U.S. Department of Commerce. U.S. Government Printing Office, p. 43.

Statistical Abstract of the United States (1978). Washington, D.C.: Bureau of the Census. U.S. Government Printing Office, p. 86.

Westoff, Charles F., and **Norman B. Ryder** (1969). Recent trends in attitudes toward fertility control and in the practice of contraception in the United States. In *Fertility and Family Planning: A World View,* eds. S. J. Behrman, Leslie Corsa, Jr., and Ronald Freedman. Ann Arbor, Mich.: University of Michigan Press.

World Population Data Sheet 1980. Washington, D.C.: Population Reference Bureau.

Zemel, Sue (1981). Choosing to parent. *Advocate* 316 (April 30, 1981): 18ff.

19

SOCIAL CHANGE, SOCIAL MOVEMENTS, AND THE FUTURE

Pat Wahrenbrock has already sold the big sofa. Bob has found a buyer for the old stereo. One of the neighbors wants the plants. The living room is beginning to look a little bare, and it is a look that gives Mrs. Wahrenbrock a little twinge. "As the time draws due and he's preparing to leave at last, it's giving me butterflies," she said, "but it's something we've got to do, and if he finds a job we're halfway there." "There" is Texas, where the jobs are, where everything is cheaper, where the kids can play outdoors all year round. Robert Roy and Patricia Wahrenbrock want to be there, too, in what sounds like an unclouded land of opportunity, to seize a future that has eluded them in economically shaky Michigan. . . .

Only two generations or so ago, the Middle West drew hundreds of thousands of Southern job seekers to its clanging factories and busy assembly lines. Now the sons and daughters of those immigrants are looking southward as the Middle West's industries stumble and unemployment rises. In the last decade, Michigan's Wayne County, which includes Detroit, lost nearly 345,000 people. . . .

At the age of 29 (Bob Wahrenbrock) . . . is earning $28,000 a year as quality control manager at an established concern that makes and installs electronic sensing devices for sewer treatment, water purification, and chemical plants. As Michigan's industrial recession continues, his company's business has fallen off by 60 percent, layoffs have begun, and he has been told that his job may have only a month to run. . . .

The Wahrenbrocks are products of the ebb and flow of opportunity across this country, and both know things do not always work out. His parents left Kansas for Detroit after World War II, when his father, a chemical engineer, was hired by the Ethyl Corporation, which makes the anti-knock additive for high-octane gasoline. Then Federal antipollution rules hit the pollutants these additives caused, the Ethyl Corporation went into a decline, and his father retired to Sun City, Arizona.

"My Dad went to the top and slowly went down as things got bad," Mrs. Wahrenbrock

recounted. The family owned a motel outside Zanesville, Ohio, on U.S. 40, the National Highway, and were prospering. But then Interstate 70 came through, and the cars did not stop for the night anymore. The motel was sold, and her father's title now is maintenance engineer at a Detroit hospital. (Peterson, 1981)*

THE NATURE OF CHANGE

All societies experience change—in the way people make a living, in the way they relate to one another, in the values they hold. Prehistoric hunters and gatherers become farmers, and farmers become merchants and city dwellers; steam and electricity replace human labor, and industrial revolutions transform human life. Empires rise and fall. Democracies replace dictatorships; and dictatorships, democracies. The deepest values of one generation are rejected—even ridiculed—by the next generation. Through all these changes in human societies, a few things remain constant: the need to make a living, whether it is by subsistence farming or by directing a sophisticated atomic research program; the need for some form of social organization; the need for norms and values that direct behavior; and the need for cultural expression in art, philosophy, and religion. Although these basic needs do not change, the *ways* in which they are met change continually.

SOCIAL AND CULTURAL CHANGE

One way of analyzing the transformation of the U.S. Midwest (or any other part of the society) is to distinguish between social and cultural changes. By **social change** we mean the change in the size, composition, and organization of society and in the relationships between individ-

---

All societies exist in a state of social and cultural change, and while a society's basic needs may remain constant, the ways in which these needs are met are always changing. As these photographs illustrate, the need for faster and more reliable means of transportation has generated dramatic advances in transportation technology.

uals and groups. For example, the population of Wayne County has been decreasing rapidly because of industrial decline. With fewer jobs, friends move away and public services deteriorate. Life styles change as income is reduced or becomes more uncertain. As with the Wahrenbrocks, families are separated as the most skilled and mobile young people move on in search of opportunity. To some degree, changed extended family ties are inevitable. Thus, in a short time the structure of Wayne County had changed.

The county has also experienced **cultural change,** a change in the skills, arts, customs, attitudes, and beliefs of a society. Changes in industrial production rendered prior skills obsolete—cars were different, and ways of making them also had to change. The whole image of a county that prided itself on being an auto capital and that had built a life around that image crumbled. Different skills were needed; different concepts developed of what a desirable automobile should be; industrial and union relationships built around earlier attitudes and beliefs had to be renegotiated. No longer was Texas seen as a faraway area of sagebrush and cowboys. All of a sudden it was a land of jobs and new living opportunities. Even Wayne County started to envy the Sun Belt.

TECHNOLOGY, ATTITUDES, AND SOCIAL STRUCTURE: THE INTERACTION

In distinguishing between social and cultural changes, we do not mean to say that they are separate phenomena. Changes in society's social organization, in the way people and groups relate to one another, influence culture; new ideas, beliefs, and inventions stimulate change in the social structure. For example, in 1447, Gutenberg invented a new type of printing process based on movable type. The printing press and the printed book not only added to the inventory of material culture in Western Europe, they have

revolutionized the values, beliefs, and knowledge systems of societies throughout the world and altered their social systems as well. To trace just one consequence: as books became available, many more people learned to read, and knowledge spread. Many began to question the authority of traditional leaders and to challenge old values and articles of faith. Declaring the supremacy of the written word (the Bible) and the individual's own conscience over the interpretations of the pope and the ecclesiastical hierarchy, Luther started the Protestant Reformation. In denying the absolute supremacy of the Roman Catholic church, Luther's followers challenged the very structure of European society. Revolutionary political changes (the decline of an absolute monarchy, for example) and economic changes (such as the rise of capitalism) have been traced in part to the spread of Protestantism. All of these changes can find their origins partly in Gutenberg's invention of movable type.

Similarly, the invention of gunpowder made possible the development of great conquest states and early experiments in rocketry. The compass made possible the development and settlement of the New World. A single change, therefore, may have far-reaching and often unforeseen consequences, and will involve complex interactions of both *social* and *cultural* factors. Consequently, a complete understanding of change requires a broad *sociocultural* perspective.

THEORIES OF SOCIAL CHANGE

Over the past 10,000 years, people have developed a vast array of societies and cultures—some large, some small, some simple, some complex. But there is one thing they all have in common— they have experienced change in some degree or form. Over the past 150 years, the United States has been transformed from a relatively stable agrarian society into a sprawling industrial giant that would astound our great-grandfathers. During this same period, however, Bushman society has apparently changed very little. But their culture has not been entirely static. At some point in their history, for example, the Bushmen were pushed out of their original home in a nearby fertile plain and forced to take refuge in a hostile desert environment. Naturally, they had to make cultural accommodations. Recently European society has made some inroads into their culture. *Nowhere do people live precisely as their ancestors did.*

Many theorists have tried to identify certain universal patterns in the phenomena of social change. Some believe that all societies pass through cycles. Others have tried to explain human history as a steady progression through recognizable stages.

Functionalist Versus Conflict Theories

The functionalist, conflict, and exchange schools of thought address themselves to the phenomenon of social change: the functionalists in the light of societal stability; the conflict theorists, as a central issue; the exchange theorists, in terms of modified exchange networks.

The functionalist view. As we have noted in other discussions, the functionalist point of view emphasizes the maintenance of balance and equilibrium in the social system. From the early work of Durkheim through the current writings of Parsons, the functionalist school has attempted to show that every element of society serves to maintain the order and stability of the society as a whole. Disruptive forces may buffet this stable system, but they are ultimately absorbed in the essential equilibrium of the total system. For this reason, cultural values, norms, and interactions tend to be conservative and resistant to change.

Obviously, functionalism must immediately confront a philosophical dilemma. How does a theory which emphasizes societal order explain the realities of social change? This problem became particularly pressing during the radical social upheaval of the last twenty years.

Before his death in 1980, Parsons continued to refine the functionalist approach to account for the seeming contradiction. Change is now seen as a shift from one stable order to another different stable order. The forces of change may come from inside or outside the society. They may be the product of internal development or of contact with other societies. In each case, he

The Japanese have successfully adapted to modern technology without giving up their unique heritage and cultural values.

argues, new social institutions will develop to accommodate the emerging norms and values. Because social institutions are necessarily conservative, a new static social system is evolved.

The conflict view. As we have outlined elsewhere, Karl Marx's theory of history as the story of conflict between the economic classes gave rise to the interpretation of society as essentially dynamic rather than stable. Conflict theorists see conflict not as a bridge between one static order and another, but as an integral and ongoing feature of society. They point not only to class conflict, but also to conflict between political groups, racial and ethnic groups, social interest and power groups, and so on. They see this constant conflict as the source of social change and the process that accounts for the evolution of societies.

Interestingly, these theorists also see conflict as the source of social cohesion. Although two groups may be driven apart in conflict, the individual members of these groups are prompted to draw together in their mutual interest. Furthermore, conflict is itself a form of interaction. Although two people or groups may view each other with hatred, they are indeed mingling their points of view, acting as reference groups for one another, delineating ideas, stimulating action, and in many other ways actually cooperating intimately. When viewed in this way, conflict loses its negative and abnormal characteristics, and is seen as a normal and essential element for social evolution.

The exchange view. The norm of reciprocity, which exchange theorists see as basic to social systems, builds in opportunities for social change. This is likely to occur in two ways. One involves altered exchanges caused by new needs of one or both of the social units involved in the exchange process. For example, when a wife begins to work the nature of her exchanges with her environment generally change. The new demands on her time make it less possible for her to provide child-rearing services in return for her husband's economic support. On the other hand, she has less need for his support since she now can generate economic resources herself. This may alter her willingness to defer to her husband as the breadwinner. These changes in the nature of family exchange patterns can have profound effects on the whole family unit. When many families are undergoing these changes, society as a whole is affected. The result may be changed sex roles, new patterns of family relationships and family forms, increased divorce rates, modified child-rearing patterns, and so on.

A second way in which modified exchanges can lead to social change is when unequal exchanges occur that create dominant and subordinate relationships among social units involved in the exchange process. For example, population changes shift the political power that groups have, which can be exchanged for prestige, economic resources, and so on. Ecological changes can also affect exchange relationships. The oil crisis in the United States in the 1970s drove up demand for natural gas and coal as alternative energy sources. Groups controlling these resources suddenly had greatly increased power in exchange relationships. Both of these events indeed led to social change. The elderly, an increasing segment of the population, have fought for and obtained a range of social programs to better meet their needs. Energy concerns have led to the acceptance of smaller cars, slower speed limits, and major industrial dislocations. Like structural-functional and conflict theories, exchange theory contributes to our understanding of social change.

Cyclical Theories: Spengler and Toynbee

The German historian Oswald Spengler believed that societies, like biological organisms, passed through stages of birth, growth, maturity, decay, and death:

Cultures are biological organisms, and world history is their collective biograph. . . . Every culture passes through the age-phases of the individual man. (Spengler, 1964: 21, 22)

Spengler estimated the average life span of most societies at about 1000 years. Most enter the period of youth at almost 50 years. He collected thousands of examples of "youthful," "mature," and "disintegrating" traits from dozens of cultures. Roman society, for example, showed youthful qualities in the early days of the empire, and signs of senescence during the later years of the empire.

In somewhat similar fashion, the modern historian Arnold Toynbee identified certain cycles of social development. Initially every society faces a "challenge"—how to conquer the environment. If the social "response" to this challenge is successful, the society goes on to tackle the next challenge. If it is unsuccessful, the society is destroyed. While Spengler believed that all societies decay and die, Toynbee more optimistically believed that for some cultures the cycle of challenge and response is a steady upward progression toward a perfect civilization. Toynbee's theory has been criticized, however, for its ethnocentrism—its assumption that modern Western society is the most successful ever achieved.

Evolutionary Theories

Many other social theorists have shared the view that cultures and societies progress upward. But instead of continual cycles, they have identified specific stages of development. According to this theory, societies develop from simple to more complex forms. Lewis H. Morgan, an early cultural evolutionist, outlined an elaborate series of seven stages. He believed that as a culture developed more advanced techniques and social institutions, it would progress from the lower, middle, and upper levels of savagery, through the lower, middle, and upper stages of barbarism. Finally, with the invention of phonetic writing, culture achieves its seventh stage—civilization.

The early evolutionists believed that such sequences were necessary and preordained.

Twentieth-century evolutionists, however, have modifed these early ideas. Some theorists have identified a few widespread master trends: *technological development,* based on an improved mastery of the environment; *social differentiation,* based on an increasing diversity of social positions and on specialization; and *functional interdependence,* based on a complex division of labor that makes it necessary for individuals and groups to rely on each other impersonally for specific social tasks. But modern evolutionary theorists point out that no single sequence of stages can be applied to all societies. Japan, for example, did not follow the same path of modernization as the United States. In fact, because modernization was already fully developed, Japan was able to skip many intermediate processes, leaping from a feudal to a fully modernized industrial society in a few generations. Other societies, however, may develop along still different lines. While in the West urbanization and industrialization have gone hand in hand, Iran has become relatively modern and urbanized without developing significant manufacturing industries. Iran has used the income from vast oil and mineral deposits to invest in modern agricultural techniques rather than industry and now exports many agricultural products to its Middle Eastern neighbors. In other words, no particular trend is inevitable. Societies may control or modify the course of their development.

The concept of progress. Finally, modern evolutionists do not equate evolution with progress, or *social improvement.* While accepting the notion that humanity has generally increased its ability to master the environment, they do not suggest that this trend has increased human happiness or has produced societies that are better at filling their members' emotional and psychological needs. Our ability to travel faster than the speed of sound does not mean that we have mastered the art of living.

Progress implies an unscientific value judgment about the desirable direction of change. Whether a change is considered "progress" depends on personal standards and opinions. Most of us would probably agree that industrial and economic development represent progress, but many others would question that view, pointing to industrial pollution, misuse of resources, loss of small-town communal values and the inconveniences of city life as evidence of anything but progress. Some see the easing of social and legal restrictions on sexual behavior as liberating, progressive developments, while others see these tendencies as signs of moral degeneration.

Both the cyclical and the evolutionary theories of change are an attempt to develop a framework for comparing whole societies and for understanding large-scale processes. With many Third World nations beginning to modernize and Western societies changing at an accelerated rate, there is a growing need to find certain general guidelines.

THE DIMENSIONS OF CHANGE

Dramatic overnight transformations are the exception rather than the rule. Some changes—for example, the agrarian revolution of our distant past—are centuries in the making. Some changes alter the course of history; others affect only a limited number of people; still others are only temporary. One aspect of a society may change very rapidly while other aspects do not, sometimes throwing a society off balance for a time.

The Rate of Change

Most of the truly significant changes in human societies in the past took place over long periods of time. People spent hundreds of thousands of years as hunters and gatherers before discovering agriculture. Tens of thousands more years passed before the next great change—the building of cities and the birth of civilizations. People began to use iron for tools in about 2500 B.C., probably in the Middle East; only after thousands of years did iron-working spread to Asia, Africa, and Europe. The compass and gunpowder were invented in China, but it took several centuries for news of these inventions to reach Europe. The changes associated with the Industrial Revolution took place over several hundred years in Europe and the United States. Today, however, the pace of change has accelerated enormously. Why?

The rate of sociocultural change in a society is directly related to the **culture base**—the technology and accumulated information that

This huge minicomputer installation is used by a major New York bank to handle foreign exchange transactions. Already, the fast-growing computer industry has brought significant changes to our society. With their capability of placing a limitless wealth of knowledge at the disposal of the masses, computers hold the key to unforeseen social and political consequences.

people have at hand. Imagine, for example, a town whose hardware store carries only red and blue house paint. The person who wants to be innovative has only one choice—to mix the red and the blue to make purple. But if the store adds yellow paint to its stock, the painter can then have purple *or* green *or* orange *or* even a sort of brown. The number of possible combinations increases geometrically with every addition to the paint shelf. By analogy, the more tools and knowledge a society has, the more new knowledge and technology it is likely to develop.

One classic example of this knowledge is the wheel. At first this simple discovery provided only an easier means of rolling heavy objects. But combined with other technological advances, it now provides the basic design element for the internal combustion engine of cars (while the tires still perform the wheel's original function).

The problem of demographic transition in India is a good example of the effects of cultural lag. Until well into this century, the Indian birth rate was very high, but so was the death rate. A couple might have ten or twelve children, but only two or three of the children would survive to adulthood. Under these circumstances, Indian cultural values naturally stressed having as many children as possible; it was too risky to have only a few children who might die at any time. The population problem in India springs directly from the fact that a technological development—the introduction of modern medical techniques—has drastically reduced the Indian death rate, while attitudes about child-bearing, and thus the birth rate, have not changed. Traditional religious values and social pressures still encourage large families; in many parts of India it is still considered disgraceful to have no children or only a few. As a result, the population of India has multiplied enormously in the last few decades, but the traditional economy of India cannot support all these people. In an attempt to avert famine, India has spent large sums to import food, money that might otherwise be spent on building new industries. Until cultural values are adjusted to take into account the new rate of population growth,

overpopulation will continue to be a serious problem in India.

The rate of technological change is geometric. This relationship is often called the **exponential principle.** In our own society, we have become accustomed to seeing the impossible come true—from heart transplants to landings on the moon. And each of these achievements adds to our technology and knowledge, and theoretically makes possible innumerable new achievements. In fact, some observers feel that the rate of technological change in modern society has outpaced humanity's ability to adapt.

It is all very well to talk about a modern human's unusual ability to cope with change and even to define her or him by that unusual ability, but surely there is some upper limit on a human's ability to adjust to rapid radical changes. If we presently undergo radical social transformations roughly once every quarter century and gear our education for an unknown future to such a rate of change, can we up that rate to once in two decades, to once a decade, to once a year . . . ? One of the questions about which we rarely speculate and know nothing definitively is the following: What is the upper limit—to what rates and scales of change are human beings capable of adjusting? Right now most of us speak of the problems of modernization as though we mean the problems of becoming highly modernized. The problems of staying highly modernized and simultaneously staying alive in any bearable way of life may be much greater. Our ecological threats may only scratch the surface. (Levy, 1972: 54–55)*

Cultural lag. Sociologist William F. Ogburn called the gap between advances in material culture and the consequent adjustment in nonmaterial culture **cultural lag.** Cultural lag occurs when one part of a culture changes more rapidly than other, related parts of the culture. Because all aspects of a culture are related, adjustments need to be made, and the delay in adjustment

---

* From *Modernization: Latecomers and Survivors* by Marion J. Levy, Jr. © 1972 by Marion J. Levy, Jr. By permission of Basic Books, Inc., Publishers, New York.

causes problems for society. In Ogburn's view, technology generally changes faster than social values and norms. Industrialization, for example, changed the material conditions under which people labor. By 1870, many people were working in factories where industrial accidents were common. Yet, it was not until 1915 that the United States laws gave protection to working people through legally enforced safety standards and workmen's compensation. It took that long for people to recognize and act on the problem of safety in factories. Still, safety lags behind technology as shown in the high incidence of lung cancer among the workers in asbestos factories.

THE ORIGINS OF CHANGE

A number of social and ecological processes increase the likelihood that social change will occur. For example, ecologists may warn of the long-run dangers of increasing water pollution but their warnings may be ignored. At the same time, researchers may be seeking ways to avoid the inherent dangers of water pollution. All of these potential sources of social change—ecological changes, as well as inventions and discoveries aimed at preventing them—can be occurring simultaneously, although relatively few people may be aware of any of them. And, of course, none may in the final analysis lead to social change; attempts at changes may not materialize.

In this section, we will look at six processes that have often generated social changes: social movements; ecology; interventions and discoveries; cultural predispositions; cultural diffusion; and acculturation. We will begin with social movements, an important source of often dramatic changes.

Social Movements

One year ago . . . the solidarity trade union was born. After 18 days of strikes, under floodlights from television crews from around the world and to the strains of the Polish national anthem, Lech Walesa

and a deputy prime minister signed a document that, for the first time, ceded representation of the workers to an organization outside the control of the communist party. . . . (Poland) seems to be a different country. . . . Over the past 12 months the three institutions that are the pillars of national life—the Communist Party, the Roman Catholic Church and now, Solidarity—were vastly transformed. . . . Solidarity has grown from a protest labor union into an awesome social and political movement of nearly 10 million dues-paying members. . . . So dominant is Solidarity in the political landscape that no government, either national or local, can effectuate any decision that the union disagrees with. (Darnton, 1981)*

The rise of Solidarity in Poland is a particularly dramatic example of a **social movement:** a relatively sustained collective effort to achieve or to block social change. Other social movements with which most people are familiar include "The Moral Majority," women's liberation, the Civil Rights movement, and the antiwar movement during the Vietnam war. Social movements form around a desire to influence the way people think and act. They are self-conscious and ideological, and, when successful, result in long-term social change. Solidarity, as noted above, was a long-term collective effort of millions of people that led to fundamental changes in the institutional fabric of Polish society. Whereas something like a riot is spontaneous and short-lived, a social movement develops over time.

For discontent, confusion, and alienation to be shaped into a social movement, several things are needed. Individuals must become aware of the fact that others share their dissatisfaction (see Table 19.1). This seems to occur in regular social networks, with people who have relatively few other commitments most likely to join social movements (Snow et al., 1980). Ideas about why people are uneasy and what can be done must develop. Programs, organizations, and channels of communication have to be worked out in

---

* © 1981 by The New York Times Company. Reprinted by permission.

TABLE 19.1 / EXTENT OF KNOWLEDGE OF, ATTRACTION TO, AND PARTICIPATION IN NEW GROUPS*

Number of groups	Percentages who know about, are attracted to, or have taken part in each number of groups		
	Know at least a little about	Attracted to	Taken part in
None	21	48	79
At least			
1	79	52	21
2	66	30	8
3	55	18	3
4	45	10	2
5	35	4	1
6	26	2	†
7	20	1	†
8	14	1	0
9	4	0	0
10	6	†	†
11	4	†	0
12	1	0	0
13	†	†	0
(Number)	(1,000)	(1,000)	(1,000)

† Less than .5 percent.

* New groups include Hare Krishna, Yoga, Satanism, Transcendental Meditation, Zen, Scientology, Tongues, Children of God, Jews for Jesus, Campus Crusade, and others.

Source: Robert Wuthnow, "The New Religions in Social Context," in Charles Y. Glock and Robert N. Bellah, eds. *The New Religious Consciousness* (Berkeley: University of California Press, 1976), p. 275. Reprinted by permission.

ways that inspire people to press for change. Morale needs to be maintained, and movement leaders should be prepared to implement their programs when they obtain power.

Phases of social movements. In the *incipient phase,* people often are anxious and uneasy (Turner and Killian, 1972). Agitators are useful in calling attention to discrepancies between the ideals and reality of some aspect of the social system; they ask pointed questions and verbalize feelings that others have found difficult to express. Lech Walesa, for example, asked why workers had so little power and access to so few material goods in a communist state which was supposed to exist for their benefit. When discontent is popularized, and anger and frustration are expressed openly, the *popular stage* has been reached. A

sense of group identity begins to develop, along with a consciousness of the dividing line between "us" and "them." In Poland, Solidarity members openly challenged the authority of their bosses by staging strikes at will.

At this point in the movement goals are established and demands may be issued, although organization is still loose. Those in power may seek to suppress further development by removing the movement's leaders; however, suppression may only serve to strengthen determination in the movement's membership. An exiled, imprisoned, or dead leader may exercise as much or more power than he or she did when free or alive. Bobby Sands, a leader in the Irish Republican Army's efforts to liberate Northern Ireland, was imprisoned and subsequently died during a hunger strike. However, he was elected to the

The funeral of Bobby Sands, the most famous of Northern Ireland's hunger strikers, was an important public event. The Irish Republican Army (IRA) used it to popularize the social movement advocating the independence of Northern Ireland from Britain.

British Parliament while in prison, and his death sparked riots and renewed resistance efforts.

A movement's long-run success depends on the attainment of the *formal stage* in which specific programs and strategies for achieving the goals of the movement are developed. This channels energy and enthusiasm into a relatively formal organization that can utilize resources in a planned way. The development of Solidarity as a union resulted from a series of strikes that would never have had an impact society-wide if they were not formalized into a structure that was able to mobilize millions of people to work toward identified, long-range goals. This has proven to be true even in the face of the imposition in late 1981 of martial law aimed at severely limiting— or even destroying—the union. The *institutional stage* is reached when a social movement achieves its purpose. At this point the character of the movement may change dramatically. Putting ideals into practice is sometimes a difficult and frustrating experience. The Socialist candidate, François Mitterand, was not expected to win the French presidential election in 1981. When he did, the general surprise was so great that there

was a period of inaction while the newly elected president and his party learned how to form a new governing structure.

Ironically, the success of a social movement may lead to greater conservatism among its leaders. They now find themselves on the side of the law, and they face the possiblity of new social movements from other quarters. They also now have a vested interest in maintaining their position. For example, after Solidarity had been successful in attaining its goals, it was described as follows: "Its leadership is moderate at the top, radical in the middle, and mixed at the bottom" (Darnton, 1981). It was also sometimes forced by its membership to support strikes it originally tried to discourage (Markham, 1981).

Types of social movements. Sociologists Ralph Turner and Lewis Killian (1972) classify social movements according to whether they stress ideology (or values), power, or participation. *Value-oriented movements* grow out of a belief that something is wrong and must be changed. The labor movement demanded the right to collective bargaining; the Moral Majority espouses a return to traditional family structures and the view of the Bible as the literal truth; and the Irish Republican Army has been demanding freedom from British rule for Northern Ireland. Value-oriented movements are *causes,* being ideological rather than personal. Because they are dedicated to righting certain wrongs, they must try to maintain the appearance of the rightness of their strategies for doing so. For example, many people became disenchanted with the Islamic revolution in Iran under the Ayatollah Khomeini when he used highly repressive measures to achieve goals that were supposed to espouse freedom.

Power-oriented movements are those which focus on obtaining control, recognition, or status for their members. These movements stress control, and their members believe that the ends justify the means. The black power movement in the United States which emerged after Civil Rights leaders had won many of their legislative objectives is a case in point. Stokely Carmichael was concerned about *who* controlled those aspects of the system that relate to the lives of Black Americans. As reported by Adoff (1968), "Black

Power means, for example, that in Lownes County, Alabama, a black sheriff can end police brutality. A black tax assessor and tax collector, and county board of revenue can lay, collect, and channel tax monies for the building of better roads and schools serving black people."

The third type of social movement is quite different from those already discussed. *Participation-oriented* movements are those grounded in fantasy: the belief that the end of the world as we know it is at hand (millennial movements); the conviction that a messiah will appear, bringing peace and harmony (messianic movements); the idea that historical forces make change *inevitable.* Movements of this type do not offer the tangible rewards of social reform or uplifted status; rather, they suggest a reinterpretation of individual fate. Activities in participation-oriented movements center around preparing for the New Age, but in a sense these activities are ends in themselves. Simply participating in the movement may compensate for existing hardships. Within the structures of the movement people find status and hope which the outside world denies them (see Table 19.2). Although

TABLE 19.2 / PARTICIPANTS IN MOVEMENTS

The following data demonstrate that respondents with specific characteristics are more likely to join the types of movements shown. The figures are a subjective discontent index developed by the author of the research: the higher the figure, the more likely one is to join as a result of the characteristics shown.

	Counter cultural movements	Personal-growth movements	Neo-Christian movements
Never married	2.0	1.2	1.3
Looking for a job or working part time	2.2	1.5	1.7
Moved twice or more in last two years	1.7	1.8	1.3
Bothered about work or work plans	1.4	1.4	.9
Bothered about sex life	1.5	1.1	1.0

Source: Robert Wuthnow, "The New Religions in Social Context," in Charles Y. Glock and Robert N. Bellah, eds. *The New Religious Consciousness* (Berkeley: University of California Press, 1976), p. 291. Reprinted by permission.

they do have general goals, these movements are more important for the gratification that members feel by participating. This seems to be the case with the Moral Majority, for example, many of whose members are poor women with little education (Marty, 1981). For them, a vision built on literally interpreted biblical events may offer more than the life they experience on earth.

Social movements and the future. Social movements perform a number of important functions for society and its members. People are mobilized to participate actively in social issues and groups. Prevailing values, attitudes and practices are examined and challenged, helping to prevent stagnation. Social movements also provide an outlet for the disenchanted and alienated members of society, enabling them to work for change in a way that also minimally disrupts the daily operation of the social system. Vietnam war veterans provide an especially interesting example of these effects. They have begun to organize to ". . . fight for their interests, provide mutual support, and foster the sense of pride that they feel society has denied them" (Martin, 1981). In doing so, they help each other function better in social institutions like the family, schools, and work. However, by working to take over traditional veterans organizations like the American Legion and Veterans of Foreign Wars, they have the potential for changing our society's view of the war and their place in it.

Social movements, then, are powerful sources of social change and as such, they affect the future. New social movements are continually developing; gay liberation, "La Raza" Hispanic power groups, and independence movements in several Third World nations are recent examples. Any social movement that is successful has an impact on the future. It is impossible to predict what movements will occur and what their effects will be. We can expect, however, that there will always be social movements and that they will change their society in some way.

Ecology

When the Reagan Administration proposed transferring control over Matagorda Island from the Federal Interior Department to the state of Texas, conservationists were outraged. They feared that the state, not bound by the Endangered Species Act of 1973 as is the federal government, would permit recreational uses of the island that would disturb the area for the endangered species that live there: the last of the nation's whooping cranes, brown pelicans, Southern bald eagles, Arctic peregrine falcons, American alligators, and several species of sea turtles (*The New York*

An ecosystem is a balanced interrelationship of living organisms with their environment. Changes to any feature of the system will have far-reaching consequences, until a new balance is established or the ecosystem is destroyed.

Times, 1981: A10). However, the island is on Texas's popular Gulf of Mexico coast. With the state's population burgeoning as a result of population shifts to the Sun Belt areas, it needs more recreational lands. But can humans, eagles, and sea turtles all coexist?

Such a situation highlights the close link between social change and ecology. The study of the interrelationship between living organisms and their environment is the subject of the science of **ecology**. Ecology examines the balance that exists in these relationships, or *ecosystems,* and **human ecology** specifically focuses on human life as part of ecosystems. In an ecosystem, energy (ultimately derived from sunlight) and inorganic matter are converted into organic matter by green plants through the process of photosynthesis. Plants are consumed by animals, which are consumed by other animals, and so on, in what are known as *food chains.* Their waste products and the dead organisms (both plants and animals) are broken down by such organisms as bacteria and fungi. Reduced to basic components, once-living matter again becomes the nutrient source of green plants.

Clearly, the balance within an ecosystem is complex and delicate. As living organisms, we humans depend on this balance for our own survival. By working great changes on our environment, we are tampering with the ecosystem that supports us. By destroying forests, we eliminate the vast energy-converting power and the animal shelter provided by green plants; by polluting water supplies, we threaten everything that depends on that water; by using poisons to solve crop "problems," we introduce poisons into the food chain which we ultimately depend on (see Fig. 19.1).

Sociologist Gerhard Lenski (1970) of the University of North Carolina has suggested that particularly harsh environments—a desert, the Arctic—probably do inhibit cultural change and innovation. Survival is so time-consuming, and access to resources so limited, that living alternatives are very restricted. In many cases, however, the restrictive effect of ecology on cultural development and social change can be modified through the use of our increasingly sophisticated technology. **Technology** is the application of scientific knowledge to the solution of human problems. For example, we can talk of medical technology to solve health problems, biogenetic technology to solve problems caused by genetic inheritance, and industrial technology to solve problems related to the production of goods like steel or automobiles.

Technology is a critical link between ecology and social change in a number of ways. Much of our *technology uses the environment* in new ways. We dam rivers for hydroelectric power; we exploit oil reserves to operate automobiles; we "farm" trees to create paper needed for part of our media explosion; and we create types of waste—such as plastic—that are practically impervious to natural processes of organic decomposition. *Technology also alters the environment* as a byproduct of growth and development. We pollute the air around many types of industrial plants; we create drainage problems by replacing grass with concrete; we tear down hills in order to extract coal. As the members of our society—and others as well—have gone about the business of technological development, we have radically altered the environment as well as the relationship between human life and other plant and animal life forms. Quite simply, humans now dominate all other life forms, and the majority of inanimate ecological processes as well. Although natural events such as earthquakes, floods, tornadoes, and heat waves can still drastically affect human life and all other ecosystems, even they are coming increasingly under control through better forecasting techniques, special architectural techniques, and other technological processes.

Population is an important stimulus to technological development; hence it affects ecology. Population growth has traditionally exerted tremendous pressure on the environment and on

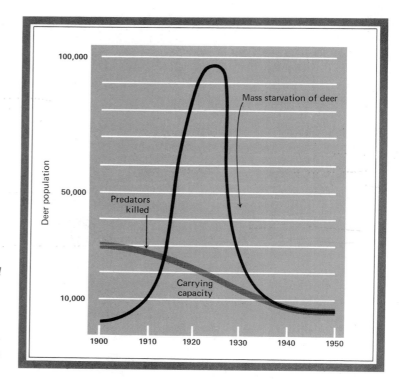

Fig. 19.1 / Mule Deer Population Curve

The dramatic effects of killing the natural predators of the mule deer on the Kaibab plateau. The subsequent damage to the carrying capacity of the plateau is apparently permanent.

Source: Reprinted with permission of Macmillan Publishing Co., Inc. from *Our Ecological Crisis* by J.C. Grahame Smith *et al.* Copyright © 1974 J.C. Grahame Smith.

technology to try to adapt the environment to the needs of larger populations. Developments result in such varied new species as higher-bearing corn and high-rise apartment buildings, which then must be supported by complex sewage, electrical, and water distribution systems. Population distribution interlocks with these factors. When people move from farms to cities, or from the Midwest to the Southwest, the environment is affected. Even a societal value which demands that human life be preserved and protected has implications for population size, population composition, and, of course, medical technology. However desirable huge medical complexes for research and treatment may be, they have their ecological and technological costs: animals bred for research purposes; people kept alive who will need life-long care and treatment; buildings which use tremendous amounts of energy and water 24 hours a day.

All of these events are a part of social change and society's response to its sense of its own future. They are also relatively recent. Preindustrial societies made many fewer demands on their environments, but, of course, the nature of social life was also quite different. So far industrial nations have chosen to change toward greater complexity and to make increasing demands on the environment even while worrying about the need for conservation. Indeed, we have now come to the point in humankind's domination of ecology that we have the capacity to destroy the whole planet.

The impact of ecology on social change. Obviously, changes in the natural environment or changes in the size of a population will affect a society. Sometimes these changes are drastic. The depopulation of men in Germany as a result of World War I undoubtedly changed the social system by affecting the family structure and economic productivity. The poisoning of the land and water at Love Canal near Buffalo, New York, because of chemical wastes dumped there seriously disrupted residential patterns and family life in the area. And the whole downtown section of Butte, Montana, had to be moved when the copper mines—basic to the area's economy—expanded and took over the original downtown land. All of these examples show how basic ecology is to patterns of social life, and how ecological changes lead to social changes.

Inventions and Discoveries

Human beings have sometimes been characterized as "toolmaking animals," and technology is generally acknowledged to be an important factor in social and cultural changes. Technological innovations are often listed as landmarks in human history that have had profound consequences for human life: the invention of the wheel; the domestication of plants and animals; the development of written languages; inventions

that used wind and waterpower, steam, electricity, and, finally, atomic power.

Technological changes may result from **invention**—that is, from the creation of new ways of using existing knowledge or new ways of combining existing artifacts. The wheel, the bow and arrow, the plow, the steam engine, and the computer are examples. Universities, democracy, the assembly line, and Freudian analysis are another kind of social invention. Innovations may also result from **discovery**—that is, a new perception of some feature of the environment.

Even a single invention can produce large-scale changes in a society. The classic example is the automobile. Cars have greatly increased individual mobility and in many ways have changed the way people live. Courtship customs and leisure-time activities have changed since horse-and-buggy days. Moreover, cars have opened up whole new categories of government activity: building and maintaining highways, controlling traffic, and urban planning to accommodate the "car culture." Many new economic activities are directly related to cars. People make cars, repair cars, and sell cars, drive trucks and taxis, design

A single invention can lead to profound changes in a society. Although originally the subject of much ridicule, the automobile soon became a permanent fixture of modern society, encouraging industrial expansion, providing employment for millions, and facilitating expansion into the suburbs.

and build highways and parking lots, operate roadside motels and restaurants; others supply the steel, glass, and plastic used to make automobiles. Today there is a huge demand for petroleum and other irreplaceable resources. In addition, Henry Ford, one of the founders of the automobile industry, was the first to apply the principles of the assembly line on a large scale to meet the demand for his new product. This method was so efficient that it was rapidly adopted by most other industries.

Yet, inventors and their inventions are not always welcomed in a culture. Galileo was persecuted; Mendel's research findings on heredity and Leonardo da Vinci's designs for flying machines and submarines were largely ignored; Fulton's steamboat provoked laughter when it first appeared on the Hudson and was dubbed "Fulton's Folly." Those who have proposed social or religious innovations have often had an even more difficult time winning social acceptance. Christ, for example, was put to death for his radical religious teaching, and for centuries his followers were persecuted. Utopian social planners such as Jeremy Bentham (who developed communes for his mill workers) were regarded as eccentric and slightly suspicious characters. Many dismissed Woodrow Wilson's proposal for a League of Nations as a visionary scheme. In our own day, Betty Friedan's belief that sex roles can be restructured to achieve equality between men and women has been attacked as anti-family, anti-feminist, and "unnatural" (Friedan, 1981).

For every successful invention that has been taken up and used by a society, thousands of others have fallen by the wayside. The invention of the steam engine in the eighteenth century has been counted as one of the most significant technological developments of all times, producing enormous changes in Western societies and ultimately in all human life. Yet, some of the scientists of ancient Greece not only understood the principles involved, but built small model steam engines which they treated as interesting intellectual toys. The steam engine, however, was never used in a practical way and had no effect on Greek society. The invention itself was forgotten for some 2000 years because the Greeks did not *perceive* the need for a new power source. The economic life of Greece was based largely on the muscle power of slaves and animals—and there was no shortage of slaves or animals. The Greeks had few complicated machines to which steam power could be successfully applied. Added to this was the upper-class Greek attitude toward scientific speculation and physical labor. It was fine for a "gentleman-scientist" to engage in scientific speculation, but science was not expected to have any practical applications. Physical labor was "vulgar." Greek scientists were not concerned and saw no need to make human labor easier or more efficient.

The values of Greek society prevented the adoption of steam as a new source of power; the values of Western European societies prior to the 1700s made the "reinvention" of the steam engine almost inevitable. As Lynn White put it:

By the middle of the thirteenth century . . . a considerable group of active minds, stimulated . . . by the technological success of recent generations . . . were beginning to generalize the concept of mechanical power. They were coming to think of the cosmos as a vast reservoir of energies to be tapped and used according to human inventions. They were power-conscious to the point of fantasy. But without such fantasy, such soaring imagination, the power technology of the Western world would not have been developed. (White, 1962: 134)

Cultural Predispositions

Technological innovations, then, are factors in social and cultural changes. But they do not take place in a vacuum; they are the products of particular cultures at particular points in time. And the effects of a single innovation may vary from culture to culture. Technological changes are themselves determined in part by a society's needs, customs, attitudes, and system of knowledge.

In the area of science, new discoveries are invariably based on a long chain of past discoveries, an accumulated body of scientific knowledge. Henry Ford, for example, could never have developed his Model T before the discovery of the wheel, or without knowledge of internal combustion engines, or before scientists had learned how to generate electricity using a battery or to vulcanize rubber (for tires). Ralph Linton has speculated that "if Einstein had been born into a primitive tribe which was unable to count beyond three, lifelong application to mathematics probably would not have carried him beyond the development of a decimal system based on fingers and toes" (1964: 434). Sir Isaac Newton said that he saw so far because he stood upon the shoulders of giants—the many scientists whose work provided the basis for his discoveries. In other words, even radically new insights or discoveries do not come out of the blue; they are firmly tied to a cultural base.

Hundreds of scientific discoveries have been made almost simultaneously by two or more scientists working independently of one another. As suggested earlier, scientific discoveries or technological innovations have a multiplier effect—the broader the base of scientific knowledge and the more scientists there are in a society, the more likely it is that new discoveries will be made (Ogburn, 1922).

The attitudes of a society toward scientific inquiry may stimulate or inhibit change. In medieval Europe, church leaders were powerful and respected. These individuals regarded scientific speculation as heretical. They encouraged unquestioning faith in church doctrines, including the belief that God had made Earth the center of the universe. In questioning this and other beliefs, Galileo and his contemporaries risked the harsh punishments inflicted on heretics, and Galileo was, in fact, tried for heresy. In contrast, the United States and most modern societies actively encourage technological change. The successful scientist is rewarded with honors and prestige and sometimes with money. Governments, private industries, and foundations employ many scientists and sponsor research in the hope that the new knowledge will have practical applications, and the high value placed on science encourages many young people to dream of scientific careers. This change in values has contributed to the accelerated rate of change.

Cultural Diffusion

Jazz was "born and raised" in the United States, but most of the music we listen to, the clothes we wear, the food we eat, the words we speak, and the thoughts we think come from other cultures. Spaghetti, for example, was brought here by Italian immigrants whose ancestors developed a taste for pasta in China. The idea of democracy originated in ancient Greece, was revived in Western Europe in the seventeenth and eighteenth centuries, and then became the central idea in the founding of the United States government. It also inspired revolutions in Latin America and France, and has become so popular in the twentieth century that even nations that do not practice democracy give lip service to democratic ideals. Every society borrows and learns from its neighbors.

Cultural diffusion—the process by which social and cultural elements are transferred from one society to another—takes many forms. Imperialists carry their ideas and ways with them, often imposing their culture on the colony. Missionaries, migration, trade, tourism, transported labor (for example, slaves or indentured servants), intellectual exchanges, and diplomacy also play a role in cultural diffusion. Whether or not a society accepts new technology, new forms of government, or a new religion depends on their utility, on whether the new elements are consistent with their traditions, on "the prestige of the bearers of novelty," on the degree of cultural integration, and on the extent of contact with the new culture (Arensberg and Niehoff, 1971).

Diffusion can be a very slow process. The art of ironworking, for example, took thousands of years to spread from somewhere in the Middle East to all of Asia, Africa, and Europe. Today, because of vastly improved means of transportation and communication, diffusion is very rapid. News of important technical breakthroughs, developments in international politics—even the latest scores in international sporting events—spread quickly to even the remotest villages. Societies which are barely out of the stone age are caught up in the processes of industrialization and urbanization.

Acculturation

In 1519, Cortez arrived in Mexico with an army of 2500 Spaniards. They found an urban society that extended throughout central and southern Mexico: large cities supported by a highly developed system of garden cultivation, extensive trade networks, a high degree of economic specialization, and a well-developed class system. This society was dominated by the Aztecs who had established loose political control over a far-flung network of peoples through military conquest. Within three years, the Spaniards had organized a large army of disaffected natives and had destroyed the Aztec capital. The Spaniards then moved into the social positions previously occupied by the Aztec upper class. They continued to exact tribute from the peoples formerly dominated by the Aztecs but allowed friendly Indian rulers to keep their positions of local authority. For a period of time many Indians not only accepted the Spaniards peaceably as the successors to the Aztecs, but actually embraced Spanish culture eagerly. The official Spanish policy was to convert the Indians into Christian subjects of the Spanish crown. Christianity was a welcome respite from the bloody human sacrificial rites of the Aztec religion and was accepted at all class levels; many members of the native

nobility migrated to Spain where they were accepted among the upper classes.

In areas of Mexico where the Spaniards acquired large landholdings, however, the Indians were gradually exploited and more rigidly controlled. Traditional language, dress, and life styles were abandoned under pressure and, finally, lost. On the other hand, the Spaniards adopted many of the agricultural practices, food habits, and architectural techniques of the Indians. Gradually, the cultural distinctions between the Indians and the Spaniards disappeared as the two societies merged. Today Mexico is a blend of Spanish and Indian culture.

The modification of cultures that occurred in Mexico exemplifies a special kind of change called *acculturation*. In contrast to diffusion, which simply involves adapting new elements to the existing structure of a culture, **acculturation** is a basic restructuring of cultures that have come into contact. Usually one culture holds a superordinate position and exerts some sort of pressure—either through direct force, economic pressure, technological superiority, or prestige.

The United States has sometimes been held up as a model of acculturation. In addition to the Indian societies who were the first-known inhabitants, our society has received a steady stream of immigrants from other cultures. As we said in the last chapter, this process continues. Americans have taken pride in the "melting pot" nature of the society—many different cultures melted into one new and distinctive culture (Gordon, 1964; Handlin, 1966). However, acculturation has its disadvantages as well as its advantages. While the new composite culture can draw on and preserve desirable aspects of each of its parts, other cultural components are lost. America blends the artistry of Italians, the reverence of learning of Jews, the love of the land of Scandinavians, the respect for the elderly of Hispanics, and the strength of spirit of Blacks. Yet each of these groups has also lost some of its distinctiveness by having to blend into the whole, with a diminishing of identity as a result.

The United States continues to struggle with the balance between acculturation and pluralism, which, as you recall from Chapter 9, is when the various cultural groups making up a larger culture such as the United States coexist, but with limited acculturation. In part, the future direction of our society will be shaped by the way the whole and its component subcultures decide to work together.

Summary of Change Processes

Summarizing the sociocultural factors which often lead to social change, we have seen that social movements, ecology, inventions and discoveries, cultural predispositions, cultural diffusion, and acculturation all play a part. It is important to remember, however, that the adoption of change is strongly influenced by its compatibility with the existing culture and the society's willingness to accept change. Prohibition is the classic example of this point. In 1932, the United State Congress finally repealed Prohibition. After almost 13 years of bootlegging,

bathtub gin, speakeasies, and gang wars, reformers had to admit that Prohibition had not created a teetotaling population. The effort to change our drinking habits had been a failure. Why? Perhaps the most important reason was that Prohibition had never been widely supported. It was a decision imposed on the country by a small minority. The lesson of Prohibition is that people often resist changes that are forced on them. In the next section we will look at the way societies respond to change which has begun to be integrated into its social structure.

THE RESPONSE TO CHANGE

Why is it that the Japanese have accepted birth-control techniques so readily, while the Egyptians and Indians have resisted any attempts to alter traditional attitudes toward child-bearing or to limit family size? Why have new manufacturing practices been adopted so rapidly in the South, while racial practices have changed so slowly and with great resistance? As we discussed earlier, not all changes are made at the same rate. Some

If change is to be successful, it must be compatible with a society's way of life. Prohibition, in its attempt to halt the consumption of alcohol, was a highly unsuccessful reversal of a society's predisposition. Here, law officers confiscate one of the innumerable stills that supplied an active underground market.

changes are more easily accepted than others. And different societies may have different reactions to proposed changes. Change is never automatic; rather, it is always a selective process.

Selective Acceptance

Individuals set out to change their own lives because they believe the change will be for the better. People migrate to new lands in hopes of finding better economic or social conditions. People change jobs or cars—or even spouses—in the expectation that the new condition will be better than the old. In somewhat the same way societies adopt changes when the change is generally perceived to be for the better. Material objects, skills, and techniques are among the most readily acceptable elements of change, because their usefulness is easily demonstrated and immediately recognized.

Change comes to Vicos. The village of Vicos is located in an isolated spot high in the Andes Mountains in Peru. Its people are of Indian ancestry, and up until the early 1950s they were essentially serfs bound to the land of a hacienda. This system dated back to Spanish colonial days, and it left the people of Vicos powerless, poverty-stricken, disease-prone, illiterate, and almost completely cut off from the modern world. Fear and suspicion were a natural part of life. They feared the hacienda supervisor, who administered beatings and other punishments with little regard for justice. They feared the outside world, for non-Indian people of the region sometimes hunted Indians as they would hunt wild animals. They feared famine and illness; and they feared a god who obviously thought that Indians deserved to be hungry, ill, and ignorant. They feared their neighbors for, with things so bad, a neighbor would automatically try to take advantage of you if you showed weakness; only family members could be trusted.

In 1951 a group of anthropologists from Cornell University took over the lease of the Vicos hacienda; they wanted to see if they could improve the lives of the Indians and to study the changes that took place. New agricultural techniques were introduced. After some hesitation, the changes were enthusiastically adopted; the new techniques worked. The harsh rules of the hacienda were abolished, and people were paid for work on communal projects. The anthropologists did not force changes; they made suggestions and offered help and advice. The people of Vicos selected and adopted their suggestions and knowledge.

They embraced changes that seemed beneficial to them. They started to grow cash crops and to trade with surrounding areas. They were able to build a new school and a new health center, to form a democratically elected community council, and to take care of community affairs. Today the people of Vicos own their own land and direct their own lives. They vote in national elections. They travel regularly to the capital city of Lima to shop, to work, or just to see the sights. Young people go away to college. Economic development continues; in fact, the people of Vicos now provide technical advice and assistance to neighboring villages.

The economy, the social and political life, and the attitudes and beliefs of the people of Vicos have changed radically. Other changes, however, have been rejected. Suggested hygienic measures have not been adopted. A government-sponsored forestry project failed for lack of local interest. The villagers refused to invest in a small tourist hotel nearby—no one could see the value of owning nonagricultural property. Nor do they see any purpose in sending girls to school (Holmberg, 1958). The Vicos project succeeded in large part because the Cornell scientists started by introducing a change that the villagers regarded as immediately beneficial—a technique for improving their potato crops. Gradually they accepted other useful innovations. However, if the Cornell scientists had first tried to convince the people of Vicos to ignore the hacienda supervisor and to organize a farming cooperative, these proposals would have been rejected outright. Such changes would have been completely incompatible with the existing social structure and with cultural attitudes and values.

In their selectivity, the people of Vicos are no different from members of any other society. Americans, for example, continue to struggle with the concept of sex-role equality in the 1980s. Many changes have been accepted: women in the workforce, women as single parents, and women in occupations previously reserved for men, such as driving taxicabs and working in coal mines. On the other hand, our society continues to struggle with the roles of men and women in the family, fearing that major role redefinitions will destroy the ability of families to perform their societal functions (Friedan, 1981). Change is usually gradual and selective, becoming a part of the overall societal structure in ways that tie into existing social networks. Nevertheless, the women's movement serves to remind us that even gradual change can involve conflict and the use of power.

Compatibility with the social structure. The fewer the changes required in role behavior and social organization the more acceptable an innovation will be. Thus, while physicians might readily adopt a new drug that does not change existing medical practices, many would balk at delegating routine medical procedures (such as taking a medical history or making simple diagnoses) to a paramedical staff because of the change it would make in their roles. Similarly, many educators who see classroom lecturing as a basic part of the professor's role oppose proposals to offer course work in the community for academic credit (Fairweather, 1972). Such changes that involve alterations in personal or political power are very likely to be resisted.

Yet change does occur even if power relationships are threatened when other parts of the social structure are benefitted. More and more doctors are utilizing physicians' assistants to take medical histories and make simple diagnoses because the high cost of medical care demands more specialized use of the time of highly paid doctors. And there is more outreach into the community by schools in order to include nontraditional student populations and thereby compensate for a decline in the number of traditional students.

It is not always the wealthiest or most powerful members of a society who have the greatest stake in maintaining present conditions. Working people may oppose automation because it threatens their jobs. It has frequently been noted that white people in the lower socioeconomic levels, in both North and South, have opposed racial integration with greater fervor than middle-class whites. The lower-class whites see integration as a direct threat to their economic and social position.

Almost everyone has some vested interest in the status quo—from millionaires with oil depletion allowances, to farmers with tax subsidies, to the poor with their welfare checks. However, even the most conservative groups may become enthusiastic supporters of an innovation if it supports their interests. Social scientists have usually regarded peasants as among the most conservative and unambitious members of society. Yet, many studies show that if the opportunities are right, peasants may become lively innovators. In a study of cacao farmers in Ghana, economist Polly Hill (1963) found that the peasants migrated on their own initiative to new lands suitable for cacao growing at a time when world markets were ripe. Through foresight and shrewd investment, they developed a thriving commerce with little outside encouragement.

FROM TRADITION TO MODERNITY

Some feel that social change has begun to spin out of control. Others feel that it is simply progress, that social change is moving toward the creation of a better world. We will now turn to this issue of modernization and progress.

Modernization is the process by which traditional, agriculturally based societies become urbanized and industrialized. In the West, this process occurred gradually over several centuries following the Industrial Revolution. But in many parts of Asia, Africa, and Latin America today, there is pressure to move from ox cart to jet planes in a generation or two. Japan was transformed from an essentially feudal society to a powerful industrial state in about a century. In our own society, immigrant groups often arrive from agricultural societies and have to make rapid cultural adaptations to our highly complex industrial society (Hornblower, 1980).

Modernization

How do these changes occur? In part, societies themselves are pushing for change because they are eager to share in the material benefits they see in Western nations. In part, external pressures simply leave no choice. Once contact has been made and even a small change introduced, values, attitudes, motivations, and interpersonal relationships as well as technological processes will begin to alter. As Smelser described the process:

. . . *"modernization"* . . . *refers to the fact that technical, economic, and ecological changes ramify the whole social and cultural fabric. In an emerging nation, we may expect profound changes (1) in the* political *sphere as simple tribal or village authority systems give way to systems of suffrage, political parties, representations, and civil service bureaucracies; (2) in the* educational *sphere, as the society strives to reduce illiteracy and increase economically productive skills; (3) in the* religious *sphere, as secularized belief systems begin to replace traditionalist religions; (4) in the* familial *sphere, as extended kinship units lose their pervasiveness; (5) in the* stratification *sphere, as geographical and*

Rapid technological advances have caused profound changes in the cultures of developing nations by introducing new values, motivations, and interpersonal relationships.

social mobility tend to loosen fixed, ascriptive hierarchical systems. (1966: 111).

In other words, modernization is not simply piecemeal economic or technological changes but a total process, involving an entire sociocultural system. (Eisenstadt, 1980: 842)

Before analyzing modernization further, we should briefly reflect on a bias inherent in this concept. When we talk about something as modern, or refer to progress, we are using words that carry a favorable connotation in our society. However, not all societies would define modernization and progress as we do, nor would they necessarily feel that they are desirable (Granovetter, 1979). When Puerto Ricans reject proposals to build a factory because it would foul a beach valued for its beauty and cleanliness, they are not being backward or anti-progress. They are instead expressing a different set of social priorities and a different societal definition of progress (Steiner, 1974). Even though the factory would help the island's economy and provide badly needed jobs, its social cost is seen as too high for the benefits. Many sociologists would agree with Lenski and Lenski (1978) and Granovetter (1979) when they suggest that imposing value-laden terms like progress and modernization sometimes obscures and distorts the processes of social change. Nevertheless, modernization is the framework most commonly used to look at change that moves in the direction of increased societal complexity, the increased use of technology, and greater control over the environment. Whatever the word for it, these changes have created the type of social world in which we live—and with which we struggle. For them to have occurred, several specific processes were necessary, which we will examine in the next sections. These same processes will probably be important in other societies that also seek to move toward greater social and technological complexity.

Commitment to change.

In the late 1940s and early 1950s, many Asian and African nations won their independence. Many people assumed that ending colonial rule automatically opened the door to modernization. But the transformation is not so simple. First, people must be committed to the idea of change (Allen, 1971). Not all societies share our commitment to progress. Of course, new aspirations have appeared where people have had direct contact with Westerners (missionaries, colonial administrators, or servicemen) and have become aware of alternative ways of life. But many traditional peoples, accustomed to a stable, almost static, way of life, may not even consider the possibility of change. The idea is so alien to the Trobrianders, for

example, that they do not even have a word for change in their vocabulary. Where people are concerned with the past, with tradition, or belief in a divinely ordained social order, they may reject the idea of purposive change.

Capital.

Second, development requires money. Building new industries, highways, railroads, educational systems, hospitals, mechanizing agriculture, installing electricity, and so on—all require huge capital investments. Where is this money to come from? Some can be borrowed, some may be obtained through assistance programs or through expropriation of foreign estates. But, in most cases, during the early stages of development in an agricultural society, farmers must carry most of the burden. As the most productive segment of society, farmers pay for industrialization through price and export controls. Hence, one of the prerequisites of modernization is a relatively well-developed system of commercial agriculture.

Unity.

Third, the developing society must try to weld many regional and often culturally diverse groups to strengthen national institutions and create commitment to national development. The bloody and protracted Nigerian civil war illustrates the often disastrous consequences of trying to unify tribes who have been sworn enemies for centuries. Sometimes one tribe will be concentrated in urban areas where the members hold jobs as skilled laborers, fill most of the civil service posts, and hold positions of economic and political power. Other tribes, living in rural, isolated areas, and excluded from the power structure and benefits, may refuse to cooperate with the modernizers.

Countries such as Indonesia, Pakistan, Burma, and Sudan have experienced setbacks in their modernization efforts for just this reason. In these countries, political structures intended to represent the many varied factions of the society by unifying the people under a government able to

SOCIAL ISSUE/Science and Social Change

Norman W. Storer/*Baruch College,*
The City University of New York

Certainly the chief source of social change in recent times has been humankind's increasing ability to make use of nature to satisfy its needs. But technology—the systematic use of natural phenomena to achieve specific goals—has not always been based on general, systematic knowledge of these phenomena. The accidental discovery some 3000 years ago that blending tin with copper would produce a stronger metal (bronze) did not depend on knowledge of *why* this happened. Ancient potters could not say *how* heat hardens clay, but they knew that firing their products would make them waterproof and more durable.

The things that make our lives so different today from the lives of previous generations are more and more frequently the products of technology that relies on generalized, research-based knowledge. One could hardly discover by chance how to release nuclear energy, how to transmit television pictures by radio waves, or how to help stop the spread of cancer in a person's body. Instead, these technological achievements have depended on the development of explicit, systematic knowledge of atomic structures, of electricity, and of cellular structures and processes.

Behind the increasing pace of social change due to technology, then, lies one of the most important social inventions in history: the establishment of scientific research as a full-time occupation, or the role of the scientist.

Science (that is, the collective, continuing effort to develop trustworthy, cumulative knowledge of the natural world) has by now become central to our continued well-being. We depend on it to point the way to new sources of energy, new ways to sustain and improve health, and to solve other important problems. There is thus good reason for us to be interested in this special sector of society. The fact that the scientific community is also a unique sociological phenomenon adds further interest to exploring the structure and dynamics of this important group.

It is usually agreed that modern science began in 1543, when Copernicus argued that the Earth revolves about the sun (rather than vice versa) and Vesalius published the first accurate book on human anatomy. But the possibility of making a career of studying nature did not develop for another 300 years, and only within the last century has the scientific community grown to a respectable size.

It has been estimated (Price, 1963) that the number of people engaged in scientific research has been doubling every 15 years since 1600. This means that more than 90 percent of all the scientists who have ever lived are alive today, and there are probably more than 1 million of them now. The number who hold the doctorate and engage in original research, however, is much lower—perhaps a quarter of a million, of whom probably more than one-quarter are in the United States. While this may still seem a large number, we must remember that they are divided among more than 1000 specialized areas in the mathematical, physical, biological, and social sciences. Thus probably no more than 200 scientists are at work in any particular specialty, and often the number is closer to five or ten.

It was not until the early 1600s that the first scientific association was founded (the *Accademia dei Lincei,* or "Academy of the Lynx-Eyed," in Rome). It was only in 1662 that the Royal Society of London was chartered. These groups were formed to enable their members—they called themselves "natural philosophers" then—to meet and discuss their findings. The first scientific journal (the *Philosophical Transactions* of the Royal Society) was published in 1665, beginning the practice of recording and disseminating the results of scientific research. Today, approximately 1 million scientific journals are published throughout the world.

These early "natural philosophers" tended to be privileged gentlemen (and a few ladies) who enjoyed research as a hobby, for it was impossible then to earn a living as a researcher. Slowly, however, as knowledge of different natural phenomena developed, some sciences were added to university curricula and it became possible for a few people to earn a living through teaching—and to do research in connection with this responsibility. The link between teaching and research remains strong today, and it is still in the universities that basic research is most honored.

Although the practical value of science had been emphasized early in the seventeenth century by Francis Bacon, its usefulness did not really become apparent much before the latter half of the nineteenth century. Federal support for agricultural research began in the 1860s in this country, and by 1875 the production of synthetic chemical dyes was an important industry in Britain and Germany. However, the systematic pursuit of applied research, or research directed toward the solution of immediate practical problems, developed primarily after the First World War.

It is clear, then, that the early growth of science could not have been due to its demonstrated economic value. Yet the word "scientist" was coined in the 1840s, and we may take this as a rough indication of when the role was first recognized.

Why did science not develop earlier in history? What, if not the profit motive, inspired some people to seek careers in science, and other people to support them? The answers to these questions involve both social and cultural factors.

Several changes in the social structure of ancient and medieval societies had to occur before science could grow. A wealthy leisure class had to develop before people could have time to take up research as a hobby. Second, there had to be a change in the idea that manual labor was dishonorable before these people could engage in physical experiments without criticism. Third, control of universities by the Church had to diminish before they could become potential homes for such secular pursuits as scientific research. By 1600, these changes were well under way.

In terms of cultural factors, it was necessary that people come to view natural phenomena as occurring regularly—that is, in terms of unchanging principles rather than at random. They had to give up the assumption that things happened simply at the whim of some supernatural power. Without this view, the very idea of building a body of reliable knowledge of nature would be unthinkable. Such a change did occur in religious thought gradually, so that by the end of the seventeenth century people in some parts of Europe conceived of the Deity as quite removed from the everyday events of the natural world. He was the "clockmaker" who had created the universe, but thereafter left it to run according to its own laws. In this view, research could easily be defined as a way of glorifying God by examining His handwork—the universe.

Still, neither the desire to glorify God nor even the hope of practical payoffs was sufficient to define the role of the scientist. To "be" a scientist, after all, is to occupy a social position, and a position exists only as it is defined by a set of norms that govern its occupant's interactions with others. Two types of norms are important in outlining the scientist's role: technical norms that concern the research process itself, and social norms that control the scientist's relationships with other scientists. Here we shall be concerned only with the latter.

To begin with, science is clearly a cooperative endeavor. Scientists must draw on the findings of others as they seek to learn more about their special subject matters. And since it is always possible that someone might be wrong in interpreting the results of his or her research, scientists must also depend on each other to evaluate the validity and importance of their work so that mistakes in understanding nature are held to a minimum.

Sociologist Robert K. Merton first identified the norms of science, and he is now widely recognized as the "father" of the sociology of science. He pointed to four specific norms that provide the basic social structure of the scientific community, even though (as in every other area of social life) such norms are occasionally violated (Merton, 1973).

The first of these is *universalism,* the belief that the validity of a scientific statement is unrelated to its author's personal characteristics. Ideally, one's sex, race, religion, and nationality should be completely irrelevant to whether or not what one has said about a natural phenomenon is true. It is the connection between the statement and empirical reality, rather than between the statement and its author, that is important.

The second norm, *communality,* requires scientists to share their findings freely with each other. It should be obvious that if scientists kept their findings secret, or tried to sell them to the highest bidder, scientific progress would come to a halt. It is for this reason that scientists dislike the secrecy imposed on them in wartime and in some fields of applied research.

Organized skepticism is the third norm. It calls on scientists to take a critical look at each other's work and to call attention to errors so that mistakes will not creep into the body of accepted scientific knowledge. Because of this, scientists try hard to make sure that their own work is free of errors before it is published.

Finally, the norm of *disinterestedness* supports the other three by trying to separate research from the scientist's private interests. It discourages the scientist from seeking personal profit from what he or she has discovered, either financial or in terms of prestige, so that findings can be shared freely and criticisms accepted unemotionally because personal interests are not at stake.

Together, these norms facilitate the cooperative search for scientific truth. But why people should *want* to engage in research requires further explanation, for there have always been other careers that require less painstaking training and may pay much more. What is it that a scientist finds so rewarding in research?

Merton has suggested that the appropriate reward for scientific achievement is *professional recognition,* or the formal acknowledgement of the validity and importance of one's work by other scientists. Such recognition can be expressed in a number of ways, ranging from footnotes to the receipt of a Nobel Prize. The importance of recognition to scientists can be seen clearly in the disputes that sometimes arise between scientists when there is a question of who was the first to discover something. (Recognition, after all, can go only to the first per-

son to have made a discovery. No one today, for example, can expect praise from colleagues for announcing that $e = Mc^2$.) Newton and Leibnitz each claimed priority in the invention of the calculus; Darwin and Wallace finally agreed to publish jointly their independent discoveries of the principle of natural selection—although Darwin, having collected much more information on the topic, is today given all of the credit for the theory of evolution.

The practice of *eponomy,* or naming things after their discoverers, is another way to express professional recognition. Boyle's law, Avogadro's number, Halley's comet, and the Rorschach ink-blot test are good examples. This sort of "symbolic" ownership of one's discovery substitutes for private ownership so that the scientist can obey the norm of communality and still receive the reward of professional recognition. In another sense, such recognition is intrinsically rewarding and serves as the appropriate "coin of the realm" within science.

It should be apparent that professional recognition is not ordinarily earned on the basis of the practical value of one's contributions. Instead, it is customarily given to those who answer questions that emerge naturally from the incomplete state of present-day scientific knowledge. For instance, whether or not there would be any immediate utility in understanding the structure of the DNA molecule, it was clear by the late 1940s that such knowledge would open vast new opportunities in biochemical research—and Watson and Crick's model of that molecule (the famous double helix) did indeed earn them a Nobel Prize in 1953 (Watson, 1968).

Later, of course, answers to fundamental questions may well turn out to be of practical value, but this is rarely the immediate reason for seeking those answers. Actually, it is rare that scientists can foresee the ways their discoveries may be put to practical use in the future. Did Einstein, in 1905, foresee that his work on relativity would lead to the atomic bomb 40 years later?

All this means that the driving force within the scientific community is not simply a commitment to be helpful to society. Scientists engaged in basic research, in fact, tend to look down on those working in applied research. The latter are apparently violating the norm of disinterestedness by being employed to discover things that can help their employers solve immediate problems or increase their profits, instead of to contribute to the extension of generalized scientific knowledge.

Yet basic as well as applied research often provides the foundation for new technologies that have tangible impacts on our lives. Most of these are welcome, of course, but there are times when controversy arises over the possible dangers that may accompany the introduction of a new technology. Certainly the continuing campaign against nuclear generating plants is a case in point, as was the serious concern a few years ago that genetic engineering might accidentally create new, incurable plagues. The possible dangers of fluoridating public drinking water were hotly debated some 20 years ago.

Current attempts to require the teaching of "creationism" in public schools as well as the theory of evolution demonstrate that the mistrust of science is not limited to fear of physical dangers. If scientists' findings seem to contradict religious or political beliefs, attempts may be made to suppress them, or at least to question their validity. Research on the relationship between race and IQ has incited bitter controversy, just as the discrepancy between the Biblical and Darwinian accounts of the origins of humankind has agitated people for more than a century.

The central social problem is that experts can usually be found who will argue both for and against a new technology or the validity of a new discovery. Since the subtleties and probabilities that go into scientific reasoning are difficult to explain in public debate, and since the public may find it hard to evaluate different experts' credentials, the result is often confusion and an inability to reach a realistic assessment of the issue.

It is clear, then, that the link between the disinterested quest for knowledge and the fact that this quest may have practical consequences later on raises the serious question of how to control scientific research. New knowledge is always a potential two-edged sword, capable of leading to harmful consequences (whether or not they are intended) as well as to beneficial consequences. Out of basic physics has come the neutron bomb as well as the radioactive elements used in medical diagnostics; out of basic biological research have come poisonous viruses and defoliants as well as new medicines. Laser beams, now widely used in industry, may also become horrifying weapons in a future war.

As science continues to advance, both edges of the sword become sharper. There is a greater chance that research findings will be misused, cause unforeseen damage, or generate unwanted social change, while at the same time they promise more effective help in solving problems of health, energy, and virtually every other aspect of the human condition.

We are only now beginning to understand the dimensions of the problems that science presents, and to consider how best to handle this new, powerful force in society. To minimize its dangers without also interfering with its potential benefits will require wise policies and an enlightened public. The sociologist's understanding of the scientific community will not automatically point to the best policies, but it will be necessary if we are to succeed in mastering this fascinating modern source of social change.

REFERENCES

Merton, Robert K. (1973). *The Sociology of Science*. Chicago: University of Chicago Press.

Price, Derek J. de Solla (1963). *Little Science, Big Science*. New York: Columbia University Press.

Watson, James D. (1968). *The Double Helix*. New York: Atheneum Publishers.

address itself to many problems, were discontinued. Instead, more authoritarian and autocratic structures were established, which were limited in their views and equipped to handle a much smaller range of social problems (Eisenstadt, 1973). The civil disorders in Nicaragua and El Salvador in the 1970s and 1980s are additional examples.

THE POSTINDUSTRIAL SOCIETY

Having reached an advanced industrial stage, societies do not suddenly stop dead. Change, in fact, seems to be accelerating rapidly. Essayist Alvin Toffler spoke of a "roaring current of change" which gives rise to "future shock"—mass disorientation resulting from constant bombardment with new elements that make our learned behavior obsolete (Toffler, 1970). Sociologists Warren Bennis and Philip Slater argued that the accelerated pace of change in countries like the United States produces *temporary societies,* characterized by "temporary systems, nonpermanent relationships, turbulence, uprootedness, unconnectedness, mobility, and, above all, unexampled social change" (Bennis and Slater, 1968). Daniel Bell has characterized change as adding "layers" to a society, not necessarily displacing all of the old ways (Bell, 1976).

Our society has reached what is commonly called the postindustrial stage. A **postindustrial society** is one in which the focus of production has shifted from the production of manufactured goods to the provision of services. The most rapidly growing segment of the working population is in such service areas as office workers, medical care givers, government workers, and computer programmers (*Social Indicators,* 1980: 355). This is partly the result of advanced technology. Computers and automation have taken over many industrial processes. In doing so they have created a tremendous need for people to program and process their output. The growth in service jobs also reflects the high degree of affluence in the society. We can afford to be more concerned with the quality of life rather than simply its maintenance.

Inevitably, social change again raises the question of the quality of life. Is our postindustrial society creating better lives for most of our citizens? The question is, of course, impossible to answer. Different groups experience different living conditions: blacks are victims of more crimes; women are paid less than men; minorities still suffer prejudice and discrimination. These experiences affect people's perceptions, as is shown in Fig. 19.2. Yet fewer people live in poverty, and life expectancy for the population as a whole has been increasing. The answer all depends on what one values, as Granovetter has noted (1979). We certainly live in a society that has many more consumer goods than previously; we have what sometimes seems like limitless choices in matters ranging from sex to educational opportunities. Yet a nationwide poll taken in 1978 found 55 percent of the population believing that the following year was going to be worse than the present one (Gallup Poll, 1980: 1). As we noted at the beginning of this book, sociologists can study society and report the observable realities of people's lives. However, it is not our purpose to make a value judgment as to whether the changes that have occurred—and will continue—are either "good" or "bad." Each of us has to make that decision based on our own set of priorities and values.

Planning social change. In the decade of the 1960s, the United States planned and carried out a space program that ultimately landed people on the moon. Planning is an old and familiar process in the technological and economic field. Planning in other areas of society has not been entirely neglected, but by and large, it has been undertaken in an unsystematic and haphazard manner. We encourage birth control to keep the

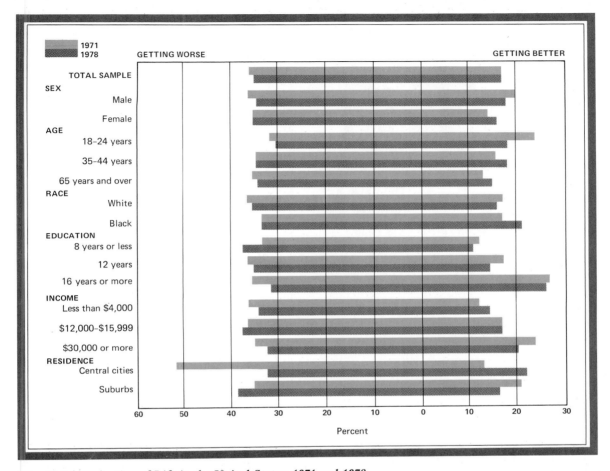

Fig. 19.2 / Evaluation of Life in the United States: 1971 and 1978

Source: 1971 data from Table 2.2 of *The Quality of American Life: Perceptions, Evaluations, and Satisfactions* by Campbell, Converse, and Rodgers. Copyright © 1976 by the Russell Sage Foundation. Used by permission of Basic Books, Inc. 1978 data from *The Sense of Well Being in America* by Angus Campbell et al. Copyright © 1980 by the McGraw-Hill Book Company. Used by permission of the publisher.

population within bounds, sponsor urban-renewal projects and the building of "new towns" as the urban population soars, and seek to equalize wealth and opportunity through progressive income taxes and social welfare programs. The civil rights laws of the 1960s were an effort to correct gross injustices in our social system. Most of the attempts at social reform, however, are reactions to existing conditions that are suddenly perceived as problems. After decades of dumping industrial wastes and raw sewage into our nation's rivers, we suddenly perceive the destructive effects and hastily pass environmental protection laws.

THE WORLD WILL END OCT. 10

RAIN DATE OCT. 17

From the Wall St. Journal,
Permission-Cartoon Features
Syndicate.

If technology is sometimes seen as the cause of many social problems, it can also provide the means of solving many of those problems. Atomic science has unleashed tremendous powers for good as well as for destruction—depending on how we choose to use it. The tremendous explosion of knowledge in modern times and the vastly improved means of processing information (computers) and communicating it (television, satellites) offer human beings the opportunity to use that knowledge not just to increase our material goods, but to improve the *quality* of human life. Part of the new knowledge is in the social and behavioral sciences—new information about the behavior of individuals and groups. The application of this kind of knowledge to the problems of human societies may yield results as impressive and dramatic as any of our technological achievements.

SUMMARY

1. The main purposes of this chapter are to explore the social, cultural, and technological aspects of change; to discuss theories of social change; to discuss the origins of change and the rate at which it occurs; to explore responses to change; to look at the process of modernization; and to describe the relationship between human ecology and social change.

2. In all societies, the ways in which societies meet basic social needs (for norms, cultural expression, social organization, and earning a living) change continually. One way to analyze change in society is to have a broad sociocultural perspective—to distinguish between social, cultural, and technological changes, and to understand the complex interactions that occur between them in the process of change.

3. Many theorists have tried to identify certain universal patterns of social change: *functionalists* see change as a shift from one stable order to another different stable order; *conflict theorists* see conflict as the source of social change and the process that accounts for the evolution of societies; *exchange theorists* believe that modifying existing exchange relationships can generate change; *cyclical theorists* assert that societies pass through cycles of social development; and *evolutionary theorists* believe that societies develop from simple to more complex (but not necessarily better) forms through a series of specific stages rather than cycles.

4. When analyzing the process of change, one must consider two important factors: the rate at which it occurs and its origins.

   The rate of change is related to the cultural base of the society and proceeds according to the exponential principle. Some parts of a culture cannot adapt to changes as quickly as they occur in other parts. This difference is called cultural lag.

Conditions and factors that cause and influence social change include ecological factors, inventors and discoverers, cultural predispositions, cultural diffusion, acculturation, and social movements.

5. As societies change, their environment is affected. Modern technology gives human populations tremendous control over their environments, including the ability to destroy ecological resources and other life forms. More harmonious ecological relationships can be achieved through social planning.

6. Societies have different reactions to proposed changes. Changes will generally be adopted when they are perceived to be for the better, and they will be most readily accepted when their usefulness is easily demonstrated and recognized. The acceptance or rejection of a change will also depend on its compatibility with the existing culture and social structure.

7. Modernization is a process by which traditional, agriculturally based societies become urbanized and industrialized. It affects the whole sociocultural system and requires that a society commit itself to change, have adequate capital, and be politically unified.

After reaching the postindustrial stage, rapidly changing societies can plan and control their futures by anticipating the consequences of change and by directing the process of change toward achieving certain goals.

REVIEW

Key Terms

Social change	Cultural lag	Technology	Acculturation
Cultural change	Social movement	Invention	Modernization
Culture base	Ecology	Discovery	Postindustrial society
Exponential principle	Human ecology	Cultural diffusion	

Review and Discussion

1. Do you believe that the United States has progressed over the past 100 years? In what ways has life improved? What situations do we face today that were not a problem for our ancestors?

2. Cultural lag is always best seen in retrospect. The resistance to birth control can be seen as an example of cultural lag, because birth control is now widely accepted in our society. Do you think the following will prove to be examples of cultural lag: The resistance to abortion? The resistance to nuclear power? The resistance to research in genetic engineering techniques like cloning? Why do you feel as you do?

3. How has the computer changed our society? Distinguish between intended and unintended consequences.

4. What do you think life in the United States will be like in the year 2000? What changes would you like to see? Can you do anything to bring them about or to stop undesirable changes?

5. If you were in a position of power, how would you deal with the problems of environmental pollution and depletion of resources? Be sure to consider the opposition you would face and how you would deal with it.

6. Do you ever get frightened by social and ecological changes in our society? What aspects of change pose personal threats? Which make you wonder about the future of the society as a whole? What role do you see yourself playing in these changes?

Experience with Sociology

This chapter has surveyed social movements, of which the Civil Rights movement has been an unusually important recent example. You might also want to review Chapter 9, which spent considerable time looking at the history and present situation of the black American. These two chapters together will provide a thorough analysis of the Civil Rights movement as an effort to reduce the most destructive aspects of the legacy of slavery. As you will recall, it attempted to address the social structures that perpetrate racism, prejudice, and discrimination, as well as the efforts of individuals to better understand and appreciate themselves.

Module 6 in *Experience with Sociology: Social Issues in American Society* focuses on the Civil Rights movement as a major turning point in the fight against the legacy of slavery. It presents data to help you assess the effectiveness of the Civil Rights movement in reducing institutionalized discrimination and improving the life chances for black Americans. It also asks you to form your own opinion: Was the movement successful? With your knowledge of social movements, you may want to think about the potential for future movements, given the results of your data analysis in this module.

References

Adoff, Arnold, ed. (1968). *Black on Black.* New York: Collier.

Allen, F. R. (1971). *Sociocultural Dynamics: An Introduction to Social Change.* New York: Macmillan.

Arensberg, Conrad M., and **Arthur H. Niefhoff** (1971). *Introducing Social Change: A Manual for Community Development,* 2nd ed. Chicago: Aldine.

Bell, Daniel (1976). *The Coming of Postindustrial Society.* New York: Basic Books.

Bennis, W. G., and **P. E. Slater** (1968). *The Temporary Society.* New York: Harper & Row.

Darnton, John (1981). Poland, one year later, is a society transformed. *The New York Times,* August 31, 1981, p. A4.

Eisenstadt, S. N. (1973). *Tradition, Change, and Modernity.* New York: John Wiley.

———— (1980). Cultural orientations, industrial entrepreneurs, and social change: Comparative analysis of traditional civilizations. *American Journal of Sociology* 85, no. 4 (January 1980): 840–69.

Fairweather, George W. (1972). *Social Change: The Challenge to Survival.* Morristown, N.J.: General Learning Press.

Friedan, Betty (1981). Feminism's next step. *The New York Times Magazine,* July 5, 1981, p. 13ff.

The Gallup Poll, Public Opinion 1979 (1980). Wilmington, Del.: Scholarly Resources.

Gordon, Milton (1964). *Assimilation in American Life.* New York: Oxford University Press.

Granovetter, Mark (1979). The idea of "advancement" in theories of social evolution and development. *American Journal of Sociology* 85, no. 3 (November 1979): 489–515.

Handlin, Oscar, ed. (1966). *Children of the Uprooted.* New York: George Braziller.

Hill, Polly (1963). *The Migrant Cocoa Farmers of Southern Ghana.* New York: Cambridge University Press.

Holmberg, Allan (1958). The research and development approach to the study of change. *Human Organization* 17: 12–16.

Hornblower, Margaret (1980). Hmongtana: Laotian tribe starts over in bewildering new world. *Washington Post,* July 5, 1980, pp. A1ff.

Lenski, Gerhard (1970). *Human Societies.* New York: McGraw-Hill.

Lenski, Gerhard, and **J. Lenski** (1978). *Human Societies,* 3rd ed. New York: McGraw-Hill.

Levy, Marion J., Jr. (1972). *Modernization: Latecomers and Survivors.* New York: Basic Books.

Linton, Ralph (1964). Discovery, invention, and their cultural setting. In *Social Change,* eds. Amitai and Eva Etzioni. New York: Basic Books.

Markham, James H. (1981). In Solidarity, a new focus. *The New York Times,* August 24, 1981, p. A9.

Martin, Douglas (1981). Vietnam veterans in Iowa town organizing to reach goals. *The New York Times,* July 16, 1981, p. A13.

Marty, Martin (1981). Morality, ethics, and the new Christian right. *The Hastings Center Report* 11, no. 4 (August 1981): 14–17.

The New York Times (1981). U.S. considers ceding control of crane refuge, July 8, 1981, p. A10.

Ogburn, William F. (1922). Are inventions inevitable? A note on social evolution. *Political Science Quarterly* 37: 83–98.

Peterson, Iver (1981). Michigan family chases American dream in Texas. *The New York Times,* June 13, 1981, p. A8.

Smelser, Neil J. (1966). The modernization of social relations. In *Modernization: The Dynamics of Growth,* ed. M. Weiner. New York: Basic Books.

Snow, David, Louis Zurcher, Jr., and **Sheldon Ekland-Olson** (1980). Social networks and social movements. *American Sociological Review* 45, no. 5 (October 1980): 787–801.

Social Indicators 1980. Washington, D.C.: Department of Commerce, U.S. Government Printing Office, p. 355.

Spengler, O. (1964). The life cycle of cultures. In *Social Change,* eds. Amitai and Eva Etzioni, pp. 21–23. New York: Basic Books.

Steiner, Stan (1974). *The Islands.* New York: Harper & Row.

Toffler, Alvin (1970). *Future Shock.* New York: Random House.

Turner, Ralph H., and **Lewis M. Killian** (1972). *Collective Behavior.* Englewood Cliffs, N.J.: Prentice-Hall.

White, Lynn Jr. (1962). *Medieval Technology and Social Change.* New York: Oxford University Press.

APPENDIX

SOCIOLOGY AS A CAREER

The development of sociology as an independent discipline in the social sciences dates to the late 1800s. Courses in sociology were first offered in American colleges in 1885. The American Sociological Society—today called the American Sociological Association (ASA)—was founded in 1905, and a membership of 115 attended its first meeting. By 1981 the ASA had a membership of 13,485, of whom 9,956 were full voting members.

TABLE A.1 / MEMBERSHIP IN THE AMERICAN SOCIOLOGICAL ASSOCIATION: 1906 and 1981

Category	1906	1981
Total membership	115*	13,485
Full members	—	9,183
Member emeritus	—	413
International members	—	313
Associate members	—	1,266
International associate members	—	603
Student associates	—	1,660
Others	—	47

* Only full-membership category existed in 1906.
Source: American Sociological Association, *Directory of Members* (Washington, D.C.), 1981.

The *American Journal of Sociology* was the initial journal of the American Sociological Society, and it remained the only publication of the Society for some time. Eventually the *Journal* was replaced by the *American Sociological Review* as the official publication of the American Sociological Association (the *American Journal of Sociology* is still one of the leading journals in

TABLE A.2 / REGULAR PUBLICATIONS OF THE AMERICAN SOCIOLOGICAL ASSOCIATION

Journal	Frequency
American Sociological Review Official journal of the ASA; publishes articles on new trends and developments in theory and research.	Bimonthly
Contemporary Sociology A journal of reviews.	Bimonthly
Journal of Health and Social Behavior Analysis of problems bearing on human health and illness.	Quarterly
Sociology of Education Concerned with research about education as a social institution and as a part of human social development.	Quarterly
Social Psychology Quarterly Interdisciplinary journal of research and theory in social psychology.	Quarterly
The American Sociologist Articles analyzing sociology as a profession and as a discipline.	Quarterly
Footnotes A newsletter on activities and news of the profession, including official reports and proceedings of ASA groups.	Nine times/year
ASA Employment Bulletin Lists current positions available for sociologists.	Monthly

Source: American Sociological Association, *Directory of Members* (Washington, D.C.), 1981.

TABLE A.3 / SECTIONS OF THE AMERICAN SOCIOLOGICAL ASSOCIATION: 1981

Undergraduate sociology*	World conflicts*
Methodology	Environmental sociology*
Medical sociology	Marxist sociology*
Criminology	Sociological practice*
Sociology of education	Population*
Family	Political economy of the world system*
Organizations and occupations*	Aging*
Theoretical sociology	Visual sociology*
Sex and gender*	Collective behavior and social movements
Community*	Racial and cultural minorities*
Social psychology	

* Sections organized since 1970.
Source: American Sociological Association, *Directory of Members* (Washington, D.C.), 1981.

sociology, however). By 1981, the ASA was publishing six journals and sponsoring additional publications such as *Sociological Methodology* and the *Annual Review of Sociology*. Such professional publications are important because they provide opportunities for sociologists to exchange data and a variety of information among themselves.

The growth and development of sociology is evidenced by, among other things, the development of regional and state societies, such as the Eastern Sociological Society, the Southern Sociological Society, the Pacific Sociological Society, and the Midwest Sociological Society. There has been a corresponding growth in sections, groups of sociologists interested in a particular aspect of the discipline who organize to work together under the auspices of the ASA. These sections demonstrate sociologists' continuing concern with theoretical and research issues confronting the world today.

From the inception of the discipline, the primary place of employment for American sociologists was in academia. This practice has continued throughout the years. In 1980 close to 70 percent of sociologists were employed in academic positions, with about 30 percent working in applied settings. The latter included government, industry, and service occupations where sociologists conducted research and applied their skills of data evaluation and analysis. In the 1950s and 1960s, the high demand for sociologists led to estimates of a continuing pressing need for sociologists in all areas. However, declining enrollments in colleges and universities, periodic economic recessions, and decreased federal funding for research have created a concern about the future employment of sociologists (a concern shared by those in many other disciplines as well). Some observers anticipate that by 1990 the demand for academic sociologists will decline, and while there will be increasing opportunities in applied fields, they are not expected to provide enough employment for all the existing M.A. and Ph.D. sociologists.†

---

† Additional information about careers in sociology may be found in American Sociological Association, *Careers in Sociology* (Washington, D.C.), 1977.

TABLE A.4 / EMPLOYMENT OF M.A. AND Ph.D. SOCIOLOGISTS: 1980 AND 1990

Place of Employment	1980		1990*	
	Number Employed	Percent of Total	Number Employed	Percent of Total
In academia	14,529	69.5	14,570	64.8
In applied fields (total)	6,382	30.5	7,917	35.2
In government (total)	1,806	28.3	3,267	41.3
Federal	533	8.4	340	4.3
State	676	10.6	2,218	28.0
Local	597	9.4	709	9.0
In services and industries (total)	4,576	71.7	4,650	58.7
Educational services	1,855	29.0	1,533	19.4
Misc. professional services	722	11.3	925	11.7
Medical health services	702	11.0	1,111	14.0
Nonprofit organizations	676	10.6	607	7.7
Business management	293	4.6	400	5.1
Other services	87	1.4	73	0.9
Misc. industry	241	3.8	1	.0

* Estimated figures.
Percentages may not add to 100 due to rounding.
Adapted from R. W. Manderscheid and M. Greenwald, Supply and demand of sociologists in 1980. Paper presented at the Annual Meeting of the American Sociological Association, September 6, 1982, San Francisco, Cal.: 1–16.

GLOSSARY

Abstracted empiricism. C. Wright Mills's concept which describes focusing so completely on the analysis of data that the researcher loses sight of the fact that sociological research should contribute in some way to the betterment of society.

Academic freedom. The liberty to study behavior without restrictions imposed by groups which have particular value positions regarding such behavior.

Acquisitive crowd. A crowd bent on possession of economic goods or some scarce resource.

Accommodation. The permanent or temporary end of a conflict that allows opposing parties to function together without open hostility, but does not necessarily resolve or settle the causes of the conflict.

Acculturation. A basic restructuring of cultures that have come into contact.

Achieved position. A position acquired through personal effort, choice, or accomplishment.

Age-specific death rate. The number of people who die at a given age per 1000 people in that age category.

Agent of socialization. A social unit that has recognized responsibility for carrying out socializing activities.

Aggregate. A number of people who happen to be at the same place at the same time, but whose interaction is limited and unstructured.

Aggressive mob. A mob that seeks a target for violence—either people or property.

Alienation. A feeling of not belonging and of powerlessness in one's social world.

Amalgamation. Complete mingling of groups through intermarriage and interbreeding.

Anomie. A state of confusion that occurs when the individual or a significant portion of the society does not feel bound to or supported by any set of norms and values.

Anticipatory socialization. Socialization that prepares people for future statuses and roles.

Applied sociology. The use of sociological knowledge and research techniques to solve specific social problems.

Artificial insemination. Impregnating a woman by mechanical means using male sperm donated for this purpose.

Ascribed position. A position assigned by society without reference to personal ability, effort, choice, or accomplishment.

Assimilation. The gradual merging of differing groups so that the distinguishing features of the groups become less and less identifiable as common interests come to outweigh points of difference.

Average. The center of the distribution.

Audience. A passive crowd that assembles for a specific event and reacts to an external stimulus.

Authority. Power that is regarded as legitimate by those whom it affects.

Average life expectancy. The number of years lived, on the average, by members of a given population.

Bilineal. Descent traced through both male and female lines.

Biotechnology. The industrial use of biological processes, including genetic engineering.

Blended family. Families composed of previously married adults and their children from those marriages as well as from the current one.

Bourgeoisie. Karl Marx's term for the ruling class in a society which owns the means of production.

Bureaucracy. A formal organization with specialized functions, fixed rules, and a hierarchy of authority.

Busing. Transporting students out of their neighborhoods for the purpose of achieving racial integration.

Capital. Goods accumulated for the production of other goods.

Case study. The in-depth study of social phenomena, often utilizing several research techniques.

Caste system. A type of closed class structure in which a person's social rank is unchangeable.

Category. A number of people who share the same characteristics but who do not necessarily interact with one another.

Census. A periodic population survey.

Centralization. The clustering of certain economic and social activities within a particular part of a city.

Channeling. Guiding students into learning experiences which will prepare them for the roles they will be expected to play as adults in society.

Charismatic authority. Authority based on extraordinary personal qualities.

Church. Any established religious organization with a stable membership and relatively fixed beliefs and practices.

City. An urban community. Sometimes city is used to refer to the most densely populated center of an urban community, distinct from outlying suburbs.

Closed class system. A social structure in which a person inherits a fixed class status or caste.

Coercion. Power (especially the use of force) that is regarded as illegitimate by those whom it affects.

Cognitive development. The growth of intellectual processes such as reasoning, language, and abstract thinking.

Collective behavior. Group activity that is spontaneous, relatively unstructured, and focused on a particular stimulus.

Collectivity. A temporary collection of people who are interacting in response to a specific stimulus.

Community. A group of people living within a specific geographic area who cooperate in many life activities and who share a sense of belonging.

Competition. The effort of individuals or groups to surpass each other in order to obtain rewards that are in limited supply.

Concentric zone model of urban growth. Urban growth viewed as a series of rings spreading outward from the city's center.

Conflict. A form of competition in which the competitors seek not only to surpass their rivals, but to eliminate them from competition, to injure them, or to control or deprive them of something against their wills.

Conflict theory. The theoretical perspective in which social interaction is viewed as being motivated by the quest for power.

Control group. A group that shares everything experienced by the experimental group except the independent variable.

Cooperation. The joining of effort for a mutual goal.

Correlation. The degree to which events or variables are related.

Craze. A form of collective behavior similar in nature to fads and fashions, but usually involving larger sums of money and tending to be more obsessive.

Crime without victims. Behavior defined as a crime in which all parties engage willingly and from which they feel they have benefited (e.g., prostitution, for example).

Crowd. A temporary, relatively unorganized group of people who interact in close physical proximity.

Crude birth rate. The number of births each year per 1000 population, including all ages and both sexes.

Crude death rate. The number of deaths each year per 1000 population, including all ages and both sexes.

Culture. A population's characteristic values, beliefs, behaviors, and artifacts which are preserved and transmitted from generation to generation.

Cultural base. The technology and accumulated information that people have at hand.

Cultural change. Alteration in the skills, arts, customs, attitudes, and beliefs of a society.

Cultural diffusion. The process by which social and cultural elements are transferred from one society to another.

Cultural lag. The gap between advances in material culture and the consequent adjustments in nonmaterial culture.

Cultural relativism. Recognition that a society's norms and values should be examined and understood within their particular cultural context.

Data. Facts that are systematically collected in the real, observable world.

Defining the situation. W. I. Thomas's belief that people define reality according to their own perceptions of it, rather than react automatically to situations.

Democracy. The form of government in which the people make the rules on how to govern.

Democratic Party. The political party generally identified as more responsive to concerns of the working class and the poor.

Demographic transition. The theory that predicts long-term population stability in developing nations which occurs when, as a result of industrialization, changing family patterns lead to lower birth rates. Until this time, however, developing societies usually experience a population spurt because death rates fall in response to improved technology more quickly than birth rates.

Demography. A branch of sociology whose practitioners measure, describe, and analyze populations and the ways they change.

Denomination. A large, well-established church that is neither officially nor unofficially linked to the government.

Dependent variable. The variable that changes in response to changes in the independent variable.

Dependency ratio. The number of dependent individuals who are supported by 100 working people.

Descriptive statistics. Statistical techniques that are used to describe, summarize, and organize data.

Deviance. Any behavior that violates social expectations.

Differential association. The tendency to internalize the norms of the group in which people spend most of their time, or the group that is most significant to them.

Discovery. A new perception of some feature of the environment.

Discrimination. The unequal treatment of individuals based on their membership in a particular group.

Division of labor. The task specialization which occurs in societies as they grow in size and complexity.

Dual labor market. A workplace which channels men and women into distinct types of jobs, each having different levels of stability and financial rewards.

Ecclesia. A church that includes all or most of the members of a society and is recognized as the official religion of the state.

Ecology. The study of the interrelationship between living organisms and their environment.

Economic institution. The social structure that provides for the production, distribution, and consumption of goods and services.

Education. The social institution providing for the transmission and the generation of knowledge.

Elementary school. A school with grades kindergarten through six.

Emotional contagion. The sharing of feelings in a crowd which stimulates behavior among its members.

Endogamy. Marriage within a particular group.

Epidemiology. The identification of types of diseases within a population and its subgroups.

Ethnic group. People who share a sense of common heritage and cultural identity.

Ethnocentrism. The tendency to consider the norms and values of other groups inferior to one's own.

Exchange. A mutually rewarding social relationship in which individuals or groups supply each other with desired goods or services.

Exchange theory. The theoretical perspective which emphasizes the exchange of valued services and benefits as the basis for ongoing, structured social behavior.

Exogamy. Marriage outside a specific group of people.

Experimental group. A group whose behavior in response to a specific variable is to be observed and measured.

Exponential principle. The proposition that states that the rate of technological change is geometric.

Expressive crowds. Highly emotional crowds that focus on the subjective experiences of the members.

Expressive leader. The leader in a group who seeks harmony and to ensure that all members are relatively happy in the group.

Expressive roles. Roles emphasizing interpersonal nurturing and emotional behavior.

Extended family. A household made up of two or more generations of blood relatives.

Fad. A behavior that enjoys short-lived popularity and usually involves rather trifling and superficial activities or expressions.

Family. A group of adults linked by blood or marriage who live together, cooperate economically, and share responsibility for bringing up their collective offspring.

Family of orientation. The family into which one is born (also called the consanguine family).

Fashion. A form of briefly popular collective behavior that involves not only variability in dress styles but also changing behavior patterns in almost any area of cultural activity.

Family of procreation. The family one creates through marriage (also called the conjugal family).

Folk community. A small, isolated, and self-sufficient agricultural settlement where relations between people are personal and are usually based on ties of kinship.

Folkways. Informal customs regarding the correct way to behave.

Formal organization. A complex and deliberately constructed group that is organized to achieve certain specific and clearly stated goals.

Fertility rate. The number of births each year per 1000 women of childbearing age.

Gemeinschaft. A primary community that is rooted in tradition.

Gender. Social and psychological sexual identity, irrespective of the biological fact of sex.

Gene splicing. The ability to alter genetic material in order to affect the characteristics of an organism.

Generalized other. The impression a person has of society's overall expectations.

Genetic engineering. The use of biotechnology to influence genetic composition and development.

Gentrification. The buying of low-cost, often physically deteriorated urban property by affluent people who displace the existing low-income residents.

Gesellschaft. A voluntary association of people who live or work together because it is convenient.

Ghetto. The oldest, least desirable residential areas of a city, generally in or near the central business district.

Government. The group of people who hold legitimate decision-making power within the structure of the state.

Group marriage. The union of two or more men with two or more women.

Group. Two or more people who interact regularly and identify with one another.

Hawthorne effect. The effect of the research process itself on the behavior being studied.

Homesteading. Allowing people to purchase deteriorated housing very cheaply in return for a commitment to rehabilitate the property.

Homophobia. Extreme, often pathological reactions against homosexuality.

Horizontal social mobility. Movement within the same social class position.

Hypothesis. A tentative relationship that experimentation will seek to prove or to disprove.

Idioculture. The knowledge, beliefs, behaviors, and customs shared by members of a group and which give the group its distinctive character.

Independent variable. The variable that the researcher controls for experimental purposes.

Industrialization. The shift from human and animal power to the widespread use of mechanical power in the production process.

Infant mortality rate. The number of infants who die in their first year per 1000 live births.

Inferential statistics. Statistical techniques that enable researchers to make predictions and estimate the probability of errors occurring.

In-group. Any group or social category to which a person feels he or she belongs.

Informal organization. A network of personal relations that emerges spontaneously among members of a formal organization.

Innovation. The development of new means to attain conventional, socially approved goals.

Institution. A system of norms, values, positions, and activities that develops around a basic societal goal.

Institutional racism. Laws and practices that both reflect and produce racial inequality.

Instrumental leader. The leader in a group who directs activities and helps a group make decisions.

Instrumental roles. Roles emphasizing concrete, task-focused behavior.

Intergenerational social mobility. Mobility between classes that occurs from one generation to the next.

Intragenerational social mobility. Mobility between classes that occurs within one generation.

Invasion. The process by which a new group of people or a new industry enters an area for the first time.

Invention. The creation of new ways of using existing knowledge or new ways of combining existing artifacts.

La raza. "The race," referring to the pride Chicanos have in their own culture.

Labeling. The assignment of an inflexible social identity to an individual.

Language. A system for communicating facts, ideas, and feelings by using standardized symbols in a grammatical framework recognized by a particular society.

Latent functions. The unintended, often unrecognized, and possibly undesirable functions of an institution.

Latent role. Role expectations that are not relevant in a particular situation.

Laws. Formalized norms enforced through specific penalties by designated authorities.

Leader. Someone who has the potential ability, the power, to influence the way other people behave.

Legal authority. Authority based on or established by a codified set of rules.

Life chances. Access to a supply of goods, external living conditions, and personal life experiences.

Life style. The attitudes, values, and patterns of behavior that typify a particular social group.

Life-table. A schedule of death rates by age.

Lobby. A group organized to influence the political structure to advance the interests of its members.

Looking-glass self. The self-concept all individuals form from the reactions other people show to their behavior.

Majority group. The group that holds the controlling social power.

Manifest functions. The intended functions for which an institution is ostensibly designed.

Manifest role. Role expectations that are relevant in a particular situation.

Mass. A large number of people whose members are physically dispersed and react independently to a common stimulus.

Mass hysteria. A kind of contagion—the spread of irrational, compulsive beliefs or behavior.

Mass society. A large social system characterized by impersonality, anonymity, and functional interdependence.

Matriarchy. Female dominance in a family.

Matrilineal. Descent traced through the female line.

Matrilocal. When the husband moves in with his wife's family, or close to it.

Mean. A descriptive statistic which averages scores by dividing the sum of the scores by the total number of scores.

Means-end inversion. The obsessive adherence to rules to the point of excluding the overriding objective.

Mechanical solidarity. Emile Durkheim's term used to describe the social cohesion resulting from homogeneous group membership and a common moral order.

Median. A descriptive statistic that is the middle value in a set of scores.

Medical sociology. The study of the behavior of physicians, patients, and nurses, as well as the organizational structures in which they interact.

Megalopolis. An almost unbroken urban region formed as metropolitan areas overlap and merge across municipal, county, and state boundaries.

Migration. The movement of people within and between countries.

Minority group. Any group with less than controlling social power.

Mob. One type of active crowd that is emotionally aroused and may openly engage in destructive behavior.

Mode. A descriptive statistic which is the score that occurs most frequently in a group of scores.

Modernization. The process by which traditional, agriculturally based societies become urbanized and industrialized.

Modified extended family. A network of related nuclear families who cooperate but maintain their autonomy.

Monarchy. A government based on the rule of one supreme individual who usually claims a divine or inherited right to govern.

Monogamy. Marriage to one person at a time.

Monotheism. The worship of one god.

Mores. The norms that a culture considers to be essential.

Multiple nuclei model of urban growth. Urban growth formed by the merging together of the business districts, entertainment areas, and the neighborhoods of what had previously been independent smaller communities.

Natural areas. Sections within the urban community where people engage in particular activities.

Natural sciences. Scientific study of the physical features of nature and the ways in which they interact and change.

Nature vs. nurture. The relative effects on human behavior of inheritance versus the social environment.

Negative correlation. A change in one variable in response to and in the *opposite* direction from a change in another variable (e.g., an increase in one results in a decrease in the other).

Neighborhoods. Places where people living near each other interact on a friendly—or at least somewhat personal—basis.

Neolocal. When a newly married couple chooses its own place of residence, not necessarily living with or near either set of parents.

New Federalism. The return of decision making and fiscal control to the states from the federal government.

New town. A community designed and built from scratch to create optimal living conditions for its residents.

Nontraditional students. Students whose age, race, ethnicity, and socioeconomic characteristics are different from those of the traditional college-age student.

Norm of reciprocity. The expectation that there will be reasonably equal exchanges between people involved in ongoing social interaction.

Nuclear family. A married couple and their children living together by themselves.

Oligarchy. An elitist government in which a small number of landowners, industrialists, and/or military leaders hold authority.

Ombudsman. An official who mediates between individuals and bureaucratic organizations.

Open class system. A social structure in which people can change their status through their own achievements.

Organic solidarity. Emile Durkheim's term used to describe social cohesion resulting from many specialized activities being coordinated to work toward a common goal.

Out-group. Any group or social category to which a person feels he or she does not belong.

Panic crowd. A crowd that seeks a rapid exit from a situation perceived as threatening.

Parochial school. A private school with a Catholic tradition.

Patriarchy. Male dominance in a family.

Patrilineal. Descent traced through the male line.

Patrilocal. When a bride moves in with her husband's family, or close to it.

Participant observation. Observing behavior using systematic research techniques while also participating in the activities being studied.

Peer group. Friends and associates who are usually of similar age and social standing.

Personality. The consistent, relatively predictable characteristics that distinguish people from each other.

Pluralism. A situation in which many different groups live together, keeping and respecting their individual identities and heritages.

Political institution. The social structure that legitimates certain ways of acquiring and exercising power, and that defines the relationship between government and the people.

Political party. A structure to recruit, select, and appoint political office holders, to socialize voters, and to transmit the wishes of the electorate to those in power or seeking office.

Polyandry. Marriage by a woman to more than one husband at a time.

Polygamy. Marriage to more than one partner at a time.

Polygyny. Marriage by a man to more than one wife at a time.

Polytheism. The worship of many gods.

Population. (1) In demographic studies: the collectivity of individuals who inhabit a specific social unit or geographical area; or (2) in survey research: the total category of people who are to be investigated.

Positive correlation. A change in one variable in response to and in the *same* direction as a change in another variable (e.g., an increase in one results in an increase in the other).

Postindustrial society. A society in which the focus has shifted from the production of manufactured goods to the provision of services.

Power. The ability to control collective decisions and actions.

Power elite. A group of leaders from the military, business, and government who have enough power to shape the policies of the nation.

Prejudice. An inflexible, stereotyped prejudgment of people belonging to certain social groups.

Prenuptial agreement. An agreement prior to marriage which specifies how possessions will be divided in case the marriage is dissolved.

Primary. An election in which party members choose among candidates within their own party to run for a particular office.

Primary group. A small, intimate group of people who relate to one another in direct, personal ways.

Primary labor market. The part of the work force in which stable, well-paid jobs offering opportunities for advancement are assigned to men.

Proletariat. Karl Marx's term for propertyless workers in a society who must sell their labor power to survive.

Propaganda. The deliberate attempt to persuade people to adopt a particular point of view.

Public. A scattered group of people who share some interest or concern over a controversial issue where norms are shifting or uncertain.

Public opinion. The newly formulated and shared viewpoint held by the members of a public.

Punishment. Preventing people from getting what they want or injuring them physically or psychologically.

Quality of life. People's perceptions about whether their lives are better or worse than in the past. Usually material benefits as well as the nature of social interaction are included in these perceptions.

Quantitative methods. Procedures intended to collect accurately data which is measurable and able to be expressed numerically.

Race. A group of people who are distinguished by their inherited physical characteristics.

Racism. Discrimination on the basis of race.

Rational legal authority. Authority based on the law.

Rebellion. The development of new means and new goals.

Reciprocity. Voluntary and informal social exchange.

Reference group. Any group that individuals take into account when they evaluate their own behavior or self-concept.

Regional articulation. Part of the impact of mass society on rural communities in which regional structures and services enter rural communities.

Reliability. The degree to which a research device yields consistent results each time it is used.

Religion. A system of beliefs and practices related to matters that are held to be sacred and supernatural.

Republican Party. The political party linked to higher income groups and generally viewed as conservative.

Retreatism. Rejection of both the means and goals society prescribes.

Reward. Giving others what they want, or enabling them to avoid what they do not want.

Ritualism. Strict adherence to socially approved means without regard to goals.

Ritualization. Formal, stylized, or carefully contained hostile exchanges.

Role. The behaviors and attitudes expected of all the individuals who occupy a given social position.

Role ambiguity. The strain that occurs because role expectations are unclear or poorly defined.

Role conflict. A role problem which occurs when an individual is expected to perform one role with built-in inconsistencies or two roles that are incompatible.

Role discontinuity. A shift from one role to another in which there is inadequate preparation or acceptance of the new role, and where there may also be a sense of loss in regard to the old role.

Role set. The cluster of social roles that are to some extent defined by their relationship to each other.

Rumor. An unsubstantiated report that tends to spread rapidly.

Rural community. A community characterized by small population size, low population density, and primary relationships among its members.

Sacred. The objects, places, people, and ideas that believers associate with special power.

Sample. In survey research: a specific group of subjects drawn from a larger population.

Scientific method. A systematic, objective, and verifiable process used by scientists to investigate a problem and to gather information.

Secondary group. A goal-oriented group of people who relate to one another in relatively formal and impersonal ways.

Secondary labor market. The part of the work force in which temporary, modestly paid jobs with few opportunities for advancement are assigned to women.

Secondary school. A school with grades 7 through 12.

Sect. A small and separatist religious group that usually emphasizes fundamentalist teachings and strict ethical codes.

Sector model of urban growth. Urban growth viewed as occurring through the outward expansion of pie-shaped sectors of business, industrial, and residential activities.

Segregation. The establishment of certain neighborhoods as residences for specific minority groups.

Sex. Genetically inherited biological sexual characteristics.

Sex roles. Socially created rules and expectations governing the behavior of men and women.

Sex ratio. The number of males per 100 females in a population.

Sex role stereotypes. Rigid definitions of sex roles that resist change regardless of empirical data.

Significant others. People whose evaluations matter enough to affect one's self-esteem.

Social category. A number of people who share the same characteristics who do not necessarily interact with one another.

Social change. Change in the size, composition, and organization of society.

Social class. The people who share the same characteristics of economic resources, prestige, and power and who are aware of their common situation.

Social control. The ways in which society encourages and enforces conformity to its norms and expectations.

Social differentiation. Distinguishing between groups of people, thus creating differences in their social experiences.

Social disorganization. A breakdown in norms, communications, and commitment.

Social margin. The social "credit" that people extend to each other.

Social mobility. The movement of an individual from one social class to another.

Social movement. A relatively sustained collective effort to achieve or to block social change.

Social position. A category of people who perform similar functions.

Social problem. A condition that a significant number of people believe is undesirable and should be changed.

Social processes. The important recurring patterns of social behavior that characterize the interactions between individuals and groups.

Social sciences. The scientific study of various aspects of human society.

Social stratification. A system for ranking individuals and groups who share unequally in the distribution of wealth, prestige, and power.

Social structure. The statuses, roles, groups, and social institutions that serve to organize behavior in a society.

Socialization. The process of learning and internalizing culturally approved ways of thinking, feeling, and behaving.

Society. A group of people living in a specific geographical territory who share a culture which forms the basis for rules that guide their behavior.

Sociobiology. The study of the biological basis of social behavior, especially in humans.

Sociogram. A method for analyzing the relationships within a group developed by J. L. Moreno.

Sociolinguistics. The study of how language affects society.

Sociology. The scientific study of the structure, the functioning, and the changes in human groups.

Sociological imagination. C. Wright Mills's concept describing a "quality of mind" that enables people to use information and to develop reason in order to achieve an understanding of events going on in the world, as well as feelings within themselves.

Standard Metropolitan Statistical Area (SMSA). A statistical unit used by the U.S. Bureau of the Census to measure changes in population in urban areas.

State. The social structure that claims a monopoly over the legitimate use of force within a territory.

Status. A position in a set of relationships.

Status attainment. The process through which individuals attain a specific position in the social class structure.

Status inconsistency. Differences in the dimensions of stratification for an individual.

Stereotypes. Fixed images and beliefs about members of certain groups.

Structural functionalism. A view of society which emphasizes its wholeness and its stability. Societal parts are seen as interdependent, so that change in one part will lead to changes in other parts.

Subculture. Variant norms and values that distinguish a group of people from others in their culture.

Suburbs. Areas surrounding center cities, and dependent on them for goods and services, which are characterized by less specialization and lower population size and density than exist in the center city.

Succession. The process by which a group that was previously dominant in an area is replaced by others.

Superordination. Presenting conflicting groups with a situation in which they can gain certain rewards only by abandoning competitive or conflicting behavior and cooperating with one another.

Surrogate father. A man who impregnates a woman at her request so that she may have a child.

Surrogate mother. A woman who bears a child for a man at his request so that he may have a child.

Survey. A research technique used to gather information about a social phenomenon involving large numbers of people.

Symbolic interactionism. The theoretical perspective that focuses on the emergence of a social structure from the daily interactions between people.

Technology. The application of science to achieve the goals of society, especially those which are industrial and commercial.

Total institution. A highly structured formal organization that controls major portions of its members' lives.

Totem. A common object to which symbolic and sacred meaning has been given.

Traditional authority. Authority based on established customs or norms.

Theoretical perspective. A systematic explanation of the relationships between experimental facts.

Urban communities. Places where large numbers of very different kinds of people live together very closely.

Urbanization. The process through which rural and subrural communities increase in population size, population density, structural complexity, and reliance on advanced technology.

Urban planning. Efforts to consciously manage urban growth and development in order to reduce social and economic problems, and to improve the quality of life in urban areas.

Values. Cultural goals and criteria for evaluating people, behavior, experiences, and objects.

Variable. Any measurable quality or condition that is subject to change.

Variability. The degree to which scores are scattered around the center point of the data.

Validity. The degree to which a research device actually measures the variable it has been designed to measure.

Vertical mobility. Movement up or down in the social class structure.

Voluntary associations. Organizations formed by persons who join freely to pursue mutual interests.

Worship. The traditional channel for communication with the supernatural.

White-collar crime. Crime within business organizations, such as embezzlement.

PHOTO CREDITS

AUTHOR INDEX

SUBJECT INDEX